DNW
RCL
LG/HB
8/13/08

Handbook of
School-Based Interventions

Jeffrey J. Cohen
Marian C. Fish

Handbook of School-Based Interventions

RESOLVING STUDENT PROBLEMS AND PROMOTING HEALTHY EDUCATIONAL ENVIRONMENTS

Jossey-Bass Publishers · San Francisco

Substantial discounts on bulk quantities of Jossey-Bass books are available to corporations, professional associations, and other organizations. For details and discount information, contact the special sales department at Jossey-Bass Inc., Publishers. (415) 433-1740; Fax (415) 433-0499.

For sales outside the United States, contact Maxwell Macmillan International Publishing Group, 866 Third Avenue, New York, New York 10022.

Manufactured in the United States of America

The paper used in this book is acid-free and meets the State of California requirements for recycled paper (50 percent recycled waste, including 10 percent postconsumer waste), which are the strictest guidelines for recycled paper currently in use in the United States.

10% POST CONSUMER WASTE

The ink in this book is either soy- or vegetable-based and during the printing process emits fewer than half the volatile organic compounds (VOCs) emitted by petroleum-based ink.

Library of Congress Cataloging-in-Publication Data

Cohen, Jeffrey J.
    Handbook of school-based interventions : resolving student
problems and promoting healthy educational environments / Jeffrey J.
Cohen, Marian C. Fish. — 1st ed.
      p.   cm. — (Jossey-Bass social and behavioral science series)
  Includes bibliographical references and index.
    ISBN 1-55542-549-6
    1. School psychology—Handbooks, manuals, etc.   2. School social
work—Handbooks, manuals, etc.   3. Problem children—Education—
Handbooks, manuals, etc. 4. Classroom management—Handbooks,
manuals, etc.   I. Fish, Marian C., date.   II. Title.
III. Series.
LB1027.55.C64   1993
371.4'6—dc20
                                                 93-3619
                                               CIP

FIRST EDITION
HB Printing   10 9 8 7 6 5 4 3 2 1   *Code 9352*

The Jossey-Bass
Social and Behavioral Science Series

GUIDEBOOKS FOR THERAPEUTIC PRACTICE
Charles E. Schaefer and Howard L. Millman
Consulting Editors

Therapies for Children: A Handbook of Effective
Treatments for Problem Behaviors
Charles E. Schaefer and Howard L. Millman
1977

Therapies for Psychosomatic Disorders in Children
Charles E. Schaefer, Howard L. Millman,
and Gary F. Levine
1979

Therapies for School Behavior Problems
Howard L. Millman, Charles E. Schaefer,
and Jeffrey J. Cohen
1980

Group Therapies for Children and Youth
Charles E. Schaefer, Lynnette Johnson,
and Jeffrey N. Wherry
1982

Contents

Contents

Contents

Contents

To my wonderful family,
Pat, Jamie, and David,
thank you for your love and understanding.
—J.J.C.

Thank you to research assistants
Christine Nucci, Adena Rosenthal, Susan Liberstein, and Tracy Lenz
for their help.

Special thanks to "my guys"
Robert, Eric, and Gregg
for their support and patience.
—M.C.F.

Preface

The period since the publication of *Therapies for School Behavior Problems* (Millman, Schaefer, & Cohen, 1980) has been tumultuous for schools. Harsh criticism of the American educational system and the quality of its teaching has stimulated much discussion about and some significant action toward stricter academic standards for all students. While Public Law 94-142 has provided the opportunity for academically challenged youngsters to be educated closer to the mainstream of school life, success within that mainstream has become harder to achieve as schools tighten academic requirements in response to local policy and governmental regulation. This change in the character of the school environment further complicates an already intricate mix of cognitive, affective, and behavioral dynamics contributing to problem behaviors in school-age children, and substantiates the need for continuing access by school professionals to the literature on effective intervention strategies. To meet this need, and to bridge the gap between research and application, the *Handbook of School-Based Interventions* offers psychologists, counselors, social workers, teachers, administrators, parents, students in training, and related professionals in and out of the schools an extended and updated guide to assist in planning school-based interventions.

As in the previous nine publications in the Guidebooks for Therapeutic Practice series, the format of this book focuses on the digest—a succinct, nontechnical summary of the intervention strategy described in the original article, emphasizing its practical utilization in the school setting. The aim of the digest is to capture the relevant information without undue entanglement in theoretical formulations or research methodologies. The commentaries at the end of each digest suggest extensions of the technique, identify cautions, or offer other comments that might enhance its utility or further define and clarify its use. The goal is to explain the procedure while encouraging the reader to explore the literature in further detail.

This book is not a text on experimental precision but a compilation of strategies with demonstrated or potential value for school settings. Thus, while every attempt was made to choose well-planned and well-executed interventions, articles were not selected solely on the basis of their methodological or statistical rigor. Techniques described in the literature might never be used in everyday practice if experimental purity were the only acceptable standard for their application. A strategy was therefore included when converging or cumulative evidence of its utility was demonstrated, despite the methodological imperfections of its parent studies. Innovative or promising techniques were also highlighted, even if evidence of their effectiveness remained tentative according to rigorous scientific standards. The intent of this book is to motivate school professionals to read about useful techniques and further evaluate their utility through thoughtfully planned field applications. In this context, readers are strongly advised to obtain the original article (and related writings) if their interest is stimulated by a given digest. This work is not intended to be a "cookbook" but rather to encourage exploration and thoughtful selection of available interventions.

Judicious use of existing strategies, however, requires more than just a knowledge of the literature. Readers are also advised to supplement their technical knowledge with an operational framework for determining the choice of techniques in a given situation. Among others, factors such as the age of the student, teacher skill and sensitivity, degree of parental involvement, urgency of the need for change, ethical/moral considerations, and extent of administrative support may influence the shape of the intervention. As one reviewer of this book correctly observed, good practice involves both knowledge *and* a model that guides the application of that knowledge for problem-solving purposes. We hope the reader will utilize the information in this text within a sound problem-solving framework.

We have made changes in the content and organization of chapters as originally presented in *Therapies for School Behavior Problems*. These modifications do not affect the integrity of the book, but they modernize it and allow it to reflect a more school-based view of problem behaviors. For example, the struggle to redefine chapter headings and subheadings vividly exposed the larger contradictions inherent in any attempt to compartmentalize the variety, complexity, and natural fluidity of human thought, feeling, and behavior. However, as classification in some form was necessary to organize the book and make it more accessible to the reader, we chose to orient categorical descriptions toward health-promoting labels rather than terms more characteristic of medical disorder and psychological deficit. We believe the goal in schools is not merely to treat pathology but to promote healthy, competent behavior and to stimulate the setting to provide optimal conditions for growth and development.

We wish to thank the authors for permitting us to digest their articles and all the authors cited in this book for their contributions to the ever-growing literature on school-related interventions.

One final point. School practitioners do not have the luxury of choosing their clients. When a student is referred for any problem covered or not covered in these pages, the school-based professional is not in a position to decide whether to "take the case." All students are our clients regardless of the nature or severity of the presenting problem. Furthermore, if the issue is not resolved, the student not successfully engaged, or the intervention not effective, next year's teacher will likely be back on our doorstep with the same concerns. To address this challenge, the school professional must have access to an eclectic storehouse of techniques drawn from the spectrum of journals and texts. *Handbook of School-Based Interventions* and its predecessor, *Therapies for School Behavior Problems,* provide this access, introducing school professionals to tested and promising strategies and enabling them to demonstrate through their successful interventions one of many valuable roles they play in the life of the school.

Reference

Millman, H. L., Schaefer, C. E., & Cohen, J. J. (1980). *Therapies for school behavior problems: A handbook of practical interventions.* San Francisco: Jossey-Bass.

June 1993

Jeffrey J. Cohen
Ardsley, New York

Marian C. Fish
Flushing, New York

The Authors

Jeffrey J. Cohen has been a school psychologist in the Ardsley Union Free School District in Westchester County, New York, since 1971. He chairs the committees on special education and preschool special education for the school district. Currently, he also teaches on an adjunct basis in the Long Island University School Psychology Program in Dobbs Ferry, New York. He received his B.A. degree (1966) from New York University in psychology and his M.A. and Ph.D. degrees (1968, 1971) from Hofstra University in school psychology.

As a field-based practitioner, Cohen has advocated a more broad-based view of school psychological service in which the activities of the school psychologist affect as many students as possible. In practice, Cohen spends much time consulting with teachers, parents, and administrators, has developed district-based special education programs for students previously placed in out-of-district settings, is the liaison for the district employees' assistance program, and is a member of the high school child study team. He also supervises school psychology interns. One of his major priorities is to educate school personnel and community members about the multiple skills of school psychologists and the varied roles they can play to enhance the educational environment for all students.

Cohen is coauthor of *Therapies for School Behavior Problems* (1980, with H. L. Millman and C. E. Schaefer), contributor to the National Association of School Psychologists publication *Best Practices in School Psychology* (1985), and coauthor of several articles on cross-sex friendships in children. He is a member of the Division of School Psychology of the American Psychological Association, and of the National Association of School Psychologists. He lives with his wife Pat, daughter Jamie, and son David, and is in big trouble if they are not mentioned.

Marian C. Fish is associate professor and coordinator of the graduate program in school psychology at Queens College of the City University of New York (CUNY). She also serves on the faculty of the Ph.D. program in educational psychology at the Graduate Center of CUNY, where she teaches courses in school psychology and supervises doctoral dissertations. She received her B.S. degree (1969) from Cornell University in child development; her M.A. degree (1970) in early childhood education and Ph.D. degree (1974) in school psychology were awarded by Teachers College, Columbia University.

Fish has taught elementary school and worked as a school psychologist for a number of years in Westchester County, New York. She has published book chapters and numerous articles in professional journals on interventions for school problems, family-school relationships, a family systems orientation to school psychology, and the use of computers in the schools. She is associate editor of the *Journal of Educational and Psychological Consultation*. Her current research involves the development of a systems instrument to measure classroom functioning.

Fish is a member of a number of professional organizations, including the American Psychological Association, the National Association of School Psychologists, the American Educational Research Association, and the American Orthopsychiatric Association.

*Handbook of
School-Based Interventions*

Introduction: Perspectives on School-Based Interventions

Ecology

A growing body of literature substantiates that schools can make
a difference in the achievement, socioemotional, and socialization outcomes of children. . . . It is apparent that the quality
of a child's school experience is important not only for the academic and achievement outcomes, but for fostering self-esteem,
self-confidence, and general psychological well-being [Linney
and Seidman, 1989, p. 336].

The impact of school on the lives of children is undeniable and powerful. School requires a concentrated effort over a sustained period of time
and demands of the student not only academic mastery but, as noted by
Weinstein (1991), mastery of the "social lessons—lessons about appropriate
behavior in various contexts, about one's self as a learner and one's position
in a status hierarchy, about relationships with students from other ethnic
and racial groups, about the relative value of competition and cooperation,
and about friendship" (p. 520). Hamilton (1983) refers to this socialization
function of school as the "hidden curriculum." While these instructional and
social skills tasks are formidable for many children, they are particularly
challenging for the youngster with behavior and emotional problems who

1

may require intensive, ongoing intervention just to survive the school experience. Yet, if school practitioners are to understand problem behavior fully and are to use that knowledge to design and implement effective interventions that benefit problem students, they will need to look beyond the traditional person-centered models of maladjustment and incorporate into their helping strategies the organizational and systems (environmental) variables contributing with equal force to the psychological distress experienced by children (see Elias and Branden, 1988, for discussion of person-centered and environment-centered approaches to primary prevention). In this regard, the research on school effectiveness (for example, Good and Weinstein, 1986) consistently demonstrates that the ecology of the school setting and the emerging "patterns of social relations, connections, or linkages" identified by Seidman (1988, p. 9) as *social regularities* are crucial factors determining how students develop academic and social-emotional competencies (see also Kasen, Johnson, and Cohen, 1990). Hobbs (1975) described maladaptive behavior in an ecological framework by indicating that the child's actions were embedded

> in the ecological system of which the child is an integral part. This system consists of the child and the settings and the individuals within these settings that are a part of the child's daily life. All parts of the system influence all other parts of the system. . . . Thus, assessments and interventions focus on the exchanges between the child, the settings in which he participates, and the significant individuals who interact with him. . . . The objective is not merely to change or improve the child but to make the total system work. Change in any part of the system, or in several parts, may accomplish this purpose [pp. 113–114].

Assessment from an ecological perspective requires examination of all the interdependent elements of the system to understand the context in which problem behaviors occur. This includes the child–setting relationships and interactions, and the system characteristics that initiate and maintain the difficulty (Fish and Massey, 1991, provide preliminary data on the extent to which school psychologists make contact with the various systems that impact the life of the student). Likewise, "ecological" intervention involves not the "repair" of internal "defects" within the child, but the establishment (or reestablishment) of a systems balance that allows each member or element of the system to benefit. Thus, when teachers substitute a systematic behavior management strategy for ineffective yelling and punishment, they are initiating a fundamental shift in their relationship with the child through the use of specific methods and materials (Maher, 1981). Similarly, when teachers rearrange students' desks to improve on-task behavior, they are in effect altering the transactional dynamics of the classroom. Finally, when teachers initiate cooperative learning strategies, they are creating a new interactive environment in the classroom in which system relationships and social linkages are restructured (Linney and Seidman, 1989).

The literature provides ample illustrations of how an ecological perspective adds new dimension to existing intervention approaches. For example, Martens and Witt (1988) highlight the *treatment-environment relationship* as an important consideration when a new reward strategy is introduced into a setting (for example, a classroom) in which background reinforcement is already operating. They note that "a given rate of reinforcement supports a higher rate of behavior in a relatively 'barren' environment than in an environment 'rich' with background reinforcement" (p. 278). Thus, the practitioner must consider the preexisting environment when assessing the possible effect of a new strategy on the target behavior. Rosenfarb and Hayes (1984) demonstrate how the outcomes of two cognitive strategies for treating children's fear of the dark — self-statements and modeling — which are believed to alter behavior primarily through their informational impact, can be significantly affected by *social influence mechanisms* operating in the experimental setting. Last, Kelly (1986) indicates how consultation meshes with an ecological framework as the consultant helps the members of the system utilize the resources of the social setting to address a problem situation.

An ecological or systems perspective is well suited to school practice in several ways: First, it enables the school practitioner to dispense with a clinical model of psychopathology and focus on effecting a match between the needs of the child and the resources of the school environment; second, it facilitates the consultation process in that the role of the practitioner changes from helping the teacher "cure" the sick child to enhancing the teacher's effectiveness in her interactions with the child; finally, it shifts the locus of the intervention to the setting where the behavior must ultimately occur. In their discussion of the ecological perspective in child cognitive/behavioral therapy, Glenwick and Jason (1984) note that "the ecological approach . . . reminds one of the need to take into account continually the influence of the environment on the behaviors . . . of those children whom we are addressing in our interventions (as well as the reciprocal influence of children on environments)" (p. 145). This ecological view is particularly important in the schools, where the setting makes the helping process quite different from traditional therapy. An ecological viewpoint is at home in school where it is virtually impossible to work with students without at the same time involving the people and settings with which the child interacts. The practitioner who ignores these crucial system relationships will find it difficult to create change at any level of the system, whether in the individual student or teacher, classroom, school, district, or community.

Clarizio (1979) described the influence of *high-impact social environments* such as the family and school on the social and emotional development of children, but he noted that the school climate had not been thoroughly investigated. The research of the past decade clearly shows how difficult it is to assess the impact of interventions without also considering how the outcomes alter, and are in turn affected by, student–setting relationships, school climate, organizational structures, and other factors that collectively make up the school ecology. Prilleltensky (1991) fervently stated the case when he argued: "It is quite remarkable that in spite of overwhelming evidence pointing to the social causes of psychological distress . . . most diagnostic and therapeutic efforts are still directed toward the individual child. According to present practices not only is there a tendency to wait until the problem reaches major proportions, but once the problem is identified there is a similar inclination to treat the single child and neglect, practically and conceptually, equally important changes required in the environmental . . . and socioeconomic conditions" (p. 205). As practitioners explore the strategies described in this book, they are reminded not only to consider the impact of the school setting on problem behaviors in students but to remain sensitive to the ecology of the intervention itself.

Competency and Classification

Writing about the school dropout, unintended pregnancy, and substance abuse among other problems, Scales (1990) indicates that "the key to preventing problems among adolescents . . . is not to focus on preventing each of these problems but to concentrate on the broad development of cognitive, behavioral, and social capabilities among these adolescents" (p. 420). Scales outlines a social policy agenda that describes how changes in ecological contexts — that is, the economic environment, the family, the schools, and community service opportunities — can develop the competencies in adolescents that prevent maladaptive behavior and promote health (see Perry , 1984, and Stokols, 1992, for further discussion of the concept of health promotion).

Throughout this book and particularly in Chapter Four, the reader will find the theme of competency revisited and consisting of such trainable components as resistance skills, assertive communication skills, coping skills, social problem-solving skills, decision-making skills, and critical thinking skills. Competent youth are viewed as well adjusted in that they possess the skills to manage, and in many ways control, the forces in their environment that may influence their knowledge, attitudes, values, feelings, and behavior.

Conversely, while maladjusted students may be differentiated according to the categories of disorder listed in the currently accepted taxonomies, these categorical differences may mask a shared absence of underlying competency skills as well as a shared need for the skills-training paradigms cited in the chapters to follow. Scales (1990) notes that "when significant problems, such as unintended adolescent pregnancy, school dropout, and alcohol and other drug abuse occur among youth, they increasingly seem to occur together rather than in isolation from each other" (p. 421). Similarly, Kazdin, Bass, Siegel, and Thomas (1989) demonstrate that children with such diverse antisocial behaviors as fighting, unmanageability, stealing, truancy, and running away altered their negative patterns when exposed to problem-solving skills training.

Finally, Edwards and O'Toole (1985) believe that "a characteristic common to most behavior disordered students is lack of effective social and affective skills" (p. 8). They describe a self-control curriculum created to remediate the skill deficits associated with these behavior disorders. These comments point to a core of capabilities underlying competent functioning which, when learned, prevent or reduce negative behaviors regardless of the traditional diagnostic labels to which these behaviors are attached. As new research refines and expands the techniques to teach these skills, many labels that have been mainstays of childhood classification may well become less relevant; intervention strategies will operate across traditional, categorical boundaries, limiting the discriminative utility of these boundaries and encouraging their replacement by more empirically valid classification schemes.

Discussing traditional taxonomies such as the American Psychiatric Association's *Diagnostic and Statistical Manual* (DSM), Edelbrock (1979) points out that "there is no evidence that the diagnostic categories offered by these systems differentiate among disturbed children in terms of important criteria such as etiology, prognosis, and differential response to treatment. Likewise there is little evidence of this kind to support the taxonomy of children's disorders offered in the recently proposed DSM-III" (p. 355).

The externalizing-internalizing dichotomy utilized in this volume is described by Achenbach and Edelbrock (1978) and Edelbrock (1979) as an example of a research-based alternative to existing diagnostic categories that is derived from factor and cluster analysis of parent, teacher, and case history reports. The externalizing pattern includes the range of classroom management problems and related conduct disorders as well as destructive behaviors, hyperactivity, and impulsivity. These disorders are symptomatically more overt and are often defined as outer-directed or undercontrolled responses. Students displaying these disorders are characteristically considered behavior problems in the classroom. On the other hand, internalizing disorders encompass anxiety and stress-related difficulties, depression, phobias, low self-esteem, identity issues, elective mutism, and others. These are the inner-based reactions whose symptoms are more covert, whose behaviors are more overcontrolled, and to which the term *emotional problem* is more often attached.

These two broad-based syndromes (Achenbach, 1966), like the competency-based interventions described above, overlap and highlight the common elements among diverse diagnostic categories, emphasizing the questionable ability of these older taxonomies to distinguish among groups of disturbed children from an etiological, prognostic, or treatment outcome perspective. If varied problems such as substance abuse, truancy, and high-risk sexual behavior all respond to related competency-based strategies, perhaps they need to be linked categorically within a more empirically developed system. As Edelbrock (1979) notes, "In order to have any impact upon the delivery of mental health services for children and youth, such empirically derived taxonomies must interface more directly with existing services" (p. 367). However, King, Hamilton, and Ollendick (1988) indicate that, "although the multivariate approach holds considerable promise in terms of the development of parsimonious, reliable, and valid classifications of child psychopathology, the clinical usefulness of the taxonomies in individual assessment and treatment is not apparent" (p. 27). Perhaps as progress is made in the simultaneous development of more practical classification systems and more broad-based interventions, these trends will merge to provide labels that more adequately differentiate problems and offer guidance for the use of appropriate strategies.

Conclusion

Ecology, competency, and classification are central themes for the school practitioner. All interventions realign the child–setting relationship no matter how individually focused they appear. Similarly, the co-variation among many problem behaviors indicates the need to identify their commonalities, develop classification systems that better reflect how these behaviors cluster together, and utilize intervention strategies that address the underlying competencies or lack thereof. The reader is asked to adopt these perspectives when using the techniques described in this book, recognizing that the orientation in schools should be less dependent on "therapy for mental illness" and oriented instead toward providing children with the skills and environmental structures that foster academic, behavioral, and social competence, reduced vulnerability to high-risk behavior, and relative freedom from psychological distress.

References

Achenbach, T. M. (1966). The classification of children's psychiatric symptoms: A factor-analytic study. *Psychological Monographs, 80* (7, Whole No. 615).

Achenbach, T. M., & Edelbrock, C. S. (1978). The classification of child psychopathology: A review and analysis of empirical efforts. *Psychological Bulletin, 85,* 1275–1301.

Clarizio, H. F. (1979). Primary prevention of behavioral disorders in the schools. *School Psychology Digest, 8,* 434–445.

Edelbrock, C. (1979). Empirical classification of children's behavior disorders: Progress based on parent and teacher ratings. *School Psychology Digest, 8,* 355–369.

Edwards, L. L., & O'Toole, B. (1985). Application of the self-control curriculum with behavior disordered students. *Focus on Exceptional Children, 17,* 1–8.

Elias, M. J., & Branden, L. R. (1988). Primary prevention of behavioral and emotional problems in school-aged populations. *School Psychology Review, 17,* 581–592.

Fish, M. C., & Massey, R. (1991). Systems in school psychology practice: A preliminary investigation. *Journal of School Psychology, 29,* 361–366.

Glenwick, D. S., & Jason, L. A. (1984). Locus of intervention in child cognitive/behavior therapy: Implications of a behavioral community psychology perspective. In A. W. Meyers & W. E. Craighead (Eds.), *Cognitive behavior therapy with children* (pp. 129–162). New York: Plenum.

Good, T. L., & Weinstein, R. S. (1986). Schools make a difference: Evidence, criticisms, and new directions. *American Psychologist, 41,* 1090–1097.

Hamilton, S. F. (1983). The social side of schooling: Ecological studies of classrooms and schools. *The Elementary School Journal, 83,* 313–334.

Hobbs, N. (1975). *The futures of children: Categories, labels, and their consequences.* San Francisco: Jossey-Bass.

Kasen, S., Johnson, J., & Cohen, P. (1990). The impact of school emotional climate on student psychopathology. *Journal of Abnormal Child Psychology, 18,* 165–177.

Kazdin, A. E., Bass, D., Siegel, T., & Thomas, C. (1989). Cognitive-behavioral therapy and relationship therapy in the treatment of children referred for antisocial behavior. *Journal of Consulting and Clinical Psychology, 57,* 522–535.

Kelly, J. G. (1986). An ecological paradigm: Defining mental health consultation as a preventive service. *Prevention in Human Services, 4,* 1–36.

King, N. J., Hamilton, D. I., & Ollendick, T. (1988). *Children's phobias: A behavioral perspective.* Chichester: Wiley.

Linney, J. A., & Seidman, E. (1989). The future of schooling. *American Psychologist, 44,* 336–340.

Maher, C. A. (1981). Interventions with school social systems: A behavioral-systems approach. *School Psychology Review, 10,* 499–508.

Martens, B. K., & Witt, J. C. (1988). Expanding the scope of behavioral consultation: A systems approach to classroom behavior change. *Professional School Psychology, 3,* 271–281.

Perry, C. L. (1984). Health promotion at school: Expanding the potential for prevention. *School Psychology Review, 13,* 141–149.

Prilleltensky, I. (1991). The social ethics of school psychology: A priority for the 1990's. *School Psychology Quarterly, 6,* 200–222.

Rosenfarb, I., & Hayes, S. C. (1984). Social standard setting: The Achilles heel of informational accounts of therapeutic change. *Behavior Therapy, 15,* 515–528.

Scales, P. (1990). Developing capable young people: An alternative strategy for prevention programs. *Journal of Early Adolescence, 10,* 420–438.

Seidman, E. (1988). Back to the future, community psychology: Unfolding a theory of social intervention. *American Journal of Community Psychology, 16,* 3–24.

Stokols, D. (1992). Establishing and maintaining healthy environments: Toward a social ecology of health promotion. *American Psychologist, 47,* 6–22.

Weinstein, C. S. (1991). The classroom as a social context for learning. *Annual Review of Psychology, 42,* 493–525.

1

![decorative divider]

Classroom Management

Disruptive behavior, particularly rebellion, noncompliance, vandalism, fighting, and stealing, continues to be a major concern of teachers at all grade levels. They are acutely aware that students achieve better in well-managed classes and that the ability to maintain order is often viewed by administrators as one indication of teacher competence. In addition, serious conduct disorders present the threat of physical harm to other students and to teachers, particularly if they are unskilled in proper methods for defusing such behavior. Finally, it is simply quite unnerving for teachers to consider the prospect of losing control of the classroom. They therefore turn to a school-based professional to assist them in planning strategies that reduce student misconduct and allow them to focus on teaching.

The practitioner must have available a variety of possible interventions to meet these legitimate teacher demands. Many such effective techniques are presented in this chapter, which includes seven subsections on classroom disturbance as well as sections on dishonest behavior, truancy, and destructive behavior. Strategies such as correspondence training, peer tutoring, social skills training, structural family therapy, cooperative learning, self-management, overcorrection, community-based treatments, and others offer the school helper numerous alternatives with which to promote classroom management of behavior. However, these procedures are designed primarily to address already existing behavior problems and are not typically employed until the misbehavior is occurring at a sufficiently high rate and degree of seriousness to motivate the teacher to seek help. Of equal importance are proactive management techniques that structure the classroom environment to *prevent* the occurrence of disruptive behavior and foster academic achievement. Teachers who have mastered these skills are able to minimize the need for more intensive and intrusive strategies; they thus spend more time assisting students with their work and creating a climate that is relaxed yet clearly oriented toward academic productivity.

Research has identified several skill clusters possessed by effective teacher-managers: (1) They establish clear rules for behavior and procedures for classroom routines, which they effectively communicate to students, systematically rehearse, monitor, and enforce. They present these with particular clarity during the first days of school. In effect, these teachers apply the skills of good teaching to classroom behavior management. (2) They direct the flow of classroom information effectively. This means, first, communicating a clear and consistent message about the importance of instruction as the primary goal and emphasizing the student's responsibility for completing assignments and classroom work. Second, it involves presenting tasks clearly, in language understandable to all students, and with an awareness of the various skill levels present in the class. Such care in expressing expectations increases the likelihood of student success and motivation. Third, part of the flow of information is an awareness of student behavior at all times and student knowledge of the teacher's awareness. The effective teacher-manager clarifies acceptable behavior for students. A clear understanding of permissible behavior allows for quick corrective action for misbehavior rather than coercive interventions that punish without helping the student learn appropriate responding. Good managers also arrange the environment to maximize attending behavior. (3) Effective managers avoid the need for later interventions by using the early days of the new school year to set the rules and procedures, monitor and provide consequences for misbehavior, establish a climate conducive to student participation, organize instructional routines with little wasted time, and have materials ready for use. They help students learn how to meet the teacher's expectations and they recognize the importance of setting the proper class tone from the first day.

Proactive management issues illustrate the importance of an ecological perspective in understanding how classroom behavior problems develop. A child's behavior is a product of many interacting variables including the conditions at school under which students attend and learn. While students need to be held accountable for their behavior, the adults need to examine the educational environment they create to ensure that it offers the best opportunity for academic success.

Finally, selection of an appropriate intervention must take into account a number of distinct student, teacher, parent, and setting variables which by themselves can influence the outcome of an intervention independent of the strategy itself. Even the meaning of disruptiveness can vary from school to school or class to class, a disparity that in turn will affect whether there is sufficient interest from the setting in reducing a given behavior. The practitioner needs to consider all these factors deliberately before taking action.

The reader is encouraged to consult the following works for further information on the issues addressed above.

References

Brooks, D. M. (1985). The teacher's communicative competence: The first day of school. *Theory into Practice, 24,* 63–70.

Center, D. B., Deitz, S. M., & Kaufman, M. E. (1982). Student ability, task difficulty and inappropriate classroom behavior. *Behavior Modification, 6,* 355–374.

Evertson, C. M. (1985). Training teachers in classroom management: An experimental study in secondary school classrooms. *Journal of Educational Research, 79,* 51–58.

Evertson, C. M., & Emmer, E. T. (1982). Effective management at the beginning of the school year in junior high classes. *Journal of Educational Psychology, 74,* 485–498.

Gettinger, M. (1988). Methods of proactive classroom management. *School Psychology Review, 17,* 227–242.

Hyman, I., Stern, A., Lally, D., Kreutter, K., Berlinghof, M., & Prior, J. (1982). Discipline in the high school: Organizational factors and roles for the school psychologist. *School Psychology Review, 11,* 409–416.

Sanford, J. P., Emmer, E. T., & Clements, B. S. (1983). Improving classroom management. *Educational Leadership, 40,* 56–60.

Dishonest Behavior

Research has indicated that children as young as two-and-one-half years of age are capable of utilizing deceptive strategies. It is not surprising, therefore, that four- and five-year-olds are reported to engage in various forms of dishonest behavior. Lying, stealing, and cheating are reviewed in this section as examples of dishonesty and are frequently associated in the literature with later adolescent and adult antisocial behavior. The stability and seriousness of dishonesty argues strongly for the development and refinement of early assessment and intervention strategies.

Rewarding Truthfulness
Through Correspondence Training

AUTHOR: Freddy A. Paniagua

PRECIS: Correspondence training as a technique to teach truthfulness to children

INTRODUCTION: There is a surprising lack of research on the treatment of lying in children, especially considering that early lying may be a precursor of later antisocial behaviors. This void in the literature is filled with speculative recommendations to reduce lying, which are often not practical or realistic. Parents often view lying as "bad" behavior requiring punishment, even though punishment is ineffective in reducing lying and has been shown to trigger aggressive, withdrawing, and even more serious pathological behaviors. The author advances a new perspective on the definition, prevention, and treatment of lying, focusing on the relationship between saying and doing. This perspective examines correspondence between the child's verbal assertion and the external or internal event to which the statement refers. For example, if the child states that he cleaned his room and he in fact did clean it, a relationship exists between the statement and the external event indicating truthfulness. On the other hand, if the room has not been cleaned, then the verbalization is not related to the event and the child may be presumed to be lying. For internal events, a verbal-internal relationship exists if the child's statement (for example, "I have a headache; I can't go to school") matches the internal cognition (a headache is in progress); lying may be inferred if there is no headache. Verbal-external event relationships are public, observable, and open to confirmation; internal states are more private, concealed phenomena that are difficult to verify. It is, therefore, easier to detect lying when the child's statements refer to external events. Correspondence training utilizing verbal-external event relationships is a procedure designed to teach honesty and reduce lying in children by reinforcing their saying-doing correspondence — that is, by rewarding children for doing what they promised to do or for making a true statement about what they have already done.

RESEARCH: The author cites several studies supporting the effectiveness of correspondence training. In the first, children promised to play with blocks and were immediately rewarded with a toy for their promise, whether or not they actually played with the blocks. In this condition, children did not typically keep their promise. However, when children were shown but not actually given the toy until they fulfilled their promise to play with the blocks, block play increased significantly. In other words, they kept their promise and were rewarded for the saying-doing correspondence. In a second study, two hyperactive children were observed and later asked to report whether they paid attention and controlled their activity level. During baseline sessions with no treatment, they were not generally truthful, but when they were rewarded only for truthful reporting of their actions, their reports corresponded to their actual behavior.

PARENT USE OF CORRESPONDENCE TRAINING: The author recommends everyday use of correspondence training by parents to develop truthfulness in a child during the preschool years before lying develops as a problem. For example, the parent can elicit from the child the promise to go to bed on time, can display and discuss the reward that will be given if the promise is kept, and then can present the reward (with appropriate verbal praise) if the child is found to be in bed on time. If the promise is not kept, the reward is not given and training is repeated until correspondence is achieved. The same format may be used with potential problem behaviors, such as when the child promises not to hit people or destroy property during a certain time period, is shown the reward for keeping the promise, and is later given the treat for telling the truth and not behaving aggressively. A "doing-reporting" correspondence may also be trained by asking the child whether he hit or destroyed things during the specified time period and then rewarding with praise and/or a treat for providing an accurate report. While the private nature of internal states makes correspondence training more difficult for verbal-internal state relations, the author indicates his belief that training truthfulness with external states may generalize to the less verifiable situations. Certain internal states can also be monitored, as when a fever is checked with a thermometer.

GENERALIZING TRUTHFULNESS: Several strategies are identified that extend truth telling to situations where training has not occurred, or which maintain truthfulness after the rewards are no longer given. In *mediated generalization* the truthful assertions arising from the original correspondence training exert a powerful controlling force by mediating continued truth telling either across new settings or after training has been discontinued in the original situation. In the technique known as *training of sufficient exemplars,* correspondence training is accomplished over enough verbal-event relationships that truthful statements occur under untrained conditions. Finally, in the method referred to as *use of indiscriminable contingencies,* rewards are given on an intermittent and unpredictable schedule during correspondence training. When children are unable to predict the occurrence of the reinforcing or nonreinforcing events, the saying-doing relationship is maintained and generalized.

ADVANTAGES/DISADVANTAGES: Correspondence training may be incorporated into daily parenting activities, making it less like treatment than more complex, time-consuming strategies such as token economies or time-out procedures. However, this training requires much adult supervision that can only be reduced over time as truth telling develops. In addition, since verbal accuracy is a goal of treatment, correspondence training may not be suitable for children who lack communication skills, although some research is now suggesting otherwise. Correspondence training is also not recommended when the external behaviors are such that lying might result in self-injury (e.g., the child promises not to hit himself in the face and then does so).

COMMENTARY: Like parents, teachers can weave correspondence training into their daily routines. For example, they may extract a promise from the student to complete homework, discussing and displaying the reward that will be given if the promise is kept and then presenting the award if the homework is in fact done. This paradigm may be applied to a variety of behaviors such as avoiding cheating on tests, organizing a messy locker, refraining from misbehavior, or other possibilities. The practitioner may work with the parent or teacher to target instances of untruthfulness that might have more negative consequences than others. A key point is that aversive punishment is avoided with this technique, enhancing its attractiveness for the school setting.

SOURCE: Paniagua, F. A. (1989). Lying by children: Why children say one thing, do another? *Psychological Reports, 64,* 971–984.

Re-Creating the Scene

AUTHORS: Ron Van Houten and Ahmos Rolider

PRECIS: Reducing theft by guiding a developmentally delayed student through the re-created stealing episode followed by punishment

INTRODUCTION: Stealing may not be discovered until long after its occurrence, making the application of immediate consequences difficult. The authors report that having the perpetrator reenact the event with punishment as the outcome can reduce its frequency in cases where consequences must be delayed.

METHOD: Karen, a seventeen-year-old developmentally delayed girl, was a compulsive stealer and hoarder who lived in an institutional setting. She stole various items from the residences and was rarely caught. For the intervention, her room was thoroughly checked every thirty minutes for stolen items while ten items per day were planted at sites from which she stole to assure a constant opportunity for the behavior to occur. A check of these sites occurred before each search of her room, with every missing item from a site always found in her possession. During the seven-day baseline period, Karen was praised each time a check of her room yielded nothing stolen. If items were found, she was held by the shoulder and in a strong voice was told, "You don't steal food." For the intervention, the stealing episode was re-created in the following manner when a theft was discovered: (1) The item was replaced in its original spot (Karen always stole at least one planted item); (2) Karen was taken to the site; (3) she was guided toward the item; (4) as she came close to picking it up, she was loudly reprimanded with "Don't steal"; (5) she was moved to a safely padded corner for a one-minute "movement/suppression time-out procedure," in which her chin was placed against a corner with her hands crossed behind her back and her feet close together touching the wall. She was not allowed to move or talk in any manner and was strongly admonished if she did so with the words, "Don't move," or "Don't talk," while being moved back into the corner with the adult's hand against her upper back. After one minute, the entire sequence was repeated twice.

(*Note:* The authors describe two case studies in the article. For Karen, they do not specifically describe the entire re-creation but indicate that the procedure was the same for both cases with two minor exceptions — namely, use of a padded corner and involvement with Karen by the second author. Thus, steps three and four of the sequence reported here represent an extrapolation from the known procedure but are considered accurate representations of the technique.)

RESULTS: Implementation of the procedure immediately reduced Karen's stealing from seventeen to thirty-two items per day during the baseline period to under ten items per day through the first eight treatment days (including four days of no stealing). Four consecutive stealing-free days were achieved by day 9. Informal follow-up observations indicated reduced stealing as compared to baseline rates. No further follow-up opportunities were available as the contract to work with Karen expired.

COMMENTARY: The authors recognize the intrusive nature of this procedure and suggest the use of less intense strategies first. For example, overcorrection is a relatively nonaversive technique that provides restitution to the victim as well as negative reinforcement to the thief. Care must also be taken when re-creating a scene to avoid placing the participants at risk for harm or emotional trauma, particularly if dangerous behaviors are involved. Finally, the authors cite several advantages of delaying consequences for misbehavior, such as enabling the better-trained practitioner to deliver the punishment and allowing time for secretive behaviors to be uncovered. While re-creating the scene plus punishment may be an appropriate delayed consequence for developmentally delayed persons, reinstatement is a similar method reported in the literature with grade-school youngsters in which delayed discipline is provided for misbehavior. Reinstatement has been shown to be most effective when a detailed verbal description of the transgression is given followed by withdrawal of a valued possession as punishment. Unlike reenacting the scene, no behavioral rehearsal of the event is included. Perhaps developmentally delayed students benefit from a concrete replay of the occurrence, although it is possible that the movement-suppression time out would be a sufficient deterrent. Further research would need to address these issues.

SOURCE: Van Houten, R., & Rolider, A. (1988). Recreating the scene: An effective way to provide delayed punishment for inappropriate motor behavior. *Journal of Applied Behavior Analysis, 21,* 187–192.

Stimulus Control Training to Reduce Stealing

AUTHORS: Howard S. Rosén and L. Alison Rosén

PRECIS: Using differential reinforcement to reduce stealing in an elementary special education classroom

INTRODUCTION: Stealing may be difficult to control when the contingencies are weak, delayed, ineffective, or inconsistently applied. If the guilty student is never exposed and the behavior reinforced by admiring friends and possession of stolen objects, then stealing behavior may become more firmly entrenched. In this study, Steve, a seven-year-old special education student, was referred by his teacher for repeatedly having items in his possession that did not belong to him. The authors applied a differential reinforcement strategy using points and fines to reduce the stealing activity.

METHOD: On each morning of the study, all of Steve's belongings were marked with a green circle. Teaching staff then checked his person, desk, and supply box every fifteen minutes and considered an item stolen when it was found in his possession unmarked. After an initial baseline period of eleven days in which no contingencies were introduced, a fifteen-day *points and fines* condition was established in which Steve earned points and verbal praise after each check in which all of his items had green circles. A five-point fine and verbal reprimand were imposed when he was found with unmarked items. Steve was allowed to trade his points for various reinforcers at a classroom store established as part of a classwide token economy system. A second baseline condition of four days was followed by another sixteen-day experimental condition. Then a twelve-day *fading* condition was instituted in which Steve's belongings were checked every two hours instead of every fifteen minutes. Finally, points, fines, and markings were ended during a *follow-up* condition and his possessions were checked only when items were reported missing by students or staff.

During the treatments, Steve's stealing was reduced from an average of six items per day to .33 items during the first experimental condition and .31 items during the second experimental condition. Fading to a checking procedure every two hours yielded just one stolen item over the entire twelve-day period, while Steve stole only three items during the thirty-one-day follow-up condition. In addition, other aggressive-destructive behaviors not directly targeted decreased to approximately one-half their pretreatment levels, and Steve's parents and teachers reported diminished stealing at home and in other locations around the school.

COMMENTARY: Defining stealing in terms of the outcome of the misdeed (possession of stolen items) rather than the act itself (taking items) allowed the investigators to identify and provide consequences for the behavior more systematically. However, this procedure might be difficult for a regular classroom teacher who does not usually have assistants or aides to check a student's possessions every fifteen minutes. Thus, help from school staff might be necessary unless, as in many special education classes, paraprofessionals are already working with the teacher on a daily basis. In addition, fading checks to every two hours did not diminish the power of the intervention in the study, although it is possible that this time span was effective because it was preceded by the more frequent fifteen-minute interval. For practical reasons, the practitioner might wish to begin with time lengths longer than fifteen minutes to determine whether longer initial checking intervals might be as effective. Finally, the authors argue for early and immediate intervention for stealing, noting that younger children are still responsive to adult-delivered contingencies while adolescents prefer peer reinforcement. Age-appropriate reinforcers are essential if stealing is to be curtailed at an early age.

SOURCE: Rosén, H. S., & Rosén, L. A. (1983). Eliminating stealing: Use of stimulus control with an elementary student. *Behavior Modification, 7,* 56–63.

The Nature of Cheating

AUTHOR: James P. Murphy

PRECIS: Identifying strategies that encourage schoolwide honesty, discourage potential cheaters, and reduce preexisting cheating behavior

INTRODUCTION: Although there is no single character profile distinguishing the student who cheats from the noncheater, cheating has been associated with certain personality traits, behavioral characteristics, and environmental influences. Cheaters are described in the literature as more neurotic, outgoing, high strung, irascible, and agitated than most other children. Furthermore, uncertainty about the future, fear of failure, and the lack of early school success seem to increase students' risk for cheating. Finally, perceived school and/or home-based academic pressure, affiliation with other cheating students, a curriculum believed to be empty of substance, teaching seen as poor, an authoritarian teaching style, and work viewed as too easy or too difficult all contribute to a climate in which cheating is more likely to occur.

PREVENTION: Strategies to deter cheating may take the form of primary, secondary, and tertiary preventive measures that the school or district may institute to promote honest behavior, target students at risk for cheating, or intervene with those who have been found to cheat. Primary and secondary activities may include (1) advocating and modeling honesty as an integral part of the school structure, which can be expressed in the day-to-day behaviors and reactions of all the adults as well as in the more formal instructional activities of the classroom; (2) developing a policy on cheating that guides school staff as they interact with students in situations conducive to cheating; (3) educating students about cheating and its consequences for everyone; (4) creating a supportive school atmosphere conducive to honesty, directly instructing students not to cheat before tests, and arranging conditions to make cheating risky; (5) organizing peer discussions with the goal of fostering moral development; (6) minimizing the chance for cheating to occur by varying assignments, keeping student papers, and creating other tasks that are difficult to accomplish through cheating; and (7) using punishment or threat of punishment to discourage cheating on a short-term basis.

Tertiary intervention for students who have engaged in acts of cheating consist of several steps. (1) The practitioner should move beyond punishment to formulate strategies that redirect the student toward honest behavior. (2) The student should be questioned so the practitioner can understand the circumstances of the cheating behaviors and evaluate the student's view of the action as either a moral transgression or a violation of social norms. The latter distinction will determine whether the interventions should address the effects of cheating on the student and others, or whether the deviancy of the behavior itself should be the focus. (3) The student should be helped to focus on the misbehavior itself and the emotional arousal engendered by cheating. The breach of rules of conduct rather than the threat of facing the authority's reaction should be emphasized within the framework of a supportive, honesty-oriented school environment. Fear of punishment has no long-term effect on cheating.

COMMENTARY: The author points out that children in our society are unavoidably exposed to situations in which cheating is rewarded. Certainly they will witness some of that in school as cheaters will at times go unpunished or other forms of dishonesty will be ignored or minimized by adults. The resulting confusion can make it difficult for certain students to identify their values clearly as they grow physically and emotionally. Providing an accepting atmosphere in which integrity and respect are valued and in which staff and students alike adhere to standards of honesty will help to deter cheating.

SOURCE: Murphy, J. P. (1987). Children and cheating. In A. Thomas & J. Grimes (Eds.), *Children's needs: Psychological perspectives* (pp. 83–87). Washington, DC: National Association of School Psychologists.

Assessing and Treating Lying

AUTHOR: Jan Hughes

PRECIS: Proper assessment of lying behavior to prescribe more appropriate, effective intervention strategies

INTRODUCTION: A lie is an untruthful statement designed to deflect criticism, gain a reward, or hurt others; it may be distinguished from other fabrications by its intentionally deceptive antisocial intent. In contrast, unintentional or prosocial falsehoods are not lies because the speaker honestly believes them to be true or states them with positive intent. For example, unintentional lying may be done by the child whose reality testing is weak, who uses denial as a defense mechanism, or who is simply misinformed; lying to protect another's feelings is an example of prosocial deception. Everyone lies sometimes, but treatment should be considered for the child who lies frequently, is socially ostracized by peers, and who may also display concomitant problems such as poor academic performance and various school behavior disorders.

ASSESSMENT: The author recommends beginning with the following steps that are designed to determine the reasons for lying and the most effective treatment strategy: (1) Utilizing the categories of falsehoods described above, the practitioner discusses specific instances of the lying with the referring adult to identify the problem behavior more clearly. (2) Once lying has been defined successfully, its baseline frequency may be estimated by asking teachers and adults to record instances of the child's lying over a seven- to twelve-day period. They are instructed to record all suspected falsehoods and to investigate some of these occurrences discreetly to monitor the accuracy of their suspicions. (3) For each lie observed, the adults are asked to note the content of the lie and the events immediately preceding and following it. For example, the child may have been criticized just before lying, or another child punished just after. These events should be recorded. (4) To understand the potential effect of the child's lying on peer relationships, classmates are asked to indicate their perceptions of which peers lie. The author suggests a technique from the literature cited in the article in which students are asked various "guess who" questions—in this instance, "Guess who says things that are not true?" (5) Because lying is usually part of a more encompassing condition (such as delinquency or poor academic performance), parents and teachers are asked to evaluate other behaviors, perhaps using formally constructed checklists or rating scales such as the Peterson-Quay Behavior Problem Checklist or the Achenbach Child Behavior Checklist. Assessment of social skills is particularly meaningful, as lying has often been attributed to lack of competence in this area. (6) A social history is taken to provide an understanding of the environmental, developmental, and socioeconomic context in which the child's sense of honesty has developed.

CASE STUDY: The author describes two case studies to illustrate how this assessment process might actually operate. One case discusses twelve-year-old Heather, referred for lying by her parents. After eliciting from the parents several examples of Heather's lies, the psychologist met with them and the teacher to determine the scope of the behavior. Heather was found to be deceiving both home and school (for example, signing her mother's name to excuse notes), and record keeping at home and school verified fifteen additional instances of Heather's lying over a two-week period. In terms of peer relationships, Heather was identified as a liar by only two classmates while two responses labeled her as a best friend. A teacher checklist indicated numerous externalizing characteristics such as disobedience; a tendency to argue, lie, and cheat; and stubbornness. Heather's grades were in the C to D range. Her parents were described as inappropriately punitive and restrictive, with much disharmony in the relationship between them and Heather. This assessment data led the psychologist to speculate that lying was a component of Heather's more global defiance of her parents' severe parenting style.

INTERVENTIONS: Although a strict behavioral approach to reducing lying is not endorsed, the author points out that contingencies should be managed in a way that diminishes rewards for lying while expanding opportunities to reward honesty. For example, an uncovered lie that was designed to avoid punishment for misbehavior should result in punishment for both the lie and the original offense, while a self-motivated confession of wrongdoing should reduce the penalty intended for the misdeed. Furthermore, as lying is typically one symptom of a larger problem, treatment strategies should address the problem rather than the individual lie. For example, contracting has shown promise as a treatment strategy for antisocial behaviors while behavioral or cognitively based social skills training has the potential to assist youngsters who must learn the basic thinking and behavior strategies necessary for social success.

When dysfunctional parent-child relationships lead to lying, parent training programs can help parents learn and practice more effective management techniques. For the child who impulsively lies for no particular gain, research with self-control training programs is demonstrating some effect on impulse control. Finally, adults can help children who assert wishes as truth by carefully rephrasing or reframing the falsehood as a true wish in a nondefensive, respectful manner. When attention is given to the broader patterns of disorder, of which lying may be a part, there may be a concurrent decrease in the child's lying behavior.

COMMENTARY: Other chapters in this book focus more specifically on the techniques briefly described here. The important point is that lying is rarely if ever a single, independent behavior. It almost always occurs as an underlying part of a larger syndrome. Thus, while adults must react appropriately to the lie itself, they must also address the bigger picture from which the lie draws its motivation.

SOURCE: Hughes, J. (1987). Children and lying. In A. Thomas & J. Grimes (Eds.), *Children's needs: Psychological perspectives* (pp. 335–342). Washington, DC: National Association of School Psychologists.

Additional Readings

Henderson, J. Q. (1983). Follow-up of stealing behavior in twenty-seven youths after a variety of treatment programs. *Journal of Behavior Therapy and Experimental Psychiatry, 14,* 331–337.

Eight different treatment approaches to reduce stealing were compared in this retrospective study utilizing the case histories of twenty-seven children. The treatments were no direct treatment; counseling, individualized combined treatment (ICT) that included relaxation, biofeedback, suggestion, covert practice, and various operant techniques; residential/hospital placement for emotional disturbance or mental retardation; day special education class; respondent/operant strategies; court-ordered punishment; and boarding school not considered under residential placement above. Children treated with ICT spent only 2.5 percent of their subsequent time stealing while those treated with other methods spent 45.6 percent of their follow-up time stealing. Special education and residential placements were the least effective of all methods. Furthermore, 20 percent of those treated by ICT returned to stealing within two years while 60 percent stole again after other treatments. For those who received no treatment, 75 percent engaged in theft within two years. The *ICT Stealing Treatment Manual* may be obtained from the Chief Psychologist, Department of Education, Private Bag, Government Buildings, Wellington, New Zealand. More detailed description of the ICT techniques is provided in Henderson, J. Q. (1981). A behavioral approach to stealing: A proposal for treatment based on ten cases. *Journal of Behavior Therapy and Experimental Psychiatry, 12,* 231–236.

Houser, B. B. (1982). Student cheating and attitude: A function of classroom control techniques. *Contemporary Educational Psychology, 7,* 113–123.

Fourth-, fifth-, and sixth-grade students were directed by a teacher to follow instructions and not cheat while taking a test. Instructions were given under five different social influence conditions: reward power, coercive power, legitimate power, referent power, and informational power. Reward and coercive power are based on the teacher's power to reward or punish behavior (for example, children who do not cheat can go to recess early, or students who cheat must go to the office); legitimate power derives from the teacher's right to direct behavior (for example, as your teacher, I am directing you not to cheat); referent power is generated by the student's desire to identify with the teacher or a particular group (for example, your friends did not cheat and I hope you wish to do as well); finally, informational power relates to the teacher's ability to change the students' perceptions (for example, completing this task without cheating will teach you something important for the future).

Students cheated the least and expressed the most favorable attitudes toward the teacher under the coercive influence condition. The author suggests that students may have viewed the teacher's use of coercive power as legitimate and within her rights as a teacher. The author recommends awareness but cautious use of coercive power, as there are limitations and potential side effects such as possible modeling of coercive behavior by students, persistence of disruptive behavior in problem youngsters, interference with learning, and loss of power over time. Other cautions are also cited.

Miller, G. E., & Klungness, L. (1989). Childhood theft: A comprehensive review of assessment and treatment. *School Psychology Review, 18,* 82–97.

Although nonconfrontive stealing is the most prevalent crime in the public schools and is associated with later delinquency, school failure, and emotional disorder, little is known about effective treatment strategies for this behavior. In addition, assessment approaches are of questionable reliability and validity, there are no clear diagnostic criteria for judging the seriousness of stealing at given age levels, detecting and defining a stealing episode is often problematic, data assessing conditions that cue stealing behavior as well as the personal and social consequences of stealing need to be further developed, and input is often difficult to obtain from parents because of their reported lack of insight and more detached parenting styles.

Given the limitations of each assessment method, the authors recommend a broad-based analysis of the child's stealing behavior encompassing the following: (1) observation; (2) interviews; (3) behavior ratings; (4) self-reports; (5) use of multiple informants; (6) assessment of possible co-varying behaviors such as lying, truancy, fire setting, and vandalism; (7) a clear definition of stealing so that those reporting the behavior may have a reliable set of criteria by which to judge its occurrence and severity; (8) full exploration of the antecedent and consequent events surrounding the theft; (9) assessment of adult stress and social supports; (10) attitudes of important people in the child's life toward antisocial behavior; (11) analysis of the effect of the child's "stealer" reputation on self-esteem, peer relationships, and adult attitudes; and (12) review of the child management skills of significant adults including degree of supervision, discipline strategies, and quality of the relationship between the adult and the child.

Having cited these diagnostic techniques, the authors then advocate the use of five specific steps to prevent stealing and treat its occurrence: (1) Giving specific instruction for all adults who have a significant relationship with the child on defining and labeling stealing events so that there is consistent and immediate response to the behavior. (2) Teaching child management skills to the adults so they may more effectively monitor free time, track occurrences of stealing, respond appropriately to positive behavior, provide reliable and suitable praise, and use effective disciplinary strategies. Providing adults with needed support and the coping skills to handle stress in their own lives will also assist them in managing the child's behavior. (3) Teaching the child self-control strategies to provide more timely contingencies, encourage self-management of stealing behavior, and allow the child to break the chain of events leading to the act of theft — for example, engaging in substitute antecedent behavior using imagery to project mental punishments as a deterrent to stealing behavior, or creating a self-instructional sequence to block stealing-related cognitions. (4) Targeting behaviors that co-vary with stealing but are more available to intervention. Rewarding positive behaviors so that the reinforcement obtained from stealing is replaced by other positive consequences, preferably of the child's choosing. (5) Altering environments in which a child operates (especially the school) so that appropriate relational and achievement needs, among others, can be met within that setting. Establishing clear rules for behavior and realistic disciplinary policies developed by all members of the school community also help create a preventive climate to deter stealing. Securing the physical premises and monitoring building areas likely to be visited by thieves is yet another deterrent. Finally, educational programs should be instituted to alter accepting attitudes regarding criminal behavior by focusing on the consequences of stealing, the available prosocial substitutes, the effect of positive role models, and the media endorsement of these activities.

Mills, R. K. (1988). Using Tom and Huck to develop moral reasoning in adolescents: A strategy for the classroom. *Adolescence: 23,* 325–329.

"Value" education involves the teaching and application of critical thinking and reasoning skills to the solution of moral dilemmas. Issues such as responsibility, fairness, right and wrong, intent, and caring raise moral questions. Moral education should help students examine alternative solutions, explore personal values, and enhance their own moral development. Research suggests that value education strategies can contribute to moral growth. The author suggests using works of fiction in the classroom to expose students to moral dilemmas. Fictional figures face many moral predicaments and are often confronted by alternative solutions in the form of other characters in the book. Using these realized creations, students are able to analyze moral issues without personalizing the problems as their own. *The Adventures of Huckleberry Finn* is cited as a fictional work well suited for this purpose. The author lists questions related to significant moral problems in the story that can be considered by students individually and in small groups. In every case, each group develops a solution and reports it to the class. Responses are listed on the board. Through this process, the author hopes that students will learn how to approach some of the crucial moral problems they will face in their own lives.

Olson, J. R. (1981). Curbing vandalism and theft. *Educational Horizons, 59,* 195–197.

A three-phase program to lessen incidences of theft and vandalism at Memorial High School in Madison, Wisconsin, was derived from Kohlberg's model of moral development; it addresses the various stages of moral reasoning present within the high school student population. Causes of vandalism are first characterized according to their association with pre-moral, preconventional, or conventional modes of moral thinking. Methods to curtail vandalism and theft are then grouped to match and respond to these three stages, resulting in a broad-based program of management, apprehension, and prevention in phase 1, deterrence through capture and punishment in phase 2, and a longer-term reshaping of attitudes and norms regarding vandalism and theft in stage 3.

To combat the vandal or thief who functions at the pre-moral stage of decision making, who has no developed sense of right or wrong, and who does not fear punishment, the school's response should consist of protecting the environment through installation, repair, and replacement of security devices and vandal-proof materials; frequent checking of buildings, particularly on weekends; and monitoring the time and location of thefts and acts of vandalism. Also suggested are cash rewards for information resulting in the capture of perpetrators, and orientation of students at the start of school to the causes and prevention of theft and protection of personal items. The vandal or thief at the stage of preconventional reasoning is influenced by rewards and punishment, making the cash incentive for information an important deterrent. The fact that those who committed these acts were caught and rewards given should be advertised as a further restraint on the preconventional thinker.

Conventional reasoning, in which group and family norms and conventions take precedence, requires a more extended process of altering attitudes in younger students so that not stealing or destroying property becomes the accepted value, and students take the responsibility to report acts of theft or vandalism. In this phase, high school students visit with elementary and middle school children to discuss controlling vandalism and theft and their role in the effort. For their work, they are publicly commended and their work is reported by the newspapers. Over five years, this program has reduced the cost of vandalism by almost 75 percent and the number of acts from ninety-seven to thirty per year.

Sauer, R. (1983). Coping with the copiers. *English Journal, 72,* 50–52.

Although it is virtually impossible to stop students from copying or reusing others' papers, steps can be taken to minimize these occurrences: (1) Be objective. Look for evidence of copying in the paper itself. Take advantage of your position as an expert with training and experience in reviewing and grading papers. (2) Develop a policy that outlines the steps taken when plagiarism is uncovered. Better yet, a building or department policy would have more force. (3) Know when there is a lack of evidence to pursue a suspected case of copying. (4) Question a student in a tactful, nonaccusatory manner when there is reasonable suspicion. Asking for a draft of the paper may be appropriate. But without evidence and/or an admission of guilt, there is little to pursue. (5) When confronted with two identical papers, the teacher can grade the first one and fail the second, grade the first, fail the second, and give the average of the two to both, or give different low grades to both, letting them come forward to discuss the situation. The teacher can notify students by attaching a note to their graded papers stating the conviction with evidence that copying has occurred, the policy in such matters, the decision regarding the consequences, and how the teacher can be contacted. The students should have the opportunity to comment as they read the note. (6) Retain student papers on file and let students know. (7) Develop new ways to teach and measure performance. This avoids the routines that may lead to increased opportunity for copying.

Schab, F. (1980). Cheating in high school: Differences between the sexes (revisited). *Adolescence, 15,* 959–965.

This survey on cheating behavior by high school students was originally done in 1969 and replicated ten years later. The author discusses cheating as reported by students to be a serious problem, becoming even more serious. Cheating is reportedly occurring more frequently with girls and so-called good students. Copying, forging parents' and teachers' signatures, plagiarism, and keeping found money or valuables are all occurring with greater regularity. Cheating on tests is indicated as more common, with fewer students willing to report a friend for cheating. More students view dishonesty as at times necessary and see adults as more dishonest than children. They often believe that crime does pay, and more frequently, they doubt the honesty of teachers. The author does not directly relate these changes to the events of the 1970s but does note their coincidence in time.

Stouthamer-Loeber, M. (1986). Lying as a problem behavior in children: A review. *Clinical Psychology Review, 6,* 267–289.

This paper reviews the limited research on lying including studies on general problem behaviors that include information on lying. Lying in children is viewed as a possible forerunner of later antisocial behavior as well as a related component of serious emotional disorder. Teachers, clinicians, and students all rank lying as highly serious behavior. Although no studies examine parents' perceptions of the seriousness of lying, parents in one study rated honesty as a highly desirable behavior for ten- to eleven-year-old children. Furthermore, while longitudinal patterns of lying have yet to be adequately researched, lying is found in all age groups beginning as young as four to five years of age. The data also suggest lower rates of lying in girls than boys. Lying is more prevalent in clinical as opposed to nonreferred children; it seems more closely but not exclusively related to covert antisocial behaviors such as fire setting, gang membership, and alcohol/drug use compared to the more overt behaviors of arguing, demanding, swearing, rowdiness, and hyperactivity.

An interactional relationship is presumed to exist between lying and other antisocial behaviors, but there is no agreement on which behaviors are more likely to lead to lying and which behaviors are in turn encouraged by lying. Available longitudinal studies reveal a moderate relationship between lying and later pathology and criminal conviction, but no evidence exists that associates childhood lying with later cultivation of close personal relationships. The article further discusses conditions that may enhance or inhibit the tendency to lie, including the degree of parental warmth/rejection, stability of the home, degree and skill of parent supervision, consistency and style of discipline, parental honesty, association with peers rated by mother as undesirable, group norms of loyalty, and pressure to achieve in school.

In regard to treatment, little research is cited, but the following suggestions are offered: (1) Rather than punishment, young children may need to be taught truth from falsehoood to help them better grasp reality-fantasy distinctions and understand how their actions affect others. (2) Older children may require contingency-oriented responses to their more knowing and sophisticated lies. In fact, rather than requiring the parent to shoulder the burden of separating truth from lie, frequent liars might be made to furnish proof of their honesty. (3) Parents need to be involved in their children's lives, not just to supervise but to help cement the bonds that might ultimately reduce their need to lie. Finally, the author indicates the need for further study of this still relatively unexplored phenomenon of lying.

Truancy

When truant children are not in school, they cannot learn and the possibility of their failing is enhanced. However, recent perspectives on truancy make it hard to view the problem as a simplistic outgrowth of individual student pathology or academic under-achievement. Multiple causes seem to influence unexcused nonattendance, among them economic and family instability, differences in learning styles, social skill deficits, in-stitutional rigidity, pregnancy and parenthood, the need to work, ethnic membership, and parental abuse. Thus, instead of counseling students for maladjustment, practitio-ners seem to be focusing their interventions more on enhancing the cognitive and social skills that enable students to better manage the problems or attitudes maintaining their truant behavior pattern.

Cross-Age Tutoring to Reduce Truancy

AUTHOR: Charles A. Maher

PRECIS: Cross-age tutoring improved the attendance of tutors as well as the academic performance of both the tutor and the student being tutored while reducing tutor behavior problems

INTRODUCTION: Cross-age tutoring in which older students tutor younger students has been found to benefit both the tutor and the recipient on a variety of academic measures. Such programs have the additional advantage of enlarging the pool of instructional providers, demonstrating the ability of the school practitioner to develop such resources, and providing added services for children with school-related problems, particularly in urban settings. However, it is less clear from the research whether the pupils taking part derive any social or emotional gain from the experience. In this applied research, the author directly replicated his previous study on cross-age tutoring with handicapped adolescents and elementary school students in order to strengthen the data base for this intervention and advocate its use with greater confidence.

STUDENTS: Eight students receiving resource support for their regular education classes were randomly selected as tutors from each of two high schools. They ranged in age from fourteen years, five months, to sixteen years, five months; all were designated under New Jersey mandates as emotionally disturbed, displaying problems such as cutting and truancy, fighting, verbal abuse of teachers, refusal to work, and general disruptiveness. Sixteen educable mentally retarded youngsters ages nine years, three months, to twelve years, one month, attending self-contained classrooms in two schools, were selected by teacher judgment to be the children tutored. They were not considered to have emotional problems.

PROGRAM: The ten-week program consisted of four components: (1) Training: Tutors were trained in three two-hour workshops conducted by counselors who were first trained by the author. Counselors used lectures, discussion formats, role-playing, simulated tutoring sessions, and feedback to teach tutors the information, skills, and attitudes necessary for program success. Tutors learned about their tutees, the special education teacher, subjects to be taught, and methods for planning and tutoring. They were instructed on how to develop goals and tutoring topics with the special education teacher, how to help tutees with their work, and how to reward work accuracy. Accepting support from the counselor-trainers and attending and participating faithfully in all aspects of the program were also addressed. (2) Planning: Weekly fifteen-minute conferences were held between the tutor and the special education teacher to review the previous tutoring sessions and develop the focus, method, and materials for the next two weekly meetings. (3) Tutoring: Two thirty-minute weekly sessions were held in which the tutor defined the goals for the session, answered questions about the materials, helped the tutee work on and complete all tasks, and provided appropriate social reinforcement. (4) Tutor support: Three two-hour meetings were held with the counselors over the ten weeks to receive feedback from the special education teachers, discuss successes and concerns, and receive advice and reassurance. Individual counselor–tutor conferences were also possible.

RESULTS: Records kept by participants and observational data gathered during the ten-week period indicated that all components of the program were carried out as planned. On the five outcome measures evaluating the program's effect on tutors, the following results were obtained: (1) Completed assignments: School A tutors were found as a group to have increased their mean percentage of completed tasks per week from 63.6 percent at baseline to 93.1 percent during the program and 91.5 percent during follow-ups. School B tutors increased from 68 percent per week at baseline to 88.6 percent and 87 percent during intervention and follow-up, respectively. (2) Tests and quizzes: For High School A, the mean weekly percentage of correct answers on tests rose from 59.5 percent at baseline to 83.4 percent and 81.9 percent during implementation and follow-up; for High School B, the 60.7 percent baseline rate rose to 87.2 percent during the program and to 84.3 percent during follow-up. (3) School attendance: High School A tutors increased their weekly attendance from a mean baseline of 72 percent to 96.5 percent during the program and 94.3 percent during follow-up; the High School B tutor baseline rate was 79 percent, rising to 96.1 percent during the program and to 91.7 percent at follow-up. (4) Disciplinary referrals: High School A disciplinary referrals averaged 4.5 per week during baseline, 1.4 during intervention, and 1.25 during follow-up. High School B referrals were 2.5 at baseline, 1.1 during intervention, and 1.3 at follow-up. (5) Tutor reactions: Tutors indicated that the program made them more aware of setting aside study time, helped them appreciate the planning done by teachers, motivated them to perform better in school, and made them more hopeful about prospects for their own academic success. They felt the program helped the tutees by assisting the teachers to provide better services, improving tutees' grades, and offering a personal relationship with an older student. Some of the tutors felt that it was not advantageous for the program to end, and thirteen of the sixteen tutors offered to continue tutoring their youngsters.

Two measures of tutee success were gathered: (1) Completed work: In Elementary School A, the mean percentage of assignments completed for the tutee group was 71.9 percent at baseline, 93.3 percent during the program, and 90.6 percent at follow-up. For School B, the figures were 73.9 percent at baseline, 85.4 percent for the intervention, and 82.4 percent at follow-up. (2) Tests and quizzes: In Elementary School A, the group mean percentage of items correct was 69 percent at baseline, 84.3 percent for the intervention, and 80.9 percent at follow-up. For School B, the results were 69.6 percent, 84.3 percent, and 81 percent for baseline, intervention, and follow-up rates, respectively.

COMMENTARY: The author stresses that the success of this direct replication and the fact that the intervention was carried through as planned allows the procedure to be recommended with considerable confidence as an effective strategy for use within a school setting. A distinguishing feature identified by the counselor-trainers was the clarity with which the program was defined and planned. The author highlights the need for those originating such programs to specify in distinct, understandable language the goals and steps involved.

If school administrators and staff are to be convinced that the program's outcome will be worth the required commitment of effort and personnel, they will need to understand fully its aims, sequence of events, and rationale. A point worth noting for such a discussion is that the program as described here is extremely cost effective, costing approximately $2,600, a figure much lower than that of many other instructional services.

Finally, there is no need to limit the tutors and tutees to the categories of students described in this study. Other populations need to become involved to test the program's range and integrity under varying conditions. From an ecological perspective, one may ask under what organizational climate conditions might a school district implement this project most successfully. While there are numerous research questions still to be answered, there is also a fairly solid empirical basis for moving ahead with this program should the practitioner be so inclined.

SOURCE: Maher, C. (1986). Direct replication of a cross-age tutoring program involving handicapped adolescents and children. *School Psychology Review, 15,* 100–118.

Training Cognitive and Social Problem-Solving Skills

AUTHORS: Irwin G. Sarason and Barbara R. Sarason

PRECIS: Reducing school truancy, lateness, and behavior referrals through the teaching of social and cognitive skills for effective problem solving

INTRODUCTION: Students who are unsuccessful in school, who achieve poorly, who have high truancy and dropout rates, and who are often disruptive in class typically lack the cognitive and social skills needed to think through and solve problems of everyday living. Skills training programs may be designed to teach these students how to engage in adaptive behaviors and thus enhance their opportunities for successful life experiences. The authors report on a social and cognitive skills modeling intervention with urban high school students at significant risk for dropping out and engaging in delinquent acts.

METHOD: Intensive interviews were conducted before the program began with students attending the targeted high schools, former dropouts, teachers, counselors, and employers to determine the specific cognitive and/or social skill deficits responsible for the problems these at-risk students often encountered. Respondents reported an inability to consider behavioral alternatives or consequences, approach teachers and employers in a suitable manner, assert themselves appropriately, postpone immediate gratification, tolerate delay in solving problems, or develop problem-solving strategies. Students self-reported impulsivity, appeared disinterested about the impact of their current behavior on their future, and considered school virtually irrelevant. They tended to give up or disappear when faced with a difficult academic task or minor problem at work, had little understanding of how their actions affected others, and could not appreciate alternative points of view.

Once the students' deficient skills were targeted, real-life scripts for role-playing were developed and refined with the help of paid students from the school. Pilot studies determined that role-play would be more effective than discussion in maintaining students' attention, so the program itself used both live and videotaped models. One hundred twenty-seven students with a mean age of fourteen years, eight months, participated in the program, which ran for thirteen health classes; in the program, trained psychology graduate students addressed a different skill area each session. They began with a brief orientation to the skill, described its importance for competent thinking, problem solving, and behavior, and elicited students' related experiences.

Following the introduction, one group observed the live role-plays while the other was exposed to videotaped performances. All were acted by students from the school. A control group attended regular health classes. The following topics were enacted through role-plays: (1) having a job interview, (2) countering peer pressure, (3) soliciting help in school, (4) asking questions in class, (5) establishing good relations with your employer, (6) handling job-related frustrations, (7) cutting classes, (8) seeking help at work, and (9) relating to parents. A sample script on cutting class was presented in the article; it dramatized a conversation in which Tom attempts to persuade Jim to cut school for an afternoon party. Jim provides reasons that he can't cut, but Tom persists, informing Jim that Lydia, a girl Jim would like to date, will be there. Jim thinks out loud that although he wants to attend the party and perhaps ask Lydia out, he also needs to be in class.

While he privately considers the possibility that he could cut and study harder on Saturday, he questions his ability to follow through. The skit ends with Jim reserving his decision.

Each role-play and remarks by group leaders addressed perspective taking, consideration of alternatives, and appropriate interactions with adults, as well as the theme itself. After students viewed the scene, some were requested to give summaries of what they had seen; next, the leaders presented those tenets of social behavior illustrated in the episode. Volunteers then role-played the more skilled behavior, using the principles discussed. All students were encouraged to join in the role-plays while leaders praised participation and corrected student enactments gently and supportively.

Eight homework assignments requiring about five minutes to complete were scattered throughout the program. They described a scenario illustrating the skill issues from the school sessions, followed by review questions. The example in the article depicts a clerical worker who does not know what "collate" means or how to file some papers when asked by her boss to do so. She thinks about asking someone but does not want to appear stupid or get fired. So she guesses what to do, is wrong, and is strongly reprimanded by her boss for not asking. The questions ask why the boss was angry, why the worker did not ask for help, why her cognitions were not helpful, what she might have considered to convince her to ask for help, how her boss would have reacted to her seeking help, and alternatives to asking her boss.

Students' completed assignments and scores on tests given at the midpoint session and at the end of the program were credited toward their health grades.

RESULTS: Five indices of program effectiveness were described: (1) performance on measures of test anxiety and locus of control; (2) the student's ability to list intermediate goal-oriented behaviors (known as *means*) leading to a successful outcome when presented with anecdotes describing only the initial problem; (3) the student's ability to think through alternative solutions when presented with two problem situations (for example, you want to watch a TV special but your brother is watching his favorite program); (4) performance on job interviews set up months later without the student's awareness of the connection between the interviews and the program; and (5) measures of absences, lateness, and behavior referrals for the year following the program. Students in both the live and videotape modeling groups listed significantly more means behaviors and realistic alternative solutions than did the control group. Furthermore, while both high and low test anxiety students in the experimental group generated significantly more means than students not in the program, high test anxiety students performed better than low anxiety students, suggesting that the former were more positively influenced by the modeled skills training experience.

While just eight students receiving the program and six students from the control group were interviewed for jobs (suggesting that caution should be used in data interpretation), only the students exposed to the live role-plays were judged significantly more effective than the control group. Live model students also displayed significantly more eye contact than either the video modeling group or the controls. However, the students involved with the video models in turn showed significantly more eye contact than the control students. Although data for absences, lateness, and behavior referrals were limited to seventy-five students and means for each area were small, significant differences were reported between role-play and control groups on all three measures.

COMMENTARY: This study demonstrates that cognitive and social skills can be taught to young adolescents in the classroom within a reasonable time period, and that they seem to have some effect in reducing the students' absenteeism, lateness, and referrals for behavior problems. The program does not attack truancy directly but attempts to strengthen skills associated with competent problem solving, thus reducing the need to resort to the maladaptive coping behavior of truancy. In this regard, cognitive and social skill training has the potential to affect a wide range of competencies for teenagers. An interesting point made by the authors is the importance of gathering information from the students regarding those life experiences most affected by their social and cognitive deficiencies. This program truly requires a cooperative interaction between providers and recipients to make the role-plays more relevant and realistic. Perhaps as the authors suggest, this is one component enhancing its success.

SOURCE: Sarason, I. G., & Sarason, B. R. (1981). Teaching cognitive and social skills to high school students. *Journal of Counseling and Clinical Psychology, 49,* 908–918.

Computerized Absence Reporting

AUTHORS: Carroll M. Helm and Charles W. Burkett

PRECIS: Reducing school nonattendance by use of a computer-assisted calling device to inform the home of daily absences

INTRODUCTION: Research consistently shows that when parents are telephoned on days their children are absent from school, attendance rates improve significantly compared with rates of students whose homes are not called. Students who do not attend school regularly may be experiencing a personal crisis or may be prime candidates for dropping out of school. By developing strategies that improve attendance, schools are not only helping

students but are also increasing their revenues, since most funding mechanisms factor daily attendance into the final formula. This study compared
attendance rates for pupils who received computer-dialed telephone messages with students who were not called.

METHOD: Fifty students were selected randomly from each of two high
schools and one middle school to serve as experimental subjects. The same
procedure was used to select the control group for a total of 150 in each group.
Letters were sent to the parents indicating that a computer-dialing instrument was being tested and soliciting their voluntary cooperation. Beginning
the first month of the school year and continuing to May, the names of absent students were programmed into the device on a daily basis. The machine
began continuous calls to the homes of these students at 6 P.M. until someone answered. The recorded message from the principal identified the caller,
indicated that the child was absent that day, and encouraged the home to
call the named contact person at the school to ask questions, comment, or
indicate that the recorded absence was an error. After thanking the parent,
the message ended. Each day the machine listed those called, who was contacted, and who was not contacted. After the study was completed, attendance records for experimental and control groups were compared. Results
showed a significant difference in absentee rate. Called students were absent an average of 6.55 days while those not called showed a mean of 11.18
absences. Sex of the student, socioeconomic status, race, and school of attendance made no difference.

COMMENTARY: In previous research digested in *Therapies for School Behavior Problems,* the attendance of elementary school students was improved
when either the principal or a school secretary called the home with increasingly serious messages after a predetermined sequence of absences. This study
extends the age range into middle and high school levels and utilizes a
computer-assisted calling device. In both instances, the principal was relieved
of the time-consuming responsibility of making the calls, while in the procedure described above, no staff person needed to spend the time. It should
be noted that the recorded message did not make critical comments regarding nonattendance; it simply stated the fact and offered the opportunity for
further discussion. This seems the best course of action, particularly if the
absenteeism is a precursor to more serious issues that would require ongoing home–school contact.

SOURCE: Helm, C. M., & Burkett, C. W. (1989). Effects of computer-
assisted telecommunications on school attendance. *Journal of Educational Research, 82,* 362–365.

Additional Readings

Hess, A. M., Rosenberg, M. S., & Levy, G. K. (1990). Reducing truancy in students with mild handicaps. *Remedial and Special Education, 11,* 14–19.

Contingency contracting was combined with group counseling in a ten-week program to reduce truancy, raise school performance, and maintain improvement after the intervention was discontinued. Twenty-six mildly to moderately handicapped students ranging in age from eleven years, one month, to sixteen years, six months, were subjects. The experimental group selected rewards for their individual weekly contract, which was then developed to include behavior criteria to be met, the rewards to be given, and the signature of the student. Daily progress was monitored. Counseling focused on the inappropriateness of truancy and encouraged the decision to attend school. Each student reported on his or her attendance and focused discussion on group members who were not attending, exploring the irrational beliefs involved. Solutions were examined and students committed to attending during the coming week. Control students did not participate in the program.

Although results indicated a significant decrease (49 percent) in weekly truancy rates for the experimental group, counseling sessions failed to maintain this improvement during follow-up. Grade point averages were unaffected by treatment, although significantly fewer students in the program were retained, compared with control students. The authors stress the importance of developing other approaches to discipline besides suspension or transfer, and describe the need to research other strategies such as parent participation, meetings with counselors, or other methods that may maintain treatment effects over time.

Lazerson, D. B., Foster, H. L., Brown, S. I., & Hummel, J. W. (1988). The effectiveness of cross-age tutoring with truant junior high school students with learning disabilities. *Journal of Learning Disabilities, 21,* 253–255.

A cross-age tutoring program had eleven- to fifteen-year-old learning disabled truant and tardy students tutor disabled elementary and intermediate grade students who were six to ten years old. Truancy was defined as illegitimate absence at least one day per week, tardiness as lateness to at least five classes per week. Tutors were trained on the general requirements of service, how to reward good performance, how to correct wrong answers, and understanding the program. The program lasted six weeks with tutoring sessions occurring three times weekly for at least twenty minutes. After the program, tutors showed a substantial increase toward an internal locus of control, and reduced their instances of truancy from a weekly mean of 2.5 to .5. Tardiness decreased from a mean of four instances per day to 1.5. Four tutors stopped truancy completely while seven were no longer late to any classes. Responses by tutors to questionnaires indicated that social ostracism from their peers and adults was the primary reason for their truancy, not academic failure. This study like others supports the importance of the social context as a significant factor in truancy, perhaps even more significant than academic status. Tutoring may be effective because of the social skills it reinforces and the sense of personal control it fosters.

Maher, C. A. (1981). Effects of involving conduct problem adolescents in goal setting: An exploratory investigation. *Psychology in the Schools, 18,* 471–474.

Adolescents in grades 10 to 12 with conduct problems (including truant students) were assigned to counselors for weekly sessions as part of a behavioral counseling program. Level 1 pupils actively participated in setting counseling goals while level 2 students had goals set for them. Goal-setting students helped identify the problems to be addressed in counseling (for example, truancy), helped set the behavioral goals (for example, improved attendance), and helped develop a scale to measure achievement of the goal. Students in level 2 had no similar involvement but knew goals were set. Counseling sessions focused on circumstances blocking achievement of the goal and the development of problem-solving competencies. Results indicated significantly higher levels of goal attainment and greater expressed satisfaction with the counseling experience by level 1 students. No follow-up data were gathered. While the author identified this research as preliminary in nature, it does suggest that involvement in goal setting enhances students' achievement of counseling goals and increases their satisfaction with the intervention.

Miller, D. (1986). Effect of a program of therapeutic discipline on the attitude, attendance, and insight of truant adolescents. *Journal of Experimental Education, 55,* 49–53.

A one-day program of therapeutic discipline for truancy is described as an alternative to traditional suspension. Students are kept in school to examine and try to change their behavior using a cognitively oriented skills training format rather than being sent home. The dean first met with the student to describe the program and his expectations for success. The student then attended the suspension center in school where she worked on a cognitively based bibliotherapy packet of stories, essays, and written exercises addressing the reasons for truancy, its self-defeating consequences, and possible solutions. The supervising adult helped the student work through the materials in a therapeutic manner, then sent the student to the dean to discuss the materials when completed. Issues from the packet related to truancy were highlighted along with steps the student might take to address the problem. A ten-day contingency contract was then drawn up; it required the student to self-monitor attendance through graphing and daily notes to the dean. After day 10 student and dean met again to discuss progress. After forty days the student was administered a survey assessing her attitudes toward attendance. Control group students were disciplined with warnings of further action, were required to do classwork in the suspension center, and received no counseling. Results showed that the therapeutic discipline produced less positive attitudes toward school attendance but better attendance, less truant absences, and more self-help insights regarding ways to reduce nonattendance. An understanding of which components of the program were responsible for change in attendance will require further research.

Schloss, P. J., Kane, M. S., & Miller, S. (1981). Truancy intervention with behavior disordered adolescents. *Behavioral Disorders, 6,* 175–179.

   An approach to motivating the return to school of three chronically truant young adolescents began with uncovering the variables linked to poor attendance. Interviews with the parents, target students, and teachers requested information about behavior and attitudes of the child when home from school, feelings about school, steps taken to return the child to school, patterns of school attendance, relations with classmates, general school behavior, willingness to participate in this program, and other issues. The responses given were used to develop strategies for the following goals: (1) increased satisfaction with school; (2) decreased satisfaction with staying home; (3) social skills training to assist the student in benefiting from the school experience. Strategies for these goals might include such activities as reducing work demands, reducing peer conflicts, increasing rewards for work done, increasing positive communications with parents, allowing the student to verbalize school-related concerns, providing work at home on days absent, going to the home to bring the student to school, administering punishment for refusal to attend, providing social skills training programs as well as specialized courses in shop, athletics, art, and others. For the three teens, attendance improved initially, then declined, then rose again after a series of home visits were made.

Svec, H. J. (1990). An advocacy model for the school psychologist. *School Psychology International, 11,* 63–70.

   Noting that dropouts do not necessarily differ from nondropouts on measures of cognitive functioning, achievement, and motivation, the author suggests that attributing dropping out to individual emotional or social maladjustment may obscure the inadequacies of the school in addressing the unique needs of the dropout population. Dropping out may result from a combination of factors such as behavior issues, physical abuse, social skills deficits, family strife, economic stress, learning styles, pregnancy, and truancy.

   The school psychologist is in a position to play a positive nonconfronting advocacy role by assisting the school in developing the flexibility required to accommodate these different needs. The first step is to define the institutional barrier preventing flexibility, identifying other more appropriate responses, understanding the reasons for the inflexible policy, planning steps to increase flexibility, providing positive consequences to reward new appropriate actions, assisting the student to develop new skills that encourage ongoing flexibility from the school, and continuing follow-up with the student and school. While traditional intervention strategies assume that change will come from the student, advocacy works to change the behavior of the institution to deal with student differences more effectively.

Classroom Disturbance

Classroom disturbance has been subdivided into the categories of boisterous or rowdy behavior, noncompliance, physical and verbal aggression, class clown, temper tantrums, annoying or bothering others, and out-of-seat (off-task) behavior. Teachers have long considered disruptive classroom behavior to be among the most debilitating impediments to effective teaching, and a wide variety of interventions, many based on the foundation research of the 1960s and 1970s, continue to be developed and refined to address these serious problems. The reader is reminded that while subsections provide a useful (if somewhat subjectively defined) method for classifying articles, human behavior is not so conveniently discrete. Articles often describe students with overlapping behavior problems, allowing any given technique to be potentially effective across categories.

Classroom Disturbance: Boisterous or Rowdy Behavior

Boisterous behavior is typically loud, intrusive, difficult to control, and disorderly. The child will call out without permission, often making inappropriate, attention-seeking, or disruptive comments. Without strategies to curb this behavior, the teacher may become trapped in a cycle of fruitless exchanges with the student.

Self-Management of Inappropriate Classroom Behavior

AUTHORS: Spencer J. Salend and Elizabeth Marie Allen

PRECIS: Externally managed and self-managed free token response cost systems equally effective in reducing inappropriate behavior

INTRODUCTION: Research has demonstrated the ability of students to self-manage their own reward/punishment contingencies for improved behavior. A free token response cost system may be self- or externally managed with success. In such a system, the student begins with a predetermined number of tokens that are given up as targeted inappropriate behaviors are displayed. Remaining tokens are then traded for reinforcers. Two learning disabled second graders were exposed to both conditions to determine their comparative effectiveness. One of the youngsters often called out and forgot to raise his hand while the other had trouble sitting still in his chair.

METHOD: The intervention was employed in the resource room during reading and math instruction. For the more boisterous student, talking without teacher permission was the targeted inappropriate behavior while out-of-seat behavior was identified for the other child. During an eleven-day baseline period, rates of these behaviors were tallied by the resource teacher. After baseline ended, the teacher described the experimental conditions in detail to the students and questioned them to make sure they understood. The first phase of intervention lasted nine days and consisted of two twenty-minute daily sessions that began with a statement by the resource room teacher as to which intervention was in effect.

Both students received both self- and externally managed conditions in a randomly determined fashion. A preset number of strips of one-by-three-inch construction paper corresponding to the number of misbehaviors allowed was taped to the students' desks (nine strips for the boisterous student, eight for the other; these were reduced to fewer than five by phase 2 of the study). For each occurrence of the target behavior, the teacher removed a token or the students themselves removed a token depending upon the condition. In the five-day second phase of treatment, the baseline and self-managed conditions were administered to the off-task student, while the boisterous student was exposed to an alternating baseline/external response-cost paradigm. Phase 3 repeated phase 1 for four days; phase 4 lasted five days and repeated the phase 2 comparisons except that the external and self-managed conditions were switched between the students. Phase 5 repeated phase 1 for five days.

Results for the boisterous student showed the self- and externally mediated free token response cost systems to be equally effective in reducing inappropriate talking out from a mean baseline of 11.3 occurrences per day to a phase 1 frequency of .44 times per day during the externally managed condition and .22 times during self-management. The interventions were equally successful during the remaining phases for both students.

COMMENTARY: Although both methods are equally effective, the authors suggest using the self-managed system for several reasons: (1) it requires students to self-monitor behavior and respond immediately; (2) self-management promotes long-term effects and generalization; (3) less responsibility is required of the teacher and the technique is less intrusive in the class; (4) there is less chance of communication breakdown between different external managers. The authors further caution against using this technique to reduce more serious or threatening behaviors that must be immediately controlled, or behaviors associated with significant cognitive impairment. This technique gradually reduces the problem behavior through differential reinforcement of low rates of responding (DRL schedule) and requires the requisite intellectual resources needed for self-management. Students with more debilitating or pathological disorders are either less able to master the appropriate skills for self-management or display behaviors that must be quickly controlled.

SOURCE: Salend, S. J., & Allen, E. M. (1985). Comparative effects of externally managed and self-managed response-cost systems on inappropriate classroom behavior. *Journal of School Psychology, 23,* 59–67.

Controlling Rowdy School Bus Behavior

AUTHORS: Brandon F. Greene, Jon S. Bailey, and Frank Barber

PRECIS: Reducing disruptive behavior on the school bus through visual feedback, contingent music, and raffles

INTRODUCTION: The need to adapt behavioral interventions for disruptive behavior on the school bus is underscored by the statistic that death in bus accidents occurs at a higher rate per million vehicle miles than general automobile fatalities. School bus drivers have been known to quit their jobs because of unmanageable behavior by students. This article presents two studies that apply behavior management strategies to reducing bus misbehavior.

STUDY I: The procedure was carried out on a forty-four-seat bus carrying sixth through eighth graders home from school. This bus was reported to have the most incidents of severe disorder during its mean run time of twenty-five minutes. Behaviors considered most offensive to the drivers were used as dependent measures, namely out-of-seat and rough behaviors such as hitting, grabbing, wrestling, and noise outbursts. Warnings by the driver to behave and related forceful comments were also tallied. A device called a noise guard was installed on the bus to record the number of outbursts above a preset noise threshold and the total length of time they lasted. In addition, a light panel above the windshield that was activated by the noise guard flashed in binary code the length of time noise outbursts remained above the threshold. Observers on the bus counted the number of children displaying the target behaviors.

After baseline rates were obtained, students were informed that the procedure was an attempt to promote bus safety. The following steps were described: (1) The lights on the display would stay on as long as noise levels remained above a certain level. (2) After a first day of noncontingent cassette music played on the bus through mounted speakers, noise levels for the bus ride could not remain above the threshold for longer than a predetermined cutoff time if the music was to be continued the next day. Tags on the light panels displayed the cutoff criterion, which was set at twenty-six seconds for day 1 of treatment (the students' best time during baseline). On day 2 this was reduced by one-half to thirteen seconds and then to five seconds each subsequent treatment day. (3) In addition to the music, four hamburger coupons would be raffled off before the bus left school if on the previous day time above the noise threshold remained below the criterion level. (4) For every five consecutive successful days, ten movie passes would be raffled. (5) Any student deliberately sabotaging the rewards would be referred to the principal.

During the treatment phaseout period, hamburgers were stopped and movie raffles were reduced to two a day contingent upon a successful preceding day. Results showed that when raffles and music were introduced, noise outbursts above threshold dropped from a baseline mean of 624.1 per trip to 27.7 per trip, with the total length of time of these outbursts reduced from 62.3 seconds per trip to 1.6 seconds. Comparable differences were recorded when baseline was reinstated followed by a second treatment condition. The phaseout stage maintained the lowered rates. Furthermore, warning and other coercive statements by drivers were lowered from an average baseline rate of 19 per trip to 2.2 during treatment 1, back up to 19.2 during the second baseline, down to 5.3 per trip during the second treatment phase, and held at 2.7 per trip during phaseout. Although not directly treated, out-of-seat behavior and roughhousing were also reduced through the intervention. Students gave positive reports about the project and felt it made for a better bus trip.

STUDY II: For this study, threshold noise levels for activating the noise guard were lowered. The authors suggested that study I students might have learned to engage in just enough disruptive behavior to avoid activating the device, thus producing a chain of events leading to more frequent above-threshold noise levels. Lowering the threshold would activate the lights earlier in the disruption process, perhaps short-circuiting the disruption while it was still relatively mild. In addition, raffles were eliminated, as this component involved soliciting community businesses, something school districts might not be willing to do. Similar students taking a similar bus run participated in study II, which was virtually unchanged from study I except for some modifications in the light panel, behavior observation procedures, and the cutoff criterion. As in study I, results showed significant reductions in the mean number and duration of above-threshold noise outbursts, even without the raffles. Furthermore, the pattern of reduction in out-of-seat behavior and roughhousing, particularly at the second treatment stage, indicated that the disruption process was blocked by lowering threshold levels.

COMMENTARY: It makes no sense to expend energy and resources maintaining a safe and positive atmosphere in the classroom and then to allow the bus ride to and from school to be uncontrolled. Students recognize that bus supervision is often minimal and some regard the trip home as an opportunity to "let loose," engage in rough behavior toward other students, and by their actions endanger the lives of peers and adults. Buses are an extension of the schoolhouse and school officials should expect the same standards of behavior they demand in the building. The procedure described here acknowledges that connection and seeks to utilize principles of classroom behavior management to reduce the threat of harm on the bus. While other steps may be required, such as placing additional aides on the bus or informing drivers about the nature of the population they are transporting (particularly with emotionally disturbed, mentally retarded, autistic, or multiply handicapped students), it is certainly best to try to break the disruption pattern before it reaches a danger level rather than responding punitively, which is often ineffective in the long run.

SOURCE: Greene, B. F., Bailey, J. S., & Barber, F. (1981). An analysis and reduction of disruptive behavior on school buses. *Journal of Applied Behavior Analysis, 14,* 177–192.

Structural Family Therapy to Modify Classroom Misbehavior

AUTHOR: Cindy I. Carlson

PRECIS: Using the structural model of brief family therapy to alter dysfunctional family patterns leading to school behavior problems

INTRODUCTION: Family dysfunction frequently contributes to the development and maintenance of school-based problems in children. Structural family therapy provides a model for evaluating and intervening in this family-school connection by utilizing time-limited directive strategies to alter the unstable patterns of family interaction that may underlie maladaptive school behaviors. In this model, the family is viewed as a system governed by a set of rules, expectations, and forces known collectively as a "structure," which determines how members of the system will relate to each other and to other systems, for example, the school. This structure has "boundaries," referring to the nature of the interactions and how they are conducted. Clearly defined boundaries with room for caring and exchange of communication are best for stable family interaction, whereas "enmeshed" or "disengaged" parent/child relationships indicate boundaries that are too diffuse or too rigid, leading to overdependence or alienation.

"Alignments" describe how family members join together to behave in certain ways and are another aspect of family structure. Dysfunctional alignments occur when parental conflicts are channeled through and reflected in the interactions with the child. For example, in "triangulation" each parent tries to align with the child against the other, while in the "detouring attacking coalition" the parents cover their conflicts by blaming all the existing problems on the child's misbehavior. A third element of family structure is "power," which refers to each member's ability to influence boundaries or alignments. Power determines the hierarchy of authority within the family, which can be harmonious or dysfunctional — for example, when children have more power than their parents. Finally, "organizational capacity" refers to the reliability and consistency of family operations. While a family's structure constantly shifts and changes depending upon the needs and stresses of living, problems arise when the structure is unbending and therefore unable to adapt to situational demands.

ASSESSMENT AND INTERVENTION: Structural family therapy begins with the psychologist obtaining information in the following areas: (1) how the family structure contributes to the problem behavior, (2) the structure's flexibility as indicated by the changing alliances and power patterns, (3) how attuned family members are to each other's needs, (4) the stresses and supports of the family, (5) the family's level of development and parent behavior, (6) the purpose of the problem behavior in maintaining or preventing relationships within the system, and (7) the home/school transactional pattern. The psychologist takes a direct role in observing, listening to, and investigating the family's relational style, developing hypotheses that are accepted or rejected on the basis of the inquiries and observations. The families are then assisted through "restructuring" or "redefining" to develop adaptive transactional structures that address the child's behavior symptoms more effectively. Restructuring techniques are designed to change the existing dysfunctional structure through changing alliances, altering power hierarchies, and other steps. Redefining attempts to help the family view symptoms from new perspectives.

CASE STUDY: Eight-year-old Douglas was referred for disruptive behavior in class, aggressive acts toward peers, and learning problems. An initial family interview yielded the following patterns of interaction: (1) no communication between father and son; (2) lack of participation by the father in reacting to Douglas's questions, disciplining him, or responding to the interviewer's questions about him; (3) Douglas's constant verbal and behavioral interruptions of the mother. On the basis of these observations, the structure of the family was hypothesized as an enmeshed mother/son and disengaged father/son relationship, with Douglas attempting unsuccessfully to align with his father against the mother and with no elements of alignment or mutual power sharing between the parents. Douglas seemed to have more power than his parents.

The presence of family routines suggested latent organizational strength, although the structure of the family was increasingly rigid. It was postulated that Douglas's behavior was a response to his anxiety regarding his distant father, weak parent controls, and rejection fears related to his adoptive status. The symptoms were therefore viewed as an attempt to challenge the parents' willingness and ability to function as a family. The family had few relatives or friendship supports. The relationship with the school was not positive, as the school's frustration with Douglas and comments by school staff lent support to the possibility that the school was blaming the mother for his behavior. From a developmental perspective, the family structure had not changed to accommodate Douglas's adoption, which had occurred one-and-a-half years before the referral.

INTERVENTION: Sixteen meetings with the family and/or the school staff were held. The first goal was to strengthen the parents as a team. This was accomplished in part through teaching them behavioral strategies they could apply together to manage Douglas's behavior and thus restore the appropriate hierarchy of authority at home. In-session tasks and homework fostered cooperative efforts between the parents. They were also helped to redefine Douglas's misbehavior as a wish for them to provide structure and communication. To clarify this concept, analogies were drawn for the parents that they were able to relate to their own life experiences. For example, Douglas's position was compared to that of a worker whose boss communicated unclear expectations for job performance. Teamwork was felt to have been achieved when the parents reported on their own plans to address management problems with Douglas.

Altering the enmeshed and disengaged relationships was the second goal. The father was helped to become more involved by emphasizing his knowledge of male behavior with peers and redefining his aloofness as a relaxed, unhurried quality during times of stress, which augmented his wife's more involved style. This approach resulted in more interaction from him during the family sessions. The mother was encouraged to let the father take over so she could relax and reprimand less. Douglas and his dad were assigned a night out together as homework; this event broadened into other such evenings and resulted in his father taking Douglas to work with him.

A final goal was repair of the relationship with the school. During a series of conferences, the staff's view of the parents was redefined to stress a "parents-in-training" perspective. Strategies for maintaining motivation were discussed with school staff, and as the year ended collaborative recommendations were made for Douglas to attend a camp for youngsters with behavior problems and for the family to stay in treatment. These steps provided a social skills training opportunity for Douglas, allowed him time away from his mother, and maintained the school's positive feelings about the prognosis for improvement.

COMMENTARY: Over the next school year, the parents continued in a parent education class and were able to handle problems with Douglas's behavior. The school reported no difficulties. Structural family therapy is a relatively brief, focused therapeutic approach with documented empirical evidence of utility. While it may be difficult to bring a whole family into school to interview them and observe their interactive style, it is an essential component of the strategy. In addition, a commitment is needed from the family to attend a minimum of eight to ten sessions, an achievement that may require careful assessment of the family's capacity to follow through.

The author stresses the need for certain preconditions to exist before such family interventions can occur in the school: (1) support from school administrators, (2) comprehensive training of the school psychologist, (3) financial ability to provide the needed services, (4) the ability of the system to manage family treatment within an educational context. While it may not be possible to utilize this specific family therapy technique in all school settings, knowledge of the structural model may provide the school psychologist with a general framework for family intervention as well as for involvement in other social systems.

SOURCE: Carlson, C. I. (1987). Resolving school problems with structural family therapy. *School Psychology Review, 16,* 457–468.

Additional Readings

Barbetta, P. M. (1990). Red light–green light: A classwide management system for students with behavior disorders in primary grades. *Preventing School Failure, 34,* 14–19.

Red light–green light is a classwide peer-mediated behavior management strategy providing immediate consequences for behavior throughout the school day. General classroom rules are first developed with student participation, from which specific behavioral expectations for given school activities are derived. Students are then taught through modeling, prompting, role-playing, and reinforcing feedback how to provide positive comments and helpful hints to peers as a way of praising or cueing good behavior. For the program itself, students can earn or lose up to seven points during each half-hour block of time for following or breaking rules, and gain other points for doing homework. After each half hour, the teacher tallies the points and indicates on the student's point sheet whether the student earned predetermined green light (seven–nine points), red light (one–three points), or yellow light (four points) privileges. The student then indicates the level earned by adjusting a "traffic light" overlay taped to the side of his or her desk to show the appropriate color. Bonus points that earn other privileges can be given by the teacher at any time for individual or group behavior. Privileges are structured by type and time required to fit the school day schedule, while other more delayed rewards can be provided, such as tokens for purchase of supplies and snacks, a no-homework night, tickets for a class lottery, a class movie when all members earn a preset number of green lights, and others. The last privilege illustrates how group contingencies can also be incorporated into the program. Students who lose more than seven points per half hour might require other more intensive contingencies or might lose points from the next time block. Furthermore, students who consistently reach the red light level may need such interventions as individual behavior contracts, social skills training, or other strategies. The authors suggest modifying the program for students who may be having more mainstream contact so that the demands of the mainstream class are more realistically portrayed — for example, extending the time blocks beyond half-hour segments (ultimately to full-day units), raising the number of points needed for each light zone, limiting rewards to those found in the mainstream, and using more mainstream-oriented behavior management approaches.

Grubaugh, S. (1989). Non-verbal language techniques for better classroom management and discipline. *The High School Journal, 73,* 34–40.

This article discusses the power of nonverbal communication in helping the teacher manage classroom behavior. Research suggests that most messages are communicated to students nonverbally and that students tend to believe the nonverbal more than the verbal message. Furthermore, proper use of body language has been shown to eliminate as much as 40 percent of the everyday misbehaviors that interfere with teaching. Body movement and position, facial expressions, and eye contact can all be used to transmit feelings of acceptance, interest, frustration, personal confidence, and other teacher messages to influence and control behavior. Students likewise give nonverbal clues to teachers about their attitudes or feelings such as difficulty with work, frustration, anger, confusion, or other emotional states, which, if read correctly, can short-circuit more serious disruption. Other techniques include use of physical proximity and silence.

Moving from the "public zone" (12 to 25 feet from the student) into the "social zone" (4 to 12 feet) is a method for controlling low-level misbehavior, while closer proximity within the "personal zone" (1½ to 4 feet) may make a more direct point or exert greater control when needed. Finally, touching the student (considered the "intimate zone") may serve yet another purpose, but should be done only under certain circumstances. When silence is used in combination with a particular body stance, the discomfort often engendered communicates a strong message to the class or individual student. Techniques for silencing a rowdy class or settling the class down for work include finger to lips in a "shh" position, use of sign language gestures, a holding breath game, a sustained silent reading program, "do now" math problems, not responding to small offenses, and waiting silently while a student vents anger before discussing possible concerns. Deliberate yet natural use of nonverbal language is a component of the effective teacher's behavior management repertoire.

Huey, W. C., & Rank, R. C. (1984). Effects of counselor and peer-led group assertive training on black adolescent aggression. *Journal of Counseling Psychology, 31,* 95–98.

Forty-eight eighth- and ninth-grade African-American male students participated in a peer-led assertive training study. All had histories of disruptive classroom behavior, low academic performance, and low family income levels. They were assigned to counselor- or peer-led assertive training or discussion groups that met for eight one-hour sessions over four weeks. Counselors and peer leaders first received assertiveness training (with appropriate cultural modifications), and then co-led their groups following a structured training guide. Discussion groups addressed such themes as anger, rules, and revenge, and students were encouraged to interact and express their feelings. Although no follow-up measures were taken, results indicated that students in both peer- and counselor-led assertive training groups learned assertive skills equally well on a short-term basis and reduced their level of classroom aggression, even though levels of felt anger and projective measures of aggression remained no different among the groups. Assertive training is not designed to alter more enduring emotional attributes but is able to influence behavior in specific situations such as the classroom.

Luce, S. C., Delquadri, J., & Hall, R. V. (1980). Contingent exercise: A mild but powerful procedure for suppressing inappropriate verbal and aggressive behavior. *Journal of Applied Behavior Analysis, 13,* 583–594.

While time out and painful consequences have successfully reduced autistic behaviors, they are not frequently used in public school classrooms because of their highly aversive qualities. Yet, as more severely disturbed youngsters are educated closer to or in the mainstream, techniques that are more acceptable in these less restrictive settings need to be developed. In this study, two emotionally disturbed students seven and ten years of age were required to perform ten repetitions of a standing up–sitting down routine whenever they demonstrated targeted verbal or physically aggressive misbehavior. For one of these students, this contingent exercise strategy was compared with a schedule of differential reinforcement of other behavior (DRO) in which the student received points for each fifteen minutes of appropriate behavior; these points were later traded for various reinforcers.

Results indicated that the contingent exercise was a more effective punishment strategy than a DRO schedule, consistently reducing the frequency of both aggressive actions and comments. This exercise strategy can be done quickly (under thirty seconds), requires minimal physical guidance, and does not need to match or be related to the target behavior as has been suggested in other research. However, the practitioner is cautioned to try milder consequences first, choose exercises the child is able to perform, avoid excessive and strenuous exertion by limiting the length of sessions to about twenty seconds, and use medical expertise to ensure that there are no contraindications for this strategy in the student's medical history.

Winborne, C. R. (1980). In-school suspension programs: The King William County model. *Educational Leadership, 37,* 466–469.

In-school suspension programs are based on the idea that students who remain in the school have a better chance for successful return to class. The model described here focuses on isolating the student from peers for an average of three to four days and providing assessment, remediation, maintenance of classroom course goals, and counseling. A program coordinator and three paraprofessionals provide services once a referred student is placed in the program by the principal. The student is evaluated, tutored, and counseled. An individual plan is prepared that integrates information from the assessments and remediation performed during the student's stay, discusses strengths and weaknesses, suggests in-class techniques, and recommends any further help. The plan is sent to the teachers and principal; if necessary, a tutor assists the teacher with the plan once the student has returned to the regular classroom. Follow-up monitoring to assess progress is conducted. During the first year of operation in the target school district, out-of-school suspensions dropped 40 percent. By the end of the school year, disciplinary referrals were also decreasing.

Witt, J. C., & Elliott, S. N. (1982). The response-cost lottery: A time-efficient and effective classroom intervention. *Journal of School Psychology, 20,* 155–161.

Teachers often object to interventions that, although effective, require an inordinate amount of time and the use of unavailable equipment.

A response-cost lottery is an effective behavior modification technique the classroom teacher can implement without an expensive commitment of time and materials. The procedures of the lottery were explained to three disruptive fourth graders, and four small slips of paper were placed on each of their desks under a three-by-five card taped on three sides to form a pocket. Each boy received a different color.

During one-half-hour treatment sessions, the teacher removed one slip of paper from the student each time he violated a previously defined classroom rule. If necessary, the teacher explained the violation to the youngster. After class, the remaining slips of paper were placed in a lottery box and on Friday a drawing was held with the winner selecting his prize from the reinforcers. The procedure resulted in a significant increase in appropriate behavior from a mean of 10 percent of the observation periods to 68 percent and 73 percent during the first and second experimental conditions, respectively. This result compared favorably with behavior of students not involved in the procedure. Substantial increases in academic accuracy were also recorded. The authors note that unlike typical response-cost procedures, the lottery system does not take away privileges already available; it provides only extra rewards. This feature might help reduce negative side effects. Further, although teachers usually removed the slips only for obvious rule violations (thus letting some occur without consequence), the procedure was still effective while not overly intrusive. This is an important balance to maintain.

Classroom Disturbance: Noncompliance

Noncompliant students can be verbally abusive to the teacher as they violate classroom rules and refuse to complete assigned tasks. Teacher reactions often inadvertently reward such disruptiveness by giving the student the attention he or she may seek. The strategies described here offer alternative approaches to this problem behavior.

Using Understandable Language
with Disruptive Students

AUTHOR: Mark S. Kiselica

PRECIS: Reducing angry, defiant behavior by helping the student analyze the events before, during, and after the misconduct

INTRODUCTION: Aggressive behavior-disordered teenagers must learn to control their anger if they are to avoid the disruptive academic, social, and personal consequences that follow their antisocial behaviors. While cognitive behavior modification can teach anger-coping skills to adolescents, it must use language the youngster can readily understand. Sophisticated terminology may be appropriate for the professional literature but it will not assist the student whose behavior the strategy was intended to help. The "before, during, and after program" adopts cognitive behavior modification strategies in a manner designed to promote understanding and participation, thus enhancing prospects for success.

BEFORE, DURING, AND AFTER PROGRAM (BDA): The author reports on the case study of a fifteen-year-old ninth grader whose behavior in school and in his community group home was so oppositional and defiant that his supervisory staff were close to placing him in a residential setting for delinquents. The counselor utilized the BDA strategy with him in twice-weekly meetings for eight weeks. During the first session, the counselor expressed an understanding of the difficulties and frustrations involved in anger control and how anxious the student must be over his possible removal from school and current residence. He stressed the student's ability to manage his anger and taught him first to graph the occurrence of each aggressive episode to make him more aware of their frequency.

In session 2, the student was asked to write about his anger-arousing experiences on five-by-eight index cards, describing the thoughts, feelings, and behaviors that occurred before, during, and after each event. For example, he entitled one such card "being criticized by a peer" and as instructed, listed the questions and answers that could help him focus on the relationship between angry thoughts and angry behavior. Under the heading "before" he wrote the questions, "What did someone else do before I became angry?" and "What was I thinking about before I became angry?" Next to the questions, he wrote his responses, which indicated that he was criticized by a peer, thought he was being put down, could not allow that to happen in front of others, and had to show others that he was tough. For the section labeled "during," he asked, "What did I do once I became angry?" To this he answered that he threatened and punched the person who criticized him and verbally abused the teacher who intervened to stop the fight. Questions for the "after" component included, "What happened to me or anyone else afterward?" "How did I feel afterward?" "What did I say to myself afterward?" His first answer revealed that the other student's nose was bloodied and he, the aggressor, was put on in-school suspension. In his two final answers, he wrote that he first felt good because he acted tough but then felt bad because he was seen as a bully and wished he could avoid getting in trouble so often.

To learn alternative cognitive and behavioral responses to these provocative events, the student was helped by the counselor to create more productive coping BDAs. On the back of the card, questions and answers were written in the same BDA format to promote more effective behavior. In this instance, the student asked what he could say to himself to avoid anger when criticized; he replied that he could just walk away, reframe the comment as helpful instead of critical, or just avoid feeling upset. As an alternate to punching, he could walk away, ignore the comment, or change the subject. In response to questions about how he felt after controlling his anger, his answers included avoiding trouble or injury to others, being rewarded by the residence director, and feeling good for not fighting.

Cards for each event were kept by the counselor and the student, who was urged to refer to them and practice the anger-coping behaviors in real-life situations. The counselor met twice weekly for two months with the student to check the graph of aggressive behavior rates, discuss problems implementing strategies, modify the BDAs when needed, and give positive feedback and encouragement. The BDA program helped the student reduce aggressive incidents dramatically during the eight-week intervention period. After a baseline week of fifteen aggressive incidents, no outbursts occurred during weeks 3, 5, and 7, with a maximum of three during week 6. The student's official status within the group home ranking system rose from the lowest to the highest level, and he had no suspensions in school during the BDA period. Follow-up after one year indicated a successful foster placement and the school no longer viewed him as a serious problem. His academics had also improved.

COMMENTARY: Reframing experimental terminology in language understandable to the student assisted him in analyzing the connections between his perceptions of events, the resulting aggressive behaviors, and the damaging consequences. This success encouraged him to participate in developing alternative BDA sequences, which guided him to more appropriate actions in the face of anger-provoking events. The author further cites the facilitating effect of the BDA cards and graphs as concrete change agents to which the student could refer. As indicated in the article, this promising case study raises future questions for research, particularly regarding the limits of BDA for less cognitively able students, the components of BDA that contributed to its effects, and the applicability of the BDA method both to other problem areas and to general adolescent developmental issues, such as dating or trying out for teams. Added to this list might be the utility of the procedure across grade levels. While the study used no control group and limited the baseline period to one week, BDA adds yet another potentially useful approach to the growing number of social and behavior skills development techniques.

SOURCE: Kiselica, M. S. (1988). Helping an aggressive adolescent through the "before, during, and after program." *The School Counselor, 35,* 299–306.

Eye Contact to Promote Compliance

AUTHORS: Carolynn C. Hamlet, Saul Axelrod, and Steven Kuerschner

PRECIS: Increasing compliance with verbal instructions through the use of demanded eye contact

INTRODUCTION: Following teacher directions is crucial to learning, and eye contact for sighted students is assumed to be a necessary prerequisite to direction following. Practitioners frequently recommend establishing eye contact as a basic teaching strategy despite the absence of confirming evidence in the literature. This study demonstrates a technique for training eye contact and documents its importance for successful instruction.

METHOD: For the study, two noncompliant eleven-year-old students with academic skill deficits heard each of ten predetermined instructions once each school day. They were required to respond within a certain number of seconds in order to be considered in compliance. During the baseline period, the teacher looked at the student, called his or her name, waited two seconds, then stated the instruction, continuing to eye the student until the instruction was finished. For the "demanded eye contact" condition, the student was required to make eye contact within two seconds after hearing his or her name. If no eye contact was made, the teacher said, "(Name), look at me," in a reasonably firm voice and waited another two seconds before giving the instruction. If the student broke eye contact, the teacher repeated the sequence. Upon compliance, the teacher thanked the student.

Eye contact was defined as a teacher judgment that the student's face and line of vision were directly oriented toward the teacher. For the first student, demanded eye contact more than doubled his compliant behavior from a baseline mean of 30 percent to a mean of 70 percent during the treatment phase. The second student tripled her 20 percent mean baseline compliance rate to a mean of 60 percent during her five-day treatment. The procedure was also effective over six replications in class, at home, in a facility for the retarded, and with students ranging in age from two to twenty-one years. Only the two-year-old's level of compliance decreased, although the authors report success with a two-year-old in a separate study. For these interventions, the teachers and parents role-played the procedures and practiced the instructions requiring eye contact.

COMMENTARY: As the authors indicate, this procedure enhances compliance without the need for more time-consuming reinforcement strategies and appears applicable over a variety of ages and settings. These are important factors considering how frequently teachers report lack of direction following in students they refer for help. Teachers often assume that following instructions is a skill students will master naturally as they move through the grades. This study indicates that direction following is a skill that may need to be facilitated through specific teacher behaviors.

SOURCE: Hamlet, C. C., Axelrod, S., & Kuerschner, S. (1984). Eye contact as an antecedent to compliant behavior. *Journal of Applied Behavior Analysis, 17,* 553–557.

Generalizing Teacher Control to Classroom Aides

AUTHOR: Howard M. Knoff

PRECIS: Improving students' playground behavior by involving the paraprofessional in a behavior-control strategy

INTRODUCTION: It is important for paraprofessionals to be able to effect stimulus control over student behaviors in the absence of the regular classroom teacher. Paraprofessionals often assume responsibility for students during specified times of the school day, but the control exerted by the teacher does not always generalize to these aides or to other settings. A specific sequence of procedures to enhance generalization of control would include identifying the behaviors under teacher control and the reinforcers responsible, having the teacher elicit and reinforce the behaviors with the paraprofessional present, continuing the teacher's prompting and rewarding while the aide takes over classroom supervision, having the paraprofessional assume stimulus and reinforcement control with periodic follow-up from the teacher, and finally giving gradual total control to the paraprofessional. A technique incorporating such steps was applied to help a playground aide exert better control over the defiant, resistant behavior of two nine- and ten-year-old third graders. Although the intervention was carried out with all third graders, data were reported for the two target students.

METHOD: These students continued their aggressive, noncompliant behaviors despite various punishments and conferences with teachers, parents, and the principal. The students believed they did not have to listen to the aide because she was not a teacher. The strategy began with the child study team detailing proper playground behavior, which broadly included treating others with fairness and respect, following the rules of games, and being good winners and losers. Students chose as a reinforcer a Friday afternoon end-of-day party; attendance was made contingent on the aide's judgment that the student had displayed appropriate behavior for 70 percent of the week's recesses. Appropriate behavior was indicated after each recess by the aide who drew either a smiling or sad face next to each student's name on a chart hanging in the classroom. Fewer than three warnings from the aide earned a smiling face.

A student was warned by the aide who took the student aside, noted the number of warnings that had been given, and told the student what the observed transgression was together with the rule for acceptable behavior. After three warnings or one instance of dangerous behavior, the student had to leave the playground and go to the classroom teacher. Students who could not attend the Friday party sat in another classroom to complete work. To effect generalization of stimulus control, the teacher explained the total procedure to the students with the aide present, continued the process by helping the aide on the playground, then gradually faded her involvement through the fifth week when she made occasional playground checkups. The program lasted from late February to June.

RESULTS: During the five-week baseline period, student 1 displayed appropriate playground behavior an average of 32 percent of the recesses attended, while student 2 averaged 56 percent. Behavior for neither student would have reached the criterion required for attendance at the Friday party. During the program, student 1 averaged 71 percent appropriate behavior, participating in twelve of the sixteen parties, while student 2 achieved a mean of 72 percent, qualifying for eleven parties.

COMMENTARY: The author indicates that this technique requires a small investment of time and resources, can be applied to a large group, and can be used in a variety of settings where aides supervise students. In addition, observations and the aide's reports suggested an increase in the respect given to the aide by the two students in the study as well as the other students. These reports need further experimental validation, but this technique for extending the influence of the classroom teacher to other supervising adults can prove valuable in enhancing the overall behavioral climate of the school. Ways to build this process into the early stages of the school year as a regular feature of the school's supervisory and disciplinary structure might be fruitfully explored.

SOURCE: Knoff, H. M. (1984). Stimulus control, paraprofessionals, and appropriate playground behavior. *School Psychology Review, 13,* 249–253.

The Good Behavior Game with Positive Reinforcement

AUTHOR: Dion X. Darveaux

PRECIS: Modifying the good behavior game to reward academic performance as well as reduce noncompliant behavior

INTRODUCTION: The good behavior game (GBG) is an effective, easily implemented group contingency for controlling disruptive behavior in the classroom. However, several drawbacks may reduce its acceptability among teachers. First, since the game requires the teacher to focus on and respond to misbehavior, such behaviors may actually increase in some students who find attention rewarding. Second, the reduction of inappropriate behaviors may generalize to other more adaptive behaviors resulting in their unwanted decrease. Third, the GBG discourages undesirable behavior without a concomitant teaching of appropriate behavior. Given that a reduction in unacceptable behavior is not functionally related to an increase in appropriate behavior and that separate planned interventions are needed to effect both changes, alterations to this intervention to foster positive behaviors would certainly increase the utility of the approach. In this modification of the good behavior game, acceptability among classroom teachers was enhanced by adding a merit system to encourage academic performance and thus demonstrate the flexibility of the technique in shaping positive as well as reducing negative behavior.

GBG PLUS M: Two male second-grade students with behavioral difficulties were placed on opposite teams when the class was divided in half for the good behavior game. The students were observed during a daily fifteen-minute period in which they worked on assignments while the teacher taught reading in small groups. When any student broke one of the predetermined class rules, a mark was recorded on the board for that entire team. Any team that remained under the five-point limit received a reward such as candy, free time, or being read a story. Under this system, both teams could win or lose. In addition to the points for bad behavior, two-by-three merit cards, each printed with the phrase "one merit" (M), were awarded to students who completed a daily math assignment at 75 percent accuracy and who raised their hands to answer a teacher's question correctly or offer a relevant comment during class discussion. Each five merits earned by the team for academic performance eliminated one point for disruptive behavior.

During the five-day baseline period, the target students' average percentage of disruptive behavior was 71.9, dropping to 11.6 percent during the first seven-day GBG plus M treatment phase. A three-day reversal period raised the level of noncompliance back to a mean of 83.8 percent; the second treatment phase lowered rule breaking to 6.25 percent. Similarly, the two target students raised their correctly completed assignment rates from 40 percent to 75 percent, while the total class rate increased from 77 percent to 88 percent.

COMMENTARY: The need to add the merit component to influence academic performance indicates that reducing noncompliant behavior does not automatically improve academic performance. Separate interventions must shape positive behaviors, although rewarding improved academic performance has been shown to reduce disruptiveness in class. The merit system also seems to capitalize on the teacher's preference for positive rather than aversive strategies; according to the teacher's reports this feature made her concentrate on productive as well as difficult behaviors in her students. Use of the merits increases the possibility that both teams will "win" and earn rewards, thus enhancing the strategy's attractiveness to teachers. While no follow-up data are reported and it is unknown whether improved behavior and academic performance generalized to other times and settings, these issues can be addressed in other research.

SOURCE: Darveaux, D. X. (1984). The good behavior game plus merit: Controlling disruptive behavior and improving student motivation. *School Psychology Review, 13,* 510–514.

Teaching Self-Monitoring to Preschoolers

AUTHORS: Edward A. Workman, George B. Helton, and P. J. Watson

PRECIS: Teaching a preschooler to self-monitor sustained school work

INTRODUCTION: Self-monitoring is one component of behavioral self-control in which a target behavior may be altered merely by having the student observe and record each occurrence of the act. In this study, a four-year-old noncompliant preschooler, who had never been involved in a behavior modification program, self-monitored his behavior to improve his compliance and sustained effort at schoolwork. Sustained schoolwork was defined as a ten-second interval of engagement in a school-related task; compliance meant following the teacher's or aide's directions during intervals when observations were taking place.

METHOD: After an initial ten-day baseline period, the student was taught through monitoring, guided practice, and practice and praise to mark a sheet of paper if he was working on an assignment from the teacher when a kitchen timer sounded a signal. On each of the six treatment days, he was given a sheet of paper by his teacher and was reminded from time to time to mark it in the appropriate way when the timer rang. The teacher set the timer to ring every five minutes during the daily half-hour sessions. A five-day reversal condition removed the treatment, followed by a ten-day reinstatement of self-monitoring. During a final four-day baseline period, the timer was set for two days but no self-monitoring occurred. It was then withdrawn for the last two days.

RESULTS: When self-monitoring was introduced, the mean daily percentage of observation intervals in which the student was engaged in sustained schoolwork rose from a baseline rate of 37.73 percent to 63.66 percent. It returned to 46.6 percent during reversal and increased to 60.63 percent during the second self-monitoring condition. The final baseline rate decreased to 46.5 percent. His compliant behavior initially rose from 59.63 percent at baseline to 82.33 percent during the first self-monitoring condition, back to 68.4 percent at the second baseline, up to 82.63 percent during the second self-monitoring phase, with a further increase to 90 percent during the final baseline. In addition, a co-varying relationship was found to exist between sustained schoolwork and compliance, suggesting that they belong to the same response class and may decrease or increase in the same direction.

COMMENTARY: This study demonstrates that children as young as four years of age who have no prior experience with contingency management systems are capable of self-monitoring their behavior to increase appropriate responding without the need for elaborate external contingencies. By monitoring and recording positive and negative teacher attention toward the child across experimental conditions, the authors were also able tentatively to rule out teacher attention as a factor in the child's improvement, although they indicate the need for further research on this variable. Whether the improvements described in the study can be maintained is another topic for future investigation. Previous research has suggested that self-monitoring has a built-in self-evaluative component and encourages more self-awareness regarding the occurrence of the target behaviors. These factors are believed to enhance the effectiveness of the procedure and may enhance a maintenance effect as well. If students at the preschool level are able to self-manage behavior change consistently, the potential options of preschool interventions are broadened. As the law directs public schools to become increasingly involved in facilitating special education programs for preschool children, the availability of empirically documented intervention strategies for these youngsters will enhance the continuity of services as these students make the transition from preschool to school-age programs.

SOURCE: Workman, E. A., Helton, G. B., & Watson, P. J. (1982). Self-monitoring effects in a four-year-old child: An ecological behavior analysis. *Journal of School Psychology, 20,* 57–64.

Additional Readings

Davis, R. A. (1979). The impact of self-modeling on problem behaviors in school-age children. *School Psychology Digest, 8,* 128–132.

An eleven-year-old fourth grader attending a self-contained special education class was referred when his fighting and verbally aggressive responses to the teacher's attempts at control were not reduced through contingency management. The student was videotaped resisting antecedent conditions that typically led to the target behaviors; he then viewed himself behaving appropriately on the tape. While he watched, comments were made to him encouraging and praising his behavior. Both fighting and unacceptable responses to teacher control were reduced substantially during the self-modeling conditions and generalized to a ten-day posttreatment follow-up. Self-modeling shows the student what is expected, demonstrates what the rewards might be, allows him the opportunity for covert rehearsal, and reduces his reluctance to perform by showing the student that he can execute the expected behavior. Self-modeling also capitalizes on the notion that imitation is effected by the perceived similarities between viewer and model.

Gootman, M. (1988). Discipline alternatives that work. *The Humanist, 48,* 11–14.

School discipline should not need to utilize corporal punishment as a method of last resort, but should acknowledge the inevitability of misbehavior and the need to teach self-control. A workable discipline program should include the following attributes: (1) Students and teachers accept responsibility for their behavior, trust each other, expect high standards of conduct, and make decisions together. (2) Time is set aside for planning a disciplinary system with the involvement of teachers, students, and perhaps parents. (3) Standards for behavior are consistent and are applied uniformly throughout the school. (4) A minimum number of clearly stated rules are defined (between four and six), including those addressing respect for self, others, and property, and preparedness. (5) Rules are applied fairly without anger and with a clear intent that the inappropriate behavior be corrected. Adults help students change inappropriate behavior. (6) Consequences are related to the misbehavior and students have the chance to work out methods of alternative action to the behavior that caused the problem. (7) Although misbehavior is not excused, its source is investigated to determine whether mental or physical health services should be provided. (8) Parents are encouraged to participate in the life of the school so that home-school contacts are not limited to problem situations. A cooperative home-school partnership is established. Proper discipline training teaches internal control. Traditional discipline fosters the continuing need for external sanctions that do not promote self-discipline and responsibility.

Rhode, G., Morgan, D. P., & Young, K. R. (1983). Generalization and maintenance of treatment gains of behaviorally handicapped students from resource rooms to regular classrooms using self-evaluation procedures. *Journal of Applied Behavior Analysis, 16,* 171–188.

Six special education students ranging in age from six years, five months, to ten years, nine months, were taught to self-evaluate their academic performance and behavior in a resource room setting and match it with teacher evaluations, earning points for accurate matching. When they achieved an appropriate behavior rate of 80 percent, the practitioner attempted to generalize and maintain the improved behavior in the regular classroom by fading the program to a less intensive level — that is, by lengthening the time between self-ratings, reducing the number of days points could be exchanged for reinforcers until no exchanges took place, and going from written to verbal to private self-evaluations. All six students improved their behavior in the resource room during the self-evaluation training phase; five of the six maintained high and consistent rates of appropriate behavior in regular classrooms during the generalization and maintenance phases. One subject showed improved but variable rates of acceptable behavior. Teachers reported the program as easy to run; students found it enjoyable, improved their work, and earned more frequent teacher praise. Future research should focus on the limitations of the procedure with more severely disturbed students and the role of accuracy of self-evaluations in maintaining improved behavior. This study revealed a relationship between accuracy of self-evaluations and higher rates of maintained appropriate behavior.

Shapiro, E. S., Albright, T. S., & Ager, C. L. (1986). Group versus individual contingencies in modifying two disruptive adolescents' behavior. *Professional School Psychology, 1,* 105–116.

Two studies compared individual and dependent group contingencies. In the first, a seventeen-year-old noncompliant, mentally retarded boy selected a reward from a predetermined menu if he switched successfully between school activities within a twenty-second time period. The criterion for reward was gradually increased from one successful transition in five to five out of five. The student was provided a card printed with the numbers 1 to 5 and was instructed to punch the appropriate number when he changed activities successfully. Praise was also given. Unsuccessful transitions were ignored, negative reactions were timed out, and the student was informed periodically which condition was in effect. For the group contingency, the reward selected by the boy was also provided to his classmates. Although the numbers of his daily successful transitions were equivalent for both contingencies, the individual contingency produced faster overall transition time.

The subject for the second study was a seventeen-year-old emotionally disturbed girl who was noncompliant and verbally aggressive when asked to perform tasks. During the individual contingency, she self-recorded the frequency and appropriateness of her verbalizations during three separate time periods. If her tally of appropriate comments was in 95 percent or better agreement with an independent observer's record, she would be able to leave school five minutes early. The group contingency followed the same format with the entire class earning early dismissal if she met the 95 percent criterion level. Again the individual contingency produced a higher percentage of appropriate verbalizations than did the group contingency, although the differences were small and both were very effective. In addition, the student achieved consistently high levels of accuracy in matching her self-recordings to the staff tally. Of note is the dramatic behavior improvements that occurred even though accuracy of tallies, not behavior change, was the target of reinforcement. Since other studies have favored group contingencies and the differences reported here are not great, the authors suggest that the practitioner examine the parameters of the total problem situation before making a decision about the intervention strategy to use. Factors such as ease of implementation and adverse peer pressure might offset the small differences in outcome.

Taylor, V. L., Cornwell, D. D., & Riley, M. T. (1984). Home-based contingency management programs that teachers can use. *Psychology in the Schools, 21,* 368–374.

To reduce disruptive behavior that is not symptomatic of severe disorder and to motivate academic performance, home-based contingency management programs have a strong record of empirical support, offer positive rather than negative contingencies, and are time and cost efficient. Parents have more latitude than schools to gear rewards to the needs of their children, although the practitioner should keep the program positive to avoid adverse reactions to students from unstable parents.

A home contingency was used in a third-grade class composed of 46 percent Caucasian, 42 percent Mexican-American, and 12 percent African-American students. Positively phrased rules were displayed and explained to parents and students. Preprinted "good behavior notes" were sent home each day to parents of children who did not break the rules that day, with instructions to parents to provide verbal and other rewards of their choosing. Notes were faded to once weekly when rule violations dropped by 80 percent, and finally were discontinued as in baseline. Daily notes reduced group rule breaking significantly, with a slight increase when notes were changed to a weekly basis and a further increase when notes were eliminated. While note fading and the change to more stringent criteria for receiving notes are methods to maintain treatment effects, applying both in this procedure may have accounted for the increase in rule breaking during fading. The authors suggest that such steps be taken with caution.

Classroom Disturbance: Physical and Verbal Aggression

This section was previously entitled "Cursing"; however, no articles were found that treated cursing in school as a single isolated behavior. It is typically embedded in a cluster of symptoms labeled collectively *conduct disorders* or *aggressive behavior*. Many interventions address the lack of social competence characteristic of aggressivity and attempt to strengthen the cognitive and affective resources that promote more competent responding. Moralistic emotional responses by adults are not effective methods for reducing aggressive reactions.

The Problem-Solving Conference:
An Alternative to Acting Out

AUTHORS: Janis Johnston, Dennis Simon, and Alice Zemitzsch

PRECIS: Addressing disciplinary concerns through problem-solving conferences that seek solutions rather than impose punishments

INTRODUCTION: Socially competent students are skilled problem solvers who seem better able to identify their problems and the conditions that evoke them. They know how to devise alternative solutions, think through the steps needed to achieve their goals, and consider the consequences of their actions. Less socially competent students are poor decision makers who do not generate alternatives and believe there is only one solution (or no solution) to a problem. Problem-solving conferences (PSCs) are responses to behavior and social disruption that focus on problem and conflict resolution, verbal communication of feelings, self-control, personal responsibility, and appreciation of another's perspective. Students learn that the school's response to behavior referrals or social conflicts need not consist only of restriction or punishment.

PROBLEM-SOLVING CONFERENCES (PSC): Any student or staff member can call a PSC by filling out and signing a form stating the problem situation and who is requested to attend. There is no limit to the size of the conference. One of a core of trained staff members serves as a facilitator to maintain the meeting's problem-solving purpose and assist students in expressing their needs and responding to adult comments. Meetings are typically brief and at times last only ten to fifteen minutes. The person calling the conference (perhaps a student) is first asked to state the problem from his or her point of view. The other party (for example, a teacher) then presents what is often an alternative perspective. Discussants are asked to talk directly to each other, and the facilitator might ask each to restate the other's position to enhance understanding. Suggested solutions are then elicited from the principals so that they take responsibility for change. Only when no ideas are put forward does the facilitator offer alternatives. Finally, a definite plan of action is negotiated and accepted. If the conference degenerates into argument, it should be terminated. Depending on circumstances, a new conference might then be attempted with other participants, or a more traditional approach to consequences might be instituted.

CASE STUDY: The authors describe Tom as an aggressive, hostile high school student who had been referred forty-eight times in one semester for cursing and other acting-out behaviors. Tom often engaged in power struggles with school authorities and no traditional disciplinary steps had been effective. During several PSCs that were called at the teacher's request, Tom's feelings were acknowledged, with the understanding that he was accountable for his behavior. Solutions to the frustrating encounters between Tom and the school staff were explored. Although Tom was resistive and hostile during earlier meetings, he eventually called a PSC on his own to explore ways to reduce his lateness to school. He considered a plan of action and seemed to understand that he had both options and responsibilities.

COMMENTARY: In addition to teaching students how to resolve problems, problem-solving conferences promote trust among students and staff, foster students' belief in their ability to solve problems, and create an awareness in all parties of the need for mutual reliance and cooperation. When opportunities are provided through these forums for all participants to express their feelings and present their positions, there may be less reason for students to communicate their needs through disruptive or defiant behavior. As the authors suggest, the purpose of these conferences is not to undo the basic authority of the teacher but to empower students with the sense that their views are important and can influence outcomes. It might be useful for the practitioner to consider the age of the child in determining how such conferences should be conducted. While the authors note that some of the initial research on cognitive problem solving was carried out with preschool children, this article describes a high school program. Further field-based research might clarify the changes required to accommodate different age levels. Finally, the structure outlined here might prove useful for many school conferences that address problems of one kind or another. While participants in any conference need some time to express feelings and present points of view, movement toward resolution helps focus on its true purpose, which is cooperative problem solving. When conferences become occasions for mutual accusation and blame, they are rarely productive.

SOURCE: Johnston, J., Simon, D., & Zemitzsch, A. (1983). Balancing an educational mobile through problem-solving conferences. *The Pointer, 27,* 33–36.

Cognitive and Behavioral Strategies for Verbal and Physical Aggression

AUTHOR: Susan G. Forman

PRECIS: Comparing cognitive restructuring and response cost to reduce aggressive behavior

INTRODUCTION: While cognitive restructuring has shown promise in reducing aggressive behavior in both individual and group work with children and adolescents, the author cites the need for more research in this area to correct selected methodological weaknesses. In this study, cognitive restructuring techniques were compared with a response cost procedure and a reading tutorial control group as methods to reduce aggressivity in third, fourth, and fifth graders in an urban elementary school. Aggressive behavior was defined as verbal aggression (for example, arguing, cursing, and teasing), physical aggression (hitting, kicking, shoving, or destroying property), noncompliance, and other actions.

COGNITIVE RESTRUCTURING: A group of seven students met for two thirty-minute sessions per week for six weeks. In the first session, leaders described the group's purpose and how thoughts can influence feelings and behavior. The group leaders then asked members about times when they had been extremely angry. One such experience was targeted each session and the youngsters were encouraged to remember the thoughts that led to their anger and to create a listing of thoughts that might inhibit or prevent the aggressive behavior. For example, they might think about the situation in an unbiased manner, reflect on why the other person might have acted as he or she did, weigh the consequences of aggression, acknowledge that feelings and behavior are under each person's control, commit to appropriate behavior, recognize the positive outcomes of avoiding anger and acting properly, and provide self-rewards. The group then relaxed with their eyes closed and pictured themselves rehearsing these thoughts in the anger-provoking episodes as the leader repeated them. Finally, practice at home was promoted as was using the thoughts in real-life anger-provoking situations.

RESPONSE COST AND CONTROL GROUPS: The seven students in the response cost group met for the same number of thirty-minute sessions per week for six weeks to play basketball, listen to records, and dance. However, for each previously defined aggressive episode, the child lost two minutes of meeting time. The student was notified of each incident, which was then recorded on a card kept by the teacher. At each meeting, the leaders checked the card and reduced the group time for the student accordingly. The four subjects in the control group (two students moved) met twice weekly for thirty-minute reading tutorials.

RESULTS: Results indicated significant decreases in aggressive behavior for students in both the cognitive restructuring and response cost programs compared to controls. It is interesting that the response cost students showed a greater reduction than the restructuring group. No follow-up data were gathered.

COMMENTARY: This program utilized restructuring of self-statements with relaxation and guided imagery to help students solve their aggressive behavior problems. The author speculates on the relationship between the cognitive and behavioral approaches, suggesting that a strategy using external contingencies may have powerful early effects while an intervention targeting the development of internal cognitive self-statements might produce more long-lasting influence. Recent reviews have suggested that overall length of treatment as opposed to number of sessions may be a factor in the success of cognitive-behavioral interventions. Longer treatment lengths of eight to twelve weeks minimum in which more practice of cognitive skills is possible seem to produce the best results. The procedure described here also included a request to students in the cognitive restructuring group to use the technique in anger-arousing situations and to practice at home. Reviews suggest that changes brought about by cognitive interventions may generalize across settings and time. However, further research is needed.

SOURCE: Forman, S. G. (1980). A comparison of cognitive training and response cost procedures in modifying aggressive behavior of elementary school children. *Behavior Therapy, 11,* 594–600.

Cooperative Learning with Emotionally Disturbed Students

AUTHORS: Spencer J. Salend and Patricia Sonnenschein

PRECIS: Improving emotionally disturbed high school students' on-task, academic, and cooperative behaviors through a cooperative learning strategy

INTRODUCTION: Traditional learning is structured so that students typically work in isolation from each other, often competing for rewards. In cooperative learning, peers work together toward a shared outcome, deriving mutual academic, cognitive, and affective benefits. The procedure described here applied a cooperative learning strategy in three self-contained classes of designated emotionally disturbed adolescents fourteen to eighteen years of age with intellectual levels ranging from borderline to bright/normal. Reading and math levels varied from significantly below to above grade level. These students were disruptive, physically and verbally aggressive, and noncompliant.

COOPERATIVE LEARNING: During a six-day baseline period, teachers taught in their customary manner using lecture, discussion, and seat work. Discipline was handled as always. On day 1 of the seven- to eight-day cooperative learning program, the teacher announced the change, specified with demonstration the rules for cooperative learning, and displayed the rules on the classroom wall. The rules were these: (1) each group must work cooperatively, (2) each group member must participate and contribute to completing the tasks, (3) group members will help each other, (4) group members will seek aid from each other if needed, (5) each group will hand in one completed assignment, and (6) a group grade will be given. The thirty-minute cooperative learning session began with the teacher rehearsing and emphasizing material from the textbook to be used in the group discussions. Students were then divided into rotating groups of two or three, with one high and one low achiever always grouped together. The group assignment was handed out to each member and the group worked together following the posted guidelines. Once all members agreed on the finished product, it was noted and submitted by the group's chosen recorder. Each student also kept a record of the group's answers to use for study.

Following the cooperative learning phase, baseline teaching conditions were reinstated for seven days, followed by a second ten-day cooperative learning format. A five-week follow-up involved weekly observations of the cooperative learning sessions. Effects of the program were measured through direct observation of on-task behavior, cooperative behavior, and academic performance. Students were recorded as on task when their eyes were focused on the teacher or another student talking, their eyes and/or pencils were on the paperwork, and their comments were related to the class work. Cooperative behaviors were identified as requests for help; friendly, positive, caring comments or gestures; cheering; and acts of assistance. Academic performance was measured by the number of problems students attempted and completed correctly. In addition, class members rated their liking of each other on a sociometric scale before and after intervention and responded to questions exploring their attitudes toward the cooperative learning technique. Results indicated clear increases in on-task behaviors, academic performance, and cooperative behaviors for all three classes. Cooperative behavior was not maintained over the follow-up period. Furthermore, 92 percent of the sociometric responses showed no change among subjects in their liking of peers although the remaining 8 percent were all more positive. Finally, 83 percent chose cooperative over traditional learning formats, indicating that it helped them try harder, complete more work accurately, get better grades, and enjoy group work aimed at a group goal. The other 17 percent felt they worked faster on their own.

COMMENTARY: This study demonstrates the ability of emotionally disturbed adolescents to benefit from a cooperative learning program. Although it appears that effects on a long-term basis are greater for performance-related behaviors (on-task and academic performance) than for social/interpersonal patterns, the authors point out that students were rotated among groups, possibly inhibiting the social influence. When allowed to work together over a longer period of time, perhaps students would develop more long-lasting positive regard for their peers. Also, in line with the authors' suggestion of examining individual subject data, it would be interesting to learn whether both high- and low-achieving students derived the same benefit from the strategy. Given that 17 percent preferred to work on their own, it might be useful to analyze future data by individual subject characteristics.

SOURCE: Salend, S. J., & Sonnenschein, P. (1989). Validating the effectiveness of a cooperative learning strategy through direct observation. *Journal of School Psychology, 27,* 47–58.

A Buddy System to Promote
Appropriate Classroom Behavior

AUTHORS: Guy Goodman, Elaine K. Powell, and Joanne E. Burke

PRECIS: Learning disabled student "buddies" helping to teach each other appropriate behavior to enhance success in the mainstream setting

INTRODUCTION: As learning disabled students spend increasing amounts of time in mainstream classes, it is crucial that they develop the social competence for successful participation. Students who achieve successfully in their resource programs are frequently reported to be disruptive, rude, and unable to maintain independent work patterns when exposed to regular education classes where academic standards are high and more independent work habits are required. These problems need to be addressed with effective interventions if students with learning disabilities are to function in regular classrooms.

BUDDY SYSTEM: This system to establish appropriate behaviors for elementary school learning disabled students in mainstream settings is first instituted in the resource room. Students attending the same regular class are paired off as buddies and are taught to observe, record, and evaluate each other's behavior for twenty-minute periods. They note the other's adherence to rules, courteous and thoughtful behavior, self-control, and avoidance of conflict. Each of these behaviors is defined and illustrated beforehand by the resource room teacher. After the twenty-minute sessions, the resource teacher reviews the records and initials evaluations with which she agrees. If she does not agree with the student's evaluations, she discusses the basis for her disagreement. Discussions also focus on preferred behaviors other than the ones displayed, with students often suggesting options on their own. Appropriate behavior is rewarded with points, and pairs with the most combined points can trade them for rewards at the end of each week. A picture of the winning team is displayed in the resource room with the title "Best Buddies." Gradually, the resource room teacher fades her help until the students are running the system. Then it is tried in the regular class with students first discussing and developing strategies to cope with the transition issues that might occur as the program is applied in the new setting (for example, how to cope with the reality that no none else in the class is involved in this program).

RESULTS: Although the regular class teacher allowed recording sessions only at the end of the day, the program was reported as effective in a number of ways. First, the authors indicated that both direct and vicarious reinforcement (receiving points and observing others earning points) encouraged a healthy rivalry and collaboration within the resource room that seemed to carry over into mainstream classes even before the program was transferred. Teachers reported behavior improvements and were enthusiastic about utilizing the strategy in their rooms. Second, receiving awards contingent upon their buddy's behavior as well as their own seemed to foster a social pressure in students to behave properly. Third, training students to control the program increased the probability of carryover from the resource to the mainstream class. As students gained self-control through a self-managed process of mutual reinforcement, they became more natural and proficient self-monitors, a skill they were able to use in classes requiring more self-imposed structure.

COMMENTARY: The authors conclude that the buddy system was "highly effective" in promoting appropriate mainstream classroom behavior. This promising approach uses a combination of empirically tested strategies including social skills training, group contingency, direct and vicarious reinforcement, and self-management. Future research might enhance the power of this technique by including a control group and greater operational specificity in the development of dependent measures. An interesting aspect highlighted by this article is the role of the resource room teacher as a principal designer of interventions. As a specialist working with learning disabled students, the resource teacher not only provides direct instruction to students but provides an equally important consultation service to classroom teachers, helping to maximize success for learning impaired youngsters trying to cope with the rigors of the regular education program. The teacher, learning disabilities (LD) specialist, and school psychologist can combine their individual expertise to develop creative solutions to the problems these students may face. By teaming the teacher's knowledge of curriculum, the resource specialist's knowledge of learning disabilities, and the school psychologist's knowledge of intervention strategies, it is certainly possible for most learning disabled students to profit from an individually determined mainstream experience.

SOURCE: Goodman, G., Powell, E. K., & Burke, J. E. (1989). The buddy system: A reintegration technique. *Academic Therapy, 25,* 195–199.

Additional Readings

Proctor, M. A., & Morgan, D. (1991). Effectiveness of a response cost raffle procedure on the disruptive classroom behavior of adolescents with behavior problems. *School Psychology Review, 20,* 97–109.

A response cost raffle was employed with four junior high school students in a resource room setting. The teacher explained and modeled the program and distributed "raffle tickets" to each student. For each inappropriate behavior, one ticket was removed by the teacher with an explanation of the transgression. If the student behaved negatively when a ticket was removed, another was taken. If the reaction continued, the youngster was referred for in-school suspension. Remaining slips were collected for the raffle five minutes before the period ended. Two were marked so that if they were drawn the entire class would win a prize. One ticket was then selected from an envelope and the winner chose a prize from a predetermined list. Results showed a clear increase in appropriate behaviors and decrease in inappropriate behavior as a result of the response cost strategy. No negative reactions to withdrawal of tickets was observed. The authors note the importance of a consistent and immediate consequence for inappropriate behavior. In light of concerns regarding the use of punishment in schools, they differentiate between response cost and other aversive procedures. Response cost does not cause physical harm, preclude rewards, remove students from class, nor cause negative side effects. It is cost effective and easy to implement.

Stefanich, G. P., & Bell, L. C. (1985). A dynamic model for classroom discipline. *NASSP Bulletin, 69,* 19–25.

The authors describe a disciplinary model for classroom management that promotes responsibility and self-motivation by adopting a "least restrictive" punishment philosophy. Four levels of disciplinary intervention move from an emphasis on independence, self-respect, and self-reliance to a fairly restrictive plan for behavior change. Level 1, preventive discipline, requires the creation of a stimulating, success-oriented, well-planned classroom in which differences are accepted, appropriate behavior is modeled by the teacher, and parents are kept informed and involved. Level 2, supportive discipline, is used in any classroom with students who need some planned assistance with behavior control, but it is applied in a manner that respects students' feelings and emphasizes praise. At this level, standards for proper behavior are created and nonintrusive control techniques are utilized to shape appropriate behavior. Level 3, corrective discipline, plans for students who misbehave and who need to hear the rules and consequences clearly so they know what they need to do to be successful. A firm discipline plan is created with specified rules, contingencies, and rewards for desirable behaviors. If possible, more supportive and preventive techniques are introduced as behavior controls are established. The authors advise practitioners to avoid group punishments, not to confront or reprimand students publicly, to make sure threats can be carried out, and not to challenge a student to misbehave. Level 4, adaptive discipline, acknowledges the need in certain cases for written individualized behavior change interventions that are more restrictive than the general classroom management strategies suggested above. If this step is not sufficient, time outs, suspension, and alternative school settings may be needed. Discipline programs need to help students find a balance between freedom and structure so that they can develop the internalized controls needed for adult living.

Classroom Disturbance: Playing the Class Clown

The literature rarely if ever refers to the term *class clown*, typically including such attention-seeking antics among a larger cluster of disruptive behaviors. While clowning may not be considered as serious as episodes of antisocial or aggressive conduct, it can interfere with teaching and distract students who are the target of jokes or those who are easily led off task.

Self-Observation by a Third Grader

AUTHOR: Wayne C. Piersel

PRECIS: Using a monitoring chart to help a third grader learn to self-monitor and improve assignment completion rates

INTRODUCTION: Self-observation, as one component of behavioral self-management, has been applied effectively to improve students' academic performance and problem behaviors. However, this strategy typically includes some form of monitoring device and meetings with an adult practitioner, and it is not known whether these elements might exert an influence on target behaviors independent of the self-monitoring effects. The author cites as an example the possible external demands or expectations that might be created through meetings with a psychologist or counselor. This study examines these variables.

METHODS: A third-grade, eight-year-old student named David was referred for not completing work and for "horseplay" and other behavioral concerns. A token reward system was tried to increase David's daily assignment completion rate to 80 to 90 percent, but it was unsuccessful. Although David's work accuracy was typically more than 80 percent, he never completed more than 40 percent of the work. After a ten-day baseline condition in which tallies were kept on the number of daily assignments completed at 80 percent or greater accuracy, David began recording on a chart taped to his desk completed assignments handed in. This twenty-day condition also included twice-weekly meetings with the school psychologist, first to review the problem and establish the self-observations, then later to review progress, examine the completed chart, and prepare a new one. At these meetings, the psychologist also addressed the need for David to complete assignments. Following a five-day return to baseline with no charts or meetings, self-observation was reinstated for fifteen days but without the meetings with the psychologist. David was instructed to continue recording his completed work each week and then turn in the chart to the school secretary who gave him a new chart. A ten-day condition followed with meetings but no charting. At these sessions, the advantages of completed work were raised, and David was urged to set goals and monitor his completions "mentally." Finally, self-observation and weekly meetings were both reinstated for ten days.

RESULTS: With the introduction of both charting (self-observation) and meetings with the psychologist, David's work completion rose from a baseline rate of 33 percent of assignments completed to between 75 percent and 100 percent completed every day. It returned to 0 to 33 percent for the second baseline. When the self-observation condition was in effect without meetings, his work completion rate rose again to a range between 70 and 100 percent. Meetings alone reduced completion to 20 to 40 percent while the final return to self-observation and meetings increased completions to between 60 and 100 percent. A six-week follow-up period that included charting and weekly progress reviews with the teacher maintained assignment completion rates at 83.3 to 100 percent.

COMMENTARY: Self-observation is an effective intervention, and the presence of the monitoring device (in this case, a chart) seems to play an important role in the success of this technique. However, the failure of the weekly meetings alone to maintain the improvements from the earlier phases suggests that external demands, expectations, or cues did not exert power over the target behavior. Thus, self-observation with visible use of a monitoring procedure is a recommended approach at this time. The student assumes virtually all responsibility for the intervention; it is considered a highly acceptable strategy by teachers, parents, and administrators; and it is relatively nonintrusive in terms of the disruption to the classroom routine required for its implementation. Self-management strategies reduce the need for external consequences and encourage responsibility and self-reliance.

SOURCE: Piersel, W. C. (1985). Self-observation and completion of school assignments: The influence of a physical recording device and expectancy characteristics. *Psychology in the Schools, 22,* 331–336.

Verbal and Nonverbal
Short-Circuiting of Classroom Misbehavior

AUTHOR: Robert L. Shrigley

PRECIS: A planned sequential model for responding to disruptive student behavior

INTRODUCTION: When strategies designed to manage classroom disruption are well planned and sequenced, effective control can be readily maintained. The author describes a disciplinary model that requires as few as eight hours of training and that is applicable for students who clown, respond defiantly, behave dishonestly, hurt others, or engage in a variety of disruptive behaviors. The model describes both nonverbal and verbal alternatives that are used sequentially depending on the situation and type of offense.

DISCIPLINARY ALTERNATIVES: The author discusses four nonverbal interventions that gradually increase the intensity of the disapproving message to the misbehaving student. These nonverbal teacher responses are typically used for less serious transgressions and make the necessary point without being too confrontive. In *planned ignoring,* the teacher is aware of the infraction but chooses to ignore it. The misbehavior may be brief, unintentional, or not particularly disruptive and often ends without incident. However, if the behavior persists, the teacher may need to give *signals* in the form of facial expressions or movements. Teachers have many signals that communicate degrees of annoyance such as slowly shaking the head "no" while maintaining strong eye contact. In *proximity control,* the teacher moves firmly but not hysterically toward the student to stand within arm's reach, often behind the student's desk, to make him or her aware of the teacher's negative reaction to the behavior. Finally, *touch control* may be used when proximity alone does not make the point. Touching the student's shoulder can function as a clear, nonverbal statement of disapproval. The teacher is alerted, however, to the limitations of this technique, particularly with older students when the teacher is male and the student female.

A broad variety of nonverbal actions are available to the teacher. Data cited by the author from a survey of teacher responses to behavior incidents suggest that 40 percent of common infractions can be eliminated by using these techniques in an orderly fashion. Yet the limitations of body language become readily apparent when the teacher must confront the more serious, chronic problem student. Here, verbal responses are needed and can again be sequenced for an orderly confrontation. Citing food throwing in the cafeteria as a sample transgression, the author indicates that the teacher can still utilize any number of nonverbal approaches while moving toward the incident. However, if these fail, the teacher can deliver either a *direct appeal* to a generally well-behaved student displaying poor judgment, or an *I message* if there is a good relationship between the student and the teacher. An *I message* states the behavior, the reasons it is disruptive, and the teacher's feelings about it (see pp. 89–90 of Millman, Schaefer, & Cohen, *Therapies for School Behavior Problems,* San Francisco: Jossey-Bass, 1980). A direct appeal also states the behavior and its disruptive qualities but then simply directs the student to stop doing it. An "is not for" directive intensifies the disapproving message without humiliating the student, for example, "food is not for throwing."

Stronger yet is the threat of a *logical consequence* such as having to sweep up the floor. This threat does not flaunt teacher authority, but follows naturally from the situation and the transgression itself. However, *contrived consequences* do flow from adult authority and include threats of detention that are not related to the misbehavior but exert the teacher's power to impose punishment for disruption. Finally, the teacher can resort to *threat* in which official school policy is imposed against a defiant student or other ostracizing consequences are initiated. In this case, assistance may also be sought with non-classroom staff (principal, counselor, parent) for long-range intervention. Other techniques for different types of misbehaviors might include humor, reward for proper behavior, assertive questioning, and tongue-in-cheek comments.

The author reports in the survey cited above that 23 percent of reported incidents were ended by threats; 35 percent were stopped with other verbal strategies. Thus, 98 percent of the incidents reported in this survey were terminated by using the steps in this model. A second survey reported on the success rate of various verbal responses used in this model to incidents of laughing, burping, arguing, visiting, or off-task behavior. Results indicated that each of the verbal confrontations was successful between 47 percent and 74 percent of the times they were used. *Contrived consequences, threats, and I messages* were most effective.

COMMENTARY: While the author acknowledges that effective teachers probably use these techniques naturally, the model consciously organizes and sequences them so that the teacher can use the least coercive intervention first and work through the model to more confrontive responses until the episode is ended. By utilizing the least aversive controls, the teacher can save serious punishments for serious behavior and maintain rapport with the class. Further, the model provides alternative response options, thus recognizing that no one response will eliminate all disruptions. Although teachers may have difficulty abandoning old methods, techniques that allow teaching to occur with minimum interference are valuable teaching assets.

SOURCE: Shrigley, R. L. (1985). Curbing student disruption in the classroom—teachers need intervention skills. *NASSP Bulletin, 69,* 26–32.

Classroom Disturbance: Temper Tantrums

Tantrums may occur as part of normal development in children one to four years of age or they may represent significant psychological or behavioral maladjustment, particularly when they linger into the elementary years. In their most severe form, they may include self-injury or aggressive acts toward others and therefore need to be treated as quickly as possible. While tantrums are traditionally viewed as bids for attention, they may also signal social skill deficits, a need to escape adversity or manipulate situations, or an inability to express needs verbally. Treatment requires a careful analysis of the motivating conditions.

Delayed Punishment for Tantrums

AUTHORS: Ahmos Rolider and Ron Van Houten

PRECIS: Reducing tantrums using delayed punishment mediated by taped recordings

INTRODUCTION: Delayed mediated punishment can be very effective in suppressing a target behavior when immediate consequences cannot be applied. Marking the child's hand with a pen for later time outs or tape recording misbehavior for later replay and punishment are examples of such mediational stimuli. This delayed strategy was applied in three separate studies to reduce tantruming in five-, ten-, twelve-, and thirteen-year-old students.

METHOD: For the first study, loud public tantrums were targeted in Michael, a five-year-old psychotic boy. Tantrums were monitored on the twenty-minute taxi ride to school, during the ten-minute wait for the bus after school with his mother, and on the twenty-minute bus ride home. Following an initial baseline period in which no special procedures were in effect, two "movement suppression" conditions separated by a second baseline period were conducted. Michael was told his behavior was being recorded by the taxi driver and his mother, and the recorder was placed in clear view. That evening Michael's parents played back a one-minute segment of the tape documenting the tantruming while the mother said, "Listen," described the tantrum, then said, "This is the way Michael behaved in the taxi (bus, etc.) today." When the tape ended, a "movement suppression" procedure was instituted. Michael had to stand in the corner with his chin pressed to the corner, hands crossed behind his back, and feet together against the wall. Any movement, however slight, brought a strong reprimand from a parent not to move or talk, accompanied by the parent's pressing Michael into the corner with a hand against his back. The parent stood behind Michael during the twenty-second suppression phase, which ended when he did not move for fifteen seconds. This entire process was then repeated three more times beginning with the playing of the tape. If tantruming occurred in two or three of the observation settings, the procedure was repeated twice for each setting. The parents received training in this procedure and were initially observed for correct implementation. In addition, the tape recorder was gradually faded during the last five sessions of the second experimental condition until it was not visible during the last session.

Follow-up observations were obtained approximately fifteen days apart for two months. Observers scored the percentage of nineteen second intervals on the tape on which the tantruming was recorded. The intervention reduced tantruming from baseline rates of 39 percent (taxi), 34 percent (waiting for bus), and 57 percent (bus), to 7.5 percent, 2.3 percent, and 6 percent, respectively, in the first mediated suppression phase. After a moderate increase in tantruming when baseline was reinstated, rates dropped to 2 percent in the taxi and less than 1 percent in the two bus settings when the intervention was reapplied. Follow-up yielded only one tantrum on the bus.

In the second study, tape recorder–mediated punishment was compared with a tape recorder playback–no punishment condition. Two tantruming boys, aged twelve and thirteen, were tape recorded for twenty-five minutes each day. Baseline was followed by a "teacher praise" condition in which the teacher praised appropriate behavior. In the tape recorder playback alone condition, the recorder was placed on the teacher's desk, started at the first tantrum, and kept on for the rest of the period. At the end of the day, the teacher played four samples of tantrum behavior for the principal in his office with the students present. After listening, he expressed a hope that the students' behavior would improve the next day. For the mediated punishment condition, the principal applied the movement suppression procedure after hearing the segments. Baseline tantrums were 50 percent and 66 percent for the two students. Teacher praise had no effect; the tape recorder alone reduced one student's rate to 30 percent while having no effect on the second student. Mediated punishment reduced both students' rates to 6 percent and 7 percent with maintenance of effects during follow-up.

In the third study, marking the student's hand, playing taped recordings, and giving live verbal descriptions were compared as mediating stimuli. Inappropriate verbalizations at home were targeted for a ten-year-old mildly retarded youngster, and delayed reprimands were delivered, mediated by one of the three actions above. Results indicated the clear superiority of the taped mediator over the marks or verbal descriptions.

COMMENTARY: Several important points are made by the authors. First, while tape recorder–mediated punishment is an effective technique for reducing tantruming, the punishment must follow the mediating stimulus. Playing the tapes alone did not reduce inappropriate behaviors. Second, the authors advise the practitioner using a punishment strategy to reward positive alternative behavior to increase the power of the strategy and to help maintain the good relationship between the adult and child. Third, they suggest using the movement suppression procedure only after other less aversive punishments prove ineffective. Ethical issues must always be considered when punishing contingencies are used. Finally, the use of videotaping is proposed when using delayed punishment for nonverbal behavior. There are many practical reasons that consequences for a given behavior must be delayed. This technique provides a method of delivering delayed punishments using a mediated stimulus that maintains the power of the effect over time.

SOURCE: Rolider, A., & Van Houten, R. (1985). Suppressing tantrum behavior in public places through the use of delayed punishment mediated by audio recordings. *Behavior Therapy, 16,* 181–194.

Contingent-Interrupted Auditory
Stimulation to Manage Crying

AUTHORS: Leigh A. Strawbridge, Lori A. Sisson, and Vincent B. Van Hasselt

PRECIS: The removal of audiotaped environmental sounds when crying and screaming occurred as a way to decrease these behaviors by a multi-handicapped girl

INTRODUCTION: There is considerable interest in finding alternatives to punitive and restrictive procedures for changing behavior of persons with severe handicaps. Recent research has supported the use of a variation of typical reinforcement programs; the reinforcement is delivered at the beginning of a session and continues until the target behavior occurs, when it is immediately terminated. Only cessation of the inappropriate behavior can reinstate the reinforcement. This approach was tried in this study using tactile stimulation (back massage) and then auditory stimulation (environmental sounds) as reinforcers.

INTERVENTION: A ten-year-old girl with multiple handicaps including mental retardation, several physical handicaps, visual impairment, cerebral palsy, and seizure disorder was the subject in this study. Her crying and screaming behavior when she was approached by an adult or when demands were made on her was disruptive and led to excessive drooling and nasal discharge, which limited the likelihood of social contacts. Previous treatment efforts over several years had been unsuccessful.

　　　Informal observation identified two possible positive reinforcers: certain types of tactile and auditory stimulation. A multiple baseline design across three settings within the classroom — sitting, kneeling, and standing — was used. Contingent-interrupted vibration was evaluated first. Following baseline, vibration in the form of back massage was applied continuously to the child until she began a crying or screaming episode. At this point the stimulus was removed; it was reinstated only when the behavior ceased. This pattern resulted in minimal behavior change. Next, an environmental sounds tape put out by Developmental Learning Materials was played at high volume until an inappropriate response occurred. The tape recorder was turned back on when this behavior stopped. In contrast to the results of the tactile stimulation, with the auditory stimulation the child's crying and screaming was reduced across all three settings. Attempts to fade the intervention by reducing the volume of the tape were successful in the sitting and kneeling positions but not in the standing position. Follow-up at five months showed that the reduction in disruptive behaviors was maintained and fading was successfully accomplished in the standing position as well.

COMMENTARY: This intervention was carried out in the classroom by the teacher with other students present. It was less aversive than many other techniques used with children with severe handicaps. Further, it was a creative approach to a difficult problem and suggests potential applicability for other students with severe disabilities.

The importance of identifying an appropriate reinforcer is underscored in this study. The continuous nature of this reinforcer provided constant feedback, unlike use of tokens or other tangible or social reinforcers.

SOURCE: Strawbridge, L. A., Sisson, L. A., & Van Hasselt, V. B. (1987). Reducing disruptive behavior in the classroom using contingent-interrupted auditory stimulation. *Journal of the Association for Persons with Severe Handicaps, 12,* 199–204.

Training Communication Skills

AUTHORS: Edward G. Carr and V. Mark Durand

PRECIS: Reducing the need for disruptive behavior by teaching appropriate verbal communication of needs

INTRODUCTION: Students may engage in serious problem behaviors such as tantrums or self-injury either to escape from an aversive situation, such as hard work, or to receive attention from the teacher or other adult. However, if more socially appropriate behaviors that serve the same escape or attention-seeking functions could be substituted for these maladaptive reactions, the best interests of the student would clearly be served. In two studies, the authors first identify situations that elicit escape or attention-seeking problem behavior, then reinforce replacement behaviors that reduce these problems.

STUDY I: Four developmentally delayed children, ages seven to fourteen, were chosen as subjects because they demonstrated a minimum of one problem behavior each hour and could produce at least single-word communications. Jim, Tom, and Sue all displayed tantrums among other disruptive conduct. Over the course of the daily ten-minute work sessions, each child was exposed to two levels of task difficulty (easy and hard) combined with two levels of adult attention (100 percent or 33 percent of the observation intervals). This produced three experimental conditions: Easy 100, Easy 33, and Difficult 100. During the Easy 100 condition, the students engaged in receptive labeling and match-to-sample tasks using Peabody Picture Vocabulary cards on which they had been pretested at perfect accuracy. In addition, attention in the form of instructions or pleasant comments was provided in 100 percent of the observation intervals. If the student left the chair and did not return within ten seconds, he or she was guided back with no comment. Physical restraint was used for risky behavior.

The Easy 33 condition used the Easy 100 match-to-sample task, collapsed instructions and praise together into every third observation interval, and eliminated the comments. This reduced attention to 33 percent while keeping task difficulty at the same level as the Easy 100 condition. The Difficult 100 condition duplicated the Easy 100 level of attention but used difficult Peabody cards on which the student pretested at chance levels of accuracy.

Having confirmed that the two levels of attention and task difficulty were established, the authors report three patterns of increase in disruptive behaviors displayed by the students: (1) those occurring more frequently during the Difficult 100 condition, suggesting a need to escape the adverse difficult task; (2) those that increased during the Easy 33 condition, indicating bids for attention; and (3) those that students displayed during both conditions, indicating multiple causation. The Easy 100 produced no disruptive behavior as the task was easy and the adults' attention constant.

STUDY II: To reduce the disruptive behaviors demonstrated in the Difficult 100 and Easy 33 conditions, students from study I were taught substitute behaviors in the form of verbal statements designed to obtain assistance with difficult tasks or solicit attention in the form of praise. The procedure from study I was duplicated except that the experimenter would ask, "Do you have any questions?" after every wrong answer in the Difficult 100 condition and at an average rate of every thirty seconds in the Easy 33 condition. Two phases defined this study. In the relevant response phase, students learned to answer the question with phrases related to the reasons for their disruptive behaviors. Thus, the students who behaved disruptively to escape difficult tasks in the Difficult 100 condition were taught to say, "I don't understand," while those who sought attention during the Easy 33 condition were trained to say, "Am I doing good work?" The experimenter would then provide the appropriate assistance or attention by pointing to and naming the correct Peabody picture or providing a statement of praise. In the irrelevant response phase, the students were taught the opposite phrase, and the response from the experimenter was likewise opposite.

RESULTS: Training in relevant communicative statements reduced disruptive behaviors in all students while irrelevant phrases produced no change. For example, Jim's percentage of disruption dropped from an average of 36.2 percent of the observation intervals to .5 during the relevant response phases, while remaining at an average 48.8 percent during the irrelevant phases. Other students had similar or better results.

COMMENTARY: This important study provides evidence that when children learn to use language to communicate their needs and receive a reinforcing response, the need to transmit the message through disruptive behavior, whether it be tantrums or other forms of acting out, is significantly reduced. However, the authors strongly emphasize that unless the replacement behavior serves the same function as the maladaptive act it replaces, the strategy will fail. Thus, study I is an essential component in that it provides a functional analysis of the problem behavior, helping the practitioner understand the stimulus conditions producing the misconduct. Clearly, verbal statements are a more socially acceptable form of communication than are tantrums or self-injury, and this form of training might be likened to a variation of social skills training. As the authors indicate, it further empowers developmentally disabled children by teaching them to assert their needs actively but appropriately, rather than being left with a choice of passively accepting reward or acting up to get their point across. Given the growing literature on the communicative intent of nonverbal behavior, it is possible that a broad population of children would abandon disruptive behavior if they were taught appropriate verbal means of stating their needs.

SOURCE: Carr, E. G., & Durand, V. M. (1985). Reducing behavior problems through functional communication training. *Journal of Applied Behavior Analysis, 18,* 111–126.

A Paradoxical Intervention to Reduce Tantrums

AUTHOR: John A. Zarske

PRECIS: Reducing tantrums by paradoxically encouraging tantrum behavior

INTRODUCTION: Tantrums have a relentless quality that creates anger and feelings of powerlessness in a child's caregivers. Paradoxical intervention, as a form of "strategic" or "communication" therapy, has effectively reduced tantruming by urging the child to perform the target behavior in a predetermined spot and for a given length of time. This case study describes the use of a two-step paradoxical strategy with Tom, a five-year-old boy with cerebral palsy who displayed one to ten tantrums per day for more than six months.

PARADOXICAL INTERVENTION: After the mother had obtained five days of baseline behavior data (frequency, duration, and location of tantrums), the parents and child aide were told to urge Tom to tantrum whenever he began. They were instructed to tell Tom that tantrums were perfectly acceptable but that he must choose a place and have them only there. Furthermore, they asked him to tell them when he was about to tantrum so he could be moved to his place. They remained with him during his tantrum.

This approach was extended to his preschool through the aide who was always with him there. During phase 2 of treatment, the adults informed Tom that he could have as many tantrums as he pleased whenever he pleased, but would now be able to have them alone in his place.

RESULTS: Over the first two weeks of the intervention, tantruming decreased significantly from a baseline mean of six per day lasting an average of 11 minutes, 13 seconds, to a phase 1 mean of 1.4 per day at an average duration of 2.2 minutes. For the next two weeks of phase 2, frequency decreased to .57 tantrums per day with none at school, while duration dropped to 40.4 seconds per tantrum.

COMMENTARY: While the paradoxical technique seems easy to use, the author cautions that it requires proper training. Further, school-based use of the technique may necessitate having an aide to monitor the child's behavior. More restrictive steps, such as imposing a time limit on the tantrums, might be needed if the behavior continues. The paradoxical method also requires a certain level of intelligence in the child for him or her to process the double message, recognize the decreasing influence of the tantrum, and evaluate the need for more adaptive responses to crises.

SOURCE: Zarske, J. A. (1982). The treatment of temper tantrums in a cerebral palsied child: A paradoxical intervention. *School Psychology Review, 11,* 324–328.

Treating Tantrums on the School Bus

AUTHORS: Barry C. Barmann, Carol Croyle-Barmann, and Bill McLain

PRECIS: Reducing tantrumlike behavior in a profoundly retarded eight-year-old through contingent interruption of music

INTRODUCTION: A variety of problem behaviors have been decreased in normal and retarded populations by contingently interrupting the playing of enjoyable music when the children display inappropriate conduct. In this study, the procedure was extended to the treatment of disruptive tantrumlike bus behavior in a profoundly retarded eight-year-old girl.

METHOD: The stimulus conditions that almost always led to the disruptive behavior were the slowing down, stopping, or turning of the bus during its fifteen-minute, twice-daily run between the student's home and school. The behavior itself consisted of the child screaming, kicking the seat in front, crying, head banging, and dropping to the floor. The adults on the bus would respond by talking or singing to her, holding her, offering toys, or giving reprimands.

Nothing was effective. After a four-day baseline period, an extinction phase was introduced for thirteen days in which the disruptive behavior was totally ignored. This condition was inserted to check for the possibility that attention from the adults was maintaining the behavior. A three-day continuous music I phase then followed in which, for the entire bus ride, the student listened on headphones to enjoyable music delivered by a portable cassette player. The music played continuously whether or not the student behaved in a disruptive manner. For the four-day interrupted music I condition, an adult discontinued the music by removing the headphones whenever the student began to be disruptive; the music was not restored until the child sat quietly for five seconds. Continuous and interrupted music conditions were then alternated twice more for the same number of days each. A fading procedure was instituted during the first two days of the final interrupted music condition, in which the following components of the program were gradually withdrawn: First, the headphones were eliminated so that music was heard from the cassette machine; second, the music was played more softly and for shorter periods; third, the practitioner gradually moved further from the client until he was totally absent. The driver then played the bus radio from time to time when the student was quiet. During an eight-week follow-up period, disruptive behavior was charted on one randomly selected day each week.

RESULTS: For the baseline, extinction, and first continuous music phases, the child displayed disruptive behavior during 93.5 percent, 99 percent, and 96 percent of the bus rides. The first interrupted phase reduced the behavior to 45 percent of the time, while the return to the second continuous music condition pushed the disruptiveness back up to 86 percent. During the second interrupted music period, the target behavior dropped to 32 percent, then rose to 91 percent for the third continuous music phase. The final interrupted music phase resulted in the student's displaying disruptive behavior for only 8.5 percent of the bus ride. Fading and follow-up maintained the effects of the intervention.

COMMENTARY: Safety requires strategies to control inappropriate behavior on a school bus. This easily administered, quick-acting treatment was successful with a profoundly retarded youngster and might also prove useful with nonretarded behavior-disordered students who often wreak havoc on the bus. These students need to realize that the standards for appropriate behavior do not end when they leave the classroom. The bus is, in reality, an extension of the school and should be regarded as such.

SOURCE: Barmann, B. C., Croyle-Barmann, C., & McLain, B. (1980). The use of contingent-interrupted music in the treatment of disruptive bus-riding behavior. *Journal of Applied Behavior Analysis, 13,* 693–698.

Additional Readings

Lexmond, T. (1987). Children and temper tantrums. In A. Thomas & J. Grimes (Eds.), *Children's needs: Psychological perspectives* (pp. 627–633). Washington, DC: National Association of School Psychologists.

When young children tantrum they tend to repeat the same behaviors; these range from sulking to self-injury. Tantrums that exceed normal expectations may affect parent-child relationships, limit social contacts, and interfere with learning at school. However, tantrums may be typical between twelve months and four years of age and can indicate age-appropriate frustration and developing independence. They become problematic when they begin to satisfy needs of the child that would not otherwise be met and thus become a manipulative tool. Interventions should match the reason for the tantrums, so observing the tantruming child and interviewing the caregivers are important preintervention activities. The interview should cover child and family background; eliminate situational or medical reasons; gather information about the frequency, duration, and chronicity of the tantrums; identify behaviors displayed during the episodes; and explore the antecedent conditions, locations of tantrums, generalizability across caregivers, behavior of caregivers during the tantrums, punishments given, and reactions of siblings. Finally, restrictions imposed on the child's normal routines and other activities as a result of the behavior should be determined. Before tantrums become well established, caregivers should be informed about their causes and dynamics, and they should be provided a clear developmental perspective. They can then manage their emotional responses to the tantrums and perhaps short-circuit the problem. Strategies for chronic tantruming include time out, planned ignoring, differential reinforcement, paradoxical intervention, and chaining/fading.

Rincover, A., & Tripp, J. K. (1979). Management and education of autistic children. *School Psychology Digest, 8,* 397–411.

As more seriously disturbed students are educated closer to the mainstream, teachers will need help developing behavior-control strategies to manage the variety of behavior problems they will encounter. Among other issues, this article addressed interventions to control tantrums, a common pattern in autistic children. Tantrums may be motivated by differing needs such as attention (positive reinforcement) or escape from adversity (negative reinforcement), and each situation requires individual analysis before treatment approaches are initiated. For example, treating tantrums through time out when the motivating need is escape may increase tantrums because it provides the negatively reinforcing removal that originally prompted the tantrum behavior. Conversely, providing attention to children who tantrum to gain such positive reinforcement will tend to maintain the behavior. In addition, differential attention may initially increase the undesirable behavior and may not work quickly enough in the case of behavior that is potentially destructive to people and property. Although punishment for tantrums has been effective regardless of the motivating conditions, the authors caution the user to consider the ethical and legal implications of punishment, be aware of possible side effects, and always provide ample positive reward for acceptable behavior, punishing only briefly and only for the tantrums.

Classroom Disturbance: Annoying or Bothering Others

Many forms of misbehavior, ranging from inappropriate comments to un-disguised aggression, prevent other students from completing their work. Sometimes students are not merely distracted but may be drawn into confrontations, which further disrupt classroom routines. Removal of the disruptive student from the room is often a temporary, if not a long-term, solution.

Overcorrection and Reward
to Reduce Inappropriate Touching

AUTHORS: Karleen K. Preator, P. Brent Petersen, William R. Jenson, and Paul Ashcraft

PRECIS: Reducing inappropriate touching through positive practice overcorrection with training and reinforcement of alternative behavior

INTRODUCTION: Overcorrection is an aversive technique in which the student is required to (1) restore a damaged situation to a better condition than when originally encountered (restitution overcorrection) or (2) practice appropriate behaviors rather than the ones that required the intervention (positive practice overcorrection). Although this strategy has been effective in reducing many maladaptive behaviors in autistic and developmentally disabled youngsters, punishment strategies are generally believed to maintain and generalize their effects better when teamed with reward for positive behavior. This study combined overcorrection and alternative response training to reduce inappropriate touching in a six-year-old autistic Native American boy.

METHOD: This youngster had made progress in his day treatment program, but his constant touching of things and people distressed his mother and impeded his learning. After a three-week baseline period, positive practice overcorrection was instituted. Whenever he touched something or someone inappropriately, the student was immediately required to raise his arms over his head and lower them to his side, repeating the motion without stopping for three minutes. At first, he was manually guided in this action, then prompted verbally. When he began to touch even during the intervention, the strategy was changed and he was instructed to sit down and stand up repeatedly, using a straight-back chair, for three minutes. After fifteen weeks, alternative response training and differential reinforcements were carried out in four steps three times weekly over four weeks. First, the therapist modeled appropriate asking behavior by holding up a toy and saying, "If you want to touch the (toy), ask me. Say, 'May I touch the toy?'" Second, the therapist prompted the student by using only the first sentence above. In step 3, the trainer briefly prompted him by saying only, "Ask me." Finally, four toys were displayed with no verbal guidance. The child was required to complete ten trials in which he asked to touch the toy, with 100 percent correct behavior, or twenty trials with 80 percent correct behavior. After that, different objects were presented anywhere in the building by any therapist to promote the child's generalization of proper asking behavior, which was praised when it occurred.

RESULTS: Baseline touching averaged twenty-six to forty-three incidents per day. Overcorrection reduced the behavior to about six instances per day. Training further decreased incidents to one per day, then to .5 per day after thirty weeks. A two-year follow-up showed maintenance of the decreased rate and generalization of reduced touching and increased question asking in the home and other places.

COMMENTARY: This study clearly demonstrates how positively reinforcing alternative behavior increases the power of an aversive technique. In these situations, it is not enough to punish for wrongdoing; the child must also be taught substitute behavior for the unacceptable actions. All children, regardless of their disability, cannot be expected to behave responsibly without learning how to distinguish responsible from irresponsible acts.

SOURCE: Preator, K. K., Petersen, P. B., Jenson, W. R., & Ashcraft, P. (1984). Overcorrection and alternative response training in the reduction of an autistic child's inappropriate touching. *School Psychology Review, 13,* 107–110.

Self-Managing Bothersome Behavior

AUTHORS: Debra J. Smith, K. Richard Young, Richard P. West, Daniel P. Morgan, and Ginger Rhode

PRECIS: Student self-management successful in reducing disruptive behavior in a resource room but not successful in generalizing to a regular education classroom

INTRODUCTION: Self-management procedures successfully place the responsibility for behavior control in the student's hands, allowing the teacher more time for teaching and helping students with their work. Self-management has been shown to maintain treatment effects from token economy programs, but there is insufficient research to demonstrate whether self-evaluation strategies can by themselves reduce behavior problems. This study examined self-evaluation as a method for curtailing disruptive classroom behavior and promoting generalization of gains from a resource room to a regular education history class.

SELF-MANAGEMENT: Four young adolescents with high rates of disruptive, off-task, annoying, and bothersome behavior served as subjects. Students were observed for thirty minutes each day in their half-day resource program. Following a baseline period, a self-management training phase was begun in the resource room. Classroom rules were described by the teacher who instructed the students to rate their adherence to the rules every ten minutes on a self-evaluation card by awarding themselves 0 to 5 points according to criteria posted in class. A rating of 0 denoted unacceptable behavior and work habits while a score of 5 indicated excellent rule following with no reprimands or reminders to behave or to work. Ratings 1 through 4 corresponded to graded levels of appropriate behavior. Every ten minutes, the students compared their ratings with the teacher's ratings of their behavior, awarding themselves the same number of points as the teacher's rating if they matched within one point. Exact matches received an additional bonus point. Points were traded for tangibles after each resource period.

The second phase of treatment (fading) was implemented when most students were earning bonus points as well as ratings of four or five points on three consecutive days. Students then compared self- and teacher ratings every fifteen minutes instead of every ten minutes. After a second baseline, in a second fading condition students compared ratings only at the end of the thirty-minute observation period. After five weeks of self-evaluation, students rated their behavior during a half-hour work period in their regular education history class. The regular classroom teachers were instructed in the rating system and asked to compare ratings with the students at the end of class. Points earned were traded for rewards in the resource room the next day.

RESULTS: Observers recorded the percentage of ten-second observation intervals during which the target behaviors occurred. Results showed all four students displaying reduced levels of off-task/disruptive behavior during self-evaluation. Baseline rates of misbehavior for the four students were 71 percent, 63 percent, 62 percent, and 74 percent; these were reduced to 17 percent, 24 percent, 25 percent, and 11 percent, respectively, during the intervention. Levels for all subjects increased during reversal conditions. No evidence of generalization to the regular education class was indicated when the modified self-evaluation procedure was introduced.

COMMENTARY: This study demonstrates that self-management can work without an initial external reinforcement strategy, such as a token economy system, to control disruptive behavior. Thus, self-evaluation can function independently to promote behavior change as well as to maintain reduced levels of misbehavior achieved through earlier strategies. According to the authors, the failure to achieve generalization to the regular education classroom was not unexpected. Teachers reported being too busy or forgetting to rate students' behavior after each class. Unfortunately, this is not an uncommon problem and requires the practitioner to carefully assess the ability and/or willingness of the mainstream teacher to carry out the intervention procedure. Strategies vary in their degree of intrusiveness into the life of the classroom, and teachers likewise differ in their tolerance for intrusion.

While new laws and new trends will require regular education teachers to accept students with a broader range of disabilities into their classrooms, practitioners will need to find ways to assist these teachers in managing behavior problems while allowing them to devote maximum time to instruction. This is a delicate balance that will tax the energy, skill, and commitment of all school professionals.

SOURCE: Smith, D. J., Young, K. R., West, R. P., Morgan, D. P., & Rhode, G. (1988). Reducing the disruptive behavior of junior high school students: A classroom self-management procedure. *Behavioral Disorders, 13,* 231–239.

Response Cost to Reduce
Inappropriate Demands for Help

AUTHORS: Spencer J. Salend and Kathy Henry

PRECIS: Two case studies demonstrating the utility of the response cost strategy in mainstream settings

INTRODUCTION: A free token response cost strategy may be able to reduce misbehavior in the mainstream with minimal time commitment from the teacher. Economy of time is crucial if such interventions are to be accepted by teachers as practical aids in managing behavior problems. Two case studies evaluate the response cost technique in regular education settings.

CASE STUDY I: A second grader constantly asked for help with assignments even though he had demonstrated the ability to master the tasks. A seven-day baseline period was first instituted in the morning language arts session after the student demonstrated that he understood the work. The thirty-day response cost strategy was implemented by first explaining the entire procedure to the boy. A set of construction paper strips, corresponding to the allowed number of assistance-seeking actions, were then taped to the student's desk. Once the child displayed an understanding of the work, he was told that any further appeal for help would require him to give the teacher one paper strip after the teacher commented, "I think you understand." If the student had any strips remaining after the two-hour period, he received a reward in the form of teacher attention (for example, lunch with the teacher, sharing a soda, or helping the teacher on various tasks). Initially, the student received eleven strips; this number was gradually reduced to fewer than five as assistance seeking declined. A second seven-day baseline period was then followed by another intervention condition lasting twelve days. Baseline 1 yielded an average of 20.3 assistance-seeking behaviors; this dropped dramatically to a mean of 1.5 during the first intervention phase. The reversal phase generated a mean of five requests for help while the second intervention reduced appeals to an average of .73.

CASE STUDY II: A fifth-grade boy attending resource room and regular education classes frequently called out and did not raise his hand in reading class. During a six-day baseline period, the teacher recorded the number of inappropriate attention-seeking comments during afternoon reading. For the intervention (nineteen days), the boy received construction paper slips corresponding to the number of nonauthorized callouts the teacher would allow. At first, the student was given five slips; this number diminished to one by the second intervention phase. If all the strips had not been used by the end of the forty-minute class, the student was rewarded with a class job. Following a reversal phase of five days, the second intervention condition lasted ten days. The average number of the student's inappropriate verbalizations during baseline was 6.1, dropping to 1.2 during the first response cost phase, reverting to 3 during baseline 2, and diminishing to .6 in the second intervention period.

COMMENTARY: Mainstream teachers are more willing to participate in a behavior management strategy when the procedure is easy to implement. Using paper slips eliminated record keeping, allowing the teacher to manage the program without losing instructional time. The authors further note that while the students could not earn back lost strips, there were no negative behavioral side effects, as had been suggested in other research. The absence of such adverse reactions may hinge on the noncontingent provision of slips at the beginning of the intervention. In contrast, when contingently rewarded tokens are lost, negative side effects are more likely. Thus, this technique seems well suited for the regular education classroom.

SOURCE: Salend, S. J., & Henry, K. (1981). Response cost in mainstreamed settings. *Journal of School Psychology, 19,* 242–249.

Additional Readings

Brown, J. E. (1986). The use of paradoxical intention with oppositional behavior in the classroom. *Psychology in the Schools, 23,* 77–81.

Three case studies illustrate the strengths and weaknesses of paradoxical strategies for controlling difficult behavior. In one case, Ron, an eight-year-old, was referred for pinching, kicking, and hitting classmates. For the intervention, adults first redefined his problem as an inability to control his behavior. He then was told that each time he behaved aggressively, he would have a chance to practice the aggressive movements with his teacher outside of class. It is interesting that no further aggressive action was reported. In the other cases, the procedure either failed because of lack of commitment by the principal, teacher, and parents, or did not generalize to other teachers and settings. The author offers the following guidelines: (1) utilize reframing to set the stage for the paradoxical instruction; (2) work toward consistency of application by the teacher; (3) obtain family support if possible, but do not abandon the technique if this cooperation cannot be secured; (4) assess family dynamics to determine whether positive behavior changes in the child can be tolerated; (5) attempt to achieve administrative support; (6) include teacher and child in all meetings related to the intervention. The author emphasizes the need for further research to develop evidence regarding this procedure.

Kehle, T. J., Clark, E., Jenson, W. R., & Wampold, B. E. (1986). Effectiveness of self-observation with behavior disordered elementary school children. *School Psychology Review, 15,* 289–295.

McCurdy, B. L., & Shapiro, E. S. (1988). Self-observation and the reduction of inappropriate classroom behavior. *Journal of School Psychology, 26,* 371–378.

Two studies evaluated the effects of self-observation on inappropriate classroom behavior. In the first study, four disruptive preadolescents were videotaped in their classroom during regular lessons. They were instructed to be on their best behavior during the taping. Three of the tapes were edited to show only appropriate behavior and each of the students viewed his or her own individual eleven-minute tape daily for five days. The control subject viewed his tape unedited, observing both appropriate and inappropriate behavior. The procedure resulted in dramatic improvement in behavior for all experimental subjects; this was maintained at a six-week follow-up. The behavior of the control student deteriorated but then improved significantly when his tape was edited and viewed. In the second study, a modified replication of study 1 occurred with the following changes: (1) Baseline data were collected for five to fifteen days after videotaping as well as before to examine the possible effects of instructing students to behave appropriately during the taping. (2) In addition to seeing the videotape of themselves, some students observed a videotape of a peer also engaging in appropriate behavior. Results indicated idiosyncratic changes in disruptive behavior of students who engaged in both peer and self-observations in the direction of study 1 but at much lower magnitudes. Thus, while self-observation shows some potential as a method for reducing misconduct, further research is needed to understand its full effects and limitations.

Classroom Disturbance:
Out-of-Seat (Off-Task) Behavior

Descriptions of off-task behavior in the literature seem to focus on three major attributes: (1) the behavior is not task oriented; (2) it does not typically involve interaction with another child; (3) if other children are distracted, it is not usually intentional. Off-task behavior that does not disrupt or distract other children (for example, daydreaming) may not cause the classroom teacher the immediate concerns that arise when actions are disruptive to the class. However, the outcome is often the same for the child: lowered academic performance. The reader is referred to other sections of this book that address inattention and other related behaviors.

Modifying Behavior Using Direct Instruction

AUTHOR: Maribeth Gettinger

PRECIS: Using direct instruction to reduce daydreaming and impulsivity and to enhance learning

INTRODUCTION: Direct instruction (DI) is a teacher-centered, academically focused, structured methodology in which the teacher controls the learning tasks, teaches in well-defined steps, works with groups, provides practice and corrective feedback, allows time for learning, and develops questions that ensure correct answers. While DI has been consistently effective with regular education students, little has been done to determine its benefits for educationally disabled youngsters. However, since children with learning deficits typically display the same negative classroom behaviors for which DI programs are developed, these youngsters may well improve through use of the DI techniques. This study demonstrates the use of DI strategies to teach a three-week phonics sequence and to reduce nondisruptive off-task behavior (doodling, looking out the window), impulsivity, and off-task verbal interactions.

METHOD: Eight learning disabled students with a mean age of seven years, nine months, were taught by two trained teachers in two groups of four for thirty-minute instructional phonics sessions. The teacher taught short *e* and short *i* sounds using a DI model with the following five components: (1) teacher-directed sequenced learning involving sound-symbol association, initial bigrams, blends, consonant-vowel-consonant (CVC) words, word discrimination, and sentences using CVC words; (2) group instruction of three to six students using round-robin individual practice and group practice; (3) mastery learning to a criterion level of one correct trial for each sequenced subskill; (4) repeated practice of words grouped by initial bigram pattern, words with mixed patterns, and sentences containing these words; (5) feedback to students preceded by teacher modeling of correct blends. Correct responses are repeated by the group, while wrong answers are repeated by the child alone.

RESULTS: Nondisruptive off-task behavior and impulsive behavior were reduced from baseline occurrence rates of 76 percent and 24 percent, respectively, to 19 percent and 6 percent for the eight students combined. Verbalizations were unchanged. Testing indicated a concomitant increase in performance on the training and transfer words.

COMMENTARY: DI reduces off-task nondisruptive behavior and is an effective format for teaching small groups of learning disabled students. As shown in other research, when intervention strategies successfully target academic performance, simultaneous improvement often occurs in associated classroom behaviors. Although DI appears to restate basic elements of good teaching, it represents a systematic empirically based approach that can help teachers better structure their efforts with children.

SOURCE: Gettinger, M. (1982). Improving classroom behaviors and achievement of learning disabled children using direct instruction. *School Psychology Review, 11,* 329–336.

Reducing Off-Task Behavior with Encouragement and Reprimands

AUTHORS: Ann J. Abramowitz, Susan G. O'Leary, and Lee A. Rosén

PRECIS: Reprimands more effective than encouragement in reducing daydreaming and hyperactivity

INTRODUCTION: Unlike reprimands that have been documented as effective in reducing daydreaming and other off-task behaviors, little research exists to determine whether encouraging or reassuring comments have similar reductive effects. Two studies were performed to determine which of these teacher responses more successfully limited inappropriate classroom behavior.

STUDY I: Subjects were two summer reading classes of eight students, seven to nine years old, who scored two or more standard deviations above the mean on measures of hyperactivity or daydreaming and/or were deficient in reading or math. Students were observed for their on- or off-task behaviors, while teacher reactions were categorized as praise, reprimands, encouraging comments, and slashes (placed next to a student's name on the chalkboard as part of a behavior management program for disruptive behavior). For baseline, the teacher looked over the class seven times during the reading group but gave no feedback except to note slashes. In the encouragement phase the teacher directed an encouraging statement to any child detected as off task (for example, "try your best," "keep trying," "I know you can do it"). No praise or reprimands were given. For the reprimand condition a statement was directed to the off-task child following the scan that indicated the behavior to be stopped, the preferred behavior, or both. Results showed that reprimands significantly lowered rates of off-task behavior while each student responded in an individual manner to encouragement. Academic performance as measured by scores on an arithmetic worksheet was not positively affected by either intervention.

STUDY II: The same two classes were exposed to both encouragement and reprimand conditions in this study. All procedures were the same as in study I. Results showed that thirteen of the sixteen students were off task less in the reprimand than the encouragement condition. For both classes reprimands resulted in significantly lower off-task rates than encouragement. In addition, the reprimand condition produced a significantly greater number of correctly completed problems than did the encouragement condition for one class but not the other.

COMMENTARY: Teachers often report that it is necessary to establish a firm, structured disciplinary style earlier in the school year; this then can be relaxed as the students become responsive. Research tends to support this position and suggests that the effects of encouragement and reprimands may change as a function of the time of year. The authors further suggest that encouragement might have a more powerful influence on off-task behavior in different situations. In the studies reported here the students were engaged in independent seat work when scanned by the teacher. A different outcome might result if reprimands and/or encouragement were delivered during a teacher-directed lesson or on occurrence of on-task as well as off-task behaviors. These possibilities require further exploration and suggest that the context within which these responses are given and the nature of the response preceding the reaction may be crucial. Perhaps, as the authors note, encouragement contingent on off-task behavior may *increase* its rate. Similarly, encouraging comments delivered on the observance of on-task behaviors may well increase their occurrence. Thus, the important issue may be to help the teacher gauge the best moment to deliver encouragement and reprimands to maximize positive and reduce inappropriate behaviors.

SOURCE: Abramowitz, A. J., O'Leary, S. G., & Rosén, L. A. (1987). Reducing off-task behavior in the classroom: A comparison of encouragement and reprimands. *Journal of Abnormal Child Psychology, 15,* 153–163.

Peer-Mediated Interventions for Off-Task Behavior

AUTHORS: George W. Stern, Susan A. Fowler, and Frank W. Kohler

PRECIS: Using peer-mediated strategies to improve the behavior and academic performance of both the peer monitor and point earner

INTRODUCTION: In peer-mediated strategies, students both administer and receive the intervention. An important question focuses on which of these two participants benefits the most from the treatment or whether both are affected equally. The following study explored this question.

METHOD: Subjects were two students in a combined fifth/sixth grade classroom referred for disruptive behavior during seat work and infrequent completion of math assignments. Other students from their math group were chosen as their partners. Behavior was recorded for a half hour on each day students were engaged in independent seat work to complete math assignments. The target students and partners alternated as peer monitors and point earners every other day and were trained in pairs as monitors. Training involved explaining why the student was chosen to participate, describing the program, modeling the use of monitoring materials, explaining the group reward strategy, providing practice for each child to 100 percent accuracy, and facilitating comments and questions. During the intervention, the monitors for that day had to finish their assignments, evaluate the point earners' behavior and attention to assignments using a Good Behavior Checklist, and distribute points for behavior and work according to preestablished criteria. At random points during the daily sessions, the checklist was filled in and given to the point earner. At the end of each session, the monitor filled in a Good Work Checklist for the point earner, awarding a point for meeting the criterion for good work. If each partner group earned their daily points on three or four consecutive sessions, the entire class earned a group reward. Observers recorded disruptive, off-task, and on-task behavior for the two subjects and seven other classmates, three who were not involved in the strategy and four "decoy" students, who participated to lessen the stigma on the two target students. Amount and accuracy of math work completed was also recorded.

RESULTS: Inappropriate behavior was effectively reduced for the two target students and the decoy students regardless of whether they acted as point earners or peer monitors. Amount of math work completed also increased for the two subjects, although accuracy varied idiosyncratically. Peer monitors matched adult observers' evaluations on the checklists 100 percent of the time for positive evaluations, and 74 to 83 percent of the time for negative evaluations. One partner never gave a negative evaluation.

COMMENTARY: It appears that both participants in peer-mediated interventions benefit from the procedure when roles are alternated and group rewards are provided. The authors advocate additional exploration when group contingencies are not provided, as well as an evaluation of the technique when roles are not switched. One subject maintained low levels of inappropriate behavior during reversal of treatment while the other did not. This too merits further study. As with self-management approaches, an advantage of this technique lies in the responsibility assumed by students, allowing the teacher to provide instruction. As the demands on teachers increase, it is important to know that students can take an active part in improving their own behaviors.

SOURCE: Stern, G. W., Fowler, S. A., & Kohler, F. W. (1988). A comparison of two intervention roles: Peer monitor and point earner. *Journal of Applied Behavior Analysis, 21,* 103–109.

Group Contingencies to Modify Inappropriate Behavior

AUTHORS: Pamela Lynne Crouch, Frank M. Gresham, and William R. Wright

PRECIS: Interdependent and independent group contingencies combined with immediate and delayed reinforcement to improve classroom behavior

INTRODUCTION: Group contingencies occur in one of three ways: an *independent group contingency* offers the same positive or negative consequence to the entire class but each member is rewarded or punished on the basis of his or her individual behavior; in a *dependent group contingency,* the behavior of one individual determines the contingency for the entire group, while an *interdependent group contingency* has the consequences determined by the combined performance of the total group. Group contingencies allow the teacher to manage the behavior of many children with one program and capitalize on the power of peer influence; but the behavior of one child can spoil the reward for many, and students can become even more disruptive if rewards are forfeited for the day. The technique reported here combined both interdependent and independent strategies with immediate and delayed reinforcement to encourage peer influence, reduce the effect of the "spoiler," and control the regression of treatment effects.

METHOD: Third graders attending a forty-five-minute art class once per week were subjects. Off-task, on-task, and disruptive behaviors were targeted for observation. After a four-session baseline phase, the ten-session intervention began with a complete explanation of the program to the children. For the interdependent contingency, the teacher observed the class about every three minutes. If 80 percent of the students were behaving appropriately, a check was placed on a prominently displayed progress chart, and immediate reinforcement was given in the form of praise. Every twelve checks earned a large check at the top of the chart. Two large checks allowed the class ten minutes of free time as a delayed reward. For the independent contingency, a disruptive student was given a gentle rebuke and his or her initials were placed on a special section of the chart. Four or more disruptive incidents by the student resulted in loss of the next morning's recess. Again, following an interdependent format, six or more disruptive students in a given period resulted in a lost opportunity for a check mark for the class and a time-out period during which students had to put their heads down on their desks. After a four-day reversal condition, the strategy was reinstated for the remainder of the school year (three sessions).

RESULTS: Although baseline rates of on-task, off-task, and disruptive behaviors did not suggest a seriously unruly class (62.29 percent, 25.56 percent, and 12.15 percent, respectively), the teacher considered these unacceptable activity and noise levels. After the first treatment condition, the percentage of children on task jumped to 85.64 percent, while off-task and disruptive behaviors declined to 13.67 percent and .69 percent, respectively. Similar changes occurred from reversal to the second treatment condition. The teacher was very pleased with the change and the program.

COMMENTARY: The authors identified the following as separate components of this procedure: rules, feedback, praise, time out, reprimands, token reinforcement, response cost, and Premack reinforcement (use of high-probability behavior to reinforce low-probability behavior). Despite the program's apparent complexity, a one-year teacher with no skills in behavioral intervention was able to carry out the program. This ease of application is crucial if behavior change programs are to be accepted in classrooms. A further analysis might eliminate the need for all eight components and present an even more simplified technique for teacher consumption. Simplification would enhance the teacher's ability to address classroom management problems without the need for separate strategies for each disruptive student.

SOURCE: Crouch, P. L., Gresham, F. M., & Wright, W. R. (1985). Interdependent and independent group contingencies with immediate and delayed reinforcement for controlling classroom behavior. *Journal of School Psychology, 23,* 177–187.

Self- Versus Teacher Assessment of Task-Oriented Behavior

AUTHORS: Daniel P. Hallahan, John Wills Lloyd, Rebecca Dailey Kneedler, and Kathleen J. Marshall

PRECIS: Demonstrating the advantages of self-assessment over teacher assessment to reduce off-task behavior and increase academic performance

INTRODUCTION: Although self-monitoring has been shown to increase on-task behavior in learning disabled students, the authors report a lack of research on whether self-monitoring is a more effective behavior change technique than external monitoring. An eight-year-old learning disabled student with problems attending to tasks served as a subject in a study comparing these two forms of observation.

METHOD: The study took place in the student's special education class during twenty-minute academic seat work sessions. Observers recorded the student's on-task behavior and scored and counted the number of arithmetic problems he completed correctly during each twenty-minute session. In the *self-assessment condition,* the student was trained to respond to a tape-recorded tone that sounded every eleven to ninety-two seconds. At the tone, the student was to ask himself if he was attending and indicate his yes or no answer on a recording sheet at his desk. In the *teacher assessment phase,* the teacher decided at the tone whether the student was attending and signaled him to record a yes or no response with either a "thumbs up" or "thumbs down" sign. He was informed by the teacher each day which condition was operating.

RESULTS: Both self- and teacher assessment resulted in significant increases in on-task behavior, but self-assessment resulted in a median on-task rate of 97 percent while teacher assessment yielded a rate of 88 percent. In addition, the student's self-assessment rates were consistently higher on a day-to-day basis and were reestablished at immediate and consistently high levels during a second treatment phase. During follow-up and fading of the procedure in which the recorded tone and then the recording sheet were eliminated, his on-task behavior was maintained at treatment levels. When the tone was faded, the student was instructed to record his attending whenever it occurred to him. After sheets were removed, he continued with his academic work. His academic rate increased modestly during both teacher and self-assessment, with small differences in favor of self-assessment. Fading had no reductive effects.

COMMENTARY: When students self-assess and self-record their behavior, they seem to show greater improvement than with teacher assessment. However, the same effects are not obtained for academic productivity, as both techniques yielded similar moderate increases in performance rates. Thus, the technique is more effectively used when the goal is to reduce off-task behavior. Teachers find this an appealing approach as it allows the student to run the program after a short training period, freeing the teacher to instruct. The authors also note that treatment effects were maintained well during fading. Thus, the intervention operates without any external indications that treatment is occurring. This is a decided advantage, particularly for adolescents who are typically quite sensitive to the comments of peers, and who would prefer to avoid drawing this kind of attention to themselves.

SOURCE: Hallahan, D. P., Lloyd, J. W., Kneedler, R. D., & Marshall, K. J. (1982). A comparison of the effects of self- versus teacher-assessment of on-task behavior. *Behavior Therapy, 13,* 715–723.

Positive Consequences to Promote Behavior Control

AUTHORS: Linda J. Pfiffner, Lee A. Rosén, & Susan G. O'Leary

PRECIS: An all-positive behavior management system to increase on-task behavior

INTRODUCTION: The frequent use and success of negative contingencies for controlling classroom behavior raises the question of whether a behavior management program that relies only on positive reinforcement can be effective. This issue was explored using eight second- and third-grade students with attention and behavior problems. On-task/off-task behavior was observed for one hour daily as the children worked independently and the teacher provided positive, negative, or neutral feedback. Number and accuracy of reading worksheets completed were also recorded. For the first five treatment days, the teacher used regular rewards and punishments; these consisted of praise, extra credit, display of work, reprimands, time out, and loss of privileges. For the next few days, regular positives only were used and all misbehavior was ignored. Then for ten days enhanced rewards were provided while no negative contingencies were applied. Enhancing rewards involved both increasing regular positives and adding new reinforcements such as song time, special recesses, a "superstar" board for display of work, comic books, use of musical instruments, writing, and drawing. A four-day return to regular positives only was then followed by another four days of regular reward and punishment combined. Then a second "enhanced positives alone" condition provided even stronger rewards than the original phase. In addition, well-behaved students could select a further reward from a daily menu. Finally, another four-day condition provided regular positive and negative consequences.

RESULTS: Results indicated that regular positive consequences alone without negative contingencies could not maintain on-task behavior. Enhanced positive consequences were generally as effective as regular positive and negative feedback, particularly when the reward menu was added. Academic performance also lessened when regular rewards alone were provided but improved and remained reasonably stable during the other conditions. Thus, in order to maintain acceptable levels of behavior without negative consequences, it appears that an extremely potent and personally oriented reward program must be used.

COMMENTARY: The authors also advise that an all-positive system may work only when earlier programs combining positive and negative contingencies have first produced and maintained high levels of acceptable behavior. This notion parallels an often-heard dictum among teachers that classroom controls can be relaxed only after clearly defined limits have been established and enforced early in the school year. These results tend to support that approach, although they also seem to suggest the importance of balancing positive and negative feedback and developing good student–teacher relationships from the very beginning.

SOURCE: Pfiffner, L. J., Rosén, L. A., & O'Leary, S. G. (1985). The efficacy of an all-positive approach to classroom management. *Journal of Applied Behavior Analysis, 18*, 257–261.

Additional Readings

Edwards, L. L. (1980). Curriculum modification as a strategy for helping regular classroom behavior-disordered students. *Focus on Exceptional Children, 12*, 1–11.

Proceeding from the theory that academic success improves problem behavior, a "modified curricular approach" was developed for underachieving students with conduct disorders who were attending a mainstream elementary class. Features of the curriculum included broadly defined curricular goals broken down into instructional objectives, adaptation of course content and teaching materials to accommodate all reading levels, immediate feedback to students on mastery of objectives through a short daily quiz, charting progress and teacher praise as forms of positive reinforcement, and adaptation of workbooks to enhance learning. These curriculum strategies were combined with three behavioral interventions: a token system with backup rewards for attending behavior, a point system for academic performance, and a no-strategy baseline. Evaluation of this package in a social studies unit revealed the superiority of the modified curriculum over a traditional approach under all three intervention conditions. While traditional curriculum students responded more positively to reinforcement of attention to task than to reward of academic performance, the modified approach showed no difference in rates of improvement under either reinforcement of attention or accurate performance. The author recommends as the best approach the use of the modified strategy with a token reward system reinforcing academic performance.

Fishbein, J. E., & Wasik, B. H. (1981). Effect of the good behavior game on disruptive library behavior. *Journal of Applied Behavior Analysis, 14,* 89–93.

A fourth-grade class described as disruptive in the library participated in the Good Behavior Game. The class was randomly divided into teams and the librarian awarded team points if each team member was following game rules when she looked up. Both teams could win by earning three of four total points; their reward was a special activity with the regular classroom teacher. The game was played with and without the reinforcer. The students' behavior improved significantly during the intervention but was not maintained when the reinforcer was withdrawn. It appears that the backup reward is an essential component of this group contingency.

Pfiffner, L. J., O'Leary, S. G., Rosén, L. A., & Sanderson, Jr., W. C. (1985). A comparison of the effects of continuous and intermittent response cost and reprimands in the classroom. *Journal of Clinical Child Psychology, 14,* 348–352.

The effects of reprimands and response cost procedures were compared using second- and third-grade children with behavior problems. Children who were off task for more than 40 percent of the time the teacher was out of the room (that is, daydreaming, calling out, being out of seat) were reprimanded on a continuous schedule (after every instance of off-task behavior) or on a fixed-ratio schedule (after 25 percent of off-task time periods) or lost four minutes of recess time (response cost), again on a continuous or fixed-ratio schedule. All four treatment conditions reduced off-task behavior, but continuous response cost was most effective. Results of the other three interventions were roughly equivalent.

Rosenfield, P., Lambert, N. M., & Black, A. (1985). Desk arrangement effects on pupil classroom behavior. *Journal of Educational Psychology, 77,* 101–108.

The variety of classroom desk arrangements reflects the personal approach of the teacher to teaching and behavior control. The on-task and off-task behavior of fifth- and sixth-grade students was observed under three different classroom desk arrangements—namely, rows, clusters, and circles. Circle configurations were found to be the most conducive to on-task behavior, verbal interaction, and participation in learning. Rows facilitated withdrawal and off-task behavior. Clusters were more effective than rows, but less of an inducement to active involvement than circles.

Williamson, D. A., Lemoine, R. L., Coon, R. C., & Cohen, C. R. (1983). A practical application of sensory extinction for reducing the disruptive classroom behavior of a profoundly retarded child. *School Psychology Review, 12,* 205–211.

While self-stimulatory behavior may be maintained by social reinforcement, an alternate hypothesis proposes that the natural sensory feedback inherent in the self-stimulation is responsible for its maintenance. Sensory extinction eliminates the sensory contingencies to reduce or extinguish the target behavior. A nine-year-old profoundly retarded student with cerebral palsy repeatedly turned door knobs to open doors and threw objects. Sensory extinction of these two behaviors involved first covering all door knobs with a device that required pulling and turning simultaneously to open the door and second, attaching objects to a twelve-inch string tied to the student's wrist so attempts to throw an item would fail. This procedure was augmented by differential reinforcement of appropriate classroom conduct. Results indicated that sensory extinction increased appropriate behavior and decreased inappropriate conduct, although the effect for inappropriate behavior was stronger. The addition of differential reinforcement to the sensory extinction process after the second baseline period caused rapid improvement in both appropriate and inappropriate behavior, but behavior deteriorated when sensory extinction was removed and differential reinforcement was applied alone. When the inappropriate behavior decreased, symptom substitution did not occur. The authors suggest closer examination of child–physical environment relationships in planning interventions.

Destructive Behavior

School vandalism costs taxpayers in excess of one-half billion dollars per year. Death from fire may be the second leading killer of children, and it is estimated that up to one-half or more of the known arson incidents are committed by youth under eighteen years of age. These statistics document the serious human and financial cost of destructive behavior and emphasize the need for effective interventions. Destructive acts by adolescents may be traced back to early antisocial tendencies that often become entrenched by the child's elementary school years. Academically and socially unskilled youth from families in which coercive behavior is reinforced develop the negative attitudes that lead to serious acting out. Although the behaviors described in the "Classroom Disturbance" section all have a destructive element, the articles in this section address behaviors in which property and possessions are destroyed or abused, or in which other people are physically harmed or threatened. The two articles below provide related information:

Kazdin, A. E. (1987). Treatment of anti-social behavior in children: Current status and future directions. Psychology Bulletin, 102, *187–203.*

Patterson, G. R., DeBaryshe, B. D., & Ramsey, E. (1989). A developmental perspective on anti-social behavior. American Psychologist, 44, *329–335.*

Living Environments for Delinquent Youth

AUTHORS: Montrose M. Wolf, Curtis J. Braukmann, and Kathryn A. Ramp

PRECIS: Providing long-term supportive environments to seriously delinquent adolescents as an alternative to short-term cure-oriented strategies

INTRODUCTION: The Teaching-Family intervention model utilizes behavioral treatment in group home settings to reduce the amount of offending behavior displayed by delinquent adolescents. Strategies used include development of social skills, establishment of positive relationships, motivational procedures, and self-government, as well as use of school notes to monitor school behavior and apply appropriate contingencies. The model has been widely adopted, is accepted by the target population, and is successful for youths during their involvement in the program. However, there has been no hoped-for "cure" for delinquency; teens improve their behavior somewhat after treatment but still act out with great frequency and are no more improved than a comparison group not involved in the process. Rather than focus exclusively on short-term approaches that try to effect a permanent cure, the authors propose the concept of "extended supportive environments" to respond to the more realistic view of serious delinquent behavior as a long-term and perhaps lifelong antisocial pattern with multiple environmental, familial, and constitutional determinants, and which is relatively impervious to current treatment technologies.

DELINQUENCY AND DISORDER: Growing evidence suggests that delinquent behavior may be part of a broader "social disability" syndrome that originates early in life and makes the youngster capable of responding to a variety of antecedent conditions with aggressive, destructive, or other antisocial behaviors. Abuse and/or neglect may arise from socially disabled parents who themselves have few response alternatives. This pattern may be maintained and displayed during the school years, in relationships on the job, in police contacts, and well into adulthood, and may be transmitted again to the next generation. Research has supported the durability of this dysfunctional pattern and the inability of affected teens and adults to cope with the everyday requirements of living. Studies also suggest a "nature/nurture" interplay, in which hereditary factors related to hyperactivity-attention deficit, cognitive/educational impairment, and other symptoms combine with parenting styles that reinforce delinquency and socially maladaptive behavior. Unfortunately, the literature provides no clear and consistent evidence that existing strategies are effective in reducing or preventing these deviant behaviors.

INTERVENTION: The above discussion argues for early identification and intervention with families; however, the parents of these children are likely themselves to be seriously at risk and may not easily become involved in treatment. Furthermore, ethical issues dictate caution in applying such highly intrusive strategies, especially when early identification is not yet reliable. Thus, the authors describe a treatment strategy in which the goal is not cure but the establishment of a long-term supportive semi-independent living arrangement akin to that provided for individuals with developmental disabilities. In this environment, relationships are established and maintained, the youngster receives educational opportunities, perhaps holds a job, conducts daily living, and receives vocational training. The youth develops to his or her best potential with the recognition that the social disability will not be cured but will be managed and controlled with the support of the structured environment.

Although the group home might provide the setting for such supported environments, the authors see the need to involve truly stable family units in which long-term intimate family-oriented relationships have a chance to develop and mature. This might be possible when parenting couples actually take a carefully matched young or middle adolescent into their home, are trained, given financial backing and consultation, and are monitored throughout the formal process, which could last through the teen years and informally into adulthood or for life. Such lifelong bonds have been witnessed in the Teaching-Family program described earlier. If the family ties offered to the youth through this plan can provide a model of family life and fill the void left by the natural parents' inability to provide such stability, perhaps some diminishing of the self-destructive, antisocial patterns would take place, and signs of coping and adjustment would appear.

COMMENTARY: Long-term supportive environments may not be appropriate for all delinquents. Dangerous youths may need other interventions first with such settings becoming an option at a later stage of treatment. The authors also point out the need for research to continue the development of short-term strategies and for careful evaluation of the type and sequencing of treatment for each individual case. The strategy described here is relatively intrusive and other less intense approaches might be tried first. Much research is needed, as little empirical evidence exists at present to evaluate properly the effects of supportive family treatment. Funding of such projects also remains an issue although a compelling argument can be made that such programs might actually be cost efficient in terms of the money that might not be spent on the teen for later treatment, welfare assistance, jail time, or institutionalization, not to mention the medical and/or insurance costs for the future victims of the delinquent's crimes, the court costs, and most significantly, the human cost to the families of the offender and the victim. Although this article does not report on an empirically validated technique, it is included because of the highly intriguing and potentially valuable treatment approach offered. Schools struggle constantly with the issues created by antisocial students and alternative strategies are not easily available. A supportive environment is one approach that bears investigation and trial.

SOURCE: Wolf, M. M., Braukmann, C. J., & Ramp, K. A. (1987). Serious delinquent behavior as part of a significantly handicapping condition: Cures and supportive environments. *Journal of Applied Behavior Analysis, 20,* 347–359.

A Home-Based Strategy for
Controlling Destructive Behavior

AUTHOR: Frank M. Gresham

PRECIS: Using notes from home for school-based contingencies to reduce destructive behavior in the home setting

INTRODUCTION: Group contingencies save teachers time, are often more effective in classrooms than individual contingencies, and require few adults to administer the technique. They are also flexible as each student can work for his or her own reward (independent group contingency), the behavior of one or more students can determine rewards for the whole class (dependent group contingency), or the class's combined performance can determine its consequence (interdependent group contingency). In this study, a daily report from home on the destructive behavior of a mildly retarded eight-year-old boy controlled rewards for his classmates. The author reports little research on control of home behavior through notes to school, although there is ample evidence supporting the effectiveness of notes to the home to improve classroom behavior. However, since most of Billy's destructive acts (fire setting, vandalism, and aggression) took place in his foster home, it was appropriate to try to control his behavior in that location.

METHOD: Billy's mother recorded the number and type of his destructive acts throughout the study. After a five-day baseline period, Billy brought a note to school each day stating whether he did or did not commit an act of destruction the previous day. Happy faces and praising comments were included in the good notes. Good notes also earned him juice time, recess, and five tokens. Five such consecutive notes resulted in a "Billy Party" for all class members, in which Billy acted as host and gave out prizes, juice, and cookies. Bad notes yielded praise for bringing it, but a scolding for the behavior and a loss of the daily rewards; no note resulted in a similar reprimand. Monday notes required a complete destruction-free weekend.

RESULTS: Destructive home behavior dropped from a total of fourteen acts over the five-day baseline to only two such acts during the entire thirty-day treatment phase. Over the five-day reversal condition, only two acts were committed.

COMMENTARY: Daily reinforcement of nondestructive behavior, a dependent group contingency operating as a differential reinforcement of low rates of responding (DRL) schedule, response cost, and the discriminative power of the note all contributed to the effects. Given the dangerous nature of the problem behavior, reduction of its frequency was extremely important. While it does not show how each component may have influenced the outcome, the study does provide continuing evidence of the value of home-school contact. When a parent participates with the school in helping the child behave appropriately, the relationship is often enhanced and there is less trepidation when further contact is necessary. It may be argued that the school's job does not extend to home behaviors and that there is enough work to occupy the practitioner's time at school. However, if by assisting the home, rapport is established and the message of home-school cooperation is communicated to the student, these actions may create a climate in which behavior and performance at school are improved. Interventions do not have to be directed at the school or class to affect those locations positively.

SOURCE: Gresham, F. M. (1983). Use of a home-based dependent group contingency system in controlling destructive behavior: A case study. *School Psychology Review, 12,* 195–199.

Fire Setting Among Children and Adolescents

AUTHOR: Melissa Gordon

PRECIS: A discussion of the juvenile fire setter with emphasis on typologies, dynamics, and interventions

INTRODUCTION: Although it is normal for children to be curious about fire, the importance of developing interventions for fire setters is highlighted by the fact that 40 to 70 percent of deliberate fires are set by youth under eighteen, and that fire is one of the leading causes of death in children. The curious youngster who accidentally sets a fire may be helped in school through educationally oriented therapeutic strategies. The more disturbed child who sets fires out of a need for stimulation, revenge, anger, satisfaction, jealousy, or other motives might need more intensive treatment outside of school.

CLASSIFICATION: Several different typologies of juvenile fire setters have emerged from the literature. Aside from the approach described in the American Psychiatric Association's *Diagnostic and Statistical Manual,* third edition (DSM-III), which considers juvenile fire setting as a conduct disorder, one particular system distinguishes four categories: (1) accidental fire setters under age ten; (2) older youngsters with multiple problems who act out as a cry for help (the most common type); (3) teens acting out against authority through a delinquent act; and (4) deeply pathological fire setters (least common). Research at the U.S. Fire Administration has characterized fire setting along a dimension of risk: (1) "low risk" fire setters who are simply curious (60 percent of reported cases), (2) "definite risk" juveniles (37 percent of cases), and (3) "extreme risk" youth (32 percent). Fire setting usually occurs as part of a cluster of other home, school, and social problems. It is rarely the reason for referral, may not be reported, and cannot be predicted with any degree of reliability. Yet, its potential danger requires immediate attention.

DYNAMICS: While psychoanalytic and social learning theorists have their unique perspectives on fire setting, no one theory can provide a clear understanding of why some children develop this symptom. Normal curiosity at ages two to seven leads to fire play for approximately 45 percent of elementary school children. By ages nine to ten, youngsters are expected to lose interest, and those who continue beyond fourth to fifth grade are no longer considered just "curiosity" fire setters. Yet early play is not a necessary predictor of later problems. Some research suggests that older fire setters may have engaged in more frequent, yet less serious misconduct at younger ages, progressing to less frequent, but more serious acts such as fire setting as they matured. Other studies emphasize the regressive nature of fire setting or suggest different motivations in boys and girls.

ACTIONS: While psychologists can alert schools and parents to the need for actions and programs that promote fire safety, they may also need to gather information to understand better the motives of the young fire setter, to assess the risk for such future behavior, and to plan a strategy to change the circumstances. Appropriate data would include background history; the materials used to start the fire; whether they are still available to the child; the child's feelings before, during, and after the act; a report by the child of his or her attempts to escape or put out the fire; the child's understanding of the consequences of the act; and the nature of the parent's response and past fire-related activities and attitudes involving the child. Also important is whether the child has plans for future fires and has matches or lighters hidden. This information coupled with projective data should assist in distinguishing the curious from the disturbed fire setter. Projective issues should focus on parental rejection, ego/superego strength, degree of reflectiveness, amount of overt anxiety, sensitivity to the needs of others, ease or difficulty expressing anger, interpersonal problems, authority conflicts, and issues related to sexual arousal.

INTERVENTIONS: Treatment can occur in several possible settings. For the low risk, curiosity offender, school-based programs are often effective. Outside referrals are more appropriate for the more serious fire setter, while residential treatment may be advisable when the home is the target. Little research exists comparing the major treatment approaches of psychotherapy, family therapy, behavioral strategies, and educational interventions. Each method has its own goals. Psychotherapy addresses the development of social and verbal mediation skills to encourage appropriate assertiveness, teach words as alternatives to destructive action, work through anger, and evaluate consequences. Fire safety lessons supplement the therapeutic experience. Family therapy can mobilize a willing family to act as helpers in the healing process. Relationship and communication issues can be addressed through structured tasks such as listing and discussing grievances. A strategic family approach works to reorder the family structure and in one case raised the status of the fire setter in the family hierarchy by retraining him as a fire safety expert. Behavioral strategies include aversion therapy, stimulus satiation, and positive reinforcement. Having the youth light large numbers of matches until satiated, and earn money finding and returning unlit matches are examples of two interventions.

In 1984, the Federal Emergency Management Agency published a *Juvenile Fire Setter Handbook* that recommended the following steps: (1) having the child supervise fire education for siblings, (2) developing contracts that reward the child for appropriate behavior, (3) establishing behavior strategies, (4) devising restitution approaches in which the child repairs or restores damage from a fire, and (5) fire safety education. The author further suggests that since fire setting does not occur frequently, the psychologist might also wish to treat collateral behavior problems that negatively impact the youngster. Education, especially for the "curiosity" fire setter, might include a talk by a respected figure to sensitize the child and the family to the serious nature of this behavior. Classroom fire safety instruction can also be provided through available published curricula and special activities, such as contests and plays with fire safety themes. The National Fire Hawk Foundation runs a program that pairs a "curiosity" fire setter with a fire fighter trained as a therapeutic helper and "big brother." This relationship can help short-circuit a predisposition toward fire setting.

COMMENTARY: The author concludes that stopping the young fire setter involves managing stress, training substitute behaviors and appropriate attention-getting strategies, helping the child become aware of the aggressive tendencies and how to express them verbally rather than through destructive action, reducing impulsivity, and raising the fear of fire-setting consequences. These strategies may effectively reduce the frequency of nonpathological fire setting, but for the disturbed youngster, they are often not sufficient.

Furthermore, a child with a reputation as a fire setter may find the door to treatment closed as schools or residential settings may be reluctant to accept the child who may act out in ways that are life threatening to others and potentially damaging to property. This writer was involved in the case management of an emotionally disturbed developmentally delayed student who was strongly suspected of fire-setting behavior. The student was able to remain in his special education program only when an aide was assigned to monitor his behavior continuously. Thus, it may be necessary in a practical sense to provide these backups while education and treatment work to improve the student's overall adjustment and potential for living within the community. The aide was required for safety reasons and was gradually faded over a two- to three-year period. As stated before, fire setting is not reliably predicted and institutions will seek to protect themselves while they attempt to treat the more seriously disturbed offender.

SOURCE: Gordon, M. (1987). Children and firesetting. In A. Thomas and J. Grimes (Eds.), *Children's needs: Psychological perspectives* (pp. 221–228). Washington, DC: National Association of School Psychologists.

Preventing School Vandalism

AUTHORS: G. Roy Mayer, Tom Butterworth, Mary Nafpaktitis, and Beth Sulzer-Azaroff

PRECIS: A three-year treatment package to reduce vandalism and disruptive behavior in elementary and junior high school students

INTRODUCTION: Vandalism is an increasingly serious school problem requiring huge expenditures for repair and security, and fostering repressive school reactions that create an atmosphere conducive to further destructive behavior. Setting events related to vandalism include assigned materials too difficult for the student's reading level, punishment as the primary behavior control strategy, and improper use of behavior management techniques. These events combine to create in students feelings of frustration, expectations of negative consequences, and the potential for counteraggression.

A three-year study evaluated a training regimen to reduce vandalism and substitute more prosocial behavior. Of twenty schools originally selected for the study, eighteen completed the first year (nine experimental and nine control schools), and by year three, five experimental and six control schools remained. Two respected, influential fourth- to eighth-grade teachers from each school were selected for direct involvement in the project; two other teachers from the same grades were randomly selected to determine any spillover effect within the school. Six students displaying off-task behavior and low scores on measures of reading comprehension and vocabulary were randomly selected from these spillover classes and observed on a predetermined schedule. Vandalism costs for each school were obtained monthly during the study. In addition, off-task behaviors for the six students in each class were observed and recorded, as was the amount and type of praise given by the teacher.

METHOD: The total three-year program combined teacher consultation at the schools, workshop training sessions, and team coordination to plan and implement a variety of programs designed to address the causes of vandalism. In the first year, consultants began working with project teachers in the experimental schools twice weekly after a three-week baseline period. Team meetings were held twice per month with the project teachers, the principal, and other interested staff to identify causes of vandalism and develop intervention activities and programs to combat it. Ten workshops attended by different combinations of the school team covered consultation skills, behavioral concepts and intervention strategies, school discipline, and vandalism. Consultants then worked with the project teachers to establish specific programs in their classrooms. Spillover teachers and others in the school could request consultation but did not attend the workshops. Project teachers received feedback on amount and type of praise given and student behavior, and were themselves praised for their efforts. No fewer than three meetings were held for this purpose.

In the second year, the procedures from the first year were implemented with the nine control schools. In addition, three workshops were conducted for the psychologists and principals from the original experimental schools to discuss and reassess ongoing activities from year 1. Projects included behavior management programs for playground and cafeteria times, strategies to reduce lateness, and outreach to the community. Consultants visited project classrooms once weekly. In some instances, workshops similar in content to those conducted the first year were held at the school for interested staff. All project teachers continued to receive information on rate and kind of praise dispensed and student behavior.

In the third year, consultation for the eleven remaining schools was faded to one-half day every other week. Team meetings ocurred every two to four weeks in which continuing programs were reviewed, positive feedback was given to staff who remained involved, and consultation skills were modeled. All interested staff, including students, were invited. Workshops to train consultation skills were taught by the first and second authors using lecture, simulation activities, and role-playing so that the principals and psychologists could continue the project after the formal program ended. One workshop focused on discussion of current programs and activities at the schools. Teachers again were informed of their praising patterns and student behavior and the information was made available to the spillover teachers.

RESULTS: During the first project year, vandalism costs decreased in six of the nine experimental schools and in one of the nine control schools. In the second year, five of the remaining seven control schools under treatment decreased their costs. Of the thirteen schools that completed at least two years of the intervention, ten decreased costs or remained at low levels. In total, vandalism costs were reduced an average of 78.5 percent for all schools. Project teachers significantly increased their amounts of praise given by midyear, while spillover teachers were not effective until end-of-year evaluations. However, in the second year of the project, spillover teachers had significantly improved rates of praise by midyear. The third year resulted in no significant effect on amount of praise. Students in classes with project and spillover teachers were off task significantly less time than control students across all three years.

COMMENTARY: The authors report a definite improvement in school climate as a result of the program. Of note is the influence on the total school of changes in a small number of respected teacher leaders, suggesting that a project such as this does not have to be implemented with all teachers, just certain influential staff who will in turn affect others positively. Such an approach is reasonable and cost efficient; therefore it should be acceptable to a central administration debating participation in a project of this type. The authors also note that this study addressed only a few of the variables influencing vandalism and off-task behavior, and the focus was limited to elementary and junior high school students. Further research might apply some of the techniques at the high school level. Nevertheless, it is clear from these results that schools can act to reduce vandalism even though the act itself may not be easily or directly observable and the perpetrator remains unknown.

SOURCE: Mayer, G. R., Butterworth, T., Nafpaktitis, M., & Sulzer-Azaroff, B. (1983). Preventing school vandalism and improving discipline: A three-year study. *Journal of Applied Behavior Analysis, 16,* 355–369.

Additional Readings

Arbuthnot, J., & Gordon, D. A. (1986). Behavioral and cognitive effects of a moral reasoning development intervention for high-risk behavior-disordered adolescents. *Journal of Consulting and Clinical Psychology, 54,* 208–216.

A moral reasoning development intervention was evaluated on forty-eight students aged thirteen to seventeen with conduct disorders and other high-risk behaviors indicative of destructive delinquency. Students met for sixteen to twenty weeks in weekly guided moral dilemma discussion groups.

The group leaders exposed the students to moral dilemmas drawn from a variety of sources. The students debated these scenarios while the leaders served as plus-one stage reasoners; they presented the issues, questions, opinions, and solutions characteristic of the next higher stage of moral reasoning and created the awareness, doubt, and self-questioning necessary for moral growth. Some sessions were devoted to role-play dilemmas and to teaching discussion and listening skills. Students in treatment increased their moral-stage reasoning by a half stage, compared with a slight decrease for a control group. While no differences were reported in teacher evaluations of behavior, disciplinary referrals dropped to nearly zero for the treatment group while increasing slightly for the control group. Lateness among both groups was also significantly different, with tardiness in the control group increasing substantially while decreasing slightly in the experimental group. Police and court contact declined to nearly zero for the experimental students while increasing slightly for the control group. Maintenance of treatment effects were evident over a one-year follow-up period. For more information on moral development programs, the reader is referred to the following: Arbuthnot, J. B., & Faust, D. (1981). *Teaching moral reasoning: Theory and practice.* New York: Harper & Row.

Durand, V. M., & Carr, E. G. (1985). Self-injurious behavior: Motivating conditions and guidelines for treatment. *School Psychology Review, 14,* 171–176.

Self-injurious behavior such as head banging, face slapping, and hand biting is self-destructive and dangerous to the developmentally disabled child and inhibits opportunities for educational progress and community involvement. It may be motivated and maintained by one or more of the following consequences: attention from others, tangible rewards, escape from aversive situations, and/or sensory feedback. Self-injury, as an outgrowth of specific organic conditions, has also been observed although social consequences may still be simultaneously operative. Assessment of the motivating conditions is crucial for effective intervention, and approaches using rating scales and simulated antecedent conditions have been helpful in evaluating the motivating forces behind the self-injurious acts.

Strategies for treatment have involved physical restraint, medication, and reliable but punishing behavioral contingencies such as electric shock, overcorrection, contingent restraint, and time out. Less aversive alternatives, such as withholding or removing rewards and reinforcing appropriate behavior, have been limited in their success. A new intervention, differential reinforcement of communication (DRC), provides the child with effective verbal communications to take the place of the self-injurious behavior. By training the child to verbalize appropriate questions and comments, the self-destructive responses are no longer needed. Treatment guidelines for use of DRC involve (1) determining the motivating condition, (2) matching the treatment contingency to the motivating condition, and (3) selecting the appropriate verbal alternative. The reader is referred to the digest of the article by Carr and Durand in the section on temper tantrums for further information.

Gaynor, J., & Hatcher, C. (1987). *The psychology of child fire setting: Detection and intervention* (pp. 122–185). New York: Brunner/Mazel.

In Chapters Six and Seven the authors focus on psychotherapy and community interventions for pathological fire setting. Outpatient psychotherapy techniques include the following: (1) Cognitive/emotional psychotherapy involves the youngster and the therapist in graphing occurrences of the child's fire setting and the accompanying feelings. The purpose is to sensitize the child to the emotions associated with the act, and thus attempt to control it. (2) Behavior therapy has primarily utilized punishment, positive reinforcement, negative practice (satiation), and operantly structured fantasies. In the last technique, the child hears a story about proper fire safety, obtains rewards for learning the story, and receives a reward from a parent for acting in the same safe manner as the story characters. (3) Family psychotherapy treats the child's fire setting as a reflection of the dysfunction within the family, and treatment is focused on family relationships and faulty communications. Community interventions focus on prevention programs through the school and prevention, early identification, and treatment programs typically handled by fire departments with interagency collaboration. Examples of prevention programs are the Children's Television Workshop's Fire Safety Project, the National Fire Protection Agency's "Learn Not to Burn" fire safety curriculum, the St. Paul, Minnesota, Fire Education Program, and programs for training of emergency fire escape procedures.

All of these are described in Chapter Seven of the book. The more intensive programs aimed at children already playing with or starting fires include the fire-related youth program of the Rochester, New York, Fire Department, the Texas Juvenile Fire Setters Program in Dallas and Houston, and the National Fire Hawk Foundation's Fire Hawk Children's Program. These are also discussed in detail. These promising approaches and programs require more empirical verification of their long-term impact as well as their effectiveness in reducing the concomitant maladjustment of which fire setting is a part.

Madanes, C. (1981). *Strategic family therapy* (pp. 65–94). San Francisco: Jossey-Bass.

In Chapter Four, the case study of a ten-year-old fire setter illustrates the use of paradoxical strategies in strategic family therapy. The therapist redirected family interactions by showing the boy how to light matches safely and by role-playing a scene (with home practice) in which he saves his mother from being burned and puts out a small fire. As he became the family "expert" on fires and fire safety, he was allowed to light the stove at home. The mother was restored to a superior position in the family hierarchy because she now controlled fire starting instead of the son. Her anger no longer needed to be directed to him, and he was recognized for appropriate skill. His maladaptive behavior lost its original purpose within the new family structure.

Webb, N. B., Sakheim, G. A., Towns-Miranda, L., & Wagner, C. R. (1990). Collaborative treatment of juvenile fire setters: Assessment and outreach. *American Journal of Orthopsychiatry, 60,* 305–310.

The Juvenile Fire Setters Intervention Program operating in New York City works quickly and aggressively to involve fire setters and their sometimes resistant families in treatment. The program has four essential components: (1) Assessment of risk by the fire marshal—if the risk for recurrence is slight, education steps are taken. If the child is rated as a definite or extreme risk, referral is made to a mental health clinic for further assessment and treatment. (2) Engagement in treatment—if necessary, home visits, and back-up by agencies involved with child abuse and neglect are helpful in pressing the family to get help. (3) Interagency cooperation—the authors describe an instance in which the therapist contacted the fire marshall who visited the home to urge the mother strongly to continue treatment. This action and others, as described in point 2 above, illustrate the importance of collaboration between agencies and aggressive support to families. (4) Preventive intervention—primary intervention can occur in the form of fire safety education in schools, while secondary prevention provides the educational component in a more intensive format with the fire marshall, the child, and the family.

If concern for the child is great, an appointment for treatment is made within forty-eight to seventy-two hours. When an assessment of the known risk factors indicates such concern, tertiary prevention involves treatment that must include the family. Children at extreme risk may require hospitalization or residential placement. Families must learn to appreciate the meaning of fire setting behavior and the importance of treatment for this life-threatening act.

2

Externalizing Responses

Two major domains of child psychopathology have been delineated: *externalizing* and *internalizing disorders*. *Externalizing disorders* are characterized by behavioral excesses and include hyperactivity, impulsivity, aggression, and conduct disorders. The nature and primary symptomatology of externalizing disorders are overt rather than covert or inner-directed. Frequently, externalizing disorders are referred to as behavior disorders while *internalizing disorders* are viewed as emotional problems. Because of their highly observable symptoms, children with externalizing disorders often come to the attention of school professionals and are referred for special services.

Two dimensions of behavior are subsumed under externalizing disorders. First, there are the hyperactive, impulsive, and inattentive behaviors; second, there are conduct problems and aggressive behaviors. Behaviors in the latter dimension are discussed in other sections of the book. For example, interventions for aggressive behavior toward peers can be found in Chapter Five, "Relationships with Peers." Likewise, treatments for conduct disorders are discussed in Chapter One, "Classroom Management."

The undercontrolled behaviors described in this chapter include impulsivity, hyperactivity, and inattentiveness. In addition, because the first three topics listed above are frequently symptoms of attention deficit hyperactivity disorder, a section on the disorder is included in this chapter.

The most effective and commonly used interventions for externalizing disorders have been behavioral and cognitive-behavioral approaches; many studies have involved peers and parents in treatment. In addition, a number of studies have demonstrated improvements for youngsters with externalizing disorders using psychostimulant medication.

Inattentive/Distractible Behavior

Attention to task is an important factor in school performance. Research has shown that academic engagement or time in which students are engaged in learning is an important correlate of classroom achievement. Inattention refers to a wide range of behaviors including problems with sustaining attention, alertness, arousal, or distractibility.

Attending is a complex behavior that has a number of components. Instructional and motivational components may play a role in attending behavior. For example, a child's attention in school may be dependent on how interesting the material is and how it is presented. Often, though not always, a more interesting or appropriate presentation of material will increase the child's motivation. Another component is the ability of the child to sustain attention or be vigilant and ignore distraction.

When referred, these children are described by teachers with such phrases as "easily distracted," "eyes wander," and "can't stay on task." These difficulties often contribute to deficits in academic performance. Interventions described in this section use behavioral and cognitive-behavioral strategies to increase on-task behavior. Contextual factors that affect attention are also discussed.

Rule-Review Procedures with Distractible Students

AUTHOR: Michael S. Rosenberg

PRECIS: Daily rule-review procedures implemented in a resource room with an ongoing token economy to improve boys' time on task and reduce disruptive talking-out behavior

INTRODUCTION: Token economy systems have been used successfully to remedy a number of classroom problem behaviors. The effectiveness of this type of structured classroom management system is largely dependent on the level of a student's knowledge of the rules and procedures of the token economy. That is, students must know those targeted behaviors that will lead to the delivery of tokens.

There is evidence that effective teachers use daily review procedures in teaching academic skills. The author suggests applying this review technique to facilitate adherence to token economy classroom rules as well.

INTERVENTION: Five boys, ages seven to nine, attending resource room for math and reading deficiencies, were identified as highly distractible and impulsive based on observational measures of time on task and talking out. Following a baseline period in which teachers used verbal reprimands and revoked recess and free time privileges as responses to inappropriate behaviors, a token system was introduced into the classroom with points being delivered at the end of the class to students who followed the rules. These rules included (1) paying attention to their assigned work, (2) looking at the board or teacher during direct instruction, and (3) raising their hands and being called on before speaking. The experimental condition involved a daily review of the rules of the group at the start of each class. The teacher asked the students to state how points could be earned, and then the group repeated the stated rule in unison. This review took about two minutes of the thirty-minute period.

Each child's attention to task increased for the token economy alone and was even higher with the introduction of the rule-review and rehearsal procedure. Talking out during the daily lessons decreased, and opportunities to respond increased most on the days when the review was implemented.

COMMENTARY: For teachers of inattentive or highly distractible students, the addition of a review and rehearsal procedure of classroom rules at the start of each class session seems to focus students' attention on their work. This simple intervention is borrowed from the literature on learning, which has shown that students perform better academically when they hear a summary of previously learned material, their homework is corrected, and they are given background information needed for the upcoming lesson. This intervention uses these findings to help children improve their attending and behavior.

A future goal for teachers would be, of course, to encourage children to internalize these rules so that they are not dependent on external direction. It would be informative to explore fading techniques to decrease teacher structuring slowly.

SOURCE: Rosenberg, M. S. (1986). Maximizing the effectiveness of structured classroom management programs: Implementing rule-review procedures with disruptive and distractible students. *Behavioral Disorders, 11,* 239–248.

Attention to Task as a Function of Context in Children with Learning Disabilities

AUTHORS: Douglas L. Friedman, Anthony A. Cancelli, and Roland K. Yoshida

PRECIS: Attention to task of children with learning disabilities found to vary by classroom setting, type of instruction, and level of peer involvement, suggesting implications for instructional practices

INTRODUCTION: The literature has reported that children with learning disabilities are frequently off task and perform poorly on measures of attending behavior. Because academic engagement or time on task is related to classroom achievement, identifying contextual variables that influence attention would be useful in developing interventions.

Though limited work has been done in this area, three environmental variables were identified that had received some attention in prior studies: classroom setting (regular class or resource room), type of instruction (teacher directed or seat work), and peer influence (total attending level of class).

RESULTS: Twenty-four students, ages eight to twelve, who were classified as learning disabled were observed in an urban public school over a two-month period. Student behavior was measured on the *Coding System for Task Orientation and Classroom Setting* in regular class and the resource room. Attending behavior included categories such as writing, reading aloud, reading silently, answering or asking a question, and raising one's hand.

The findings of the study indicate that these children were more engaged or on task in the resource room than in the regular class; there was greater attention to task during teacher-directed instruction than during seat work, and this difference was greater in the regular classroom than in the resource room. When attentional drift was refined as a category, it appears that students in the regular classroom are off task about 20 percent of the time, regardless of type of instruction. The observations of the third contextual variable, peer influence, revealed a coexistence of high academic engagement of the class and high academic achievement of children with learning disabilities. When there was lower academic engagement among the regular education students in the class (less than 75 percent of the time), the targeted children were engaged less time.

COMMENTARY: A major implication of this study is that children with learning disabilities appear to show great variability in paying attention, depending on their environmental context. This finding suggests that changes in classroom procedures might influence their attention to task. For example, classrooms where overall student interest and attention is high are more likely to facilitate on-task behavior for children with learning disabilities. Therefore, classroom management approaches that enhance regular classroom learning are essential. Working directly with the target children may be only one approach to the attention problem. Further, modification in the way classroom seat work is carried out might also be considered. Student pairings or small groupings for seat work that encourage cooperation could be considered.

SOURCE: Friedman, D. L., Cancelli, A. A., & Yoshida, R. K. (1988). Academic engagement of elementary school children with learning disabilities. *Journal of School Psychology, 26,* 327–340.

Improving Attention to Task Through Cued Self-Recording

AUTHORS: Elizabeth D. Heins, John Wills Lloyd, and Daniel P. Hallahan

PRECIS: Cued self-recording of on-task behavior using an audiotape during classroom arithmetic activities to improve attention to task and arithmetic productivity

INTRODUCTION: Self-recording is a self-management strategy that requires students to monitor a specified target behavior such as their own on-task behavior. Self-recording of attention to task has been shown to have beneficial effects in regular and special education classrooms for students of varied ages with attention problems. When students monitor and physically record their responses, greater effects are demonstrated than with monitoring alone. This study investigated the contribution of cueing to the effectiveness of a self-recording intervention.

INTERVENTION: Four boys, ages eight to nine years, who were identified as learning disabled and placed in a special education class, were chosen as subjects for this study by their teacher. They were seen as needing help with attending to their assignments during independent work periods. Two interventions to improve their attending and productivity were compared: cued self-recording and noncued self-recording. Five training procedures were used for the cued self-recording condition: (1) the teacher explicitly defined on- and off-task behavior, (2) the students were instructed on how to use the self-recording sheet on their desk, (3) the teacher modeled use of the procedure for the students, (4) the students repeated the definitions and self-recording instructions, and (5) the students performed the procedure under the teacher's direction with gradual fading. An audiotape that played tones at irregular intervals (with a mean of forty-five seconds) was placed close to the four students to cue their self-recording. During the noncued self-recording condition, the same training procedures were used except that students were asked to monitor their on- or off-task behavior "whenever you think about it" during the session.

Following a baseline period of sixteen days, using a multi-element design, the children were randomly placed in one of the two conditions for the first half of each independent arithmetic work period and in the other condition for the second half; a return to baseline conditions (to study maintenance and transfer) occurred regularly during this twenty-three-day period.

Both the noncued and cued self-recording conditions resulted in improved attention to task in comparison to the baseline conditions, but the effects of the cued self-recording were greater than the noncued for three of the four boys. This finding was maintained during follow-up observations taken once a week for seven weeks after the cessation of intervention. Arithmetic productivity improved markedly in comparison to baseline for three of the students, but there were no differences between the effects of the two self-recording conditions. These results were maintained during follow-up as well.

COMMENTARY: This study adds to the already extensive evidence supporting the use of self-recording interventions to improve attending behavior. The use of cues clearly adds to the effectiveness of the self-monitoring, at least initially. The tones are gentle reminders that are relatively unobtrusive and structure the self-recording. It would be interesting to determine how long cueing is necessary before it can be faded. It seems apparent, however, that noncued self-recording is important in promoting maintenance.

This study showed that self-monitoring must be carefully taught prior to implementation. The authors indicate that initial training could be carried out in about fifteen minutes, and that occasional reviews were important after subjects had been absent because of illnesses or school holidays. This seems like a relatively short investment of time given the effectiveness of the intervention.

Differences in student responses to this intervention suggest that students' ability to self-regulate vary and that school professionals must consider these differences when they design interventions. In general, self-recording is a practical intervention that has been shown to promote attending behavior in students and offers promise for continued use in the classroom.

SOURCE: Heins, E. D., Lloyd, J. W., & Hallahan, D. P. (1986). Cued and noncued self-recording of attention to task. *Behavior Modification, 10,* 235–254.

Reprimands as a Tool for Maintaining On-Task Behavior

AUTHORS: Maureen M. Acker and Susan G. O'Leary

PRECIS: Reprimands, given for off-task behavior, were associated with high rates of task-oriented attentiveness in a classroom for special youngsters

INTRODUCTION: The use of negative consequences such as reprimands for classroom management has been shown to be effective. This study sought to determine whether combining positive and negative consequences would further increase on-task behavior of children who were inattentive and restless. The study was conducted at the beginning of the class sessions when the teacher and students were just getting to know one another.

INTERVENTION: The nine students who participated in the study were attending a special summer reading program. All were referred because of behavioral difficulties including inattention, restlessness, and impulsivity as well as poor academic performance. They were entering second through fifth grade. Daily observations of on-task behavior were made in different situations, and academic performance was measured on a five-minute word identification task tailored to each student.

The intervention, which had a reversal design, had the following phases: students received reprimands and no praise for off-task behavior (five days), students received reprimands and praise contingent on on-task behavior (five days), students received reprimands and increased praise (discontinued after three days), students received no reprimands or praise (three days), students received no reprimands and praise (four days), and students received reprimands and praise (three days). Results clearly show that the percentage of on-task behavior was stable except for the no reprimands/no praise phase, and the no reprimands/praise phase. The results of the academic performance measure paralleled the behavior findings. Thus, the use of reprimands alone was sufficient to maintain the high rates of appropriate on-task behavior.

COMMENTARY: Although we are commonly taught to use positive approaches first to curb inappropriate behavior, it is apparent that some level of mild negative consequence is necessary to maintain these students' attention to task. Also, it seems that the addition of positive social reinforcement does not improve children's behavior. However, praise may have another role such as enhancing the teacher-student relationship or fostering interest in academic areas, so it should not be dismissed too quickly.

SOURCE: Acker, M. M., & O'Leary, S. G. (1987). Effects of reprimands and praise on appropriate behavior in the classroom. *Journal of Abnormal Child Psychology, 15,* 549–557.

Generalization of Peer Self-Reinforcement to Increase Attention

AUTHORS: John W. Fantuzzo and Paul W. Clement

PRECIS: Observation of self-administered reinforcement by a peer results in improved attending behavior for the nontreated child

INTRODUCTION: Subject generalization occurs when there is behavior change in a child who was not directly treated. In this study the authors facilitated generalization by having nontreated students observe a student who was working with the teacher and who was receiving one of three types of reinforcement for on-task behavior.

INTERVENTION: The ten second-grade boys who participated in the study were described as having deficits in sustained attention and were either disruptive or inattentive and withdrawn in the classroom. One youngster was selected as a confederate throughout the series of single-subject studies.

Each student was assigned to one of three treatment groups. During the teacher-administered reinforcers condition, the confederate received points and praise for on-task behavior; he was then able to exchange these for edible treats at the end of the session. In the self-administered reinforcers condition, the confederate praised himself and pressed a button on top of a feedback box (counter) if he was on-task when a prerecorded tone sounded. The third condition, opportunity to self-reinforce, was the same as the second condition with the addition of a feedback box on the target students' desks, giving them the opportunity to use self-reinforcement equipment themselves, though no instruction was provided as to its use. Only the confederate received contingent reinforcers based on the feedback counter score.

The results for both of the self-administered reinforcement conditions reveal improvements in attending behavior, academic achievement, and glancing behavior. There was no student generalization in the teacher reinforcement condition.

COMMENTARY: This study underscores the usefulness of peers as agents of change. There was benefit both to the confederate and the target children in this study. This approach frees the teacher from continual behavior management tasks and would probably be less costly than other, more labor-intensive strategies.

The implementation in this study, however, was in a two-person classroom and included novel instrumentation (i.e., feedback box, tape-recorded tones). Modifications would have to be made to enable teachers to extend this approach to a regular classroom.

SOURCE: Fantuzzo, J. W., & Clement, P. W. (1981). Generalization of the effects of teacher- and self-administered token reinforcers to nontreated students. *Journal of Applied Behavior Analysis, 14,* 435–447.

Additional Readings

Brown, R. T., & Conrad, K. J. (1982). Impulse control or selective attention: Remedial programs for hyperactivity. *Psychology in the Schools, 19,* 92–97.

The boys in this study evidenced difficulties on a task requiring sustained attention and accuracy, the Matching Familiar Figures Test (MFFT). They were assigned to one of four conditions; the inhibitory control training was based on the *Think Aloud* program and had children ask themselves questions to slow down their responses when confronted with a problem. The attention training condition exaggerated the critical differences on the designs and taught the children to focus on these features. The third condition combined inhibition and attention training, and the fourth condition was a control. The combination of attentional and inhibitory control strategies was most effective in improving both accuracy and latency on the MFFT. The boys receiving attention training alone made fewer errors and took longer to respond than the boys in the inhibitory control group. This result suggests that it is not enough to slow these children down; it is also necessary to focus their attention on salient characteristics of the task.

Rapport, M. D., Jones, J. T., DuPaul, G. J., Kelly, K. L., Gardner, M. J., Tucker, S. B., & Shea, M. S. (1987). Attention deficit disorder and methylphenidate: Group and single-subject analyses of dose effects on attention in clinic and classroom settings. *Journal of Clinical Child Psychology, 16,* 329–338.

The forty-two children who participated in this study were diagnosed as having attention deficit disorder with hyperactivity; they ranged in age from six to eleven. Each child received four doses of methylphenidate and a placebo in a randomly assigned order. Children's attention was measured on the Continuous Performance Test (CPT) in the clinic and in school through behavioral observation, academic work, and teacher ratings. The medication had a positive group impact on class on-task behavior, the completion rate and accuracy of academic work, teacher ratings of attention, and omission errors on the CPT. On the two classroom measures, academic performance and on-task behavior, there was a linear relationship between dosage and performance; that is, greater improvement was seen with higher doses (range was 5 to 20mg). The authors suggested that children's response to dosage is idiosyncratic and may be specific to the type of outcome measure. They recommend including academic performance as a primary outcome measure.

Impulsivity

When children have difficulty inhibiting their behavior in response to a situational demand, they are often referred to as impulsive (Barkley, 1990). In the classroom, these are the students who respond quickly in the face of uncertainty without considering the possibilities presented to them; they do not wait for complete instructions, often make careless errors, blurt out answers, and interrupt. During recess they may not wait their turn and find sharing and cooperation difficult. These children generally are inefficient at problem solving, fail to generalize newly learned strategies, and exhibit poor self-control in social situations (Kurtz and Borkowski, 1987). The structure of the school setting may exacerbate their difficulties as these youngsters are required to constrain their impulsivity. Failure to do so may impair their ability to profit from instruction and lead to poor academic performance.

Impulsivity is one of the most frequently discussed components of attention deficit hyperactivity disorder. It appears to be one of the most persistent aspects of the disorder, with continued presence at follow-up evaluations many years after initial diagnosis.

Children are frequently described as having an impulsive or reflective response style based on their pattern of responding on tasks such as the Matching Familiar Figures Test developed by Kagan (1965). Those who respond quickly and are less accurate are said to have an impulsive cognitive tempo, while those who consider their options and make few errors are said to have a reflective cognitive tempo. Interventions to improve students' performance on this task, however, do not always lead to changes in impulsivity in the classroom. Generally, strategies to reduce impulsivity have included medication and cognitive-behavioral approaches such as self-monitoring and self-instruction.

References

Barkley, R. A. (1990). *Attention-deficit hyperactivity disorder: A handbook for diagnosis and treatment.* New York: Guilford.

Kagan, J. (1965). *Matching familiar figures test.* Cambridge, MA: Harvard University.

Kurtz, B. E., & Borkowski, J. G. (1987). Development of strategic skills in impulsive and reflective children: A longitudinal study of metacognition. *Journal of Experimental Child Psychology, 43,* 129–148.

Effects of Dosage of Methylphenidate on Impulsivity

AUTHORS: Mark D. Rapport, Gary Stoner, George J. DuPaul, Kevin L. Kelly, Susan B. Tucker, and Tom Schoeler

PRECIS: Measures of impulsivity and academic performance positively affected by medication, with higher doses generally associated with greater improvement

INTRODUCTION: Psychostimulant medication is currently a widely used treatment for children with attention deficit disorder/hyperactivity (ADDH). In particular, methylphenidate has been shown to have an inhibitory effect on impulsivity in laboratory settings. In this very comprehensive study the dose level given to children was varied and measurements were taken on variables both in the clinic and in the classroom. Children's behavioral impulsivity in school as well as impulsivity as a cognitive tempo were examined. Further, group and individual analysis of the data allowed for clinical decision making.

INTERVENTION: Twenty-two children between the ages of six and ten with a primary diagnosis of ADDH participated in this study. They all had chronic problems with impulsivity and overactivity. Following baseline, the children received methylphenidate in a randomly assigned, counterbalanced sequence. The medication was administered in doses of 5mg, 10mg, 15mg, or 20mg, and there was a placebo condition. None of the children had been on medication before this study. The Matching Familiar Figures Test (MFFT) latency and error scores were used to assess cognitive tempo. Classroom measures included teacher ratings, behavioral observations, and speed and accuracy on academic work.

    Results over the six-week period clearly showed that, as a group, the children made fewer errors on the MFFT and displayed improved self-control in the classroom. The higher doses of medication resulted in the most improvement. Teacher ratings showed differences in behavior at all medication dosages whereas error reductions on the MFFT occurred only at a dosage of 10mg or higher. When the results from individual children were examined, variations in pattern were apparent, with some children exhibiting reduced impulsivity with lower doses of medication.

COMMENTARY: This is a very important study because it corroborates and refines findings on the effects of medication on impulsivity. Understandably, this remains a controversial intervention, but findings such as those reported here suggest real benefit with a wide range of symptoms. Medication is one of the only interventions to reduce impulsivity of cognitive tempo in the classroom as well as to improve the academic performance of children. The authors rightfully point out that academic success is critical in the decision to continue the use of medication. Also, only minimal side effects were reported in this study.

The necessity of looking at the individual child in prescribing a medication regimen is clear from these findings. Group results obscure some very different individual profiles.

SOURCE: Rapport, M. D., Stoner, G., DuPaul, G. J., Kelly, K. L., Tucker, S. B., & Schoeler, T. (1988). Attention deficit disorder and methylphenidate: A multilevel analysis of dose-response effects on children's impulsivity across settings. *Journal of the American Academy of Child and Adolescent Psychiatry, 27,* 60–69.

Metacognitive Training for Impulsive Children

AUTHORS: Beth E. Kurtz and John G. Borkowski

PRECIS: Children receiving strategy instructions and metacognitive training given better ratings on measures of cognitive tempo, summarization skills, and teacher assessments of impulsivity

INTRODUCTION: Children with an impulsive response style may have deficient knowledge about cognitive strategies, such as rehearsal and elaboration, or deficient knowledge about executive processes, such as monitoring performance or choosing a strategy. Often, they are deficient in both types of metacognition and this lack affects their schoolwork, such as reading comprehension. Early learning and memory strategies are posited to be related to later acquisition of these skills.

This study reports on a comparison of interventions with impulsive fourth-, fifth-, and sixth-grade children to improve their performance; it takes a longitudinal look at whether metamemory contributed to their current strategy acquisition.

INTERVENTION: The 135 children who participated in the early part of the longitudinal study were in first through third grade. Three years later, 130 fourth through sixth graders, including children from the original group and new subjects, participated. Students were identified as impulsive or reflective based on their scores on the Matching Familiar Figures Test (MFFT). There were three experimental groups: (1) a *strategy* condition in which students received summarization instructions; (2) an *executive* condition in which they received summarization instructions plus metacognitive information concerning the importance of monitoring performance, making careful strategy selection, and the need to work slowly and carefully; and (3) a control group. There were seven intervention sessions that took place approximately every two weeks; measures of reading comprehension, cognitive tempo, and teacher ratings of impulsive behavior in the classroom were collected.

Findings indicate that the children in the executive condition were better summarizers than those in the other two conditions, that the children in the executive and strategy conditions did not differ on the reading comprehension and recall measure, and that these two experimental groups made fewer errors than children in the control condition on the cognitive tempo measure. Further, early metamemory skills predicted whether children would acquire reading summarization strategies three years later.

COMMENTARY: This study shows that metacognitive skills influence the learning of new strategies from an early age. Knowledge about basic learning processes gained in the primary grades was a factor in later school performance, pointing up the need for early training of learning strategies. It is clear that the academic disadvantage resulting from this lack of knowledge can be remediated, that is, impulsive children can be taught these skills. There was no evidence, however, that the executive strategies taught to the impulsive children changed their response style. This research appears to provide support for the recent focus on "learning to learn" in schools, which refers to teaching not only content but also ways to approach a task.

SOURCE: Kurtz, B. E., & Borkowski, J. G. (1987). Development of strategic skills in impulsive and reflective children: A longitudinal study of metacognition. *Journal of Experimental Child Psychology, 43,* 129–148.

Distinctive-Feature Cues and Self-Monitoring for Impulsive Children

AUTHORS: Paul M. Smeets and Sebastian Striefel

PRECIS: Self-monitoring combined with distinctive-feature cues to help impulsive children learn a discrimination task

INTRODUCTION: This article reports the results of a series of three experiments with impulsive children. Prior work has shown that nonimpulsive children were able to learn to discriminate shapes successfully in a time delay only condition in which distinctive feature prompts were used. In time delay training, the shapes and the prompts are first presented simultaneously. A correct response by the child results in a one-second delay between the presentation of the shapes and the prompts. The delay is increased by one second after each correct response, up to a maximum delay of ten seconds. Distinctive feature prompts are those whose shape and location closely match those of the actual stimulus components. In these experiments the task was to discriminate a septagon (seven-sided figure with a straight line at the bottom) from an octagon (eight-sided figure with a wide v-shape at the bottom). The prompt for the septagon was a horizontal line, and the prompt for the octagon was a wide v-shape.

INTERVENTION: The participants in these discrimination experiments were kindergarten children who had been identified by their teachers and through assessment procedures as impulsive. They were described as children who "act before they think." A comparison was made between time delay only training and time delay plus self-monitoring. In the second treatment with self-monitoring, the children were requested to check the answer after their response and when the prompts were present. One of the experiments also compared these treatments when the prompts had distinctive features and when they had nondistinctive features.

The data show that the impulsive children did not benefit from time delay training only, regardless of the prompts. They did learn, however, with the addition of self-monitoring, but only when the distinctive feature prompts were used.

COMMENTARY: These findings are in contrast to those with nonimpulsive children in which time delay training alone produced learning about 75 percent of the time. For the impulsive children, the addition of a self-monitoring component that let them use cues to help identify critical elements of the shapes was an essential component for success. In the classroom, the type of self-monitoring used in this study (such as, Let's see if that's right) is certainly simple to use with children who act impulsively, and it seems to be a powerful intervention. The practitioner should understand, however, that the self-monitoring is a response to an adult request rather than a self-direction.

It will be important to see whether these findings generalize to tasks other than those requiring discrimination.

SOURCE: Smeets, P. M., & Striefel, S. (1988). Time-delay discrimination training with impulsive children: Self-monitoring nonwait responses and the dimensions of prompts. *Journal of Abnormal Child Psychology, 16,* 693–706.

Remediation of Impulsivity Using Self-Instruction

AUTHORS: Daniel Graybill, Michael Jamison, and Mark E. Swerdlik

PRECIS: Reductions in impulsivity among learning disabled children with an impulsive cognitive style after training in verbal self-instruction

INTRODUCTION: Verbal self-instruction is a cognitive-behavior modification procedure that teaches children to talk to themselves as a way to control their own behavior. The four-step training procedure generally involves the child (1) observing a model, (2) performing the task with a model verbalizing the instructions, (3) performing the task while verbalizing the steps aloud, and (4) performing the task while silently self-instructing. The study assessed the effectiveness of this procedure using special education learning disabilities teachers as trainers in the resource room.

INTERVENTION: The sixteen learning disabled children who participated in this study were identified as impulsive on both cognitive tempo (that is, slow response time on the Matching Familiar Figures Test) and classroom behavior (that is, teacher rating of impatience). They ranged in age from seven to twelve and attended resource rooms for academic assistance. Each of the eight children in the experimental group received self-instruction training individually for four consecutive weeks. The training task was a visually presented problem requiring the children to make choices as to the correct answer. The procedures outlined above were followed, with the teacher providing the training. On the intervening days, stimulus cards that pictorially reviewed the four-step procedure were on view to cue the students. The teacher-trainer referred to them when an appropriate task arose. Measures of cognitive tempo, classroom behavior, and self-esteem were administered before and after the intervention.

The children showed a change in response latency; they took longer before they made a response. There was no change, however, in classroom impulsivity or self-esteem.

COMMENTARY: This study underscores the need to distinguish appropriate interventions for behavioral impulsivity and for an impulsive response style. While verbal self-instruction was useful in training students to deliberate more carefully before responding, it did not affect their classroom impulsivity. Of course, the intervention was carried out over a fairly brief period of time, and there was no report of generalization training. Further exploration of this procedure with training in more than one task would seem necessary to determine whether it could have broader applicability.

The use of the teacher as trainer is important because it suggests that procedures such as these can be integrated into regular classroom activities, removing the need to pull students out for training during class time.

SOURCE: Graybill, D., Jamison, M., & Swerdlik, M. E. (1984). Remediation of impulsivity in learning disabled children by special education resource teachers using verbal self-instruction. *Psychology in the Schools, 21,* 252–254.

Additional Readings

Kendall, P. C., & Braswell, L. (1985). *Cognitive-behavioral therapy for impulsive children.* New York: Guilford Press.

The comprehensive program to overcome cognitive and behavioral impulsivity described in this book provides the reader with a theoretical approach, research evidence, and clinical application. The authors recommend the use of multiple strategies including problem solving, self-instructional training, modeling, behavioral contingencies, and role-playing to optimize treatment impact. Cooperation and coordination with parents, teachers, and peers is discussed.

Rivera, E., & Omizo, M. M. (1980). The effects of relaxation and biofeedback on attention to task and impulsivity among male hyperactive children. *The Exceptional Child, 27,* 41–51.

Boys between the ages of seven and eleven years were given the Matching Familiar Figures Test (MFFT) before and after an intervention that consisted of a taped relaxation program and electromyogram biofeedback training. After the training the boys made fewer errors on the MFFT and were more attentive to task.

Hyperactivity

Children who display excessive or inappropriate levels of activity are termed hyperactive. Most children are active, but the hyperactive child seems unable to inhibit or regulate his or her behavior and is described as restless, constantly moving, and talking excessively. Many children who are hyperactive also have attention deficits, and hyperactivity is one of the primary characteristics of attention deficit with hyperactivity disorder (ADHD).

Teachers who have hyperactive children in their classrooms report that they are frequently out of their seats, walking around the room, and/or humming or making noises. Further, these children are perceived by both adults and peers as annoying, bothersome, immature, or worse; they are often rejected by their peers. Their very overt behavior makes them easy to blame.

The number of boys referred for hyperactivity far exceeds the number of girls (estimates of six to one). The interventions described here range from stimulant medication to the use of behavioral and cognitive-behavioral strategies. The studies emphasize the increasing importance of training parents to deal more effectively with these youngsters. Overall, a multimodal approach may be necessary to effect improvement in these children.

Cognitive Training for Hyperactive Children

AUTHOR: Howard Abikoff

PRECIS: Review of cognitive training interventions used to remediate cognitive, academic, and behavioral functioning

INTRODUCTION: Interest has grown in the use of cognitive training as an alternative or adjunct to psychostimulant medication. The goal of cognitive training is to have the child develop self-control skills through procedures such as self-instructional training, cognitive modeling, self-monitoring, attentional training, and cognitive or social problem solving. Self-instruction might involve teaching the child to repeat a series of statements as he or she solves a problem. With self-monitoring, the child learns to stop at certain times and to evaluate the work completed — for example, to count the number of questions he or she has answered. This review evaluates the effectiveness of cognitive training interventions in hyperactive children and provides suggestions for improving intervention results.

INTERVENTION: The studies considered in this review all use cognitive training interventions to treat hyperactive children, primarily those diagnosed as having attention deficit disorder with hyperactivity (ADDH). Three outcome measures are examined: cognitive, academic, and behavioral functioning. Training effects on cognitive performance are equivocal with no additional improvement seen in those youngsters also on medication. Improvement in academic performance appears to occur mainly when there is an academic skills component in the training. The impact of the training on behavior is more positive, with self-monitoring and self-reinforcement proving successful in improving classroom and playground behavior. In summary, however, the generalization of training to different situations and the maintenance of improvements have not been realized.

COMMENTARY: The author makes a number of suggestions for improving the success of cognitive interventions. One of the most serious limitations of these studies has been the brevity of the training. Cognitive training requires the student to learn a new skill that necessitates adequate exposure to the skill in a variety of situations. A school professional would need to train students over an extended period of time, perhaps in different classes, and assess when mastery occurs. Second, once the skill is mastered, "booster" sessions may be needed to facilitate maintenance. Third, it is clear that the training must be directly related to the desired outcome. If academic improvement is the goal, students should be trained on academic tasks.

Finally, professionals are advised to pay careful attention to individual differences of these youngsters. Training should be tailored to the needs of the students with particular focus on their specific problem-solving skills.

For example, some children make errors because they do not take the time to read directions; others have difficulty because they do not follow task directions. The individualized training plan would, of course, be different in each case.

SOURCE: Abikoff, H. (1985). Efficacy of cognitive training interventions in hyperactive children: A critical review. *Clinical Psychology Review, 5,* 479–512.

A Token System for a Class of Hyperactive Boys

AUTHORS: P. W. Robinson, T. J. Newby, and S. L. Ganzell

PRECIS: Using a token system requiring peer cooperation in a class of hyperactive boys to improve academic achievement

INTRODUCTION: When practitioners treat children in schools, they often have restrictions that affect the nature and implementation of the intervention. In this study, for example, school district administrators imposed a number of stipulations on the project, including the requirement that the practitioner demonstrate effectiveness within four weeks and that the program eventually be handled by the single teacher in the classroom. The token system instituted here worked within these constraints because students in the class were taught to assist each other in cooperative interaction so that the program could be managed by one teacher.

INTERVENTION: Rather than target the disruptive and off-task behavior of the eighteen hyperactive boys in this third-grade class, the practitioner used an incompatible response approach. Learning to read and use new words was reinforced because increased reading behavior leaves less time available for inappropriate behavior.

The students were given reading and vocabulary assignments during the two-hour period they were in this classroom. The assignments were divided into levels and units and involved learning new words and reviewing previously learned material.

A student had to earn a total of four tokens of different colors to receive the rewards, which consisted of time on a pong machine and an electronic pinball machine. To earn the first token a student would take out the new words from his or her folder and study them with the assistance of another student who had already completed that unit; the teacher then quizzed the student and awarded a token. Then, the student was required to help another student learn the material; if this was done successfully, a second token was given. In the third step, the student learned to use the words just mastered in sentences, assisted by another student. Finally, the student helped another student with the sentences.

The design consisted of intervention (fourteen days), removal of intervention (five days), and then reinstatement of the token system (thirteen days), allowing a demonstration of effectiveness within the required time period. Results showed a ninefold increase in assignment completions during intervention in comparison to the time that the intervention was removed. The students' average completion rate on the school district weekly reading level exam also increased. All eighteen students demonstrated improved performance.

COMMENTARY: The fact that this token program could be implemented within the constraints of the classroom and restrictions of the school district underscores its practicality and flexibility. Procedures and reinforcers could easily be modified for students of different ages and for different assignments. The critical element appears to be the cooperative interaction between students. Having one student teach another reinforces the learning of the former and promotes positive social interaction. The teacher's role in this system then becomes one of monitoring and surveying the students, making it manageable for one person.

The very rapid improvement in students' performance indicates that this was an easily implemented and learned program. Students valued the token reinforcers and frequently wore them on their wrists.

Finally, the emphasis in this system was on academic performance rather than on behavior, which is the ultimate goal of education. Although not systematically recorded, disruptive behavior did decrease.

SOURCE: Robinson, P. W., Newby, T. J., & Ganzell, S. L. (1981). A token system for a class of underachieving hyperactive children. *Journal of Applied Behavior Analysis, 14*, 307–315.

Behavioral Relaxation Training with Hyperactive Children

AUTHORS: Virginia Kay Donney and Roger Poppen

PRECIS: Use of Behavioral Relaxation Training by parents in the home to decrease hyperactive behavior of three boys

INTRODUCTION: In Behavioral Relaxation Training, students are taught ten overt postures and behaviors including breathing without vocalization or movement, and with eyes closed; they learn through modeling, prompting, and performance feedback. The effectiveness of the training has been demonstrated in several prior studies, and it is viewed as an alternative to medication. Participation of parents as trainers was attempted in this study to determine the viability of having nonprofessionals implement the intervention.

INTERVENTION: Three boys—eight, nine, and ten years old—who were not responding adequately to a medication regimen for hyperactivity, participated in the study. A parent from each family was taught by the authors to use Behavioral Relaxation Training (BRT) with his or her child. First, a token reinforcement program was developed with each family to facilitate the child's sitting still. During baseline the child was asked to relax for twenty minutes and then was scored on the Behavioral Relaxation Scale (BRS). BRS scoring was discussed at each session and the parent was asked to provide feedback as the behaviors were modeled by the trainer. During the intervention the child was trained in the ten behaviors for twenty-minute periods. The authors taught the first three behaviors and then helped the parents teach two more. The last five behaviors were taught by the parent alone. Modeling, verbal instruction, and manual guidance were used as necessary. Training occurred twice a week for eight to eleven weeks and follow-up was conducted.

All three boys improved on their BRS scores and had decreased electromyogram muscle tension. Parental ratings of the boys on the hyperactivity index showed a decrease in hyperactivity by follow-up and improvement on the home situations questionnaire. Teacher ratings on the school situations questionnaire were not as positive.

COMMENTARY: Relaxed behavior is seen as a specific skill that can be taught and then applied in a problematic situation such as the hyperactivity experienced by the students described here. Two months after training, these children were able to demonstrate relaxed behaviors. Parents were able to learn the training procedure quickly and efficiently, but they did not voluntarily continue the training at the end of the study. The ease of training suggests possible usefulness in a school setting with individuals or groups.

Care should be taken to consider the individual needs of students in a training program such as BRT. For example, one child was reported to have reacted poorly when corrected for unrelaxed behavior. Further work also needs to be done in teaching children when to apply the relaxed behavior.

SOURCE: Donney, V. K., & Poppen, R. (1989). Teaching parents to conduct behavioral relaxation training with their hyperactive children. *Journal of Behavior Therapy and Experimental Psychiatry, 20,* 319–325.

Classroom Modifications for Hyperactive Adolescents

AUTHORS: Annette Shuck, Marion Liddell, and Susan Bigelow

PRECIS: Review of classroom strategies that have been shown to be most effective with adolescent students who are hyperactive

INTRODUCTION: The educational needs of many special youngsters are now being met in the regular classroom setting. With mainstreaming of hyperactive students, teachers in regular education classrooms are in need of a repertoire of classroom strategies that can improve the classroom behavior of these adolescents.

INTERVENTION: The authors reviewed the literature on five classroom strategies: classroom communication, classroom structure, noise minimization, behavior modification, and cognitive behavior modification. To enhance classroom communication, the authors stress the importance of immediate positive feedback for students on their efforts and verbal simplicity such as giving short, clear, and specific directions. Instead of telling them what not to do ("Don't run"), tell them what to do ("Please sit for ten seconds").

With regard to classroom structure, goals for the teacher are to have well-defined class rules, to have clear consequences for not following rules, to be consistent in enforcement of rules, and to respond to the disruption without embarrassing the student. Planning short-term goals and signing contracts were effective with these students. Further, allowing for productive physical movement by the student, such as arranging chairs or running errands, can be beneficial. High noise levels have been shown to be detrimental to the behavior and performance of these youngsters. Care should be taken to minimize this type of interference.

Behavioral strategies such as positive reinforcement for appropriate behaviors and time out from positive reinforcement for inappropriate behavior have been successful in changing behavior. Cognitive-behavior modification such as self-instructional techniques provides a set of strategies that teach students to control their own behavior; in most of the other strategies discussed, the emphasis is on external control, usually by an adult.

COMMENTARY: This literature review provides information on practical strategies that teachers can follow in their classrooms. For the most part, the suggestions illustrate good teaching strategies for all children, but they are particularly effective with those deemed hyperactive. While behavior and cognitive-behavior modification are covered extensively in the professional literature (see other articles in this section), the strategies concerning classroom communication and structure seem most useful. Clarity and consistency are critical in teaching these adolescent students.

SOURCE: Shuck, A., Liddell, M., & Bigelow, S. (1987). Classroom modification for mainstreamed hyperactive adolescent students. *Techniques: A Journal of Remedial Education and Counseling, 3,* 27–35.

Parent Behavioral Training for Hyperactive Children

AUTHOR: George K. Henry

PRECIS: Using a combination of medication, symbolic modeling, and parent training in behavioral strategies to increase compliant behavior of hyperactive youngsters

INTRODUCTION: Parents and teachers of hyperactive youngsters often describe them as noncompliant: the children may take a long time to comply with a request, or they may refuse outright, or they may respond with inappropriate behavior. Advances in technology have made symbolic modeling a popular training option. Symbolic modeling refers to the observation of non-live models via television, films, and other visual media. In this study modeling is presented by videotape. The study also examines the importance of parent training as an additional component in the intervention package.

INTERVENTION: Six youngsters, ages four years, six months, to ten years, six months, identified as hyperactive, participated in the study along with their mothers. The children all had an ADDH diagnosis and were on psychostimulant medication during the entire study period.

A case series design was used with baseline (A), symbolic modeling (B), and parent training (C) phases. During symbolic modeling the children were shown a brief videotaped sequence in which a child near their ages demonstrated compliance to adult demands. In a five-minute structured-task situation following the viewing, the mother made requests of the child. In the first two training sessions parents were taught attending (providing a running commentary on the child's behavior), ignoring, and rewarding behaviors. During the next four sessions they learned how to give commands and use time out for noncompliance. Each parent training session lasted about forty minutes. The students were rated on a hyperactivity index by the mothers and their behaviors were coded by observers.

Results indicate that the symbolic modeling did not result in improved compliance or decreased hyperactivity among the children. With the addition of parent training, five of the six youngsters improved compliance. At six-month follow-up, all the parents indicated improved behavior in the children.

COMMENTARY: The design of this study does not allow the reader to determine the relative contributions of symbolic modeling and parent training. However, it showed that symbolic modeling in conjunction with medication did not improve the compliance behavior of these youngsters. In fact, the behavior of some of the youngsters deteriorated during this phase. The introduction of parent behavioral training, particularly the time-out procedure, had a dramatic effect on the outcome variables. It seems that these youngsters need the external structure and guidance provided by an adult and documented in a number of other studies. Further, they seem to need a consequence for misbehavior. Asking them to change behavior after observing a model without providing rewards and consequences is unrealistic. The results also highlight the importance of family involvement in behavior change and can be extended to school involvement as well.

 While the study is limited in generalizability, it does provide very specific parent training instructions that school professionals might find useful with parents and staff.

SOURCE: Henry, G. K. (1987). Symbolic modeling and parent behavioral training: Effects on noncompliance of hyperactive children. *Journal of Behavior Therapy and Experimental Psychiatry, 18,* 105–113.

Multimodality Treatment Reduces
Delinquency Risk for Hyperactive Boys

AUTHORS: James H. Satterfield, Breena T. Satterfield, and Anne M. Schell

PRECIS: Use of a multimodal treatment program including medication, individual and/or group psychotherapy, educational therapy, and family therapy to produce lower delinquency and institutionalization rates than drug treatment alone for hyperactive boys

INTRODUCTION: This longitudinal study looks at the long-term development of hyperactive boys. An earlier article (Satterfield, Satterfield, and Cantwell, 1981; see Additional Readings) reported that multimodal therapy, compared to drug treatment alone, resulted in fewer antisocial behaviors, enhanced academic performance and self-concept, and better social relationships at home and at school at three year follow-up. This study compares the official arrest and institutionalization rates for these boys after approximately nine years.

INTERVENTION: The boys in the drug treatment condition received stimulant medication (all but one received methylphenidate) for two to three years. In addition, the parents were given brief counseling on managing behavior at the monthly medication visits.

The children and families in the multimodal treatment group were evaluated, and a very specific treatment program was designed within the clinic and in addition to the medication. The possible therapies included individual therapy with the child with the goal of building self-esteem, child group therapy, child educational therapy, parent training using behavior modification techniques to manage behavior and to help parents in their interactions with the child, and family therapy. Three psychotherapeutic approaches were available — cognitive, interpretive, or directive — and were matched to the family.

The average age of these youngsters was seventeen at follow-up. The mean number of arrests for felony offenses and institutionalizations was much lower for the multimodal treatment group.

COMMENTARY: The multimodal treatment program in this study was very comprehensive. Each child and family were evaluated from a variety of viewpoints; then one or sometimes many therapeutic approaches were selected and delivered over a three-year period. The authors speculate that drug treatment alone may not have been enough because it did little to improve the self-esteem, educational deficits, and social inadequacies of these children. Yet the medication may have been needed to ready the child for the psychotherapeutic treatment.

The obvious implication of these results is that long-term treatment may be necessary for maximizing normal development in hyperactive children. Maturation alone was not sufficient to prevent delinquency.

The study does not mention cooperative efforts with the school. This would seem a useful adjunct to the therapy (and may indeed have occurred) in that therapeutic goals and methods could be shared with practitioners working with these children in the school. Finally, while the cost of such comprehensive service seems overwhelming, the savings in terms of institutionalization of these boys would be enormous.

SOURCE: Satterfield, J. H., Satterfield, B. T., & Schell, A. M. (1987). Therapeutic interventions to prevent delinquency in hyperactive boys. *Journal of the American Academy of Child and Adolescent Psychiatry, 26,* 56–64.

Additional Readings

Brown, R. T., Wynne, M. E., & Medenis, R. (1985). Methylphenidate and cognitive therapy: A comparison of treatment approaches with hyperactive boys. *Journal of Abnormal Child Psychology, 13,* 69–87.

Thirty boys, ages six to twelve, who were identified as hyperactive were assigned to one of three treatment groups: methylphenidate therapy, cognitive training, or a combination of the two; there was a control group as well. Twelve outcome measures and ratings were used to assess efficacy after twelve weeks of training and at three-month follow-up. Results showed that medication improved attentional measures and behavioral ratings but not academic measures. Cognitive training improved only attentional deployment, and there was no indication that the combination was more effective than medication alone.

Douglas, V. I., & Parry, P. A. (1983). Effects of reward on delayed reaction time task performance of hyperactive children. *Journal of Abnormal Child Psychology, 11,* 313–326.

Hyperactive and control children in elementary school were presented with a delayed reaction time task under one of three conditions: continuous, partial, and noncontingent reward. Reinforcement occurred when the reaction time was equal to or shorter than the median time during baseline. The continuous group was rewarded for every trial that met criterion, the partial group for alternate trials that met criterion, and the noncontingent group on a random preset schedule. Results indicate that the continuous reward condition improved mean reaction times and response variability for both hyperactives and controls. The reaction times of the hyperactive children were worse under the noncontingent schedule but improved when it was withdrawn. This result suggests that inconsistent reward may impair the performance of hyperactive children.

Omizo, M. M., Cubberly, W. E., Semands, S. G., & Omizo, S. A. (1986). The effects of biofeedback and relaxation training on memory tasks among hyperactive boys. *The Exceptional Child, 33,* 56–64.

A group of forty-eight boys identified as hyperactive, ranging in age from nine to eleven, were assigned to a biofeedback and relaxation condition or a no-treatment condition. The three-session intervention consisted of a taped relaxation training program and instruction in the function and use of the biofeedback instrument (an electromyogram) used to measure muscle activity in the frontalis area. The children in the experimental condition achieved better muscle relaxation and performed better on a paired-associate memory task than the control group. There was no difference between the groups on a picture recall measure. The authors suggest that a relaxed state may facilitate attention to tasks.

Rapport, M. D., Murphy, H. A., & Bailey, J. S. (1982). Ritalin vs. response cost in the control of hyperactive children: A within-subject comparison. *Journal of Applied Behavior Analysis, 15,* 205–216.

This study compares the effectiveness of medication and a response cost strategy in two second-grade hyperactive boys. Both treatments led to improvement in on-task behavior and academic performance as measured by problem completion and accuracy rates. The response cost treatment (using free time as a reinforcer), however, led to greater improvement.

Satterfield, J. H., Satterfield, B. T., & Cantwell, D. P. (1981). Three-year multimodality treatment study of 100 hyperactive boys. *Journal of Pediatrics, 98,* 650–655.

The boys compared in this study ranged in age from six to twelve and were described as hyperactive. One group received comprehensive multimodal treatment including medication and one or more types of psychotherapy over a two- to three-year period; the other group received treatment for less than two years. At three-year follow-up, results indicated that the group treated longer was further ahead educationally, better adjusted at home and school (parent and teacher ratings), and more globally improved. They were also involved in less antisocial behavior.

Attention Deficit Hyperactivity Disorder

Attention deficit hyperactivity disorder (ADHD) is estimated to occur in 3 percent to 5 percent of school-aged children and is far more common in boys than girls. It accounts for a large percentage of the referrals made to school professionals and clinics because of its disruptive and overt nature.

ADHD children are characterized by impulsive and hyperactive behavior and inattention. Recent conceptualizations of the disorder have posited that these children have deficient rule-governed behavior — that is, problems in the regulation and inhibition of behavior, especially by rules (see Barkley, 1990 in the Additional Readings list at the end of this section on ADHD). Of great concern is the negative impact the disorder has on children's academic and social behavior. These youngsters often perform poorly and are rejected by their peers.

The diagnostic criteria for ADHD can be found in the Diagnostic and Statistical Manual, third edition, revised (DSM-III-R) of the American Psychiatric Association. In general, it is defined as a developmental disorder in which attention span, impulsivity, and restlessness are age inappropriate. The onset of the disorder is in early childhood (before age six), and it is not accounted for by neurologic, sensory, or motor impairment, or by emotional disturbance. A number of prior terms were used for this condition including brain damaged, hyperkinetic, *or* hyperactive. *The etiology of the condition is not clear at the present time although abnormalities in neurological function are suspected. There seems to be a strong biological or hereditary predisposition to the disorder, which is chronic in nature.*

The most current treatment programs for ADHD children require a multifaceted approach including medical and educational management and behavioral training.

Two categories of training programs are presented. First, cognitive-behavior modification programs have been designed to teach children internal strategies for coping with situations that require delay or self-control. Second, contingency management programs using behavioral principles have been applied in classrooms. A number of strategies to improve the instructional environment for these youngsters are available.

The Attention Training System for ADHD Children

AUTHORS: Michael Gordon, David Thomason, Shermie Cooper, and Clifford L. Ivers

PRECIS: A contingency management program using response cost and positive reinforcement was effective in reducing off-task behavior of ADHD children

INTRODUCTION: The contingency management program that is presented here is called the Attention Training System (ATS) and incorporates both awarding points for on-task behavior and deducting points for off-task behavior. The student receives systematic and immediate feedback from a small, electronic module that has a red light and a counter and is placed on his or her desk. Mr. Attention, as it is called, is regulated by the teacher from anywhere in the room.

INTERVENTION: The three boys and three girls (ages six to nine) who participated in the study were diagnosed as ADHD. They attended a once a week psychoeducational treatment program after school where they used worksheets and other educational materials. There was one teacher for four children during the fifty-minute sessions. There was a "Mr. Attention" on each child's desk, which was controlled by an observer behind a one-way mirror. When the children were off task for more than fifteen seconds, the red light was turned on, and they lost points. They received points for each minute of on-task behavior.

The first two weeks of the study provided baseline data. The ATS system was implemented from weeks 3 to 11 and then removed for the last two weeks. Results showed that in five of the six cases, on-task behavior improved during training and returned to baseline levels when the ATS program was terminated.

COMMENTARY: The ATS program provides clear and consistent application of rules and immediate consequences for behavior. It supports the most recent empirical evidence that positive consequences alone are not enough and that improvement is shown in combination with mild negative consequences—in this case, response cost.

This seems to be a program that could be implemented fairly easily by the teacher since no timers, tokens, or direct contact with the child is necessary. It appears to be more manageable than a token system. In a small, special classroom, all the children might have a "Mr. Attention" in front of them; how this would work in a regular classroom with just a few ADHD students seems more problematic.

Based on the study results, maintenance of behavior improvements are dependent on the continued implementation of the program. Thus, equipment purchased would be used over a long period of time, justifying the monetary investment. This nonmedical strategy appears to have potential for improving behavior and possibly academic performance of the ADHD youngster.

SOURCE: Gordon, M., Thomason, D., Cooper, S., & Ivers, C. L. (1991). Nonmedical treatment of ADHD/hyperactivity: The Attention Training System. *Journal of School Psychology, 29,* 151–159.

Classroom Behavioral Interventions for ADHD Students

AUTHORS: Ann J. Abramowitz and Susan G. O'Leary

PRECIS: Techniques for improving behaviors of ADHD children in the classroom using both antecedents and consequences of behavior

INTRODUCTION: Students with ADHD often present real challenges to teachers wishing to modify student classroom behavior. The design of effective classroom intervention is an important component of a comprehensive treatment approach that may include parent education, pharmacotherapy, and/or cognitive-behavioral procedures. This article examines the evidence for a wide variety of behavioral approaches dealing not only with contingency management (managing the consequences of behavior), but also with antecedents of behavior such as the setting and environmental design.

INTERVENTION: Characteristics of the classroom environment and the required task may contribute to inappropriate behavior by ADHD youngsters. Classroom seating arrangements, for example, can affect social interaction and on-task behavior. During independent seat work, row seating may increase students' productivity and reduce off-task behavior yet limit social interaction; clustered seating may facilitate social interplay but limit on-task behavior. Noise generally detracts from the on-task behavior of ADHD youngsters, as do tasks that are difficult and tasks that are paced by others. Novelty and stimulation on easy and repetitive tasks is reportedly beneficial, but not on new or difficult tasks.

Contingency management refers to the application of consequences based on the student's behavior. Contingent teacher attention and classroom token economies are proven viable options for use. A less frequently discussed intervention is home-based contingencies that involve joint school and parent efforts through daily communication between teacher and parent. A checklist is sent home with the child each day indicating whether the student has met his or her behavioral goals. Contingencies are applied by the parents. There are a number of advantages to this approach, but teacher training and the ability of parents to engage in a home program must be considered before implementation.

There are three types of group contingencies and peer-mediated reinforcement: interdependent, independent, and dependent. An interdependent contingency occurs when the behavior of the entire group determines whether the group will receive reinforcement; an independent contingency occurs when each child's behavior determines whether he or she will receive the reinforcement; in a dependent contingency, the behavior of one or more children determines the reinforcement for the whole group.

Time out from positive reinforcement procedures involves removing the child in some way from ongoing classroom activities. It has been shown to be effective, but its recommended use is with the most disruptive classroom behaviors and only when there is a highly trained staff. Other reductive procedures based on reinforcement that can be used to reduce rates of inappropriate behaviors include differential reinforcement of low rates of behavior (DRL), differential rates of other behavior (DRO), differential reinforcement of incompatible behavior (DRI), and differential reinforcement of alternative behavior (DRA).

COMMENTARY: This article reviews a wide range of classroom behavioral interventions to be used as part of a multifaceted treatment program for students with ADHD. The complexity of implementing a classroom token economy or a home-school contingency plan is often underestimated. Careful training, selection of reinforcers, and degree of commitment are all factors that influence the choice of intervention. Individualization of intervention approaches is crucial as the chronic nature and cross-situational occurrence of ADHD suggests long-term planning will be necessary.

SOURCE: Abramowitz, A. J., & O'Leary, S. G. (1991). Behavioral interventions for the classroom: Implications for students with ADHD. *School Psychology Review, 20,* 220–234.

Parent Training for Noncompliant Children

AUTHORS: Robert F. Newby, Mariellen Fischer, and Michael A. Roman

PRECIS: Comparison of three well-known parent training programs that deal with problems parents face daily such as children's noncompliant and defiant behavior and coercive parent-child interaction

INTRODUCTION: The three programs reviewed in this article rely on behavior management techniques to remediate children's behavior problems.

All are applicable to children who display noncompliant or defiant behavior alone or in combination with other childhood disorders. These target behaviors are among the most frequently cited by parents and lead to a cycle of negative parent-child interactions. The specific emphasis in this article is the application of these programs to families of children with ADHD. The three programs were developed by Russell Barkley, by Gerald Patterson and colleagues, and by Rex Forehand and colleagues. All three are based on social learning principles and are most appropriate for preschool and elementary school children.

INTERVENTION: Barkley's program, published in *Defiant Children* (Barkley, R. B. New York: Guilford Press, 1987), trains parents either individually or in groups. The goals are to improve parental management skills, to increase parental knowledge of the causes of childhood misbehavior, and to improve children's compliance to rules and commands given by parents. Parents are taught how to attend to children's positive behavior while ignoring their negative behavior. Behavioral principles such as shaping and reinforcement are introduced, and eventually a formal token system is established, making children's privileges contingent on their compliance. A time-out procedure is also introduced for unacceptable behavior.

Patterson and his colleagues from the Oregon Social Learning Center describe their program in several sources including *A Social Learning Approach to Family Intervention,* Vols. 1 and 3 (Patterson, G. R., et al. Eugene, OR: Castalia, 1975, 1982). Their approach is designed to stop coercive interactions between parents and children. The focus of the program is on teaching parents to issue requests effectively; a point program is also introduced. Time-out procedures are used, but here the children are put in a separate room with a timer whereas in Barkley's program an isolated chair serves as the time-out area.

Forehand and colleagues developed a program that is fully described in *Helping the Noncompliant Child* (Forehand, R. L., and McMahon, R. J. New York: Guilford Press, 1981). They begin with direct observations of parent-child interaction and emphasize the importance of shaping parent expectations so that they are not unrealistic. Training methods include instruction, role-playing, and cued practice. Differential attention, compliance training using the Parent's Game (where commands are given and consequences are applied), and a time-out procedure similar to Barkley's are presented. This is the most highly structured program of the three.

A comparison of the three programs indicates considerable overlap in that they all teach differential attending and use reinforcement, time-out procedures, and detailed assessments. They all introduce positive procedures before negative ones. They vary, however, in their emphasis on informal social reinforcement, the use of more formal contingency systems such as token economies, their approach to time out, and the focus on the parent-child dyad. Some research supports each of the programs, but no study directly compares them.

COMMENTARY: This very comprehensive article reviews parent-mediated approaches to behavior management. The obvious advantage of such an intervention is that parents act as therapists in the natural environment and that they can use the techniques across settings and situations. While parent training has been shown to reduce children's noncompliance, at the present time there is no evidence that the parent training has altered children's behavior in schools. Collaborative home-school programs or adaptations of these programs for school settings are possible future approaches.

The authors also note that variables such as careful initial assessment, good therapeutic rapport, flexibility and pacing in intervention delivery, and "therapist variables" such as warmth have been shown to impact outcomes. These are not cookbook approaches; they require great skill to implement.

SOURCE: Newby, R. F., Fischer, M., & Roman, M. A. (1991). Parent training for families of children with ADHD. *School Psychology Review, 20,* 252–265.

Methylphenidate for Attention Deficit Disorder

AUTHORS: V. I. Douglas, R. G. Barr, M. E. O'Neill, and B. G. Britton

PRECIS: Short-term treatment with methylphenidate resulting in positive effects on academic, cognitive, and learning performance as well as behavior of ADD-H children.

INTRODUCTION: Many medication studies have not taken into account the wide range of symptoms associated with attention deficit disorder with hyperactivity (ADD-H). Often studies examine the impact of stimulants on a single measure such as academic performance or cognitive functioning or acquisition of new learning or classroom behavior. Also, classroom performance measures are frequently not included. This study addresses the need for measurement of outcomes in the diverse domains of functioning of ADD-H youngsters.

INTERVENTION: The sixteen children (fifteen boys and one girl) who participated in this study ranged in age from seven to twelve and met the criteria for ADD-H diagnosis. The children received pretesting and screening about a week prior to the intervention. Each child was given medication or a placebo in the morning and then tested; all received medication again before lunch. In the afternoon they returned to the classroom where they were given additional testing and their behavior was rated by the teacher. The drug and test order combinations for the morning test battery were random. Methylphenidate (Ritalin) was prepared in 5, 7.5, 10, 12.5 and 15mg/kg dosages. The outcome measures included arithmetic and spelling tasks, word discovery and paired associates tasks, and ratings on the Conners Rating Scale.

Results indicate that the medicated group attempted more items and answered more items correctly on the arithmetic task. These differences were also seen on an arithmetic self-correction task where the medicated youngsters found and corrected more errors. On the other academic tasks, spelling and spelling study tasks, there were no differences between groups except in the examiner's ratings of student effort. When the children were asked to produce as many words as possible from a long word, only the effort rating for the medicated group was higher than for the placebo group. The paired-associates task required students to recall pairs of words over three trials and measured the acquisition of new learning. Results showed that the medicated group recalled more pairs than the placebo group on the second and third trials and across the three trials. Again, effort was greater for this group. Finally, children in the medication condition had lower examiner ratings of hyperactivity than did those in the placebo group. On the three classroom measures — arithmetic, word discovery, and teacher ratings — strong differences were obtained in favor of the group receiving medication.

COMMENTARY: The findings from the laboratory and classroom testing in this study were very consistent and suggest greater accuracy and effort for students taking medication. With the exception of the spelling tasks, these improvements were in academic, cognitive, and behavioral domains. There was also some evidence that the medication did not simply "slow the children down," but allowed them to be more effective in the use of their time.

The major limitation in considering these findings is the short-term nature of the treatment. While the improvements are promising, this was a very brief intervention period.

SOURCE: Douglas, V. I., Barr, R. G., O'Neill, M. E., and Britton, B. G. (1986). Short-term effects of methylphenidate on the cognitive, learning and academic performance of children with attention deficit disorder in the laboratory and the classroom. *Journal of Child Psychology and Psychiatry, 27,* 191–211.

Group Parent Training to
Improve Behavior of ADDH Preschoolers

AUTHORS: Susan Pisterman, Patrick McGrath, Philip Firestone, John T. Goodman, Ikuko Webster, and Risa Mallory

PRECIS: Parent participation in group training improves compliance of their preschoolers, parental style of interaction, and management skills

INTRODUCTION: One of the most common complaints of parents of a preschooler is noncompliant behavior, particularly when the child is diagnosed as having attention deficit disorder with hyperactivity (ADDH). This behavior is stressful to parents and contributes to unsatisfactory interactions between parent and child. Neither medication nor cognitive-behavioral interventions have improved behavior in these preschoolers, despite the more positive impact of these methods with school-aged children. Parent training has been used successfully with some preschool disorders and with older students; group parent training is employed here to improve compliance of ADDH preschoolers.

INTERVENTION: The parents of forty-six preschool children diagnosed as ADDH were assigned to an immediate (experimental condition) or delayed (control condition) group parent training program. In all but one case, the parent who participated was the mother.

The twelve-week training program, adapted from R. L. Forehand and R. J. McMahon (*Helping the Noncompliant Child: A Clinician's Guide to Parent Training.* New York: Guilford, 1981) and R. A. Barkley (*Hyperactive Children: A Handbook for Diagnosis and Treatment.* New York: Guilford, 1981) (see also Newby, Fischer, and Roman, 1991, reviewed in this chapter), included ten evening group sessions and two individual clinic sessions with parent and child. The fathers were encouraged to participate also and attended over half the sessions.

The first three training sessions were didactic; they provided information about ADDH and introduced basic concepts about the bidirectional nature of parent-child interactions as well as behavior management principles. The three important strategies that were taught in sessions 3 through 11 were how to give differential attention to children's appropriate behavior, how to issue appropriate commands, and how to use time outs for noncompliance. Training sessions incorporated modeling, role-playing, and rehearsal. A manual, distributed to all parents, included readings and homework assignments. The final session reviewed earlier material and discussed handling of future problems. At parent-child individual sessions, videotape feedback was given to parents in the experimental group only.

Results of the training were evaluated at the end of the intervention and at three-month follow-up. Looking first at the children's behaviors, child compliance as measured by percentage of compliance and frequency of noncompliance improved for those children whose parents participated in the training program. The behavior of parents in the treatment group was positively affected as well. They made fewer inappropriate commands and reinforced compliant behavior more frequently. Parents' style of interaction and their management skills were greatly improved, compared to those of the control group.

COMMENTARY: The group parent-mediated intervention described here was very successful in modifying parent and child behavior in the clinic setting. It supports an interactional view, suggesting that changing parent behavior management skills can change children's behavior. Similar interventions might be carried out with school personnel who interact with these children.

One advantage of having parents carry out the treatment is that they can use it in a wide variety of settings and situations. However, in this study, no generalization to other child behaviors occurred, such as time on task during a parent supervised activity. This absence suggests that parents may need to be reminded and/or trained to generalize their new behaviors.

The use of parent group training rather than individual training appears to be beneficial. Parents can provide support for one another, share experiences, and discuss practical issues and realistic expectations for their children.

SOURCE: Pisterman, S., McGrath, P., Firestone, P., Goodman, J. T., Webster, I., & Mallory, R. (1989). Outcome of parent-mediated treatment of preschoolers with attention deficit disorder with hyperactivity. *Journal of Consulting and Clinical Psychology, 57,* 628–635.

Multimodal Approaches for ADHD Children

AUTHORS: Carol K. Whalen and Barbara Henker

PRECIS: Discussion of the importance of considering a multimodal approach to intervention that might include stimulant, behavioral, and/or cognitive-behavioral treatments for ADHD

INTRODUCTION: In recent years a number of studies have compared pharmacologic (stimulant medication) and psychosocial therapies for youngsters with attention deficit with hyperactivity disorder (ADHD). The authors of this article raise a number of issues that mitigate against looking for a single treatment that is most appropriate for ADHD children. They view ADHD children as multiproblem youngsters with difficulties in diverse areas of functioning.

INTERVENTION: Three of the major treatment approaches used with ADHD children are stimulant medication (usually methylphenidate), behavioral treatment including classroom contingency management and parent training, and, more recently, cognitive-behavioral treatments emphasizing self-regulation.

Most children with ADHD receive stimulant medication, but there are limitations in this therapy. Some children cannot take the medicine, some do not benefit, some have only short-term benefits, and for many, improvements disappear when the medicine is discontinued. Concerns about side effects have also been raised. Behavioral approaches, as described in a number of articles in this section, have been shown to be effective alone and in conjunction with medication. The importance of teaching behavioral skills to parents and teachers who interact with these youngsters has recently been emphasized and is currently under study. Finally, cognitive-behavioral treatments (see Abikoff, 1985, reviewed in this chapter) appear to address the self-control deficits of ADHD children but have not as yet demonstrated their expected promise. Thus, while each of these treatment approaches has potential, some combination of approaches seems to make sense.

The authors suggest that the ADHD population, because of its heterogeneity, requires individualized planning to match the child to intervention procedures.

COMMENTARY: This thought-provoking article raises a number of theoretical and methodological issues regarding ADHD treatment research. It summarizes the difficulties with comparative treatment studies and encourages the reader to expect that some combination of procedures, a multimodal approach, has the potential for the greatest treatment impact. An exciting line of thinking that school professionals might consider is whether there are subgroups of ADHD that might require different treatment approaches. In general, this article reminds us to view each child as an individual when planning treatment.

SOURCE: Whalen, C. K., & Henker, B. (1991). Therapies for hyperactive children: Comparisons, combinations and compromises. *Journal of Consulting and Clinical Psychology, 59,* 126–137.

Additional Readings

Barkley, R. A. (1990). *Attention-deficit hyperactivity disorder: A handbook for diagnosis and treatment.* New York: Guilford Press.

This second edition of Barkley's book is probably *the* most comprehensive and up-to-date work in the field. It covers the history of ADHD, theoretical issues, etiology, and its primary symptoms; it provides extensive information on assessment. Barkley concludes that the primary symptom of ADHD is "behavioral disinhibition, or the inability to adequately regulate behavior by rules and consequences" (p. 73).

Seven chapters, written by Barkley and other contributors, are concerned with treatment. Any one of these chapters could easily have been selected for a digest in this book. Barkley sees working with parents as critical; he covers counseling, parent training, and family systems approaches. The chapter specifically focused on educational placement and classroom management is of most relevance to school personnel. Medication therapy and treatment to improve social skills and peer relationships are also detailed in this volume.

Children with Attention Deficit Disorders. (1988). *Attention deficit disorders: A guide for teachers.* Plantation, FL: Author.

This six-page manual for teachers emphasizes a multimodal approach to treatment of attention deficit disorder (ADD) children that includes educational planning, medical management, psychological counseling, and behavioral modification. Specific recommendations are provided for teachers working with these youngsters with regard to the classroom environment and teacher instruction. This short pamphlet could be very useful to staff members working with an ADD child. It is available from local chapters or from the national organization of Children with Attention Deficit Disorders (CH.A.D.D.), 1859 N. Pine Island Road, Suite 185, Plantation, FL 33322.

Coleman, W. S. (1988). *Attention deficit disorders, hyperactivity and associated disorders: A handbook for parents and professionals* (5th ed.). Madison, WI: Calliope.

This is a small, readable paperback that provides good background information on ADHD, learning disabilities, and affective disorders. The treatment sections on medication and management techniques are presented clearly. The book would be a useful reference to many parents.

DuPaul, G. J., Guevremont, D. C., & Barkley, R. A. (1992). Behavioral treatment of attention-deficit hyperactivity disorder in the classroom: The use of the Attention Training System. *Behavior Modification, 16,* 204–225.

The study examined the efficacy of response cost contingencies alone (Attention Training System) and in combination with directed-rehearsal procedures with two boys, ages six and seven. The students were in a special class where the intervention was carried out during independent work periods. Results indicate that response cost contingencies led to improvement in task-related attention and ADHD behavior. The researchers could not determine whether directed rehearsal contributed to additional improvement.

Kirby, E. A., & Grimley, L. K. (1986). *Understanding and treating attention deficit disorder.* Elmsford, NY: Pergamon Press.

This book presents an overview and description of children with ADD and then a comprehensive discussion of assessment procedures. The intervention approach provided is based on cognitive-behavioral training and includes verbal self-instruction training, cognitive monitoring, and social skills training. It also incorporates behavior modification procedures such as response cost. Specific guidelines for implementation are provided along with a discussion of limitations and suggestions for generalization.

3

Internalizing Responses

In 1990, *School Psychology Review* (vol. 19, no. 2) presented a miniseries entitled "Internalizing Disorders in Children." This series focused attention on a category of problems often overlooked by teachers and practitioners struggling to manage the more overtly disruptive externalizing behaviors of students. *Internalizing disorders* covers a relatively broad grouping of psychological problems, alternatively referred to as internal, covert, inner-directed, overcontrolled, emotional, unobservable, and subtle. Unlike external reactions in which behavioral acting out is a core feature, the symptoms associated with these responses are more closely identified with covert psychological states, a characteristic that places them at a lower priority for teacher attention and most likely explains why the externalizing dimension initially received greater attention in the literature during the 1970s. However, this situation has been rectified during the past ten years as interest in these patterns sparked research that continues into the current decade, and which has provided school practitioners with techniques for addressing these areas.

The internalizing responses considered in this chapter are anxiety and stress, fears and phobias, obsessive-compulsive behaviors, low self-esteem, identity crises in homosexual youth, procrastination, elective mutism, depression, and suicidal behavior. While this grouping parallels the chapter on insecure behaviors from *Therapies for School Behavior Problems,* modifications have been made in terminology and focus to reflect a different understanding of the problems. For example, only in the past few years has the literature revealed the true extent of the homophobia directed toward gay and lesbian teenagers and its effect on their developing self-identity. Arguments have been advanced, and continue to be made by some, that homosexuality *by definition* denotes instability and deviancy. A change in the section's title from "Gender Disturbance" to "Identity Crises in Homosexual Youth" is meant to refocus the issue to the identity problems encountered by youth whose sex-role development differs from that of their peers. Unlike earlier articles that offered strategies to develop "masculine" behaviors, or revise "inappropriate" sex-role attitudes, the work cited here builds on current understandings and addresses the need to create a supportive environment in which all teens can work toward a healthy self-identity regardless of sexual preference. Similarly, while there was no section on suicidal behavior in the earlier book, the current section literally explodes with information discussing prevention, postvention, warning signs, coping techniques, crisis intervention, handling the returning suicidal student, the contagion hypothesis, suicide in preschoolers, and managing the aftermath of a teacher suicide.

Finally, the chapter heading itself was changed from "Insecure Behaviors" to "Internalizing Responses" to bring a greater degree of operational precision to the classification scheme utilized in the original book. Of course, the term is not without its own limitations; as noted by Reynolds (1992), there is no commonly agreed-upon grouping of internalizing problem areas. For example, obsessive-compulsive behavior, depression, and anxiety all present a mixture of symptoms, some of which may easily be labeled externalizing. Conversely, while externalizing disorders are characterized by more dramatic behavioral manifestations, most practitioners would not deny that both emotional and cognitive states underlie their occurrence. Despite these considerations, the work of T. M. Achenbach and others on symptom classification has provided some measure of empirical justification for use of the externalizing-internalizing dichotomy.

Consistent with the emphasis on internal states, interventions for internalizing responses frequently target the core cognitive and affective processes as well as the behavioral outcomes through which these dynamics are ultimately channeled. Thus, children with these problems may be exposed to strategies such as anger control training, problem solving, stress inoculation training, relaxation training, in vivo desensitization, thought stopping, family systems therapy, and other techniques, often as part of a multicomponent package combining cognitive, affective, and behavioral methods. Although internalizing reactions may be harder to identify than the more blatant externalizing patterns, practitioners may find that students who display internalizing patterns respond more effectively to treatment. Further research will be required to understand better the meaning and utility of this dichotomy. For further information on problems addressed in this chapter, the reader may consult the following references:

References

Achenbach, T. M. (1966). The classification of children's psychiatric symptoms: A factor-analytic study. *Psychological Monographs, 80*(7), Whole No. 615.

King, N. J., & Hamilton, D. I. (1988). *Children's phobias: A behavioural perspective.* New York: Wiley.

Morris, R. J., & Kratochwill, T. R. (1985). Behavioral treatment of children's fears and phobias: A review. *School Psychology Review, 14,* 84–93.

Ollendick, T. H., & Francis, G. (1988). Behavioral assessment and treatment of childhood phobias. *Behavior Modification, 12,* 165–204.

Reynolds, W. M. (1990). Introduction to the nature and study of internalizing disorders in children and adolescents. *School Psychology Review, 19,* 137–141.

Reynolds, W. M. (1990). Depression in children and adolescents: Nature, diagnosis, assessment, and treatment. *School Psychology Review, 19,* 158–173.

Reynolds, W. M. (1992). *Internalizing disorders in children and adolescents.* New York: Wiley.

Thyer, B. A., & Sowers-Hoag, K. M. (1986). The etiology of school phobia: A behavioral approach. *School Social Work Journal, 10,* 86–98.

Anxiety and Stress

Stress and anxiety are often used synonymously but are in fact distinguishable. Stress may be viewed as having three components: the stressor or stimulus condition (a school test), one or more intervening variables (for example, an interpretation of the stressor as "overwhelming"), and a response that may be physical (elevated blood pressure), behavioral (withdrawal), or psychological (anxiety). Anxiety is thus one consequence of stress, and in school-age children it is commonly classified as either separation anxiety, overanxious disorder, or avoidant disorder. Stressful life experiences have been linked with adjustment problems in children, and this section describes interventions for three such events: divorce, surviving tragedy, and transferring to a new school.

In addition, the stress felt by teachers no doubt impacts significantly on their students, and stress management strategies for school-based adults are presented. Given that up to 90 percent of all teachers report job-related stress, coping techniques provided to the staff may well translate into better teaching and a more positive school climate. The literature on school-related anxiety is quite extensive, and a "Further References" section has been added for readers to explore this topic further.

An Intervention for Children of Divorce

AUTHORS: JoAnne L. Pedro-Carroll and Emory L. Cowen

PRECIS: The Children of Divorce Intervention Program combines affective and cognitive components to facilitate better adjustment and behavioral competence in children of separated parents

INTRODUCTION: Research has documented how the stress of divorce can impact significantly on the school performance and psychological well-being of children. The problem is serious: Each year, the parents of more than one million children terminate their marriages, a figure more than double the 1970 and triple the 1960 rates. The Children of Divorce Intervention Program (CODIP) described here was designed to help children in grades 4 to 6 cope with the emotional and behavioral consequences of divorce.

Seventy-five suburban middle-class children of parents separated for an average of almost two years participated. Students were divided into immediate (treatment) and delayed intervention (control) groups, with further subdivision of the treatment group into sets of eight or nine. These smaller groups met for ten weekly one-hour sessions at school. Each group was co-led by trained and regularly supervised leaders.

CODIP: A complete description of the CODIP program can be obtained from JoAnne Pedro-Carroll at the University of Rochester. The main elements are as follows: (1) Affective component — the first three sessions focused on getting to know each group member; using role-plays to bring out feelings, experiences, and anxieties regarding divorce and other life events; correcting inaccurate ideas and information about divorce; and understanding the effect of divorce on parents. A filmstrip was shown addressing the feelings of children of divorced parents, why marriages end, the issue of blame, and the future. These sessions were intended to provide support and reduce self-consciousness and feelings of distance from others. (2) Cognitive component — in sessions 4 through 6 children practiced interpersonal problem solving, self-statements, and strategies. They role-played solutions to divorce-related problems and discussed the feelings these generated. They learned about problems they could control or solve, and those they could not (for example, parents getting back together). Addressing solvable issues was aimed at increasing the children's sense of competence to help them return to their own growth and development and not get "stuck" in their parents' problems. (3) Anger control — sessions 7 through 9 focused on situations that trigger anger as children described events that made them angry and considered the consequences of expressing anger in acceptable or unacceptable ways. Positive ways to deal with anger were role-played with feedback from group members. (4) Conclusion — in session 10 the program was evaluated, and feelings about termination and ways to maintain the supports and friendships that had developed were discussed.

RESULTS: Measures of adjustment, competence, and problem areas were completed by teachers, parents, group leaders, and the children. All the ratings showed significant improvement in adjustment and competence and significant reductions in problem areas such as self-blame and anxiety. One exception was students' perceived self-competence, which seemed too stable to be altered by a ten-week program.

COMMENTARY: Children seemed to benefit from the reduced sense of isolation and guilt resulting from their association with others with similar experiences. However, the groups were not merely vehicles for support and sharing of feelings. The authors point out that specific problem-solving and anger control skills were learned and practiced to help students cope with the day-to-day realities of membership in a divorced family. Thus, both the emotional and cognitive components were necessary ingredients in the total package. Efforts need to be directed toward extending the positive impact of the program through booster sessions or whatever methods prove effective. As the authors note, coping with divorce is a long-term, ongoing process that will not be accomplished with a "one-shot" program. In a later study (1989, *Journal of Consulting and Clinical Psychology, 57,* 583–589), a modified version of the CODIP achieved positive results with a second- and third-grade urban multiethnic population of students. These findings suggest that the basic elements of this program may also be applicable through the elementary and secondary school years.

SOURCE: Pedro-Carroll, J. L., & Cowen, E. L. (1985). The Children of Divorce Intervention Program: An investigation of the efficacy of a school-based prevention program. *Journal of Consulting and Clinical Psychology, 53,* 603–611.

Crisis Intervention Following a Student Death

AUTHOR: Richard B. Weinberg

PRECIS: A schoolwide plan to help students cope with sudden death

INTRODUCTION: When a student dies or a major accident claims the lives of school community members, crisis intervention in the school can help address the resulting feelings that occur among the victim-survivors. Anxiety, sadness, and fear are common after such a traumatic event, and available resources may not be sufficient to provide psychological support to students in need. The following intervention plan is based on five experiences over a three-year period and includes a meeting to define specific steps, large-group assemblies, and group counseling. While individual counseling is an important component of this overall strategy, it is not discussed in this article.

INTERVENTION PLAN: On the day of the event or as soon as possible, a meeting is held with the principal, key administrators, counselors, volunteer teachers, security personnel, and others involved in the intervention to arrange for the assemblies and for counseling of groups and individuals. In the meetings, adults in shock may need comfort and support, and arguments against intervening may need to be resolved. The principal then announces the facts of the tragedy to the school during the first period in a careful, sensitive manner, avoiding glorification of a suicide. The principal also stresses that anxiety, sadness, shock, and other feelings are normal at such times and describes the planned opportunities for students to discuss their feelings and responses in the assemblies and group counseling experiences.

LARGE GROUP ASSEMBLIES: Assemblies are conducted for each grade level and are led by trained crisis/grief counselors. They describe common emotional, physical, and cognitive reactions (for example, disbelief) to such events, and how these reactions help us work through the grief. To promote appropriate expression of feelings, they also discuss the wide range of emotions that may normally occur during these times. Some students will feel intense pain; others may feel less or nothing. Crying is accepted as a natural way to cope with loss, as are verbal expressions of grief. Fears that may result from vicariously experiencing another's tragedy are described, with suggestions for dealing with these reactions. Assistants assigned to watch groups of ten to twenty students identify those who are extremely distressed and/or wish to leave, and supportively, but assertively, urge them to see one of the counselors alone or with a friend in whom they may be seeking comfort. If the student declines, he or she is closely watched and approached again when the assembly ends. If counseling is again not accepted, the student is encouraged to go later if he or she is still distressed. Those who leave in distress and will not return to the assembly are taken back to class and their names given to a counselor who follows up later with the student.

After the grief discussion (fifteen to twenty minutes), the leader discusses healthy coping skills. Students are asked how they cope with loss in their lives and are reinforced for their contributions. If unhealthy coping behaviors (drinking, acting out) are described, the leader asks others to comment on the solution, asks the original student if other alternatives were possible, and praises a better response. Finally, the issue of suicide is raised. Students are asked whether they have tried to hurt themselves and which, if any, adaptive behaviors they have used to avoid self-destructiveness. Alternative actions to self-harm are praised if any are given, and the leader concludes with the idea that healthy solutions are always possible and can be discovered. Sometimes the help of a counselor is needed and one is available to them. The point is made that the anxious, sad feelings will diminish over time, and that students have the ability to cope with the situation.

SMALL GROUP COUNSELING: Students who react very intensely are seen in groups of four to twelve. A typical session lasts about one hour. These groups deal with topics similar to those discussed in the assemblies and are observed for possible outside referral. Students introduce themselves and discuss their reactions to the tragedy. Each student has a chance to speak before emotions are released and expressed, to facilitate involvement by each participant. Group support of each member's feelings is encouraged, as is extension of the support beyond the meeting time. Guilt related to this or other tragedies is addressed, and the group is supported in its efforts to help a member work through this feeling. If self-blame is intense, an outside referral may be appropriate. Healthy coping is discussed and praised, and self-harm is discouraged.

Because of the small size of the group, individual concerns, such as embarrassment over expression of feelings or how to react to the dead teen's sibling, are often raised. If time permits, relaxation techniques are introduced and the positive effects of exercise, using the support system, and expressive activities such as art or dance are discussed. Sessions are ended optimistically but the leader acknowledges that sad or anxious feelings may return, although they will cease over time. The availability of counseling in school is restated. The group leader may refer students for outside help if they were close to the victim or incident but display no emotion, cannot control their feelings, blame themselves excessively, entertain suicidal ideation, display evidence of emotional disturbance, or seem overly concerned with interpersonal problems.

COMMENTARY: The author indicates that many occurrences can alter the original plan. During assemblies or small groups, students may bring up earlier losses not yet resolved, or angry episodes may erupt, or ongoing tensions may be exacerbated by the tragedy, leading to fights or threats. These issues need to be addressed at the initial planning meeting.

This plan offers a helpful framework for the development of an individualized approach for each school. Additional steps may be added while others may be modified. For example, a "sudden death plan" in Jeffrey Cohen's high school includes support to adult staff members who may have been close to a student or a fellow teacher who has suddenly died. There may also need to be serious discussion of what kinds of events should or should not activate the plan. However the program is customized, there should be a strategy at all grade levels, and a plan that includes a response to other traumatic events besides suicide (teacher death, natural disaster) is advisable.

SOURCE: Weinberg, R. B. (1990). Serving large numbers of adolescent victim-survivors: Group interventions following trauma at school. *Professional Psychology: Research and Practice, 21,* 271–278.

Stress Inoculation Training for Teacher Stress

AUTHORS: Marc A. Cecil and Susan G. Forman

PRECIS: Comparing stress inoculation training and co-worker support groups as techniques for reducing stress in teachers

INTRODUCTION: Occupational stress can be attacked at either the individual or organizational level. From an individual perspective, people can be taught personal coping strategies through such techniques as stress inoculation training; an organizational approach can involve increasing social support to workers through the formation of co-worker support groups. This study compared the effectiveness of stress inoculation training and co-worker support groups in reducing teacher stress. Fifty-four regular elementary and middle school teachers were randomly assigned to a stress inoculation group, co-worker support group, or no-treatment control group.

STRESS INOCULATION TRAINING: Teachers in this group met for six weekly ninety-minute sessions. This cognitive-behavioral strategy was presented in three phases: an educational phase in which the theoretical basis of the technique was described, a rehearsal phase in which relaxation and cognitive restructuring were taught, and an application phase in which the skills were practiced. Session I covered definitions, causes, and effects of stress on students and teachers. Session II provided training in deep muscle and cue-controlled relaxation. Session III introduced rational restructuring and the ABC model of emotions, which attributes emotional reactions (C) to the person's belief systems (B) through which life events (A) are filtered and interpreted. Session IV addressed the common irrational beliefs and the five questions from Maultsby's 1975 book, *Help Yourself to Happiness* (Maultsby, M. C., Jr., New York: Institute for Rational Living), for assessing the rationality of a thought. Session V focused on applying coping skills through the creation of "stress scripts" that guided effective responses to stressful events. Session VI included additional rehearsal of the scripts with use of the "barb" technique in which stress-managing self-statements were developed to cope with hypothetical stress situations. Homework assignments required daily practice of coping skills and self-recordings of daily stress levels.

CO-WORKER SUPPORT GROUP: This group also met once weekly for six ninety-minute sessions to share problems, provide mutual assistance and support, and describe successful coping behaviors. Each meeting followed a consistent format: (1) introductory circle — a question or topic was presented to which each member responded for about two minutes (for example, share something you have done to make you proud). This facilitated the sharing of personal experiences and fostered group solidarity; (2) revolving focus time — each member presented a current problem to which the group brainstormed alternative solutions; (3) open meeting — past issues and proposed solutions were reviewed with general announcements and sharing of resources; (4) closing — final thoughts were expressed about the session; (5) socialization — relaxed discussion and refreshments.

RESULTS: Stress inoculation training reduced self-reported stress and improved coping skills while co-worker support groups were not effective. Neither treatment affected motoric indicators of anxiety (for example, speech dysfluencies or fidgeting with objects) during teaching time.

COMMENTARY: Stress inoculation training teaches specific skills that can be used after the training program ends to manage stress. In the understandable haste to assist anxious students in school, it is important not to overlook the needs of the stressed teacher. Viewed from an ecological perspective, an overburdened teacher will almost certainly have a negative impact on students' school experiences. School practitioners can therefore exert a positive influence on the learning environment of many students by organizing and coordinating staff stress reduction programs. Note that only two of the fifty-four teachers in this study were male. Whether gender influences willingness to admit to stress, participation in stress reduction programs or some other grouping of variables is a question for future research.

SOURCE: Cecil, M. A., & Forman, S. G. (1990). Effects of stress inoculation training and co-worker support groups on teachers' stress. *Journal of School Psychology, 28,* 105–118.

Stress Within Schools: Causes and Interventions

AUTHOR: Maurice J. Elias

PRECIS: To reduce stress, schools must balance academic course work with instruction in competencies that promote responsible behavior and feelings of self-efficacy and self-worth

INTRODUCTION: The many behavioral problems displayed by school-aged children reflect the stress-producing emphasis on academic performance that has increased in recent years as schools attempt to address public concerns over their effectiveness. As the role of the school psychologist expands beyond evaluation to encompass a more ecologically oriented preventive and educational service, the needs of the stressed youngster will surely become a specific focus of attention.

CAUSES: Causes of student stress in schools are many, and the school psychologist is the professional with the training needed to educate the school community about the severity of the problem. School stress has many sources: (1) The extreme emphasis in some schools on grades and test scores and the rewards given to the "best" students leave others feeling excluded and unsuccessful. (2) The pressure to improve our educational system in response to international competition has led to calls for a return to basics, resulting in the introduction of people with little teaching background into the schools and the use of standardized tests as measures of successful educational reform. (3) Schools are pressured to teach more at earlier ages. (4) The pressures of school-related performance expectations reduce students' feelings of self-efficacy, with no provision for teaching them coping and stress management skills. (5) The responsibility for having and dealing with stress is placed on the child or adult. (6) Teachers are not trained in relating to and communicating with students.

CONSEQUENCES: When students feel unable to meet the expectations of significant adults, the stress they experience can result in physical symptoms, alienation from preferred socializing influences, loss of motivation, reduced achievement, lowered self-concept, depression, suicide, delinquency, and substance abuse. The entrance of the preadolescent into middle or junior high school illustrates the attributes of school-related stress and the essential coping prerequisites. As with any life change, starting a new school requires youngsters to adjust to a change in role and expected behaviors, reposition themselves within the social matrix, restructure their personal and social support system, reassess their actions in the new setting, and handle the stress that may arise in new and unpredictable surroundings. These readjustments are taking place in the context of physical, hormonal, cognitive, and psychosocial changes associated with preadolescence. Middle schools have developed operating structures that attempt to address these stress-producing issues, such as availability of a counselor, attention to personal development, a learning strategies approach, intense staff training, and teacher input into policies and program. The result has been improvements in morale, parent participation, test scores, responsible student behavior, and feelings of self-efficacy.

RECOMMENDATIONS: Reducing stress in schools is an ongoing process in which the school psychologist can play a major role. Schools can take a number of steps to facilitate the process: (1) encouraging multiple competencies, not just academic achievement; rewarding competence in any one of the linguistic, logical-mathematical, spacial, kinesthetic, musical, intrapersonal, and interpersonal "intelligences"; (2) teaching students coping skills to deal with the life stressors they will inevitably encounter; broadening the concept of "academic time" to include the teaching of such competencies as critical thinking, decision making, and problem solving; (3) integrating this expanded concept of curriculum into the life of the school and adopting it as a philosophy of instruction rather than as a disconnected series of programs or interventions; (4) providing a safe learning environment free from the threat of physical harm; (5) encouraging thoughtful educational planning by scheduling enough preparation time for teachers to plan their instruction and on a more long-term basis, by allowing sufficient time for planning major initiatives—for example, expanded use of computers or an acquired immune deficiency syndrome (AIDS) prevention program—which allows planners to consider all the variables affecting new programming, such as staff training, material needs, financial resources, and evaluation of outcome; (6) supporting well-planned, thoughtfully conceived action research in which realistic programs can be introduced, examined, improved, or discontinued in a systematic fashion, and in which the talent and competencies of the staff can be utilized, promoting feelings of control and confidence; (7) promoting the skills and approaches outlined here as relevant aspects of teacher-training programs, helping new teachers to understand and recognize stress, and account for developmental processes as they develop their instructional goals.

COMMENTARY: The author concludes that as schools place more emphasis on academic achievement as the criterion for school success, they may achieve the opposite result of stressing students to the point that they feel unable or unwilling to follow the plan and reject the values of responsible citizenship, family life, and work. In other words, "more" is not necessarily "better." Rather than pushing for more course work and skill development, school administrators need to find a balance between the teaching of content and the teaching of coping skills and self-efficacy. Only with this balance can the schools improve academic performance without overdosing students in a manner that will only turn them away from the intended goal.

SOURCE: Elias, M. J. (1989). Schools as a source of stress to children: An analysis of causal and ameliorative influences. *Journal of School Psychology, 27,* 393–407.

Developmental Facilitation Groups
for Students from Divorced Families

AUTHORS: Neil Kalter, Jeffrey Pickar, and Marsha Lesowitz

PRECIS: Developmental facilitation groups to help children cope with divorce and its aftermath

INTRODUCTION: Group work in schools with children of divorce is a relatively recent development. For children from separated families, adjustment to divorce is an ongoing process that may require repeated interventions at various points in the youngster's life, as normative developmental stressors (for example, starting school, adolescence, or high school graduation) cause dormant emotional issues to resurface. The overall goal of the developmental groups described here is to assist children in working through these developmental tasks—more specifically, to reduce the feeling of being different, to reduce confusion around divorce issues, to offer an environment in which they can work through the pain of divorce, to teach them coping skills, and to help them share concerns with their parents.

METHOD: Fifth- and sixth-grade children of divorced parents met one hour per week for eight weeks in groups of five to nine with male and female adult co-leaders. In session I, feelings and ideas about divorce were evoked as leaders began to build group cohesion. The purpose, time, length, and rules of the group were explained. Children were requested to speak one at a time, to respect one another's feelings, to decline to speak if they wished, and to maintain confidentiality. The leaders began a group story of a family with a boy and girl, one in fifth or sixth grade, whose parents were considering divorce. Each group member was encouraged to add to the ongoing story while the leaders wrote everything down on large, displayed sheets of paper.

In session II, the leaders role-played an argument between the parents while the group members imagined themselves as the children in the family overhearing the fight. Through discussion of feelings and thoughts during breaks in the role-play, the members addressed issues relating to anxiety, helplessness, loyalty conflicts, confusion about why divorce occurs, and coping mechanisms to work through these feelings.

For sessions III to VI, the format of session II was repeated, with the leaders acting out similar divorce-oriented role-plays, stopping periodically for discussion. Scenes such as the mother going on a date, custody issues, or visiting the parent who lives somewhere else were enacted. Again, members were supported as having normal feelings, coping behaviors were described, and misperceptions corrected.

In session VII, students interviewed each other for a divorce newspaper, reviewing the issues they discussed during the sessions. The leaders then put the paper together for distribution during the final session, with a photograph of the group. A party was held during session VIII with time for good-byes.

THEMES: During the meetings, the following themes most readily surfaced: (1) Anxiety over parents' fighting—when the leaders role-played the fight in session II, kids first took sides, then described with evident anxiety the emotional intensity of the fights they witnessed between their parents. Some youngsters went to a friend's house to cope; others had a friend over to ease the level of fighting. Leaders stressed the appropriateness of feeling fearful at such times, and explained that such fights stem from parent problems that are unrelated to the children. (2) Custody issues—children experienced conflict over having some choice about living arrangements and not wanting to hurt one parent. Leaders empathized with these feelings, indicating that both parents have good and bad qualities that make choosing hard, but that other factors were also considered by the court in deciding custody. This knowledge seemed to relieve members. (3) Sadness over family breakup—members were upset that their family was no longer together, that they were teased by some peers, and that one parent (usually the father) was no longer there. Reconciliation fantasies surfaced, despite the negative climate in the pre-divorce home. Leaders suggested that even if one parent sees them infrequently, it is not because of the children or something they did. (4) Feelings about mother's dating—this raised feelings of excitement and loyalty conflicts, as children were very curious about their mother's new relationships. They were angered and saddened by the loss of attention from the mother, and competition with the boyfriend, although the need for contact with a male adult also surfaced. (5) Stepfathers and live-in boyfriends—members felt pressure from their mothers to like the new person and were angered by it. They also did not like being disciplined by someone who was not their real parent. Liking the stepparent created loyalty conflicts and guilt over betraying the father. Leaders normalized these feelings and suggested that the children express to their mothers their need for time to develop a relationship with the new spouse or friend.

RESULTS: Parents (primarily mothers) reported that their children enjoyed the groups and were more willing to discuss divorce-related issues with the parents after participating in the group sessions. In response to interviews and questionnaires one week following the last session, the children indicated that the group was a positive experience and reported reduced needs for parents to reconcile, less confusion about the divorce, less self-blame over the divorce, and more motivation to do better in school. A tendency for less sadness and insecurity was also noted. Scales measuring self-competence and school maladaptation were not significantly different between pre- and post-testing.

COMMENTARY: The authors interpret these preliminary results as suggesting that while an eight-week course may well influence specific attitudes toward divorce, it cannot alter the children's broader, more enduring be-havior patterns and personality attributes. However, the groups revealed much about helping children cope with life after divorce — for example, deal-ing with issues of child support, visitation, custody arrangements, loss of one parent, divided loyalties, mother's dating, and a stepfather. The need to provide support to children as they adjust to post-divorce living is as im-portant as helping them through the initial traumas of hostility and separation.

SOURCE: Kalter, N., Pickar, J., & Lesowitz, M. (1984). School-based de-velopmental facilitation groups for children of divorce: A preventive inter-vention. *American Journal of Orthopsychiatry, 54,* 613–623.

Relaxation Training for Elementary Students

AUTHORS: Linda B. Zaichkowsky and Leonard D. Zaichkowsky

PRECIS: Relaxation training to enhance stress control among fourth graders

INTRODUCTION: Practitioners need to focus on preventing stress-related disorders in children at younger ages, rather than waiting until high-risk behaviors create stress-induced conditions that must then be treated reac-tively. Although stress management programs have been instituted with chil-dren in schools, they have not been effectively evaluated. This study sys-tematically measured the outcome of a six-week relaxation training program provided to fourth-grade students. Measures of heart rate, skin tempera-ture, respiration rate, state, and trait anxiety were used to assess the effects of the intervention.

Children were first exposed to one twenty-minute lesson that defined and described the body's response to stress and students' perceptions of the condition. Seventeen ten-minute lessons followed, focusing on abdominal breathing, progressive muscle relaxation, and mental imagery exercises. After the third week of lessons, students practiced at home using a cassette tape produced for the study. They were urged to involve parents and siblings and practice the techniques during stressful events.

RESULTS: Students exposed to the program demonstrated significantly posi-tive changes in heart and respiration rate, skin temperature, and state anxiety. For the control group, only skin temperature showed a significantly positive change. Furthermore, significant differences between the experimental and con-trol group were demonstrated for heart rate, respiration rate, and temperature.

COMMENTARY: As in other studies previously cited, short-term programs do not affect the more entrenched personality characteristics such as trait anxiety. In addition, further research is needed to determine how to maintain both the physiological controls and self-reported feelings associated with lowered tension. While working as a middle school psychologist, Jeffrey Cohen introduced relaxation techniques to eighth-grade health classes as part of a unit on blood pressure, hypertension, and cardiovascular disease. Discussions emphasized that students had the power to manage their stress, that they were not helpless in the face of stressful events, and that they could master techniques to control the effects of stress in their lives. This message of self-efficacy seems an important counterbalance to the perception that one must endure stress and "get by" as well as possible. If students believe they are capable of controlling stress, they may be more willing to learn the enabling techniques.

SOURCE: Zaichkowsky, L. B., & Zaichkowsky, L. D. (1984). The effects of a school-based relaxation training program on fourth grade children. *Journal of Clinical Child Psychology, 13,* 81–85.

An Intervention for Transfer Students

AUTHORS: Victoria J. Sloan, Leonard A. Jason, and G. Anne Bogat

PRECIS: An orientation program for transfer students to ease their adjustment to a new school setting

INTRODUCTION: Life transitions are environmental events that require the individual to adapt to new circumstances. The stress associated with these adaptational demands can impair physical and psychological health, and methods to reduce such stresses are needed. For a child, transferring to a new school is such a potentially stressful experience, but few schools provide programs to smooth the process. This study tested a two-day orientation program for new students in grades 1 through 8 that included peer-led discussion groups and a slide presentation. Students were assigned to either a discussion only group, a slide presentation only group, a discussion and slide presentation group, or a no-treatment control group.

METHOD: The orientation program began one month into the new school year. On the first day, all students had the same experience. Four trained peer guides (sixth to eighth graders) welcomed them and asked them to introduce themselves and name their previous school. The guides then briefly described a positive experience they had had as students in their current school, handed out and discussed information booklets about the school, and answered questions. On the second day, students were exposed to the treatment conditions. For the slide presentation, students viewed thirty-five scenes from various school sites, showing students enjoyably occupied in site-related activities. Important school staff were also presented on the slides. A peer guide read from a prepared script as the slides were shown; discussion and questions were welcomed. The discussion group focused on the students' recent transfer; it began with the peer guide introducing the topic and asking students to identify themselves and describe in two or three words their feelings about transferring. The guides supported the feelings the transfers expressed and stimulated ongoing discussion. Students in the slide and discussion group received both strategies. Pre- and posttesting was done using an information questionnaire about the school, an anxiety scale, and a school sentiment inventory measuring attitudes toward school, teachers, and peers. Measures of school conduct and student evaluations of the program were also taken.

RESULTS: All groups, including the control group, showed significant increases on the information questionnaire, but only the discussion and slide/discussion groups scored significantly higher than the controls. Although all groups except controls showed a statistically significant reduction on the anxiety scale compared to themselves, only the slide/discussion group scored significantly lower than controls. On the school sentiment measure, significant positive changes in attitude toward school subjects, peers, social climate, and school in general were evidenced for the discussion group; positive changes toward school subjects and teachers were registered for the slide/discussion group. No significant difference existed among any of the groups on conduct, attendance, and lateness. As a result of the orientation sessions, many of the new students reported feeling less scared and more knowledgeable about school rules. They seemed to enjoy the program, found the peer guides helpful, and would recommend program continuation.

COMMENTARY: The discussion and slide/discussion groups were more effective than the slide group, although all were more effective than the no-treatment controls. However, only the slide/discussion group showed significantly reduced levels of anxiety compared to the control group. It appears that providing new students the chance to discuss the transfer and their related feelings is a powerful component of the orientation process. In addition, students with higher levels of anxiety had less favorable attitudes toward school, peers, and the social structure/climate of the school; they also performed lower on the information test. The authors indicate that a new student with a higher level of anxiety may have a more difficult time adjusting to the new setting, developing new friendships, and learning school rules. This student may need more opportunities for discussion, perhaps on an individual basis with a school psychologist or counselor. Finally, orientation programs may be beneficial for students within a district who are moving up to a new school (for example, preschool to elementary school, elementary to middle school, or middle school to high school). Students may be nervous about expectations in the new building and might also benefit from the information and discussion format.

SOURCE: Sloan, V. J., Jason, L. A., & Bogat, G. A. (1984). A comparison of orientation methods for elementary school transfer students. *Child Study Journal, 14,* 47–60.

Additional Readings

Forman, S. G., & O'Malley, P. L. (1985). A school-based approach to stress management education of students. In J. E. Zins, D. I. Wagner, & C. A. Maher (Eds.), *Health promotion in the schools: Innovative approaches to facilitating physical and emotional well-being* (pp. 61–71). Binghamton, NY: Haworth Press.

Stress in students has been associated with emotional, physical, academic, behavior, and social difficulties. Stressors create stress reactions (anxiety) to the extent that the student feels threatened and unable to cope with the environmental demands created by the stressor. Home, school, and peers are major stressors for youth, as are life transitions and developmental or physical problems. Approaches to stress management in schools involve eliminating stressors by altering the environment or teaching the child coping skills to reduce anxiety. Coping skills programs include relaxation and self-instructional training, stress inoculation, and rational-emotive therapy, with its classroom derivative rational-emotive education. Development of an effective stress management education program involves use of the strategies identified above; participation of students, staff, and parents in training programs; the assistance of trained program providers from pupil personnel and health services; the availability of support groups; examination of environmental sources of stress such as student's workload, schedules, and decision-making opportunities regarding school procedures; and building attributes such as space, lighting, crowding conditions, and noise.

Genshaft, J. L. (1982). The use of cognitive behavior therapy for reducing math anxiety. *School Psychology Review, 11,* 32–34.

Math-anxious seventh-grade girls were exposed to tutoring and cognitive restructuring in the form of self-instruction training. The tutoring group met for forty-minute math tutorial sessions twice weekly, while the self-instruction training group received the strategy in addition to tutoring. The self-instruction method was modeled; then students wrote down their self-statements when anxious and were instructed to change them to positive goal-oriented statements to help them focus on the math task rather than their stress. Practice was provided in simulated math-anxious situations as well as in other anxiety-provoking experiences until self-statements were spontaneously created. Practice in covert self-instructions occupied the remaining four weeks. The self-instruction group showed significant improvement in math computation compared to the tutorial and control group, and they developed more favorable attitudes toward math. School psychologists should become familiar with cognitive restructuring techniques and teach them to teachers for use in class.

Herzfeld, G., & Powell, R. (1986). *Coping for kids: A complete stress-control program for students ages eight–eighteen.* West Nyack, NY: Center for Applied Research in Education.

This publication presents a program of stress control in twenty-eight lessons for students eight to eighteen years of age. All or some of the lessons and activities may be used at the adult's discretion to help students relax and deal with stresses arising from school, home, peers, and other sources. Lessons cover the nature of stress, breathing, muscle relaxation, imagery, movement awareness, physical fitness, knowing your limits, assertiveness, anger, patience, behavioral manifestations of stress, type A behavior, friendships, creative problem solving, expressing feelings, self-esteem, coping phrases, nutrition, leisure, biofeedback, healing practices, and desensitization. Each lesson begins with background information for the teacher followed by detailed procedures for working with students. Two cassette tapes contain lessons for relaxation. A separate workbook provides additional activity worksheets.

Jason, L. A., Betts, D., Johnson, J., Smith, S., Krueckeberg, S., & Cradock, M. (1989). An evaluation of an orientation plus tutoring school-based prevention program. *Professional School Psychology, 4,* 273–284.

An orientation plus tutoring program was provided to third-, fourth-, and fifth-grade transfer students considered high risks for school failure because of low socioeconomic status, academic lags, and experiences with two or three life stressors. The orientation program attempted to reduce the anxiety of these students in their new setting by disseminating general school information, answering questions about the school, and sharing feelings about transferring in a group discussion format led by sixth-grade peer leaders. Criterion-referenced testing was used to pinpoint areas in which students needed tutoring, which was given twice weekly in forty-five-minute one-on-one sessions using direct instruction techniques. Math, phonics, spelling, and reading were targeted for remediation. Results indicated very positive reactions to the program by the children, parents, teachers, and principals. However, only on standardized achievement tests were positive program effects found. Self-esteem, sociometric measures, teacher ratings of behavior, and grades, absences, and lateness showed no positive movement. Limitations of the study were discussed by the authors who suggested that improvement in school and behavioral skills would be best accomplished by direct intervention in those areas rather than by spillover effects from tutoring.

Kane, M. T., & Kendall, P. C. (1989). Anxiety disorders in children: A multiple-baseline evaluation of a cognitive-behavioral treatment. *Behavior Therapy, 20,* 499–508.

Four children, ages nine to thirteen, diagnosed with over-anxious disorder, received a cognitive-behavioral intervention in sixteen to twenty one-hour individual sessions twice weekly. Students were taught to recognize anxious feelings and accompanying physical responses, clarify unrealistic or negative cognitions in situations provoking anxiety, develop skills to manage the situation such as coping self-talk, and evaluate and self-reward successful coping strategies. Training included in vivo experiences, role-play, relaxation training, reinforcing contingencies, and homework. Training and practice occurred in anxiety-provoking situations, with the anxiety level gradually escalated; social praise was provided continuously. Practice during anxious experiences at home or in school was encouraged. Results indicated reduction of anxiety and improvement in target behaviors on parent reports, clinician's ratings, and child self-reports. Maintenance of effects was recorded for two children but was equivocal for two others. Analysis of behavior suggests that identification of cognitions may require a level of development not yet achieved by all the youngsters in this study.

Leal, L. L., Baxter, E. G., Martin, J., & Marx, R. W. (1981). Cognitive modification and systematic desensitization with test anxious high school students. *Journal of Counseling Psychology, 28,* 525–528.

Tenth-grade test-anxious students were exposed to either a cognitive modification or systematic desensitization procedure. For cognitive modification, the students examined how their thoughts and self-statements create anxiety; they were taught to identify arousal and replace anxiety-provoking reactions with more effective alternatives. In systematic desensitization the instructors paired deep muscle relaxation with anxiety-laden images such as a mildly anxious test situation. Results provided mixed support among the students for the superiority of systematic desensitization; the cognitive strategy was more effective. Cognitive modification seems the treatment of choice.

Long, B. C. (1988). Stress management for school personnel: Stress-inoculation training and exercise. *Psychology in the Schools, 25,* 314–324.

This stress-management study assessed the combined and separate effects on teachers of stress inoculation training and an unsupervised aerobic exercise treatment. In the combined condition, teachers spent one hour of each of eight weekly one-and-a-half-hour sessions in stress inoculation training with exposure to the theory, training in cognitive restructuring and positive self-statements, and rehearsal-application. The last half-hour involved an individually tailored exercise program with weekly monitoring of progress, discussion of the benefits of exercise, dissemination of related instructional materials, and ongoing encouragement to continue exercise. Teachers in the delayed treatment group took part in an unsupervised exercise program consisting of a bicycle ergometric test, educational information, and encouragement to begin a program of exercise. After eight weeks, teachers received stress inoculation training separately.

Results showed that the combined group was more effective in reducing anxiety. Both groups increased their overall positive coping skills (prevention of problems) while decreasing emotion-focused coping (denial, wishful thinking, and self-blame). Neither group improved their rates of exercise or fitness levels. The author speculated that timing may play a role in the success of these interventions, as teacher stress is more intense at different times of the school year. In general, the combined program seemed most effective with high anxious–low physically fit teachers.

Lord, J. H. (1990). *Death at school: A guide for teachers, school nurses, counselors, and administrators.* (Available from Mothers Against Drunk Driving, P.O. Box 541688, Dallas, TX 75354-1688.)

Schools can help students deal with the death of a peer, parent, or other loved one. When practitioners discuss death of a peer's family member in the elementary classroom, they need to be truthful, give only necessary information, allow for expression of feelings, accept all emotional reactions, provide opportunity for written messages to be created for the grieving child, plan for the child's return, and watch for signs of difficulty once the child is back in school.

If a teacher or classmate dies, many of the above steps are also applicable with the class. In addition, the desk of that person should remain empty for a few days to help students acknowledge the death, as much information as possible should be shared with the class before it is given to the rest of the school, a recess time should be given after the discussion, and the funeral and a memorial should be discussed. Deaths of grandparents, pets, and other loved ones should at least be acknowledged with some sharing of memories, particularly if the stress in the family temporarily removes the grieving parents from a supportive role.

With middle or high schoolers, talks may need to be private, but they should occur. For children who witness traumatic deaths, psychological and physical reactions may occur such as helplessness, fear, anxiety, withdrawal, depression, and guilt. Schools need to assess this situation, respond to the needs of staff and students, keep communication open, monitor and intervene with traumatized students and teachers, and help teachers identify students needing help.

The article ends with different reactions of students to trauma and possible "first aid" responses by practitioners and other adults. Information for families is also given. Advance preparation by the school is considered essential. Books on death for children and adults are listed. When children who had suffered a family death were asked what comments from others were most helpful upon returning to school, they listed the following examples:

"I can't know how you feel, but I want to help you in any way I can"; "I care about you"; "I can see that you're very sad"; "If you feel like sharing any of your writing with me, I'd like to read it"; and finally, "I'm sorry that (name) died."

Remer, R. (1984). Personal approaches to stress reduction: A workshop. *School Psychology Review, 13,* 244–248.

Topic areas for workshop presentations on stress reduction for teachers might include some or all of the following: definition and types of stress; life-style strategies to reduce stress; nutrition and stress; exercise; developing social support systems; relaxation responses to stress; and communication skills. Through the workshop format, in which interaction between the leader and participants is enhanced, learning takes place in an enjoyable, comfortable atmosphere. If the presenter involves the audience in activities, exercises, or other active strategies, they will be more likely to apply in their own lives what they have learned.

Saigh, P. A. (1987a). In vitro flooding of an adolescent's post-traumatic stress disorder. *Journal of Clinical Child Psychology, 16,* 147–150.
Saigh, P. A. (1987b). In vitro flooding of a childhood post-traumatic stress disorder. *School Psychology Review, 16,* 203–211.

These two studies used in vitro flooding; first of a fourteen-year-old Lebanese adolescent boy, then of a ten-year-old Lebanese girl, both of whom suffered from post-traumatic stress disorder. The boy had been abducted and tortured by the militia; the girl had experienced an artillery attack. The principal of the boy's school described the boy's academic and behavioral difficulties following the incident; the girl complained of memory and concentration deficits. Both reported great anxiety on recollection of the events. In each case, four anxiety-arousing chronological scenes from the actual occurrence were developed for use during the flooding intervention. After a baseline period in which presentation of the scenes was accompanied by muscle relaxation exercises, flooding was initiated for two sessions per week over four weeks. Each week for sixty minutes, the student was instructed to imagine vividly the most unpleasant aspects of one of the four scenes using stimulus and response imagery cues. Relaxation exercises were practiced for five minutes (the girl) or ten minutes (the boy) following the in vitro flooding. After this the remaining three scenes were presented for six minutes each, alternating with five minutes of relaxation exercises. Probes conducted every two minutes assessed anxiety levels.

Results indicated a dramatic reduction in anxiety with the flooding procedure and maintenance of effects over a four- and six-month follow-up, respectively. Other cognitive, behavioral, and affective measures were equally encouraging. For the girl, self-monitored thoughts about the trauma (excluding the ones elicited during treatment) also declined markedly. The author suggests possible application of this technique for students who have experienced traumatic events, such as crimes, and who may suffer post-traumatic stress reactions.

Tunnecliffe, M. R., Leach, D. J., & Tunnecliffe, L. P. (1986). Relative efficacy of using behavioral consultation as an approach to teacher stress management. *Journal of School Psychology, 24,* 123–131.

The authors compared relaxation training, as a clinical-individual approach to teacher stress reduction, and collaborative behavioral consultation (CBC), as a systemic-organizational model of problem solving and stress management. The CBC group learned to identify school stressors and the range of possible problem-solving techniques available to handle them. They were guided in exploring behaviors in the workplace and in creating solutions to problems using previously validated problem-solving procedures. Teachers met once weekly for five weeks in ninety-minute sessions; these covered stress theory, sources of stress, maladaptive stress among teachers, and the problem-solving approach — that is, identifying stress sources, determining possible solutions, and starting self-help stress groups in the schools. The relaxation group also identified stressors and learned some stress theory and sources of personal and school stress. Fifty minutes of each ninety-minute session were devoted to group relaxation training and completion of homework. Leaders functioned as "experts," giving answers to questions rather than collaboratively guiding participants toward solutions. Following the intervention, teacher stress declined most effectively for the CBC group, compared to the relaxation training group and controls. This effect was maintained at a three-month follow-up.

Further Reading

Drake, E. A., & Shellenberger, S. (1981). Children of separation and divorce: A review of school programs and implications for the psychologist. *School Psychology Review, 10,* 54–61.

Forman, S. G., & O'Malley, P. L. (1984). School stress and anxiety interventions. *School Psychology Review, 13,* 162–170.

Gittelman, R. (Ed.). (1986). *Anxiety disorders of childhood.* New York: Guilford Press.

Hembree, R. (1988). Correlates, causes, effects, and treatment of test anxiety. *Review of Educational Research, 58,* 47–77.

Hodges, W. F. (1986). *Interventions for children of divorce.* New York: Wiley.

Hughes, J. N. (1988). *Cognitive behavior therapy with children in schools* (chap. 4). Elmsford, NY: Pergamon Press.

Kendall, P. C., Howard, B. L., & Epps, J. (1988). The anxious child: Cognitive-behavioral treatment strategies. *Behavior Modification, 12,* 281–310.

Klingman, A. (1987). A school-based emergency crisis intervention in a mass school disaster. *Professional Psychology: Research and Practice, 18,* 604–612.

Lewis, C. E., Siegel, J. M., & Lewis, M. A. (1984). Feeling bad: Exploring sources of distress among pre-adolescent children. *American Journal of Public Health, 74,* 117–122.

Moracco, J., & McFadden, H. (1981, October). Principals and counselors: Collaborative roles in reducing teacher stress. *NASSP Bulletin,* pp. 41–46.

Sharp, J. J., & Forman, S. G. (1985). A comparison of two approaches to anxiety management for teachers. *Behavior Therapy, 16,* 370–383.

Sterling, S., Cowen, E. L., Weissberg, R. P., Lotyczewski, B. S., & Boike, M. (1985). Recent stressful life events and young children's school adjustment. *American Journal of Community Psychology, 13,* 87–98.

Strauss, C. C. (1987). Anxiety. In M. Hersen & V. B. Van Hasselt (Eds.), *Behavior therapy with children and adolescents: A clinical approach* (pp. 109–136). New York: Wiley.

Strauss, C. C. (1988). Behavioral assessment and treatment of overanxious disorder in children and adolescents. *Behavior Modification, 12,* 234–251.

Strauss, C. C. (1990). Anxiety disorders of childhood and adolescence. *School Psychology Review, 19,* 142–157.

Thoresen, C. E., & Eagleston, J. R. (1983). Chronic stress in children and adolescents. *Theory into Practice, 22,* 48–56.

Toubiana, Y. H., Milgram, N. A., Strich, Y., & Edelstein, A. (1988). Crisis intervention in a school community disaster: Principles and practices. *Journal of Community Psychology, 16,* 228–240.

Ultee, C. A., Griffioen, D., & Schellekens, J. (1982). The reduction of anxiety in children: A comparison of the effects of "systematic desensitization in vitro" and "systematic desensitization in vivo." *Behaviour Research and Therapy, 20,* 61–67.

Waddell, D., & Thomas, A. (1989, November). Children and responses to disaster: Formulating a disaster plan. *Communiqué: National Association of School Psychologists.*

Waddell, D., & Thomas, A. (1989, November). Children and responses to disaster: Teacher handout. *Communiqué: National Association of School Psychologists.*

Zatz, S., & Chassin, L. (1985). Cognitions of test-anxious children under naturalistic test-taking conditions. *Journal of Consulting and Clinical Psychology, 53,* 393–401.

Fears/Phobias

In Therapies for School Behavior Problems, *this section was entitled "Phobias," but here it was broadened to reflect the distinction between the two terms.* Fear *is the feeling of being afraid, an adaptive mechanism that represents a normal, common, age-appropriate reaction to real or imagined threats. Fears change with age and are thus of usually short duration.* Phobias *are fears that become excessively intense, persist beyond normal age expectations, result in avoidance, signal maladjustment, and usually require some form of intervention. To further complicate the matter,* fear and anxiety *are often used interchangeably even though anxiety differs from fear, representing an intense state of subjective worry or unease, accompanied by heightened physiological responses, faulty thinking, and maladaptive behavior.*

King and Ollendick (1989) point out that school-based helpers may unintentionally reinforce youngsters' fears in their efforts to protect or reassure them. In contrast, the prevalent intervention strategies expose the student to the fear-arousing situation so that he or she can develop appropriate coping skills. The articles cited here focus on such exposure techniques.

Finally, while school refusal (which includes school phobia) is commonly described as an outgrowth of separation anxiety, more recent writings report multiple causes for this behavior, which extend beyond separation issues. Thus, digests for this problem area have not been included in the "Anxiety and Stress" section; they are placed here since readers are more likely to look for them under "Phobias."

Reference

King, N., & Ollendick, T. (1989). Children's anxiety and phobic disorders in school settings: Classification, assessment, and intervention issues. *Review of Educational Research, 59,* 431–470.

Storytelling as a Primary Prevention Strategy

AUTHOR: Avigdor Klingman

PRECIS: Bibliotherapy to reduce fear of the dark in kindergarten students

INTRODUCTION: Maladaptive fears may be prevented when youngsters develop the coping skills necessary to master stressful occurrences. Biblioguidance, in which stories are used therapeutically, was utilized with forty-two kindergartners to reduce their fear of the dark.

METHOD: Students in the treatment group met for five twenty-minute sessions over five weeks to hear a story that depicted the dark in a positive manner and presented one or more coping models. A group discussion followed in which students shared their reactions to the story and recounted individual experiences while the leader praised the positive experiences and coping statements. Questions from the leader, asking how certain coping behaviors helped them, were designed to elicit such strategies from the children. A control group heard stories unrelated to fears of the dark.

RESULTS: Students in the bibliotherapy group self-rated their fear of the dark as significantly less than that of the control group immediately following the last session and at a three-week follow-up. In addition, the pretest to posttest self-rating of the experimental group showed a significant decrease while the control group showed no change in self-perceived fear of the dark. Parents of the experimental students reported that the children's fear had lessened significantly following the intervention; no changes were reported by parents of the control group. Finally, the group exposed to bibliotherapy made significantly more coping statements in the later stages of the intervention than they had in the beginning.

COMMENTARY: Storytelling can play a primary preventive role regarding children's fears of the dark by depicting the dark in positive terms and portraying coping models behaving in ways that reduce the stress associated with the situation. The author points out that since storytelling is a well-accepted component of the preschool routine, the activity as a fear-reducing technique can be easily incorporated into any classroom curriculum. It is interesting that middle school teachers often report that their students still love for someone to read them stories. The practitioner may wish to capitalize on this important attribute and use storytelling to decrease the impact of various other age-appropriate fears.

SOURCE: Klingman, A. (1988). Biblioguidance with kindergartners: Evaluation of a primary prevention program to reduce fear of the dark. *Journal of Clinical Child Psychology, 17,* 237–241.

In Vivo Desensitization for School Phobia

AUTHORS: Daniel D. Houlihan and Robert N. Jones

PRECIS: Desensitization in the natural environment to improve student's attendance and academic performance

INTRODUCTION: Approximately 69 percent of children referred for treatment of fearfulness are diagnosed as school phobic. Type I or *neurotic crisis* school phobia is usually the first episode, tends to occur acutely on a Monday, is most common in early grades, is associated in a real or imagined way with the mother's health, and typically involves good communication between parents. Type II, the *way of life* phobia, has a history of episodes, usually displays a more chronic pattern of development, occurs more often in older students, is not related to the mother's health, and reveals poor parental communication.

Behavior interventions to address this disorder have included systematic desensitization, flooding procedures, modeling, self-control, and contingency management. In vivo desensitization was used in this case study with a thirteen-year-old seventh-grade boy who had been out of school for nearly a year. Applying the strategy in vivo (in the actual setting as opposed to an office or laboratory) exposed the student to the real-life fear-provoking situations rather than requiring them to be imagined and increased the opportunity for generalization of the boy's fear reduction.

CASE STUDY: William's attendance deteriorated at the end of grade 5 and throughout grade 6, suggesting a *way of life* Type II phobia. He did not avoid social contact as in avoidant disorder, nor was separation from the parent the issue as in separation anxiety disorder. His social and academic performance were the clear targets of his anxiety, with reinforcement, home-school, and psychiatric interventions proving unsuccessful. In vivo desensitization was tried to increase his school attendance and reduce his depression.

For William, a five-level fear hierarchy was developed, then systematically attacked at each level. During level I, which lasted one day, the school psychologist walked with William for one hour in the school halls during classes, talking and relating to him in a relaxed manner. After returning to the psychologist's office, they discussed for five minutes the fun experiences of school and were then joined by the homeroom teacher for a further five-minute discussion about how much fun school could be.

During level II (four days long), William came to school for the last three hours of the day and stayed in his homeroom class. The psychologist spent a decreasing amount of time in class with William over the four days, fading his presence from fifty minutes, to thirty minutes, to ten minutes for the last two days. William was dismissed for home with all other students. For day 1 of the five-day level III strategy, William and the psychologist ate lunch in the cafeteria, talking with some students. William then attended for three hours in his homeroom without the psychologist. After a small crisis on day 2 was resolved, the psychologist faded his presence at lunch over the remaining three days, from thirty minutes, to twenty minutes, to ten minutes on days 3, 4, and 5.

For level IV (five days), William attended a full day but remained in the homeroom. The psychologist attended for the first ten minutes of two periods per day according to a prearranged schedule. Level V lasted five weeks, with William attending a new class outside his homeroom each week. Teachers were sensitized to possible reluctance from William, and the psychologist accompanied him to class and spent the first ten minutes in the room on the first day of his attendance there. The psychologist also spent ten minutes in one other class on the first day and made contact with him during one other five-minute break. Finally, after level V ended and William requested a regular schedule, the psychologist attended one class for ten minutes each week for the rest of the school year.

RESULTS: During grade 6, William attended 21 out of 180 school days, while in grade 7, he was present 152 of 180 days. For grade 8, his record was 166 of 180. He achieved a C average for grade 7, which improved to a B the following year; he reported less depression, even though his score on the Beck Depression Inventory improved from the extreme range only to the mild to moderate range. Examination of his hands and parent report suggested less compulsive hand washing.

COMMENTARY: For William, the strategy increased attendance, decreased depression, improved academic performance, social involvement, and a more positive relationship with his parents. While the authors note several ways in which the study's limitations could be addressed, they concur that the desensitization was responsible for the improved outcome. When implementing this technique, the psychologist needs to remain aware of the social implications of interacting with the student in public locations, such as the hall, classroom, or lunchroom. Younger students tend to be less sensitive in this regard, but older students are more protective of their social image and may feel uncomfortable in the public company of the school psychologist. This issue may be heightened in smaller schools where the prolonged absence of a student is more noticeable to others who might then question the phobic student as to why he or she was absent. Students may want to work with the psychologist, yet feel concerned about the stigma their interaction may impose. The practitioner should tune in to these concerns and incorporate them into the strategy.

SOURCE: Houlihan, D. D., & Jones, R. N. (1989). Treatment of a boy's school phobia with in vivo systematic desensitization. *Professional School Psychology, 4,* 285–293.

A Treatment Model for School Refusal

AUTHORS: Christopher A. Kearney and Wendy K. Silverman

PRECIS: Analysis of contributing causes to select appropriate strategies for school refusal behavior

INTRODUCTION: Refusal to attend school has multiple causes, is displayed in a variety of ways, and is influenced by different treatment approaches. This diversity creates a need to examine on a case-by-case basis the individual precipitating factors that lead to school refusal and the specific approach that may be most effective in improving attendance. For example, not all youth who avoid school show fearful behavior while others may be depressed or oppositional. Similarly, school refusal may be maintained by either negative or positive reinforcement, leading to the use of such varying interventions as desensitization, contingency management, or contingency contracting. To assist the practitioner in separating out the motivating conditions for school refusal, the authors developed the School Refusal Assessment Scale (SRAS), which evaluates four possible reasons for students' nonattendance: to avoid fearful or anxiety-provoking school experiences (negative reinforcement), to escape negative social interactions (negative reinforcement), to attract attention or avoid separation anxiety (positive reinforcement), or to obtain tangible reinforcement (positive reinforcement). The practitioner can then select the intervention strategies that most accurately reflect the motivating causes of the disorder.

CASE STUDIES: Seven school-refusing youths aged nine to sixteen were exposed to strategies developed through this prescriptive format. All had shown symptoms for less than one year and were referred by school psychologists to the School Refusal Program at the Center for Stress and Anxiety Disorders in Albany, New York. Each child received a clinical diagnosis based on a semistructured interview instrument known as the Anxiety Disorders Interview Schedule for Children; a variety of other scales, surveys, and inventories were used to assess behavioral factors associated with their school refusal.

The School Refusal Assessment Scale for Children (SRAS-C) was administered to each child to identify the conditions motivating his or her refusal to attend school; from these, specific intervention strategies were then developed. The SRAS-C contains sixteen questions scored on a Likert-type scale of 0–6 with 0 indicating *never* and 6 indicating *always*. Four questions are designed to assess each of the four possible motivating factors affecting nonattendance. For example, one question tapping general fearfulness reads, "Are you afraid of the teachers or others at school?" Another question exploring separation anxiety and attention-getting behavior asks, "How often do you feel that you would rather be with your parents than go to school?"

Scores in each of the four areas result in the assignment of a category to the child based on the most influential motivating condition. Parents also completed questionnaires (including the SRAS-P), while a school adult (teacher, counselor, or school psychologist) answered the SRAS-T (the SRAS is available from the first author, Christopher Kearney). Each child was then identified under one of the four motivating antecedents on the basis of the combined scores of the self, parent, and teacher scale.

This analysis identified four students as refusing school to avoid aversive social experiences, one refusing for general fearfulness, one refusing as an attention-getting strategy, and one looking for tangible reinforcement. The students avoiding social interactions received cognitive behavior therapy and/or modeling techniques with role-play and feedback to improve their social skills and restructure their negative thoughts. Overanxious/fearful avoidance of school was treated through in vivo desensitization with relaxation training and imagery techniques. The student using attention-getting behavior was exposed to a schedule of differential reinforcement of other behaviors (DRO schedule) to decrease tantruming and physical complaints; the student who avoided school because of the reinforcing attributes of nonattendance participated in contingency contracting. All strategies occurred in one or two thirty- to forty-five-minute sessions per week.

RESULTS: Six of the seven students returned to school for a minimum of two weeks at posttreatment. However, regarding changes in the motivating variables, results were mixed. Student 1, who fell within the overanxious category, did not show a decrease in general anxiety on posttreatment questionnaires, but his daily self-ratings of distress showed a decrease as did parent ratings of anxiety and distress. Subjects 2, 3, 4, and 5, who refused school to avoid social adversity, decreased their social anxiety and improved their social competence questionnaire scores. Subject 6, who refused school in order to gain attention at home, obtained questionnaire scores representing a significant decrease in fear of separation, aggression, and demanding attention, while subject 7, who avoided school because of the rewards of staying home, improved on measures of oppositional and externalizing behavior. At a six-month follow-up, all students except one who avoided for social reasons maintained attendance without significant distress.

COMMENTARY: If asked, most school practitioners would probably indicate that school phobia arises from the mother-child relationship. The results reported here refute that as the only reason. By demonstrating the utility of a prescriptive approach based on an analysis of the contributing variables to school refusal, the authors broaden its etiological base and allow for the intervention to fit the cause. School psychologists should find this information particularly valuable as it directs them toward strategies with empirically validated effectiveness and allows them to understand that school phobia has social, cognitive, and affective components that must be considered when planning a procedure. A preintervention assessment as done here might prevent the psychologist from selecting an ineffective strategy and wasting time while the child remains out of school.

SOURCE: Kearney, C. A., & Silverman, W. K. (1990). A preliminary analysis of a functional model of assessment and treatment for school refusal behavior. *Behavior Modification, 14,* 340–366.

Self-Control Desensitization to Reduce Multiple Fears

AUTHORS: Philip H. Bornstein and Michael Knapp

PRECIS: Reducing separation, travel, and illness fears in a twelve-year-old through a cognitive application of systematic desensitization

INTRODUCTION: Cognitive self-control procedures have been employed individually and as part of multicomponent packages to treat childhood fears. While systematic desensitization has not traditionally been viewed as a self-control procedure, some writers regard it as an active cognitively mediated mechanism for coping with anxiety. The study cited here attempted to apply this self-control desensitization process to reduce fearfulness in a twelve-year-old boy. John's fears of separation, automobile travel, and illness had severely disrupted his school attendance, caused friendships to end, and made him more reclusive.

METHOD: John's parents were trained to record his fear-related comments as the main dependent variable. A fear survey was also completed and his fear-related behaviors were recorded. During a two-week baseline period, John saw the senior author (Bornstein) for relaxation training and creation of initial hierarchies. For treatment, desensitization was presented as a coping skill and John constructed and utilized three separate fear hierarchies (separation, travel, and illness) based on analysis of previous interview material. Each hierarchy contained ten to fifteen items. As examples, one item in the separation hierarchy was an invitation to a friend's house for the weekend. While John knew it would be fun, he had not been apart from his parents for two days in over two years. A travel item depicted John riding in the car with his parents in icy blizzard conditions, seeing a car that had gone off the road. An illness image suggested that he felt all the symptoms of something as he watched "Quincy" on television. He worried he would die.

As John imagined these and other anxiety-provoking experiences on the hierarchies, he was instructed to apply his relaxation skills to cope with the anxiety rather than stop the image. After he had worked through the hierarchies, he applied his new skills to actual in vivo situations. Each hierarchy was addressed in two weekly sessions; each of the ten to fifteen items in the hierarchies was presented until the distress level associated with the item was effectively reduced.

RESULTS: John's fear-related comments in all three areas decreased significantly during treatment—from four to five comments daily to one and one-half or fewer (.03 per day for separation). A one-year follow-up yielded zero comments for separation and travel and .14 per day for illness. In addition, his fear survey scores decreased and John was able to separate from his parents when they traveled to Hawaii, take a 2,500 mile auto trip, and engage in activities that previously caused him to worry over his health. He was attending school regularly and socializing effectively with peers.

COMMENTARY: The authors note that self-control desensitization is easy to apply and is effective in a relatively short time. For further discussion of desensitization as a self-control technique the reader is referred to the 1971 seminal article by M. R. Goldfried entitled "Systematic Desensitization as Training in Self-Control" (*Journal of Consulting and Clinical Psychology, 37,* 228–234). This article expands on helping the individual generalize to real-life situations the learned coping-relaxation skills. The school practitioner is in an excellent position to train a student and monitor in vivo generalization to anxiety-provoking school situations.

SOURCE: Bornstein, P. H., & Knapp, M. (1981). Self-control desensitization with a multi-phobic boy: A multiple baseline design. *Journal of Behavior Therapy and Experimental Psychiatry, 12,* 281–285.

Reducing Fear of Fire

AUTHORS: Russell T. Jones, Thomas H. Ollendick, Kimberly J. McLaughlin, and Cathy E. Williams

PRECIS: Elaborative rehearsal with elementary students to train fire emergency skills and reduce fire-related fears.

INTRODUCTION: Latch-key children are more at risk for injury from fire than children who are with an adult. Although programs to teach emergency skills are effective, few efforts have addressed children's fears of such occurrences, even though the fear may inhibit the child's learning and use of appropriate safety skills. This study compared the effects of behavioral training and elaborative rehearsal on third-grade children to determine whether their fears associated with fire could be reduced while they enhanced their learning of proper action during a fire. The children selected had scored below 50 percent on an assessment of emergency skills in a simulated fire emergency and reported significant fire-related fears.

METHOD: All children in groups of three to four were trained in daily one-hour sessions for three consecutive days. A simulated bedroom was set up at school with a cot, rug, chair, and other items such as an alarm, window, and make-believe fire. Three fire-escape situations were presented, one each day by trainers who described and modeled the sequence of escape behaviors, praising and correcting the youngsters as they practiced the steps. Half the children then participated in a *four-step elaborative rehearsal* format. In step 1 the children answered questions related to the escape behavior sequence previously practiced. In step 2 trainers provided reasons for correct answers that the children had to repeat. For step 3 children restated how each correct answer helped in a successful escape from a fire. Step 4 allowed for questions about the procedures with answers given by the trainer. Children receiving only behavioral practice learned new fire safety information and answered factual questions. They were not given any reasons that particular escape behaviors were important and were not asked to restate answers to questions.

RESULTS: A direct behavioral assessment of children's fire skills was obtained in the simulated environment. Results showed a significant increase in skills for both the elaborative and behavioral groups but not for a control group receiving no training. On the self-report of fear measures, only the elaborative group showed a reduced fear of fire; on tests of the children's understanding of why certain escape behaviors are necessary, only the elaborative group improved pre- to posttesting.

COMMENTARY: Children can learn fire emergency skills through behavioral rehearsal without the need for elaboration on the reasons they are necessary. However, only through elaboration are fears about fire reduced, a condition that may enhance retention of skills and use during actual emergencies. While the outcome requires further study, it is important to establish the potential power of fear-reducing techniques to enhance behavioral competencies, particularly in life-threatening situations such as fires. Considering that students often do not take fire drills seriously, it might be useful to spend a few hours teaching younger elementary students fire emergency skills and reducing the fears that might interfere with their ability to act in a real crisis.

SOURCE: Jones, R. T., Ollendick, T. H., McLaughlin, K. J., & Williams, C. E. (1989). Elaborative and behavioral rehearsal in the acquisition of fire emergency skills and the reduction of fear of fire. *Behavior Therapy, 20,* 93–101.

Additional Readings

Barlow, D. H., & Seidner, A. L. (1983). Treatment of adolescent agoraphobics: Effects on parent-adolescent relations. *Behavior Research and Therapy, 21*, 519–526.

Three adolescent agoraphobics attended ten weekly group therapy sessions with their mothers. Panic management, cognitive restructuring, and between-session practice with gradual exposure to fearful situations was used with the youths while the mothers learned about agoraphobia and ways to address the anxiety that were neither punitive nor anxiety reinforcing. Parents were urged to support practice by their children and to practice with them once weekly. Results showed two of the three students reporting reduced levels of anxiety and avoidance and improved communication with their parents. The correlation between reduction of anxiety and improvement in the parent-child relationship as well as the inability of the adolescents to accept the unreality of their fears underscores the value of parental involvement in the treatment of adolescent agoraphobia.

Blagg, N. R., & Yule, W. (1984). The behavioural treatment of school refusal—a comparative study. *Behavior Research and Therapy, 22*, 119–127.

Three strategies for school refusers were compared. The first was the behavioral treatment approach (BTA), which addressed child, family, and school issues and consisted of five steps: (1) clarification of factors causing and maintaining nonattendance, (2) agreement by all involved on a strategy and return to school plan, (3) instruction to parents and teachers on maintaining attendance once return is achieved, (4) providing the child an escort if necessary, (5) ongoing follow-up with the school and parents for at least six weeks. A second approach was inpatient hospitalization, which required attention to several issues: separation anxiety, an appropriate therapeutic milieu, schooling and occupational therapy, type and degree of medication, and discharge planning. Home tutoring and psychotherapy was the third strategy. Of the BTA group, 93.3 percent successfully returned to school compared with 37.5 percent of the hospitalized students and 10 percent of the tutored psychotherapy group. The BTA group also evidenced significantly less separation anxiety. These students averaged 2.53 weeks of treatment, while hospitalization was 45.3 weeks and tuition therapy was 72.1 weeks. BTA is therefore quicker, less costly, and more effective.

Boyd, L. A. (1980). Emotive imagery in the behavioral management of adolescent school phobia: A case approach. *School Psychology Review, 9*, 186–189.

Emotive imagery was used to desensitize Ricky, a sixteen-year-old, mildly retarded school phobic. A behavioral contract required Ricky to come to the psychologist's office at school each morning for emotive imagery training. Beginning the next week he was to attend school for a half day for two weeks, then begin for a full day the week after that. He was denied television and radio for nonattendance, while two or fewer absences during the two weeks earned him a trip to the circus. Ricky and the school psychologist developed a hierarchy of school-related behaviors; he was taught relaxation skills related to mental images of each item in the hierarchy. He was required to practice this sequence once each hour. With some difficulties Ricky earned his circus trip and began full-time attendance with no further flare-ups. His motivation to succeed was cited as an important factor.

Bryce, G., & Baird, D. (1986). Precipitating a crisis: Family therapy and adolescent school refusers. *Journal of Adolescence, 9,* 199–213.

The authors describe school refusal and treatment issues from a family systems perspective. Assessment of the refusal problem is used to understand family patterns. For example, differing perceptions of the refusal behavior within the family can illustrate family dysfunction. The therapist works to establish a collaborative relationship with the family; he or she also tries to understand what function the refusal serves within the family and why it is needed at this time.

The therapeutic strategy in this case involves precipitating a crisis by insisting that the teenager return to school, then helping the family manage the crisis in a healthier manner. A day for return is chosen with the family and a strategy developed. Here the therapy can be undermined by a number of occurrences: the adolescent objects or threatens to harm himself, the family fights one another, the family challenges the therapist, or professionals mirror family dysfunction by disagreeing and arguing. At this time the therapist can use the collaborative relationship to explore the family concerns or can use a technique such as paradoxical intervention, which works around the relationship. Once the adolescent's attendance is accomplished, other areas of possible improvement might also be evaluated, such as his or her psychological and physical symptoms, maturational development, and the family dynamics.

Kolko, D. J., Ayllon, T., & Torrence, C. (1987). Positive practice routines in overcoming resistance to the treatment of school phobia: A case study with follow-up. *Journal of Behavior Therapy and Experimental Psychiatry, 18,* 249–257.

A six-year-old first grader tried to avoid school and tantrumed if the parent attempted to leave the classroom. When the principal escorted her to class, she followed but then tantrumed when he tried to leave. A positive practice intervention was applied in which she could remain in the principal's office but had to follow the classroom academic routines in the areas of general hygiene and grooming, postassignment work habits, physical exercise, and preacademic and academic skills. Each day she could choose whether to go to class or work in the office. The principal gave her instruction during lunch and after school. By the fifth week she was spending all her time in class, interacting with peers and improving her grades, having found the office work less fun than work in class. One month and one year follow-ups in a new school showed no problems despite the death of her mother.

Guidelines for overcoming resistance to treatment as displayed here include the following: (1) Allowing the problem behavior to take place in the natural location, thereby permitting the adults to gain control by not fighting the resistance to change. (2) Reframing the behavior to provide for a new set of responses to it. By reframing the behavior as a lack of skills arising from missed classes rather than as resistance to attending, the response of providing instruction becomes more appropriate than engaging in a power struggle to return her to class. (3) Changing the consequence of the behavior so that the behavior is no longer reinforced. By providing daily instruction, the principal made the consequences of remaining out of class no longer rewarding.

Pollitt, G. (1984). School phobia. *School Social Work Journal, 8,* 80–89.

This interpretation views school phobia as a form of separation anxiety rooted in a hostile, dependent mother-child relationship. By contrast, the truant child is more independent and has parents who are underinvolved. Puberty and the start of the less personal junior high school experience can aggravate an adolescent's separation anxiety. The child comes to fear that something will happen to the mother (a projection of the child's hostility) and so stays home. For the school phobic, fixation, repression, denial, displacement, and projection are the major defense mechanisms, and the school becomes the symbolic parent to defy. School phobics have not yet established their identity. They need to be back in school as soon as possible. Family therapy may be a very helpful component in treating school phobia as the therapist becomes deeply involved in the family to encourage healthy separation of the child. However, individual therapy is also important. Psychoanalytically oriented psychotherapy has been used to treat school phobia by helping the family understand the child's unresolved dependency needs, aggressive components, and subsequent anxiety.

Obsessive-Compulsive Behavior

The repetitive, unwanted thoughts and ritualized behaviors of children with obsessive-compulsive behavior can seriously interfere with their school and social life. As in the adult, washing, checking, and counting are among the most frequent behaviors, although a wide variety of others may appear. Interventions for these children are a relatively new occurrence, as this disorder was earlier considered rare in this age group. However, recent evidence suggests a more frequent incidence than previously believed. Furthermore, one-third to one-half of all adult cases report onset before age fifteen. These facts together with the resulting distress experienced by the families and children themselves and the possible relationship of the disorder to Tourette syndrome validate the importance of developing effective treatments. A variety of approaches are described in this section.

Thought Stopping for Compulsive Behavior

AUTHOR: Raymond L. Ownby

PRECIS: Using thought stopping to disrupt anxiety-provoking obsessive thinking leading to compulsive behavior

INTRODUCTION: Obsessive-compulsive patterns may be treated successfully in children with cognitive-behavioral interventions. In this case, a thirteen-year-old with a fear of contamination from a classmate washed his hands thirty to forty times per day, changed clothes after school, showered for up to one hour, and brushed his teeth eight to ten times daily.

CASE STUDY: In the boy under study, his compulsive behaviors were becoming more intense and frequent, causing him personal embarrassment and social isolation. The cognitive-behavioral intervention was applied in two stages, training and maintenance, over three, one-half-hour sessions. For training, the student learned self-recording, discussed with restatement the irrationality of his fears and compulsions (with emphasis on the power of cognitive techniques), and received instruction in the strategy known as thought stopping. In this method the therapist encouraged the student to verbalize the obsessive thoughts that preceded the compulsive behaviors and then shouted "Stop!" at the point the student reported the anxiety. This command was designed to break the anxiety-compulsion pattern. The student overtly, then covertly, rehearsed this procedure with instructions to imagine a relaxing scene just after stopping the thought. Phone contacts with parents, cooperation with the school, and monitoring by the therapist help to maintain the child's self-recordings.

After three weeks when his hand washing decreased from twenty to twenty-five instances per day to an average of eight per day, the maintenance phase began with weekly fifteen-minute meetings (faded to biweekly during the final six weeks) in which self-recordings were checked, the average number of hand washings per day was determined, the success of the strategy was discussed, and the student was praised. Parents and teachers continued to check on his self-recording compliance. Finally, self-recording was ended and he was encouraged to continue thought stopping. After three weeks the student estimated his hand washing frequency to the therapist.

RESULTS: The program continued for several months with a set goal of six hand washings per day. During the first three weeks of treatment, hand washing rates dropped from baseline weekly averages of twenty and twenty-three (over two weeks) to thirteen, then nine, then eight. During the last six weeks the average was six or fewer. At the three-week follow-up the student reported no increase in hand washing, a lowered level of fears, and a feeling of confidence in controlling them. Phone contacts six and eighteen months later revealed maintenance of effects and good academic and social adjustment in high school.

COMMENTARY: This strategy contains several components: attention to symptoms, self-recording, thought stopping, mental imagery, rational-emotive-type discussion, and parent contact. It is difficult to know how each component contributed to the success of the treatment, but the author notes that hand washing dropped significantly when thought stopping was introducd. It would be interesting to see whether younger children could benefit from this procedure.

SOURCE: Ownby, R. L. (1983). A cognitive behavioral intervention for compulsive hand washing with a 13-year-old boy. *Psychology in the Schools, 20,* 219–222.

Response Prevention and Cognitive Techniques to Reduce Obsessive-Compulsive Behavior

AUTHORS: Christopher A. Kearney and Wendy K. Silverman

PRECIS: Alternating response prevention and cognitive therapy procedures to assess the effects on compulsive checking and associated affect

INTRODUCTION: The literature on treatment of obsessive-compulsive disorder (OCD) in children is sparse, even though symptoms appeared before age fifteen in up to one-third of all adults with this disorder. In addition, the application of cognitive techniques for affected children is virtually nonexistent. This study compared response prevention and cognitive therapy in the treatment of a fourteen-year-old with two checking behaviors: checking windows for bats and examining himself for bat saliva to avoid rabies and death. The youngster performed these activities almost constantly. He was also depressed and engaged in suicidal ideation. Eating, sleeping, and attending school were seriously affected for him.

METHOD: Following interviews with the child and his mother, and completion of surveys and questionnaires to measure fear, general anxiety, depression, self-concept, and behavior issues, the therapist alternated response prevention and cognitive therapy in a predetermined sequence; each phase lasted one week and consisted of two thirty- to forty-five-minute sessions. When one method was in use, the child was told not to use the other. For response prevention, the student had to reduce his checking behavior on his own by a predetermined percentage, decided by the youngster and therapist. At the second session, progress was reviewed and the requirement was modified, if needed. In cognitive therapy, the obsessions were examined and identified as irrational; contradictory information was presented and the child was asked to check his fears with reality — for example, guessing his chances of actually seeing a bat, then reporting at the next session if he had seen one. Reading how people contract rabies and are treated provided him with another reality check. Between sessions, parents rated his daily anxiety and depression levels while the student rated his own distress and monitored his compulsive checking.

RESULTS DURING TREATMENT: During the first week of response prevention, window checking decreased over 90 percent from baseline and disappeared by week 4. For saliva checking, a decrease of about 45 percent occurred by week 2, with 99 percent elimination by week 5 and total disappearance by the last session. Self-reported distress, anxiety, and depression decreased to an extremely low level by the end of treatment. Parent ratings of depression showed no significant problems after the first week; however, anxiety never improved by more than about 70 percent, and worsened during a three-week period, rising a bit near the end of treatment. Each treatment technique improved different variables — that is, response prevention reduced window checking, distress ratings, and parent ratings of daily depression. Cognitive therapy reduced saliva checking, parent anxiety ratings, and the child's self-reported levels of daily distress.

RESULTS POSTTREATMENT: At this point, the boy's levels of fear and anxiety were reduced but his depression and self-esteem were unchanged. His parents reported improvements in his obsessive-compulsive behavior, somatic complaints, immaturity, and schizoid behavior. His social measures remained below normal. At six-month follow-up, his checking behaviors were gone, anxiety and depression were minimal, but self-esteem was no different. The child reported involvement in school, sports, and social life without distress.

COMMENTARY: Both treatments work equally well. The authors note this study to be one of the first to explore with empirical rigor the use of cognitive and behavioral techniques with childhood OCD. They suggest that alternating treatments may be preferable to using one approach to avoid what they discovered to be some extinction effects when the same strategy was continued into the second week. This suggestion will require further research.

SOURCE: Kearney, C. A., & Silverman, W. K. (1990). Treatment of an adolescent with obsessive-compulsive disorder by alternating response prevention and cognitive therapy: An empirical analysis. *Journal of Behavior Therapy and Experimental Psychiatry, 21,* 39–47.

A Family Systems Approach
to Reduce Obsessional Thinking

AUTHOR: John J. O'Connor

PRECIS: Applying various strategic family techniques to the treatment of unwanted obsessions

INTRODUCTION: Psychoanalytic psychotherapy has not proven effective in the treatment of childhood obsessive-compulsive disorder (OCD). More short-term interventions are needed, such as the strategic family systems approach described here. The obsessions of a ten-year-old boy, Michael, focused on his preoccupation with vomiting and the panic he experienced at the thought of it. Michael required constant morning reassurances from his parents that he would not vomit, even though they were not allowed to use the word. This fear required his mother to take him home early from school twice weekly. He also could not tolerate his parents' absence from the home. During the initial interview the mother talked most while the father was passive yet overtly affectionate with Michael. Michael made occasional hostile remarks aimed at his mother as she spoke, yet he was generally a well-behaved child. The author contrasts the psychodynamic and strategic approaches to this case, and then describes the intervention from a systems perspective.

PSYCHODYNAMIC APPROACH: At a simplistic level this model would describe Michael as confused by his obsessions but unable to clarify them because of his inability to use his verbal prowess rationally. Instead he sees words as magical—for example, feeling he will not vomit if his father simply says so. He also fears the thought as well as the act of vomiting. His relationship with his mother is hostile-dependent, and while he relies on his parents' words, which are overtly comforting, their tone is one of anger. Michael uses various defense mechanisms. His fear of vomiting is a symbolic "spitting out" of his parents' overprotection. Treatment would focus on his penchant for detail, acknowledging emotional expression, undoing defenses, and other areas. It would probably last two to four years, three to four times weekly, with no indication of improved symptoms or interpersonal success.

STRATEGIC MODEL: This model views the main problem as Michael's obsessions; the dysfunctional family pattern triggered when he tells them to his mother and father; his fear of vomiting and thinking about vomiting, which increases his sense of helplessness; and his attempts to manage the unwanted thoughts by seeking reassurance from his parents, avoiding the words, and perpetuating the morning ritual, all of which are ineffective. Given these issues the focus of treatment was to redirect his problem management strategies.

INTERVENTION: Five sessions over three months were conducted to help Michael master his fears. In session 1 the therapist stressed Michael's strength of resolve and suggested he take control of the thoughts by deciding when and where he would vomit or think about it. He was instructed to sit in a kitchen chair for one hour each day, thinking hard about vomiting and cleaning up if he did. If he thought about vomiting at other times, he was to stop and tell himself to save it for his hour in the chair. The therapist then gave a button to Michael from his father's sweater, told Michael that in wearing it he now possessed his father's strength and reassurance and would not vomit. Morning reassurances from his parents were to stop and his father would remind him of the button instead. His parents were instructed to go out together one evening during the week and hire a sitter for Michael. They were also to assign him age-appropriate household chores.

By session 2 Michael had stayed in school every day, morning reassurances had stopped, and his parents had gone out. Michael had trouble with the chair task and when asked to think about vomiting during the session, he could not maintain the thoughts. He reported that the button was helping him. The therapist then gave him a penny from his father, asking him to think of it in the same way as the button. The parents were told to keep going out once a week and to have Michael continue his chores.

In session 3 Michael reported fleeting thoughts of vomiting, visiting a friend's house, and possibly sleeping over. The therapist gave Michael a nickel from his father with the instruction to treat it like the button and penny. By session 4 Michael had spent the night at his friend's house and had forgotten the nickel on several occasions. The therapist praised his strength and told him he could use any change from his father in that way. Session 5 one month later had Michael symptom free and socially interactive. Fear of vomiting was not mentioned. Parents had been able to maintain a caring but appropriate distance from his age-related concerns. A follow-up two years later revealed that he was free from symptoms and was experiencing academic and social success.

COMMENTARY: The therapist used a paradoxical approach to address obsessional thoughts about vomiting by having Michael think about them and try to vomit in a particular spot. Michael's inability to make himself consciously think about these previously involuntary behaviors and the need to postpone the thought consciously until he was sitting in the chair helped him gain control. Having his parents stop reassuring him and giving him his father's button and coins were intended to interrupt the dysfunctional over-reactive family response to the obsessional thoughts, and encourage Michael's feelings of independence and self-efficacy. As he acted more on his own, his parents could loosen their control. Instructions to the parents to go out and to assign Michael chores were included to further develop and reinforce appropriate interactions within the family in which parents have time together as adults and children are seen as capable and independent.

A strategic approach used symptoms in terms of how they mirror and influence family interactions. The intervention sequence described here not only ameliorated symptoms but also made use of and positively affected the family's transactional style. This model is therefore able to help the school practitioner improve the child's situation and influence family relationships in a brief period of time.

SOURCE: O'Connor, J. J. (1983). Why can't I get hives: Brief strategic therapy with an obsessional child. *Family Process, 22,* 201–209.

Planned Ignoring in Family Therapy

AUTHOR: Patricia Dalton

PRECIS: Family treatment that ignores compulsive behavior while promoting more functional alternatives

INTRODUCTION: Psychodynamic, behavioral, and family treatment approaches to childhood obsessive-compulsive disorder (OCD) each emphasize a different etiological and treatment perspective. In previous research, a combined approach using behavioral strategies to influence family process has effectively eliminated or modified obsessive-compulsive behavior. This report focuses on ignoring obsessive-compulsive symptoms in favor of developing more productive responses.

CASE REPORT: Nine-year-old Philip was referred for hand washing, checking behind doors, daydreaming, disorganization, and poor academic performance. After interviewing the family in session 1, the therapist identified the following goals for therapy: (1) to ignore Philip's compulsive behaviors, (2) to reestablish more successful family interactions by involving the father more with his son and the mother in less obsessive ways, and (3) to promote healthy behavior in Philip. In session 2 these goals were pursued by instructing the father to help Philip with homework for one-half hour each night and to help him select his clothes for the next day. These behaviors were stressed as special contributions by a father. Other morning goals were identified by the mother, and the therapist paradoxically expressed doubt that Philip could do it all. Philip, of course, insisted he could, and a chart was created to monitor his responsibilities. The mother was urged to redirect her behavior from Philip to other activities, such as preparing breakfast or having a cup of coffee.

In session 3 the mother displayed some difficulty using the chart to reduce her overinvolvement with her son, but she was praised for the progress she had made. The father stated that his son did not want help with his home-work, but he was urged to keep trying because "boys need their fathers." Philip then volunteered that he had stopped checking behind doors. At session 4 the mother reported that her involvement with Philip had decreased and that the father had helped with homework most nights. The therapist quickly passed over Philip's comment that he had twice checked behind doors. Session 5 was a teacher conference. Charts were made for the teacher to report home on Philip's attention, participation, and organization in class. Philip had to bring the charts home for his parents to sign and he forfeited his allowance money for forgetting them.

In sessions 6, 7, and 8 Philip was charting independently, his school-work was improving, and he was able to discuss the teasing he still experienced at school. His father was helping with homework, and his mother finally stopped the foot playing she and Philip often did during sessions. She also announced that she was going back to work. This important session indicated that the family was beginning to function more independently. Session 9 continued the progress, but by sessions 10 and 11 Philip had become careless with schoolwork, was late in the morning, and was daydreaming. The parents had reacted by reverting to their original patterns.

By session 12, however, the situation had improved and the therapist reframed the setback as Philip's trying out different ways of behaving for comparison. He was paradoxically encouraged to finish his experiment by doing more checking and hand washing. In session 13 Philip had followed the therapist's suggestion and behaved more symptomatically, behavior that increased the mother's worrying again. The therapist reassured her that Philip would give up his symptoms and directed Philip to wash his hands for ten minutes each morning so he would not forget how to do it. The next session was canceled by the mother because things were going well. Philip had become bored with hand washing and had gone camping; the mother found this hard to cope with, but she did. The therapist praised her. The final two sessions were uneventful. The mother mentioned some issues but the therapist commented that problems present themselves as a natural part of life.

COMMENTARY: A one-year follow-up showed Philip to be symptom free and involved with school and friends. This relatively brief therapy lasted only fifteen sessions over seven months and relieved Philip's symptoms rapidly. Speed of improvement is important considering how obsessive-compulsive behaviors can isolate a child from the mainstream. More productive behaviors replaced the old ones; the family relationships remained intact and in fact improved. Techniques that aided success included, first, encouraging and praising the efforts made by the parents while not labeling the child as disturbed or feeding the mother's self-criticisms; second, giving directions that pulled the father in and decreased the mother's overinvolvement, thus restructuring the family's interactional patterns; third, charting functional behaviors while ignoring the obsessive-compulsive reactions.

SOURCE: Dalton, P. (1983). Family treatment of an obsessive-compulsive child: A case report. *Family Process, 22,* 99–108.

Additional Readings

Berg, C. J., Rapoport, J. L., & Flament, M. (1986). The Leyton Obsessional Inventory — Child Version. *Journal of the American Academy of Child Psychiatry, 25,* 84–91.

The Leyton Obsessional Inventory — Child Version (LOI-CV), a modified version of the original adult LOI, was used to differentiate adolescents with obsessive-compulsive disorder from normal adolescents and other psychiatric patients with some obsessive symptoms but different primary diagnoses. The inventory consists of forty-four symptom cards that the youths sorted into a "yes" or a "no" category, depending on whether they felt the symptom applied to them. The "yes" cards were then sorted by the teens according to the strength of their resistance to or acceptance of the symptom as well as by the degree to which they felt the symptom interfered with their lives. The inventory differentiated obsessive adolescents from normal controls on all three measures. Obsessive teens also showed higher resistance and a tendency toward higher interference scores than did psychiatric controls. Psychiatric and normal controls showed no differences. Test-retest reliability was demonstrated, and the inventory's ability to distinguish changes in drug treatment versus placebo groups further illustrated its validity. Its use is suggested in conjunction with other assessment instruments.

Flament, M. F., Rapoport, J. L., Berg, C. J., Sceery, W., Kilts, C., Mellström, B., & Linnoila, M. (1985). Clomipramine treatment of childhood obsessive-compulsive disorder. *Archives of General Psychiatry, 42,* 977–983.

Clomipramine hydrocloride was evaluated as a psychopharmacologic treatment for obsessive-compulsive disorders (OCD) in children ten to eighteen years old. Nineteen inpatient and outpatient children participated in both drug and placebo conditions. Psychotherapy was provided with counseling and feedback to the parents. The subjects were encouraged to resist impulsive behaviors; they kept a regular school and ward (or family) routine. A variety of rating scales measured changes in their obsessive-compulsive symptoms and other attributes such as depression and anxiety. Clomipramine significantly improved self-reported obsessions and compulsions but had no significant effect on depression, anxiety, or general symptomatology ratings. Depression scores at baseline were generally low and unrelated to changes resulting from the drug. About 75 percent of the subjects improved dramatically or moderately during treatment, with effects on symptoms occurring in three to five weeks. No predictions about which patients would respond most readily were possible from examination of baseline data. Relapses were typical on withdrawal of the drug. Improvement with drug treatment averaged about 45 percent to 60 percent on the rating scales, and not all patients benefited. Ritualizers responded better than obsessional thinkers. Early intervention for OCD is strongly recommended for children, with clomipramine the drug of choice.

Green, D. (1980). A behavioural approach to the treatment of obsessional rituals: An adolescent case study. *Journal of Adolescence, 3,* 297–306.

    A package of three techniques was employed to assist a fifteen-year-old boy with an obsessive-compulsive disorder. He had a need to repeat a given act until it was properly done to avoid harm or death he thought would come to his family. He was given autogenic (relaxation) training for five sessions utilizing a sequence of self-instructions; satiation training (three sessions) required him to maintain the obsessional thought without acting to relieve the resulting anxiety while attempting to achieve a more relaxed frame of mind. Success with this exercise decreases the emotional intensity of the thought making it easier to resist; response prevention (two sessions) took the form of an agreement between the boy and the therapist that the boy would resist the ritualistic urges and prevent himself from engaging in the checking behavior. On various self-assessments, his checking behaviors had markedly decreased and his mood had clearly improved. These effects remained at a six-month follow-up. The self-control methods may be important to an adolescent who is also dealing with issues of independence.

Liebowitz, M. R., Hollander, E., Fairbanks, J., & Campeas, R. (1990). Fluoxetine for adolescents with obsessive-compulsive disorder. *American Journal of Psychiatry, 147,* 370–371.
Riddle, M. A., Hardin, M. T., King, R., Scahill, L., & Woolston, J. L. (1990). Fluoxetine treatment of children and adolescents with Tourette's and obsessive-compulsive disorders: Preliminary clinical experience. *Journal of the American Academy of Child and Adolescent Psychiatry, 29,* 45–48.

    Both studies report on the effects of fluoxetine with preadolescents and adolescents diagnosed with obsessive-compulsive disorder. The second study includes youngsters experiencing obsessive-compulsive symptoms associated with Tourette's syndrome. In the first study, four of eight youngsters responded to treatment while two responded more equivocally. In the second study five of ten were considered responders. It is not known how long treatment must continue before subjects respond. However, as fluoxetine is the only medication of its kind commercially marketed in the United States, further research on it would prove extremely valuable.

Rapoport, J. L. (Ed.). (1989). *Obsessive-compulsive disorder in children and adolescents.* Washington, DC: American Psychiatric Press.

A comprehensive up-to-date account of obsessive-compulsive disorders in children. Following an introduction by the editor, chapters address diagnostic procedures, first-person accounts from parents and children, treatment strategies, and theory and research. A summary chapter closes the book. Of particular interest is the chapter on behavioral treatments, which discusses the research with response prevention, positive reinforcement, in vivo desensitization, and thought stopping. Family dynamics and the involvement of parents in the treatment process are noted as common components of the obsessive-compulsive pattern. Also considered are treatment issues such as the developmental level of the child, the needs and motives of the parents, treatment duration and frequency, the home or hospital as the setting for the intervention, training the parents as co-therapists, the importance of the therapist's guidance and support, planning the treatment and discussing it with the family, informing and involving school staff, and maintenance strategies. An appendix offers guidelines for planning the intervention. Finally a case study of a young college student with obsessive-compulsive disorder is presented and analyzed from a cognitive-behavioral perspective.

Low Self-Esteem

The debate continues over whether enhanced self-esteem is a cause or an outcome of improved academic achievement, but there is little argument about the multifaceted nature of self-attitudes, particularly when research shows that learning disabled students do not have lower than average general self-concepts, but substantially lower academic self-concepts. Further, recent writings have drawn parallels between the differentiated components of self-concept and the notion of competence as a multidimensional construct, pointing out that youngsters' self-perceptions of their own cognitive, social, and behavioral competencies may be quite different from adult perceptions. Although programs such as those described in this section expose students to specific activities designed to raise their self-esteem, the attitudes of teachers, the relationships they form with students, and the nature of the classroom environment may be equally powerful facilitators of self-esteem enhancement.

A School-Based Self-Concept Enhancement Program

AUTHOR: Paul C. Burnett

PRECIS: An eight-session self-concept development program to improve measured self-concept in seventh graders

INTRODUCTION: Self-concept enhancement programs have been created for use by teachers in the classroom, but not all teachers have the training or temperament to address affective development. Thus the school counselor has often taken on that responsibility, running small groups for students with behavior problems, gifted youngsters, children from divorced families, and others. The program described here is for regular classroom students, utilizing materials from several sources and consisting of eight weekly one-hour sessions. Its goal is to enhance children's awareness of their personal qualities, their feelings and ways to cope with them, their responsibility for their thoughts and behavior, reasons for and consequences of behavior, and others' feelings. Each session begins with the counselor encouraging students to express their thoughts and feelings through a review of the previous session. A story is then presented to introduce the theme. Discussion, role-plays, and other activities by the students are encouraged, and finally the counselor assigns homework so that students might better examine the ideas presented during the session. For this study a class of twenty-eight seventh graders participated in the program.

PROGRAM: Session 1 deals with personal characteristics. The leader introduces the program and helps the children develop group rules such as staying positive, not interrupting, and sharing feelings. A story from the source material about self-acceptance is read and the children discuss their feelings about the characters and how they might respond in similar situations. The children talk about why they are glad to be who they are, and discuss issues related to feeling good about themselves. For homework, children write down the positive qualities of a group member, themselves, and family. Session 2 discusses feelings. A story about feelings is presented and children are asked how they would feel in certain situations, such as finding no one to play with or being pushed off a new bike. They tell stories about personal experiences and related feelings, and complete a structured activity from the prepared materials. Homework involves tuning in to others' feelings.

Session 3 addresses negativity. Stories and activities stimulate strategies for dealing with negative statements, such as maintaining feelings of self-worth, or using I-messages. Their homework is to note negative statements made to them and to use the coping techniques from the session. Session 4 focuses on individuality. Situations are used to discuss when adult help should be sought and when independent effort is appropriate. A story from a source book is read by the students. For homework they are to say something positive to someone each day and note its effect.

Session 5 treats trust and belonging. A story is discussed and children take turns being led around the school while blindfolded to illustrate trust issues. Reasons that youngsters are rejected by a group are explored. For homework the group writes about how a rejected child can reenter a group. Session 6 looks at playing with others. The UNGAME is used to examine each player's personal qualities. For homework the game is played with family at home. Session 7 describes the purpose of behavior. Reasons that some children misbehave are discussed and put on the board. For homework, the children note behaviors they were punished for and why they misbehave. Session 8 stresses cooperation and goals. A story is read and discussed. Children take ten minutes to complete the statement "I wish," or "I wonder," and respond to questions about how wishes reveal a person's feelings and how others can help them realize their goals.

COMMENTARY: Children participating in this short-term program increased their self-concept compared to a control group, as measured on the Piers-Harris Children's Self-Concept Scale. Furthermore, the small group size allowed each child the chance to participate, and the teacher who is not comfortable with such activities did not have to lead the program. While no long-term follow-up was conducted, the use of periodic booster sessions might be helpful in maintaining the program's effects. It would also be helpful if in assessing the value of such a program, the practitioner would include behavioral indicators of improved self-concept. This would enhance the power of the program and help convince school authorities of its worth.

SOURCE: Burnett, P. C. (1983). A self-concept enhancement program for children in the regular classroom. *Elementary School Guidance and Counseling, 18,* 101–108.

Rewarding Positive Self-Statements

AUTHOR: Robert H. Phillips

PRECIS: Enhancing self-esteem by verbally praising positive self-references in third, fourth, and fifth graders

INTRODUCTION: Research has linked self-esteem to academic achievement, emphasizing the importance of teacher behavior and a positive school climate in enhancing students' self-feelings. Behavioral techniques may be used to influence such covert states through their effect on covert behaviors related to these internal processes. In this study third-, fourth-, and fifth-grade African-American and Puerto Rican students were rewarded for positive self-statements, which in turn were examined for their effect on the children's measured self-concept.

METHOD: During a seven-day observation period, teachers learned to listen, record, and praise instances of positive self-statements made by the children during a preselected daily forty-five-minute activity. Statements involving feeling happy, proud, and/or satisfied with one's good work were examples of the self-references recorded as positive and verbally reinforced. A seven-day baseline period was followed by the seven-day experimental phase. During the forty-five-minute play period, teachers immediately praised the positive self-statements with comments such as, "I'm proud of you too," "yes, you did do well," or "that's excellent thinking." A control group received no praise, but self-statements were recorded for later comparison. A second experimental phase followed an extinction phase in which all praise was withdrawn.

RESULTS: Students receiving contingent praise for positive self-statements verbalized significantly more such statements than did controls, and they scored significantly higher in the administration of the self-concept measure than either the control group or an "inventory" group not involved in any experimental or control procedure.

COMMENTARY: These results indicate that systematic teacher praise can influence the production of positive self-references in children. The author notes the possibility that the simultaneous increase in control students' positive self-statements may have resulted from a modeling effect whereby students not directly receiving praise modeled the reinforced behavior of other students. Other research has suggested this effect, which has important implications for classroom management. In terms of the self-esteem scores, these results lend support to the notion that self-statements reflect internal levels of self-esteem, and that reinforcing the overt behaviors can influence these states. Previous research has shown that rewarding positive self-statements in kindergarten through fourth-grade students enhances their measured self-esteem. This study extends this easy-to-use technique to an older group. It would be interesting to learn whether preadolescents and teenagers respond in a similar manner.

SOURCE: Phillips, R. H. (1984). Increasing positive self-referent statements to improve self-esteem in low-income elementary school children. *Journal of School Psychology, 22,* 155–163.

SAY IT STRAIGHT

AUTHORS: Paula Englander-Golden, Joan Elconin Jackson, Karen Crane, Albert B. Schwarzkopf, and Patricia S. Lyle

PRECIS: Enhancing self-esteem by helping students act on the basis of their true wishes and needs

INTRODUCTION: The SAY IT STRAIGHT classroom program helps students enhance their self-esteem and improve their interpersonal skills by teaching them to resist the urge to say "yes" in difficult social situations in which they would rather say "no." They are taught to feel comfortable with their decision and communicate their desires clearly and directly. This program has reduced reported substance abuse in middle schoolers and in this study curtailed juvenile offenses in high school students. Students discover their shared fears of rejection, embarrassment, or of hurting a friend's feelings as reasons they agree to participate in situations in which they would rather not be involved. They explore their real wishes and learn the skills to communicate them through such techniques as body sculpting, guided imagery, role-play, shared feedback, and use of videotapes.

Factual information about specific issues (for example, drugs or alcohol) is not part of this program. Simulated situations such as drug use, drinking and driving, cheating, stealing, vandalism, and sexual behavior are used to develop the skills to say "no" to a friend or express displeasure at a friend's behavior, or to say, "I have quit" to a group. In this report 357 ninth through twelfth graders took part in the training, which was voluntary, required parental permission, and consisted of five fifty-minute periods over five days in groups of twenty or fewer.

PROGRAM: From the first session students addressed the question, "Have you ever found yourself in a situation in which you very much wanted to say 'no' but for whatever reason you said 'yes' instead?" To assist them in understanding why they might have said "yes," sculpting and guided imagery were used. In sculpting, students are physically postured in body positions that express various communicated messages. In this instance they were placed in a kneeling position to represent "placating" and through imagery were instructed to imagine agreeing to any behavior just to please and keep the friend. After this exercise they shared their fears of rejection, embarrassment, and losing a friend associated with this situation. The trainer indicated how they could learn to say "no" effectively in these circumstances. In other sessions sculpting various messages, role-playing, making "movies" (role-playing), reviewing the videos, and providing feedback were used to train direct communication (leveling) rather than blaming, placating, using irrelevant comments, or trying to be super-reasonable. A SAY IT STRAIGHT workbook was used each day for a few minutes as a journal.

RESULTS: Except for eleventh graders, training significantly increased students' reported willingness to implement constructive decisions in tough situations and to feel comfortable doing so. Furthermore, for one-and-a-half years following training, juvenile offenses recorded by the police were significantly fewer for trained students than for untrained classmates. The untrained students evidenced 4.5 times the number of offenses as trained peers and participated in more severe crimes as rated by the police. In questionnaires students reported leveling (honest, direct, respectful expression of thoughts and feelings) as the only self-esteem–enhancing form of communication, with lecturing and blaming the least effective.

COMMENTARY: Training helped students feel willing to communicate difficult messages despite peer pressure. During role-plays students reported positive feelings of self when they leveled with a friend despite the pressure not to. If they gave in to the pressure, they learned that the friend lost respect for them. Leveling clearly was the most powerful communication. This program incorporates training of refusal skills and assertiveness, which are often used to address substance abuse and sexual behavior. In this instance the focus was on the internal state of self-esteem accompanying the learning of new skills. Although the program does not use an objective measure of self-esteem enhancement, it might be argued that changes in behavior of a positive nature such as reduced juvenile offenses and self-reports by the students are sufficient indicators in a school setting. This is a decision to be made by those implementing the program.

SOURCE: Englander-Golden, P., Jackson, J. E., Crane, K., Schwarzkopf, A. B., & Lyle, P. S. (1989). Communication skills and self-esteem in prevention of destructive behaviors. *Adolescence, 24,* 481–502.

Rational-Emotive Education in the Classroom

AUTHOR: Ann Vernon

PRECIS: Presenting Rational-Emotive Education (REE) concepts to teachers as a preventive consultation strategy

INTRODUCTION: Consultation allows school psychologists to use their time more efficiently and to provide services to a larger number of students than they could reach through a traditional model of direct testing and counseling. In this context Rational-Emotive Education (REE) is a preventive emotional education program for all students based on rational-emotive therapy principles, and one the practitioner can introduce to teachers.

RATIONAL-EMOTIVE EDUCATION: REE in its various forms is a structured curriculum that teaches rational thinking to children to enhance their emotional and behavioral coping and problem-solving skills. Its basic concepts include (1) awareness and acceptance of oneself independent of others' opinions, realistic acceptance of one's strengths and weaknesses, and self-tolerance of imperfections; (2) distinguishing between rational and irrational beliefs, understanding how irrational beliefs lead to disturbed emotions and behaviors and limit achievement of goals, and learning to challenge irrational beliefs and replace them with rational ones; (3) understanding that emotions come from beliefs not events, and learning how a change in negative emotions arises from a change in thinking; (4) knowledge of the event-thought-feeling-behavior sequence helps change self-defeating behavior through rational self-analysis. REE can be readily applied in the classroom, can be integrated with lessons, can help students deal with the issues underlying a problem, and can be applied to new situations once training is completed.

IMPLEMENTING REE: To help teachers minimize problems in the classroom, the practitioner can teach teachers REE prevention approaches through a six-hour workshop organized into three two-hour sessions. In session 1 the rationale for REE is presented as an emotional education program to help students develop healthy coping responses to stressful life events in order to prevent negative feelings and self-defeating behaviors. The practitioner explains the basic REE concepts and emphasizes the need to address the irrational beliefs underlying students' emotional distress. REE is described as a self-help approach that provides students with skills to prevent inappropriate reactions to events.

Session 2 focuses on implementation in the classroom and stresses the following: (1) Lessons are to be organized around an objective that is related to a corresponding REE concept. (2) A fifteen- to twenty-five-minute activity is to be used to illustrate the concept. Activities may include a role-play, simulation or feeling games, reading, writing or art projects, or group activity. (3) A fifteen- to twenty-minute discussion following the activity addresses understanding of the activity, relevance to the child's personal life experiences, and application to future behavior. (4) REE concepts explored in the lessons are to be sequentially related and built upon each other from lesson to lesson. (5) Lessons must be consistent and ongoing. (6) Trust and group bonding should be developed to facilitate sharing of personal events through rules that stress respect and sensitivity. In session 2 the practitioner also distributes and reviews sample lessons from a fifth/sixth-grade curriculum and an eleventh/twelfth-grade program.

In session 3 REE is applied to at-risk students who have low self-esteem, low frustration tolerance, poor coping skills, and a tendency to overexaggerate problems and make inappropriate demands on themselves and others. A case example is a high school junior who attempts suicide because he could not cope with his belief that he was a total failure when his girlfriend asked that they see each other less frequently, and when he could not maintain his standards of academic performance. REE techniques may have helped this youth develop rational thinking and coping skills.

COMMENTARY: The author comments that little research exists on the effects of REE with children. Studies suggest that children as young as those in grade 4 can understand the lessons and alter their beliefs; however, there is no indication in this article of how REE influences students' coping in real-life situations. Perhaps a workshop for teachers might also incorporate more information on integrating emotional education concepts into the instructional curriculum. One can imagine discussing motivations of a literary character from an REE perspective or applying the lessons of history in a similar manner. Teachers as a whole may be more comfortable and more amenable to the idea of teaching affective educational concepts using their own subject matter.

SOURCE: Vernon, A. (1990). The school psychologist's role in preventative education: Applications of rational-emotive education. *School Psychology Review, 19,* 322–330.

A Self-Concept–Enhancing School Transition Program

AUTHORS: Robert D. Felner, Melanie Ginter, and Judith Primavera

PRECIS: Altering the school structure to provide a supportive transition period for entering high school students

INTRODUCTION: As with many life transitions, entrance into high school can stress a student's coping mechanisms to their limit. The result is increased vulnerability to maladjustment. Factors affecting successful coping during transitional periods include personal coping style, the nature of the task, and the degree of support available. This study did not address the enhancement of the student's coping skills; instead it targeted the support structures of the environment (school) the student was entering. Fifty-nine students participated in this transition project as they prepared to enter a multiethnic urban high school with a population of about 1,700. As this was considered a preventive program, all the target students had shown satisfactory adjustment in their previous schools.

TRANSITION PROJECT: The project sought to redefine the role of the homeroom teacher and restructure the environment to reduce the unpredictability of the setting with which the student had to cope. Four project homerooms were defined containing only students in the program. The teachers' roles were expanded to include many support functions commonly assumed by counselors, nurses, and administrators. For example, they helped students choose classes, counseled them around problems, called home when students were absent and dealt with excuses, and contacted parents before the school year began to discuss the project and urge participation. This role redefinition was meant to increase support from someone the students saw daily; increase their feeling of being personally known by and account-able to one person; and provide easier access for them to information about school rules, routines, and expectations. Project students attended classes only with other project participants to stabilize peer group contacts and pro-vide a sense of consistency, support, and belonging. Classes were also lo-cated in close physical proximity to each other. Both project and control students were evaluated at midyear and at year's end on self-concept, per-ception of school climate, attendance, and grade point averages.

RESULTS: All midyear evaluations showed little differences between project and control students. Control students were absent significantly more often by the end of ninth grade than were project students (25.1 versus 16.7 days per year, respectively); they also had significantly lower grade point aver-ages than project students at the end of the school year. Self-concept mea-sures for project students remained relatively stable, while those for control subjects showed a clear decline over the year. Regarding perceptions of the school climate, project students reported more stable teacher relationships, a more stable view of the personal growth–enhancing qualities of the school climate, and a more consistent feeling about the clarity of rules, teacher con-trol, and general order and organization of the system.

COMMENTARY: Students in the transition project adjusted more success-fully to high school than did control students. Of note, the differences were due to declines in the control subjects' self-concept and social climate ratings, not to an increase in project students' scores. It seems that the program created a climate in which either the coping skills already in the students' repertoires could continue to be effective, or in which new skills to meet the new demands of high school could be learned and developed. Both outcomes were proba-bly operating. In regard to long-term effects it would be interesting to know how project students performed during the following school year and whether such an ecological alteration should be continued throughout the students' high school careers. Teacher teams, a middle school concept in which a group of teachers work together over the year with a given group of students, is a similar model that has been adapted by many middle schools to achieve the same goals described here (group cohesion and an enhanced relationship between students and teacher). As schools examine their ecology and its effect on student behavior and performance, perhaps such a structure will be found valuable by more of them beyond the transition period.

SOURCE: Felner, R. D., Ginter, M., & Primavera, J. (1982). Primary prevention during school transitions: Social support and environmental structure. *American Journal of Community Psychology, 10,* 277–290.

Additional Readings

Bogat, G. A., Jones, J. W., & Jason, L. A. (1980). School transitions: Preventive intervention following an elementary school closing. *Journal of Community Psychology, 8,* 343–352.

Children who transferred to a new elementary school because of the closing of their parochial school participated in a two-day orientation program prior to beginning the new school year. On day 1 students enjoyed juice and cookies while the two-day program was described. After receiving school information booklets, the students had a tour of the building, conducted by peer guides. Peers then held discussion groups focusing on the students' feelings about the closing of the private school. Finally a review of rules and general information about clubs, organizations, and school personnel was provided.

On day 2, students met the principal and vice-principal, then played a treasure hunt game requiring exploration of the school. A game involving school rules and regulations was followed by a peer-led discussion of differences between public and private schools and feelings about transferring. Students then visited their homeroom classes and went outside to review playground and morning lineup routines. Evaluation done at the end of the previous school year and two weeks after school opened for the new year indicated that the orientation program helped transfer students in areas of peer-related competencies, knowledge of school layout and rules, and teacher ratings of their conduct. Students, principal, and parents all rated the program highly.

Davies, J., & Haatvedt, L. (1990). Life skills seminar: A guidance program that seeks to prepare for life. *Middle School Journal, 21,* 36–37.

Sixth, seventh, and eighth graders at Miami Country Day School participate in a nonacademic course entitled Seminar that focuses primarily on self-esteem and making good choices through consideration of such topics as communication, values, drug education, human sexuality, and marriage and family. Once a week meetings in the course and with a small "advisory" group allow for problems to be identified and addressed. Students' self-esteem is enhanced through role-playing, guided imagery, identification of mutual strengths, goal setting, and the seminar motto, "I'm special and unique." A point system rewards students for completing assignments and helps them understand cooperation and competition. A caring, trusting atmosphere is developed in the class and strong relationships develop between teacher and student who remain together in the seminar for three years. A buddy is assigned to each new fifth grader who helps that student understand the seminar concept. Although there are several structured units, the content of each class is determined by the level of student maturity. The seminar program is a core feature of this middle school.

Gurney, P. (1987). Self-esteem enhancement in children: A review of research findings. *Educational Research, 29,* 130–136.

This article reviews self-esteem interventions as applied through curriculum, special classroom methods, modification of teacher behavior, and alterations in student behavior. While curriculum-based programs to enhance self-esteem have their intended effect, teacher/parent involvement and motivation are particularly important. In addition, special classroom procedures such as role-play and rational-emotive techniques are successful, and the research illustrates the need to examine behavior changes as well as scores on self-esteem measures. Although not extensively studied, changes in teacher behaviors have been shown to increase student self-esteem; the change in pupil behavior is achieved primarily through teachers' increasing their positive self-statements to students as an effective self-esteem–enhancing strategy. Academic achievement and self-esteem co-vary, although it is difficult to establish a clear cause-and-effect relationship between them. Thus teachers should target both simultaneously. Other suggestions to teachers include providing attention to low self-esteem students, obtaining ongoing information about the student's background and progress, encouraging self-monitoring and self-rewarding in students, encouraging parental participation in school life, planning schoolwide self-esteem programs, and rewarding themselves, each other, and their supervisors.

Locke, D. C. (1989). Fostering the self-esteem of African-American children. *Elementary School Guidance and Counseling, 23,* 254–259.

Counselors need to incorporate into their work activities and experiences that meet the cultural needs of all children, including African-American students. Suggestions for the counselor include the following: (1) remaining open to cultural differences and encouraging honesty in relationships with African-American children; (2) understanding one's own culture to foster sensitivity to others; (3) displaying respect for and recognition of cultural differences; (4) participating in community activities and inviting representatives from the African-American community to come to the school; (5) remembering that African-American children are individual people as well as members of a cultural group; (6) banishing racism from oneself and not tolerating it in others; (7) encouraging schoolwide activities that recognize the African-American culture; (8) maintaining high expectations for African-American children; (9) learning about African-American culture and sharing the knowledge; (10) fostering the psychological development of African-

American children through such methods as developing interdisciplinary programs that are an integral part of the curriculum and match the children's maturity levels.

The programs should focus on home and school experiences for the early elementary student and community activities for the older children; they should address cognitive and affective development and utilize school and community resources. Example activities are presented for different age levels, covering such topics as recognizing physical similarities and differences among children of varying racial groups; enhancing self-concept through exploring self, family, and friends; encouraging awareness of famous African and African-American individuals; and encouraging expression of ethnic and racial feelings. Methods are suggested to aid in evaluating the effectiveness of self-esteem programs for African-American children. Counselors can foster self-esteem by encouraging others to acknowledge and respect cultural diversity.

Mitchum, N. T. (1989). Increasing self-esteem in Native-American children. *Elementary School Guidance and Counseling, 23,* 266–271.

Traditional counseling techniques are not successful with Native American students who must often board away from home at schools run by the Bureau of Indian Affairs, or who compare themselves unfavorably to the dominant white culture. Cultural awareness programs often complicate the problem by accentuating the differences between American Indian culture and mainstream society. The value within Indian culture of group cooperation and harmony and the devaluation of competition limit the effectiveness of such often used self-esteem–enhancing strategies as positive self-talk, the self-disclosing shield, and strength bombardment. These approaches focus on praise and uniqueness, values inconsistent with Indian culture, which does not encourage speaking out about one's achievements. For these reasons behavior management programs that stress levels of reward are also of limited assistance. Furthermore, eye contact, which is fostered in counseling groups, is viewed as a sign of disrespect for the Native American. Finally, Indian culture values reserve, which is contrary to the verbal interaction encouraged in counseling sessions.

Given these cultural attributes, counseling for Native American children should deemphasize individual exploration and focus on the group identity. Self-disclosing exercises should help identify a group personality and give each child a sense of belonging to the group. Instead of stressing their individual identities, children are helped to see their contribution to the group personality and to identify themselves as part of a group. Feedback by the leader or members would be to the group, not to individuals. For example, if the group decides to do more homework, each child enhances his or her self-esteem by contributing to the group's new effort. Pride in the group's success is valued, not pride in individual accomplishment. Counselors, whether Native Americans or not, should run these groups in a more structured, directive fashion but with less required verbal input from the student. Use of play and art are helpful. Acceptance of Indian culture is essential.

Robertson, E. B., Ladewig, B. H., Strickland, M. P., & Boschung, M. D. (1987). Enhancement of self-esteem through the use of computer-assisted instruction. *Journal of Educational Research, 80,* 314–316.

Eighth- and ninth-grade students in a home economics course, Home and Personal Management, were exposed to computer-assisted instructional materials. Teachers were trained in the use of the microcomputer and in the development of the computer-based materials. Pre- and posttesting indicated that students who had computer-assisted instruction scored significantly higher on self-esteem measures than did control students taught in the traditional manner.

Schaughency, E., Frame, C. L., & Strauss, C. C. (1987). Self-concept and aggression in elementary school students. *Journal of Clinical Child Psychology, 16,* 116–121.

The relationship between elementary students' self-concept and aggression was explored using self- and teacher reports and sociometric ratings. The children's low self-concept and aggression were found to operate independently of each other, negating the notion that aggression is a product of low self-concept. Thus, although aggressive behavior would not be successfully reduced using self-concept enhancement strategies, it may be responsive to social skills training techniques. On the other hand, the suggested relationship among low self-concept, anxiety, and depression points toward the use of self-concept interventions for depressed or anxious children.

Stolberg, A. L., & Garrison, K. M. (1985). Evaluating a primary prevention program for children of divorce. *American Journal of Community Psychology, 13,* 111–124.

The Divorce Adjustment Project is a primary prevention program for children of divorce from seven to thirteen years of age. One phase is a twelve-session children's support group (CSG) in which students discuss divorce-related topics (for example, whose fault the divorce is) and learn problem solving, anger control, communication, and relaxation skills. A second phase is a single parents support group (SPSG), a twelve-week program emphasizing self-enhancement as mothers and individuals. Topics such as "the working me," "the sexual me," "disciplining my child," and "communicating with my former spouse about child-rearing matters" were addressed. Children who participated in the CSG groups alone displayed the most improvement in self-concept and adaptive social skills, while SPSG parents alone enhanced their adjustment to divorce. The combined CSG-SPSG subjects did not benefit from the treatment, perhaps because of the more negative circumstances surrounding their divorce situations.

Zeeman, R. D. (1982). Creating change in academic self-concept and school behavior in alienated secondary school students. *School Psychology Review, 11,* 459–461.

Tenth-, eleventh-, and twelfth-grade alienated high school students were divided into four groups. One group was exposed to a seventeen-week psychology course taught by the school psychologist and principal; the focus of the course was personal and human development, presented from a cognitive and affective perspective. A second group tutored elementary school students in math twice weekly for fifteen weeks. Group three did both, and group four served as a control. Results indicated that the most improvement in academic self-concept occurred with the students taking only the psychology class. The students doing only tutoring or exposed to both treatments improved equally, and for those in all treatment conditions measures of school behavior were affected positively. The elementary students who were tutored also benefited. For control students, however, academic self-concept declined over the same period, accompanied by increased expressions of inability by these students.

Identity Crises in Homosexual Youth

While many lesbian and gay youth are healthy, well-functioning individuals, there is little doubt that the identity struggles of adolescence are compounded for homosexual teens who must face these developmental challenges in an atmosphere of ignorance, rejection, homophobic fears, and at times, violence. These attitudes often create confusion, fear of discovery, and a sense of deep isolation that can lead to academic failure, alcohol and drug abuse, high-risk behaviors, and suicide. The school practitioner needs to become knowledgeable about these issues, provide a setting in which gay and lesbian teens will risk seeking help, and, as with all students with problems, work to develop a healthy self- and sexual identity within the framework of each student's individual life-style. To accommodate the growing literature in this area, a "Further Reading" section has been added following "Additional Readings."

The Practitioner and Homosexual Youth

AUTHOR: Barbara R. Slater

PRECIS: Issues and barriers the practitioner must confront in working with gay male and lesbian students

INTRODUCTION: Although research has substantiated that many lesbians and gay males are as well-adjusted as heterosexuals, psychologists face obstacles as they attempt to work with troubled homosexual youth. These barriers arise first from negative moral beliefs in the general population regarding homosexuality, and second from homophobic attitudes among psychologists and some homosexuals, who may have internalized this negativity before or after realization of their sexual preference. Among gay men and lesbians, homophobia may become self-directed and redefined as self-hatred, further damaging an already fragile identity and sense of self. While homosexual men and women are not generally confused about their biological sex, caring but misinformed adults who confuse gender identity with sexual orientation typically attempt to reassure the youth that his or her same-sex preference is a confusion that will pass. This response only aggravates the young person's self-doubt, further disrupting the development of a healthy, reality-based self-concept. Psychologists should know that while adolescent same-sex exploration does not necessarily predict later homosexuality, stable same-sex preferences may already be established by the teen years. A third barrier exists in the form of fear among psychologists that addressing homosexuality among teenagers will threaten their jobs, reduce their standing in the community, or bring legal action by parents. This fear prevents the school-based practitioner from dealing with the topic of homosexuality in sex education or family life courses. To work with homosexual youths, psychologists must address their own homophobia and attempt to lessen these barriers within the limitations imposed by the attitudes of their communities and employers.

ETIOLOGY AND DEVELOPMENT: The causes of homosexuality probably lie in a combination of biological, psychological, and social factors. Theories regarding the development of a stable homosexual identity stress the movement from confusion to exploration to identification. In working with gay male or lesbian students, the therapist who assists their awareness of these stages and of the coming out process can be of great value to them. Furthermore, as there is no homosexual "personality," the practitioner must be careful not to attribute problems experienced by a gay or lesbian teen to homosexuality itself but to deal with these difficulties as he or she would with the problems of any youth in distress. Homosexual youth have the same variety of problems unrelated to sexual orientation as do heterosexual youth. Finally, the psychologist must work to discourage myths about homosexuality (for example, it's a sickness, or one can pick out a homosexual by his or her behavior) and replace these with factual information.

PROBLEMS: Four major problems confronting gay male and lesbian youth are homophobia, the absence of appropriate role models, coming out, and acquired immune deficiency syndrome (AIDS). When homophobia seriously impairs a youth's development, referral to a gay affirmative therapist may be necessary. Referral information is available through the American Psychological Association, state psychological associations, and gay/lesbian organizations and agencies. Because of the small number of well-functioning, healthy gay and lesbian adults who have come out publicly, role models for youths are scarce. Television, movies, and literature have improved their portrayal of homosexual adults, but real-life models are needed. Psychologists working with gay and lesbian youth need to identify for them healthy, successful, living figures and individuals from history and the arts as well as agencies, centers, organizations, and other resources they can identify with and turn to for support.

Coming out to oneself and others is a third issue. Ideally, homosexual youth should be able to explore their sexual values and behaviors in the same manner as heterosexual youth and accept their orientation surrounded by a supportive family and community; the reality, however, is that most lesbian and gay teens experience confusion, internalize the society's homophobia, and either remain closeted or come out in such a negative manner that others who hear their "confusion" react just as the teen expects them to. The result for the homosexual teen is isolation, stress, and possible suicide. In coming out to others, the adolescent needs a support network to buttress him or her against the rejection that may follow. For the youth thinking of coming out but at the same time struggling with self-esteem issues and confusion, the psychologist needs to focus on building positive self-regard, providing information on homophobia, helping the young person build a support network, and helping him or her decide to whom he or she should come out and how it should be done. The reasons for coming out need to be addressed. Coming out must be for healthy reasons, not for revenge or anger.

Regarding AIDS, the psychologist must be current on the latest information, and this article lists a variety of sources to consult. The practitioner might also access gay and lesbian community centers in urban locations. He or she should have reliable information sources on the disease, counseling sources for young gay men who are well but worried, and resources for individuals who have tested positive for the virus. Workshops for staff should also be considered.

INTERVENTION: Depending on the restrictiveness of the setting, psychologists may be able to provide one or more of the following: direct counseling, informational and referral services to youths and families, and information to school staffs; resource materials only to homosexual teens and staff; or perhaps only printed materials. In any event psychologists need to evaluate their personal attitudes, knowledge, skills, and motivation when assessing the possibility of working with lesbian and gay male adolescents. One therapeutic approach involves bibliotherapy, the use of selected readings to provide information and stimulate therapeutic interactions between the practitioner and client. The appendix to this article provides a partial sampling of reading material available for bibliotherapeutic work. Psychologists can address the isolation felt by school-aged homosexuals and attempt to provide a setting in which these youths can explore the issues they face.

COMMENTARY: Since as many as 10 percent of youth are homosexual, it is likely that many school practitioners will have contact with gay and lesbian students and will need to confront their own attitudes. They will need to weigh their feelings against the prevailing atmosphere in the community in which they work and determine the extent to which they will offer their services to these children. They may be helped in their decision by knowledge of the loneliness, confusion, fear, guilt, and potential for suicide characteristic of many lesbian and gay teens. One can hope they will respond as compassionate professionals to this or any other group of students in need.

SOURCE: Slater, B. R. (1988). Essential issues in working with lesbian and gay male youths. *Professional Psychology: Research and Practice, 19,* 226–235.

Counseling a Gay Student in School

AUTHOR: Donna Tartagni

PRECIS: Counseling guidelines to help a gay student cope with his sexual orientation and regain self-esteem

INTRODUCTION: Because of entrenched homophobic attitudes, schools are mostly reluctant to address the reality of homosexual youth. These students must therefore exist as isolated, lonely teens, unable to seek assistance for their confused feelings. The following case study illustrates how practitioners can assist adolescents who believe they may be homosexual.

CASE STUDY: Jimmie's first few sessions with the counselor focused on issues commonly encountered with youths concerned about their sexual orientation, namely the hostile reactions of others, negative self-feelings, and the need to come out to someone. As a general rule, practitioners should not be quick either to label the student as homosexual or to negate the possibility, but they should be sensitive and nonjudgmental as the student expresses his or her fears. In helping students deal with hostility from others and with self-dislike, counselors must first confront and eliminate their own ingrained homophobic attitudes. They must help students accept their sexual orientations without the self-disgust and guilt the counselors' own unrecognized homophobia might cause them to display. Second, they must act as advocates for gay teens, encouraging them to use their talents and skills, and pointing out the contributions of gay persons to our culture.

Third, they need to substitute real information for myths among both homosexual and heterosexual students. For example, Jimmie had heard that homosexuals could not believe in God, and he was experiencing guilt and self-hatred as a result. The counselor showed him articles about religious leaders who supported homosexual rights and encouraged him to write to gay-oriented religious organizations.

Fourth, the counselor used rational-emotive techniques to promote positive self-talk and to counteract the negative self-statements Jimmie made when he was depressed by the rejection he experienced. Coming out to oneself and others is an important step toward self-acceptance. Jimmie wanted the counselor to tell his mother he was gay, but the counselor agreed only to tell her of Jimmie's concern that he might be gay and of Jimmie's wish to share his anxieties with her. Counselors are urged to explore with the student all the possible positive and negative consequences of coming out before the step is taken. A bibliotherapeutic approach may help the student at this point; it may also help the parents cope with the disclosure. For Jimmie, coming out helped him to realize that there are other gay youth to whom he could relate and who have had similar experiences. This knowledge aided his adjustment and helped him develop a positive self-concept.

COMMENTARY: Homosexual students are often totally cut off from heterosexual peers and other gay youth who may also need to stay closeted. The counselor may be the only help available to assist the student in working out these issues and strengthening a sense of self.

SOURCE: Tartagni, D. (1978). Counseling gays in a school setting. *The School Counselor, 26*, 26–32.

Crisis Intervention with Homosexual Adolescents

AUTHORS: Gary Ross-Reynolds and Barbara S. Hardy

PRECIS: Counseling techniques for the crisis counselor dealing with a homosexual student

INTRODUCTION: Although attitudes toward homosexuality in the United States make it difficult to obtain accurate demographic information, it is reasonable to assume that in a high school with 500 male students, up to 185 have engaged in a homosexual act leading to orgasm. Yet no theory of homosexuality has received empirical support, and no psychological variables have been uncovered that distinguish homosexuals from heterosexuals. No therapy to "treat" homosexuality has been successful, and given that homosexuality is no longer categorized as a mental illness, such therapies might be justifiably questioned on an ethical basis. Still, gay adolescents must develop their homosexual identity in a generally hostile social climate where homophobia, a lack of role models and support systems, and the issues associated with coming out create feelings of isolation, fear of discovery, and guilt. School psychologists must free themselves of homophobic tendencies and become knowledgeable about the gay life-style if they are to help homosexual adolescents develop a positive self-identity.

CRISIS COUNSELING: The first test in counseling is identifying the problem. Given that adolescent and adult sexual behaviors are not necessarily related, it is important that the practitioner not over-interpret same-sex sexual activity in adolescence; on the other hand, he should not disregard it. An attitude of respect for both heterosexual and homosexual orientations, without the need to answer the question, "Am I gay?" is an appropriate stance. Thus the psychologist helps the confused student address this issue by providing information and supporting the student through continued contact if desired. For students who are certain they are gay and whose frequency, intensity, and duration of same-sex behavior supports their feelings, the important task is helping them establish a positive self- and sexual identity. Again, homophobia and the absence of role models inhibit positive self-feelings, especially when teachers themselves may be negatively inclined toward a gay life-style. Furthermore, gay students are likely to possess homophobic feelings as well, devaluing homosexuality and, by extension, themselves. These issues require the counselor to maintain an attitude of acceptance, perhaps press for a change of teachers for the student, provide the teen with reading materials from gay organizations, help the student develop relationships with other adolescents, and explore with the student any mannerisms that are role-played as part of a preconceived image of effeminacy supposedly characteristic of the gay male. Coming out requires a realistic discussion of the risks (for example, rejection by friends and family, banishment from home) and speculation about which outcomes are more or less likely in a given situation. The therapist may need to work with the parents to help them deal with their anger, rejection, and self-blame.

PREVENTION: Counseling is directed at an actual crisis confronting the gay adolescent; school psychologists, however, should not wait for these to occur. They can engage in prevention activities to avoid or minimize crises by advocating that topics on homosexuality be taught in sex education classes, by teaching such units, by encouraging discussion on the issue in class, by providing inservice training to staff and individual consultation to teachers who are teaching a gay student, by dispelling myths about homosexuals, and by refusing to tolerate gay jokes or condone inappropriate comments. Practitioners may receive negative feedback or worse for their efforts. If they can obtain administrative support, this may provide them with needed backup, and presenting all perspectives on homosexuality may counter much suspicion and hostility.

COMMENTARY: Acceptance, offering alternatives, and enhancing coping skills are three essential elements of the school psychologist's role in counseling the gay student. Although the authors focus exclusively on gay males and do not mention lesbian students, it is likely that females have the same struggles and need the same openness, respect, and advocacy from the practitioner.

SOURCE: Ross-Reynolds, G., & Hardy, B. S. (1985). Crisis counseling for disparate adolescent sexual dilemmas: Pregnancy and homosexuality. *School Psychology Review, 14,* 300–312.

Project 10

AUTHORS: Friends of Project 10, Incorporated

PRECIS: A description of the first school-based program in the United States to focus on the concerns of lesbian, gay, and bisexual students.

INTRODUCTION: Project 10 is a school-based dropout prevention program aimed at homosexual students; it has been in operation at Fairfax High School in Los Angeles, California, since 1984. Its purpose is to provide counseling, information, referrals, and a support network to students who identify themselves as gay, lesbian, or bisexual, and to offer inservice training to school personnel, outreach to parents, and coordination with school programs teaching responsible sexual behavior to lesbian, gay, and bisexual youth. The inability of schools to recognize and address the needs and problems of homosexual youth, which arises from institutionalized homophobia and fear of community reaction, have left the homosexual teenager isolated, confused, and fearful of discovery and rejection. These additional strains come at a time when the normal stresses of adolescence compound the students' already difficult search for sexual and self-identity. The compound result for these young people is often damaged self-esteem, school failure, substance abuse, and suicide. The program adopts the premise that homosexuality is a normal variation in sexual orientation and behavior, but that societal attitudes stigmatize homosexuals, forcing them to remain closeted and denying them opportunities for personal growth. Through its various activities, Project 10 attempts to counteract these feelings.

HANDBOOK: The handbook from which this digest is taken covers such issues as the "denied" adolescence of the homosexual teen, suicide, families of gay and lesbian adolescents, health and minority issues, starting a program, homophobia, and class lessons to stimulate discussion of issues related to homosexuality. Appendices describe suggestions for a homosexual library, a bias self-evaluation for teachers, techniques for dealing with homophobia and heterosexism, and ways to handle community opposition. Of particular interest for this digest, is the chapter on intervention guidelines.

Whether a student refers himself or is referred by someone else, the following suggestions should guide individual conferences: (1) Find privacy but not off campus; remain visible to others. (2) Guarantee confidentiality. (3) Stay calm and balanced despite the student's cause for distress. (4) Be honest with yourself. Homosexuality is a sensitive topic; monitor your own reactions and if you are too overwhelmed, transfer the student to another person. (5) Acknowledge and help clarify the feelings of the student; gently probe for additional information using more targeted questions if appropriate. (6) Provide information but at the appropriate time and in a nonlecturing manner. (7) Identify the student's available resources and supports and help decide when and how to access this network.

An interview with a high school crisis counselor who uses Project 10 as a resource reveals that students are often afraid to discuss their concerns about their homosexuality; they may make a first contact because of their distress over sexual arousal while stripping for gym or emotional reactions to same-sex teachers or classmates. The counselor discusses how students may use flamboyant behavior (for example, cross-dressing) to force parents to acknowledge their homosexuality, and how the practitioner can help the parent and student deal with the issue in a neutral place (the counselor's office) and in a manner that can preserve if not improve the relationship. Students may also internalize society's view of homosexual behavior, regarding themselves as members of the opposite sex (in a psychological sense) because of the expectation to act that way. When students want to know whether their past same-sex experience means they are gay or lesbian, the counselor explores their discomfort to help them understand its meaning with the possibility of referral for further help. However, problems with private therapy or agency service are the expense and the need for the student to tell the parents why help is wanted.

In workshops with school staff, lists of phrases, behaviors, and words that are and are not acceptable were developed. It is not permissible for staff to name call or allow name calling among adults and students, to use terms such as *queer, fairy, dyke, fag, butch, queen,* or others, or to tell jokes with homo-sexual content. It is not acceptable for them to ask students the following kinds of judgmental questions: "Are you sure you are gay or lesbian?" "Have you tried dating the opposite sex?" "Do you feel God is punishing you?" "Have you tried to change?" "Do you want to have children?" "Is something wrong with you?" Also to be avoided are inappropriate statements: "You'll get over it." "You're not normal." "You don't look like one." "I don't want to listen." "You'll get AIDS." "You won't have a happy life." "You'll embarrass your family." "You need counseling." Parents should not say, "Where did I go wrong?" or "Why are you doing this to me?" It is all right for school personnel to use terms such as *homosexual, gay,* or *lesbian*. They must discourage jokes about homosexuality, raise the topic of homosexuality where appropriate in class discussions, and be open when a student tells them he or she is homosexual. Counselors should use gentle questions or statements to bring out students' feelings, such as "Tell me more." "Can you share your feelings?" "Are there others you can also talk to?" or "What are your concerns?"

COMMENTARY: The name Project 10 is derived from the estimated 10 percent of the population believed to be homosexual. In a book chapter by Virginia Uribe (the founder of Project 10) and Karen Harbeck ("Address-ing the Needs of Lesbian, Gay and Bisexual Youth: The Origins of Project 10 and School-based Intervention." In K. M. Harbeck (Ed.), *Coming out of the Classroom Closet: Gay and Lesbian Students, Teachers, and Curricula.* Bingham-ton, NY: Haworth Press, 1992), isolation, family violence, school homopho-bia, stress, shelter, and sexual abuse were identified in conversations with gay and lesbian teens as their primary concerns. Interviews with self-identified homosexual students at Fairfax High School revealed that concerns with AIDS and other sexually transmitted diseases was a main reason for the teens to contact Project 10 and that those in the program the longest seemed to be modifying their sexual practices.

Most of the families of the boys reacted negatively to knowledge of their sons' homosexuality; almost all the boys were alcohol or substance abusers, and half had attempted suicide. Harassment in school was frequent and came from teachers as well as students. The boys recalled coming out to themselves without support as intolerably painful. Early sexual experiences were compared to "date-rape."

For lesbian students, sexual experiences had not been violent, but com-ing out to themselves was also painful. Few reported harassment, but all knew of anti-gay responses directed to others. When these female students came out to their parents, they were told it was a passing phase—a very different response from those made to the gay males. Lesbian students ex-pressed strong feelings of isolation and fear of discovery.

Interviews with the general student population revealed a climate of acceptance of the Project 10 program. When students were provided an educational experience based on homosexuality and bisexuality, their understanding and tolerance increased. Practitioners should be aware that students will not likely present themselves with an open admission of homosexuality but that these concerns may be hidden behind the presenting problem. Gentle encouragement in a nonjudgmental manner provides the best opportunity to establish a relationship with a teen who is feeling confused, isolated, and unsupported.

SOURCE: Friends of Project 10, Incorporated. (1989). *Project 10 handbook: Addressing lesbian and gay issues in our schools* (available from Virginia Uribe, Ph.D., Fairfax High School, 7850 Melrose Avenue, Los Angeles, CA 90046).

Additional Readings

Chng, C. L. (1980). Adolescent homosexual behavior and the health educator. *The Journal of School Health, 50,* 517–521.

In regard to homosexual behavior among youth, the health educator has a role as instructor, referring source, and change agent. As instructor, teaching about the range of human sexuality, discussing the homosexual aspects of everyone's sexual identity, and exposing students to well-functioning homosexuals humanizes the concept and demonstrates that healthy living is possible regardless of one's sexual orientation. The health educator should also learn about community resources and professional services and refer students in need of therapeutic help. By instructing others and referring those in need, the health educator fulfills a role as a change agent, modeling openness and acceptance, using role-playing to sensitize students to others' feelings, and dispelling myths and stereotypes about homosexuals. While health educators should not counsel emotionally distressed students, they can help students better understand and tolerate the various life-styles they will encounter.

Krysiak, G. J. (1987). A very silent and gay minority. *The School Counselor, 34,* 304–307.

This article addresses many of the issues already discussed in this section, but also adds information from interviews with homosexual students who have gone on to college. They indicate that a counselor might become familiar with college and university settings most amenable to gays and lesbians by contacting homosexual organizations in cities. The counselor may also facilitate the gay/lesbian students' participation in intramural activities and in courses in which homosexual role models are more likely to surface.

Makki, D. L. (1991, June). Counseling the gay adolescent student. *Communiqué: National Association of School Psychologists,* p. 12.

To counsel homosexual students, the school psychologist needs to be as nonhomophobic as possible, sensitive, and informed. Important areas for counseling are recognition and acceptance of a homosexual identity, confidentiality, and acquired immune deficiency syndrome (AIDS). The goal of counseling is not to change students' sexual orientation, but to help them discover, understand, and accept their sexual and self-identity. Coming out is extremely difficult, and questions are listed for teens to consider before revealing their orientation to parents. Contact with the family may occur when parents discover their child's sexual orientation. Fears and concerns need to be addressed as they would be for any student. School psychologists can be part of the support network needed by homosexual teens as they come out. They must maintain confidentiality and leave the decision on coming out to the youth. AIDS education and information to the school as a whole may help to counteract the misconceptions about AIDS as a "gay disease." Counseling a student with AIDS involves open and honest expression of feelings, contacting sex partners, and providing support.

Savin-Williams, R. C. (1989). Gay and lesbian adolescents. *Marriage and Family Review, 14,* 197–216.

This article distinguishes the terms *sexual orientation, sexual behavior,* and *sexual identity.* Homosexual orientation refers to "a preponderance of sexual feelings, erotic thoughts or fantasies, and/or behaviors desired with respect to members of the same sex." Homosexual behavior consists of sexual interaction between members of the same sex. Sexual identity refers to the ways in which individuals interpret and represent their sexual orientation and behavior to themselves. Usually a homosexual identity involves some degree of self-recognition of this identity. In adolescence these three dimensions may not necessarily overlap; that is, students may admit to same-sex sexual behavior but not identify themselves as gay or lesbian. Similarly, there are teens who have never engaged in sexual activity with same-sex partners yet who identify themselves as homosexual (homosexual virgins). This is not as unusual as it seems, considering that many teens who have never engaged in heterosexual behavior routinely identify themselves as heterosexual. Identity is not defined only in terms of behavior. These confusions often make it difficult to label an adolescent as lesbian or gay based on sexual behavior or self-identification, and suggest that health education and AIDS prevention programs be targeted for all adolescents, not just those who are self-labeled homosexuals. Finally, the problem-oriented focus on gay and lesbian youth in the literature has overshadowed other data, indicating that many homosexual teens are healthy, resilient, have positive self-images, have few negative feelings about their sexual orientation, and are generally satisfied with their lives. Homosexuals should not be viewed as a clinical population but as a varied group of individuals with problems and promises.

Further Reading

D'Augelli, A. R. (1988, June). The adolescent closet: Promoting the development of the lesbian or gay male teenager. *The School Psychologist,* Division of School Psychology Newsletter, American Psychological Association, pp. 2, 9.

Marantz, S., & Coates, S. (1991). Mothers of boys with gender identity disorder: A comparison of matched controls. *Journal of the American Academy of Child and Adolescent Psychiatry, 30,* 310–315.

Moses, A. E., & Hawkins, R. O. (1982). *Counseling lesbian women and gay men* (chap. 5). St. Louis: C. V. Mosby.

Powell, R. E. (1987). Homosexual behavior and the school counselor. *The School Counselor, 34,* 202–208.

Price, J. H. (1982). High school students' attitudes toward homosexuality. *The Journal of School Health, 52,* 469–474.

Remafedi, G. (1987). Adolescent homosexuality: Psychosocial and medical implications. *Pediatrics, 79,* 331–337.

Ross-Reynolds, G. (1982). Issues in counseling the "homosexual" adolescent. In J. Grimes (Ed.), *Psychological approaches to problems of children and adolescents* (pp. 55–88). Des Moines: Iowa Department of Public Instruction. (ERIC Document Reproduction Service No. ED 232 082)

Procrastination

Procrastinators delay or avoid to the point of distress. Their fear of failure, perceptions of task aversiveness, evaluation anxiety, perfectionism, and lack of self-confidence cause them to perpetuate their self-defeating pattern for the sake of temporary short-term relief. Thus, poor organization of time and deficient study skills are only partly responsible for procrastination. Affective, cognitive, and behavioral components also operate to influence this reaction, and interventions have reflected this diversity by emphasizing multicomponent formats, utilizing cognitive-behavioral techniques, guided imagery, self-control strategies, anxiety reduction techniques, and self-awareness training, among other approaches. With one study reporting more than 40 percent of college students nearly always or always procrastinating on test preparation (with accompanying feelings of intense anxiety), the need to assist procrastinating students at younger ages is critical.

Multimodal Treatment of Procrastination

AUTHOR: Linda A. Morse

PRECIS: Group multimodal counseling to address the fears and feelings of procrastinators as well as their habits and skills

INTRODUCTION: When traditional methods to reduce procrastination such as behavior management programs and study skills instruction do not work, other methods must be sought that address the fears, attitudes, and affective distress of procrastinators. Students who procrastinate have the following characteristics in common: (1) they honestly intend to do their homework; (2) they focus on what they cannot or do not do rather than what they can or did do; (3) they do not profit from low grades or teacher feedback to improve performance; (4) they display a short attention span; (5) they perceive themselves as more productive when pressured; (6) they use lack of understanding or inability as excuses for not working; (7) they become annoyed when reminded of incomplete homework; (8) they say they will improve but never do. These attitudes are also characteristic of procrastinating elementary school children and suggest that these youngsters might benefit from counseling interventions that address procrastinating behavior. Procrastination may be employed to protect an established self-image, avoid the risk of failure, postpone an imperfect outcome, evade the pressures of success, defy authority, be rescued from overwhelming tasks, and demonstrate frustration over a lack of skill. The major interventions for procrastination share a common core of strategies that include promoting awareness of the causes and behaviors associated with procrastination and encourage reframing, internal self-talk, enhancing self-esteem, and goal setting. However, research on the value of these methods is limited and no data for elementary-age students has been reported.

In contrast, a multimodal intervention strategy is described that approaches the process from a broad-based multidimensional view of personality, encompassing health, emotion-feeling, learning-school, personal relationships, imagination, need to know, and guidance of action variables. Students in grades 3 through 6 who were turning in less than 75 percent of their assignments over a two-week period before treatment (for reasons other than their inability to do the work) were defined as procrastinators and considered for participation in the multimodal group counseling program.

MULTIMODAL GROUP COUNSELING: Twenty-nine sessions each lasting twenty-five minutes were conducted three times weekly, then twice weekly during the final three weeks. Each session focused on one or more causes of procrastination, which was addressed through a group activity based on the modes of personality model described above. Causes encompassed low self-esteem, fear of failure, perfectionism, fear of success, rebellion against authority, lack of problem-solving skill, and locus of control. As an example, one session, derived from the health aspect of personality, addressed locus of control concerns through relaxation exercises; another session, based on the learning-school modality, dealt with rebellion, fear of failure, and fear of success through a discussion of problems in completing assignments. The sessions utilized such strategies as discussion and expression of feelings, worksheets on procrastination, guided imagery, role-playing, and goal setting. Goal setting was used to stimulate students' learning about themselves and to focus on acquiring new skills rather than achieving the goal itself. No punishment or negative consequence of any kind was imposed for unmet goals, and emphasis was placed on discovering why the goal was hard to accomplish and looking toward success with the next goal.

RESULTS: Students in the treatment group completed significantly more homework assignments during the two weeks following the end of the counseling than did the waiting list students. Students made great progress in goal setting, attitude, and behavior. Their grades improved and they reported feeling better about themselves and about progress in learning to get work in on time. This broad-based treatment strategy, in which students gain self-knowledge and new skills, can bring positive change when more specific problem-solving, time-management, or behavior programs are not effective.

COMMENTARY: The author has prepared a manual that provides a detailed description of the group activities as well as the forms, surveys, and letters needed for the program. Additional comments by the author suggest that individual contacts with students and parents to address the causes of procrastination may also be helpful in reducing this problem behavior. In addition, she notes the possibility that creating and reaching a daily goal with praise from the teacher and/or counselor may be sufficient to effect a change in the student's procrastinating pattern. The author also indicates a variety of possible reasons other than procrastination for students to fail to complete work on time: (1) the work is truly difficult; (2) the child has vision or hearing problems; (3) emotional disturbance or other disabling conditions interfere; (4) the student is emotionally overloaded due to a stressful transition experience such as divorce, relocation, or death; (5) the student lacks information and/or skill regarding proper study habits; and (6) he or she is a substance abuser. This article provides support for the idea that procrastination is not merely a time management problem but has its roots in the feelings and self-concept of the youngster.

SOURCE: Morse, L. A. (1987). Working with young procrastinators: Elementary school students who do not complete school assignments. *Elementary School Guidance and Counseling, 21,* 221–228.

Self-Control Techniques to Reduce Procrastination

AUTHOR: Leon Green

PRECIS: Self-monitoring and self-reward in combination to significantly reduce procrastination in academic behavior

INTRODUCTION: Procrastination has not been well researched in college students, and no study has examined the effect of self-monitoring and self-reward on the procrastination patterns of disadvantaged minority college students. This study hypothesized that self-monitoring plus self-reward would increase academic behaviors and decrease procrastination; that self-monitoring alone would have a similar effect, but not as strong as the two procedures combined; and that students would be able to follow through on multiple, simultaneously operating self-reward contracts to reduce procrastination.

METHOD: Six economically and academically disadvantaged minority freshmen taking a "reading improvement" course were subjects. They had been admitted to college as part of a special program, and had ranked in the lower-fiftieth percentile of their high school class. Each subject was exposed to three conditions: baseline, self-monitoring, and self-monitoring plus self-reward. The first two conditions lasted for two weeks each; the third was divided into three two-week periods during each of which a new self-reward contract was initiated. During the two-week baseline, academic behaviors of attendance in the course, assignment completion, and amount of studying in the study center were observed and recorded. For the self-monitoring condition, the students were taught to observe and record these behaviors on their own. For self-monitoring plus reward, students learned the self-reward contract procedure. They selected one accessible highly rewarding activity for each of the three contracts (for example, watching television, shopping, playing sports, and others). They then committed to each contract at two-week intervals, agreeing to perform the rewarding activity only when they had achieved criterion performance of a predesignated academic behavior. As each new contract was begun, the previous one remained in effect so that all three were operating and all three academic behaviors were under contract during the last two-week period. Subjects continued self-monitoring during this condition.

RESULTS: Self-monitoring plus self-reward resulted in a significantly higher attendance rate, a significantly more prompt assignment completion rate, and significantly more studying than either baseline or self-monitoring alone. Procrastination, defined as tardiness, postponed assignment completion, and postponed studying, was also significantly reduced across all three behaviors under the self-monitoring plus self-reward condition, compared to baseline and self-monitoring alone. Grades on assignments and exams were also significantly higher during the self-monitoring/self-reward condition than during the other phases. Finally, subjects were able to maintain multiple contracts simultaneously. At a six-month follow-up all subjects were still in school. One year later, two subjects had dropped out of school but none had been terminated by the college. Four of the six graduated.

COMMENTARY: Contrary to the author's initial hypothesis, self-monitoring alone had no significant effect on the subjects' academic procrastination. However, it is encouraging that these disadvantaged students were able to reduce avoidance and delay of several behaviors simultaneously during the contract period. These self-control techniques may be applicable to much younger children, as research has established the ability of the elementary school student to self-monitor and reward behavior. While a broad definition of procrastination would include an affective dimension as well as the behavioral components of delay and avoidance, it is important to have shown these behaviors to be amenable to recognized intervention strategies.

SOURCE: Green, L. (1982). Minority students' self-control of procrastination. *Journal of Counseling Psychology, 29,* 636–644.

Additional Readings

Burka, J. B., & Yuen, L. M. (1983). *Procrastination: Why you do it, what to do about it.* Reading, MA: Addison-Wesley.

This book addresses understanding and overcoming procrastination. Procrastination is viewed as a delaying mechanism that protects individuals from facing their fears of failure, success, isolation, over-attachment, and/or loss of control to others. The authors present the Procrastinator's Code, which consists of twelve irrational statements that guide the behavior of many procrastinators: (1) I must be perfect; (2) everything should be easy and effortless; (3) doing nothing is safer than risking failure; (4) I should have no limitations; (5) if it cannot be done right, it should not be tried; (6) challenges should be avoided; (7) my success will hurt someone; (8) I must always do well; (9) others' rules take away my control; (10) never let go of anything or anyone; (11) my real self is not likable; (12) I must find the one right answer. These rigid, self-critical rules perpetuate the individual's procrastinating behavior; awareness of their influence is the beginning of overcoming the problem. Procrastination is fear.

Knaus, W. J. (1985). Student burnout: A rational-emotive education treatment approach. In A. Ellis & M. E. Bernard (Eds.), *Clinical applications of rational-emotive therapy* (pp. 257–276). New York: Plenum Press.

This chapter relates procrastination in students to burnout in school. When students experience burnout, some engage in avoidant behaviors such as procrastination as a result of the self-doubt and critical self-evaluation that accompanies stress overload, loss of control, and boredom. Procrastination interferes with the development of problem-solving skills and academic competencies, even though it might provide temporary short-term relief. Thus its relationship to burnout is reciprocal; these two alternate as cause and effect. Rational-emotive education, offered as a counteracting force to procrastination, involves five steps: consciousness raising about procrastination, self-awareness training, problem-solving training, self-confidence development, and frustration-tolerance training. Other time management techniques such as goal setting, prioritizing, and creating subtasks are utilized but only in conjunction with the five steps. Counselors who help children deal with procrastination should model problem solving, use the child's strengths, employ positive reinforcement, monitor and help students correct misconceptions, and use humor. Using characters to illustrate procrastination, such as the Wheedler who tells children to avoid discomfort and the Time Thief who steals time, captures youngsters' interest, allowing the counselor to introduce problem-solving techniques. As always, it is important to consider the child's level of developmental maturity when planning interventions.

Lamwers, L. L., & Jazwinski, C. H. (1989). A comparison of three strategies to reduce student procrastination in PSI. *Teaching of Psychology, 16*, 8–12.

Students in a psychology course, taught under a personalized system of instruction (PSI) format, were exposed to one of four conditions. The *baseline* or *self-paced* condition (SP) provided no intervention; in the *contracting* (C) condition, students failing to meet deadlines for completing chapters set up contracts with the teacher to complete units and take tests; the *Doomsday* (D) condition required students to withdraw or fail if they did not complete two chapters by the Christmas break; *Doomsday with tokens* (DT) resulted in the same consequences as Doomsday but students received bonus credits for completing units within specified times.

Procrastination as measured by delay of first testing was least evident in the Doomsday with tokens group; the contracting group was in second place. Delay was most prevalent among the self-paced students. Outcomes in the three contingency conditions did not differ statistically from each other on delay of first testing attempt. Students in the contracting group made significantly more progress in completing units than did those in the other three groups; they also had the lowest withdrawal rate, while the two Doomsday conditions had the highest. Ninety percent of the contracting group students who contracted with the teacher completed the course. The Doomsday with tokens condition produced the highest number of A's with the contracting group second; the largest percentage of failures occurred in the self-paced condition. Although contracting is the most time-consuming strategy, it appears to be the most effective strategy overall and provides the most help to students who do poorly under the PSI format.

Ottens, A. J. (1982). A guaranteed scheduling technique to manage students' procrastination. *College Student Journal, 16*, 371–376.

Procrastinating college students are taught a guaranteed scheduling technique (GST) that addresses four needs: the need for a reasonable, flexible schedule; the need for concrete accomplishment; the need for awareness of one's self-defeating behaviors; and the need to work and play effectively. GST centers around preparation (with counseling) of a daily contract (including weekends) that commits students to spend a reasonable amount of time on relevant academic work; requires them to write down interfering thoughts, feelings, or behaviors that prevent work completion; and asks them to describe the methods they attempted to overcome any problem. Consistent daily guaranteed accomplishment of goals is stressed, with realistic planning based on students' daily responsibilities. Charts help students compare the contract with the actual time they spent studying, regulate the contract length, and develop realistic goals. Self-awareness of one's procrastinating style is pursued in counseling where students learn techniques such as rational disputation, self-talk to set self-rewards for completion of tasks, self-reminders, and realistic self-evaluation. Students reportedly have responded favorably to the GST format.

Zinger, D. J. (1983). Procrastination: To do or not to do? *The School Guidance Worker, 39,* 9–15.

The author describes a program of six two-hour weekly sessions he conducts to help students and adults reduce procrastination. Participants have ranged in age from fifteen to fifty. Sessions 1 and 2 focus on group cohesion, time and behavior management strategies, weekly goal setting, and recording a log of personal thoughts and feelings that precede, accompany, and follow procrastinating behavior. In sessions 3–6 goal setting and management strategies are further taught and practiced. Reasons for procrastination are explored; these typically go beyond simplistic explanations such as laziness, lack of organization, or irresponsibility. Through exercises and group discussion, members examine attributes associated with procrastination, such as unrealistic absolute thinking, perfectionism, fear of failure or success, low self-esteem, family expectations, rebellion, using small tasks to avoid more important ones, and self-labeling.

Methods to address procrastination are included; an example is the use of a balance sheet or brainstorming session in which consequences of procrastinating and not procrastinating are listed and/or discussed. Other techniques involve guided imagery, reframing as a rational-emotive strategy, scheduled breaks, and avoidance of self-labels. A major goal is to help procrastinators establish an internal locus of control that allows them to see themselves as responsible for their actions and to attribute success to their own behaviors, not to luck or circumstance. In working with procrastinators, the author suggests grouping them, teaching time and behavior management strategies, setting specific goals, examining underlying causes, monitoring absolute thinking, identifying nonprocrastinating behaviors in members, using reframing, encouraging deadlines, and being creative with ideas.

Elective Mutism

Electively mute children talk only in selected situations and with certain people, even though they are quite able to speak and understand language. Often they are completely mute in the classroom, sometimes communicating through gestures or one-syllable sounds. Although this disorder is considered rare, it may be more prevalent than commonly assumed. Furthermore, while its origin has been traditionally regarded as psychogenic, there is evidence of speech and other developmental immaturities, electroencephalograph irregularities, and more frequent occurrences of enuresis and soiling in children with this disorder. Other research highlights the importance of early treatment, as improvement seems more difficult to achieve after a child reaches age ten.

Self-Modeling to Eliminate Elective Mutism

AUTHORS: Thomas J. Kehle, Steven V. Owen, and Elizabeth T. Cressy

PRECIS: Electively mute students viewing videotapes of themselves responding to questions quickly begin verbal interactions

INTRODUCTION: In self-modeling, students observe themselves on videotapes that have been edited to show only appropriate behavior. In a series of studies, self-modeling reduced disruptiveness in behaviorally disordered youngsters and improved affect in depressed students; it also increased question answering, volunteering, and classroom verbal interactions in electively mute children. The technique has also demonstrated superiority over peer modeling techniques. This study presents the case of a six-year-old academically competent boy who had been electively mute in school for several years, although he was reportedly verbal at home. While he was accepted by classmates and apparently enjoyed and participated nonverbally in all activities, he would not talk.

METHOD: Baseline observations of the boy during class and recess revealed no verbal interactions, sounds, or responses of any kind from him, even under provocation. For the intervention, his mother came to school to videotape a session with no one present except her and her son. She asked him nine questions and, with encouragement, he answered. The teacher then, without success, asked the boy the same questions with all children present. The tape was edited to make it appear as if the child was responding to the teacher's questions in class. During the six-minute tape the child was actually depicted talking for less than four seconds. Over a one-week period, the child viewed the tape three times, receiving a reward (baseball card or candy) for each response he made on the tape and the promise of a toy for improvement. Further, the entire class saw the tape (with his permission) and students were happy to see their classmate talk. Unfortunately, these procedures yielded no results. Therefore, the mother was called back and a second five-minute tape was made in which the child talked for about 13.5 seconds. The child saw this tape twice and was given rewards similar to those he received in viewing the first tape.

RESULTS: No rewards were needed after the first viewing of the second videotape as the child suddenly began talking freely and introduced his classmates on request. He was able to talk about himself to a graduate psychology class and received an award at school for his academic participation and performance. A seven-month follow-up showed no loss of his verbal skills.

COMMENTARY: The authors speculate that self-modeling increased the child's self-efficacy in relation to talking. As he viewed himself responding to the teacher, he came to believe he could actually do it and thus behaved accordingly, obtaining rewards as a consequence. This is an easy-to-use, cost- and time-effective technique that, as indicated in the introduction, may be applied to other behavior problems. In a later article in the September 1991 newsletter *Communiqué,* published by the National Association of School Psychologists, the senior author, Kehle, provides further suggestions for this intervention: (1) Try to get the child to respond to the mother in the classroom. For this effort the author has used a McDonald's lunch as a reward. While this strategy frequently works, a space at the child's home may need to be set up as the simulated classroom if the attempt in the classroom is unsuccessful. The home simulation is difficult, however, and should be avoided if possible. (2) For ease of editing, use separate tapes for teacher and mother and be sure they adhere to the question sequence. (3) During playback of the tape, give the child reinforcement for each verbal response he makes on the tape. (4) With the child's permission, show the tape to classmates; this tends to alter their expectations in a positive way. (5) Make more than one tape and vary them during treatment to monitor the child's interest. (6) Try to show the child talking for more than thirty seconds. This number is somewhat arbitrary, but in the study cited above, a longer talk time seemed to make a difference in the child's reaction from tape one to tape two.

SOURCE: Kehle, T. J., Owen, S. V., & Cressy, E. T. (1990). The use of self-modeling as an intervention in school psychology: A case study of an elective mute. *School Psychology Review, 19,* 115–121.

Reinforcing Verbal Responses in a Child with Reluctant Speech

AUTHORS: Charly Morin, Robert Ladouceur, and Renaud Cloutier

PRECIS: Using tangible rewards and social praise to increase question answering

INTRODUCTION: While elective mutism is characterized by the absence of any speech in certain situations, children with reluctant speech are occasionally verbal in these settings. A six-year-old kindergarten boy would not speak to his teacher or his classmates and did not take part in classroom activities. With out-of-class treatment involving the teacher and three children, he began to speak, but there was no carryover to the classroom and only infrequently would he answer teacher questions.

METHOD: Treatment lasted for twenty-two sessions. For each of five baseline sessions the teacher asked the child ten questions relating to kindergarten activities and requested a verbal answer. He was questioned when alone, in close proximity to a group of peers, and with the group. The number of his responses was recorded by the teacher as the dependent measure. A four-session treatment phase followed in which the child received a dollar in "school money" and social praise for each verbal answer given to a question from the teacher. Once he earned a certain amount of money—and the amount increased as the study progressed—it could be traded for predetermined arts and crafts materials. A second baseline of four sessions was followed by another treatment phase that continued until the target behavior was achieved 100 percent of the time. This required an additional four sessions. In a final phase, the teacher presented the reinforcer on an intermittent variable ratio schedule.

RESULTS: During baseline the youngster responded about 20 percent of the time to teacher questions. This number jumped to 95.4 percent when the reinforcement contingency was introduced, declined to 66.6 percent during the second baseline period, and rose to 100 percent for the second reinforcement phase. A drop to 70.8 percent occurred when the intermittent reinforcement schedule was introduced. Follow-up at one year showed maintenance at 100 percent.

COMMENTARY: A background history of shyness developing in some children has been linked to elective mutism; from its description, reluctant speech apears to have some behavioral similarities to shyness. The authors indicate that the differences between elective mutism and reluctant speech may extend to intervention strategies. Thus the practitioner should carefully assess the pattern of verbal interaction to determine which label most effectively describes the problem.

SOURCE: Morin, C., Ladouceur, R., & Cloutier, R. (1982). Reinforcement procedure in the treatment of reluctant speech. *Journal of Behavior Therapy and Experimental Psychiatry, 13,* 145–147.

Additional Readings

Kupietz, S. S., & Schwartz, I. L. (1982). Elective mutism: Evaluation and behavioral treatment of three cases. *New York State Journal of Medicine, 82,* 1073–1076.

The article describes three cases in which stimulus fading is applied for treating elective mutism. Four phases characterize this technique: in phase 1 the parent engages the child in conversation in the school; in phase 2 the teacher gradually moves closer to the child as the parent and child talk; in phase 3 the teacher asks the child questions through the parent, gradually taking over the situation until the child is responding more directly to the teacher; in phase 4 the teacher and child speak, first with one or two other children present, then with increasing numbers until the whole class is involved.

In case 1, treatment of a four-year-old boy was successful with his mother's participation over a half year of school. By year's end he spoke freely to his teacher in a whisper. In case 2, a fourteen-year-old emotionally handicapped boy with organic impairment was treated with the father as participant. The teacher's presence disrupted communication with the father; the connection was repaired and new plans for continued treatment were formulated after a break resulting from scheduling problems. In case 3, a nine-year-old boy with "arrested hydrocephalus" was treated successfully with the mother in thirty-one sessions over three months. The authors recommend evaluation and treatment for elective mutism with attention to cognitive, psychological, and neurological issues. They recognize, however, the difficulty of specifying the relationship between these factors and elective mutism.

Lazarus, P. J., Gavilo, H. M., & Moore, J. W. (1983). The treatment of elective mutism in children within the school setting: Two case studies. *School Psychology Review, 12,* 467–472.

Two case studies of elective mutism are presented. In the first, six-year-old Tracey was referred for a psychoeducational evaluation for lack of verbal communication in school. During the evaluation, the school psychologist recommended the following steps: (1) transfer from an open, team-taught class to a traditional classroom; (2) encouragement and praise in all areas including normal conversation, even if she did not respond; (3) use of a classroom pet to stimulate conversation; (4) use of a tape recorder and puppets in speech sessions. Tracy began to verbalize in response to these strategies, and for the remainder of the evaluation the psychologist used play materials and behavioral strategies therapeutically to establish and maintain a safe, supportive relationship with her. Behavior techniques were also applied in class and in speech therapy. Four months later the child was regularly engaging in spontaneous conversation.

In the second case seven-year-old Karen was electively mute and had peer interaction problems. Treatment first included three sixty-minute family sessions over three weeks dealing with dysfunctional family relationships. Behavior therapy was applied in the fourth through ninth weeks, and a tape recorder was used to help Karen rehearse conversing with the school psychologist, then with a child, then with a few children, the teacher, and finally her whole reading group. Transfer was gradually achieved from the tape recorder to direct conversation with the psychologist and to the classroom. More students were added to the reading group and they asked Karen questions, facilitating conversation with her.

In both cases, Tracey and Karen showed dependence on their mothers, and both mothers displayed passive-aggressive resistance to the treatment. In similar cases the psychologist can stress the seriousness of the problem, encourage the family to seek help, work with school staff, and help reduce the child's anxiety related to speech.

Paniagua, F. A., & Saeed, M. A. (1987). Labeling and functional language in a case of psychological mutism. *Journal of Behavior Therapy and Experimental Psychiatry, 18,* 259–267.

For an eleven-year-old girl who spoke to no one in any setting, a treatment package was employed to produce productive labeling of picture cards and functional language (defined as her describing features of the cards or initiating a verbal exchange with her parents or the therapist). For productive labeling the child was first praised for imitating the therapist, who named each picture. She was next required to label an increasing number of cards in order to keep tokens with which she could purchase snacks. In one strategy for functional language she received tokens for answering questions about the picture cards. She also answered questions about her age, how she was feeling, and other simple inquiries. Another intervention, begun after the productive labeling treatment ended, used response cost and modeling to encourage her to ask and answer questions. Following this, a method to generalize use of functional language without picture cards and to parents was implemented. The child's productive labeling and functional language increased with these procedures and her general verbal interactions also changed significantly.

Pigott, H. E., & Gonzales, F. P. (1987). Efficacy of videotape self-modeling in treating an electively mute child. *Journal of Clinical Child Psychology, 16,* 106–110.

A nine-year-old African-American child had been electively mute in school for four years and would speak only when his mother and brother were with him. He was videotaped over many sessions answering questions from the teacher with classmates present while his mother and brother were present in class but off camera. Two edited videotapes were produced, one of the child answering direct questions and one of him volunteering to answer, being called on, answering, and receiving praise. He viewed these tapes at home each day for two weeks before school. The youngster also self-recorded his own hand-raising behavior during the last month of school and was rewarded at home for more than six occurrences per day. The self-modeling videotape for direct answering of questions substantially increased his responding in class while the tape of him volunteering to answer produced mixed results. Self-monitoring of his hand raising increased his volunteering to a consistent level.

Depression

Prior to the 1980s the existence of childhood and adolescent depression was not taken seriously, even though current estimates of clinical depression in adolescence range from 6 to 12 percent. During the past decade this inattention has given way to some research on assessment and school-based intervention strategies, although less than might be expected given the importance of this problem area. Case studies periodically appear in the literature illustrating psychodynamic therapeutic approaches with depressed children, but much of the research to date has attempted to modify adult cognitive-behavioral strategies for use with depressed youth, using such treatment components as self-management (self-control) techniques, cognitive restructuring, activity scheduling, social skills and relaxation training, and parent involvement. Perhaps the next ten years will see a greater proliferation of interventions for depressed school-aged youngsters now that depression in children and adolescents has been acknowledged in its own right as a serious, perhaps life-threatening, condition and the need for multicomponent strategies has been documented. It is also important to note that while suicide and depression are related, they appear to be independent problems; that is, many depressed youngsters are not suicidal, while many youth at risk for suicide do not appear to be depressed. Thus practitioners should always be alert to suicidal behavior in depressed students but should not confine their concerns about suicide only to this group. For further information on this topic the reader should consult the reference section following the chapter introduction and the following resources:

Further Reading

Gotlib, I. H., & Colby, C. A. (1987). *Treatment of depression: An interpersonal systems approach.* Elmsford, NY: Pergamon Press.

Kolko, D. J. (1987). Depression. In M. Hersen & V. B. Van Hasselt (Eds.), *Behavior therapy with children and adolescents: A clinical approach* (pp. 137–183). New York: Wiley.

Matson, J. L. (1989). *Treating depression in children and adolescents.* Elmsford, NY: Pergamon Press.

Reynolds, W. M. (1992). Depression in children and adolescents. In W. M. Reynolds (Ed.), *Internalizing disorders in children and adolescents* (pp. 149–253). New York: Wiley.

Stark, K. D., & Brookman, C. S. (1992). Childhood depression: Theory and family-school intervention. In M. J. Fine & C. Carlson (Eds.), *The handbook of family-school intervention: A systems perspective* (pp. 247–271). Boston: Allyn & Bacon.

A Multicomponent Program to
Reduce Depression in the School Setting

AUTHORS: Kevin D. Stark, Cathy Simmons Brookman, and Randy Frazier

PRECIS: A school-based, cognitive-behavioral intervention program for individuals or groups to reduce depression in school-age youth

INTRODUCTION: The literature is filled with techniques to identify depression in children and adolescents, but there is practically nothing on effective school-based interventions. For this program, nine- to thirteen-year-old depressed children are identified during three stages: (1) completion of a self-report screening instrument (Children's Depression Inventory), (2) a second identical administration less than one week later (for those scoring 16 or above), and (3) an interview with those scoring above 16 a second time. The Schedule of Affective Disorders and Schizophrenia for School-Age Children is used for this purpose. Youngsters meeting the criteria for depression then participate in a multicomponent program derived from adult interventions but modified extensively to meet their developmental needs. The program is presented in twenty-six sessions over an eighteen-week period and consists of cognitive strategies, self-control training, behavioral techniques, and parent training/family therapy. The particular program components are selected for a given child after he or she has received an extensive evaluation that uses projective techniques, questionnaires, and other cognitive and behavioral assessment instruments listed in the article. Almost all children participating in the program will need the components of cognitive restructuring, self-control training, and parent training; the behavioral strategies, however, will vary from child to child, reflecting individual needs. Because much of the program involves components needed by all participating students, group work is relatively easy to conduct.

PROGRAM COMPONENTS:

1. *Cognitive Strategies*—Cognitive restructuring, attribution retraining, and modeling make up the cognitive strategies part of the program. Restructuring is designed to alter the distorted negative self- and worldviews common in depressed youngsters. Through stories, coaching, games, and completion of thought records, students learn to identify depressed thinking, challenge these thoughts, develop alternative ways to view positive and negative events, take action to reduce their sense of helplessness, and gain control of their lives. Attribution retraining addresses their tendency to blame themselves for negative events while minimizing their role in positive outcomes. Students learn about positive and negative causes and consequences; they see how depressed people emphasize the negative, and they find ways

to develop realistic, adaptive attributions. The program therapists provide modeling by problem solving out loud and verbalizing coping thoughts as issues arise during the therapeutic process.

2. *Self-Control Training* — The second phase of the program teaches students self-monitoring, self-reinforcement, and self-evaluation — techniques that encourage them to focus on positive daily events, evaluate their behavior in more realistically positive terms, reinforce themselves more, and punish themselves less. The children learn to self-monitor and self-record pleasant events within and outside of therapy sessions using Pleasant Events Schedules. With their parents' participation, they then identify rewards and learn to reinforce their own monitoring actions, acquiring the information and skills that reduce depression. They also learn to evaluate their behavior more accurately by examining personal standards, evaluating them more realistically, setting achievable goals to meet the new standards, and rehearsing the skills needed to reach these goals.

3. *Behavioral Techniques* — Activity planning, assertiveness training, social skills training, and relaxation/imagery training are among the behavioral techniques used to help youngsters reduce learned helplessness and passivity, impact their environments more actively, improve their social responding, and derive more pleasure from their lives. Activity planning teaches students how to influence their own feelings and increase the pleasant activities they engage in. Assertiveness training legitimizes appropriately assertive behavior by teaching students (1) how to ask family and peers to participate with them in pleasant activities, (2) how to provide rewarding feedback to others for doing something with them they like, and (3) how to tell others to stop doing something unpleasant. Social skills training follows the familiar strategies of teaching, modeling, rehearsing, coaching, and feedback to promote (1) initiating and responding to social overtures, (2) maintaining social contact, and (3) managing conflict. As the group works together to write a movie about friendship, they apply many of the skills required for social participation. Relaxation and imagery exercises combat the anxiety depressed youngsters frequently feel; they also help the students develop self-control. Training in deep muscle relaxation and imagining pleasant past experiences is modified to make these more interesting and accessible activities for younger children.

4. *Parent/Family Training* — The program component addressing parent and family training acknowledges the depressive effect on children of parents' depression, their lack of emotional involvement with their children, parents' marital instability, and life stresses in the family. Parents and students attend three meetings; other siblings may take part if their participation is considered helpful. In the first meeting the therapist describes the program, seeks agreement with the parents regarding the presenting problem, evaluates the parents' management skills, encourages parents to prac-

tice positive behavior management, and obtains their agreement to help their child complete the homework assignments. In meeting 2 the student's sessions are reviewed and he or she is urged to show off newly learned skills. Homework completion is evaluated, parental involvement is reemphasized, and parents are asked to encourage appropriate assertiveness in their child. Meeting 3 includes additional review and display of the student's new skills as well as instruction for the parents on identifying and helping their child reduce negativism and restructure his or her thoughts.

COMMENTARY: Noting that these components were originally designed as interventions for depressed adults, the authors describe the changes made to adapt this program for children: (1) use of cartoons to make concepts more understandable; (2) use of more enjoyable, entertaining formats such as stories, activities, and videotapes; (3) use of materials that facilitate organization and retention such as review outlines and reminder homework sheets; (4) a strong early emphasis on establishing group cohesion and identity to encourage openness about emotional concerns; (5) reduction in group size to four students and two therapists to provide more individual attention and better behavior management; (6) use of well-structured sessions beginning with homework review, followed by discussion of concerns and skill training, and ending with homework assignments; and (7) flexibility in the number of sessions scheduled to accommodate children who may require more time to learn and use the new skills. In making these modifications, the authors acknowledge that children are not easily involved in the therapeutic process and that depressed youngsters may be even tougher to engage. Finally, the authors wisely note that this complex and time-consuming program will be successful in a school setting only if teachers and administrators are actively consulted at all phases of its implementation. Issues such as the importance of reducing depression, securing parental permission, setting meeting times, and managing the classroom performance and behavior of depressed children will need to be addressed in a spirit of collaboration. It is particularly important to enlist the teacher's ongoing cooperation so that the child may complete the entire program. For the first effort, the school professional might consider selecting children from classrooms in which teachers have historically provided reliable support for such interventions, moving to teachers with a less cooperative history after the success of the program has been demonstrated. While this plan might delay earlier involvement for some students, it might offer a greater opportunity for their ultimate success.

SOURCE: Stark, K. D., Brookman, C. S., & Frazier, R. (1990). A comprehensive school-based treatment program for depressed children. *School Psychology Quarterly, 5,* 111–140.

Restoring Self-Worth in Depressed Adolescents

AUTHOR: Jules R. Bemporad

PRECIS: Psychodynamically oriented strategies help depressed teens rebuild self-esteem and master the developmental tasks of adolescence.

INTRODUCTION: As adolescents make the transition from the safe and familiar world of childhood, they face the major developmental task of reinventing a sense of self capable of finding age-appropriate satisfaction and fulfillment in the new activities, relationships, and demands of teenage life. Their struggle with the inevitable psychosocial pressures of adolescence requires them to abandon their childhood behaviors and fantasies; appraise their strengths, limitations, and goals more realistically; and develop new standards by which to evaluate their developing competencies.

These life-altering changes create a normative despair peculiar to yet not at all uncommon in adolescence. Most teenagers work through this malaise (with the usual mood swings, periods of authority testing, and experimentation), but some become overwhelmed by their dysphoria and seek unhealthy outlets through suicidal behavior, substance abuse, gang or cult involvement, sexual behavior, or criminality. To determine the level of risk for a particular teen, the therapist should explore thoroughly the youngster's previous functioning to determine whether the current depressed mood is a temporary reactive aberration in a typically healthy child or a more entrenched clinical pattern with a force and intensity independent of situational circumstances. In either case, a major goal for the therapist is to steer the youngster away from a self-defeating (or destructive) course of action and promote openness to alternative options, while the depression reduces and the self reorganizes. For the majority of teens who emerge from their "stage" depression and eventually find self-worth in new pursuits, therapy is a time-limited supportive experience in which they discover and establish their new sense of worth. On the other hand, those who do not manage this transition have usually entered adolescence with an already precariously distorted sense of self, unable to leave the childhood patterns behind and find new sources of psychological and social gratification. For them, therapy involves a longer and more complex process of generating a stable self-image capable of coping with these developmental changes.

ANACLITIC AND INTROJECTIVE DEPRESSION: Two forms of adolescent depression are identified; both of these, from a psychodynamic perspective, signify the teenager's inability to cope with the challenges of adolescence. Anaclitic depression arises from the failure to separate psychologically from one's family role and move out into the world at large as a fully functioning, distinct individual with an independent sense of self-worth. Thus, the idea of independent behavior free of adult structure, restriction, and/or support becomes a feared prospect and a threat to the self; it is consequently avoided or accompanied by intense anxiety and somatic manifestations, among other symptoms. While the syndrome may be triggered suddenly by a traumatic occurrence (such as the loss of a friendship), in reality the explosion has likely been building for a long time. The author cites a case study of a shy, withdrawn sixteen-year-old girl raised by nannies and an older sister in a materially comfortable but emotionally barren family setting. In this environment she nurtured a passive, dependent orientation that proved ineffective as she entered adolescence and began experiencing pressures to interact with people and to take initiative for directing her life. As friends abandoned her to become involved in more active social experiences and as her isolation and self-perceptions as a misfit grew, so did her panic.

In therapy, interpretation and advice giving were subordinated to establishing a supportive, safe, reassuring relationship in which the therapist communicated to the teenager unconditional concern, understanding, acceptance, respect, and accessibility in times of crisis. While exploring the girl's strengths and encouraging creative independent action, the therapist accepted setbacks, focused on building a positive therapeutic relationship, and kept interpretation to a minimum; only gradually did the therapist begin unearthing the teenager's past and its connection to her present fears of adolescence. Over time the girl was able to enter and experience more of her true adolescence. The author strongly advises preventing teens from making choices that give the appearance of independence but in reality block individuation and growth.

Introjective depression is represented by the adolescent who has been able to separate from family but whose behavior is directed and controlled by internalized and often unrealistic parental expectations and sanctions ingrained in childhood. These youngsters feel trapped by their developing awareness that their actions based on personal needs arouse the guilt and anxiety associated with betrayal of family values, while adherence to parental ideas sacrifices their emerging freedom and breeds a sense of personal emptiness. This form of depression is illustrated by the case of an eighteen-year-old college student who revealed to her parents an intimate relationship she was having with a young man whom she loved deeply. Her parents' hysterically negative reaction led her to feel unfathomable shame which their later apologies could not undo. On returning to college she ended her affair, shut herself off from others, and gradually came to view her life as empty and without purpose. Her wish to rekindle her loving relationship with her boyfriend created guilt and anxiety, and when she entered therapy, she was isolated and depressed. Again the therapeutic strategy emphasized an alliance with the therapist based on acceptance, support, and understanding rather than interpretation, and through which she could begin to assert her personal desires without fear of criticism or abandonment. In this context she could begin to explore how her past helped shape her values and subsequent self-perceptions.

COMMENTARY: The author points out that in both types of depression the youngster is overwhelmed by the tasks of adolescence because the self from childhood can not be relinquished and continues to govern behavior. In therapy this unrealistic self needs to be acknowledged, understood for its inability to meet the challenges of the teen years, and finally left behind for new age-appropriate self-perceptions.

Although the strategies described here are not expressly written for the school-based professional, they are certainly applicable in school settings. In particular, the author identifies the following steps: (1) considering all instances of depression, however transient, as serious and worthy of intervention; (2) exploring background history to distinguish true clinical depression from temporary stage-related unease; (3) matching the therapy to the form and intensity of the depression; (4) forming a trusting alliance between client and therapist; (5) helping the teen avoid destructive solutions to ease the pain; (6) emphasizing unconditional understanding, acceptance, and reassurance while using interpretation and advice giving sparingly; (7) gradually exploring and rebuilding the student's self-image. This psychodynamic process is not incompatible with other multifaceted programs combining cognitive, behavioral, and parent training components. Approaches are not necessarily mutually exclusive even though they address depression from different perspectives.

SOURCE: Bemporad, J. R. (1988). Psychodynamic treatment of depressed adolescents. *Journal of Clinical Psychiatry, 49*(Suppl), 26–31.

Brief, Intense School-Based Interventions for Depression

AUTHORS: James S. Kahn, Thomas J. Kehle, William R. Jenson, and Elaine Clark

PRECIS: Comparing cognitive-behavioral, self-modeling, and relaxation strategies for reducing depression in middle school students

INTRODUCTION: School-based interventions for depressed middle school students have been virtually nonexistent. In recent studies cognitive-behavioral packages such as the Coping with Depression course have been effective with adults, adolescents, and elementary school children, while self-modeling has been used successfully with adults and relaxation has been helpful to older adolescents. This study compared these three techniques with depressed sixth, seventh, and eighth graders.

METHOD: Using self-reports, parent reports, and structured interviews, the population of a middle school produced 68 subjects meeting the criteria for moderate and severe depression. These students were divided into the three treatment conditions and a wait list control group. All students were seen in groups of two to five for twelve fifty-minute sessions over six to eight weeks.

For cognitive-behavioral treatment, the Coping with Depression course was adapted for the middle schooler. The course is a skill-based program focusing on the teaching of strategies to cope with depression-related problems. Such strategies include constructive thinking, self-reinforcement, scheduling pleasant events, and social skills. For the middle school students, the program was modified to include the teaching of self-control strategies, simplification of terms, examples, role-plays, and practice at home.

In session 1 the meaning of cognitive-behavioral treatment was introduced, workbooks and folders were distributed, and self-observation and monitoring were discussed; session 2 addressed skills such as targeting problems, identifying antecedent and consequent conditions, setting goals, and self-reinforcement. Sessions 3 and 4 covered pleasant events scheduling; sessions 5 and 6 dealt with positive and negative thoughts and constructive thinking; session 7 presented communication skills; sessions 8 and 9 demonstrated problem solving; sessions 10 and 11 covered social skills; and session 12 discussed maintaining the skills and using them in varied settings.

Relaxation students first discussed how stress is associated with depression and heard a description of progressive relaxation. Activities helped them identify anxiety-arousing situations and symptoms of tension. Sessions 2 through 5 taught progressive relaxation techniques, while sessions 6 through 11 addressed refinement of, and variations in, relaxation skills such as using fewer muscle groups, recall, counting, mental imagery, breathing, and generalization of skills to other tension-producing situations. Session 12 reviewed the learned skills. For self-modeling, students learned and practiced behaviors incompatible with depression, such as making eye contact, maintaining body posture, smiling, using an animated voice tone, and verbalizing positive self-statements. A three-minute video was produced showing the student engaged in nondepressed behavior. Students viewed their own tape twice weekly for six to eight weeks.

RESULTS: All three intervention procedures significantly reduced the students' depressive symptoms and raised their self-concepts. This change was evident immediately following treatment and at one-month follow-up. Furthermore, while more experimental than control students moved from the dysfunctional to the nonclinical range of depression, the change was more pronounced for the cognitive-behavioral group than for the self-modeling students. Up to one-half the self-modeling group also returned to the clinically depressed range at their one-month reevaluation.

COMMENTARY: In their 1986 study ("A Comparison of Cognitive-Behavioral Therapy and Relaxation Training for the Treatment of Depression in Adolescents," *Journal of Consulting and Clinical Psychology, 54*[5] 653–660),

William Reynolds and Kevin Coats used cognitive-behavioral and relaxation techniques to reduce depression and enhance self-concept in adolescents. The study cited here extends their findings to preadolescence and further supports the efficacy of short-term school-based group treatments for depressed youngsters of varying ages. In addition, the successful treatment of depression with self-modeling broadens its use to students with internalizing disorders. Previously, self-modeling had addressed only externalizing behavior problems. The success of these three approaches provides the practitioner with a rare opportunity to choose among three workable techniques. Perhaps future studies will be able to delineate factors mediating the choice of a given method. Consideration of such issues as available time, degree of staff involvement, parent motivation, school structure, and other variables in addition to student characteristics may be important elements in the equation.

SOURCE: Kahn, J. S., Kehle, T. J., Jenson, W. R., & Clark, E. (1990). Comparison of cognitive-behavioral, relaxation, and self-modeling interventions for depression among middle-school students. *School Psychology Review, 19,* 196–211.

Additional Readings

Butler, L., Miezitis, S., Friedman, R., & Cole, E. (1980). The effect of two school-based intervention programs on depressive symptoms in preadolescents. *American Educational Research Journal, 17,* 111–119.

Fifth- and sixth-grade students identified as depressed were exposed to ten one-hour sessions of either role-playing, cognitive restructuring, or attention-placebo interventions. In role-play students acted out relevant themes such as peer relations, loneliness, and guilt to develop social and problem-solving skills, personal insight, and sensitivity to others. Cognitive restructuring involved recognizing irrational, self-demeaning thoughts, and substituting more effective ones, improving listening skills, and understanding the thought/feeling connection. The attention-placebo group answered research questions by working cooperatively to gather and present information. A control group remained in their classes. A more favorable outcome was reported for the role-play students, although some positive changes occurred with the cognitive restructuring and control groups. Teacher interviews revealed most favorable behavior changes in the role-play students. The authors recommend exploration of role-play as an intervention for depression.

Emery, G., Bedrosian, R., & Garber, J. (1983). Cognitive therapy with depressed children and adolescents. In D. P. Cantwell & G. A. Carlson

(Eds.), *Affective disorders in childhood and adolescence: An update* (pp. 445–471). New York: S. P. Medical and Scientific Books.

In the section entitled "Depressed Adolescents" the authors point out that, with the exception of suicidal behavior, adolescent referrals are rarely made for depression directly but typically focus on poor school performance, substance abuse, sexual acting out, or defiant behavior. Depression is not often recognized as the underlying dynamic, and the therapist needs to help the family reinterpret the youngster's behavior as depressed rather than simply rebellious, hostile, or destructive.

When treating adolescents with cognitive therapy, the following guidelines are suggested: (1) make sessions brief; (2) take time to build rapport with the teen and reduce his or her sense of being threatened; (3) expect some noncompliance and tolerate it; (4) maintain contact with the student's family; (5) respect the teen's privacy; (6) collaborate with him or her on therapy goals; and (7) assign concrete behavioral tasks rather than overly complex homework assignments. Use of games helps reduce the adolescent's discomfort and provides useful information to the therapist while alternate modes of communication (letters, tapes, songs) may help the youth express his or her concerns. Family participation is crucial to reduce placing blame on the teen and to correct unrealistic expectations of him or her.

McKnew, Jr., D. H., Cytryn, L., & Yahraes, H. (1983). *Why isn't Johnny crying? Coping with depression in children.* New York: W. W. Norton.

Written for professionals and lay people, the book describes in two of its chapters available treatment options and guidelines for parents for managing depression in their children. The authors discuss how to distinguish serious depression from temporary, expected periods of unhappiness, how to recognize the symptoms of depression, how and when to seek professional help, and ways to help the child at home. The writing avoids scientific jargon and thus may appeal to parents who need more understanding of depression and its varied manifestations. In this sense the book acknowledges the important role of parents in treating their child's depression.

Reynolds, W. M. (1988). Major depression. In M. Hersen & C. G. Last (Eds.), *Child behavior therapy casebook* (pp. 85–100). New York: Plenum.

This chapter describes "cognitive-behavioral" interventions for depression, drawing together a variety of theoretical models into one unified package of sequenced procedures. A fictional case of a sixteen-year-old boy identified as depressed through a three-stage assessment process is presented. The assessment process involves a self-report measure administered schoolwide to identify at-risk students, a small-group retesting on the same instrument one to two weeks later, and an individual clinical interview. The intervention strategy consists of twice weekly fifty-minute group sessions with four students over five weeks. Techniques used include self-monitoring, homework assignments, discussion of mood-behavior relationships, focus on positive attitudes, self-evaluation, attribution retraining, setting realistic goals, developing a plan for changing behavior, developing feelings of self-efficacy, social and self-reinforcement, relaxation, and use of positive self-statements. These strategies are presented sequentially over the ten sessions. Self-reports and interviews immediately following the program and at five-week and one-year intervals indicate few depressive symptoms.

Several modifications are suggested when treating children or adolescents as opposed to adults: (1) briefer treatment to demonstrate the possibility of a quicker positive outcome, but flexibility to allow for added practice and clearer presentations; (2) an emphasis on fun activities to promote involvement; (3) a group format to take advantage of social interaction among youngsters; (4) parent participation to facilitate activities outside of sessions and reduce the negative effects of parental problems. The professional is cautioned to determine suicide risk, the presence of other pathology, and the need for pharmacological supports.

Saklofske, D. H., & Janzen, H. L. (1987). Children and depression. In A. Thomas & J. Grimes (Eds.), *Children's needs: Psychological perspectives* (pp. 157–165). Washington, DC: National Association of School Psychologists.

Depressive symptoms in children include mood changes; helplessness; low self-esteem; self-criticism; guilt; suicidal thoughts and behavior; loss of interest in activities; physical complaints; lethargy; social withdrawal; slowness of action; reduced attention, concentration, and memory; academic and behavior problems; and loss of motivation. Depression is a multidimensional disorder involving genetic, affective, cognitive, behavioral, biological, social, and environmental components. The school psychologist may receive referrals for behavior that are later found to be indicative of depression, such as school phobia, anxiety, hyperactivity, passivity, and antisocial behavior. The practitioner can use interview, observation, testing, and measures of depression to verify his or her diagnosis.

The article describes a multistage assessment format that can identify depressed students within a total school population while treatment approaches can address the correlates of depression as well as the disorder itself. Samples of techniques for treating depression include the Crystal Ball Technique; Write, Read, and Burn; Doing Something Different; Coverant Control Technique; and Reward, Punishment, and Impersonal Distractions. Elements of therapy involve encouraging the teen to engage in self-directed activity, realistic self-appraisal, improved social relationships, and increased positive feelings and self-statements. The therapist may find it necessary to collaborate with outside professionals. The reader is referred to the article for a more detailed description of the interventions cited above.

Stark, K. D., Reynolds, W. M., & Kaslow, N. J. (1987). A comparison of the relative efficacy of self-control therapy and a behavioral problem-solving therapy for depression in children. *Journal of Abnormal Child Psychology, 15,* 91–113.

Twenty-nine depressed elementary school children (fourth, fifth, and sixth graders) were exposed to self-control or behavioral problem-solving therapy. Self-control training involved teaching self-monitoring of pleasant activities and self-statements, realistic self-evaluation, an adaptive attribution style, and increased overt and covert self-reinforcement. Therapy was conducted in a carefully sequenced format. Behavior problem-solving focused on self-monitoring, pleasant activity scheduling, problem-solving skills, and discussion of feelings and social behavior. Both interventions significantly reduced the children's self-reported depression and anxiety while a wait list control group showed nonsignificant differences. The self-control group alone reported improvement in self-concept. Follow-up posttesting eight weeks later showed maintenance of these effects.

Wilkes, T.C.R. (Chris), & Rush, A. J. (1988). Adaptations of cognitive therapy for depressed adolescents. *Journal of the American Academy of Child and Adolescent Psychiatry, 27,* 381–386.

Depressed adolescents need to be approached differently from adult clients during cognitive therapy. Teens are usually brought to therapy unwillingly by their parents, a situation that complicates the development of a therapeutic alliance. The therapist should approach the teen as a collaborator to help uncover the young person's negative interpretations of self and the world. The therapist needs to be open to different modes of communication and utilize them by remaining aware of the youth's level of cognitive development. If the teen can generate alternative points of view, less modification of cognitive techniques is needed. Similarly, dichotomous thinking inhibits discussion of alternatives and restricted vocabulary may stifle discussion.

The therapist must teach the student about a range of responses and alternatives. The therapist can counter suicidal ideation by understanding its different meaning for teens, which may stem from their failure to understand its finality. Rather than rejecting the idea of suicide, the therapist reframes it as ineffective in achieving the young person's desired goals and helps the teen explore and discover the pros and cons of a contemplated act.

Parental needs are also influential and may affect the adolescent's reactions in significant ways, particularly if the relationship between child and parent is characterized as enmeshed. Helping parent and child examine their individual moods can help disentangle them. Treatment of the parents' relationship also aids in understanding how family issues impact the adolescent.

Suicidal Behavior

The research on youth suicide during the past ten years has proliferated at an astounding rate. This level of interest parallels the growing concern over the increasing numbers of teens who think about killing themselves (1 in 4), attempt to kill themselves (perhaps as high as 1 in 8), and succeed (1 in every 200 attempters). Even those who do not attempt to end their lives are affected by those who do. Sixty percent of teens surveyed in a recent Gallup Poll reported knowing personally a peer who had attempted suicide, while 15 percent knew someone who had completed the attempt. These figures indicate that schools, as one of the major socializing institutions, need to search for ways to prevent this irreversible act of self-destruction, and failing that, help students cope with the loss of a peer without imitating the behavior.

Suicidal behavior in adolescents is reported by the students themselves to be caused by home stresses, depression, interpersonal problems with peers, low self-esteem, male-female relationship problems, and feelings of rejection. Children six to twelve years of age who are prone to suicidal behavior also have persistent thoughts about death, become increasingly stressed as they get older, and are extremely angry. Suicidal patterns in preschool children arise from a need to escape, reunite with a loving person, reverse an unbearable circumstance, or inflict self-punishment. No age range is immune.

The articles presented here cover prevention and postvention and stress the need to respond to suicide at all levels of the school-community, from the individual child to the board of education and the community at large. The scope of the literature on suicide requires a supplementary listing, "Further Reading," presented following the "Additional Readings."

Primary Prevention of Adolescent Suicide

AUTHORS: John M. Davis, Jonathan Sandoval, and Milton P. Wilson

PRECIS: A description of school-based individual and institutional strategies designed to reduce the risk of student suicide

INTRODUCTION: Completed suicides among adolescents have risen 300 percent since 1950. Ten to 13 percent of high school students attempt suicide while approximately 60 percent of teens engage in suicidal ideation. These statistics require the school practitioner to develop skills to intervene with suicidal students and to develop primary prevention strategies for the school. Primary prevention can occur in a person-centered or institutional context. Aspects of each approach are presented in this article.

PERSON-CENTERED APPROACHES: These approaches are directed at students, school staff, and parents, and may involve any of the following steps:

1. Education—in-class suicide prevention programs may be taught by teachers, school psychologists, or outside personnel, either independently or as part of a social studies, health, or physical education course. Topics include warning signs, listening skills, and ways to get help for a peer. The five warning signs of suicide are a verbalized intent or wish to die, a previous attempt, depression, dramatic behavior changes (for example, acting out, major drug use, risky behavior), and final preparations such as giving away possessions or saying good-bye. While recent research has suggested that such programs may not alter the attitudes and behavior of high-risk students, further evaluation is needed. Peer counseling programs involve students helping other students get help. Establishing a peer program requires consideration of the appropriate grade levels, the criteria for selection and training of peer counselors, the counselors' roles, program content, organization and materials, and evaluation procedures. Programs directed at staff may also be developed to help them identify at-risk students and act as referral agents. Learning how to talk to students about suicide may reduce adult fears about such discussions, while training in listening skills and available school and community resources may allow staff to fulfill their roles more effectively. Finally, presentations to parents may sensitize them to troubled sons and daughters and can be accomplished through the Parent-Teacher Association (PTA) or other community organizations.

2. Screening—screening to identify high-risk students can occur in two ways: first, *psychometric screening* utilizes self-reports; peer, teacher, and parent ratings; and/or personality inventories that profile either a variety of personality characteristics or more narrowly defined areas such as depres-

sion or suicidal ideation. Second, *peer screening,* which operates within the peer counseling format, capitalizes on the evidence that the suicidal student will likely tell a peer of his or her contemplated attempt before telling an adult. Thus, selected peers need training to detect warning signs and act appropriately to refer their troubled classmates.

3. Mental Health Consultation — the school psychologist may consult directly with teachers and other school personnel around a given case to provide information about suicide, bolster skills, strengthen confidence, and reduce fears about confronting the issue. Direct contact with the student may also be necessary followed by later discussion with the staff member to share steps taken and educate for possible future encounters.

4. Competence Enhancement — programs on stress management, social skills enhancement, problem solving, constructive thinking, parenting skills, and others may be provided to students, parents, and staff as a preventive strategy to reduce the sense of helplessness that often leads adolescents to thoughts of suicide.

INSTITUTIONAL APPROACHES: The following approaches to primary prevention target the school, district, community, government, media, and other organizational structures: (1) A school district policy on suicide commits the district to a program of awareness that enhances student safety and provides legal protection. Staff receive a copy of the policy and review it at staff meetings. The policy can provide guidance for a number of issues: the appropriate person to inform about an at-risk student, the person to take charge in a crisis, available community resources, procedures for notification of parents, conditions under which a student is taken to a hospital or other facility, a post-suicide response plan, and guidelines for informing staff about the policy. The article offers suggestions in each area. (2) School-community coordination at the local level can result in well-organized suicide prevention programs jointly created by schools and local community mental health centers. State-level departments with overlapping interests in suicide prevention can also avoid "reinventing the wheel" by integrating their efforts to develop coordinated projects. (3) School-based professionals can lobby as advocates for prevention to restrict the tools of suicide such as guns and poison. Educating the media to the possible contagion associated with glorified reports of suicide may also be helpful.

BARRIERS: Prevention efforts may be hampered by adolescents' cognitive development in several ways. First, teens may harbor ideas of how their death would punish or otherwise affect others without considering that they would not be alive to witness these reactions. Second, they often believe that nothing bad can happen to them, only to others. Thus, risk has a different meaning for many teens who cannot conceive of their own injury or death. This issue must be addressed directly in prevention programs.

Prevention efforts may be further counteracted by group dynamics that exclude some teens from the peer group, heightening their isolation and risk. Other youth identify strongly with their group and fear discovery as "fakes" and consequent exclusion. These teens are also at risk.

Sex-role stereotyping may foster suicide by viewing male attempters as cowardly unless they complete the actual suicide; on the other hand, the same stereotyping in a subtle way stamps as more acceptable suicide attempts by females.

Contagion is yet another barrier to prevention that has generated much controversy. Research suggests that contagion is more likely when suicidal behavior is modeled *without* discussion. Discussion may reduce the contagion effect. This supposition requires further evaluation. Finally, some argue that prevention can be manipulated by teens who threaten suicide because they know they will be taken seriously. However, it seems self-defeating to suggest that prevention efforts should cease because some would abuse their intent.

LEGAL ISSUES: When providing prevention programs, practitioners should be aware of the possible need for parent permission, the potential limitations of confidentiality, and the possibility of malpractice or negligence suits resulting from failure to provide a program, or providing one that invades privacy or fails to prevent a suicide. This dilemma is not easily resolved and reinforces the need for appropriate confidentiality and a well-defined school policy.

COMMENTARY: School-based prevention programs have a mixed track record, suggesting either that prevention is not possible within a school setting, or that all elements of effective programming have yet to be uncovered. Assuming the second option is more likely, it is clear that programs require at least peer involvement, nonsuicidal role models, less glorification of suicide in the media, direct communication between adults and teens, an understanding of adolescent cognitive development, and consideration of the legal issues surrounding program delivery. Perhaps suicidal behavior represents a failure to master the coping skills associated with adaptive living and in this sense might respond to the same program components utilized for substance abuse, sexual behaviors, and other maladaptive patterns. Further research is needed to answer these questions.

SOURCE: Davis, J. M., Sandoval, J., & Wilson, M. P. (1988). Strategies for the primary prevention of adolescent suicide. *School Psychology Review, 17,* 559–569.

The School's Response to Adolescent Suicide

AUTHOR: John Kalafat

PRECIS: Elements of a suicide response program within the school setting

INTRODUCTION: There is little doubt that the incidence of teen suicide is rising, that suicide attempts are increasing at an even faster rate than completions, and that children are demonstrating suicidal behavior at increasingly younger ages. While many suicide attempts are not successful, the result to the attempter is often brain damage, paralysis, or other serious injury. These facts make it impossible for schools to ignore the suicide issue, as attempters are likely to be present within the student population. Although substance abuse, antisocial behavior, learning deficits, family suicide, and previous self-destructive attempts are more common in suicide victims than in others, there are no characteristics that *reliably* distinguish suicidal from nonsuicidal youth. Thus, implementing consistently effective prevention programs may not yet be practical.

Current information about suicide, however, can still help schools develop effective responses. For example, suicide attempts seem to occur under crisis conditions in which isolated teens see no other option. Yet these youngsters give off warning signals that, although observable in nonsuicidal youth, may still signal trouble. Signs include feelings of helplessness, guilt, sadness, anxiety, anger, or restlessness; death themes in speech or written material; changes in personality, eating habits, and sleep patterns; loss of interest in activities; sudden elevation in mood; suicide-related statements; gestures (cutting wrists); and the making of final plans. Practitioners may use these symptoms to identify and monitor at-risk students. Peers are an important information source as they often know of a student's impending attempt before adults do, even though they may not tell. Students must be taught what they should do with such information and must be convinced of the importance of taking action. Certain triggering events such as trouble with authority and fear of consequences, disappointment and rejection, a stressful life transition, the anniversary of the death of a loved one, and knowing someone who tried or succeeded in killing himself are all incidents that can push a vulnerable teen over the edge. Based on this knowledge schools can set the following goals: (1) to identify at-risk students; (2) to help students in crisis develop options, to provide supports, and to push for their use; (3) to provide students, parents, and staff with the knowledge and methods to respond to the teen, have professional help on hand, and communicate a message to use it; (4) to respond to attempters and to victim-survivors after a completion.

CONTAGION: When planning suicide programs, counselors must address the question of contagion. In the planning, the following points should be made: (1) When television programs dealing with suicide emphasize responsible behavior and publicize local referral services (for example, hot lines), suicides do not increase. (2) The method of suicide reported may be modeled by suicide-prone youngsters. (3) Most students have already been exposed to suicide information or an experience through knowledge of someone's attempt. Class discussion will not be their first exposure but may be the first balanced presentation in which emphasis is placed on preventive actions, coping strategies, and resources. (4) Factors promoting contagion can be a situation that is intensely emotional, perceived similarity between the youth and the model, and achievement of a goal through the suicidal act. Programs, therefore, need to be low keyed, free of suicidal models, and focused on reducing imitation.

PROGRAM ELEMENTS: A comprehensive program for suicidal youth should include the following components: (1) specific policies and procedures for dealing with at-risk students, attempters, completions, and the returning student; (2) education of staff about suicide, responses to students, aftermath programs, and resources; (3) outreach to parents about suicide and the school's response; (4) programs for students about suicide, available resources, and what they can do if they or a friend develop suicidal feelings; and (5) liaison with community agencies who may receive school referrals, and help return the attempter to school. Schools can schedule such programs for students within existing class schedules (for example, health classes), ensure that the lessons are educationally rather than clinically oriented, use trained volunteer school personnel (for example, psychologists and teachers) who see the students daily and feel comfortable with the topic, and present materials that are developmentally appropriate for the age group and relevant to their concerns.

COMMENTARY: The author notes that to date, the only behavior influenced by suicide education programs is a reported increase in the willingness of some students to use a hot line; these are students who had earlier indicated they would not tell anyone about an at-risk peer. The unfortunate reality is that attitudes and behavior among students remain essentially unchanged by school efforts. Perhaps the school is not a potent enough force to address suicidal feelings on its own. This position is supported by an article, "Youth Suicide: A Psychodynamic Perspective," that appeared in a recent special issue of *Reaching Common Ground,* a publication of Common Ground, the Center for Adolescents at the Stamford Hospital in Stamford, Connecticut. In the article Dr. Herbert Hendin, executive director of the American Suicide Foundation, observed that the suicide rate among youth has continued its steady rise through the calm of the 1950s, the energy of the 1960s, and the drug and economic problems of the 1970s. In his view this pattern provides additional support for the conclusion that the breakdown of the family unit is the root cause of the suicide problem. If this is so, then the schools will need to rethink the extent of their influence and work to develop new and creative relationships with the families in question. It appears that the elements of these relationships have yet to be discovered.

SOURCE: Kalafat, J. (1990). Adolescent suicide and the implications for school response programs. *The School Counselor, 37,* 359–369.

Mutual Storytelling in a Suicidal Crisis

AUTHORS: Kathy Stiles and Terry Kottman

PRECIS: The therapist elaborates on the child's created story to demonstrate understanding of the problem and offer alternative coping strategies

INTRODUCTION: Each year in the United States about 200 children under the age of twelve commit suicide, and many more engage in suicidal ideation. Suicidal children display the following signs: (1) anger directed at themselves and/or others; (2) loss of an important object or person; (3) dangerous behavior; (4) destructive play; (5) incorporation of unrealistic superheroes into their repetitive play; and (6) comments about suicide and death. At-risk children pass through three stages: The first stage is the occurrence of a stressful life event; the second is an increase in stress, feelings of helplessness, and loss of control; the third is a perception of a threat to their well-being. During the third stage the child's self-destructive tendencies are heightened. Although suicidal children are often hospitalized, outpatient treatment (utilizing play and art techniques, among others) is possible if parents are supportive and nurturing, if therapy lasts at least a year, if the relationship with the therapist is deep, and if the child's aggression can be expressed appropriately. Mutual storytelling is an aspect of play technique used by the therapist to help suicidal children cope with self-destructive thoughts and survive the suicidal crisis.

MUTUAL STORYTELLING: Mutual storytelling capitalizes on the metaphorical richness of stories. The child creates a story on any topic as the therapist interprets its meaning. The therapist then tells a similar story with the same characters, but has them solve their problems in more adaptive ways, showing the child more effective coping strategies. This approach works best with verbal children over five years of age who can comfortably tell stories, and particularly with preadolescents nine to fourteen years old. It is also more productive when the practitioner and child have established a trusting relationship and the therapist understands the child's metaphors. Mutual storytelling is not recommended for children with expressive language impairment, limited reality contact, or reduced intellectual capacity.

CASE STUDY: Three years earlier seven-year-old Nathan was playing with his sister when she fell, broke her neck, and died instantly. Since then he had not cried and was disruptive in class. He believed his parents blamed him for the accident and he talked of joining his sister. In his play therapy, burial themes were prevalent as was aggression covered by a need to be happy at all times. Nathan buried toy animals then "rescued" them, suggesting he had not yet accepted his sister's death.

During consultation with the therapist, Nathan's parents began talking openly about his sister, an occurrence that had a positive effect on him. However, improvements in the initial sessions evaporated as Nathan began losing control, tearing his clothes, destroying his schoolwork, and hitting his head against a wall. These actions coincided with the anniversary of his sister's death. When the school suggested a self-contained special education program, Nathan was convinced he was unwanted and uncontrollable; he engaged in self-denigrating and heightened self-destructive behaviors such as scratching himself until he bled and expressing self-hatred. The counselor advised removal of all tools of suicide and saw Nathan for an emergency session.

The practitioner began the storytelling technique by asking Nathan to tell a story using the animals from his burial play. Nathan's story reflected his crisis by depicting a zebra acting wild, being forced to go to the zoo in a cage, and escaping by kicking open the door. However, no one would pay attention to him. The therapist then asked to tell his story in which the lion, pig, and horse urged the zebra to calm down so no one would take him to the zoo and put him in a cage. They liked him and felt scared when he acted wild. The zebra decided to change his behavior so he could stay with them. Nathan spontaneously suggested the zebra could let out his energy racing or playing, and that there was a time and place for acting wild.

The therapist ended the session by telling Nathan how important he was, and that he should not try to hurt or kill himself. He indicated that Nathan could talk to his mother, dad, school counselor, or the therapist when he had these feelings. Nathan chose him, and hugged him. Further promises not to kill himself were elicited from Nathan during later sessions until the suicidal crisis had passed. By session twenty Nathan had stopped burial play and was displaying more adaptive behavior. Therapy ended six weeks later.

COMMENTARY: The authors stress that children in serious suicidal crisis should be referred for psychiatric evaluation and possible hospitalization. Mutual storytelling is not a substitute intervention for children in this state. It is a technique used in a positive play therapy relationship to bring out a child's thoughts and feelings and through which more productive coping strategies can be offered to the child in an atmosphere of understanding. In this sense, mutual storytelling may have broader application over a range of problems and can allow the therapist to show that the child's message has been heard and accepted.

SOURCE: Stiles, K., & Kottman, T. (1990). Mutual storytelling: An intervention for depressed and suicidal children. *The School Counselor, 37,* 337–342.

Are Suicide Prevention Programs Effective?

AUTHORS: Ann Garland, David Shaffer, and Barry Whittle

PRECIS: Serious questions are raised about the value and safety of school-based suicide prevention programs; more research is needed

INTRODUCTION: A survey of existing suicide prevention programs produced 115 school-based curriculum programs for adolescents. The oldest continuing program had been operating for approximately twenty years. Nine out of ten programs trained school staff; seven of ten often included a parent program. Ninety-eight percent targeted adolescents. Average program length was almost four hours, with 66 percent reporting some standard manual or descriptive literature. Topics included facts and warning signs, accessing community resources, breaking confidentiality, stress reduction/coping strategies, psychological development in adolescents, signs of emotional disturbance, interviews with attempters, and death/dying education. Half the programs were taught by combined school and mental health agency personnel, with most others run by agency staff exclusively. Only 2 percent were taught by school-employed mental health practitioners. Ninety-five percent of the programs described suicide as a response to intense stress that can affect anyone.

ISSUES: The major issue raised by the authors is whether the goal of prevention is being realized through these programs. They cite the following points in support of their concerns:

1. Although most programs view suicide as a consequence of stress to which everyone is susceptible, few teens actually commit suicide (10 per 100,000). In addition, since these programs reach less than 1 percent of the fifteen- to nineteen-year-old population, only eighteen of the expected 1,849 suicide completers would be exposed to any program. The authors suggest that strategies be aimed at already identified at-risk youngsters rather than targeting the entire population of a school, most of whom have no serious suicidal inclinations.

2. The authors question whether these programs are "effective, safe, or necessary" (p. 933). First, most students know suicide warning signs and

are quite willing to seek help for related problems. Second, those most likely not to seek help are not typically influenced in a positive manner by such programs and do not usually find them helpful. In comparing attempters who attended a program versus attempters who did not attend, more attenders would not reveal suicidal intentions, did not believe a mental health professional could help them, and viewed suicide as a reasonable solution.

3. Ninety-five percent of the programs take the position that stress can lead anyone to suicide; in reality, suicide has its roots in more complex emotional disturbance, involving significant affective and cognitive distortions among attempters. This inaccurate portrayal of suicide may actually promote modeling of suicidal behavior while its link with mental illness may decrease its attractiveness as a "mainstream" solution to problems.

4. Evaluation efforts have measured knowledge and attitude changes after exposure to programs, but have yet to deal with their effect on suicidal behavior itself.

COMMENTARY: The authors have no problem with program components that sensitize and train teachers and other staff to identify at-risk teens and help them find needed resources. However, they dispute the value of broad-based programs that target whole populations that do not need them in the hope of influencing a few who apparently are not influenced, and who may in fact be inclined to imitate suicidal behavior as a result of the program's emphasis on a shared vulnerability faced by many stressed teenagers. In related articles these issues are pursued in greater depth and the reader is referred to the following resources: Shaffer, D., Garland, A., Gould, M., Fisher, P., and Trautman, P. "Preventing Teenage Suicide: A Critical Review." *Journal of the American Academy of Child and Adolescent Psychiatry*, 1988, *27*, 675–687; Shaffer, D., Vieland, V., Garland, A., Rojas, M., Underwood, M., and Busner, C. "Adolescent Suicide Attempters: Response to Suicide-Prevention Programs." *Journal of the American Medical Association*, 1990, *264*, 3151–3155.

The authors state that efforts to address teenage suicide might be more productive if high-risk students could be more reliably identified and provided help. This of course requires a better understanding of the factors that increase the risk for suicide. In the meantime they do not feel that current prevention programs meet the need for which they were designed and cannot be evaluated in terms of actual changes in suicidal behavior among the target population.

SOURCE: Garland, A., Shaffer, D., & Whittle, B. (1989). A national survey of school-based, adolescent suicide prevention programs. *Journal of the American Academy of Child and Adolescent Psychiatry, 28,* 931–934.

Responding to Suicide

AUTHOR: Iris M. Bolton

PRECIS: Guidelines for responding to suicidal youth

INTRODUCTION: Awareness of the suicide crisis is highlighted by the statistic that every ninety minutes in the United States a youth completes a suicide. Schools are being asked to take on the challenge of developing prevention, intervention, and postvention programs. Before interventions can be developed, sound information must be provided. The following information answers many of the important questions about suicide:

- Eighty percent of suicidal youth talk about or threaten suicide.
- Substance abuse is involved in two-thirds of all suicides.
- Suicidal youth seem to see only two choices — pain or escape.
- Youngsters may be suicidal for only a short time and if prevented from killing themselves, may not remain suicidal.
- Raising the issue of suicide does not cause it to happen.
- Hopelessness is a major factor in adolescent suicide.
- Biological, emotional, intellectual, and social variables operate together to create conditions conducive to suicidal behavior.
- Warning signs include personality, behavioral, and physical changes, new self-destructive behaviors, death themes in conversations or writings, depression (although depression is not by itself a sign of impending suicide), preparing for dying, having a suicide plan, previous attempts, changed relationships, moodiness, self-criticism, poor concentration, changed sleep and eating patterns, anger, sudden absence of depression, major life transition events (birthdays, graduation, holidays, divorce), and a felt loss.

Several points should be remembered when you are assisting potentially suicidal youth: (1) Don't ignore signs; take every threat seriously. (2) Let the person know you have gotten the message and are concerned for his or her well-being. (3) Be calm and listen to the person. (4) You can help someone look at alternatives but you are not responsible for that individual's life; you can't force someone to live. (5) Let the person know that suicide is irreversible. (6) Tell the youth that many people contemplate suicide but never attempt it. (7) Discuss the suicide plan, namely method, weapon, and steps. (8) Offer your own personal experiences of feeling unhappy and hopeless. (9) Never commit to secrecy. (10) If you decide to inform someone, tell the person you are counseling that you have made this decision; call with the counselee present. Stay with the person until someone comes. (11) Learn the available referral and treatment resources. (12) Be aware that some youth take their lives without warning; no one can stop someone who is determined on suicide.

AFTERMATH: After a suicide, many left behind will feel guilt and anger. They need to understand that their reactions are common, that each person recovers in an individual way, and that the grief will slowly pass. Postvention is a form of prevention in which survivors are helped to feel hope for the future. The following steps are suggested for a school response to suicide:

- Calmly tell students the truth. Allow them to attend their friend's funeral with their parents' permission. Homeroom and small group discussions are helpful to allow students to vent their feelings. Writing letters to the dead student's family is also appropriate for students.
- A large group assembly led by a grief counselor helps support students, especially vulnerable ones, and lets them know what kind of personal reactions to expect. Similar meetings for teachers and/or parents may be advisable. Teachers can be available just to talk to students informally. Teachers can also incorporate into their teaching self-esteem building, improving communication skills, relationship building, stress management, and profiting from mistakes.
- Teachers, parents, students, and community referral agencies need to be part of the healing process.

COMMENTARY: Not all of these points will find total support in the literature. For example, not all counselors are willing to state categorically that raising the issue of suicide will not trigger an act. The contagion issue has made schools cautious about initiating comprehensive programs as they try to understand the conditions under which students will imitate suicidal behavior. In addition, the author indicates that preventive programs have not been comprehensively evaluated. Until such assessment takes place it will be difficult to determine their true impact.

SOURCE: Bolton, I. M. (1986, Spring). Educated suicide prevention. *School Safety*, 8–11.

A Student Death Response Plan

AUTHOR: Richard B. Weinberg

PRECIS: A consultant assists an intervention team in managing a death-related crisis in the school

INTRODUCTION: In the aftermath of a teen suicide, school staff and members of the school community may feel intimidated by the awesome task of responding to saddened, anxious, and vulnerable youth. Thus a district may often arrange for outside consultants to counsel students through the crisis. These consultants can best serve the district by teaching school-based practitioners the skills with which to manage these events rather than directly servicing the students themselves. This article describes a consultation and training process by which consultants assisted the district in developing and implementing its own postcrisis plan.

CRISIS INTERVENTION TEAM: When a young girl was found dead several weeks after being abducted from a parking lot, school psychologists, social workers, and a nurse from various schools in the district volunteered their aid to the student's school, forming a crisis intervention team (CIT). The author also offered his assistance as a psychologist with expertise in postcrisis counseling; he subsequently became the team's consultant and trainer when the first meeting revealed the inexperience and discomfort of the team in facing the situation.

DEVELOPING A PLAN: First, a communication mechanism was established to bring the CIT together from the various district schools during a crisis. The consultant helped the group problem-solve this task by raising issues and questions, encouraging discussion, and clarifying disagreement. Next, he provided training in crisis theory, assessment of suicidal risk, and crisis intervention/grief counseling strategies. Training techniques included role-plays, a simulated interview of a suicidal student, and observations of experienced trainees by their less-experienced colleagues.

In three subsequent teen suicides, the CIT and the consultant were summoned to the schools. The consultant's role involved helping the team plan the intervention; providing support and encouragement; planning, demonstrating, and evaluating counseling techniques in vivo; and acting as a backup counselor. The goal was to develop the expertise of the team who then worked with the principal, assistant principal, a security staff member, counselors, and on occasion a few teachers to plan the strategy and serve as a source of leadership to a typically shocked, numbed, and anxious staff.

The consultant remained attentive to signs of stress and fatigue in CIT members, sharing their ordeals as they counseled students and reminding them to take needed breaks. However, the consultant delayed focusing too much attention on the team until the debriefing, which took place at the monthly CIT meeting following the crisis. Here, members recounted intensely stressful experiences with students and adults as the consultant attempted to draw out the full range of their feelings through empathetic comments and feeling-oriented questions. Fellow members consoled and supported one another as team members told of actions they regretted. The consultant took care to commend the team and instill in them a sense of pride for taking on such a tough job.

COMMENTARY: CIT members are reportedly planning to train practitioners from district schools as crisis counselors so that those most familiar with the home school can be available during periods of crisis. As the author suggests, postvention is in reality a form of prevention, designed to block the occurrence of new tragedies in response to the triggering event, whether suicide, violent crime, or other misfortune. Although no person can stop a student intent on self-harm, one may limit the damage among those impacted by the situation. It is particularly important to attend to the emotional needs of the crisis counselors, providing them an opportunity to express feelings that have no outlet during the time of their greatest activity. The consultant's less-intense involvement with students allowed him the emotional distance needed to manage this process, an important and necessary backup function.

SOURCE: Weinberg, R. B. (1989). Consultation and training with school-based crisis teams. *Professional Psychology: Research and Practice, 20,* 305–308.

A Suicide Prevention Program Manual

AUTHORS: Marion E. Breland, Paul Brody, Judy Hunter-Ebeling, Janet A. O'Shea, and Pat Ronk (for the Rockland County, New York, Task Force on Adolescent Depression and Suicide)

PRECIS: A school-based suicide prevention plan involving students, teachers, and parents developed jointly by school, community, and county mental health department personnel

INTRODUCTION: *Depression and Suicide in Youth: A Comprehensive Approach for Schools* is a program designed and presented in manual form by the Rockland County Task Force on Adolescent Depression and Suicide under the auspices of the Rockland County, New York, Department of Mental Health. This cooperative venture among community mental health providers, school personnel, and department of mental health staff helps schools respond to depressed and suicidal students, increase their knowledge of warning signs, and learn what to do and where to get help when crises occur. The program comprises the following components:

1. *Development of a referral plan* — this involves selecting a contact person knowledgeable about depression and suicide who can receive referrals from staff, assess the level of risk for the student, refer the youngster to appropriate resources, contact parents, follow up on any action taken, and provide linkage between school- and community-based services. The manual suggests particular staff members for this role and provides a brief section on informing staff (including secretaries, custodians, cafeteria workers, bus drivers, etc.) about the position, and about the inservice training component.

2. *Mandatory inservice training for school personnel* — the training includes a general presentation to the entire staff and more intensive small group workshops. The large group program addresses facts about youth suicide, warning signs, the issue of denial, and preventability. It includes a movie (from a suggested list provided in the manual), to be followed by discussion of its informational components and emotional impact as well as steps to take when facing a suicidal student. In smaller groups the presentation for students (see number 4 below) and the role of the teacher in this process are reviewed in detail. Teachers are asked to remind students of the presentation, encourage them to be present, remain in class during the presentation, follow up the next day by allowing students to ask questions and voice their concerns, remind students of the availability of certain staff members if they need to talk to someone, and contact absent students to determine if they need to be referred to a counselor.

3. *Parent presentation* — in this presentation school and community experts provide information to parents about depression and suicide in young people, the school referral plan, and the content of the student presentation. Parental concerns are then addressed. An expected outcome of the evening presentation is that parents will gain some knowledge, be able to discuss the issue with their children, and know when to get help.

4. *Student program* — this program, which runs for one class period, is not designed for students below eighth grade. It should be offered in conjunction with the staff and parent components and after establishment of the referral plan described above. Furthermore, it should be conducted by two presenters so that one is available to deal with upset students who might need to leave the room. As a result of the presentation, students should have learned accurate information about depression and suicide, including causes and warning signs; understand their feelings and be able to discuss suicide with their peers; recognize when to break confidentiality and tell an adult about a suicidal friend; know how to identify and talk to a depressed or suicidal peer; and know what to do for themselves or others if suicidal feelings arise.

Handouts for parents, teachers, and students are provided in the manual as well as questionnaires with which parents and students can evaluate the presentations made to their groups. Section II of the manual is a guide for assessing suicidal risk in which the following questions or topics are suggested for the interview between the contact person and the referred student: (1) recent loss or trauma; other background information such as academic performance, substance abuse, loss of interest; (2) whether the student is considering suicide (to be asked directly); (3) previous suicidal thoughts or attempts; (4) knowing someone who has committed suicide; (5) suicidal plans — that is, how lethal (fast acting), how realistic, how detailed, chosen method; (6) supports and resources available; for example, parents, former therapist.

The guide also stresses the importance of establishing a direct, honest but gentle and patient tone for the interview. Furthermore, students should not be left alone if they are judged to be at serious risk or if they indicate feeling suicidal. Parents should be contacted and students should be immediately taken to an emergency room or crisis center. If parents do not cooperate, the contact person may need to act independently. After the referral or other action, follow-up by the school is important to continue the helping process if it has stopped, and ensure that everything possible is being done to prevent a suicidal act.

Section III includes guidelines for a stress management program, a substance abuse program, a children of alcoholics program, and faculty awareness programs covering these areas; section IV offers a postvention plan for responding to the aftermath of a suicide. It outlines the plan for formation of a crisis intervention team and a response plan for informing and mobilizing staff, informing students, addressing the needs of upset students, responding to the media, calling parents of particularly distraught youngsters, providing an emotional outlet for the staff at an end of the day debriefing, and listing students needing further monitoring. The school staff should consider making a visit to the home of the student who committed suicide, take precautions not to glorify the death, and return to normal operations as soon as possible. A final section of the manual lists books and movie resources.

COMMENTARY: Once again, it is important to note that few data are available in the literature to document the effectiveness of prevention programs. However, as with so many other societal problems, schools are often targeted for blame when students kill themselves, creating tremendous pressure for them to "do something." Prevention and postvention programs represent some level of response, and until research uncovers all the factors involved, these programs remain one of the only actions available to the schools.

SOURCE: Breland, M. E., Brody, P., Hunter-Ebeling, J., O'Shea, J. A., & Ronk, P. (1986). *Depression and suicide in youth: A comprehensive approach for schools.* (Available from the Rockland County Department of Mental Health, Community Mental Health Center, Pomona, NY 10970.)

Additional Readings

Appel, Y. H. (1984). *Adolescent suicide awareness training manual.* (Report No. PTM-400-18). Trenton, NJ: State Department of Education. (ERIC Document Reproduction Service No. ED 261 281)

This suicide prevention training manual addresses an issue no other article mentions: procedures to assist the student who returns to school after an attempt at suicide. The following suggestions are offered: a pupil personnel staff member should have access to as much pertinent information about the situation as possible; teachers who need to know about the circumstances should be informed in confidence; the youth should be treated like any other absent student returning to school and should resume normal activities; communication among pupil service staff, parents, and the outside therapist should focus on helping the student deal more effectively with school stress; consultation should occur with teachers and other staff to encourage ongoing discussion of concerns about how to react to the student. Such support among colleagues is crucial, and monitoring of the student's adjustment and progress should take place through checks with teachers, review of attendance, disciplinary reports, and academic performance; contact should be maintained with the parents to provide information and support, and to maintain their involvement. It is important that a relaxed sense of confidence be maintained in dealing with the situation and that open communication within the school be encouraged. The clear message to all is that the school is coping with the crisis effectively.

Brent, D. A., Kerr, M. M., Goldstein, C., Bozigar, J., Wartella, M., & Allan, M. J. (1989). An outbreak of suicide and suicidal behavior in a high school. *Journal of the American Academy of Child and Adolescent Psychiatry, 28,* 918–924.

Research on the contagion hypothesis suggests that teens closest to a suicide victim may be at increased suicidal risk. To evaluate this evidence the authors profiled adolescents in one school in which two suicides occurred within a four-day period. The school district called in outside professionals who obtained "psychological autopsies" to correct misinformation and identify exposed students, met with and referred needy kids for additional mental health screening, and monitored referral sources for self-referring students and families. This process identified a suicidal cluster of thirty-two students including the two who committed suicide, seven who attempted, and twenty-three who manifested suicidal ideation, all within an eighteen-day period. The study produced several noteworthy findings: (1) The existence of this cluster was more than a chance occurrence, supporting the contagion phenomenon. (2) Close friends of the victims tended to have a higher rate of emotional instability, existing before the suicides occurred. (3) Past and current depression and a history of suicidal behavior were better predictors of suicidal behavior among exposed students than closeness to the victims. However, a history of emotional disorder was not a necessary prerequisite for becoming suicidal if the exposed teen was a close friend of a victim prior to the suicide. (4) Attending the funeral did not seem to trigger suicidality. (5) For the suicide to elicit emotional instability, the intensity of exposure would have had to include witnessing the death or discovering the body. The authors recommend screening exposed students for suicide risk as a reasonable step, particularly students who have a psychiatric history or were close friends of the victim. Further, they suggest that the clinical team leave as soon as the process is complete, and they offer a three-week time frame as the point by which newly suicidal students will likely be identified.

Carter, B. F., & Brooks, A. (1990). Suicide postvention: Crisis or opportunity? *The School Counselor, 37,* 378–390.

The Youth Suicide Prevention Services in the Department of Psychiatry at Albert Einstein Medical Center in Philadelphia offers school-based post-suicide crisis intervention services to survivors of a completed suicide. The following guidelines were developed from the experiences of this program: (1) provide evaluation and therapy for survivors; (2) provide inservice training for staff; (3) use support groups; (4) use community resources; (5) develop procedures for coping with the media; (6) develop a postvention plan prior to emergencies; (7) utilize outside consultants who can assess school resources, screen survivors for significant risk, and implement interventions; (8) act quickly, alleviate fear, and take a proactive approach; (9) strengthen existing support systems and offer new resources; (10) utilize a group therapy format of ten to twelve weeks in duration; and (11) pursue survivors rather than waiting for them to ask for help.

The authors describe a postvention group of six teenagers left behind by the suicide of a close friend. The goals of the first sessions were to assess the students' needs, provide immediate support, provide access to more in-depth therapy, and prevent additional suicides. Students vented their feelings in a nonjudgmental atmosphere, were asked to discuss plans for short-term support, and met for additional sessions (a total of twelve). Parental reactions to the group process illustrated the role of family issues in suicidal behavior. One group member made a suicidal gesture, illustrating how adult support systems will often be tested in extreme ways. The group addressed themes of permanent and reversible loss, discussed religion, death, God, emotional honesty, group relations, problem-solving techniques, and feelings around holiday time. Countertransference issues were described, and the help of an auxiliary therapist was suggested. One and one-half years later all six group members were alive and doing well. Three of the six had entered therapy.

Contagion in the form of distress may occur among survivors, increasing the risk of suicidal behavior. However, postvention can be a counteracting process, allowing potentially self-destructive feelings to be expressed, tolerated, and thus diminished.

Kneisel, P. J., & Richards, G. P. (1988). Crisis intervention after the suicide of a teacher. *Professional Psychology: Research and Practice, 19,* 165–169.

A one-day postvention following the suicide of a fifth/sixth grade teacher is described. Its goal was to help the students and school staff through the mourning process and limit future psychological problems through acknowledgment and understanding of the tragedy and the feelings created in the survivors. Information was provided to prevent rumors; fire prevention was discussed as the suicide was by self-immolation; support and referral for additional therapeutic help was offered. A faculty meeting provided information to teachers about the intervention for students and allowed teachers to share information, express concerns, and offer suggestions. Classroom discussions with intervention teams helped children acquire information, minimize their feelings of self-blame, ask and answer questions, and share their feelings and fears. Children asked many questions as an indirect way to express their feelings, displaying confusion as to the teacher's reasons, projecting blame, and in some cases perhaps feeling guilty for her death. Individual sessions for teachers and students were also available, with referral for follow-up assistance if needed. A follow-up meeting between the principal and the intervention team provided additional steps. The school sent a letter home to parents giving complete information about the suicide, the funeral, and a community memorial service. The letter also identified mental health resources in the community. A school memorial service was held. Other steps included inservice training for the school psychology staff on responding effectively to such crises, establishing a crisis hot line, and forming a crisis team. Suicide prevention guidelines were also written for the school district. Steps were taken to provide financial coverage for mental health services for teachers through their union. The authors offered suggestions for improving the postvention response.

Rosenthal, P. A., & Rosenthal, S. (1984). Suicidal behavior by preschool children. *American Journal of Psychiatry, 141,* 520–525.

Sixteen suicidal preschoolers with an age range of two and a half to five years were compared with nonsuicidal age mates with significant behavior problems. The suicidal groups showed more self-aggression, attempts to run away, and depression. Child abuse/neglect was more prevalent among these children, and they expressed feelings of abandonment, a wish for reunion, despair, and hope for reversing their loss. Four motivations for suicidal behaviors were described: self-punishment, escape, reunion with a nurturing figure, and undoing an intolerable life situation. Three case studies were presented to illustrate these dynamics. Most of the children in the suicidal group displayed no pain or crying when they were injured. A lack of loving caretakers was evident in this group, with disturbed attachments being most characteristic of the suicidal youngsters. Suspicion of suicide in this age group should be heightened by the presence of injuries, repeated events involving injury, intense family stress, abuse/neglect, loss of a nurturing relationship, and aggressive behavior. Children should be asked about accidents as they will readily admit suicidal motivation if it exists.

Wellman, M. M. (1984). The school counselor's role in the communication of suicidal ideation by adolescents. *The School Counselor, 27,* 104–109.

To help school staff identify at-risk students, the author offers a five-stage model of suicidal behavior, illustrated with case material. Stage 1 describes a history of problems extending to early childhood, in which the child views the parents as uncaring. He has overwhelming feelings of isolation and helplessness. In stage 2 new problems compound existing issues and escalate into the child's adolescence. Stage 3 finds the adolescent more isolated and unable to cope with the stresses of living. By stage 4 remaining social relationships have disintegrated, the teen sees no hope, and a "last straw" event takes place. Finally, stage 5 involves justifying the suicide. Suicidal intent may be communicated in two stages. In the first stage the teenager toys with death (suicidal gestures), while "crying for help," through behaviors, comments, and perhaps a suicide letter. In the second stage the young person makes a lethal attempt, following a period of silence in which help is no longer sought.

Teens communicate suicidal intentions through affective and behavioral systems such as sadness, lethargy, belligerence, sexual behavior, running away, academic failure, social isolation, changed eating and sleeping habits, verbal self-denigration, themes of death in writings or art, collecting lethal tools, giving away possessions, and previous suicide attempts. School practitioners need to be aware of these signs so they may provide help and support quickly. Other suggestions include holding inservice sessions for staff on an emotional and cognitive level. Intervention involves referring a student to a multidisciplinary planning and placement team, having meetings with parents, dealing with parental resistance and denial with the help of the team, referring the student for further therapeutic help or hospitalization, providing help for parents, and coordination with teachers and the school psychologist.

Further Reading

Blumenthal, S. J. (1990). Youth suicide: The physician's role in suicide prevention (editorial). *Journal of the American Medical Association, 264,* 3194–3196.

Brent, D. A., Perper, J. A., Goldstein, C. E., Kolko, D. J., Allan, M. J., Allman, C. J., & Zelenak, J. P. (1988). Risk factors for adolescent suicide. *Archives of General Psychiatry, 45,* 581–588.

Cole, D. A. (1989). Psychopathology of adolescent suicide: Hopelessness, coping beliefs, and depression. *Journal of Abnormal Psychology, 98,* 248–255.

Crespi, T. D. (1990, June). Self-poisoning and suicide in adolescents. *NASP Communiqué* [publication of the National Association of School Psychologists], p. 24.

Davis, J. M. (1985). Suicidal crises in schools. *School Psychology Review, 14,* 313–324.

Freiberg, P. (1991, July). Suicide in family, friends is familiar to too many teens. *APA Monitor* [publication of the American Psychological Association], pp. 36–37.

Grob, M. C., Klein, A. A., & Eisen, S. V. (1983). The role of the high school professional in identifying and managing adolescent suicide behavior. *Journal of Youth and Adolescence, 12,* 163–173.

Hahn, W. O. (1987). Children and suicide. In A. Thomas & J. Grimes (Eds.), *Children's needs: Psychological perspectives* (pp. 602–608). Washington, DC: National Association of School Psychologists.

Hahn, W. O. (1990, June). Children and suicide. *NASP Communiqué.*

Mazza, J. (1989). Review of *Preventing teenage suicide: The living alternative handbook. School Psychology Review, 18,* 137–138.

Overholser, J. C., Hemstreet, A. H., Spirito, A., & Vyse, S. (1989). Suicide awareness programs in the schools: Effects of gender and personal experience. *Journal of the American Academy of Child and Adolescent Psychiatry, 28,* 925–930.

Pfeffer, C. R. (1981). Suicidal behavior of children: A review with implications for research and practice. *American Journal of Psychiatry, 138,* 154–159.

Pfeffer, C. R. (1991, Summer). Suicidal behavior in young children. *Briefings: The Newsletter of the New York Hospital-Cornell Medical Center, Westchester Division,* pp. 3–6. (Available from the New York Hospital-Cornell Medical Center, Westchester Division, 21 Bloomingdale Road, White Plains, NY 10605.

Ritter, D. R. (1990). Adolescent suicide: Social competence and problem behavior of youth at high risk and low risk for suicide. *School Psychology Review, 19,* 83–95.

Ross, C. P. (1980). Mobilizing schools for suicide prevention. *Suicide and Life-Threatening Behavior, 10,* 239–244.

Saffer, J. B. (1986). Group therapy with friends of an adolescent suicide. *Adolescence, 21,* 743–745.

Smith, K. (1990). Suicidal behavior in school aged youth. *School Psychology Review, 19,* 186–195.

Spirito, A., Overholser, J., & Stark, L. J. (1989). Common problems and coping strategies II: Findings with adolescent suicide attempters. *Journal of Abnormal Child Psychology, 17,* 213–221.

4

Cognitive and Social Competence

Competence refers to those cognitive, behavioral, and affective attributes that enable the individual to respond adaptively and effectively, creating positive outcomes in a given environmental context. Terms such as *social-cognitive problem solving, social decision making, social skills,* and *social-behavioral competence* have become identified with this construct which, through its emphasis on adequacy and enhancement, has helped to refocus school-based interventions toward coping and resolving problems rather than reliance on reducing pathology.

The importance of helping all youngsters develop competencies is underscored by the research documenting (1) the relationship between socially responsible behavior and academic performance, (2) the importance of social competence in developing peer relationships, and (3) the negative consequences of poorly developed competency skills (for example, juvenile delinquency and high-risk sexual behavior). Even the behavior of youngsters with such identifying labels as mental retardation must not be excluded from discussions about competence, as numerous researchers (for example, Landesman and Ramey, 1989) have emphasized the importance of teaching children with limiting conditions about generating solutions, evaluating the probability of successful outcomes, judging feelings, and learning when they need help. Recent additions to the literature have expanded this issue by questioning whether intelligence as currently understood is adequate to encompass a proper understanding of the behaviors of individuals with mental retardation. Matarazzo (1992) in his *American Psychologist* article, "Psychological Testing and Assessment in the 21st Century," predicts growth and refinement in competence assessment, with particular consideration given to different cognitive styles of individuals from varying backgrounds, and special focus on the ecological context of each individual's actions. In fact, it is not possible to discuss the issue of competence independent of ecological considerations, as behavior judged to be effective in one setting may be totally inappropriate or inadequate in another. Thus, to teach students competencies one must teach skills that enable students to determine the most effective responses *in given situations.*

Problems addressed in this chapter have been conceptualized as competency-based in the sense that competency in a given area enhances children's potential to manage the environment more effectively, while lack of competency diminishes their coping effectiveness and increases the likelihood of a negative outcome. For example, the nursery school teacher may respond inappropriately to a language impaired preschooler because she is unable to decipher the child's unintelligible comments. Similarly, the high school student who comes to class drunk and falls asleep at his or her desk or who must be carried home every weekend from the neighborhood party is establishing a potentially self-destructive pattern in addition to risking alienation from previously accepting and sympathetic peers. Finally, the encopretic elementary student may exude an odor that leads to peer ridicule and avoidance even by adults.

Interventions directed at substance abuse and risky sexual behavior among adolescents continue to deemphasize a traditional counseling approach, focusing instead on the cognitive and behavioral competencies and feelings of self-efficacy these young people need to modify maladaptive patterns. Thus, they should have training in resistance, communication, and decision-making skills as well as health services with counseling and education to help them develop more responsible behavior. The approach to assisting students with communication disorders deemphasizes language as a structural system that must be drilled in pull-out programs and instead highlights its importance as a vehicle for expressing intentions, feelings, and needs. Its value in helping the user influence and elicit responses from the environment requires its practice and use in naturalistic everyday settings. This shift has led to the current stress on classroom-based strategies in which teachers pool their resources to integrate language development into all aspects of the curriculum.

Techniques to improve students' academic performance have been accompanied by research findings that affirm the value of homework and the importance of providing students with opportunities to respond correctly in class. The literature also stresses the need for teachers to target academic performance directly (rather than related behaviors assumed to affect performance), the power of direct teaching methods, and the importance of adequate instructional time. Cooperative learning, peer and cross-age tutoring, curriculum-based assessment, self-instruction training, goal setting, corrective feedback, relaxation and desensitization, group contingencies, and contracting are among the strategies described for addressing problems in academic performance.

For masturbation and thumb sucking/nail biting, efforts have been directed away from punishment strategies to such approaches as self-management, influencing co-varying behaviors, competing response training, utilizing preferred behaviors as rewards, hypnosis, and differential reinforcement of other behaviors (DRO) schedules. Milder forms of aversive contingencies such as facial screening, systematic use of commercially prepared nail coatings, and overcorrection have also been used, all with the goal of helping the youngster develop the competencies that will allow for greater participation in social and community activities. Methods for reducing children's soiling and wetting continue to utilize the bell and pad, dry-bed training, retention control training, positive reinforcement, logical consequences, and family participation. A multicomponent package known as Full Spectrum Home Training is cited, as is an interesting strategy described as cognitive-behavioral play therapy. Again, competence is closely tied to social participation and acceptance.

Research in school-based interventions continues to deemphasize the more psychodynamically oriented therapeutic approaches in favor of a more direct focus on the presenting problems. This trend does not, in this writer's judgment, devalue the importance of counseling and therapy or the relevance to behavior of internal affective states, but it reflects a practical need for the school professional to help the teacher and student cope *at the moment* with behaviors that inhibit learning. For further information, the reader should consult the following sources:

Further Reading

Elias, M. J., & Allen, G. J. (1991). A comparison of instructional methods for delivering a preventive social competence/social decision making program to at risk, average, and competent students. *School Psychology Quarterly, 6,* 251–272.

Juvonen, J., Ratekin, C., Keogh, B. K., & Bernheimer, L. (1992). Children's and teachers' views of school-based competencies and their relation to children's peer status. *School Psychology Review, 21,* 410–422.

Landesman, S., & Ramey, C. (1989). Developmental psychology and mental retardation: Integrating scientific principles with treatment practices. *American Psychologist, 44,* 409–415.

Matarazzo, J. D. (1992). Psychological testing and assessment in the 21st century. *American Psychologist, 47,* 1007–1018.

Merrell, K. W., Merz, J. M., Johnson, E. R., & Ring, E. N. (1992). Social competence of students with mild handicaps and low achievement: A comparative study. *School Psychology Review, 21,* 125–137.

Sundberg, N. D., Snowden, L. R., & Reynolds, W. M. (1978). Toward assessment of personal competence and incompetence in life situations. *Annual Review of Psychology, 29,* 179–221.

Wentzel, K. R. (1991). Social competence at school: Relation between social responsibility and academic achievement. *Review of Educational Research, 61,* 1–24.

Cognitive Competence

This section defines two aspects of cognitive competence: academic performance and communication development. It is essential that youngsters master academic and communication skills if they are to access higher education, compete in the work force, and/or advance to higher levels of career success. In addition, a crucial component of environmental mastery is the ability to express needs in a manner that others can understand and to which they can respond. Although there is ongoing debate about whether schools can or should teach social decision making and problem solving, few would argue against a primary emphasis on academic skill and language development.

Cognitive Competence: Academic Performance

Much attention has been directed to improving academic performance for good reason. First, academic achievement is considered by many to be the single most important goal of the school experience. It is in a sense the "business" of schooling. Second, few would disagree that school mastery and generalization of mastery to settings outside of school are essential prerequisites for meeting the challenges of adulthood. Third, poor performance may arise from or cause other school-related problems, heightening in either case the risk of failure and promoting a progressive decline in the child's ability to rebound adaptively. Interventions to improve academic performance have focused more directly on enhancing performance rate and/or accuracy rather than attacking behavior problems; strategies that reduce classroom misbehavior have not produced a simultaneous improvement in performance rate/accuracy, while those that target academic performance do show a concomitant improvement in behavior. Other issues remain regarding the measurement of academic performance and whether strategies for increasing performance have long-lasting positive effects. Despite these concerns, practitioners have a variety of techniques from which to choose, and interventions discussed in other sections of this book should also be explored for their power to produce concomitant increases in academic functioning.

Student-Directed Versus
Teacher-Directed Spelling Instruction

AUTHOR: Maribeth Gettinger

PRECIS: Improving spelling accuracy through student-directed self-instruction aided by visual and verbal cues

INTRODUCTION: Spelling difficulties have multiple causes and are not confined to students who are learning impaired. Certain instructional methods seem to promote spelling accuracy, although other techniques have not been adequately researched. This study evaluated two strategies for improving spelling with nine poor spellers in grades 3 to 8.

METHOD: During the baseline period, each student received a pretest on six selected words, studied the words for five minutes, and was then post-tested. Four treatment conditions were then applied:

1. *Teacher-directed (TD) without cues* — The child was pretested using six words, with the teacher checking correct words and commenting, "Good. this is how you spell _____ ." For each incorrectly spelled word, the teacher stated, "This is how you spelled the word," and rewrote the word using the student's incorrect spelling. The teacher then said, "This is the right way to spell it," and pronounced and wrote it correctly next to her incorrect imitation. For each of the six words, the teacher then displayed a card showing the word, said the word, took the card away, had the child write it, then checked the child's spelling. This card practice was repeated until the child spelled the word correctly twice. Posttesting was then conducted.

2. *Teacher-directed (TD) with cues* — Condition 1 was duplicated except that the teacher circled in red both the misspelled piece of the word in her imitation and the corrected portion in her properly spelled revision. Referring first to the misspelled imitation, she said, "This is the part of the word you need to remember. Look carefully at this part." She then pointed to the circled segment of the correct word saying, "Here's how this part should be spelled." Pointing back to the circled error she said, "Not like this." After instructing the child to study the difference, the teacher practiced the card display with the child, emphasizing the misspelled parts and instructing the child to remember the correct spelling.

3. *Student-directed (SD) without cues* — Students self-corrected their pretests using word cards and checked each correct word. They wrote imitations of their misspelled words, then wrote and repeated the correct word. They also practiced using the card displays on their own following the teacher-directed format.

4. *Student-directed (SD) with cues* — After self-correcting their pretests, students circled in red both their own misspellings and the correctly spelled models saying, "This is the part of the word I need to remember." They then studied the corrections and practiced with the cards by pointing to the corrected parts and circling them.

RESULTS: While all four treatments improved the children's spelling accuracy over baseline, student-directed was more effective than teacher-directed practice. Furthermore, adding cues did not enhance the teacher-directed training but did improve accuracy on student self-correction. Thus, student-directed practice with cues was the most effective procedure, resulting in accuracy rates of between five and six correct words for each six-word list during the final phase of the study. Students' retention of words after one week was also higher for the student-directed treatment (4.25 to 5.50 for student-directed versus 2.25 to 3.75 for teacher-directed). The addition of the visual and verbal cues did not enhance the retention effect for either condition.

COMMENTARY: As the author notes, the students received individual training in this procedure and did not self-correct in the context of regular classroom activity. Thus, its practical effectiveness remains untested. However, it seems apparent that students can improve their spelling on their own once they are taught a sequential format that combines specific cues for self-instruction. The advantage for teachers lies in their freedom to work with other students. Further, while a one-week follow-up found more accurate retention for student-directed training, one week is not a particularly long period over which to assess maintenance of effects. Whether long-term retention is enhanced by this procedure remains to be seen.

SOURCE: Gettinger, M. (1985). Effects of teacher-directed versus student-directed instruction and cues versus no cues for improving spelling performance. *Journal of Applied Behavior Analysis, 18,* 167–171.

Contracting and Goal Setting for Academic Improvement

AUTHORS: Mary Lou Kelley and Trevor F. Stokes

PRECIS: Contingency contracting increases academic performance while self-managed goal setting maintains the improved productivity

INTRODUCTION: Studies show that self-management has been as effective as externally managed contingencies in improving academic performance. Student goal setting is a form of self-management in which students participate in determining the criteria for their own rewards. However, adolescents seem to require a transition period in which they gradually shift from ongoing externally controlled contingencies to self-management of behavior. The authors utilized contingency contracting as a transition vehicle to improve students' academic productivity since it requires them actively to negotiate performance standards and consequences, yet leaves the application of the consequences to the adult. The authors then introduced self-managed goal setting to evaluate its effectiveness in maintaining the improved performance. Subjects were eight students sixteen to twenty-one years of age with histories of significant conduct disorders and academic deficiencies. They attended an occupational education program, spending a half-day in vocational training and a half-day preparing for their general equivalency diploma (GED) examination. The study was done in their academic class where they worked in skills workbooks.

METHOD: During the baseline period, students were paid for attendance as they completed workbook assignments. Teaching aides graded answers and recorded the number of right and wrong responses on progress sheets. Teachers disciplined the children as usual. For the *contracting* phase, students were paid up to $6 daily for correct workbook items. Each week they negotiated with the teacher the number of items they would answer correctly each day in each subject. Work demands were reasonable but not open for further discussion once finalized. Students could work ahead but could not make up work once the day was over. They could earn an extra $13.50 for meeting all daily goals in a given week. This bonus was prorated for students meeting goals on four or fewer days. In the negotiations, the teacher and student stated reasons for the performance criteria they believed to be fair, discussed differences, and reached a compromise. In early contracts, the teacher pressed for a 10 percent increase in performance over baseline, with 5 to 10 percent increments each week. When *goal setting* was initiated, students set their own daily and weekly work standards, were paid as in the contracting phase, but were expected to complete the same number of problems as during the contract period.

RESULTS: Contracting with contingent pay clearly increased students' academic performance. Goal setting maintained their performance at a higher level than baseline although neither performance standards nor academic productivity were as high as during contracting. The effect of the goal setting lasted through the six-week condition.

COMMENTARY: The contracting sessions taught the students how to set appropriate goals for the self-management phase and thus fulfilled their transitional role. In fact, the authors note that contracting resulted in dramatic increases in students' correct workbook answers, suggesting that they increased their attention to the instructional materials substantially in order to respond accurately to the questions. However, pay-for-work is not a typical contingency employed by schools. Therefore, consistent with the authors' suggestions for future research, this procedure should be evaluated with more frequently used contingencies. If students could be assisted in maintaining an acceptable performance level through setting their own goals, the teacher would be more available to provide instructional assistance, especially when students are attempting to pass examinations for the high school diploma.

SOURCE: Kelley, M. L., & Stokes, T. F. (1984). Student-teacher contracting with goal-setting for maintenance. *Behavior Modification, 8,* 223–244.

Group Self-Instructional Training with Retarded Students

AUTHORS: Thomas Whitman and Mary Beth Johnston

PRECIS: Applying self-instructional training in group settings with cognitively impaired students to improve their math performance

INTRODUCTION: Mentally retarded children have been shown to use self-instruction training successfully to decrease their off-task behavior. The study reported here extended this training regimen to a group setting to evaluate the use of self-instructions to teach children addition and subtraction with regrouping. Participants were nine developmentally disabled special education students ranging in age from ten years, two months, to thirteen years, eight months.

METHOD: During baseline, in daily thirty-minute sessions, students worked on math sheets containing addition and subtraction problems, using a number line that had been explained to them. In the initial ten minutes the teacher observed and recorded the number of problems each student completed for the study. A "good worker" contingency was in effect throughout, which rewarded students for remaining on task nine out of the ten minutes. The teacher instructed students to do as many problems as they could and collected the papers after ten minutes. Each day the children received their scores from the day before. The remaining twenty minutes was devoted to instruction.

For self-instruction training, the students first completed their ten minutes of problem solving, then they received the training in groups of three in the following steps: (1) The teacher solved a math problem for the youngsters while self-instructing out loud. (2) The teacher and students rehearsed solving problems together while she verbalized the self-instructions.

(3) The students were prompted while reciting the self-instructions and solving problems. Their increasingly accurate repetitions were shaped with social praise and/or food. (4) Practice occurred in groups and with each child performing verbally while the others followed the instructions to solve the problem. (5) The difficulty level of the problems was increased. (6) Reinforcers were faded as students mastered the instructions to solve problems. (7) Children worked alone at their desks using the instructions, solving problems and being checked and reinforced by the teacher.

Students learned to self-instruct in the following format: First, they asked themselves what kind of problem they had to solve. They answered, "Addition" or "Subtraction," noting the presence of a plus or minus sign as the clue. Second, they asked what to do, and then talked themselves through every step of the problem beginning with adding the top and bottom numbers in the ones column, using the number line to count spaces, carrying the number when the sum was more than nine, and adding the tens column. Finally, they self-reported solving the problem and gave themselves verbal praise. After the students learned the procedure, they were allowed to use their own words as long as the problem-solving strategies were included in their self-instructions. Training for subtraction was begun when two of the three children in each group performed addition with 70 percent accuracy.

RESULTS: Tapes revealed that all the children learned the self-instructions for addition and subtraction but varied considerably in their use of them during the ten-minute daily problem-solving period. Self-instructional training significantly increased the overall mean problem-solving accuracy rates. Baseline rates ranged from 11.6 percent to 64.6 percent accuracy, increasing to more than 88 percent accuracy for seven students, over 75 percent for one student, and 69 percent for the ninth child during the last five training days. Interestingly, the number of problems completed declined from baseline to the final five training days. With self-instructional training, all children increased their accuracy rates in addition with regrouping (27.4 percent during baseline versus 82.4 percent during training) and in subtraction with regrouping (2.9 percent versus 85.2 percent); they also decreased the number of problems they solved in both instances. Addition and subtraction without regrouping showed similar patterns, although the number of such problems presented to the students was small.

COMMENTARY: These mentally retarded preadolescents, with measured intelligence levels ranging from 53 to 78 and Wide-Range Achievement Test math scores ranging from 1.2 to 3.5, were capable of mastering self-instructions in a group setting and using them to improve their skills in addition and subtraction with regrouping. The reduction in the number of problems solved seems to be an outgrowth of self-instruction rehearsal and a more careful approach to the problem-solving task. Self-instruction training is both an intervention strategy and a teaching technique that teachers can incorporate into their instructional approach across many subjects. It is a process-oriented skill that focuses less on task outcome and more on the cognitive process involved in mastering the task. Its effectiveness with mentally retarded students in a group setting suggests that as developmentally delayed students increase their time in the mainstream, teaching techniques such as this can make that time productive.

SOURCE: Whitman, T., & Johnston, M. B. (1983). Teaching addition and subtraction with regrouping to educable mentally retarded children: A group self-instructional training program. *Behavior Therapy, 14,* 127–143.

Corrective Feedback to Improve Reading Performance

AUTHORS: Darlene Pany and Kathleen M. McCoy

PRECIS: Improving word recognition and reading comprehension with learning disabled students using corrective feedback

INTRODUCTION: Research on corrective feedback provided during oral reading has yielded inconclusive results. While most of the studies have evaluated the effects of feedback on decoding skills, the few that are known to have assessed comprehension have only tentatively suggested a facilitative effect. This study examined three feedback conditions for their effect on students' word recognition accuracy and reading comprehension. Subjects were sixteen third graders designated learning disabled, with total reading scores between the tenth and thirty-fifth percentile on the California Achievement Test, and an error rate between 10 and 15 percent on an oral reading passage one minute in length.

METHOD: Students read orally one passage per day that had been preselected as yielding a 10 to 15 percent error rate as above. They were told whether they would receive feedback for a given passage and were also apprised of the comprehension questions to follow. After reading the passage, they were instructed to retell everything they could remember about the story, then answered eight literal comprehension questions and finally read aloud a list of all words they had mispronounced in the passage. Two to three days later, they reread the same list. In the *total feedback condition,* the reader received a feedback response on every oral reading error after a five-second delay. Prompts were sequenced until the student repeated the word accurately. Prompts included (1) pointing to the incorrectly pronounced word saying, "Try another way"; (2) pointing to letter groups within the word saying, "What sounds does _____ make?"; and (3) supplying the word with the comments, "The word is _____ ." In the *meaning change feedback con-*

dition, feedback was given as above, but only on words whose mispronunciation changed the meaning of the sentence in which they appeared. A *no feedback condition* provided no correction on errors. Students were simply instructed to try their best or skip words they could not pronounce.

RESULTS: When students received corrective feedback on every error as opposed to no feedback, they showed better word recognition both in context and on isolated lists, and better literal comprehension of passages. As conditions progressed from no feedback to meaning change feedback to total feedback, their overall performance improved.

COMMENTARY: It appears that corrective feedback enhances students' reading comprehension at least in part by improving their word recognition. The notion that feedback inhibits students' comprehension by utilizing information-processing channels that would ordinarily be devoted to comprehension is not supported by these data. Although further research is needed to evaluate corrective feedback with different populations of students reading at different levels of proficiency, teachers might wish to employ this technique as part of their reading instruction. More than half the sixteen subjects reported a preference for reading without the corrective help, but this did not seem to affect the overall outcome.

SOURCE: Pany, D., & McCoy, K. M. (1988). Effects of corrective feedback on word accuracy and reading comprehension of readers with learning disabilities. *Journal of Learning Disabilities, 21,* 546–550.

Self-Instruction Training for Homework Completion

AUTHORS: Marian C. Fish and Leonard R. Mendola

PRECIS: Self-instructional training to improve homework completion by special education elementary students

INTRODUCTION: Self-instruction training is a self-control technique in which students use their own overt or subvocal verbalizations as mediating guides for behavior. This study evaluated self-instruction as a method for improving students' homework completion. The relationship between time spent on homework and school achievement has been documented in the literature, suggesting that homework itself may be used as an intervention strategy to improve students' grades. Using self-instructions to increase homework time may therefore increase the time students spend practicing skills, preparing for new lessons, applying skills to new settings, and thinking creatively. All these activities can help to improve their classroom performance.

METHOD: Subjects were three students designated emotionally disturbed; in age they were eight years, eleven months, to nine years, eleven months. They were enrolled in a special education program. Among other academic and behavioral problems, their percentage of homework completed each week fell under 50 percent. They were given homework four days a week in math, reading, and language arts. Each morning, a homework review was the first task, with the teacher recording complete or incomplete assignments. After six weeks of baseline observation, the training sequence was begun and followed Meichenbaum and Goodman's model, as described in their 1971 article, "Training Impulsive Children to Talk to Themselves: A Means of Developing Self-control" (*Journal of Abnormal Psychology, 77,* 115–126). The procedure comprised five steps: (1) the adult modeled the self-instruction out loud for the student while performing the homework task; (2) the student did the task to the adult's self-instructions; (3) the student self-instructed while doing the task; (4) the student did the task while whispering the self-instruction; (5) the student self-instructed silently. The teacher praised the students for correct use of the instructions and provided corrective feedback for errors. The following verbatim self-instruction illustrates what students were taught:

> Now, what time is it? Oh! Time for me to do my homework. Where am I going to do it? I know, I'll do it in the _____ [whatever room subject usually does homework in]. Now, what homework do I have for tonight? Okay, first I'll do _____ , then _____ , and then _____ . Good! It looks like I have a lot to do, but I'll do the best I can. If my mind wanders, I'll tell myself, "Back to work!" After I'm finished, I can play.

The self-instructions were designed to engage the child in the homework activity, not encourage completion of individual questions or problems.

RESULTS: Mean percentages of homework completions rose from baseline rates of 29.1 percent, 34.3 percent, and 40 percent for the three students, to 75 percent for all three during the two-week self-instruction training period. Posttreatment means were 66.6 percent, 90 percent, and 91.7 percent, respectively. Follow-up data, collected in the fall of the following school year for two of the three youngsters, showed rates of 96.8 percent and 87 percent, which were consistent with completion levels for their classmates.

COMMENTARY: The authors note as important the maintenance of improved homework completion after the summer break. However, the accuracy of the completed assignments was not examined, and since completion does not by definition connote accuracy, practitioners may need to plan separate or related strategies to increase certain students' accuracy rates. Finally, the literature indicates that homework time is second only to ability as a determiner of grades. Thus, the practitioner may wish to work with the classroom teacher and the principal to rethink homework practices for the school, and also work with parents and students to increase the chances for follow-through on homework outside the school setting.

SOURCE: Fish, M. C., & Mendola, L. R. (1986). The effect of self-instruction training on homework completion in an elementary special education class. *School Psychology Review, 15,* 268–276.

Curriculum-Based Assessment

AUTHOR: Edward S. Shapiro

PRECIS: Integrating, with case study examples, several curriculum-based assessment formats into a global model that assesses needs, intervenes, and evaluates performance outcomes

INTRODUCTION: Curriculum-based assessment (CBA) operates on the simple notion that the best way to determine students' instructional needs is to observe their progress in the local curriculum of their school. Traditional standardized tests are not appropriate for this task because they often do not reflect the individual school's educational standards. Furthermore, they yield scores that categorize and rank students but do not provide information directly relevant to planning instruction. CBA requires a knowledge of the school's expectations for subject mastery at each grade level so that the student's actual performance can be measured against local criteria. This procedure allows for a closer link between assessment and instruction. In this article, the author describes a model of CBA that integrates elements of several existing models, each responsive to a different aspect of the CBA process. He then illustrates the application of the model with two case studies.

CBA MODEL: The model described here represents a method of curriculum-based assessment that utilizes the contributions of earlier CBA formulations. Four steps are proposed:

1. *Assessing the academic environment* — this step acknowledges the importance of an ecological assessment in which the setting is evaluated for its ability to provide effective instruction. Other purposes include identifying where instruction may not be working for the student and beginning to explore remedial techniques. Using a model of direct assessment, structured interviews with teachers and students, observation of classes, and inspection of the student's papers, tests, projects, and other materials are employed to evaluate the problem in the context of the student-setting relationship.

2. *Determining grade level placement within the local curriculum* — after the academic environment has been explored for its contribution to the student's progress, this step helps provide the student with instructional materials appropriate for his or her skill level so that success is maximized and the student is not exposed prematurely to more advanced elements of the curriculum. Using rate of correct performance as a documented measure of the student's skill attainment and drawing on materials directly from the class curriculum, levels of achievement are determined for the student to effect a match between the student's skills and the appropriate curriculum materials and to decide on the components of the curriculum that need modification to meet the student's needs.

3. *Instruction/curriculum modification* — once the appropriate grade level has been identified within the curriculum, the evaluator determines specific instructional levels and teaching strategies using accuracy-based measures. The author notes that materials vary in their degree of difficulty even within the same grade level, and the student's level of accuracy should be examined so that the appropriate materials and techniques will be utilized.

4. *Evaluating progress* — to measure student progress, rate-based skill probes are conducted at various points in the instructional sequence using sample one-minute performances on randomly selected materials currently being taught or from materials just ahead of the current instruction.

CASE STUDY I: Scott, a first grader, displayed problems in reading and math but had no behavior or social difficulties. Teacher and student interviews, class observations, and examination of his worksheets indicated no severe problems with the academic environment. Rate probes using the reading series in which he was instructed determined his level to be lower than the level at which he was being taught, but after discussion with the teacher no change in level was made. For reading remediation, words known and unknown to him were identified and drilled daily with a technique known as "folding-in," or the "sandwich technique" that mixed the presentation of known and unknown words in a fixed ratio (8:2) until the reading task was completed. Scott was evaluated on one-minute probes given one to three times weekly; he showed a jump from a baseline of twenty correct words read per minute to about forty per minute during the six-week remediation period, then to about seventy-five per minute two weeks after the intervention. His score on the test given at the end of the unit was 94 percent.

CASE STUDY II: Steps 1 and 2 of the CBA process indicated that Joel, a fourth grader, did not have skill problems in math but was frequently off task, disruptive, and noisy during independent seat work, completing only 60 percent of his assignments with 100 percent accuracy. Thus, the learning environment was altered to increase feedback to Joel in three ways: (1) through a self-monitoring system, (2) through immediate correction of errors, and (3) through positive or negative consequences for improved or unimproved daily performance. Two daily probes revealed substantial improvement for Joel in correct performance on daily math worksheets from the very beginning of the twenty-day intervention.

COMMENTARY: The model described here is a product of the collective inputs from several distinct CBA formats, each with its own unresolved research questions. Thus, the author's point is well taken that much is still unknown about the workings of this integrated approach and the contributions of the various components to the overall treatment effects. However, CBA challenges the practitioner to examine the process by which he or she evaluates student needs. CBA eschews reliance on standardized testing, the traditional backbone of individual and group assessment; it stresses an evaluation of the student-environment relationship, an ecological focus different from the intrapsychic emphasis on the individual student practiced by most school helpers; and it argues for a truly systematic approach to evaluation in which a sequenced series of steps develops the needed data, plans the remediation, and monitors the outcome. Clearly, the responsibility for implementing these steps must be shared by the practitioner and teacher, and not all school professionals will be enthusiastic about this approach. However, using what the student is learning and will learn to evaluate his or her learning needs is an inherently logical idea that requires further study.

SOURCE: Shapiro, E. S. (1990). An integrated model for curriculum-based assessment. *School Psychology Review, 19,* 331–349.

Behavior Therapy for Reading Avoidance

AUTHORS: Penny Word and Vitali Rozynko

PRECIS: Using systematic desensitization and relaxation to countercondition a learned avoidance response to reading

INTRODUCTION: While desensitization has been used to reduce fears associated with a variety of events, objects, and activities, the case reported here utilized relaxation, desensitization, and reinforcement of reading behavior to decondition a fear response in an eleven-year-old that resulted in reading difficulty.

CASE STUDY: Eileen was experiencing severe reading problems in school and was afraid to take part in her reading group. During the first of ten sessions, Eileen reported that in an earlier class the teacher gestured as if she were going to hit her and made distorted facial expressions whenever Eileen read hesitantly. The therapist explained what she and Eileen would be doing in the sessions; then she asked Eileen to lie down and read to her a thirty-minute relaxation script. Session 2 consisted of a short discussion about school and a second reading of the script. In session 3, the therapist and Eileen developed a desensitization hierarchy that the therapist called a "story" to help Eileen understand the procedure. The story began as follows:

> You don't like reading in school. When you were in Mrs. _____'s class, you were punished for not doing what the teacher liked. Now you feel uncomfortable when you must read in school You are right, but so is the teacher. You could not behave in any other way than you do in reading group. Reading can be fun. You can learn to be comfortable and enjoy learning to read.

The remainder of the story consisted of a hierarchy of ten situations ranging from minimally anxiety provoking to intensely fearful for Eileen. Each situation began with the phrase, "Vividly imagine," first depicting a benign event (receiving a book in the mail for Christmas), then ending with an event of intense anxiety (reading for a substitute teacher, reaching an unknown word and having the teacher look angry and raise her arm as if to strike). Each of the ten statements in the hierarchy ended with the phrase, "You are calm and relaxed." Following the creation of this "story," the therapist read aloud a fifteen-minute version of the relaxation script. Eileen then asked for help with a library poster on which she wrote, "Happiness is reading." This act by Eileen suggests that she was developing a more relaxed feeling about reading. In session 4, the therapist read the relaxation script and the first six statements in the hierarchy. After the presentation, Eileen imagined a previously selected enjoyable scene, then picked up a book and read to the therapist. Over the next sessions, the entire hierarchy was gradually utilized and repeated until Eileen reported no difficulty hearing any of the statements.

RESULTS: During treatment, Eileen came to enjoy relaxing. She also became less distractible and more independent and persevering. On several occasions, she asked her mother to read her the relaxation script. Her attitude toward reading also changed. The therapist never corrected her when she read and expressed enjoyment in hearing Eileen read. Eileen would come to the therapist's house to read to her and began going to the library. By session 9, Eileen reported no fear of her reading group. Her report card grade was also much improved, with a teacher comment describing her as more interested in her work. One year later, Eileen reported she was reading on grade level. Eileen's fear and defensiveness regarding reading seemed to have dissipated.

COMMENTARY: Although this anecdotal case study appeared approximately eighteen years ago, it is included here because of its provocative subject matter. Most problems with reading are attributed to skill deficits in decoding and/or comprehension, and are frequently labeled learning disabilities. Fear, anxiety, frustration, or other emotional reactions associated with reading are typically viewed as outgrowths or results of the educational disability, with better feelings about reading assumed to occur as skills improve. This intervention described the fear and avoidance of reading as the primary problem with no associated skill deficits.

Before proceeding in such situations, the practitioner must be careful to rule out cognitive, neurological, or other educationally related causes of the reading problem. In many instances, intervention may need to address psychological, educational, ecological, and other dimensions of the problem simultaneously. With the emphasis in schools on learning disability and neuropsychological concomitants of behavior, it is important to keep in mind that psychological and behavioral dynamics are powerful determinants that can operate independently to affect academic performance.

SOURCE: Word, P., & Rozynko, V. (1974). Behavior therapy of an eleven-year-old girl with reading problems. *Journal of Learning Disabilities, 7,* 551–554.

Classwide Peer Tutoring to Facilitate Mainstreaming

AUTHORS: Kenneth Bell, K. Richard Young, Martin Blair, and Ron Nelson

PRECIS: Classwide peer tutoring to improve the academic performance of behaviorally disordered adolescents in a mainstream setting

INTRODUCTION: As increasing numbers of special education students are mainstreamed into regular education classes for greater portions of the school day, strategies for effective instruction will need to be developed to make the experience productive. This study extended the use of classwide peer tutoring (CWPT) to behaviorally disordered students attending a mainstream high school class and further evaluated the CWPT technique with high-, middle-, and low-performing regular education students.

METHOD: Subjects were fifty-two nondisabled and seven designated disabled students attending a high school history class. Five of the seven students attended a special education program for severe conduct problems and two were in resource classes. During the baseline period, students read a history chapter, worked alone and in groups on study sheets whose questions were reduced to about four key words, corrected the sheets, heard a lecture, and studied for, took, and corrected a chapter test. These activities spanned seven to eight days.

For CWPT, the schedule was collapsed somewhat to allow for three twenty-minute tutoring sessions per week. The students were all divided evenly by previous test performance into red and blue teams. Tutor/learner pairs were then formed with one high and one low test performer in each pair. Each student was a tutor for ten minutes, then a learner for ten minutes during the twenty-minute tutorials, which focused on the questions from the study sheets. In the sessions, student tutors were taught to model the right answer for the learner, ask the question, obtain an answer, then either acknowledge the right answer or interrupt a wrong answer. They then modeled the correct response again and retested the question. They earned points for adhering to the teaching procedure and answering questions correctly on the chapter tests. Teachers circulated among the tutor/learner pairs, calling out point awards for the blue or red team and recording the points on a displayed chart. Incorrect procedures were retaught with no points. Daily reports on point totals were made to the students and the weekly test scores were also converted to points. The winning team was announced the following week.

RESULTS: All seven disabled students increased their mean weekly test scores over baseline, and most showed a decrease in variability from week to week. Furthermore, the disabled students increased their test scores an average of 29.6 percentage points during the peer tutoring while the nondisabled students increased by 12.9 points. Disabled students were more strongly influenced by the treatment than were the full-time regular education students, to the point that the differences in test scores between the two groups in one of the two classes were statistically nonsignificant. Finally, the four groups of students — the disabled, and the high-, middle-, and low-achieving nondisabled groups — all increased their test scores above baseline by a significant margin. Again the disabled students showed the biggest gain while the highest achievers had the smallest.

COMMENTARY: Although peer tutoring appears to be an extremely effective procedure, teachers may view it as requiring extensive changes in their teaching style. Actually, the technique is meant to be integrated into the teacher's approach, and practitioners considering this strategy may need to educate staff to its benefits. Peer tutoring helps both the tutor and the learner and, especially for adolescents, capitalizes on the power of peer contact. It is applicable over a wide variety of student populations and with many different subject areas. It does not require many years of teaching experience to implement. However, before it is implemented, the teacher and/or counselor should determine whether the peers are competent to carry out the tutoring process and whether peer pressure might produce adverse effects.

SOURCE: Bell, K., Young, K. R., Blair, M., & Nelson, R. (1990). Facilitating mainstreaming of students with behavioral disorders using classwide peer tutoring. *School Psychology Review, 19,* 564–573.

Group Contingencies for Spelling Improvement

AUTHORS: Edward S. Shapiro and Ronald Goldberg

PRECIS: Dependent, independent, and interdependent group contingencies are found to improve spelling performance with equal effectiveness

INTRODUCTION: Research comparing the effectiveness of independent, dependent, and interdependent group contingencies has been inconclusive. Furthermore, little information exists on the acceptability of these procedures to the students involved, although some preference for the independent strategy has been noted in the literature. Two sixth-grade classes using a token reward system with response cost acted as subjects to evaluate the effect of these group modes on their spelling performance.

METHOD: Students took daily spelling tests, then marked each other's papers, obtaining a percentage score. The students received the ten spelling words the day before the exam and were told which group contingency would be in effect during the test. They were reminded of the condition just before the test; and to ensure their understanding, each condition was color coded, with the appropriately colored piece of paper displayed each day. Spelling word lists were also color coded. The teacher administered the test by saying each word twice and giving a sentence with the word in it. Students then exchanged and marked the papers while the teacher spelled each word out loud. The teacher collected the papers, checked the grades, and gave each student a score.

The six-day baseline provided no contingencies. During the *independent group contingency* phase, each student scoring 90 percent or above received five points as part of the token economy system. For the *interdependent group contingency,* all students received five points if the mean of all scores was 90 percent or better. During the *dependent group contingency* condition, one student's name was drawn from a box containing all the tests. If that student's score was 90 percent or better, all students earned five points.

RESULTS: Students were divided into low, middle, and high groups based on their baseline spelling test scores. For all three groups, no differences in effectiveness among the three group contingencies were found. Students in all three groups improved their spelling performance under all treatment conditions, although the low initial performance group displayed far more variable performance under the interdependent condition than under the independent or dependent treatments. Students also rated the independent contingency as significantly more acceptable than the others.

COMMENTARY: Given these results, the major question is which group contingency should be selected for classroom use. Since peer pressure may be a significant factor if one student loses the reward for others, the age of the target group might be a consideration in choosing the particular group treatment. Peer pressure may also have a stronger influence in smaller groups where each score has a potentially greater influence on the delivery of the reward. Thus, group size may also be a determining factor in the choice of the intervention. The authors noted that the lower spelling test performers during baseline had more variable spelling scores under the interdependent condition. This suggests a third factor, student performance, as an issue to examine before deciding which contingency to use. Finally, student acceptability emerges as a fourth variable. The independent condition was considered by students to be more acceptable based on their actual experiences as subjects. This important finding cannot be ignored in treatment determination. Further research is needed to clarify these and other treatment issues.

SOURCE: Shapiro, E. S., & Goldberg, R. (1986). A comparison of group contingencies for increasing spelling performance among sixth grade students. *School Psychology Review, 15,* 546–557.

Additional Readings

Andrews, P. E., Beal, C. R., & Corson, J. A. (1990). Talking on paper: Dialogue as a writing task for sixth graders. *Journal of Experimental Education, 58,* 87–94.

To assist sixth-grade regular education and special needs students with the writing process, dialogue writing was introduced. Children wrote stories in a dialogue format by imagining characters engaged in normal conversation and writing down their talk using a different colored pen for each character's comments. No expository writing was involved. They also engaged in a free-writing task utilizing a traditional story-writing structure. With dialogue writing, children wrote significantly longer stories. Reading ability or motivation had no effect on story length, and vocabulary was similar for both writing modes. Children reported enjoying dialogue writing more than free writing, yet chose free writing during the last session when a choice was allowed. The technique may aid writing because it tends to mimic normal conversation in which a discussion partner prompts continuing reciprocal dialogue. It appears useful with a variety of student populations.

Ayllon, T., Kuhlman, C., & Warzak, W. J. (1982). Programming resource room generalization using lucky charms. *Child and Family Behavior Therapy, 4,* 61–67.

Transfer of students' performance skills from a resource room to a mainstream class was accomplished using a discriminative stimulus backed by a token economy reward system. Eight students ages eight to eleven attending a resource program completed more than 95 percent of their assigned reading and math work in the resource room, while finishing less than 60 percent in their regular classrooms. To facilitate generalization of task completion from one setting to the other, students brought from home small items of personal value such as a small family picture or an award; they kept the items on their resource room desks as "reminders" to do good work. These were their "lucky charms" and could not be taken from the resource room for the eight baseline days. On day 9, students were allowed to take their lucky charms to either their math or reading regular education class, and finally to both classes for the last six sessions of the study. The charms effectively increased reading and math performance for all students. One representative student increased his reading performance from 48 percent to 99 percent, and math performance from 32 percent to 92 percent. The authors note that "lucky charms" will only generalize already existing skills.

Duffy, G. G., Roehler, L. R., & Rackliffe, G. (1986). How teachers' instructional talk influences students' understanding of lesson content. *The Elementary School Journal, 87,* 3–18.

Analysis of two teachers' lessons indicated that the way in which the teachers communicated the content of the instruction determined how well students reported understanding the topic. The more effective teacher (1) concentrated more on helping students *understand* the goal of the lesson (for example, how to use context clues) than on teaching them the correct label (learning the word "context"); (2) showed students how to use the process to achieve the instructional goal rather than rigidly defining the discrete steps; and (3) described how the skill could be generalized to all reading activities, as opposed to describing it as an artificial shortcut, and utilizing examples drawn from real-life reading experiences. There were also differences in the way the more effective teacher structured the lesson, explained the process, encouraged students to activate their own knowledge base as a tool for understanding, and utilized student answers to build the lesson. Similar differences were found in another set of lessons taught by these two teachers as well as in the lessons of two other teachers. What teachers say during teaching and how they say it is clearly important to the instructional process. In addition, the way that identical teacher training experiences affect teachers differently needs to be further explored.

Fantuzzo, J. W., Polite, K., & Grayson, N. (1990). An evaluation of reciprocal peer tutoring across elementary school settings. *Journal of School Psychology, 28,* 309–323.

       Low socioeconomic status fourth and fifth graders with academic and behavior problems and arithmetic scores below the fiftieth percentile on the California Achievement Test were trained in reciprocal peer tutoring (RPT) techniques. Students took part in five-minute arithmetic drill sessions, completing worksheets and exchanging papers for correction. During the *teamwork only* condition, student dyads were trained and reinforced in goal setting, cooperative teamwork, and achieving team goals. They applied these team strategies to completion of a school improvement project. In the *teamwork-plus-group-contingency* phase, training extended to teaching a self-managed interdependent group contingency, in which the paired students set a team goal, discussed strategies for successful performance on the drills, prompted each other, and monitored, recorded, and rewarded their goal achievement. The RPT group contingency doubled the average baseline rates of correct math performance and significantly increased attendance while teamwork training alone had no systematic effect. Teaming students and rewarding cooperative behavior was not sufficient to enhance performance. RPT with peer-managed group contingencies was effective in producing behavior change.

Heron, T. E., & Catera, R. (1980). Teacher consultation: A functional approach. *School Psychology Review, 9,* 283–289.

       This article stresses the value of skillfully conducted consultation in devising and implementing behavior management strategies with the teacher in the classroom. Guidelines for the effective consultant include (1) emphasizing the joint contributions of the teacher and consultant while deemphasizing the consultant's role, leaving the decision to use or reject ideas to the teacher; (2) promoting later use of strategies without the consultant by having the teacher run the intervention; and (3) evaluating outcome in terms of usefulness and practicality. Three case studies illustrate the consultation process in action. Positive contingencies, the principal as a reinforcing agent, and a work-race game format were used to increase learning disabled students' completion of assignments. It is important that (1) the consultant and teacher agree on a plan and give it time to work, (2) the teacher play an active decision-making role, (3) strategies be selected from the various possibilities after appropriate consultation, and (4) teachers take the lead in operating the procedure in the class (which they will do if the outcome is worth the effort). The authors note that teachers in these case studies found the procedures nonintrusive. The last recommendation is that, for students being mainstreamed, strategies should be implemented in the special education setting prior to the students' regular education placement, with planning for generalization before the student is reintegrated.

House, J. D., & Wohlt, V. (1991). Effect of tutoring on voluntary school withdrawal of academically underprepared minority students. *Journal of School Psychology, 29,* 135–142.

Academically underprepared African-American, Latino, and Asian-American college freshmen volunteered to be tutored during their freshman year by upperclassmen and graduate students. Tutors were trained in study and test-taking skills, reducing math and text anxiety, and communication skills. For Latino and African-American students, a significantly higher percentage of tutored students (71.1 percent and 76.6 percent, respectively) than untutored students (54.8 percent and 68.3 percent) returned for their sophomore year. For Asian-Americans, the percentages of returnees were 82.5 percent of the tutored group and 81.3 percent of the untutored group, a nonsignificant difference. Peer tutoring is a cost-effective method of improving persistence of academically unprepared minority college students.

Idol-Maestas, L., Ritter, S., & Lloyd, S. (1983). A model for direct, data-based reading instruction. *Journal of Special Education Technology, 6,* 61–76.

This model of remedial reading instruction is designed to improve students' reading accuracy, reading rate, and reading comprehension. It includes curriculum-based assessment, direct instruction of the deficient skills, systematic ongoing observation of operationally defined reading behavior, repeated practice, and use of behavior management strategies. CBA is utilized instead of standardized testing to define more precisely the point in the teacher's curriculum at which instruction should begin. Instruction strategies focused on (1) formalized error correction, (2) measurement of progress through a timed reading sample, (3) comprehension questions that assess knowledge of story content and inferencing skills at advanced levels, (4) a charting system to self-monitor improvement in reading ability, (5) an instructional plan, (6) sound sheet to practice sound-symbol relationships derived from the reading, (7) sight word drills, (8) improving reading speed through behavioral contingencies, (9) prompts and self-timed repeated readings, (10) "skip and drill" technique, (11) backward chaining to improve comprehension, and (12) transfer of oral questions and answers to written form. Use of this model over a five-and-one-half-year period resulted in a two- to three-month gain in reading for students for every month of instruction, despite the student's type of disabling condition, with maintenance of gains over time. This improvement represents a rate two to three times higher than that achieved by traditional teaching and indicates that, no matter what the diagnostic label, there are reading problems common to all students.

Kapadia, E. S., & Fantuzzo, J. W. (1988). Effects of teacher- and self-administered procedures on the spelling performance of learning-handicapped children. *Journal of School Psychology, 26,* 49–58.

Four learning disabled students with behavior problems worked on independent spelling tasks daily for twenty minutes. An aide graded papers and awarded students a point for each correct answer on their spelling worksheets. They could exchange points for reinforcers displayed on a poster board. When training was begun, the aide guided the students, with focused questions, feedback, repetition, and verbal praise, to grade and reward themselves until they independently self-administered 90 percent of the steps in the process. Each child then self-administered the spelling assessment and reward without prompts. Results showed the superiority of the self-administered over the teacher-directed strategy in the students' achieving gains in spelling performance. The number of self-administered components seems related to the effectiveness of the procedure. In this case, five components (self-observation, self-recording, self-evaluation, and self-administration of both secondary and primary reinforcers) combined to create a powerful self-management intervention.

Kirby, K. C., Holborn, S. W., & Bushby, H. T. (1981). Word game bingo: A behavioral treatment package for improving textual responding to sight words. *Journal of Applied Behavior Analysis, 14,* 317–326.

Third-grade students played word game bingo each day to improve their sight word vocabulary. The adult drew a word card from a previously constructed set of cards, called out the word, and visually displayed the card for fifteen seconds (visual display was quickly faded over approximately four days). The children were instructed to find the word on their bingo cards and place a chip over it. Help from others seated next to them was encouraged. After each child had covered the word, the next word was prsented. The game continued until one child reached the preset criterion and called out "bingo." Play continued for forty-five minutes. Winning students received stars traded for reinforcers at the end of the week. The bingo game increased children's sight word recognition from baseline rates of 45 to 60 percent to more than 90 percent, with data for individual students generally consistent with overall rates. Posttreatment retention was highly stable. This group intervention is enjoyable, easily taught, and extremely time efficient as it can be applied to a small number of children or an entire class.

Ladouceur, R., & Armstrong, J. (1983). Evaluation of a behavioral program for the improvement of grades among high school students. *Journal of Counseling Psychology, 30,* 100–103.

At-risk high school students were exposed to a ten-session behavioral treatment regimen that included self-monitoring of study time; study skill training in reading, memory, scheduling time, note-taking, and exam preparation; relaxation training and desensitization; and assertiveness training for the classroom. Training techniques utilized modeling, feedback, rehearsal, and coaching. Results indicated that the treatment significantly improved students' math and French grades and grade point average over the school year.

Maher, C. A. (1984). Handicapped adolescents as cross-aged tutors: Program description and evaluation. *Exceptional Children, 51,* 56–63.

Maher describes a cross-age tutoring program in which designated emotionally disturbed adolescents tutored elementary educable mentally retarded youngsters. The program had four components: (1) cross-age tutor training in which tutors were provided information, specific skill training, and a positive attitudinal orientation toward the student to be tutored and the program; (2) planning for tutoring, including discussion of subject content, teaching methods, and materials; (3) twice weekly thirty-minute tutoring sessions in arithmetic, reading, and language arts; (4) tutor support conferences in which tutors received feedback on their tutoring, discussed positive and negative experiences related to the tutoring, and listened to suggestions from the trainer.

After planning, tutoring, and support conferences were implemented, the tutors' performance as students in their own classes improved. Their rates of assignment completion rose from a baseline mean of 61.7 percent to 94.7 percent during tutoring, with a follow-up completion rate of 93.1 percent; performance on tests went from 56.4 percent at baseline to 88.3 percent during tutoring and 85.1 percent during follow-up. Disciplinary referral means were 5.5 at baseline, 1.6 during tutoring, and 1.3 during follow-up. Assignment completion for those tutored was 66.1 percent to 93.8 percent in tutoring and 90.2 percent at follow-up. Correct test items for this group rose from 65.2 percent at baseline to 88.3 percent and 82.1 percent during tutoring and follow-up. The program was enthusiastically supported by the school administration; fourteen of the sixteen tutors enjoyed participating, and teachers of the educable mentally retarded felt it was a rewarding experience for their students.

Mevarech, Z. R., & Rich, Y. (1985). Effects of computer-assisted mathematics instruction on disadvantaged pupils' cognitive and affective development. *Journal of Educational Research, 79,* 5–10.

In traditional teacher-centered mathematics instruction, teaching mastery of skills seems incompatible with maximizing personal development. However, computer-assisted instruction (CAI) may relieve some of the pressures associated with mathematics drill and practice and provide some opportunity for teachers to focus on the affective growth of their students. In this study, academically disadvantaged elementary school students in grades 3, 4, and 5 were taught math either with traditional instructional methods or with a traditional approach augmented by a computer-assisted instructional package known as TOAM. (TOAM is the Hebrew acronym for computer-assisted testing and practice.) TOAM diagnosed students' math skills in fourteen areas, then provided a customized instructional sequence of drill and practice using computer-generated problems in the appropriate skill domains. This program resulted in significantly higher arithmetic achievement test scores for the students than did traditional instruction. Similarly, measures of math, self-concept, and perceived satisfaction with school, school work, and teachers all favored the computer-instructed group. No gender differences were found. Computer-assisted instruction can simultaneously affect cognitive and affective components of school life in a positive direction.

Pressley, M., Johnson, C. J., Symons, S., McGoldrick, J. A., & Kurita, J. A. (1989). Strategies that improve children's memory and comprehension of text. *The Elementary School Journal, 90,* 3–29.
    Six empirically validated strategies to improve reading comprehension and memory for students in grades 3 through 8 are recommended for use by the classroom teacher.

    1. *Summarization* — summaries can be as small as single sentences and are typically created through a series of rules that emphasize deleting trivial or redundant information, integrating items and events with superordinate terms, creating topic sentences, and identifying main ideas.

    2. *Mental Imagery* — representational images are direct representations of the narrative content, while mnemonic images utilize associative key words to aid understanding and recall.

    3. *Story-Grammar Training* — this technique teaches students the structure and sequence of events underlying most story lines, such as identification of main characters, location and time of the story, actions of the important players, ending of the stories, and feelings of the main characters.

    4. *Question Generation* — students are taught to construct integrative questions regarding the major ideas of the reading; answers to the questions transmit a great deal of meaningful information. Teacher feedback regarding the relevance of the questions is an important component of training.

    5. *Question-Answering Strategies* — answering questions following the reading of a passage enhances learning only if the reader reviews and rehearses appropriate information after answering a question incorrectly. A look-back strategy focuses the reader on relevant parts of the text and helps him or her extract and integrate important information. Training students to distinguish different types of questions (literal, inferential, self-knowledge based) aids their comprehension.

    6. *Prior Knowledge Activation* — a more complex strategy that capitalizes on information already in the student's knowledge base to assist his or her comprehension and memory.

    The authors note that each of these strategies is useful at different points in the reading process. Some are applicable before reading (prior knowledge activation), some during reading (story-grammar summarization, question generalization, imagery), and some after reading (question answering).

Among them, they cover the entire reading act. Finally, strategy training is not remedial in nature but is designed to train effective comprehension in all readers. It should be taught slowly, in small doses, thoroughly, and in the context of content areas. The article provides an outline of the teaching components.

Shapiro, E. S. (1987). Academic problems. In M. Hersen & V. D. Von Hasselt (Eds.), *Behavior therapy with children and adolescents: A clinical approach* (pp. 362–384). New York: Wiley.

This chapter begins with a general discussion of issues related to academic performance. The amount of material students actually learned and amount of time they spent engaged in academic activities are two critical factors influencing their performance. Also influential are behavioral interventions and sequenced, clearly defined instructional strategies that have been found to increase students' academic engaged time and their opportunities to respond in ways intended by the instructional materials. Procedures such as peer tutoring, response-contingent performance feedback, modeling, self-management of performance, and contracting are cited as strategies to enhance academic responding, all of which seem to have in common a contingent reinforcement component. The author describes other techniques that have been applied to improve student performance in specific content areas. For example, previewing and contingent reinforcement are two of many strategies used to improve reading. However, generalization of skills from instructional texts to content areas such as social studies or science is an important yet relatively untouched area of investigation. In math, self-instructional training and strategy training, among other approaches, have been applied successfully but here also generalization of skills is a problem. For spelling, programs combining prompting, modeling, feedback, and rehearsal have shown promise. Team games, self-managed correction, and positive practice overcorrection have been used with success. Writing strategies have used self-management packages with modeling, strategy training, practice, and feedback in addition to self-instruction and self-managed goal setting. A case study illustrates the use of contingent reinforcement to improve performance on measures of oral reading.

Skinner, C. H., Beatty, K. L., Turco, T. L., & Rasavage, C. (1989). Cover, copy, and compare: A method for increasing multiplication performance. *School Psychology Review, 18,* 412–420.

Four behavior-disordered students (two fourth graders and two tenth graders) practiced the cover, copy, and compare (CCC) technique to increase their proficiency in multiplying one digit by one digit problems. CCC has five steps: (1) looking at the solved problem, (2) covering it with an index card, (3) writing the problem and solution, (4) uncovering the problem with solution, (5) comparing responses. Students completed the CCC procedure and were assessed the following day before the next CCC session. All three students who completed the study improved their rate of correct problem solving, and two of the three maintained the effects over follow-up and maintenance periods. Faster responding did not decrease their accuracy. CCC is a cost-efficient, self-directed strategy that provides students much opportunity to respond to the stimuli and immediate feedback. These two factors are closely associated with effective learning.

Stevenson, H. C., & Fantuzzo, J. W. (1986). The generality and social validity of a competency-based self-control training intervention for underachieving students. *Journal of Applied Behavior Analysis, 19,* 269–276.

Fifth-grade African-American students with poor math performance and low socioeconomic status took part in a self-control training procedure. Students were paired with a control subject, worked on math worksheets in school and at home, and were trained in a self-control procedure involving goal setting, choosing a reinforcement, self-recording math scores, self-evaluating, and self-rewarding. Self-control training increased arithmetic accuracy for the trained students with effects generalizing to the untreated partner. In most cases, both treated and control subjects improved their math performance to a level equal to or above the mean performance of their classmates. Teachers noted the intervention as very helpful and easy to use.

Williamson, P. A., & Silvern, S. B. (1986). Eliciting creative dramatic play. *Childhood Education, 63,* 2–5.
Williamson, P. A., & Silvern, S. B. (1990). The effects of play training on the story comprehension of upper primary children. *Journal of Research in Childhood Education, 4,* 130–134.

In the first article, second graders planned and acted out a familiar story to facilitate recall, language comprehension, and story comprehension. Research yields the following recommendations for the teacher who involves the class in this form of creative dramatics (also known as thematic fantasy play or TFP): (1) Start small, perhaps with the students most able to handle this task. (2) Make a long-term commitment to the technique rather than using it as a gimmick. Incorporate it gradually into classroom activity. (3) Start with familiar stories so the students feel comfortable and experience a successful first effort. (4) Be directive at first, gradually relaxing the teacher-directed structure. Train students in dramatic reenactments through reviewing the characters and events to be dramatized, choosing parts, assembling props, and narrating while the students act out the story. (5) Encourage adaptations by the children, for example, an added character, once they have mastered the process. (6) Create a casual atmosphere in which students can plan and be flexible, perform for classmates, and return to other activities.

In the second article, the same authors cite evidence to show that this technique is useful for older primary children whose level of cognitive development still requires them to engage in such concrete reenactment. This activity assists them in forming the cognitive schemes needed for effective story comprehension. The authors recommend use of TFP for the upper primary student with low comprehension skills and suggest establishing a "dramatic play center" in higher primary grade classrooms.

Wilson, N. S. (1986). Counselor interventions with low-achieving and under-achieving elementary, middle, and high school students: A review of the literature. *Journal of Counseling and Development, 64,* 628–634.

Counseling interventions conducted with low-achieving and under-achieving students K–12, and published between 1960 and 1983, were reviewed for their effects on students' grade point averages. In addition to the above attributes, criteria for selection of articles included presence of a control group in the studies and statistical analyses of data. The author concludes that the general quality of research in this area is poor. However, the existing evidence suggests that group counseling may be more effective than individual counseling; that structured, directive, and behaviorally oriented interventions may be more effective than person-centered approaches; that longer treatments (twelve or more weeks) fare better than shorter ones; that voluntary programs are more successful than nonvoluntary procedures; that counseling with study skills training is more productive than counseling alone; and that parental involvement strengthens treatment effectiveness. The trend over the past twenty-five years has been toward fewer studies, more structured behavioral approaches, and more complex methodologies.

Cognitive Competence: Communication Development

The 5 to 10 percent of preschoolers with communication deficiencies will likely carry these problems into their school years and are at increased risk for learning, behavior, and emotional difficulties. Many of the articles presented in this section acknowledge that "catch-up" interventions are not realistic and reflect two apparent trends in the literature on speech/language interventions. First, they emphasize the communicative intent and purpose of language rather than its structure, with a corresponding shift away from teaching discrete components to a focus on helping students use language to convey needs and influence the environment. Second, to emphasize that language is a part of virtually all experience, including academic performance, they advocate classroom-based, as opposed to pull-out, models of service delivery to provide the help in the location where it is used naturally. In *Therapies for School Behavior Problems,* this section was entitled "Speech Disorders." The change to "Communication Development" reflects the shift in the field to a more functional view of language acquisition.

Teaching Language-Based Learning Strategies
to Language Learning Disabled Students

AUTHORS: Judith Buttrill, Judy Niizawa, Carole Biemer, Candace Takahashi, and Stella Hearn

PRECIS: Meeting the needs of language-impaired, learning disabled students through strategy training, a classroom-based alternative to traditional pull-out service

INTRODUCTION: Students with receptive and expressive language disabilities often do not outgrow their disorder when they reach adolescence. Thus, they need a model of service that supports and accommodates them as they cope with the language demands of the secondary-level curriculum. A pull-out approach is not responsive to their needs for several reasons: first, they resent having to leave their regular education class to receive service; second, they miss the work presented while they are absent; third, they receive no credit for pull-out language assistance; fourth, scheduling them into workable groups is difficult; and fifth, they require more help than a secondary-level pull-out service can provide. This article describes a classroom model that focuses on teaching language-based learning strategies to enhance academic performance in mainstream classes. Curriculum for this program is derived from an ecological assessment that examines the setting demands as well as the learning styles and disabilities of the language learning disabled (LLD) student.

ASSESSMENT AND CURRICULUM: Evaluation of the secondary school setting reveals a variety of specific performance expectations of all students. These include the ability to work independently, organizational competence, listening skills, note-taking skills, reading and comprehension facility, critical thinking skills, social and other pragmatic skills, writing ability, and test-taking ability. Assessment of LLD students reveals deficits in the communicative skills they need to meet the demands of secondary school. Impairments in students' receptive and expressive language interfere with their textbook and lecture comprehension, test performance, unassisted assignment completion, effective use of learning strategies, adherence to class rules, and facility in class discussions, among other competencies. Thus, the curriculum for the classroom program discussed below emphasizes mastery of learning strategies intended to help LLD students meet the demands of the school setting. Students learn to choose the best strategy for a given task, monitor each step in the application of the strategy, and assess its effect after use.

CLASSROOM STRATEGY TRAINING MODEL: Referral, assessment, and identification of students who may benefit from this language/study skills class are accomplished according to established procedures. The students' individualized education plan (IEP) goals and objectives facilitate their mastery of subject area content by focusing on both remediation of specific skill deficits and mastery of learning strategies that enhance receptive/expressive language processing. The class meets daily, contains eight to ten students, offers credit, and gives grades like any other subject. The speech/language specialist acts as both class teacher and resource person; he or she teaches students how to use the learning strategies to improve their listening, speaking, writing, and thinking skills. The teacher also consults with mainstream staff, parents, and students to help make the accommodations needed to enhance the students' academic success. Counseling is also provided to help students plan their post–high school direction.

STRATEGIES: The following strategies taught in the special class are designed to help students master the language skills they need for high school level performance:

1. Academic organization—to manage the differing work and time demands of each class, students learn to break down assignments, plan the time for each step, organize subject sections in their binders, write down assignments on an assignment sheet, develop a study schedule, analyze time spent in various academic and social activities, create an appropriate study space at home, and monitor their study habits. A consistent form of classroom discipline is also established by the teacher.

2. Study skills—students are taught text analysis to improve their comprehension of material, active study and memory strategies, note-taking techniques, test-taking strategies (for example, making appropriate preparation, learning test terms, asking the teacher about the type of test, answering easier questions first, and proofreading), use of reference skills to facilitate access to information and library resources that help them create research papers and written reports. Instruction in paraphrasing skills prepares them for oral discussions as well as written assignments.

3. Critical thinking—verbal learning cannot take place unless students have the ability to process, interpret, and apply factual knowledge for problem solving. LLD students are not able to use language to think through issues and develop and express conclusions. This program provides exercises and activities to teach students how to think and how to monitor their thinking. They practice general thinking strategies, such as conceptualizing, comparing, hypothesizing, and explaining. Students learn to problem solve by analyzing problem situations, developing the steps to a decision, and evaluating the outcome. Finally, they are introduced to higher-level thinking skills, such as inductive reasoning, analogies, and abstract relationships.

4. Listening—students are trained to distinguish and attend to important information. In *prelistening,* students learn to "tune in" while "tuning

out" distracting stimuli. For *literal listening,* students review methods to enhance their understanding of orally presented material, such as recognizing cues to important information given by the lecturer, identifying main ideas, improving semantic-syntactic understanding, and listening for details and "wh" information. *Evaluative listening* trains the student to listen critically and to judge information, for example, to separate fact from opinion, recognize propaganda, or discern incorrect information.

5. Oral language production — students improve their oral expression by practicing discussion skills in small groups; the teacher facilitates and prompts such verbal skills as paraphrasing, questioning, responding, enumerating, comparing, and analyzing. Students may interact around tasks that require giving oral directions, brainstorming, committee involvement, and games; around topics that are presented orally to group members; or around personal events that may arise during these experiences.

6. Written language — LLD students may avoid writing because of the difficulties they have with this process. Students are first motivated in small group discussions to think about exciting, controversial topics. Then their remediational skill development focuses on such areas as idea and content organization, development of sentence structure, use of compound sentences, and proofing.

7. Pragmatics — three areas are stressed: (1) adapting to the language demands, subject matter, and general context of the interaction, and using language to express relevant related ideas at the appropriate time to the appropriate person; (2) interpreting the meaning of conversation — that is, sarcasm, joking, opinion versus fact, or other nuances; (3) beginning and continuing a conversation, taking turns, questioning, returning discussion, and changing a topic. Stating rules for discourse and role-playing help students practice pragmatic skills, although many LLD students are already proficient and therefore socially successful. Others have less interpersonal contact because their disability causes them to misperceive the verbal content of social interaction.

COMMENTARY: The daily scheduling of the language/study skills class provides a great deal of support to language-impaired students without conflicting with other subject area classes. Offering the class for credit emphasizes the value of the program and provides an inducement for students. While the focus for middle school youngsters is on specific learning strategies, high school students work on applying these techniques to their content area subjects. As students move into the upper middle school grades and into high school, they seem less amenable to leaving class for speech/ language therapy sessions. While they tend to see the value of resource programs that more directly support subject mastery, they often have a difficult time appreciating the connection between speech/language therapy and success in the classroom. The model presented here makes language development more relevant to their academic success by teaching them language-based strategies and helping them apply these techniques directly to their studies. To strengthen this sense of relevance, perhaps a closer working relationship between the resource teacher, the speech/language therapist, the classroom teacher, and the school psychologist might be of greatest benefit to the LLD youngster. Such an alliance exists in program form at the elementary school in the district in which this writer works as a school psychologist. Known as the K/1 PASS Program (Program of Assisted Studies and Support), this special education program features a structure combining regular and special classes that provides academic and language development experiences to kindergartners and first graders with learning and language disabilities. The special education teacher, regular education teacher, and speech/language therapist work as a team to infuse the curriculum with language development activities and experiences, while students attend regular academic classes for the majority of the day. Although no formal analysis of the program's effectiveness has yet been conducted, year-end testing and anecdotal reports by teachers and parents indicate noticeable progress by the participating students. Such models provide continuing service to students without segregating them from mainstream school experiences.

SOURCE: Buttrill, J., Niizawa, J., Biemer, C., Takahashi, C., & Hearn, S. (1989). Serving the language learning disabled adolescent: A strategies-based model. *Language, Speech, and Hearing Services in Schools, 20,* 185–204.

A Behavioral Treatment Package for Stuttering

AUTHORS: Chantal Caron and Robert Ladouceur

PRECIS: A multicomponent strategy involving the parent as co-therapist to reduce stuttering

INTRODUCTION: Stuttering has been treated with both direct and indirect methods. Direct methods have included operant approaches and fluency training; counseling with parents or instructing parents to speak to their child slowly, clearly, and in simple language are examples of indirect techniques. Concern about raising the child's awareness of stuttering and thus making him or her afraid of speaking have prompted development of indirect methods. Neither strategy has proven more effective than the other in reducing dysfluency; this study utilized both to assess their combined influence.

METHOD: Subjects were four stutterers ages six to nine with a 5 percent minimum percentage of stuttered syllables. Stuttering was defined as hesitations, prolongations, repetitions, and blocking. During baseline, background information was obtained. For treatment, three separate strategies were employed as a way of interrupting the automatic quality of stuttering. First, an awareness training procedure was implemented to make students aware of their stuttering for 50 percent of their dysfluent episodes (most stutterers are aware of only 28 percent of their stuttering episodes on average). Stuttering was defined for parent and child followed by modeled examples and visual display of different types of stuttering episodes. Child and parent signaled each time an instance of stuttering was presented. The therapist also suggested providing verbal feedback to the child when stuttering occurred and use of audio recordings to recognize stuttering. The parents received information about the causes of stuttering, its prevalence, and similar demographics; they also learned positive communication techniques to use with the child (for example, speaking slowly, giving the child time to finish talking, maintaining eye contact, not finishing words for the child, avoiding difficult questions). These techniques were reviewed throughout the study, with the therapist providing corrective feedback.

In a second treatment strategy, regulated breathing, the therapist taught the child to stop speaking when he or she began to stutter and to take a deep breath. The child was further instructed to say words while exhaling. In gentle contact, a third technique, the stutterer learned to tense and relax his or her facial muscles to reduce tension during speech. Relaxed speech was extended from single to multisyllable words, to short then complex sentences, with a criterion of fewer than 3 percent stuttered syllables required for movement to the next step. Parents learned these strategies and supervised fifteen-minute daily practice sessions with their child. Graphed visual feedback on progress was shown to the child at each treatment session. Intervention ended when the rate of stuttered syllables dropped to 3 percent.

RESULTS: Dramatic decreases in stuttering were obtained for three of the four youngsters in only twelve to twenty-four sessions. The other child showed less striking improvement. Parents also developed more positive communication styles toward their children, confirmed by therapist report. Treatment effects were maintained at a six-month follow-up.

COMMENTARY: This multicomponent strategy effectively reduced a resistant behavior problem in a relatively short time period. The authors consider parental involvement to be a significant factor, allowing treatment to continue away from the sessions. In addition, gentle contact and regulated breathing are considered powerful modifiers of stuttering. In other areas as well, parents are becoming more active participants in procedures to help their children. It is important, however, for the practitioner to assess the parents' ability to follow instructions, their willingness to follow through with consistency, and their emotional stability to avoid punitive reactions to slow progress or resistance by the child. Disturbed, noncompliant, or simply impatient parents can not only cancel out the beneficial effects of an intervention but can also do much psychological harm to a child who may be looking to them for support.

SOURCE: Caron, C., & Ladouceur, R. (1989). Multidimensional behavioral treatment for child stutterers. *Behavior Modification, 13,* 206–215.

Home Tutoring by Mothers to Improve Children's Language Skills

AUTHORS: Janet W. Wedel and Susan A. Fowler

PRECIS: Mothers read to their language-impaired children at home to improve sight word and letter recognition skills

INTRODUCTION: When parents tutor their children at home, they are providing many extra hours of instruction over the course of the school year and giving the child increased opportunities to respond to academically related materials. Since active responding by children to such academic concepts has been strongly linked to their mastery of skills, home tutoring has the potential to be a powerful supplement to their school experience. Reading to children as a home tutoring activity has been shown to improve their language, vocabulary, and fund of information; it also circumvents problems of finding suitable materials or selecting appropriate tutoring experiences within the limited time available to working or single parents. Parents often read to their children anyway, and in this study, story reading was used by parents who had never tutored at home to teach letter and word identification skills to their language-delayed children.

METHOD: Four mother-child pairs took part in the study; the children ranged in age from four years, one month, to six years, eight months. The children were mildly to moderately language impaired with one student learning English as a second language. Students were read a total of four stories at home by their mothers four evenings a week. The readings were tape recorded and brought to the teacher each week; at this time she gave the parents new storybooks. Parents also received a training list of Dolch sight words or letters that the student was not able to identify on pretesting.

During a one- to three-week baseline period, parents read stories and asked the children general questions at home while the teacher tested them on a weekly basis for letter and sight word recognition. For the intervention, each child received a set of training items consisting of letters and sight words. The teacher gave the parents a sheet with letters or sight words to teach the children. After each page of reading, the parent was instructed to point out one training letter or word for the child to identify. Correct answers were validated and praised ("Yes, that's a C."). Incorrect answers were correctly labeled and rehearsed. During the first treatment week, the teacher met with the parent to review and model the tutoring method. After that, they met to share results of the weekly class testing and for the teacher to give the parent feedback based on review of the tapes. Teachers then answered any questions from the parent. Students continued to be tested on the training items each week by the teacher. If the child labeled every item correctly, the teacher gave the parent a new set of training items for the next week.

RESULTS: Although results for some of the students were more rapid and dramatic than for others, all students learned their letters and words to 100 percent criterion, except one who reached a 50 percent and 75 percent level of accuracy on two sets. Interestingly, the mother who spent the greatest amount of time in tutoring each day (an average of twenty minutes) obtained the best outcome; the parent who tutored the least and presented the smallest number of learning trials achieved the least stable results. Results of the Peabody Picture Vocabulary Test suggested but did not establish the beneficial effect of this procedure on the children's receptive vocabulary.

COMMENTARY: This home tutoring technique clearly helped the language-impaired and English as a second language (ESL) youngsters learn sight words and letters, and did so in a manner potentially beneficial to the parent-child relationship. Given the number of word or letter trials presented (over 1,300 for one student), the students' opportunities to respond to instructional materials were also greatly enhanced, a factor empirically linked to improved academic mastery. However, while the authors rightly point out that tutoring is not a substitute for school instruction, it is an extension of the school experience and can be quite reinforcing for parent and child. In fact, the article suggests that rewarding the parents for improvement in their child's performance might further enhance the gains recorded. Techniques that actively involve parents offer many advantages, among which are extension of the strategy to a new setting, increased interest by parents in their child's school performance and behavior, and a potentially more cooperative relationship between home and school.

SOURCE: Wedel, J. W., & Fowler, S. A. (1984). "Read me a story, Mom": A home-tutoring program to teach prereading skills to language-delayed children. *Behavior Modification, 8,* 245–266.

A Free Token/Response Cost Intervention for Stuttering

AUTHORS: Spencer J. Salend and Marilyn J. Andress

PRECIS: Use of a free token/response cost strategy to reduce stuttering in an elementary school student

INTRODUCTION: Response cost is one of a variety of behavioral techniques used to decrease stuttering in adolescents, college students, and adults. These two studies examined the effectiveness of a modified free token/response cost system in reducing an elementary student's dysfluencies during reading and storytelling. Stuttering was defined as repetition or prolongation of sounds, syllables, words, and phrases.

METHOD: A twelve-year-old learning disabled boy receiving twice weekly speech therapy for stuttering was the subject. Two and one-half years of treatment had produced almost no change. During the baseline of each study, the frequency of stuttering in the therapy sessions was counted for seven days. For the eleven-day intervention, the student received eleven tokens (small slips of construction paper). The therapist removed one slip each time the student stuttered during reading (study I), or storytelling (study II). If slips remained at the end of therapy, he earned a mutually determined reward, such as a positive note home, a pen, or other items. Eleven tokens were chosen as representing the number of times per minute the average person stutters (0.5) times the number of minutes per session (20), plus one to allow for an average stuttering rate without loss of the reward. After a five-day return to baseline, the intervention was repeated for nine days in study I and eight days in study II.

RESULTS: For both studies, the response cost procedure resulted in a considerable decrease in the student's stuttering. In the baseline period, the student averaged 1.41 stuttering episodes per minute while reading. By the second intervention, this number dropped to a mean of 0.21. For storytelling, the baseline mean of 1.49 dysfluencies per minute dropped to a mean of 0.29 during the second intervention.

COMMENTARY: In these studies, the elementary student earned a reward by limiting his stuttering to less than a preset frequency. This free token/response cost procedure differs from other response cost strategies in which each episode of the unwanted behavior results in a loss of reward. Perhaps the free token technique would be consistently more successful with elementary age youngsters because they experience less frustration with free tokens than with the loss of previously earned tokens, as happens in the more traditional response cost procedure. Such a comparison would require further research. As the authors suggest, the free token system facilitates a positive rapport between the therapist and the child through the giving of noncontingent tokens and the eventual reward. This strategy is easy to use in a therapy session and is certainly cost effective.

SOURCE: Salend, S. J., & Andress, M. J. (1984). Decreasing stuttering in an elementary-level student. *Language, Speech, and Hearing Services in Schools, 15,* 16–21.

Delay as a Technique to Increase Language Production

AUTHORS: James W. Halle, Donald M. Baer, and Joseph E. Spradlin

PRECIS: Teaching teachers to delay responses as a way of stimulating spontaneous language in language-impaired developmentally delayed children

INTRODUCTION: Adults often inhibit children's use of language by responding to the child before he or she makes a request or expresses a need. Delay is a strategy designed to induce handicapped students to use language by withholding a response or other help until the child verbalizes the request. Delay is an easy procedure to implement and was used in this series of two studies to encourage developmentally delayed language-impaired youngsters to initiate language.

METHOD: In the first study, subjects were six children aged three to five years old. During two months of initial observation, free play, snack time, and lunchtime were selected as activities during which teachers could provide language opportunities through delay. For example, during play an opportunity to delay occurred as the teacher assisted the children with gross motor toys. A snack time delay situation arose as the teacher approached the children to pour juice or help zipper and button coats for outdoor recess. Finally, the lunchtime delay opportunity came as the teacher approached the children with a tray of food. Under typical free-play conditions (and during baseline), the teacher would help the children with toys without vocalizing. During the delay condition, the teacher was trained to approach to help but to delay her assistance until the children requested her aid. At snack time, the teacher normally poured juice without waiting for a request, or verbally requested the children to tell her what they wanted. Under delay, the teacher made no move to pour until the children verbally initiated the request for juice. Similarly, during delay, the teacher waited for a verbal request before helping the children zip up or button their coats. At lunch, the children had to initiate a verbal request for lunch during the delay condition before they were served.

When the teacher acted on a delay opportunity, she was instructed to (1) delay for five seconds or until the child initiated a vocal request, (2) not vocalize during the five seconds, (3) situate herself within three feet of the child, (4) orient her head toward the child, and (5) have the child's head oriented toward her enough to assume that the child was aware of her delaying action. The teacher could also engage in a visual prompt, maintain an expectant look, orient her body to the child, and/or kneel down at the child's eye level. The child's verbalization had to occur within the five-second delay, be uttered without a verbal prompt from the teacher, and have relevance to the delay situation.

DELAY I: After baseline in which no delays occurred, the teachers were told about the play, snack, and lunch delay opportunities and learned the five-second delay technique to use during these times. Teachers could model a verbal request for the children if they did not initiate one during the delay, but the child had to repeat the vocalization before the request could be honored. During baseline, the percentage of teacher delays and student initiations ranged between 5 and 10 percent. On the first day of the intervention, teacher delays rose to a range of 67 to 100 percent while student initiations increased to 44 to 83 percent. A check for continued use of the strategy over ten weeks following the study showed teacher use of delays averaging 60 percent, with student initiations closely paralleling these percentages early in the maintenance period.

DELAY II: The second study duplicated the first but focused on generalization and maintenance of delay effects. The subjects were six developmentally delayed children with language impairments; they were five years, eleven months, to nine years in age. Academic time, snack time, and show-and-tell time were events selected for their delay opportunities. Teachers were trained on eight of twenty delay opportunities, were told that other such opportunities existed, and that they should use the five-second delay whenever appropriate. Observers recorded delays and child vocal initiations on all twenty events to chart generalization to untrained situations. Maintenance was evaluated at one-month, two-and-a-half month, and five-month intervals. As in study I, use of delays and child vocal initiations increased immediately when teachers were instructed to begin using the five-second strategy. Teacher delays rose to a group mean of 93 percent while child initiations increased to a mean of 73 percent (baseline means were 18 percent). Use of delay during generalization to untrained opportunities rose from a 7 percent baseline mean to 56.5 percent during the intervention. Over five months a gradual reduction in use of delay was recorded, beginning with a dramatic decline during the first month.

COMMENTARY: Teachers easily learned and implemented the delay technique and were able to integrate it smoothly into their class routines. They generalized the use of the technique to other delay opportunities, then gradually reduced their use of delay over five months after an initially large reduction during the first month. Final maintenance use rates remained well above baseline rates. The delay strategy can be taught to any caregiver interacting with retarded individuals under naturally occurring conditions to stimulate use of language. It can also be used to determine whether language skills learned in structured sessions are being applied in the "real world." Teaching children to use spontaneous language encourages them to be active participants in verbal exchanges rather than remaining dependent on the words of others to provide them cues to express their needs.

SOURCE: Halle, J. W., Baer, D. M., & Spradlin, J. E. (1981). Teachers generalized use of delay as a stimulus control procedure to increase language use in handicapped children. *Journal of Applied Behavior Analysis, 14,* 389–409.

Language Therapy in a Naturalistic Setting

AUTHORS: Janet A. Norris and Paul R. Hoffman

PRECIS: Naturally occurring activities and events are used to stimulate the emergence of more effective language

INTRODUCTION: Language has a function as well as a structure. Its content and manner of use influences the behavior of others as readily as its form. This basic principle guides the whole language approach to communication development. Learning language means learning to organize and interpret the important components of one's physical and social surroundings, learning to communicate to achieve desired outcomes, and learning to expand one's language skills to express a developing understanding of the world. Naturalistic therapy utilizes a whole language philosophy by guiding the child's communicative development within noncontrived activities and social situations. The child learns to use increasingly complex language to bring meaning to an ever-widening experiential base and to exert some control over these events. The child also learns the value of language through the effect it has on others. This approach is contrasted with traditional language therapy in which students practice individual skills repetitiously in an artificial setting, without developing a simultaneous understanding of their function, value, and contextual meaning.

INTERVENTION: The naturalistic therapy model comprises three steps:

1. The therapist structures developmentally appropriate play activities for the child. These may range from the most basic sensorimotor explorations to complex language-infused inference-oriented novel events. As the

child plays, the therapist maintains and expands the experience by helping the child use the play materials in new and more refined ways, with accompanying language that adds further new meaning to the events. For example, if a child rocks a baby doll then abandons it, the therapist may talk about the doll's messy hair, how it may need to be brushed, how pretty it looks when brushed, and in this way lead the child into hair brushing as a new, more complex experience with the doll. As this occurs, the therapist encourages the child to expand communications around the act of hair brushing, such as discussing how well the doll looks with brushed hair or suggesting to someone else that their hair be brushed. The course of the language intervention is thus directed by the child's behavior and level of interaction within the naturally occurring activity rather than with a lesson plan predetermined by the adult. The language needed to interpret or guide these events will increase in complexity as the activities become more complex; as other children take part; as behaviors take on symbolic meanings (the doll's smile symbolizing happiness); and as motives, intentions, temporality, and perspective taking become relevant. The therapist must continue to integrate these diverse elements into the structure of the activity while maintaining its thematic focus and organization.

2. Having organized an environment conducive to communication, the therapist uses the ongoing events and interactions to stimulate more mature language. The child initiates a statement, comment, request or gesture, or other language-related behavior during the naturally occurring activity; the therapist helps the child clarify, expand, or interpret this behavior to make the communication more effective. This *scaffolding* process helps the child better understand the purpose of language and provides a wider range of alternatives for expressing new ideas. Returning to the doll example, the therapist may model talking to the doll while brushing her hair, expand the child's comment into a more complete sentence, or talk to the doll with the child. Various scaffolding techniques to help expand the child's communications include starting a sentence and pausing to have the child fill in blanks (Cloze technique); using gestures, pointing, and other nonverbal cues; use of relational terms such as "but" or "next" to cue the child to add to what he or she has said; using preparatory sets that cue the child about the appropriate language or concept needed in the situation (for example, the need to *ask*, not just *take*); using "wh" and comprehension questions requiring a summary of the events; giving the child choices; providing initial parts of a word the child must then complete.

3. The therapist provides feedback to the child on the effectiveness or ineffectiveness of the communication. Effectiveness means whether the environment responds to the intent of the message. The therapist provides positive consequences that demonstrate the effectiveness of the utterance through validating the child's comment, repeating it with more complex language (expansion), altering its content and context slightly (expatiation),

or adding a new idea to it to stimulate new play (extension). Techniques that provide these kinds of positive feedback include acknowledging the accuracy of the child's statement, using nonverbal reactions to show agreement or surprise, verbatim restating, rewording the child's comment to show other ways of stating it, summarizing the events leading to the child's words, modeling the child's dialogue through self-talk or parallel talk, responding directly to the child's request, stating feelings relating to the activity, asking questions to stimulate the child to add new information to the event, and projecting to future actions. When the child uses ineffective language the therapist must make a *communicative repair,* which provides the child with information needed to revise the message so that it achieves its purpose. The therapist supplies the information through such strategies as having the child repeat the message under more favorable conditions (such as waiting for the receiver's attention), informing the child what is inaccurate about the comment, asking for clarification, expressing doubt about the comment through the tone of the feedback, requesting more information, correcting speech patterns, reinterpreting comments for greater relevance to the activity, and helping the child integrate events into an overriding concept. Repair helps the child refine language productions to make them more relevant and influential on the setting. The child is required to repair the utterance before the play continues.

This three-step process is designed to increase the child's level of play and social interaction, and the language that goes with it. Goals and objectives are phrased to emphasize the sequential development of more appropriate complex language within the context of the play experiences. The therapist organizes the experiences, then helps shape and refine the child's emerging communications.

COMMENTARY: This naturalistic whole language approach to language intervention fits well with the trend toward providing therapy within the classroom rather than in the therapist's office. The therapist can use the naturally occurring events, whether focused on play or academic assignments, to encourage the production of more sophisticated language using the strategies outlined. The therapist's job is not to teach language but to structure the environment, stimulate communication, and supply feedback in order to help the child accomplish the purpose of language. It is strongly recommended that the reader consult the article for further clarification.

SOURCE: Norris, J. A., & Hoffman, P. R. (1990). Language intervention within naturalistic environments. *Language, Speech, and Hearing Services in Schools, 21,* 72–84.

Additional Readings

DiLorenzo, T. M., & Matson, J. L. (1987). Stuttering. In M. Hersen & V. B. Van Hasselt (Eds.), *Behavior therapy with children and adolescents: A clinical approach* (pp. 263–277). New York: Wiley.

In the American Psychiatric Association's *Diagnostic and Statistical Manual* (3rd ed.) (DSM-III) stuttering is characterized by repetitions or prolongations of sounds, symbols, or words, hesitations and pauses that result in dysfluent speech, and an increase in stuttering severity when stress accompanies the need to communicate. Males stutter more than females, and 80 percent of stutterers spontaneously remit by late adolescence. Poor parenting skills are associated with stuttering, which rarely begins after a child is age nine. Behavioral assessment of stuttering reveals four possible dysfluencies: repetitions, blocks, prolongations, and fillers that can be measured through a percentage dysfluency rate. Analysis of the controlling variables indicates that the following conditions influence stuttering: positive or negative reinforcement, anxiety, dysfluent speech patterns, rapid or slow speech, the belief that stuttering is inevitable in certain situations or with certain people, and anticipatory anxiety. Linguistic treatment strategies target stuttering directly; behavioral techniques often address the underlying distress. Use of the metronome to promote rhythmic speech and delayed auditory feedback are two linguistic methods whose outcomes have not been satisfactory. Behavioral approaches that have targeted the anxiety associated with stuttering have included systematic desensitization, cognitive therapy, and assertion training. Operant techniques frequently have been combined for treatment. Positive reinforcement, token economies, time out, extinction, response cost, and self-management have all appeared in the literature. The basic format of treatment has been establishing fluency, achieving transfer, and maintaining effects. A case presentation illustrates the steps in problem identification and application of treatment using desensitization, positive reinforcement, and programming to generalize and maintain gains.

Hoffman, L. P. (1990). The development of literacy in a school-based program. *Topics in Language Disorders, 10,* 81–92.

Communication disorders affect children's academic, social, and cognitive development. Language influences virtually all academic behavior, and research suggests that children do not outgrow their language and speech problems. The prekindergarten through twelfth grade communication development program described here integrates social and cognitive theories of communication development, and infuses six elements of literacy—reading, writing, listening, speaking, spelling, and handwriting—into all content areas. Students learn to monitor and be aware of their own learning styles, strengths, and weaknesses; to understand why they are learning a given topic; to become literate (that is, to know more about the world they live in); to operate in least restrictive settings; and to make good decisions about their future.

A team composed of a speech/language practitioner, teacher of the deaf, social worker, career educator, and aide (with appropriate consultants) develops the individualized education program (IEP) and works with fourteen students, teaching all academic subjects to groups of two to five students in a classroom-based format. All team members use and share their expertise in concert with the other specialists while furthering the primary goal of language and social skills development through academic instruction, group counseling, or other activities. The team provides training opportunities to help staff expand their roles. Students are mainstreamed as much as possible with regular education teachers receiving help from team members. Language intervention is infused into all areas by all team members.

Student progress is measured in several ways: through descriptions of students by teachers; by checklists, observations, and testing; and later through attendance, job success, life skills development, and parent feedback. Results show that participants made gains in language, reading, and math of five to twelve months per school year; they also showed growth in life skills, zero dropout rates, and 100 percent success in securing jobs or further training.

Konstantareas, M. M. (1984). Sign language as a communication prosthesis with language-impaired children. *Journal of Autism and Developmental Disorders, 14,* 9–25.

Fourteen cognitively impaired students with telegraphic speech — aged three years, ten months, to eleven years, one month — were presented with drawings depicting scenes representing the use of pronouns or prepositions. Relevant sentences using these functors were presented with the drawings. For training, the experimenter either said the functor or said and signed it simultaneously. Results indicated that both acquisition and recall of these speech components were superior under the "say and sign" condition as compared to the "say" condition. Signing is a definite aid in helping children with limited speech improve their speech production and complexity.

Kriegsmann, E., Gallaher, J. C., & Meyers, A. (1982). Sign programs with nonverbal hearing children. *Exceptional Children, 48,* 436–445.

Teaching signing to nonverbal hearing children to enhance their language production requires first a careful screening of candidates. Students should be at least at the early preoperational level, preferably over two-and-a-half years old with solid verbal comprehension, ability to express needs, independent manual dexterity, ability to imitate and retain signs, and interest in signing. They should have unintelligible or poorly developed phonetic skills; a history of poor responsiveness to other speech interventions; family support and commitment to training; and a school staff with knowledge, readiness to train, and some signing ability. The program for each child is individualized, based on the child's cognitive, linguistic, motoric, and motivational attributes. Like most language interventions, this one is focused on meaningful communication of intentions that are relevant to the child's life, emphasizing the three areas of acquisition, transfer, and maintenance. Feelings of awkwardness that anyone can feel while signing, reactions of the extended family, and day-to-day teaching issues such as the amount of teaching time needed and rate of sign acquisition need to be addressed.

Masterson, J., Swirbul, T., & Noble, D. (1990). Computer-generated information packets for parents. *Language, Speech, and Hearing Services in Schools, 21,* 114–115.

Computer-generated information packets for parents (CIPPs) can help parents gain a better understanding of their child's communication disorder and the helping role they can play in remediation for it. In the program reported here, Appleworks was used to create a master file for each major speech/language disorder, with one section describing the disability and its causes and a second section providing suggestions and activities for the parent to use at home. Individual client packages were created by accessing the appropriate master file for the child's disorder, selecting the parent suggestions and activities pertaining to the child's needs, and personalizing the packet with the names of the child, teacher, and therapist. With the availability of microcomputers in the school, CIPPs can be easily generated.

Meline, T. J. (1980). The application of reinforcement in language intervention. *Language, Speech, and Hearing Services in Schools, 11,* 95–101.

In naturally occurring situations, language-based communications are socially reinforced to the extent that their purpose is achieved. If the consequence of a communicative act achieves its intent, it will continue to be used. During language therapy, less natural reinforcers, such as tokens, food, or other objects are used and are typically preplanned, do not operate consistently for all children, usually reward a correct language form rather than the communicative intent, and may actually interrupt the act of communication. These characteristics of clinical reinforcers often make it quite difficult for students to generalize learned language skills to spontaneous use in the real world. It is important that natural reinforcers be identified through an examination of the youngster's real environment and used in clinical settings. While it is not necessary to eliminate clinical intervention totally in favor of a naturalistic approach, clinicians can "naturalize" the therapy session to facilitate transfer of training. Therapists can make clinical settings more natural by using realistic tasks and objects to facilitate language, selecting natural reinforcers, and using familiarization techniques. There are many language intervention programs that fall along the continuum of naturalness. A plan must be developed for each child individually.

Miller, L. (1989). Classroom-based language intervention. *Language, Speech, and Hearing Services in Schools, 20,* 153–169.

The primary mode of service delivery for speech/language therapy has been the pull-out model. With newer theories stressing language use in all areas of life, service models have shifted to classroom-based programs to assist students in their natural settings. Examples of classroom-based formats include (1) the language therapist teaching a self-contained language class; (2) a team-teaching approach with the regular education, special education, or resource teacher; (3) individual work with students in the classroom; (4) consultation service to the regular or special education or resource teacher; and (5) indirect service on a school or districtwide basis through staff training and curriculum and/or program development. Classroom intervention allows the therapist to use materials and tasks from the class in therapy, facilitates teacher-specialist coordination, allows students to remain in class, avoids the problem of generalization from therapy office to the classroom, avoids use of materials irrelevant to the student's needs, and allows students to be present to keep up with classwork. Changing from a pull-out to a classroom-based format requires reorienting professionals who are trained in traditional modes of intervention, abandoning the catch-up model in favor of strategy-based and systems approaches, and acknowledging the importance of language needs across subject areas with all age levels, preschool through adolescence. In addition, lines of authority for new programs and responsibility for developing the child's individualized education program (IEP) must be clarified; administrative, financial, and colleague support must be obtained; grading and credit policies must be established; and procedures for identifying students for service must be developed.

Norris, J. A. (1989). Providing language remediation in the classroom: An integrated language-to-reading intervention method. *Language, Speech, and Hearing Services in Schools, 20,* 205–218.

A transcript of a classroom language therapy session conducted with a small reading group of fifth- and sixth-graders illustrates the technique known as communicative reading strategies (CRS). This approach provides language intervention in the context of classroom-based reading instruction. The clinician organizes an appropriate unit of written material for the child to communicate, listens for indications of language difficulty as the child reads, and gives feedback through verification, requests for clarification, restatements by other students, and other consequating responses to assist the reading group in enhancing the communicative nature of reading. The purpose of the approach is not reading instruction per se but facilitating the student's ability to use linguistic aids to improve understanding of the written material and its communicative intent. CRS can be used in any subject without the child's leaving the classroom for therapy; it utilizes materials relevant for the classroom, facilitates social interaction to aid learning, enhances generalization of skills, promotes communication between the teacher and therapist, is cost effective, and promotes accountability of the therapist as she uses the reading process to develop measurable language goals and objectives.

Telzrow, C. F., Fuller, A., Siegel, C., Lowe, A., & Lowe, B. (1989). Collaboration in the treatment of children's communication disorders: A five-year case study. *School Psychology Review, 18,* 463–474.

A five-year educational program to improve the language skills and social behavior of a youngster with a severe communication disorder illustrates the importance of collaborative consultation skills for the school psychologist. Over the five-year period, the child showed significant progress from receiving behavioral interventions at home and in school, individual tutoring, involvement in a total communication program, attention to his interpersonal weaknesses and behavioral ridigity, careful use of mainstreaming, corrections of unrealistic perceptions of adults, and collaborative program planning and consultation among parents, educators, and psychologists. By age six, the youngster was attending a regular first grade with related speech, occupational therapy, and counseling services. With knowledge of communication disorders and the techniques of collaborative consultation, school psychologists can greatly assist in providing appropriate services to severely language-impaired youngsters.

Social Competence

Youth who effectively practice social competence strategies manage life experiences to their advantage and avoid potentially negative outcomes. For example, by reducing or avoiding participation in unprotected sexual intercourse or by refraining from misuse of cigarettes, alcohol, or drugs, these youngsters minimize their risks of unwanted pregnancy, dropping out of school, or serious health impairments such as AIDS. Likewise, youngsters who do not suck their thumbs, bite their nails, or masturbate under inappropriate circumstances are more likely to maintain their appearance, avoid infection, avoid social ostracism, and increase their opportunities for involvement in and acceptance by various community settings. They have learned to monitor their behavior and respond in a self-enhancing manner to the demands of the settings in which they operate. As the components of social competence become better identified, more focused interventions will follow to help students learn and refine their competency skills.

Social Competence:
Inappropriate Masturbation

A distinction should be made between masturbation as a natural, appropriately private expression of sexual interest and as a compulsive public behavior that may interfere with an individual's desired goals and outcomes and/or which may suggest a history of sexual abuse. For example, excessive public masturbation by some developmentally delayed individuals may prevent their successful integration into community activities; repeated sexual victimization may cause other youngsters to masturbate to excess as a sign of genital preoccupation or in an effort to cope somehow with the abusive encounters. Both retarded children and their more cognitively able peers need information about their growing sexual interests. Adults must teach youngsters more than what is inappropriate; they must help them learn how to express their feelings acceptably.

Substituting High-Probability
Behaviors for Masturbation

AUTHORS: R. M. Foxx, Martin J. McMorrow, Sarah Fenlon, and Ron G. Bittle

PRECIS: Reducing genital self-stimulation by providing and rewarding opportunities to engage in higher priority stereotypic behaviors

INTRODUCTION: Public masturbation by retarded individuals inhibits their progress toward community involvement as well as their educational achievement. However, efforts to reduce the frequency of this behavior have been limited. Possible reasons are that (1) punishment has been the main experimental approach; (2) some studies have not described their procedures in verifiable terms; (3) some of the strategies have required advanced behavioral knowledge and skill not usually possessed by school personnel or parents. In the procedure described here nonpunitive measures were applied (DRO schedules) to reduce the individual's genital stimulation, with the reinforcer removed after the goal was achieved.

METHOD: Zeke, a sixteen-year-old retarded boy with a history of touching his genitals, was the subject. Efforts to reduce his self-stimulatory behavior by various punishments and other contingencies had not been successful. After an eleven-day baseline period in which frequency of his self-stimulation was reported, a three-day noncontingent condition began in which Zeke was allowed to engage in a variation of a stereotypic hand behavior he frequently displayed. The behavior consisted of picking up and dropping small objects or switching them repeatedly between his hands. Interestingly, he did not touch his genitals while so engaged.

In the study, rice was selected as the item for him to drop, as he seemed to prefer it to other objects and dropped it more frequently. Every three minutes during morning classes he was summoned by the observer to leave his classroom seat and play with a tablespoon of rice. For thirty seconds the observer counted rice drops then returned Zeke to his regular seat. For the twenty-two-day DRO schedule, Zeke was praised and could play with the rice if he did not touch his genitals during the three-minute intervals. He was informed of the contingency before class began and allowed one thirty-second play period as an illustration. In addition, he was rewarded with a Cocoa Puff placed in a transparent cup each time he dropped the rice during play. After the thirty-second play period, he was allowed to eat the cereal. If he touched his genitals during the three-minute interval, he was reprimanded and told there would be no rice. If he touched himself during rice play, play was immediately terminated.

When his rate of touching was equal to or lower than the rate of the previous day, the interval between play periods was increased, with thirty seconds of rice play still given for each three minutes without touching. The DRO intervals began at three minutes and rose to six minutes, then to nine minutes, to fifteen minutes, twenty-one minutes, thirty minutes, and finally to forty-five minutes. If no touching occurred during the forty-five-minute period, Zeke earned seven minutes and thirty seconds of play.

Beginning with the forty-five-minute DRO, reinforcer displacement was introduced. Behavior incompatible with genital touching (rice play) had been rewarded with Cocoa Puffs; now the food was abruptly removed to reduce Zeke's stereotypic response. Finally, a maintenance period was implemented in which rice play was ended and Zeke received Cocoa Puffs after each forty-five-minute period free of touching.

RESULTS: Zeke's baseline self-touching averaged 13.2 percent during the morning and 17.1 percent in the afternoon, decreasing during the three-minute DRO condition to 4.1 percent and 3.9 percent, respectively. The rates decreased as DRO schedules were lengthened until they averaged .6 percent in the morning and .5 percent in the afternoon for the forty-five-minute interval. For thirteen mornings and ten afternoons, Zeke did not self-stimulate. His stereotypic rice dropping seemed unaffected by the edible reward or its removal.

COMMENTARY: Rewarding higher probability stereotypic behavior as a method to reduce genital self-stimulation seemed a quite effective alternative to punishment. In addition, the technique was administered almost entirely by classroom staff after the twenty-eighth day, and required them to have no particular behavioral expertise. The authors note with interest that providing both reinforcements and reinforcer displacement had no effect on the subject's rice-dropping behavior. This conclusion calls into question the value of these components, particularly when the Cocoa Puffs maintained low levels of self-touching after the stereotypic behavior was ended. Perhaps a DRL-DLO schedule with edibles as a reward might effectively reduce self-touching without recourse to stereotypic behavior as an element of the strategy. This change might simplify the procedure. A well-designed study with properly detailed procedures would shed light on the answer to this question.

SOURCE: Foxx, R. M., McMorrow, M. J., Fenlon, S., & Bittle, R. G. (1986). The reductive effects of reinforcement procedures on the genital stimulation and stereotypy of a mentally retarded adolescent male. *Analysis and Intervention in Developmental Disabilities, 6,* 239–248.

Additional Readings

Barmann, B. C., & Murray, W. J. (1981). Suppression of inappropriate sexual behavior by facial screening. *Behavior Therapy, 12,* 730–735.

Facial screening was used to reduce self-stimulation by a severely retarded fourteen-year-old. Teachers, bus aides, and parents were taught to place a nonabrasive terrycloth bib loosely over the student's face and hold it in place from the back of the head for five seconds whenever he rubbed his genitals for five seconds or longer. The statement, "No touching in public," was made to the boy prior to the procedure. If his self-touching continued with the bib in place, it was held there until he stopped the behavior. Application of this technique decreased his genital rubbing by 98 percent in the classroom, 91 percent on the bus, and 92 percent at home. Effects were maintained over a six-month follow-up. The student was subsequently involved in a sex education program to assist him in utilizing appropriate sexual outlets.

Morgan, S. R. (1984). Counseling with teachers on the sexual acting-out of disturbed children. *Psychology in the Schools, 21,* 234–243.

While sexual feelings are quite normal, disturbed youngsters often act out these feelings in overelaborated ways that pose concerns for the classroom teacher. Teachers need help understanding the dynamics of these behaviors so that they may better manage them when they occur. Compulsive masturbation has been interpreted as a method of anxiety reduction, a depressive reaction to unmet affectional needs, a form of guilt-relieving self-punishment, a way to reduce fears associated with sexual stimulation, and most basically as an impulsive need to increase the pleasure arising from sexual arousal.

A case study is described of a six-year-old compulsive masturbator deprived of emotional nurturance from her parents and looked after by a loving grandmother who provided little structure or controls. Her sexual behavior was viewed as an outgrowth of depression related to the loss of parental love, which caused her to feel anger and hostility, then guilt and anxiety. Masturbation was thus a form of self-punishment, the need for which also arose from her guilt over her freedom to act out on her grandmother without consequence (hitting, kicking, and biting) when limits were attempted.

Guidelines for assisting teachers who work with sexually acting-out children include the following:

1. Not raising sexual countertransference issues unless the teacher expresses some initial awareness, and then providing only enough understanding of the issue to facilitate the teacher's action
2. Helping teachers consider emotional, parental, religious, moral, and societal constraints as they show the child that sexual feelings are acceptable but must be displayed in appropriate ways, under proper circumstances, and in appropriate settings

3. Providing information about the child
4. Not isolating sexual behavior for special treatment that would not also be used with other acting-out patterns
5. Setting limits for acceptable action
6. Avoiding recasting the behavior in a humorous light
7. Not using planned ignoring
8. Giving teachers an understanding of the child so that they may in turn provide insights to the youngster
9. Involving parents, not to punish the child but to alert him when problems are becoming too intense for classroom management

Polvinale, R. A., & Lutzker, J. R. (1980). Elimination of assaultive and inappropriate sexual behavior by reinforcement and social-restitution. *Mental Retardation, 18,* 27–30.

A multicomponent treatment package was applied to a thirteen-year-old severely retarded Down's syndrome boy who engaged in assaultive acts, provocative or coercive sexual behavior with classmates, and self-touching. Differential reinforcement of other behavior (a DRO schedule) gave him verbal praise for not displaying the target behavior and directed praise at a peer if the behavior was evident. Social restitution (overcorrection) required him to apologize to his age-mates or adults individually when he behaved inappropriately. Control of the procedure was gradually shifted from trainer to teacher and intervals between praise were lengthened. For all target behaviors, the DRO schedule alone produced a slight decrease, which became dramatic immediately upon addition of the social restitution strategy. Transfer of control to the teacher was successful, and follow-ups at one and six months showed no reappearance of inappropriate sexual behavior. The teacher was quite satisfied with the technique.

Social Competence:
Thumb Sucking/Nail Biting

Although thumb sucking and nail biting may not be among the most serious problems, their chronic display may nevertheless cause great concern among parents, interfere with learning in retarded and autistic youngsters, lead to various medical and dental conditions, and precipitate withdrawal from interpersonal contact. Thus, the school practitioner must consider many issues in deciding whether intervention is warranted. While it would be inappropriate to conclude that intervention is necessary for all children who bite their nails or suck their fingers, it is equally clear that for some, routine neglect of these behaviors will surely exacerbate the psychological, social, and medical consequences.

Self-Recording Age-Inappropriate Thumb Sucking

AUTHORS: Richard Cohen, Hope Monty, and Deborah Williams

PRECIS: Self-management to decrease instances of thumb sucking

INTRODUCTION: A ten-year-old child self-recorded instances of his thumb sucking under parental supervision. After a seventeen-day baseline period in which the parent observed and recorded the child's thumb-sucking activity, a ten-day demand characteristic/praise condition was instituted in which the parent requested the child to avoid thumb sucking, provided reasons for the request, and praised the child for refraining. A fifteen-day self-recording period then began in which the child was given eight and one-half by eleven inch sheets of paper divided into fifteen squares. For forty-five minutes each evening, four days per week, the child placed a checkmark in one of the squares at the end of each five-minute segment if he sucked his thumb during that time period. The parents signaled the start and finish of each interval and they also recorded the child's thumb sucking to validate his accuracy. A baseline thumb-sucking rate of 37 percent was reduced to 16 percent during the demand/praise period and to 6 percent during self-recording. The 6 percent rate remained unchanged during a thirteen-day withdrawal phase in which all interventions were terminated. Agreement between the child's and parent's recordings was 90 percent.

COMMENTARY: The authors suggest a cautious interpretation of these results in light of the design of this preliminary study. They further note the lack of follow-up data, which is important, considering that self-recording strategies often yield temporary behavior changes that require continuing intervention to solidify progress. However, self-recording may represent an important step in the change process by demonstrating to the child that improvement is possible and that the child has control in the situation. Self-recording is also a practical technique for classroom use as it requires minimal teacher involvement and makes the child an active participant in the treatment. Whether it is necessary for the adult to signal the start and finish of segments is a question for further research.

SOURCE: Cohen, R., Monty, H., & Williams, D. (1980). Management of thumb-sucking using self-recording with parent as observer and experimenter. *Perceptual and Motor Skills, 50,* 136.

Reducing Thumb Sucking Through
Response Prevention of a Co-Varying Behavior

AUTHOR: Patrick C. Friman

PRECIS: Preventing thumb sucking by removing the opportunity to engage in a co-varying response

INTRODUCTION: Interventions for thumb sucking frequently involve punishment that may inhibit their usefulness as a widely accepted strategy. Response prevention, a method of preventing rather than punishing behavior, may be one acceptable alternative to aversive techniques. This study investigated whether eliminating behavior that co-varied with thumb sucking would prevent a youngster from sucking her thumb. If two concurrent behaviors are co-variants, then elimination of one should prevent the display of the other.

METHOD: Five-year-old Sue was a chronic thumb sucker, most frequently at home in the evening while watching television in bed. She had not responded to scoldings and loss of privileges, and her parents reported that she regularly held a special doll when she sucked her thumb. They also observed that she rarely sucked when not holding the doll. During the baseline period, the parents observed Sue once every thirty minutes beginning at 8 P.M. and averaging five observations per evening. For the intervention, Sue's special doll was removed; she was told that she was older now and should play with other items before bed. For a withdrawal phase, the doll was replaced on Sue's bed with no comment. However, on the third withdrawal day, Sue told her parents to remove the doll because it caused her to suck her thumb. This was followed by four more treatment days, then a three- and six-month follow-up, with no further return of the doll. Results clearly showed almost complete elimination of thumb sucking through the follow-up.

COMMENTARY: While this study did not deal with thumb sucking in school, it is quite conceivable that certain classroom-based behaviors may co-vary with thumb sucking. The practitioner may wish to observe a child for such concurrence following his or her referral for this problem. Depending upon the co-varying behavior, the same or similar response-prevention format may then be adapted and utilized. In fact, as the author suggests, a better understanding of how co-variation develops may allow the practitioner to develop a strategy that deliberately establishes a co-varying relationship between appropriate substitutes for thumb sucking.

SOURCE: Friman, P. C. (1988). Eliminating chronic thumb sucking by preventing a covarying response. *Journal of Behavior Therapy and Experimental Psychiatry, 19,* 301–304.

School-Assisted Home Treatment of Thumb Sucking

AUTHORS: Viv Clowes-Hollins and Neville King

PRECIS: Combining positive and negative contingencies to reduce thumb sucking

INTRODUCTION: Since thumb sucking often occurs at home, parents may be helped by the school practitioner to provide the interventions after school or during evening hours. In this case, eight-year-old Fiona sucked her thumb only while watching television and sleeping. She was developing malocclusion of her front teeth and a slight lisp.

METHOD: The parent checked Fiona for thumb sucking three times during her television watching, three times between her and the parent's bedtime, and once in the morning when they awoke. After a two-week baseline period, the intervention began with a direction to Fiona to stop sucking her thumb. Her two brothers were requested to help by also telling her to stop. The television was turned off for five minutes if she was observed thumb sucking during a check. After three weeks, a second baseline was conducted followed by reinstatement of the five-minute television time out. With this second treatment phase, Fiona earned a star each time she was not thumb sucking when checked; she could put the award on her "star chart." Three stars a night for three weeks earned her a set of books. In the final week of the intervention, Fiona's mother modeled self-instructions by pretending to be Fiona and saying, "I don't have to suck my thumb." Following a self-instruction training format, Fiona was prompted to practice the self-statement during the week, gradually fading to whispering, then subvocalizing.

RESULTS: Time out from television and encouragement from her brothers reduced Fiona's television thumb sucking by 65 percent. Her thumb sucking was virtually eliminated when reinforcement was added in the form of stars and books. Results generalized to her nocturnal thumb sucking. No thumb sucking was evident at a six-month follow-up, and Fiona began her own chart to help maintain her progress.

COMMENTARY: As the authors indicate, this strategy illustrates the value of augmenting punishment with positive reward. Children are more inclined to work to receive positive contingencies than to avoid negative outcomes. It is also not uncommon for parents to ask the school practitioner for assistance with home-based difficulties. Home problems can have a significant effect on a child's school performance even if they are never overtly manifested in class as problem behaviors. Working with a parent to relieve a concern at home may not only improve the child's school behavior and performance but can also demonstrate the value of home-school contact, and more specifically the importance of support and input from the school psychologist or counselor. Helping the parent with a thumb-sucking problem may increase the likelihood that the parent will call again if more serious problems arise. Such home-school cooperation in the treatment of problem behaviors may also strengthen the effect of an intervention by allowing for generalization of treatment effects across settings. It is almost always in the best interests of the school, the practitioner, and the family to promote a positive relationship between the school and the home.

SOURCE: Clowes-Hollins, V., & King, N. (1982). Parents and siblings as behavior modifiers in the control of a common developmental problem (thumbsucking). *Journal of Clinical Child Psychology, 11,* 231–233.

Relaxation and Competing Response Training for Hair Pulling and Nail Biting

AUTHORS: Rayleen V. De Luca and Stephen W. Holborn

PRECIS: Comparing the effectiveness of relaxation and competing response training in eliminating hair pulling and nail biting

INTRODUCTION: A seventeen-year-old girl engaged in both hair pulling and nail biting. She reported biting her nails when she became anxious in public; hair pulling she always did alone. Research has demonstrated the effectiveness of behavioral strategies for these two problem areas. More recently, habit reversal training, a thirteen-component intervention package that includes competing response training as part of its format, has been used to reduce hair pulling. This study selected two elements of the habit reversal approach—relaxation and competing response training—and evaluated their ability to reduce nail biting and hair pulling simultaneously.

CASE STUDY: Roxanne's embarrassment about her thin hair and partially bald scalp, and her swollen, unsightly, nailbitten fingers resulted in her often being absent from school, putting her high school graduation in jeopardy. Her condition made her depressed. For baseline, she recorded the number of hairs she pulled and nails she bit each day for twenty-four days. Then, on a twice weekly basis for three weeks, she was trained in relaxation through the progressive tensing and relaxing of various muscle groups. During training, she was informed of the ameliorative effects of muscle relaxation on hair pulling and was provided data each day by telephone by the therapist. The therapist praised her for improvement. Following the relaxation training, she was given competing response training once weekly for three weeks.

She was instructed to clench her fists for three minutes if she felt the urge to pull her hair or bite her nails, or if the behavior occurred. Relaxation practice continued, as did phone contacts with and praise from the therapist. After three weeks of complete suppression of both behaviors, monthly follow-ups continued for six months, then contact every three months for a total of two years.

RESULTS: Relaxation training reduced Roxanne's hair pulling from a baseline mean of 107.5 hairs per day to 34 hairs per day, but had no effect on her nail biting; the baseline mean of 8.25 nails bitten per day increased to 9.3. However, competing response training lowered hair pulling to .8 hairs per day and completely eliminated nail biting. After three weeks of total cessation of both acts, Roxanne reported no further problems over the two-year follow-up. Examination of her hair growth and fingernails confirmed her self-reports.

COMMENTARY: Competing response training seems to be a potentially powerful intervention for nail biting, although further validation with larger subject pools would seem appropriate. In addition, while relaxation training seemed to have no effect on Roxanne's nail biting, this study does not make clear whether it may have influenced the dramatic results obtained when competing response training was introduced. This too requires additional inquiry. The study also highlights the question of client age and motivation in regard to the competing response approach. The authors report that Roxanne did not like clenching her fists but followed through with the procedure in spite of her dislike. Research may need to address the relative merits of utilizing the competing response technique with a younger and less mature population as well as with individuals of any age who may not respond as compliantly as Roxanne.

SOURCE: De Luca, R. V., & Holborn, S. W. (1984). A comparison of relaxation training and competing response training to eliminate hair pulling and nail biting. *Journal of Behavior Therapy and Experimental Psychiatry, 15,* 67–70.

Additional Readings

Barmann, B. C. (1979). The use of overcorrection with artificial nails in the treatment of chronic fingernail biting. *Mental Retardation, 7,* 309–311.

The article reports how nail biting was eliminated in a nine-year-old retarded girl. First, artificial nails were placed over her severely bitten fingernails to provide a more immediately reinforcing demonstration of pretty nails.

Then, two overcorrection procedures were implemented. For positive practice, she had to raise her hands just to her lips without touching them, then return her hands to her side and fold them for two seconds. This movement was repeated twenty times. Immediately following positive practice, restitutional overcorrection required her to file, shape, and paint the nail she bit, all her other nails, and all her mother's nails. The parents were taught this intervention and applied it on their own during the second and third treatment weeks. By the end of the third week, her nail biting was eliminated. A ten-week follow-up revealed maintenance of treatment effects. This procedure is easily learned by parents and future research should establish whether all components are needed.

De Francesco, J. J. (1987). Children and nail biting. In A. Thomas & J. Grimes (Eds.), *Children's needs: Psychological perspectives* (pp. 378–382). Washington, DC: National Association of School Psychologists.

Nail biting usually begins at about age four and is most prevalent at ages thirteen for boys and eleven for girls. While mild cases do not necessarily require treatment, severe nail biting can cause infections, social discomfort, parental distress, and dental problems; it may also signal emotional difficulties. Before planning an intervention, the psychologist should do a comprehensive assessment to determine historical, family, academic, social, or other factors that may be contributing to the behavior. Hypothesized causes of nail biting have focused on unresolved oedipal conflicts, regression, displaced masturbatory needs, genetics, modeling of family members, habit formation, stress, and high parental standards. Treatments are equally diverse and include less successful approaches such as psychotherapy, hypnosis, play therapy, use of gloves, chewing gum, and applying bad-tasting substances to the nails. More effective are stress-reducing techniques and behavioral interventions. Relieving the underlying causes of nail biting with stress reduction may take time; behavioral approaches yield more immediate short-term results, but they do not address the internal stresses. Used together, however, stress reduction and behavioral methods represent a promising approach to this problem. Overcorrection, negative practice, contracting, covert sensitization, self-monitoring, and aversive measures have all been used, with habit reversal training showing the most significant effects.

Freeman, B. J., Moss, D., Somerset, T., & Ritvo, E. R. (1977). Thumbsucking in an autistic child overcome by overcorrection. *Journal of Behavior Therapy and Experimental Psychiatry, 8,* 211–212.

Thumb sucking was eliminated in a two-year-old autistic child through positive practice overcorrection applied at school. Each time thumb sucking occurred, he was told, "Put your hands down," and his hands were held to his side for thirty seconds. Praise and attention were given for appropriate behavior and no thumb sucking. Thumb sucking was reduced from over 200 instances during day 1 of the baseline period to 31 on day 1 of the intervention, to zero after thirteen days. Over fourteen months, the thumb-sucking behavior remained completely suppressed. Similar results and improved social responding were obtained with the child on the ward where he stayed although no treatment had been implemented there. Over the same period, his intellectual testing showed steady positive change, suggesting to the authors that his contact with external experience was improving.

Friman, P. C., Barone, V. J., & Christophersen, E. R. (1986). Aversive taste treatment of finger and thumb sucking. *Pediatrics, 78,* 174–176.

The thumbs of seven chronic thumb suckers, three to twelve years of age, were coated with a commercially prepared bitter-tasting liquid (Stop-Zit, Pure Pac Pharmaceutical Company) when they awoke in the morning, just before bedtime, and each time they were seen thumb sucking. When no sucking was observed for five consecutive sessions, the parents stopped the morning application. The evening coating was terminated after five more consecutive nonsucking sessions. For all seven children, both daytime and nocturnal thumb sucking was eliminated completely and remained at zero at three- and six-month follow-ups. Total instruction time with parents was less than two minutes. The authors caution against recommending this technique unless more severe emotional disturbance is ruled out, as thumb sucking may be just one of a cluster of symptoms requiring more intensive treatment.

Jenson, W. R., Kehle, T. J., & Clark, E. (1987). Children and thumb-sucking. In A. Thomas & J. Grimes (Eds.), *Children's needs: Psychological perspectives* (pp. 643–650). Washington, DC: National Association of School Psychologists.

Thumb sucking is the most common problem habit of childhood. It can occur during the day or at night and may be related to other habitual problems such as nail biting. Prevalence seems to peak between ages two and four, with a sharp drop-off after age six. Hypothesized causes include oral stage gratification, unsatisfying feeding experiences, effect of cup versus bottle versus breast feeding, the role of teething, maladaptive habit formation, and early prenatal reflexive actions. No one cause seems primary. Although thumb suckers do not appear to be more predisposed to psychological disorder, they may suffer more social distress if they continue the behavior into middle childhood. In addition, dental and other medical problems are more prevalent among chronic thumb suckers, and the self-stimulatory sucking of autistic or retarded children may inhibit their learning. Symptom substitution has not been reported as an aftereffect of treatment.

Following a child's referral for thumb sucking, a thorough background history on him or her should be gathered to determine the appropriate intervention. Antecedent conditions, chronicity, effect of the habit on the child's adjustment, past efforts to curtail the problem, and times when the thumb sucking occurs with greatest frequency are some of the data that will assist the practitioner. Strategies for reversing this habit include self-monitoring, psychotherapy, hypnosis, differential reinforcement of other behavior (DRO schedule), response cost, time outs, use of distasteful substances on the thumb, response prevention (such as use of gloves), overcorrection, and habit reversal training. Each has its own advantages and disadvantages, although the DRO schedule avoids punishment and is therefore a desirable method. While habit reversal training has yielded the highest success rates, it is a complex procedure that might not always be practical to use.

Tilton, P. (1980). Hypnotic treatment of a child with thumb-sucking, enuresis, and encopresis. *The American Journal of Clinical Hypnosis, 22,* 238–239.

Hypnosis was used in four fifteen-minute sessions to eliminate thumb sucking, enuresis, and encopresis in an eight-and-a-half-year-old boy. At the first session, the boy, J., agreed to the therapist's suggestions to suck a different finger each day and to hold his urine and feces as long as he could before eliminating. His aunt was instructed to praise him for a clean bed and pants. The Television Screen Technique for trance induction was then used with the therapist role-playing Buck Rogers (J.'s favorite character). "Buck" made the same suggestions that the therapist made when the boy was awake. After one week, soiling and wetting were reduced, but their pretreatment rates resumed during the month between the first and second sessions. At session 2, a new suggestion was made to J. under trance to suck all his fingers each time he sucked his thumb. The suggestion to hold his urine and feces remained, with emphasis on the prospect of a clean bed and pants. At the third session, the suggestions were again repeated under trance with the comment that sucking all his fingers would become boring and that he would soon be able to sleep at a friend's house. The final session revealed four days of no thumb or finger sucking, no wetting, and one small soiling episode. The suggestions were stated again while J. was awake and in trance, and he was told he could suck all or none of his fingers. One month later, only nocturnal thumb sucking was reported. A six-month follow-up found all three problems eliminated. The author suggests that the fatherlike authority of the therapist and "Buck Rogers" aided the treatment.

Social Competence:
Enuresis–Encopresis

While the large majority of enuretics wet at night, most soiling occurs during the day. Thus, the school practitioner may be more likely to have direct contact with encopretic children either through teacher reports of odor or perhaps on referral from the school nurse when the child is sent to clean up. However, this possibility may be slight, as many children do not soil during school and only 1.5 percent of seven- to eight-year-olds display encopretic behavior. Given the prevalence of nocturnal over diurnal wetting, if a child comes to school smelling of urine, other possibilities should be considered such as a more serious concern over parental neglect, which may necessitate further inquiry.

Reinforcing Continence with Logical Consequences for Soiling

AUTHOR: Mark A. Lyon

PRECIS: Decelerating positive reinforcement combined with logical consequences to reduce incidents of soiling in an eight-year-old, mentally retarded youngster

INTRODUCTION: Encopresis has been treated with family therapy as well as varying combinations of positive and negative behavior contingencies, counseling, logical consequences, and discrimination training. However, studies in this area have been criticized for their use of aversive techniques, their lack of methodological rigor, and their employing experimental designs that validate strategies by reversing the effects of treatment. The choice of intervention and the design of the study reported here attempted to alleviate these problems through the school-based treatment of an eight-year-old mentally retarded special education student.

METHOD: Larry had been soiling since age four for no medical reason and efforts to eliminate the problem were unsuccessful. During a ten-day baseline, the teacher and aide recorded soiling incidents upon detecting fecal odor. They also noted situational variables related to the behavior, such as time of day, location, and other factors. The first treatment phase began with a conference attended by Larry, his special education teacher, and the school psychologist. They discussed the problem (which Larry understood), the social consequences, and their desire to help him. Each day Larry received a sticker and was praised by his teacher each time he was clean when checked at 10 A.M. recess, 11:45 lunch time, 1:30 P.M. recess, and 2:45 dismissal. He could also earn one sticker each morning and/or afternoon for asking to use the bathroom in an appropriate manner. The possible number of daily stickers he could earn was six. Stickers were posted on a chart displayed in class, a procedure previously discussed with his classmates. Three stickers in a day earned twenty minutes of private time with the teacher. Seven clean days were rewarded with an ice cream cone (both contingencies chosen by Larry). If he soiled, logical consequences were applied and he had to clean up, rinse his clothes, and change.

The second phase of treatment began after the first clean seven-day period. In conference, Larry was praised and urged to continue his success. The two recess checks were eliminated and verbal praise was substituted for stickers when Larry appropriately requested to use the bathroom. Thus, two daily stickers were now possible with four needed to see the teacher individually. This reward required two days of continence instead of part of one day. The ice cream cone reward and logical consequences for soiling remained in force.

In the third phase, one cleanliness check was performed at dismissal and five stickers were needed to see the teacher, raising the required number of clean days to five. A final conference occurred after seven consecutive clean days to praise Larry's progress. He received a letter acknowledging his success which he was told to show to his mother.

RESULTS: Larry soiled eight out of ten baseline days; the incidence diminished to one of eleven days during treatment 1, and one of nine days during treatment 2. Phase 3 and the subsequent five-month follow-up period yielded no incidents.

COMMENTARY: Soiling carries significant social and psychological consequences as the isolated encopretic child withdraws or is ostracized and teased. Treatment needs to be quick, and this strategy reduced the problem dramatically as soon as it was introduced. Furthermore, continence generalized to the home with no reports of soiling after treatment. This finding is unexplained but quite interesting, as generalization is not seen as an automatic outcome; typically generalization must be planned if it is to succeed. The author makes the final point that as reward criteria are tightened in this intervention, students should be helped to see it not as punishment but as an indication of their improved behavior.

SOURCE: Lyon, M. A. (1984). Positive reinforcement and logical consequences in the treatment of classroom encopresis. *School Psychology Review, 13,* 238–243.

Treating Encopresis with
Cognitive-Behavioral Play Therapy

AUTHORS: Susan M. Knell and Douglas J. Moore

PRECIS: Combining play therapy, cognitive-behavioral therapy, and behavior management techniques to reduce the incidence of soiling

INTRODUCTION: This article describes a unique combination of cognitive-behavioral therapy, play therapy, and a parent-run behavior management strategy to reduce soiling in a five-year-old. The authors note the importance of modifying therapeutic interventions when appropriate to suit the developmental needs of the youngster under treatment. Utilizing cognitive-behavioral strategies in a play therapy format represents an attempt at such accommodation.

INTERVENTION: This youngster, one of a set of triplets, had expressive language and articulation disorders and became angry when he could not be distinguished from his brothers. He indicated that he did not want to bowel train on the toilet as his brothers did. No medical basis existed for his incontinence, and diet changes proved ineffective in correcting the problem. He soiled frequently each day and would not change himself. During twelve days of baseline, his parents checked for soiling at 12:30 P.M., 3:30 P.M., 6:30 P.M., and bedtime, and recorded the percentage of checks in which soiling was detected. Soiling was recorded if they saw fecal material and discoloration of his underpants.

The child then began cognitive-behavioral play therapy with an initial period of free play. When his play revealed themes of toileting fears and competition with his siblings, they were addressed through cognitive-behavioral techniques. For example, in his play, a stuffed bear constantly fell into the toilet and was "flushed away." The therapist repeatedly identified this irrational fear for the child despite the child's early denials. The therapist began to counter this belief and shape appropriate toileting in the bear by assuring the bear that he would not fall in and be flushed down, and by using positive self-statements for the bear such as, "I can use the toilet," "I will not get flushed down the toilet," and "I feel good when I use the toilet." These statements were intended both to neutralize the child's fear and to reinforce in him the desired realistic thoughts while the therapist gradually moved the bear toward the toilet, having him sit on the toilet and defecate without getting flushed away (exposure and response prevention). In addition, the therapist had the bear model direct expression of feelings rather than acting out through soiling.

Also, the parent-managed behavioral program for the child was tied to a similar one for the bear; the bear was rewarded for defecating in the toilet and for maintaining dry pants. As a result, the child began competing with the bear for stars. In the behavior management program, the child received a sticker from his parents for each clean pants check and use of the toilet. As a prompt, he was seated on the toilet three times daily for ten minutes, about one-half hour after each meal. He was also taught how and expected to place his soiled pants in a pail of soapy water and change to new underwear.

By week 8 of treatment, his soiling had decreased but he was still not having bowel movements in the toilet. The child was then informed calmly that if he was toileting appropriately by the third day he would not be given an enema. Three enemas were used over nine days with praise both from his parents and a preselected list of "friends-who-care" when he went to the toilet after each enema. He was also given small toys after the first two movements.

RESULTS: The child's soiling went from 77 percent of the pants checks during the baseline period to zero after session 14 (approximately thirteen weeks into treatment). He consistently used the toilet for bowel movements after session 12. Treatment effects were maintained at eight- and forty-five-month follow-ups.

COMMENTARY: In this structured intervention, behavioral, affective, and cognitive dimensions were targeted simultaneously in treating the encopretic problem. The child was involved in the treatment through play, from which he was able to learn appropriate alternative toileting behavior. Two issues are important. First, as the authors point out, it is impossible to know which components of the package had the most effect and therefore whether each piece was necessary. This is important for situations in which one or more elements cannot be implemented—for example, if the parent cannot or will not apply the behavioral contingencies, if the practitioner is not skilled in cognitive-behavioral therapy, or if the child is language disordered and thus restricted in verbalizing his feelings and/or cognitive understanding. Second, with no control subjects, the exact relationship between the treatment and the outcome remains unclear. For school professionals who use play therapy, this technique offers a method of structuring the play experience and actually teaching the child new skills. Further research seems appropriate to deal with the many questions raised by the introduction of this integrated strategy.

SOURCE: Knell, S. M., & Moore, D. J. (1990). Cognitive-behavioral play therapy in the treatment of encopresis. *Journal of Clinical Child Psychology, 19,* 55–60.

Bell and Pad Variations to Reduce Enuresis

AUTHORS: Steward L. Kaplan, Miranda Breit, Bernard Gauthier, and Joan Busner

PRECIS: Comparing dry-bed training, tangible rewards with fading, and simple bell and pad technique for their ability to reduce nighttime wetting

INTRODUCTION: Although the bell and pad technique for treating enuresis is considered the most effective of all strategies, the authors report that only two-thirds of those treated respond. There is a one-third relapse rate requiring additional training. To enhance treatment outcome, the bell and pad has been combined with various reward and punishment strategies with mixed but promising results. This study evaluated an enhanced bell and pad technique (tangible rewards with fading), compared with the more complex dry-bed method and the basic bell and pad procedure.

PROCEDURE: Subjects were three groups of enuretic children over six years of age, most of whom came to an enuresis clinic after unsuccessful attempts to reduce nighttime wetting by having their liquids restricted, being waked at night to urinate, using the bell and pad, or being given medication (imipramine). Each group received one of the three interventions. After screening to rule out organic causes, the clinicians met with the families to review the particular strategy and give them the bell and pad and a descriptive parent manual. In the *dry-bed condition,* the child drank a great deal at bedtime and was awakened each hour during the night to practice toileting twenty times (positive practice). The child was urged to wait until the next hour to urinate and was given more liquid to drink. If wetting occurred and the alarm sounded, the child had to clean up (cleanliness training) and engage in the positive practice routine. Following this intensive training night, posttraining supervision began in which positive practice and cleanliness training were undertaken with each accident and positive practice was repeated at bedtime the night following a wetting incident. After seven consecutive dry nights, the bell and pad was terminated but positive practice and cleanliness training continued until fourteen continuous dry nights were achieved. Two wet nights in seven resulted in reinstatement of the bell and pad with the accompanying procedures. Social rewards and punishments were also utilized in this complex program. (For further details, the reader is referred to Azrin, N. H., Sneed, T. J., and Foxx, R. N. "Dry Bed: Rapid Elimination of Childhood Enuresis." *Behavior Research and Therapy,* 1974, *12,* 147–156.)

For *tangible rewards with fading,* the parents and child together chose a reward and punishment for a dry or wet night. If wetting occurred, the child engaged in cleanliness training with parent supervision and received the positive or negative contingency the next day in conjunction with praise or disapproval. The bell and pad were removed after fourteen consecutive dry nights and the program was faded by adding a day of "no program" each week if no wetting occurred the week before (for example, six days on, one day off, then five days on, two days off, etc.). The program would end after six weeks if no wetting occurred. However, an accident required morning cleanliness training and no additional day off the next week. More than one accident in a week resulted in a return to the bell and pad and a new fourteen-night criterion. For the basic *bell and pad treatment,* supervised cleanliness training took place during the night, praise and disapproval were delivered for dryness and wetness, and no accidents for fourteen consecutive nights led to termination of the program.

RESULTS: No differences in effectiveness were revealed among the three treatment procedures. However, 85 percent of the children receiving tangible rewards with fading achieved fourteen consecutive dry nights, while only 67 percent of the basic bell and pad subjects did so. Furthermore, 67 percent of the bell and pad youngsters relapsed within six months of treatment compared with 37 percent of the "tangible rewards" group.

COMMENTARY: The authors indicate that the complexity and intensity of the dry-bed method is not justified by the outcome and do not recommend its use. They prefer the tangible reward with fading approach over the bell and pad alone because of the results cited above in addition to its minimal drawbacks. It is important, however, to reassure the family that punishing the child for wetness is not intended to imply his or her willful noncompliance, and that the procedure is designed to train the body, not chastise the child. Further, it is essential to provide parents feedback on responding to wet and dry nights so that their consequent actions do not further aggravate the situation they are trying to alleviate.

SOURCE: Kaplan, S. L., Breit, M., Gauthier, B., & Busner, J. (1989). A comparison of three nocturnal enuresis treatment methods. *Journal of the American Academy of Child and Adolescent Psychiatry, 28,* 282–286.

A Family Approach to Enuresis

AUTHORS: Sam Goldstein and Robert Book

PRECIS: A model of family-based treatment for wetting that incorporates known intervention components in a prearranged sequence

INTRODUCTION: A sequenced family approach is described for reducing primary enuresis. Phase 1 consists of problem assessment and preparation of the family for intervention, while phase 2 teaches and implements the procedure and monitors progress. When bed wetting is an outgrowth of significant pathology (secondary enuresis), the authors recommend consideration of an outside referral and possible use of this model as a component of the therapeutic treatment. With primary enuresis, the psychologist can apply this procedure on its own as a school-based intervention.

PHASE 1: The practitioner meets with the family for one or two sessions to gather background information for diagnosing primary or secondary enuresis. If primary bed wetting is identified, the psychologist explores, among other issues, the family's attitude toward the problem, results of previous treatments, and subsequent parent reactions. These data give the professional insight into the parents' commitment to treatment, the most effective way to present the treatment strategy, the outlook for success, and other relevant treatment variables.

Once background is obtained, the psychologist discusses possible causes of wetting, such as capacity and control problems resulting from a weak bladder muscle. This instruction is provided in a noncritical manner to redefine the problem as unintentional and developmentally based. If needed, drawings, models, or other materials can be used by the therapist to augment the discussion.

The helper then introduces retention control training in which the child attempts to increase bladder capacity by holding the urine as long as possible. The parents record when the child urinates and how much. Volume is then compared against standardized charts. This technique reveals for the parents the child's urinary capacity, provides a baseline measure of volume, and promotes a cooperative child-parent alliance against the problem, which is the intent of this phase. The psychologist also discusses the hypothesized influence of sleeping habits on wetting and describes wake-up techniques, such as periodic walks to the toilet and the bell and pad. Finally, the parents receive a card with assigned tasks to be carried out until the next session two or three weeks later. Tasks include allowing the child no liquids in the hour before bedtime, walking the child to the toilet one hour after bed, retention control practice daily after lunch, obtaining three measures of urine volume after retention practice over a two-week period, buying a bell and pad device, making the child responsible for cleaning the bed, and checking each morning with an appropriate reward for a dry bed. The psychologist cautions the child not to expect a dry night for a few weeks, that the process will probably require about three months, and that periodic wetting may still occur. However, the child is assured that this is typical for most children and that the bell and pad is available if needed.

PHASE 2: Two to three weeks later, the therapist sees the family to review the assignments and check the child's bladder capacity. If the family has not completed the assignments after two sessions, it may be advisable to suggest that they wait six months to try again. If phase 1 tasks have been done, the psychologist suggests that restriction on liquids, night walks, and self-cleaning be continued, but retention control training can be ended if the child's bladder capacity is adequate. The bell and pad is then demonstrated, with a chart to track dry nights. Parents are instructed to wake the child when the alarm sounds for the first few nights and to continue if necessary to wake and walk the child during the procedure. During the first two weeks, the child receives reinforcers (privileges and other nontangibles) for any three dry nights per week, reduced to two to three consecutive dry nights during weeks 3 and 4, and finally to five dry nights in a row by the sixth week. After about four weeks of dryness, the bell and pad can be removed, but they may be needed to handle expected relapses. The child is reminded to be patient and to remember the support available through the psychologist. Parents are telephoned one week into phase 2 to clear up any procedural issues. One or two subsequent sessions may occur, perhaps once per month, so the therapist can check the child's progress and praise dryness.

COMMENTARY: No data accompanied the presentation of this model and the individual treatment components have been tested with varying degrees of success, as reported in other studies. For example, the bell and pad is considered a successful strategy, while retention control training is much less effective alone but potentially useful in combination with the bell and pad. The article reinforces the importance of a structured enuresis program, the benefits of building rapport with the parents, and the need to encourage a cooperative effort between parent and child. In effect, the authors provide a framework for integrating separate treatment strategies into a workable intervention model.

SOURCE: Goldstein, S., & Book, R. (1983). A functional model for the treatment of primary enuresis. *School Psychology Review, 12,* 97–101.

Additional Readings

Grimes, L. (1983). Application of the self-regulatory model in dealing with encopresis. *School Psychology Review, 12,* 82–87.

The article describes a self-regulatory model of soiling control in which the encopretic third grader chose major components of the intervention, which were implemented by the parents after training from the school psychologist. The child set the conditions for the contingency contract, decided on the nature of the overcorrection procedure, determined the parameters for positive practice, and decided how much his classmates should know about his condition. The school psychologist taught the child a visual imagery sequence in which he imagines feeling the urge to defecate and leaves a ball game to obey the bodily sensation. He uses the bathroom and feels good and in control. Results showed a drop in soiling from one incident per day at school to one, two, or no accidents per two-week contract period and into the next school year. Parents reported a similar decrease in soiling at home. When children are offered the chance to participate in planning their own treatment, they tend to take more responsibility for their improvement.

Houts, A. C. (1987). Children and enuresis. In A. Thomas & J. Grimes (Eds.), *Children's needs: Psychological perspectives* (pp. 194–201). Washington, DC: National Association of School Psychologists.

Enuresis is defined as any unintentional or uncontrolled wetting after age three and a half. Primary nocturnal enuresis in which dryness has never been achieved encompasses 80 percent of all bed wetting. Secondary enuresis identifies resumed wetting after dryness lasting two or more months and arises from more intense medical or emotional problems in the child five to eight years of age. Primary enuresis is the focus of this chapter. About 14 to 16 percent of bed wetters become continent spontaneously each year between the ages of five to nineteen. Thus, one child in seven or eight will be dry a year later without treatment.

Enuresis seems to result from the inability of the child to "attend and respond" while he is asleep to the need to urinate. Infections, bladder and kidney defects, emotional disturbance, and deep sleep are not adequate explanations for the problem. Thus, strategies to reduce bed wetting focus on behavioral approaches although medication has also been used. Imipramine (brand name Tofranil) given one hour before bedtime has been the drug of choice, but it has had a lasting cure rate no better than the spontaneous remission rate cited above — and with unpleasant side effects. The most common behavioral methods include bell and pad training, retention control training, dry-bed training, and Full Spectrum Home Training. All require cooperative and motivated parents and child. Bell and pad achieves a 75 percent initial success rate in about eight to fourteen weeks, with one-third of these children relapsing within one year; they can, however, be retrained.

In overlearning the child drinks lots of fluids one hour before bedtime starting after two consecutive dry weeks and continuing until the child is dry two additional consecutive weeks. When incorporated into bell and pad training, this strategy results in half the relapse rate of bell and pad training alone and has a permanent cure rate over 60 percent. Retention control training by itself has a less than 30 percent lasting cure rate, but it may add power to the bell and pad procedure. Dry-bed training is a rather intense treatment regimen that includes nighttime waking, positive practice of toileting, bell and pad, and cleanliness training. There is some question of whether the strenuousness of this night training procedure is worth the outcome.

Full Spectrum Home Training also uses the bell and pad, cleanliness training, retention control training, and overlearning with a contract signed by the parents and child committing everyone to the process. Initial changes have been reported for 81 percent of the children using this method, with a 24 percent one-year relapse rate, and a 61 percent permanent success rate. The author recommends Full Spectrum Home Training. Medication may provide some short-term relief, allowing the child to participate in sleepover activities. Families need to realize that children are not willfully enuretic.

Houts, A. C., & Liebert, R. M. (1984). *Bedwetting: A guide for parents and children.* Springfield, IL: Thomas.

This publication discusses the problem of bed wetting in children, its causes, available treatments, and the authors' home-implemented training program known as Full Spectrum Home Training. The training involves an initial screening procedure to determine whether treatment is appropriate, and an explanation of bell and pad training, retention control training, and overlearning. Step-by-step instructions are provided with tips to parents for dealing with children's noncompliance, equipment problems, discouragement at the slow pace of progress, and relapses. The book includes an important document, the Family Support Agreement, which explains all the steps and commits the family to the process. The authors report that 81.4 percent of the children from sixty families who tested the program achieved a dry bed within eight weeks. Twenty-four percent relapsed at the one-year follow-up with permanent dryness accomplished by 61 percent of the participating children.

Kaplan, S. L., Breit, M., Busner, J., & Gauthier, B. (1991, February). Helping a child overcome enuresis. *Medical Aspects of Human Sexuality, 25,* 36–38.

The authors describe a behavioral treatment for use by the physician that combines the bell and pad, reward and punishment, and a fading procedure. Steps include (1) taking a bed-wetting history, including frequency, duration, family bed-wetting history, current efforts to manage the problem, and the family's views of the problem; (2) screening for organic causes; (3) screening for psychological problems with referral for therapy concurrent with the treatment described here; (4) assessing the need for treatment by examining the degree of family distress and the age of the child; (5) describing the problem and the program in a nonblaming, training-oriented fashion to enlist the child's cooperation; (6) demonstrating the bell and pad device; (7) describing the steps to follow when the bell rings — the cleaning up procedure and resetting the alarm under parent permission; (8) choosing the reward and penalty and applying them consistently for dry and wet nights; (9) describing the self-monitoring procedure of marking wet or dry nights on the calendar until fourteen consecutive dry nights are achieved; (10) describing the fading process that accompanies removal of the bell and pad after the fourteenth dry night. Fading involves one less day on the program each week for each previous all-dry week; (11) calling the family weekly to monitor and provide encouragement. If there is no change after eight to twelve weeks, the treatment can be stopped for six months, different contingencies can be tried, or rewards can be contingent on reduction in the number of wet episodes per night. A success rate of 85 percent is reported with reduced relapse rates resulting from the fading strategy.

Rolider, A., & Van Houten, R. (1985). Treatment of constipation-caused encopresis by a negative reinforcement procedure. *Journal of Behavior Therapy and Experimental Psychiatry, 16,* 67–70.

Retention of feces over time can cause impaction and psychogenic megacolon, resulting in seepage of fecal liquid into the clothing. This form of encopresis is believed to account for 80 to 95 percent of all soiling cases. Three treatment procedures for reducing this constipation-based soiling were evaluated. Parents of a twelve-year-old encopretic girl checked her underwear for soiling each hour. In the differential reinforcement of other behavior (DRO) condition, each clean check earned her a chocolate candy and a coupon. She could trade five coupons for tangible reinforcers. In the DRO plus overcorrection procedure, DRO was continued, but for each soiling incident, the girl had to wash her dirty underwear and five other pairs of underwear. Also, she had to enter the bathroom from several different locations in the house and sit on the toilet for a few moments. The negative reinforcement phase required her to sit on the toilet upon awakening for twenty minutes or until she moved her bowels. If she did not defecate, she had to sit at 1 P.M. for forty minutes or until she defecated. If she was not successful, the time went to ninety minutes at 7:30 P.M. Defecation at any time terminated the need to sit anymore that day. While sitting, she was not allowed to do anything else.

The DRO and DRO plus overcorrection lowered the average percentage of soiled checks from 28 percent at baseline to 16 percent. Negative reinforcement lowered this further to 1.6 percent. A second negative reinforcement phase after reversal completely eliminated soiled underpants, and this behavior was maintained over a ninety-five-day follow-up. Bowel movements went from one during the six days of baseline to two during the eight days of DRO and DRO plus overcorrection to one per day during negative reinforcement. A call at fourteen-months follow-up revealed regular bowel movements and no soiling.

Simonson, D. T. (1987). Children and encopresis. In A. Thomas & J. Grimes (Eds.), *Children's needs: Psychological perspectives* (pp. 189–194). Washington, DC: National Association of School Psychologists.

Children are not diagnosed as encopretic until after age four when bowel control is usually established. While nighttime soiling is rare, soiling occurs most often during the latter part of the day and may occur as frequently as several times daily or only a few times per month. By the time a child is sixteen, soiling is almost nonexistent. Retentive soiling accounts for 80 to 95 percent of all cases, often resulting in impaction, psychogenic megacolon, loss of sphincter muscle tone, and leakage into the underpants. Etiology varies at differing age levels because of individual, familial, and experiential factors. Treatments include positive reinforcement for proper toileting and/or no soiling (DRO schedules), punishment, negative reinforcement, overcorrection, self-regulation, and strategies combining behavioral and medical approaches. In school, encopretic students may need a special bathroom, the freedom to go to the toilet at any time, a change of clothing, and to be excused from gym and showers. Treatments take time and must stress teaching the child to defecate in the toilet as well as to reduce soiling. While the latter may occur well before the former, patience from the participants is required for the total process to succeed. A multidisciplinary approach involving the practitioner, teacher, physician, parents, and child will produce the most beneficial outcome.

Sluckin, A. (1989). Behavioral social work treatment of childhood nocturnal enuresis. *Behavior Modification, 13,* 482–497.

Given the importance of social, developmental, and family history data in the assessment and treatment of nocturnal enuresis, the author considers the contribution of the social worker to be crucial. After describing such treatments as contingency management, retention control training, bell and pad, overlearning, and the effectiveness of the bell and pad in residential children's homes, she describes three case studies. In the first, a ten-and-one-half-year-old is treated with a combination of bell and pad and desensitization of anxiety associated with urinating at school. In the second, an eleven-year-old is helped with the bell and pad after a star chart reward contingency was ineffective in reducing his almost nightly wetting. Case 3 was initially treated unsuccessfully with medication, then with the bell and pad. Although blind, the mother was able to implement the strategy.

A child's achieving continence often improves family relationships by relieving stress and odor and removing blame from the child. However, the bell and pad is not recommended for dysfunctional families with a potential for increased hostility toward the child as a result of the treatment effect. In addition, individual family circumstances such as inadequate living conditions or sexual abuse within the family may make enuresis management more complex and may even shift the focus of intervention to these pressing issues. Lack of parent cooperation, inability to handle the sound of the bell at night, and pathological conditions in the child that take priority over enuresis are some of the situations leading to failure or the need to postpone treatment. Social workers have the skills to work in the home and facilitate outreach to community resources to help the enuretic child and his or her family.

Social Competence: Substance Abuse

The seriousness of substance abuse cannot be overstated. Statistics speak for themselves as they assault the reader with grim reminders of the societal consequences of this epidemic. Three million teenagers in the United States are alcoholics, 56 percent of junior high school students have used alcohol, and in one survey 37 percent of high school seniors reported heavy drinking within the previous two weeks (five or more consecutive drinks). About 20 percent of seniors smoke cigarettes daily and more than one in twenty report daily marijuana use. In an Oklahoma survey, 13 percent of third-grade boys had used smokeless tobacco. One in ten occasional drug users has tried crack cocaine; 26 percent of callers to the National Cocaine Hotline (800-COCAINE) reported committing a crime while on crack, 95 percent of which were violent crimes. Alcohol is implicated in 40 percent of adolescent suicides and 45 percent of fatal car accidents involving teens. Thirty percent of all cancer is now believed to be caused by cigarette smoking. Interventions have focused on teaching children and adolescents resistance to drug-related social pressures and broad-based competencies such as decision-making skills, assertiveness, and anxiety reduction. These strategies were first applied to smoking prevention but have been expanded to address alcohol and drug abuse. Recent writings also discuss responsible or controlled use as a more realistic intermediate strategy, with abstinence as an eventual goal. The literature for this section is so vast that "Other References" have been added after the "Additional Readings" to provide the reader with an extended list of resources.

Counseling Alcohol-Abusing Children of Alcoholics

AUTHOR: Ellen R. Morehouse

PRECIS: Obstacles to overcome when treating adolescent alcohol abusers who are children of alcoholics

INTRODUCTION: Given the relationship between parent and child drinking patterns, it is not surprising that many teenage alcohol abusers and alcoholics are themselves children of alcoholics. Alcohol abuse disrupts the adolescent's ability to function in all areas of living, but the consequences are less severe than they would be if the teen were alcoholic; there is no physical addiction, bodily damage, loss of behavior control, or blackouts. Thus, not all teenagers who suffer the effects of their drinking can be labeled alcoholic, and techniques for working with abusers and alcoholics are different. This article focuses on abusers and some of the barriers to treatment for them.

IDENTIFICATION: Identification of the teenage alcohol abuser may be inhibited by several factors. The severity of the teen's problem may be denied by one or both alcoholic parents who also deny their own drinking, as recognition of the child's situation would force them to acknowledge their own disease. At the other end of the spectrum, a recovering alcoholic parent or nonalcoholic spouse may regard any drinking, however nonabusive, as a sign of potential alcoholism and press for unnecessary treatment, perhaps angering the child who then reacts to the mistaken assumption by drinking more. In addition, alcoholic parents who refuse treatment for themselves may provide an opportunity for adolescent abusers to avoid help with the rationalization that if their parents do not need help, neither do they, or that they do not drink as much as their parents and therefore do not need the same treatment. Guilt may also fuel a teen's abuse if the teen breaks a self-made promise not to drink like his or her parent(s), becomes an abuser, then denies the problem to relieve the guilt.

ASSESSMENT: Assessment of the adolescent's drinking problem requires an accurate and complete background history. However, alcoholic parents may not be accurate respondents, either because their drinking absented them from significant events or because their guilt regarding their role in their child's problem causes them to minimize it.

MOTIVATION: Motivating the adolescent child of an alcoholic to stop drinking is also problematic. Some do not admit that drinking has been detrimental to their parents and do not see why they should stop. Others do not believe there are alternatives to drinking because they have no experience with adult nondrinking role models. Still others do not see improvements at home when a parent stops drinking, or they blame Alcoholics Anonymous for its importance in their parent's life. Alcoholic parents are usually a main focus for the abusing teen who worries about their health and safety; is confused by their unstable behavior; is angry at their inconsistent physical care and affection; is concerned about fights between both parents and the possibility of violence, criminal, or improper sexual behavior; feels neglected; and perhaps feels responsible for their alcoholism. The teen needs the opportunity in counseling to express these feelings while the counselor educates him or her about alcohol abuse and alcoholism. The goal is to motivate an interest in treatment by having the adolescent understand the negative outcomes associated with drinking and the available alternatives. The counselor also helps students learn why they drink and how it creates problems with school, boyfriends or girlfriends, or other experiences. These steps may encourage the teen to seek treatment.

TREATMENT: A major problem in treatment is the effect on the family dynamics when one member changes. The teen may abandon a role that has maintained the family's status quo (for example, scapegoat), causing the family to pressure the child into resuming the role. The family may also try to undermine treatment by urging the teen to drink; criticizing the new, more healthy behavior; refusing to drive the adolescent to sessions; creating situations that cause missed or late appointments; and criticizing the therapist or other involved practitioners. The counselor can prepare the teen for these attempts by discussing the dynamics of such behavior and what might be done when parents are alcoholic. Attempts to involve the nondrinking spouse might lessen the sabotage but other living arrangements for the teen might need to be made if all else fails.

COPING: Drinking helps the adolescent cope with the pain of an unstable family and can lead him or her to substitute drugs during treatment. In treatment, all substance abuse must stop if the problems are to be confronted. Sometimes the counselor will stop treatment if there is no reduction in drinking after several months and allow the teen to face the outcomes of drinking, such as jail or suspension from school. Sometimes this approach contributes to positive changes.

ISSUES: Once drinking is eliminated, the adolescent child of an alcoholic can explore issues related to the situation such as his difficulty separating from home if he is concerned for younger siblings, unresolved needs for parental care, and worries about an unpredictable response; these are identity conflicts related to the lack of consistent parental role models, peer problems (resulting in dependent, demanding, overly sensitive, and confused reactions to friends as the teen transfers conflicted home relationships to his social experiences), embarrassment or rage at having an alcoholic parent and withdrawal from activities in which parents might participate, abuse of the parents to make them change, depression over the reality of a deprived family life, or guilt over having to take over a parenting role from the alcoholic parent.

COMMENTARY: The author considers groups (including Alcoholics Anonymous and Al-Anon) the most effective modality for treating adolescent alcohol-abusing children of alcoholics. Groups reduce the sense of isolation felt by these youngsters, offer peer support and influence, provide a forum for dealing with relational conflicts, give them feedback on behavior, and act as a buffer against the undermining behavior of alcoholic parents. Family sessions can be useful in helping parents see the need for help, but they are difficult if one parent is an active alcoholic. The school is a particularly appropriate place for such groups to meet. Teens congregate at school, and programs to assist alcohol-abusing students and children of alcoholics can be applied in the schoolhouse with the greatest consistency. The author of this article, Ellen Morehouse, heads a countywide program, the Student Assistance Program, which intervenes with substance-abusing students in school settings. For further information, contact Morehouse at Ardsley High School, 300 Farm Road, Ardsley, NY 10502. The reader is also referred to the following articles that discuss children of alcoholic parents and describe the student assistance model:

Chambers, J., and Morehouse, E. R. "A Cooperative Model for Preventing Alcohol and Drug Abuse." *NASSP Bulletin,* 1983, *67,* 81–87.

Morehouse, E. R. "Working in the Schools with Children of Alcoholic Parents." *Health and Social Work,* 1979, *4,* 144–162.

SOURCE: Morehouse, E. R. (1984). Working with alcohol-abusing children of alcoholics. *Alcohol Health and Research World,* *8*(4), 14–19.

A Cognitive-Developmental Approach to Smoking Prevention

AUTHORS: Robert S. Hirschman and Howard Leventhal

PRECIS: A cognitively based antismoking program to prevent students from progressing to more established smoking habits

INTRODUCTION: Unlike many smoking prevention programs that focus on resisting peer pressure, this three-session intervention induces students to reinterpret initial smoking experiences as negative, thus preventing them from progressing to habitual smoking. The developmental-stage model proposes four states of smoking development: (1) a preparatory stage in which attitudes toward smoking and smoking self-image are shaped; (2) an experimental stage in which expectations about smoking are confirmed or refuted and continued use is determined through positive or negative early smoking experiences; (3) a regular smoking stage wherein smoking becomes established at certain times and places; and (4) an addictive stage characterized by a strong need to smoke, heavy smoking, and withdrawal symptoms. This study attempted to capitalize on the aversive bodily sensations associated with initial smoking behavior to deter further smoking. The fact that 85 to 95 percent of students try one cigarette, but only as few as 32 percent try a second, suggests that initial experiences are a good starting point.

METHOD: Sixth, seventh, and eighth graders were exposed to three forty-five-minute class sessions, each of which began with a ten- to fifteen-minute slide presentation with accompanying tape. The presentations showed eight student actors and a physician moderator discussing smoking. These three edited discussions were rewritten and scripted from a two-and-a-half-hour talk involving six adolescents who responded to questions about their first smoking experience, developing the smoking habit, and entering the addiction stage. During the re-creation, three pathways to smoking were depicted in the students' behaviors: smoking due to peer pressure, smoking to control tension and stress, and smoking to create a self-defined, risk-oriented adultlike image.

Following the slide show, a thirty-minute directed discussion was conducted by a teacher. The discussion following the first presentation addressed why the first cigarette might be so physically unpleasant, possible body damage from these unpleasant sensations, and their value in deterring a second cigarette. The second discussion focused on the individual's growing accustomed to these symptoms, the continued damage occurring to the body, and the importance of stopping, despite the lessening of bodily warnings. Discussion 3 looked at addiction and the smoker's inability to judge when addiction is occurring. During all sessions, motivations to smoke or techniques to resist were described. Role-plays illustrated how to avoid smoking with minimal social fallout. Students were praised for their involvement and interest in trying out their newly acquired refusal skills. A control group saw films on health consequences of smoking and had their questions answered. To assess the program's effects, students were questioned about their smoking habits, their intent to smoke, possible pathways to smoking, understanding of first cigarette symptoms, adaptation to symptoms and addiction, knowledge of health consequences, and perception of smoking norms.

RESULTS: Results indicated that the program had no reductive effect on first cigarette triers or on those moving on from their second cigarette to experimentation and regular smoking, but it had clear effects on reducing the move from first to second cigarette at one-week, six-month, and eighteen-month follow-ups. Experimental students also tended more frequently to delay smoking the second cigarette by a week or more at the eighteen-month follow-up. At eighteen months, students from the program reported less experimentation (smoking within the previous six months) than did controls at a marginally significant level. Among self-described nonsmokers at the beginning of the program, significantly fewer described themselves as occasional or regular smokers at eighteen-month follow-up except those who were influenced to smoke by social pressure (having a best friend who smokes). It appears that the effect of the program operates over time rather than producing immediate differences. Experimental students also demonstrated superior gains in understanding first cigarette symptoms (at one week, six months, and eighteen months), adaptation issues (also at one week, six months, and eighteen months), and addiction (at one week and six months but not at eighteen months).

COMMENTARY: After only three sessions, students involved in the program demonstrated reduced progression of smoking eighteen months later. It appears that they successfully reinterpreted the smoking experience as intended. The authors note that the program was not successful with students whose best friend smoked, suggesting that peer pressure is a powerful force and that a social skills component may be an important addition to the treatment. However, students definitely changed their view of smoking sensations and improved their understanding of initial symptoms, adaptation, and to a lesser extent, addiction. This change in the interpretation of smoking suggests that altering interpretations of other experiences may cause these experiences to become powerful cognitive and behavioral modifiers.

SOURCE: Hirschman, R. S., & Leventhal, H. (1989). Preventing smoking behavior in school children: An initial test of a cognitive-development program. *Journal of Applied Social Psychology, 19,* 559–583.

Resisting Drug-Related Peer Pressure Through Assertion Training

AUTHORS: John J. Horan and John M. Williams

PRECIS: Assertion training to teach students resistance to peer pressure to use drugs

INTRODUCTION: Peer approval (or disapproval) is of tremendous importance in determining whether a student will smoke, drink, or use drugs. Coupled with evidence that assertiveness skills are poorly developed in drug users and that peer influence affects children's attitudes toward drugs, it is possible that peer pressure can render a nonassertive youngster susceptible to drug use. Assertion training may help such youths exercise their own free will independent of social pressure.

METHOD: Seventy-two eighth graders, ranked as least assertive on an Assertive Behavior Test, were subjects for this intervention. The test consisted of two role-plays to which the students responded and were scored for behavioral indications of assertiveness. Selected students met in small groups for five forty-five-minute sessions over two weeks and were exposed to an assertion training format. The counselor first discussed various attributes of assertiveness, followed by student modeling through live role-plays of assertive responses to ten non-drug assertiveness training stimuli and five stimuli involving peer pressure to use drugs. All students assumed each of the roles of speaker, listener, and responder twice for each training stimulus. The counselor supervised the training while modeling, instructing, and critiquing where appropriate. Three episodes were role-played during each session. The ten non-drug situations consisted of such scenes as friends interrupting your study, the laundry losing your clothes, or the waiter serving you steak that is too rare. Other students took part in discussions relating to peer pressure, drugs, and assertiveness without experiencing the training component. A control group had no experience of any kind.

RESULTS: Trained students were significantly more assertive on posttesting than were either the discussion or control groups, and at a three-year follow-up maintained a greater ability to resist drug-oriented peer pressure than either set of nontrained subjects. Furthermore, from pre- to posttesting, only the assertive training group was less willing to drink and use marijuana. After three years, there was less drug use among the experimental subjects than among the others.

COMMENTARY: The authors point out that assertion training helps the student refuse drugs when pressured by peers but that other factors are implicated in the decision to use or abstain. Thus, a multicomponent strategy is advocated that would include problem-solving and decision-making strategies. This intervention highlights the inadequacy of a "Just Say No" approach. While saying no is an important response, those most susceptible to drug use through peer pressure seem in most need of training that teaches them *how* to say no. It should not be assumed that the skill is present and need only be brought forward.

SOURCE: Horan, J. J., & Williams, J. M. (1982). Longitudinal study of assertion training as a drug abuse prevention strategy. *American Educational Research Journal, 19,* 341–351.

*Comparison of Curricula Stressing Short- and
Long-Term Influences for Smoking Prevention*

AUTHORS: Rise Morgenstern Arkin, Helen F. Roemhild, C. Anderson
Johnson, Russell V. Luepker, and David M. Murray

PRECIS: Smoking prevention programs with adult and peer leaders to prevent onset of smoking

INTRODUCTION: The health risks associated with smoking underscore
the need for effective smoking prevention programs. Social influences significantly impact the decision to smoke, and many interventions address this
as the primary issue. Two smoking curricula are contrasted here, one of
which deals specifically with social pressures to smoke.

CURRICULA: Seventh graders in eight junior high schools participated
in the program and were initially assessed for their smoking rates using self-
reports and saliva thiacyanate analysis. They were then assigned to one of
the following interventions:

1. Short-Term Influences Curriculum — students learned how peers,
family, and the media all create pressures to smoke and how to combat these
pressures. In two schools, health educators led the discussions; in four schools,
three students were selected by their peers in each class to be trained as
leaders. After two half-day workshops in group process, leadership training, and practice for the class activities, these leaders ran the five-session
program in each of their classrooms, with the health educator acting as su-
pervisor. For session I, students discussed disadvantages of smoking and
why seventh graders start. Methods to resist pressures to smoke were role-
played. In two of the four peer-led schools, media were utilized in the program and the video, "Why Do People Smoke?," from the Minnesota Smoking Series, was shown. It depicted short-term physical effects of smoking
and provided resistance techniques to pressure. Session II emphasized that
most students do not smoke, after students overestimated the number of
seventh graders who smoke regularly. More role-playing was done, followed
by a second film in the series for the schools using media; the film showed
students refusing cigarettes. For session III, students took turns role-playing
offering and refusing cigarettes to explore both sides of the smoking argument and to develop resistance responses. In session IV, students made antismoking collages from cigarette ads and displayed them throughout the
school; in the school using media, students saw the final tape in the series,
which discussed the messages in smoking ads and the influence of family
smoking on students. In session V, half the students publicly committed in
a videotaped session not to smoke; this group saw the entire video in class
to reinforce their efforts. The other half of the group did not make a no-
smoking commitment.

2. Long-Term Influences Curriculum—the health educator led all five sessions of this curriculum, which addressed the long-term physical effects of smoking. Session I examined effects on the lungs with the film, "Breath of Air," from the American Cancer Society. Session II discussed cardiovascular damage, and the students viewed, "Smoking: A Report on the Nation's Habit," from Pelican Films. In session III students played Password using smoking and health-oriented terms, while session IV focused on effects of smoking on the unborn child. The film, "I'm Sorry, Baby," from Pelican Films was shown. In Session V, some classes made a public commitment not to smoke while some constructed thematic collages.

RESULTS: Use of a standard curriculum was least effective in preventing nonsmokers from trying smoking. Furthermore, students in this group had the highest rate of experimental and weekly smoking when posttested. The Long-Term Influences Curriculum was more effective than the Short-Term curriculum in discouraging nonsmokers from experimenting with cigarettes. The adult-led short-term strategy was most effective in reducing weekly smoking. Experimental smoking was reduced 37.3 percent by all experimental programs, while weekly smoking declined by 58.8 percent. Peer-led strategies and use of media were no more effective than adult-run or no-media approaches.

COMMENTARY: It is not clear which components of these programs actually prevent smoking, but the authors note first that resistance to pressure has been shown in other research to be enhanced when individuals create and practice opposing viewpoints. Second, they point out the importance of public commitment in fostering adherence to a goal. Both of these findings from the literature are incorporated into the program and demonstrate the importance of linking research with application. It would have been interesting if a comparison of groups making a public commitment with those who did not had been pursued in the study. In a later study in which these curricula were replicated, peer-led groups were more effective than teacher-instructed groups. Perhaps the superiority of peers as teachers depends upon which adults are used. Health educators may be expected to be more skilled than classroom teachers in presenting such programs. However, if health educators are not available, trained peers may be preferable to classroom teachers.

SOURCE: Arkin, R. M., Roemhild, H. F., Johnson, C. A., Luepker, R. V., & Murray, D. M. (1981). The Minnesota Smoking Prevention Program: A seventh-grade health curriculum supplement. *The Journal of School Health*, *51*, 611–616.

Reducing Drug Use Through Inoculation Techniques

AUTHORS: Howard Shaffer, James C. Beck, and Phyllis Boothroyd

PRECIS: Inoculation strategies to prevent, reduce, and stop smoking and marijuana use

INTRODUCTION: Analogous to medical practice, inoculation against smoking involves exposing the student to a weakened form of the disease agent (social pressure to smoke) in order to develop resistance to the disorder (skills to combat the pressure). Inoculation procedures were tested with seventh graders to determine whether they could be prevented from smoking.

METHOD: The program focused on helping students view smoking as an affective and behavioral response to demands of a particular setting; it can be prevented if students recognize the cues to smoking and develop coping strategies to manage the behavior. The program was implemented in three stages — cognitive preparation, skill acquisition, and skill rehearsal — over six forty-five-minute class periods. The instructor was guided by a manual that gave detailed instructions for each session (available from the authors).

　　1. Cognitive preparation — reasons for smoking, health dangers, and the need for prevention programs were presented with handouts. Students explored the antecedent conditions leading to smoking (feelings, situations, and specific people), their own desires about smoking, the general reasons students begin, the self-statements that reduce the need to smoke, awareness of the physical and psychological signals that cue smoking, and the possible use of inoculation as a preventive technique.

　　2. Skill acquisition — three sets of inoculation procedures were learned: a cognitive set, an affective set, and a behavioral set. The cognitive set enabled students to learn what occurrences trigger conflict and the need to smoke, and how to redefine these occurrences to manage the triggering effect. Two specific skills, maintaining a task orientation and developing self-efficacy, were taught through a film, slides, and role-plays in which students learned to develop their own ideas and coping responses to smoking pressure from friends and media. The affective set of inoculation skills was taught in the form of relaxation training; the behavioral set included the ability to communicate feelings accurately, respond effectively to various situations, and problem solve in a task-oriented manner.

　　3. Skill rehearsal — in this final stage, the students practiced their newly acquired skills (the article did not treat this stage separately from stage 2).

RESULTS: Information about smoking behavior was obtained through a questionnaire given in a pre- posttest format. Students exposed to the program reported significantly less smoking behavior at posttesting than did a control group exposed only to cognitive preparation. The control group actually increased their use of cigarettes. The program was also effective in preventing the onset of smoking in some students and in inducing others to quit.

COMMENTARY: Students can learn alternative responses to the conforming patterns imposed by peer pressure. Interestingly, the program also effectively retarded initial marijuana use (but not alcohol consumption), suggesting to the authors that certain "interactional nets" (p. 182) exist in which user groups will focus on certain clusters of drugs and not others. Cigarettes and marijuana may be one such cluster. The effectiveness of this program and the influence of modeling on substance abuse suggests that inoculation against peer pressure will be more productive than presentation of the long- or short-term risks associated with specific drugs. As the authors further suggest, booster sessions might be needed to maintain effects over time. Further research is needed.

SOURCE: Shaffer, H., Beck, J. C., & Boothroyd, P. (1983). The primary prevention of smoking onset: An inoculation approach. *Journal of Psychoactive Drugs, 15,* 177–183.

A Psychosocial Approach to Smoking Prevention

AUTHORS: Gilbert J. Botvin, Nancy L. Renick, and Eli Baker

PRECIS: The Life Skills Training Program as a method of smoking prevention and a strategy to address other health-compromising behaviors

INTRODUCTION: Informing students of the health consequences of smoking may increase their knowledge and promote attitudes unfavorable to smoking, but it does not reduce their smoking behavior. The program presented here is a multicomponent classroom-based approach to smoking prevention that focuses on social competence and broad-based coping skills.

METHOD: Subjects were seventh graders, 92 percent of whom were considered nonsmokers at pretesting. They were exposed to the fifteen-session Life Skills Training (LST) smoking prevention program conducted by trained classroom teachers in either a once-weekly format as part of the health or science program, or as a daily minicourse for approximately one month. Each session lasted for a one-hour class period. In addition, one of the schools using the minicourse approach received eight booster sessions between post-testing and a one-year follow-up.

LIFE SKILLS TRAINING: The LST program begins with an orientation session in which a pretest questionnaire is completed by each student, saliva is collected from participants for analysis, and the program is introduced and described. The following topics are covered during the course: smoking attitudes, prevalence of smoking, the pros and cons of smoking, becoming addicted, the growing societal intolerance for smoking, short-term respiratory and cardiovascular consequences, developing a positive self-image, decision making and independent thinking, resisting advertising techniques that encourage smoking, managing anxiety, communication skills, social skills, assertiveness, and a concluding session for saliva collection, a posttest questionnaire, and general wrap-up. A control group received no special smoking prevention activities. A complete description of the program with lesson plans may be found in the following: Botvin, G. J., and Eng, A. *Life Skills Training: Teachers' Manual.* New York: Smithfield Press, 1980.

RESULTS: The LST program reduced new smoking by 50 percent by the end of the first year, with a 32 percent reduction evident after the one-year follow-up. A 49 percent reduction in regular smoking was also evident by the end of the second year. Interestingly, the superiority of the more intensive minicourse format did not become evident until the end of the second year, producing about one-half the number of new smokers as the weekly course. Booster sessions held during the second year helped extend the effects of the minicourse by producing 60 percent fewer new smokers than among the students who received no booster. Altogether, when compared to the control group, the minicourse LST program using booster sessions resulted in an 87 percent reduction in new regular smokers. Furthermore, smoking-related knowledge and other attitudes and personality variables associated with enhanced psychosocial competence were significantly increased as a result of the LST program. Specifically, assertiveness, positive self-image, and antismoking attitudes were increased, while social anxiety, external locus of control, and susceptibility to social pressure all decreased.

COMMENTARY: This complex program certainly would benefit from a component analysis to determine whether all its elements are required to produce the goal of reduced smoking or prevention of onset, as acceptance of any program by an already overscheduled teaching staff is often determined by the amount of time required for implementation. If a program such as this is to be utilized, it will need to demonstrate its practicality. One selling point is the co-varying relationship of many health-compromising behaviors, allowing them to be correlated with each other, such as smoking, drinking, use of drugs (for example, marijuana), and/or sexual activity. This relationship suggests that a psychosocial program like LST might be able to attack several related problems simultaneously by addressing their common causes. In these instances, vulnerability to social influences may be an underlying variable requiring intervention to strengthen the students' appropriate resistance mechanisms. For a more thorough discussion of the

LST format and its application to alcohol misuse, the reader is referred to the following articles:

Botvin, G. J. "The Life Skills Training Program as a Health Promotion Strategy: Theoretical Issues and Empirical Findings." In J. E. Zins, D. I. Wagner, and C. A. Maher (eds.), *Health Promotion in the Schools: Innovative Approaches to Facilitating Physical and Emotional Well-being* (pp. 9–23). Binghamton, NY: Haworth Press, 1985.

Botvin, G. J., Baker, E., Botvin, E. M., Filazzola, A. D., and Millman, R. B. "Prevention of Alcohol Misuse Through the Development of Personal and Social Competence: A Pilot Study." *Journal of Studies on Alcohol,* 1984, *45,* 550–552.

SOURCE: Botvin, G. J., Renick, N. L., & Baker, E. (1983). The effects of scheduling format and booster sessions on a broad-spectrum psychosocial approach to smoking prevention. *Journal of Behavioral Medicine, 6,* 359–379.

Additional Readings

Best, J. A., Flay, B. R., Towson, S.M.J., Ryan, K. B., Perry, C. L., Brown, K. S., Kersell, M. W., & D'Avernas, J. R. (1984). Smoking prevention and the concept of risk. *Journal of Applied Social Psychology, 14,* 257–273.

The article describes the Waterloo Smoking Prevention Project. Sixth graders participated in six one-hour weekly sessions consisting of (1) information about smoking and its consequences, settings likely to trigger social pressures to smoke, and resistance techniques; (2) resistance training to inoculate students against smoking pressures; and (3) a decision by participants regarding whether to smoke and a public announcement of the decision to the class. Two maintenance sessions were held near the end of grade 6 followed by two booster sessions in grade 7 and one in grade 8. Students were divided according to their smoking experience and their risk level (no smoking parents, siblings, or friends, to smokers in at least two of these groups). Results indicated that experimental smokers in the program stopped smoking earlier than those in a comparison group receiving a traditional smoking curriculum. Further, for students with little or no smoking experience, there was no difference between treatment and comparison groups until the grade 8 follow-up. The program was more effective with students exposed to a greater number of smoking models.

This article is described as a fourth-generation study in a comprehensive review of psychosocial approaches to smoking prevention. Such studies are more methodologically rigorous than earlier generations of studies, yet they still leave open questions regarding why social influences work, for whom, and under what conditions. More research is needed. The reader is referred to the following article:

Flay, B. R. "Psycho-social Approaches to Smoking Prevention: A Review of Findings." *Health Psychology,* 1985, *4,* 449–488.

DeRicco, D. A., & Niemann, J. E. (1980). In vivo effects of peer modelling on drinking rate. *Journal of Applied Behavior Analysis, 13,* 149–152.

At a tavern, friends of a drinker modeled reduced drinking to influence the drinker to lower her consumption of beer. After a baseline drinking rate for the subject was established, three intervention phases were conducted. In the first, one of the friends drank 50 percent less beer than the subject's baseline rate. In the second, two confederates drank at the 50 percent rate and in the third, four friends reduced their level to 50 percent. Only when all four modeled reduced drinking did the subject reduce her rate to match theirs. Peer modeling in this real-life drinking situation effectively reduced a high rate of consumption.

Forman, S. G., & Linney, J. A. (1988). School-based prevention of adolescent substance abuse: Programs, implementation, and future directions. *School Psychology Review, 17,* 550–558.

Three types of school-based substance abuse prevention programs are described. The first are education/information programs that work with adults but not adolescents. The second type are social resistance programs that use role-play and assertiveness training to teach teens (primarily seventh to ninth graders) resistance skills in response to peer pressure to use drugs. Other social influences, such as the family, advertising, and the media, are also addressed. The last type is coping skills training, which teaches a broad range of competency skills through lectures, discussion, role-playing, self-instruction, relaxation training, and assertiveness training. Programs for students already experimenting with drugs are few in number, but they include goal setting with teachers, rewards for meeting goals, regular parent contacts, general coping skills training, and teacher and parent training.

Issues to address when implementing such programs in the schools include administrative, parent, staff, and student acceptance; personnel requirements and staff training; scheduling; materials; promoting generalization through parent and community participation; parent training in family management skills; community programs to provide alternative behaviors to drug use; and coordinated media involvement in school/family programs. Future programs need to address the complex causes of substance abuse through multilevel strategies.

Hansen, D. M. (1991, Summer). The window of sobriety: Chemical dependency and adolescent development. *Mental Health Perspectives.* (Available from Craig House Hospital, Howland Avenue, Beacon, NY 12508), pp. 2, 5.

Although adolescents nearly always regress to chemical dependency within a year after treatment, the author argues that this is an inevitable outgrowth of the adolescent need to experiment, coupled with the ego deficits and weak coping mechanisms of the teen abuser. However, each repeated treatment experience provides a window of sobriety for the teen, during which developmental maturity occurs as the benefits of treatment are assimilated. Although the relapse halts the developmental process, it is important to open the "window" as many times as necessary so that development of the self can be restarted and eventually reach a point where drug use is not resumed. Outpatient group treatment combined with parent education and support groups is seen as filling the gap between long-term inpatient treatment and the twelve-step programs.

Hawk, D. E. (1985). Substance abuse prevention: Components of program planning. In J. E. Zins, D. I. Wagner, & C. A. Maher (Eds.), *Health promotion in the schools: Innovative approaches to facilitating physical and emotional well-being* (pp. 99–112). Binghamton, NY: Haworth Press.

Responsible substance use rather than total abstinence is a legitimate and practical goal for substance abuse prevention programs. This goal involves encouraging delay of first use, limited amounts per use, reduced frequency of use, use at appropriate times and in appropriate settings, and emphasis on no use as a responsible choice. Programs should include a knowledge component; a values or attitudinal component; decision-making, self-esteem, assertiveness, and communication skills components; and a range of alternative enjoyable activities to replace substance use. In addition, schools, families, and community need to participate in program development and implementation. When planning a prevention program it is essential to gain support from varied sources in and out of the school; conduct a needs assessment; identify a program philosophy that addresses school-community needs; set goals and objectives; tie program activities to the goals and objectives; identify personnel needs, funding sources, and needed program materials; identify training needs; construct an evaluation procedure; and determine what modifications may be required to overcome program weaknesses and/or barriers to success.

Hays, R. D., & Ellickson, P. L. (1990). How generalizable are adolescents' beliefs about pro-drug pressures and resistance self-efficacy? *Journal of Applied Social Psychology, 20,* 321–340.

Adolescents who are taught resistance skills to combat pressure to use drugs seem to be able to generalize these resistance techniques as well as their belief in their ability to resist across alcohol, cigarettes and marijuana, and situations in which drug use might occur (for example, a party or a date). However, perceived self-efficacy is reported by teens to drop as pressure to conform increases. This is particularly true for alcohol and may relate to the greater acceptance of alcohol use in this country (64 percent of high school seniors report drinking; 18 percent and 29 percent report marijuana and tobacco use, respectively). The authors suggest that prevention programs need to teach adolescents how to avoid high-pressure drug situations, reduce the felt pressure imposed by others or generated internally, and model successful resisters; they also need to provide realistic information about the majority of peers who do not use drugs. Furthermore, the training of resistance skills may need to be associated with various situations and settings to promote generalization.

Schinke, S. P., & Gilchrist, L. D. (1985). Preventing substance abuse with children and adolescents. *Journal of Consulting and Clinical Psychology, 53,* 596–602.

Efforts at substance abuse prevention focus on controlling or eliminating the substance or access to it, altering the environmental conditions that influence use, or strengthening the individual's ability to avoid use. In this study, sixth graders met in ten one-hour group sessions and were exposed to a coping skills strategy that included films, slide presentations, antismoking information from peers, problem-solving techniques, self-instruction, and communication skills training to manage pressure to smoke. The multicomponent intervention was effective in preventing students from smoking at posttesting and at six-month, one-year, and two-year follow-ups, and in enhancing the coping skills targeted by the training. An attention-placebo group who did not receive training in problem solving, self-instruction, and communication development performed better than the control group but did not match the results of the experimental group.

Smith, T. E. (1983). Reducing adolescents' marijuana abuse. *Social Work in Health Care, 9,* 33–44.

Occasional moderate use of marijuana by basically healthy persons is not seen as a public or personal health hazard, but use by increasingly younger adolescents who do not easily regulate their intake can have negative health and psychological consequences and possibly lead to abuse, as so often happens with tobacco and alcohol. Programs that require total abstinence or conditions that permit unrestricted use do not inhibit or promote moderate use. Teaching adolescents guidelines for responsible controlled use rather than aiming for total elimination might represent a more constructive approach to reducing dangerous levels of ingestion. The ultimate stated goal is abstinence, but responsible use may be viewed as a progression toward that goal, one that reduces the hazards of abuse.

The intervention described includes an information component that is value free and accurate, a cognitive component focusing on problem-solving (decision-making) skills, and a behavioral component that helps students act on their decisions by addressing such social skills as refusal techniques, assertiveness, and expression of feelings. The model is illustrated with an example of a school-based adolescent group of marijuana abusers who learned from each other through discussion and role-play to identify problems resulting from marijuana use, develop solutions, and choose the best alternatives. Compared to a delayed-training control group, the trained group was absent from school less, achieved higher grades, had more friends who were not users, and used and abused the drug less. The model is easily adapted for use with abusers of other drugs.

Van Meter, W., & Rioux, D. (1990). The case for shorter residential alcohol and other drug abuse treatment of adolescents. *Journal of Psychoactive Drugs,* 22, 87–88.

The authors argue that although residential treatment for adolescent alcohol and/or drug abusers is at times necessary, shorter-term placements can be effective despite the reported traditional length of stay of forty-two days to six months. They cite the College Hill Medical Center in East Strouds-burg, Pennsylvania, which offers a twenty-one-day program to teens thirteen to eighteen years of age. The center provides individual counseling, intensive group therapy, recreation therapy, Alcoholics Anonymous and Narcotics Anonymous meeting opportunities, a school experience including coordination with the home school district to prevent students from falling behind in their studies, family therapy separate from and with the teen, and a well-designed aftercare plan. During their stay, the youngsters interact with adult recovering clients, hearing about the catastrophes awaiting them if they pursue their addiction. A telephone survey to former clients validated the effectiveness of this short-term approach.

Youngstrom, N. (1991, September). Psychology helps curb cigarette sales. *APA Monitor,* p. 1.

A community psychologist and police sergeant in the Chicago suburb of Woodridge, Illinois, teamed to influence passage of a law that required merchants to be licensed to sell cigarettes. If the merchants sold cigarettes to minors, the law allowed their licenses to be revoked for one day and a fine of $400 to be imposed on them. They also had to lock cigarette machines and obtain proof of age from purchasers before unlocking them or making sales. Before the new law, 60 to 79 percent of local merchants sold cigarettes to youths in defiance of the original law. With enforcement of the new law, sales dropped to zero and have remained so. Stores that are not selling to minors when randomly checked receive a commendation letter from the mayor. After two years under the new law, the proportion of seventh and eighth graders who were involved in experimental/social smoking had dropped from 60 percent to 23 percent; those who were regular smokers decreased from 15 percent to 5 percent. Such a law must exist in adjoining communities for greatest effectiveness; however, many teens reported that the law in their community alone helped them cut down on smoking.

Further Reading

Botvin, G. J. (1986). Substance abuse prevention research: Recent developments and future directions. *Journal of School Health,* 56, 369–374.

Clarke, J. H., MacPherson, B., Holmes, D. R., & Jones, R. (1986). Reducing adolescent smoking: A comparison of peer-led, teacher-led, and expert interventions. *Journal of School Health, 56,* 102–106.

Duryea, P. E., Kreuter, M. W., & Braza, G. F. (1981). Cognitive perceptions of importance in students' decisions about smoking. *Health Education, 12,* 4–8.

Evans, R. I., Rozelle, R. M., Maxwell, S. E., Raines, B. E., Dill, C. A., Guthrie, T. J., Henderson, A. H., & Hill, P. C. (1981). Social modeling films to deter smoking in adolescents: Results of a three-year field investigation. *Journal of Applied Psychology, 66,* 399–414.

Forman, S. G., & Randolph, M. K. (1987). Children and drug abuse. In A. Thomas & J. Grimes (Eds.), *Children's needs: Psychological perspectives* (pp. 182–188). Washington, DC: National Association of School Psychologists.

Horan, J. J., & Straus, L. K. (1987). Substance abuse. In M. H. Hersen & V. B. Van Hasselt (Eds.), *Behavior therapy with children and adolescents: A clinical approach* (pp. 440–461). New York: Wiley.

Hurd, P. D., Johnson, C. A., Pechacek, T., Bast, L. P., Jacobs, D. R., & Luepker, R. V. (1980). Prevention of cigarette smoking in seventh grade students. *Journal of Behavioral Medicine, 3,* 15–28.

Klepp, K., Halper, A., & Perry, C. L. (1986). The efficacy of peer leaders in drug abuse prevention. *Journal of School Health, 56,* 407–412.

McDermott, R. J., & Marty, P. J. (1982). Athletes score a hit with kids in grades four through eight. *Journal of School Health, 52,* 94–96.

Perry, C. L., Killen, J., Slinkard, L. A., & McAlister, A. L. (1980). Peer teaching and smoking prevention among junior high school students. *Adolescence, 15,* 277–281.

Perry, C., Killen, J., Telch, M., Slinkard, L. A., & Danaher, B. G. (1980). Modifying smoking behavior of teenagers: A school-based intervention. *American Journal of Public Health, 70,* 722–725.

St. Pierre, R. W., Shute, R. E., & Jaycox, S. (1983). Youth helping youth: A behavioral approach to the self-control of smoking. *Health Education, 14,* 28–31.

Schinke, S. P., & Gilchrist, L. D. (1983). Primary prevention of tobacco smoking. *Journal of School Health, 53,* 416–420.

Seffrin, J. R., & Bailey, W. J. (1985). Approaches to adolescent smoking cessation and education. In J. E. Zins, D. I. Wagner, & C. A. Maher (Eds.), *Health promotion in the schools: Innovative approaches to facilitating physical and emotional well-being* (pp. 25–38). Binghamton, NY: Haworth Press.

Severson, H. H. (1984). Adolescent social drug use: School prevention program. *School Psychology Review, 13,* 150–161.

Social Competence:
Sexual Behavior

Each day in the United States, about three thousand adolescents become pregnant. Ten percent of the 500,000 teenagers who give birth each year are fifteen years old or younger. One-third of all abortions are to teens. The incidence of acquired immune deficiency syndrome (AIDS) among thirteen- to twenty-one-year-olds is doubling each year. Twenty percent of all AIDS cases occur among adults in their twenties, suggesting that original transmission may well have occurred during adolescence. More than half of all teens have had intercourse by age nineteen. Teenagers often engage in high-risk sexual behaviors, often delay use of contraception for up to one year after their first sexual experience, and may not have the knowledge, values, communication, and decision-making skills needed to manage their developing sexuality. Coupled with peer pressure, impaired relationships with parents, academic difficulties, and social-cognitive deficits, these factors may precipitate early risky sexual activity. Schools remain an important setting in which teenagers may learn the skills needed to alter their risk-taking sexual behavior.

Skills Training to Avoid Unplanned Pregnancies

AUTHORS: Lewayne D. Gilchrist and Steven Paul Schinke

PRECIS: A cognitive-behavioral program to encourage contraceptive use

INTRODUCTION: Many teenagers do not use any form of birth control for at least a year after becoming sexually active. Given that 50 percent of unintended pregnancies occur within six months of initial sexual activity, the need to teach young people the skills associated with contraceptive use is evident. Skills to promote contraception seem to involve communication, interpersonal problem solving, planning, and assertiveness. In this study, the authors exposed groups of twenty or more tenth, eleventh, and twelfth graders to a cognitive-behavioral treatment package that had been previously tested in small groups.

METHOD: Two groups of twenty-seven teens met in fifty-minute daily sessions for two weeks led by a trained male/female team. For two sessions, they discussed factual information about reproduction and birth control. One session described problem solving, focusing on defining the main concern, developing alternative solutions, working through the consequences of each proposed solution, choosing the option, and implementing it. Another session dealt with elements of effective interpersonal communication, stressing verbal and nonverbal approaches, and refusal and request skills. Six sessions were devoted to practice exercises, role-plays, and covert behavior rehearsal in which leaders instructed, coached, and provided feedback on the teens' problem-solving and communication skills. The students practiced using facts to make decisions about contraception that applied directly to their own lives. They role-played discussions about birth control with partners, buying contraceptive devices, refusing sexual demands, and obtaining needed information. They practiced relaxation, then imagined discussions with a sexual partner regarding birth control. They completed homework assignments, including writing a dialogue of the imagined conversation, which was then role-played in the sessions. They completed readings, took quizzes, and wrote up results of assignments in which they had to price birth control products, obtain information from a retailer, discuss contraception with a date, and solicit opinions from adults. These were read anonymously in class and praised by group members who offered corrective suggestions (materials and a treatment manual are available from the first author).

RESULTS: Compared with control subjects, the experimental groups demonstrated more contraceptive knowledge, had more positive attitudes toward contraception, were more intent on using birth control, and demonstrated more effective problem-solving and communication skills. Group members were also judged as demonstrating these skills in a more realistic fashion.

Finally, after treatment had ended, experimental group members viewed themselves as more effective and less anxious than controls.

COMMENTARY: The success of this cognitive-behavioral treatment package with groups larger than many academic classes indicates that, given proper planning and support, such programs can be implemented in school settings to reduce unplanned pregnancies. Often claims are made that such programs encourage sexual activity; these arguments are refuted, however, by the finding that in this study, conducted in a middle-class suburban public high school, nearly one-third of the students already reported at least one experience of sexual intercourse, and about one in twenty indicated having been pregnant or having gotten a girl pregnant. None of these students was indicated as having academic or psychological problems. As in many other interventions with multiple components, determining which parts of the strategy contribute most to its effectiveness would be helpful, allowing schools to apply it in its most economical form. Possibly the program could be conducted with fewer sessions or with different leaders, including peers. These issues require further research.

SOURCE: Gilchrist, L. D., & Schinke, S. P. (1983). Coping with contraception: Cognitive and behavioral methods with adolescents. *Cognitive Therapy and Research, 7,* 379–388.

Teaching Adolescents to Refuse Sexual Advances

AUTHORS: William J. Warzak and Terry J. Page

PRECIS: Refusal skills training with two handicapped teenagers to reduce instances of sexual intercourse

INTRODUCTION: The academic, vocational, psychological, and health consequences of teenage pregnancy and parenthood, both for the parents and child, demand that methods be developed to reduce pregnancy rates. Interventions focusing on information, decision making, and values education have not been effective. Competency-based approaches teach problem solving, communication skills, and assertiveness to help teens clearly communicate their refusal of sexual advances. In this study, two sexually active teenage girls — a deaf sixteen-year-old (Amy) and a developmentally delayed fourteen-year-old (Karen) — were taught refusal skills at their request.

METHOD: Role-play scenarios in which a confederate made sexual advances were created from the girls' "who, what, when, and where" descriptions of situations in which they had actually engaged in sexual intercourse. Each daily training session began with the girls performing one of the scenes during which their refusal skill deficits were assessed and identified. Then, following a review of the skills they had already learned, three role-play scenes were used to teach them new refusal skill components through a five-step process: providing a rationale, modeling use of skills, rehearsing skills, providing corrective feedback, and giving reinforcement. Each session ended with another assessment role-play. Measures of effective skill training were establishment of eye contact, a clearly stated or a visible "no," a statement indicating the inappropriateness of the sexual behavior, and walking away from the confederate after the sexual advance.

RESULTS: During baseline, Amy demonstrated use of eye contact, perhaps because of her deafness, but no other refusal skills. Karen utilized verbal refusal but no other components. As each skill was trained, the girls displayed high rates of the behavior. A two-week follow-up with different staff showed continued high-level use of the skills, and a one-year follow-up by telephone yielded reports of decreased sexual activity by each girl. A social validation of the girls' use of refusal skills indicated clearly that they had acquired the skills and were using them.

COMMENTARY: As with substance abuse, the authors do not unrealistically advocate the use of refusal skills training to eliminate sexual intercourse but to provide the skills needed when a person chooses to resist sexual offers. The suggestion here is that teens may engage in sexual behavior when they would rather not because they do not know how to say no, are embarrassed or pressured into engagement, or are afraid to refuse. Refusal skills allow them a choice, even though the consequences of teenage pregnancy and the health risks associated with unprotected intercourse make refusal a desirable decision. The authors also point out that refusal skills can be used to set the parameters of sexual activity — for example, use of birth control. Given the existence of AIDS, such skills can have a potentially life-saving effect.

SOURCE: Warzak, W. J., & Page, T. J. (1990). Teaching refusal skills to sexually active adolescents. *Journal of Behavior Therapy and Experimental Psychiatry, 21,* 133–139.

Pregnancy Prevention in the Schools

AUTHOR: Kathleen D. Paget

PRECIS: The components of potentially effective pregnancy prevention strategies and the psychologist's role in program planning

INTRODUCTION: Schools are an appropriate setting for pregnancy prevention programs, and school psychologists can coordinate these efforts if they are knowledgeable about correlates of teenage pregnancy, existing prevention programs, and applications of these to the school environment.

CORRELATES: Factors related to teenage pregnancy include membership in a minority group, low socioeconomic status, life stresses, low educational performance and career goals, living in a single-parent home, family strife, and many foster care placements. Although pregnant teenagers are more likely to have a history of academic difficulties, those with higher achievement and career goals are more likely to choose abortion. In addition, most who give birth do not return to or complete school, further depressing their economic status and leading to dependency on government assistance programs. While teenage mothers are able to find jobs, the responsibilities of parenting cause them to put off employment and then to accept easily available positions that pay little and offer no real advancement opportunities.

Regarding birth control, many adolescents do not consider future consequences of their present risky behaviors and therefore do not consider using contraceptives. Others have little knowledge of contraceptives or believe they will not get pregnant, or think that contraceptives are either not effective or immoral. Some teens may wish to become pregnant. The nature of the mother-daughter relationship also influences birth control use. All these factors collectively suggest that pregnancy prevention programs must urge students to complete high school; must include development of employability skills, that is, choosing, securing, and maintaining an acceptable job; and must focus on the cognitive, attitudinal, and psychological issues that increase a teenage girl's vulnerability to pregnancy. Providing information about birth control is not by itself useful.

SCHOOL-BASED PROGRAMS: Although not widespread, school-based family-planning services offer education, counseling, clinic referral services, and general and reproductive health examinations, including lab tests and contraceptive distribution accompanied by ongoing education sessions. Two successful programs are the Adolescent Health Services of the St. Paul/Ramsey Medical Center Maternal and Infant Care Project in St. Paul, Minnesota, which operates in several St. Paul high schools, and the Johns Hopkins University Medical Center Program running in two junior and two senior high schools in Baltimore, Maryland.

School-based programs that promote more reflective and responsible sexual behavior are increasing in number although there is a lack of evaluative data to judge their effectiveness. Approaches such as the Iowa State University "Sexuality and the Adolescent" curriculum encourage students from all socioeconomic backgrounds to explore and more clearly define their sexual values, while the "Postponing Sexual Involvement" curriculum from Atlanta, Georgia, teaches resistance and assertive responses to social/sexual pressures, involves parents in the learning process, and emphasizes personal rights in relationships. The "A Community of Caring" curriculum developed at the Joseph P. Kennedy, Jr., Foundation promotes sexual self-discipline as the correct value and attempts to instill the view that commitment and love, not pleasure, should be the paramount attribute of sexual intimacy. Other cited educational resources include Planned Parenthood and the Institute for Family Research and Education at Syracuse University.

COMMUNITY-BASED PROGRAMS: Community support to schools has been provided through several programs:

1. Girls Club of Dallas—for females eleven to eighteen years of age, this program provides assertiveness training; mother-daughter classes for sexual communication; courses in planning, budgeting, health, and employment; a focus on advantages of postponing sexual relationships; career and leadership education through a field-based female mentor program; and dropout prevention.

2. Early Adolescent Helper Program—offers after-school community improvement activities to eleven- to fourteen-year-olds, coinciding with the time of day when many early pregnancies occur. Pre-employment experiences and career exploration combine with parenting seminars that promote discussion and reflection about early and appropriate parenthood.

3. El Puente—empowers Hispanic youth, twelve to twenty-one years old, to move from adolescence to adulthood, to attain economic independence and a personal sense of self-sufficiency. The program provides physical and sexual health services, experiences in the arts, counseling, legal services, job placement, and classes in English as a second language. In return, participants are empowered by planning with a counselor to contribute to the program through assisting with community projects or through other activities. Members of the community who have grown up and been successful sit on an advisory board, act as role models, and help fund the program.

Collectively, these programs utilize various strategies, rely on collaboration among agencies, emphasize a reciprocal give-and-take relationship between the program and the clients, include peer support, focus on future planning, and aim toward health promotion.

PROGRAM PLANNING: In planning prevention programs within school settings, the author highlights certain essential steps a school psychologist can take: (1) Include nonproblem as well as at-risk groups to establish normalization of services as a framework. (2) Target groups, not individuals. (3) Utilize an ecological framework when planning interventions. (4) Be proactive. (5) Use face-to-face interactive methods. (6) Promote empowerment and competency. (7) Develop plans that take into account and therefore are aligned with community values, school structures, community cultural backgrounds, and other ecological variables. For example, pregnancy prevention strategies can take nonsexual formats if necessary, such as using math to discuss budget and family planning, or other activities naturally incorporated into existing curricula. (8) Provide staff training. In addition, the school psychologist can participate in political and legislative action through collaboration with other professional groups who advocate family planning and pregnancy prevention programs and lobby for research funding to help build an empirical foundation for effective programming.

COMMENTARY: The reader is referred to the end of Paget's article, listing national organizations that address adolescent pregnancy and parenting issues. An important, if often overlooked, point is that pregnancy prevention does not have to focus directly on sexuality education. Given community sensitivities, programs that stress high school completion, vocational awareness and training, family budgeting, parenting skills, and personal empowerment are also assisting young women in postponing the risky sexual behaviors that lead to early pregnancy. As the author points out, perhaps such programs will more systematically begin to include young males.

SOURCE: Paget, K. D. (1988). Adolescent pregnancy: Implications for prevention strategies in educational settings. *School Psychology Review, 17,* 570–780.

Additional Readings

Dryfoos, J. G. (1984). A new strategy for preventing unintended teenage childbearing. *Family Planning Perspectives, 16,* 193–195.

Adolescents gain the *capacity* to avoid parenthood through knowledge of reproduction, contraception, counseling, and abortion. However, *desire* to avoid maternity involves understanding the negative consequences of teenage childbearing, such as loss of educational and employment opportunities. This message never reaches many disadvantaged teens. The article proposes a strategy to push for access to educational and career opportunities as a vehicle for pregnancy prevention and reproductive health, through formation of a "life options" coalition of pregnancy prevention and youth advocates. Such an alliance can raise public awareness of these needs, lobby for legislation and funds to improve the educational and career opportunities of disadvantaged youths, publicize related research, assist in establishing school-based reproductive and educational services utilizing the resources of outside agencies, and encourage community-based programs that help teens stay in school and find jobs. A "life options" coalition can marshal the resources of the total community to reduce teenage childbearing.

Flora, J. A., & Thoresen, C. E. (1988). Reducing the risk of AIDS in adolescents. *American Psychologist, 43,* 965–970.

Adolescents risk contracting acquired immune deficiency syndrome (AIDS) because they engage in such high-risk behaviors as unprotected sexual activity, intravenous (IV) drug use, and sexual activity with IV drug users. AIDS education programs have yet to demonstrate the ability to reduce high-risk behaviors. Preventing human immunodeficiency virus (HIV) infection involves helping students minimize their risky behaviors, reduce habits that endanger their health, and/or delay starting risk-taking, unhealthy behaviors.

Experience in developing and testing other substance abuse programs, particularly smoking prevention approaches, can provide guidelines for structuring an effective AIDS-prevention program. Successful programs generally include resistance skill training, a knowledge of immediate physiological effects of smoking, a public commitment to change behavior, correcting views about the number of smokers, an examination of family influences, inoculation against mass media, and use of peer leaders. Programs may be grounded in a cognitive/affective, behavioral, or environmental approach, but social marketing uses a consumer orientation to reach individual consumer groups, to encourage the acceptability of new ideas and behaviors, to pretest new programs, to engage in needs analyses, and to provide communication links to disseminate information. Thus, effective AIDS-prevention programs will need to be directed to a specific population; promote delay-of-onset behavior; match the target population with the type of intervention; analyze the antecedents and consequences of sexual activity; utilize the results to identify and role-play the conditions, pressures, and language associated with sexual behavior; apply creative techniques; and educate adults.

Foster, C. D., & Miller, G. M. (1980). Adolescent pregnancy: A challenge for counselors. *The Personnel and Guidance Journal, 58,* 236–240.

Many factors contribute to increased adolescent pregnancies including a greater number of teenagers, lowered age of first menstruation, earlier sexual experiences, lack of appropriate sexuality education, misinformation regarding contraception, less self-control in younger adolescents, peer pressure, belief by the teen that having a baby will provide her with missing love and foster a commitment by the baby's father, media representations of sexuality, greater access to urban centers where teen sexual behavior may be influenced by a relatively freer social climate, and the developmental struggles associated with adolescence. Pregnancy and early childbearing carries medical and psychological risks including earlier marriage, divorce, economic instability, loss of educational opportunities, a second pregnancy within three years, and increased risk of child abuse.

Pregnant teens need peer acceptance, freedom from total dependence on their own parents, an opportunity to express their feelings, knowledge about mothering and bodily changes, and continued educational involvement. The pregnant teen needs support to face the issues of adolescence and pregnancy. This help can come from teams of physicians, nurses, social workers, and other professionals, including counselors, who help the teen work through the six major pregnancy crises, which include discovery and confirmation of the pregnancy, informing others, making decisions about the pregnancy, making decisions about education, labor and delivery, and making decisions about caring for the baby.

Lawrance, L., Levy, S. R., & Rubinson, L. (1990). Self-efficacy and AIDS prevention for pregnant teens. *Journal of School Health, 60,* 19–24.

Minority teens at an alternative school for pregnant students were administered the AIDS Self-Efficacy Scale and the AIDS Awareness Test. The Self-Efficacy Scale is an eighteen-question survey assessing the student's self-perceived ability to engage in AIDS-preventive behaviors; the Awareness Test, developed by Louis Harris and Associates and the Metropolitan Life Insurance Company, taps knowledge of AIDS symptoms, methods of transmission, and contagion. Results indicated that the greatest perceived self-competence was in avoiding multiple sex partners, avoiding others who have had multiple partners, and not using drugs to enhance sexual experience. Lower self-efficacy was reported in terms of discussing or revealing homosexual/bisexual and anal sex experiences, asking a sex partner to use a condom, or buying and carrying condoms to give to a partner.

Although the level of AIDS-related knowledge demonstrated by these teens was higher than the national average, they were deficient in areas that could increase risky behaviors. AIDS education, specifically communication-skills training and decision making, may be needed to address the identified areas of low self-efficacy while factual instruction can address information gaps.

Lewis, G. M. (1982). Adolescent pregnancy: An interdisciplinary challenge for school psychologists. In J. Grimes (Ed.), *Psychological approaches to problems of children and adolescents* (pp. 387–424). Des Moines: Iowa Department of Public Instruction. (ERIC Document Reproduction Service No. ED 232 082)

A particularly informative section of this article discusses the necessary response of the practitioner to each of the following six emotional crises associated with teenage pregnancy: (1) Confirmation of and reaction to pregnancy — the counselor allows the teen to express her feelings and establishes an atmosphere of trust and support. Referral to a family planning clinic may be appropriate. (2) Informing parents — the counselor helps the teen find a way to tell parents and is present if necessary. The prospective father may be included. If the teens decide to marry, marriage counseling is suggested. (3) Deciding on the pregnancy — the counselor helps the student explore the available options of keeping the baby, releasing it for adoption, or having an abortion. He or she provides support to the teen before and

after an abortion. If the counselor finds the option of abortion unacceptable, he or she refers the student to another professional. The youth is helped
to deal with the many issues of adolescent pregnancy. (4) Deciding on
education—the counselor helps the teen locate alternative programs, deal
with peer reactions, and plan for a return to school if she drops out. (5) Planning for delivery—the counselor learns about the availability of birthing
classes, helps the teen understand body changes, acts as monitor during delivery, or asks a family member. (6) Deciding about the baby's care—after birth,
the counselor is there to support the student who keeps the baby or chooses
adoption.

Ross-Reynolds, G., & Hardy, B. S. (1985). Crisis counseling for disparate
adolescent sexual dilemmas: Pregnancy and homosexuality. *School Psychology Review, 14,* 300–312.

Adolescent pregnancy risks the health and safety of both mother and
child. Primary prevention can begin with helping upper elementary school
children understand the future physical changes they will experience. Junior
and senior high school programs that address dating, premarital intimacy,
contraception, marriage and family life, and personal rights in relationships
can be integrated into the curriculum. Trained personnel are required to
teach these topics, and coordination with community agencies may be helpful. Parent training may improve parents' communication with their children regarding decisions about sexual behavior. School psychologists can
help in training staff, discussing responsibility and values in sex education
classes, developing parent groups, and coordinating services for the adolescent parent. The psychologist can also counsel the pregnant adolescent, provide support, direct her to resources, and help her think through options
and make decisions. The counselor can attempt to locate the adolescent father,
provide him group counseling, help him find parenting skills programs, prepare him for the frustrations and experiences of teen fatherhood, assist him
in defining educational goals, and generally help him cope with a situation
for which he is more than likely emotionally unprepared.

Schoenholtz, S. W., Horowitz, H. A., & Shtarkshall, R. (1989). Sex education for emotionally disturbed adolescents. *Journal of Youth and Adolescence,
18,* 97–106.

Fifteen emotionally disturbed students, fifteen to eighteen years of age,
enrolled in a special education school attached to an inpatient adolescent
treatment facility, were presented with a sex education program over eight
one-hour sessions. The article does not describe the specifics of the course
but indicates that the structure was tight and task oriented, that reading and
writing demands were minimal, and that a multimodal format was employed.

Results indicated age-appropriate reactions by students to the course;
they showed an increase in their knowledge, particularly on topics directly
treated in the sessions such as contraception. Furthermore, some students

reported greater clarity in their sexual values, while others felt increased uncertainty. While students' responses to a questionnaire indicated no greater comfort discussing sex with parents or peers after the intervention, hospital staff reported greater openness and ease discussing such issues with them. Figure drawings made by the students after the course were less aggressive, more secure, and revealed greater sensitivity. Staff also reported more willingness by students to discuss a personal topic and seek advice regarding gynecological concerns, a request for examination, a rape, personal relationships, and an overall better ability to handle physical closeness. Some carryover of sexual awareness to nongroup members was also noted. The psychiatrists treating them noted no problems. A carefully designed and implemented sex education program is valuable for emotionally disturbed adolescents, especially given the developmental emergence of their sexuality at this point in their lives.

Strouse, J., & Fabes, R. A. (1985). Formal versus informal sources of sex education: Competing forces in the sexual socialization of adolescents. *Adolescence, 20,* 251–262.

Formal sex education programs have not prevented pregnancies among teenagers for several reasons: (1) knowledge alone does not necessarily lead to behavioral change; (2) young teens do not have the cognitive sophistication to determine what constitutes responsible sexual behavior; (3) values discussions may reinforce immature reasoning; and (4) parents and television often send informal but powerful alternative messages about sexual behavior. Through its polished, alluring presentation, television displays sexuality as casual and fun-filled with no potential consequences. It also stereotypes women's roles while simultaneously portraying physically attractive women as role models. Parents can intervene and directly influence their children's developing sexuality even though youth do not tend to see their parents as strong sexual role models.

The authors recommend that parents and educators first accept television's power to influence and use it for learning purposes in school, such as analyzing the negative messages in many commercials. Second, parents must acknowledge the primary importance of the home as a source of sexuality education. Third, professionals must attempt to influence TV program content, and help parents preview programs critically and supervise their children's viewing habits. Fourth, parents can use programs as starting points for discussions with their children. Fifth, teachers must be able to teach "universal" values without sounding moralistic. Sixth, unattached parents need to be aware of how their teens view their sexual behavior, and be discreet. Seventh, all adults need to publicize positive models of responsibility.

5

Relationships with Peers

The development of social competence is critical to the successful adjustment of all children and adolescents. Although social competence has been defined broadly and includes many diverse components, all conceptualizations include social relations as a necessary component (Eisenberg and Harris, 1984). Most often children acquire relationship skills from their interactions with one another; adults also may play an important role in facilitating these interpersonal interactions. Social skills are not only important for the social-emotional development of children but also for their academic performance. Peer acceptance and friendships are widely regarded as measures of positive social relations. Examples of inappropriate relationships include aggressive and prejudiced behavior toward peers, shyness, withdrawal, and social isolation.

There is considerable evidence that children who experience difficulties with peer relationships tend to have low self-esteem, problems adjusting to the classroom environment, and poorer academic performance. Further, they appear to be at risk for serious future problems during adolescence and adulthood. Estimates vary as to the number of children who have difficulties with peer relationships. Asher and Renshaw (1981) report that in studies using sociometric techniques about 5 to 10 percent of elementary school children are not named a friend by anyone in their class. Other estimates run as high as 20 percent. There is reason to believe that exceptional children may be overrepresented in this group; both retarded and learning disabled children have been shown to experience greater rejection than their nonexceptional peers.

In choosing interventions to improve children's social skills it is important to consider the variable of age and its contribution to skill development. The nature of friendships and expectations of friends change with age. Children will need to possess different social skills and understand the obligations inherent in friendship as they grow (Eisenberg and Harris, 1984).

There is general agreement that difficulties in peer interaction can result from social skill deficits or social performance deficits. Children with social skill deficits have not learned the necessary skills, or they have failed to learn a critical step in the performance of the skill (Elliott, Gresham, and Heffer, 1987). When children have a social performance deficit, they have learned the skills but do not perform them at acceptable levels. Often shy and withdrawn behavior is associated with social skill deficits and aggressive behavior with social performance deficits. This conceptual classification is used to select appropriate interventions based on the type of deficit. Generally, the most effective interventions combine the manipulation of antecedents or consequences along with modeling/coaching procedures.

The recognition that social skills are an important component of the social-emotional development of the child can also be seen in the proliferation of formal social skills training programs that are now available. These packages can be used both for prevention of social skills problems and for intervention once skill or performance deficits are identified.

Disturbed peer relations provide a signal to school professionals of youngsters at risk for short- and long-term problems. Without intervention, these children will continue to display the same interaction deficits in new classrooms and with new peer groups. Thus, intervention is critical to breaking this cycle.

Each section in this chapter includes "Additional Readings" and "Further Reading." The first part, "Shyness and Withdrawal," is followed by a list of social skills packages that provide systematic approaches to social skills training that can be used in schools. The section on prejudice includes names and addresses of some organizations that have educational materials and programs for fighting prejudice.

References

Asher, S., & Renshaw, P. (1981). Children without friends: Social knowledge and social skill training. In S. Asher & J. Gottman (Eds.), *The development of children's friendships*. London: Cambridge University Press.

Eisenberg, N., & Harris, J. D. (1984). Social competence: A developmental perspective. *School Psychology Review, 13,* 267–277.

Elliott, S. N., Gresham, F. M., & Heffer, R. W. (1987). Social-skills interventions: Research findings and training techniques. In C. A. Maher & J. E. Zins (Eds.), *Psychoeducational interventions in the schools* (pp. 141–159). Elmsford, NY: Pergamon.

Shyness and Withdrawal

Shy and withdrawn youngsters have fewer interactions with their peers than do other children their age, and the quality of these interactions is poorer. They avoid social interactions and rarely initiate social contact. Once in a social situation, the behaviors they display are often not appropriate. Many people report having been shy at some time in their lives, and this helps explain the estimates of shyness in the school-age population of around 40 percent, with equal prevalence in boys and girls. Youngsters who are extremely shy and withdrawn make up a much smaller percentage of the population. Explanations for shyness include both social anxiety, which may be accompanied by negative cognitions, and social skills and performance deficits. Shy and withdrawn behavior affects overall social development of children and puts them at risk for psychological adjustment problems in later years.

Increasing Social Initiations of Withdrawn Preschoolers

AUTHORS: James Fox, Richard Shores, David Lindeman, and Phillip Strain

PRECIS: Social initiations of withdrawn preschoolers increased by teacher prompts and praise and maintained using a response-dependent fading tactic

INTRODUCTION: Behavioral interventions have been shown to facilitate peer interactions of withdrawn preschoolers. These interventions are under adult control, however, and once the contingencies are removed, the preschoolers' behaviors often return to baseline levels. It is important that the social consequences of the interaction be powerful enough to maintain and extend the interactions. This study examined three social behaviors — sharing, assisting, and verbally organizing play — in terms of how they were affected when a teacher-implemented, response-dependent fading procedure was used to move from teacher prompting and praising of children to their independence from teacher control.

INTERVENTION: Three withdrawn preschoolers between the ages of thirty-four and forty months were identified as displaying little or no interaction with classmates. The two boys and one girl (a Down's syndrome child) were in an all-day preschool program of twenty children. In the intervention, the teacher gave verbal and physical prompts and contingent praise for five minutes daily during the children's free play. The purpose was to increase the children's positive social initiations to their classmates. The response-dependent fading refers to the gradual reduction of teacher prompting and praise as long as the initiations to peers continued at a frequency equal to or greater than 75 percent of each child's mean for the previous three days.

A multiple-baseline-across-subjects design was used to evaluate the effects of the prompting, praising, and fading on the frequency of the children's social initiations and the percentages of their extended interactions. As in prior studies, the teacher's prompting and praising increased social initiations of all three preschoolers over baseline levels. These higher frequencies were maintained with response-dependent fading of prompting and praising whereas complete withdrawal of teacher prompting resulted in reductions in the children's social initiations. Two of the three children continued to initiate interactions at levels above baseline after fading was completed.

COMMENTARY: The promise of fading tactics as a means of maintaining social interaction when adult contingencies are removed is demonstrated in this study. The children's initiations generally led to positive responses from their peers, thus encouraging them to interact even after teacher praise was reduced.

Of further note is the need to consider differences in response to fading for handicapped and nonhandicapped children. The Down's syndrome child in this study did not demonstrate sustained benefits from this intervention at follow-up. The authors suggest that adjustments in intervention or fading tactics, such as longer intervention periods, might be needed to facilitate generalization for a special child.

SOURCE: Fox, J., Shores, R., Lindeman, D., & Strain, P. (1986). Maintaining social initiations of withdrawn handicapped and nonhandicapped preschoolers through a response-dependent fading tactic. *Journal of Abnormal Child Psychology, 14,* 387–396.

Social Skills Training for a Shy Adolescent

AUTHORS: Daniel P. Franco, Karen A. Christoff, Daniel B. Crimmins, and Jeffrey A. Kelly

PRECIS: Intensive social skill training with an extremely shy adolescent to improve conversational skills during unstructured situations with unfamiliar persons

INTRODUCTION: Peer relationships during adolescence take on great importance. Students become involved in school social activities and develop new friendships away from the family; they become interested in heterosocial interactions. Generally, social interaction skills are devleoped at an early age, but they change qualitatively as children grow. Recent studies indicate that many adolescents perceive themselves as shy or as having social interaction difficulties. Limited work has been done with shy adolescents that is focused on the actual problematic situations teens face. The social skills intervention described here occurred in an applied mental health setting, but it attempts to provide real-life applications of the skills.

INTERVENTION: The fourteen-year-old student in this study had a long-standing history of few friends in school and poor conversational skills; he was referred to in a derogatory fashion by other students (e.g., *nerd*). Despite his extreme shyness and unhappiness, he showed no evidence of social anxiety; rather, he was described as a somewhat depressed young man with a socially isolated life-style. During twice-weekly twenty- to thirty-minute training sessions in a mental health clinic, the student learned four different components of conversational skill: asking questions, making reinforcing/acknowledging comments, making eye contact, and showing affective warmth. At each session over the fifteen-week training period the rationale for the skill was explained by the therapist who then modeled the behavior; the behavior was rehearsed by the boy and the therapist gave him feedback on his actions. Following each training session the young man was asked to engage in a ten-minute conversation with a person he had never met before, and this encounter was videotaped. Improvement was judged through changes in his conversational behaviors; rating scales completed by the student, his parents, and his teachers; and ratings of the videotaped conversations by popular peers who did not know the young man. Results show considerable skill improvements in all four areas over baseline rates; these were maintained at a three-and-a-half-month follow-up. The sustained improvement was confirmed by the peer ratings. Further evidence was provided by higher ratings by his parents, teachers, and conversational partners in such areas as social adjustment, ease of interaction with friends, and participation in extracurricular activities.

COMMENTARY: Although this intervention did not occur in a school setting, the authors provided continual skill practice in a realistic conversational situation for this shy adolescent. They varied his conversation partners and used unstructured content to prevent his memorizing specific responses. This technique seems to have helped him generalize the newly learned skills into the school setting as evidenced by the teacher and parent reports. This method seems applicable for use in schools as well. Perhaps, as is seen in some of the other interventions described in this section, some focus might also be given to enhancing peer acceptance of these new conversational skills.

It is important to note that this adolescent did not have physiological arousal or fearful cognitions that sometimes accompany shy behavior. If he had, additional components of treatment may have been necessary, such as relaxation or desensitization to target the anxiety.

SOURCE: Franco, D. P., Christoff, K. A., Crimmins, D. B., & Kelly, J. A. (1983). Social skills training for an extremely shy young adolescent: An empirical case study. *Behavior Therapy, 14,* 568–575.

Behavioral Consultation with Parents and Teachers for Withdrawn Students

AUTHORS: Susan M. Sheridan, Thomas R. Kratochwill, and Stephen N. Elliott

PRECIS: Conjoint behavioral consultation to improve social initiation behaviors of withdrawn children at home and school

INTRODUCTION: Behavioral consultation has been effectively used in school settings for a variety of problems. Of great importance, however, is the generalization of these treatment effects across settings and time. Since children are involved in two major systems—the family and the school—parent and teacher involvement would seem essential to effect behavioral change in withdrawn students. Thus, the study reported here compared a teacher-only consultation intervention with a teacher-parent (conjoint) consultation intervention to determine the effects on home and school social initiation behaviors of withdrawn students.

INTERVENTION: Four elementary school students between the ages of nine and twelve were identified as being socially withdrawn both at home and at school. Specifically, they had difficulty initiating social interactions with peers, although these children were not outcasts. The intervention for all four students was behavioral consultation for social withdrawal; for two of the students it was with the teacher only, and for the other two students, the mother and the teacher met jointly with the consultant. The four stages of behavioral consultation were followed in all cases: problem identification, problem analysis, treatment implementation, and treatment plan evaluation. The actual treatment lasted for about twenty-one school days and involved the consultant implementing a social skills training package with the students. The skills addressed included approaching a peer and making a statement or asking a question, requesting a response from a peer or suggesting participation in an activity together. Techniques used were goal setting, self-report procedures, and positive reinforcement. In the conjoint consultation meetings there was emphasis on home-school communication. Both the teacher and parent reviewed progress in the other setting and reinforced the student where appropriate. Changes in behavior were measured by direct observation, behavioral interviews, checklists, rating scales, and self-reports.

The results showed that social initiations increased for all four students in school to a level that met or exceeded their individual goals. Changes in social initiations with peers at home were seen most clearly for the students in the conjoint behavioral consultation condition. These findings were maintained at four-month follow-up for all subjects, though they were most obvious for those in the conjoint condition.

COMMENTARY: The importance of this intervention lies in its extension of a teacher-only approach to a conjoint approach. This conjoint method allows the school professional to work across settings to benefit the student as well as to facilitate parent-school relationships through a cooperative effort. Research has shown that parent-school collaboration is beneficial to the child's school experience. This article presents a framework to help professionals achieve such a collaboration.

Of concern are some logistical and practical issues inherent in the more complex conjoint approach. For example, there may be scheduling difficulties and the time commitment on the part of parent and teacher is substantial. Further, the authors suggest that joint consultation would probably require greater skills on the part of the consultant who must consider the interpersonal and interactional dynamics that occur.

SOURCE: Sheridan, S. M., Kratochwill, T. R., & Elliott, S. N. (1990). Behavioral consultation with parents and teachers: Delivering treatment for socially withdrawn children at home and school. *School Psychology Review, 19,* 33–52.

Skill Training and Peer Involvement to Improve Social Adjustment

AUTHORS: Karen Linn Bierman and Wyndol Furman

PRECIS: The combination of social skills training and a peer group experience with goals to improve both social interaction skills and peer acceptance in preadolescents

INTRODUCTION: Social skills training programs have been shown to improve children's social behavior, but they do not necessarily result in peer acceptance. This lack is especially apparent with preadolescents when, despite the acquisition of more appropriate social skills by unaccepted youngsters, their peers may continue to behave negatively and be less responsive to these youngsters. The authors of this article have focused on both improving the target students' conversational skills and changing the responses of their peers.

INTERVENTION: Fifth- and sixth-grade students who were rated low in sociometric status and conversational skill performance were subjects for this study. The fifty-six students were randomly assigned to one of four treatment conditions. The *individual coaching* condition involved skills training by an adult in three conversational skills: self-expression, questions, and leadership bids. Students were trained using instruction, rehearsal, and feedback techniques over ten half-hour sessions. In the second condition, *group experience,* the unaccepted student met with two high-status peers over the ten sessions. The three were asked to make "friendly interaction films" together, which provided a group goal. The third group combined this *group experience* with *social skills coaching,* and the fourth group served as a *no-treatment control.* Dependent measures included conversational skills assessed in dyadic and peer group situations, peer acceptance rating scales, rates of peer interactions, and self-perceptions of competency on social skills and social competence. Results support the use of the combined intervention of coaching and peer group experience. Students in the combined intervention showed improvement in social skills, peer acceptance, and peer interactions; these results were sustained after six weeks. The individual coaching alone improved their conversational skills and the group experience alone increased peer acceptance and the children's self-perceptions of their social efficacy.

COMMENTARY: The authors emphasize the importance of developmental considerations when designing interventions. It may not be necessary, for example, to include the peer group experience for younger children. During preadolescence, students become more peer oriented, and group pressures, norms, and standards play an important role in their lives. Student behavior change alone does not result in peer acceptance. Thus, for this age group, making environmental changes to encourage peers to "take another look" at these unpopular students is essential.

SOURCE: Bierman, K. L., & Furman, W. (1984). The effects of social skills training and peer involvement on the social adjustment of preadolescents. *Child Development, 55,* 151–162.

Assigning Manager Roles to Withdrawn Children

AUTHORS: Diane M. Sainato, Larry Maheady, and Gerald L. Shook

PRECIS: Socially withdrawn preschoolers placed in classroom leadership roles to increase positive peer interactions and sociometric ratings

INTRODUCTION: Many of the interventions for shy and withdrawn young children involve significant amounts of teacher time for training or contingent reinforcement. To shift this responsibility from the teacher, these authors placed withdrawn youngsters in charge of leading or directing popular activities so they would be associated with these preferred activities (reinforcers) and consequently would be given status with their peers. This study, using a multiple baseline design, is an attempt to show that environmental manipulation results in the subjects' increased interactions with peers and greater popularity.

INTERVENTION: Three four-year-old children — two boys and one girl — in a kindergarten classroom were identified as being socially withdrawn based on observation, teacher rankings, and peer sociometric measures. The intervention was implemented by having the teacher announce to the class that the first youngster would be a classroom helper for the next two weeks. He was given a "manager" button in front of all the children and was placed in charge of activities such as directing the feeding of the guinea pig, collecting milk money, ringing the bell for clean-up, and handing out "keys" to class play areas (e.g., the barber shop). These were highly preferred activities as rated by the class. The importance of the job was highlighted by daily review of the manager's duties and a visual display of the tasks in front of the classroom. The manager was changed every two weeks until all three subjects had held the position.

Results showed that during the period that each child was manager, increases in positive social contacts occurred during free-play periods, both contacts initiated by the child and those directed by peers toward the child. Negative social contacts were reduced as well. These improvements in social contacts declined when each child was no longer manager and at four-week follow-up, but they still remained above initial baseline levels. Similarly, the children's peer ratings were more favorable during intervention, and they were selected more frequently as best friends. There was partial maintenance of these improvements at follow-up.

COMMENTARY: One explanation for the success of this intervention suggests that the leadership position of these youngsters increases their personal attraction. Further, they are a source of reinforcement in the classroom as they have direct control over access to many desirable activities. Studies have shown that interpersonal attraction is enhanced under these conditions, which leads to greater social interaction. Although this intervention might appeal mainly to those who work with young children, the underlying principle of giving high status and control of reinforcers to a withdrawn youngster might be applied to other age youngsters as well. It would also be important to ascertain whether this intervention is equally effective with youngsters with social skill deficits and performance deficits.

As the authors note, this type of intervention is conducted within the classroom, requires limited teacher time, and does not remove children from the classroom, making it both cost and time effective.

SOURCE: Sainato, D. M., Maheady, L., & Shook, G. L. (1986). The effects of a classroom manager role on the social interaction patterns and social status of withdrawn kindergarten students. *Journal of Applied Behavior Analysis, 19,* 187–195.

Peer-Mediation to Increase
Acceptance of Unpopular Students

AUTHORS: Helene Middleton, Jake Zollinger, and Richard Keene

PRECIS: Training popular students to use social skills interventions with socially neglected students to improve their acceptance

INTRODUCTION: Social skills training has been used with children who are not accepted by their peers. Generally, an adult instructs these students who have few, if any, friends by teaching them socially desirable behaviors such as sharing, complimenting others, helping, and initiating relationships. As an alternative approach, this study trained popular students in social skills intervention techniques that they then used to engage unpopular students in interaction in order to improve acceptance of these students in the classroom.

INTERVENTION: A sociometric questionnaire was used to identify students who ranked highest and lowest in social acceptance in eighteen fifth- and sixth-grade classrooms. The most popular four to eight students from each class, who were known as Student Peer Facilitators (SPFs), met once a week for approximately twenty minutes for instruction in intervention techniques. The topics covered over the seven-week period were greetings, praise (compliments), affective responsiveness, communication (including eliciting and providing information), social initiations (joining the activities of other children or inviting others to join into one's own activity), task participation (interaction with peers in a shared task or activity), and reinforcement of prosocial behavior. During the instructional session each topic was introduced and examples were elicited from the SPFs; this was followed by rehearsal of the skill.

SPFs were assigned to work with one or more of the forty-eight unpopular students within their own classrooms on a rotational basis. Confidentiality was discussed, and they were told not to inform the target child of the intervention. Although new skills were introduced each week, those learned in prior weeks were continued so that the program was cumulative in effect. A control group of forty-seven unpopular students was used for comparison.

When the sociometric questionnaire was administered at the end of the training period, the social acceptance of the experimental group students had increased significantly while that of the control group remained stable. No significant decline was found in the acceptance of the SPFs. It appears that the combination of modeling and controlling antecedent (e.g., greetings) and consequent (e.g., praise) events as carried out by the SPFs was successful in improving peer acceptance of the target students.

COMMENTARY: It is important to take into account the entry-level behavior of the socially neglected student when using this intervention. For example, if the lack of peer acceptance stemmed from inadequate behavioral controls, other techniques such as self-instruction or relaxation might have been more appropriate. Also, if social skills were markedly deficient, direct shaping or differential reinforcement procedures might be required.

The use of peers in this intervention seems effective because of the age level of the students. By preadolescence, peer group behavior becomes very important. Thus, this type of intervention might be less successful with younger children.

Finally, this intervention is appealing because it allows the adult professional to serve in a consultant role, thus reaching many more students. It is both time and cost efficient in this regard.

SOURCE: Middleton, H., Zollinger, J., & Keene, R. (1986). Popular peers as change agents for the socially neglected child in the classroom. *Journal of School Psychology, 24,* 343–350.

Effects of Cooperative Learning on Isolated Teens

AUTHORS: Debra Mesch, Marvin Lew, David W. Johnson, and Roger Johnson

PRECIS: Eighth graders participate in cooperative learning groups with group-academic and social skills contingencies to improve peer relationships and academic performance

INTRODUCTION: Individualistic and competitive classrooms provide limited opportunities for student interaction whereas cooperative learning situations encourage students to interact constructively. It is not enough, however, to place socially withdrawn or isolated students in a cooperative learning situation without teaching them the social skills necessary for interaction. This study examined the relative contribution to social interaction and student achievement of three processes: making academic rewards contingent on the level of student learning, training students in social skills, and giving rewards for engaging in actions required for effective collaboration.

INTERVENTION: Five eighth graders identified as socially isolated, withdrawn, and academically deficient participated in cooperative learning groups in math and foreign language classes daily over a six-month period. These cooperative learning situations emphasized that students would achieve their own learning goals if others in the group achieved theirs. The groups were randomly assigned but stratified for ability, attitudes toward class, and level of social integration into the peer group.

There were four conditions. The group-academic contingency condition specified that if all students answered correctly 80 percent or more of the weekly test questions, each group member would receive five bonus points on their test grade. The second condition added social skills training to the group-academic contingency. The skills taught included sharing ideas and information, asking questions, praising, and checking with others for understanding. The third condition, group-academic contingency and social skills contingency, gave an additional five bonus points if students used the social skills in the group situation. Also, there was a no contingency condition in which the academic tests reflected individual performance.

Clearly the combination of group-academic and social skills contingencies resulted in the highest levels of verbal participation by the five subjects, and this generalized to free-choice situations. Sociometric measures indicated that their peers increased their liking for and decreased their rejection and avoidance of these five teenagers as well. Finally, academic performance was best in this condition.

COMMENTARY: This study provides strong support for the use of cooperative learning for improving the social interaction of adolescents who are rejected by their peers and who have serious academic deficits. Specifically, it involves facilitating peer collaboration by rewarding everyone for the group's academic performance and training students in relevant social skills and rewarding the group for their use. This cooperative learning approach varies from the more individualistic one that predominates in American education and may require greater effort to implement on the part of the professional.

SOURCE: Mesch, D., Lew, M., Johnson, D. W., & Johnson, R. (1986). Isolated teenagers, cooperative learning, and the training of social skills. *The Journal of Psychology, 120,* 323–334.

Teacher's Role in Training Behaviorally Handicapped Children to Share

AUTHORS: Lorrie E. Bryant and Karen S. Budd

PRECIS: Using a training package to teach young children with behavioral, social, and academic handicaps to share in a classroom setting

INTRODUCTION: Sharing is an essential component of childhood play and involves exchanging toys and materials with other children as well as offering them opportunities to participate in games and activities. Many studies have looked at improving sharing behaviors with normal youngsters, but only a few have involved special needs children. Often, these children have difficulty making friends and have limited social skills. This study focused on training behaviorally handicapped young children using the actual classroom setting and the teacher as trainer.

INTERVENTION: The six children in this study ranged in age from four to seven years; four of them had developmental delays. They attended a special class for behaviorally handicapped youngsters.

A comprehensive training package for teaching young children to share, developed by E. J. Barton and F. R. Ascione ("Sharing in Preschool Children: Facilitation, Stimulus Generalization, Response Generalization, and Maintenance," *Journal of Applied Behavior Analysis, 12*, 417–430), was used for this study. The training included teacher instructions, modeling, and behavioral rehearsal in sharing followed by teacher prompts and praise during a free-play activity. Specific behaviors taught were offers to share, requests to share, and responses to requests or offers. Negative behaviors identified were taking something without asking, opposing play, and aggression; these were incompatible with sharing. Training in sharing occurred on four consecutive days during the first ten minutes of free play. This was followed by the teacher prompts and praise, which occurred over approximately forty-eight days. Sharing was measured through direct observation, and a multiple-baseline design was employed. Results show that five of the six children increased all the sharing behaviors and decreased the negative ones during the treatment phase. Requests to share were used more frequently than offers to share, and children accepted the sharing initiatives more frequently.

COMMENTARY: Learning that a sharing skills package can be applied successfully with special needs children is an important finding for school professionals, although the generality of these findings must still be assessed. Once again the school professional can serve as a consultant to the teacher who is carrying out the actual intervention. Of concern is the feasibility of using this intervention in classrooms with many children and few staff members. The eight-student classroom in this study had a teacher and two aides, allowing the teacher the opportunity to train the youngsters.

This program seemed to provide the kind of intensive intervention necessary for special needs children and for very young children. It could be modified for use with shy children as well.

SOURCE: Bryant, L. E., & Budd, K. S. (1984). Teaching behaviorally handicapped preschool children to share. *Journal of Applied Behavior Analysis, 17*, 45–56.

Additional Readings

Bergsgaard, M. O., & Larsson, E. V. (1984). Increasing social interaction between an isolate first grader and cross-cultural peers. *Psychology in the Schools, 21,* 244–251.

The social interaction of a white, six-year-old boy with his American Indian peers was increased within a first-grade classroom by the use of instructions and reinforcers. Initially, the youngster did not interact with any of his peers, cried often, and complained of physical ailments. The subject was told he would receive tangible reinforcers at the end of each day for every ten positive social interactions he engaged in. His rate of positive social interaction increased to socially significant levels and was maintained at follow-up six months later.

Biemer, D. J. (1983). Shyness control: A systematic approach to social anxiety management in children. *The School Counselor, 31,* 53–60.

This article presents a structured stepwise program, the Shyness Control Program, to help children cope with shyness in individual or group formats. It views shyness as normally developed behavioral, cognitive, and emotional habits.

The program includes identifying events and persons precipitating the shyness, weighing the pros and cons of overcoming shyness, teaching verbal and nonverbal social skills, teaching relaxation, and evaluating progress.

Elliott, S. N., & Ershler, J. (1990). Best practices in preschool social skills training. In A. Thomas & J. Grimes (Eds.), *Best practices in school psychology II* (pp. 591–606). Washington, DC: National Association of School Psychologists.

This chapter provides a classification scheme for conceptualizing social behavior problems of young children. It reviews basic assumptions and strategies for promoting social skills including operant, social learning, and cognitive-behavioral intervention procedures and provides guidelines for selecting interventions.

Elliott, S. N., Sheridan, S. M., & Gresham, F. M. (1989). Assessing and treating social skills deficits: A case study for the scientist-practitioner. *Journal of School Psychology, 27,* 197–222.

This article provides a hypothetical case study of a withdrawn third-grade child to show how a multimethod approach to intervention could be effective in remediating social skills problems. The treatment combined the manipulation of antecedents and consequent events with modeling and coaching procedures. A review of the assessment and treatment literature for social skills is also presented.

Gresham, F. M. (1985). Utility of cognitive-behavioral procedures for social skills training with children: A critical review. *Journal of Abnormal Child Psychology, 13,* 411–423.

This article reviews thirty-three studies that have used cognitive-behavioral social skills training procedures including modeling, coaching, treatment packages, and social problem solving. It concludes that modeling and coaching are effective in teaching social skills to children and claims that the success of self-instruction and social problem solving have not been clearly demonstrated. The author criticizes the failure of the research to demonstrate changes on socially valid outcome measures.

Morse, C. L., Bockoven, J., & Harman, M. A. (1987). DUSO-R and AC-CEPTS: The differential effects of two social skills curricula on children's social skills and self-esteem. *Child Study Journal, 17,* 287–299.

This study compared two treatment programs — the Developing Understanding of Self and Others-Revised (DUSO-R) and the Walker Social Skills Curriculum (ACCEPTS) — offered in a family education center with a control group. The six- to ten-year-old children were randomly assigned to one of the groups; each treatment group had two hours of instruction a week for eight weeks. Some limited support was found for use of the ACCEPTS program to improve social skills using measures of social adjustment and behavior.

Orlick, T. D. (1981). Positive socialization via cooperative games. *Developmental Psychology, 17,* 426–429.

Children in two kindergarten classes participated in an eighteen-week cooperative games program designed to elicit cooperative behavior among two or more students. A control group was exposed to a traditional games program emphasizing individual activity over the same period of time. Candy sharing behaviors remained stable or increased in the cooperative games group but tended to decrease in the traditional games group.

Schneider, B. H., Rubin, K. H., & Ledingham, J. E. (Eds.). (1985). *Children's peer relations: Issues in assessment and intervention.* New York: Springer-Verlag.

The third and fourth sections of this book are devoted to interventions for children. The chapters cover issues such as matching appropriate interventions to the target group, peers as intervention agents, social skills training for adolescents, and social problem-solving programs for the classroom. All the chapters present theoretical perspectives and research findings as well as applied information.

Strain, P. S., Guralnick, J. J., & Walker, H. M. (Eds.). (1986). *Children's social behavior: Development, assessment and modification.* Orlando, FL: Academic Press.

This comprehensive volume provides a theoretical overview of research on social behavior. The section on modification of children's social behavior emphasizes the importance of beginning intervention early, selecting interventions carefully, and using parents and other children in the change process. Current trends including the use of multifaceted intervention strategies with more diverse populations in naturalistic settings are discussed.

Social Skills Packages

Hazel, J. S., Schumaker, J. B., Sherman, J. A., & Sheldon-Wildgen, J. (1981). *ASSET: A social skills training program for adolescents.* Norman Baxley & Associates. Distributed by Research Press, Champaign, IL.

Hops, H., Guild, J. J., Fleischman, D. H., Paine, S. C., Street, A., Walker, H. M., & Greenwood, C. R. (1978). *PEERS: Procedures for establishing effective relationship skills. Consultant manual.* Eugene: Center at Oregon for Research in the Behavioral Education of the Handicapped, Center on Human Development.

Jackson, N. F., Jackson, D. A., & Monroe, C. (1983). *Getting along with others: Teaching social effectiveness to children.* Champaign, IL: Research Press.

Further Reading

Asher, S., & Renshaw, P. (1981). Children without friends: Social knowledge and social skill training. In S. Asher & J. Gottman (Eds.), *The development of children's friendships.* London: Cambridge University Press.

Eisenberg, N., & Harris, J. D. (1984) Social competence: A developmental perspective. *School Psychology Review, 13,* 267–277.

Elliott, S. N., Gresham, F. M., & Heffer, R. W. (1987). Social-skills interventions: Research findings and training techniques. In C. A. Maher & J. E. Zins (Eds.), *Psychoeducational interventions in the schools* (pp. 141–159). Elmsford, NY: Pergamon Press.

Gresham, F. M., & Elliott, S. N. (1984). Assessment and classification of children's social skills: A review of methods and issues. *School Psychology Review, 13,* 292–301.

Kohler, F. W., & Fowler, S. A. (1985). Training prosocial behaviors to young children: An analysis of reciprocity with untrained peers. *Journal of Applied Behavior Analysis, 18,* 187–200.

Aggression

Aggressive behavior toward others may be physical or psychological and results in personal injury or the destruction of property. Aggressive children generally show high rates of inappropriate and aversive social behaviors toward their peers. Examples of aggressive behavior include verbal or physical assaults or threats. These children may tease their victims or fight with others, generally ignoring the rights of their peers. Often these inappropriate behaviors are effective and achieve the desired ends for the aggressive child. Unlike shy or withdrawn children who rarely interact with their peers and are usually ignored by them, children who are aggressive with their peers and disruptive in school are actively disliked and rejected. A particularly virulent type of aggressive behavior is bullying. This behavior has received attention mainly in the Scandinavian countries but now appears to be generating interest in other countries including the United States. Bullying is found at all school levels and its manifestations are wide ranging—from name calling and teasing, to intimidation, extortion, and assault. There is great concern for the victims who suffer enormously from this abuse.

Aggressive behavior toward peers is quite resistant to change and hard to treat. The short-term consequences of this behavior are that these children have few friends and that their victims are negatively affected by the aggressiveness; long-term findings indicate a high risk for their future pathology.

Instructions and Prohibitions for Aggressive Boys

AUTHORS: Karen Linn Bierman, Cindy L. Miller, and Sally D. Stabb

PRECIS: Prohibitions and response cost for negative behaviors, and instructions and coaching in positive behavior with reinforcement used to improve social behavior and sociometric ratings of peer-rejected, aggressive boys

INTRODUCTION: Previous work has shown that social skills training programs that include instructions, modeling, and rehearsal are useful in teaching skill-deficient children to interact with their peers; often they lead to greater peer acceptance. Because these children are frequently neglected socially, as their social skills improve, they become more popular. For children who are verbally or physically aggressive, however, learning prosocial behaviors alone does not always lead to a reduction in these negative social behaviors, and they continue to be socially rejected. On the other hand, direct prohibitions of negative behaviors may reduce the children's aggression but may not lead to increases in prosocial interaction. This study looks at these two strategies alone and in combination to see how they can be used most effectively.

INTERVENTION: Thirty-two boys in first, second, and third grade were identified through behavioral observations and an aggression rating inventory as having negative social behavior. Sociometric measures indicated that they were rejected by the other students. These boys were randomly placed in one of four treatment groups: (1) instructions, (2) prohibitions, (3) instructions and prohibitions, and (4) no treatment. Nonaggressive peers also participated in the groups, which met for ten half-hour sessions. In the instruction condition, three target skills were taught: questioning others, helping, and sharing. The adult coach praised and rewarded appropriate behaviors. In the prohibition condition rules were presented, including no fighting, arguing, and yelling, but there was no instruction in specific social skills. The boys received general praise for not breaking the rules and were rewarded with tokens; however, when a rule was broken they were not allowed to receive a token for one minute. The combined condition included both the instruction and the prohibitions.

Results showed that negative behavior initiated by the boys in the prohibition-response cost group declined immediately and remained lower at six-week follow-up; there were temporary increases in positive interactions. The instruction-reinforcement group boys had stable increases in positive behaviors. The combination of prohibitions and instructions resulted in immediate decreases in negative behaviors and stable positive peer interactions. Of importance is that only in the combined group did peer acceptance increase.

COMMENTARY: This article shows how very difficult it is for youngsters who are perceived by their peers as aggressive to free themselves from this label. Peer stereotypes, even at this young age, appear very hard to change. Although the subjects modified their social behaviors, neither a decrease in their negative actions nor an increase in their positive actions was sufficient for these children to be accepted by their peers. Only the combination of instructional strategies and prohibitions resulted in enough behavioral change to shift peer ratings. Professionals working with aggressive children must consider both their social behavior and their sociometric status.

SOURCE: Bierman, K. L., Miller, C. L., & Stabb, S. D. (1987). Improving the social behavior and peer acceptance of rejected boys: Effects of social skill training with instructions and prohibitions. *Journal of Consulting and Clinical Psychology, 55,* 194–200.

Training Alternative Social Responses to Reduce Aggression

AUTHOR: Dennis R. Knapczyk

PRECIS: Using videotaped examples to model, rehearse, and provide directed feedback of appropriate social behavior alternatives to reduce the frequency of aggressive peer interactions of two junior high school boys

INTRODUCTION: There is evidence that children in special education classes who are aggressive to peers may be excluded from regular education classes or may have unsuccessful mainstream experiences and be returned to special education classrooms. The two junior high school boys in this study—seventh- and eighth-grade students attending a part-time special education program—typify this type of youngster. Their aggressive behavior did not meet the performance standards set for regular education classrooms, and they were in danger of being removed from their regular education placements. This study used videotaping to assess the types of setting events that served as antecedents for the performance of their aggressive behaviors in regular and special classes. Through analysis of the videotape it was learned that these boys became aggressive toward their peers when they initiated an interaction such as a greeting or a request from a peer and their peers either ignored the greeting, denied the request, or made a derogatory comment. Once the trigger for the aggressive behaviors was established the teacher was able to develop and implement the intervention.

INTERVENTION: The training in this study focused on developing social skills in the two students that were appropriate alternatives to the ones they were using. Observations were made of the boys' peers in the setting to see how they behaved in the same or similar circumstances. This observation revealed that if a student requested a pencil of another student and was refused, his alternative might be to ask another student or the teacher for a pencil, or engage in another activity that did not require a pencil. Ten-minute videos for each of the three experimental settings — regular education gym and shop classes, and special education study period — were prepared for the training based on these observations. Peer actors from the school simulated the aggressive responses and then the acceptable alternative responses.

The special education teacher viewed and discussed the videotapes with each student individually and then had them present their own examples and rehearse alternatives for the first three days of intervention. Feedback on the alternatives was provided. For the remaining five days of intervention, the boys' behavior was monitored by the special education teacher, who reviewed their performances with them at the end of each class. She praised and encouraged them and arranged for further discussion and rehearsal if they continued to display aggressive actions.

A multiple-baseline-across-settings design was used to evaluate changes in the occurrence of aggressive behavior for the two junior high school students during special education study periods and regular education shop and gym classes. For both students the frequency of aggressive behavior declined and remained lower during follow-up, five to fourteen days after treatment had been discontinued. Also, negative responses to their initiations of peer interactions declined and positive responses increased, suggesting a greater willingness of peers to interact with them.

COMMENTARY: The increased occurrence of positive peer interactions with the two students is an important result of this study. As seen in numerous other studies, changing behavior does not necessarily result in peer acceptance. Support from the natural environment is essential to maintain the change of behavior. It is interesting that the increase in acceptance by peers was slow to come and occurred only after the boys' aggressive behavior declined considerably.

Several components of this intervention are notable. First, using videotape technology to gather data about events in the actual setting and for modeling and rehearsal is apparently an efficient and highly effective means of training students. Second, this technology was easily used by the classroom teacher who actually implemented the intervention. Finally, consideration was given to both regular and special education settings in training, suggesting a concern of the study designers with generalization.

SOURCE: Knapczyk, D. R. (1988). Reducing aggressive behaviors in special and regular class settings by training alternative social responses. *Behavioral Disorders, 14,* 27–39.

School, Parent, and Student Education
to Reduce Bully/Victim Problems

AUTHOR: Dan Olweus

PRECIS: A program based on principles developed from research on aggressive behavior including a booklet for school personnel, a folder for parents, a videocassette and questionnaire on bullying, and an evaluative feedback session to schools used to reduce the incidence of bullying in schools

INTRODUCTION: In direct response to an incident in which extreme bullying resulted in the suicide of several youngsters, the Ministry of Education in Norway initiated a nationwide campaign against bully/victim problems. The results of this intervention with a subsample in one city are reported in this chapter.

In this study a bullied person is defined as one who is repeatedly exposed to negative actions by one or more other persons; an unequal power balance is suggested. Data from a nationwide sample indicated that approximately 9 percent of students reported they were victims, and 7 percent reported they had bullied other students "now and then." Victimization decreased from second to ninth grade; more boys than girls were exposed to bullying and most of the bullying occurred in school. The typical male victim was an anxious, insecure youngster, often alone, who was physically weak. The bully stereotype was substantiated in that bullies were aggressive toward peers, but they displayed aggression toward teachers, parents, and siblings as well.

The existing problem in Scandinavian elementary and junior high schools was not being addressed by schools or parents when the intervention was implemented. The goal of the program was to reduce current bully/victim problems and prevent future problems.

INTERVENTION: The primary goal of this intervention was to create a warm school environment with involved adults that also set firm limits for unacceptable behavior. When violations occurred, for example, sanctions were to be nonhostile and nonphysical.

The four subgoals of the intervention were (1) to increase awareness of the bully/victim problem and advance knowledge about it, (2) to achieve active involvement of teachers and parents, (3) to develop clear rules against bullying behavior, and (4) to provide support and protection for victims. These goals were reflected in the five components of the program: (1) a booklet for school personnel on bullying with specific intervention and prevention suggestions, (2) a folder on bullying for all parents providing advice for both victim and bully families, (3) an inexpensive videocassette with episodes about two bullied children, and (4) an anonymously completed questionnaire for students that asked questions about bully/victim problems in the school.

Fifteen months after the program was initiated, the final component was introduced. This was a two-hour meeting with the staff of each school in which feedback on the level of problems and the school's reactions to the problems was compared to the other participating schools. Also discussed were the basic principles of the intervention.

A quasi-experimental design was used to evaluate the effects of the intervention program in forty-two primary and junior high schools (grades 4 through 7) in Bergen, Norway. Approximately 2,500 students participated. Baseline data were collected before intervention; outcome measures asking how often students had bullied or been bullied in school as well as how often students spent recess alone because others did not want to be with them (indirect bullying) were collected after eight and twenty months and compared with baseline. Results from these data collections indicated that bully/victim problems had decreased after eight and twenty months of intervention. There was an increase in student satisfaction with school life. Also reported was a general reduction in antisocial behavior such as vandalism, theft, and truancy.

COMMENTARY: This study presents very impressive results for a widespread and serious problem. Although the data were self-reported, the anonymity and the agreement across findings help alleviate concerns in this area.

The basic resources needed for this intervention are not expensive and are very simple to provide. Most important in an intervention of this type is the willingness of the school staff, parents, and students to participate. The intervention is primarily a restructuring of the social environment. Perhaps having the weight of the government behind it was beneficial.

While bullying was dramatically reduced, it was not eliminated. It is of interest that there is still apparently a hard core group of aggressive youngsters who have not been reached by this intervention. Additional treatment would be needed to help decrease their aggressive behavior.

SOURCE: Olweus, D. (1991). Bully/victim problems among schoolchildren: Basic facts and effects of a school based intervention program. In D. J. Pepler & K. H. Rubin (Eds.), *The development and treatment of childhood aggression* (pp. 411–448). Hillsdale, NJ: Erlbaum.

Behavioral Consultation to Decrease Negative Interactions

AUTHORS: Linda Zwald and Frank M. Gresham

PRECIS: Decreasing the frequency of teasing and name calling in a junior high school resource room, using differential reinforcement of low rates of behavior (DRL) within the context of an interdependent group contingency

INTRODUCTION: Behavioral consultation, a problem-solving approach to intervention, has four stages: (1) problem identification, (2) problem analysis, (3) plan implementation, and (4) problem evaluation. A consultant guides a teacher through these stages using a series of interviews. Behavioral consultation has been used successfully with young children, but little evidence was available as to its effectiveness with adolescents. The problem chosen was a common one: teasing, name calling, and put-downs of one student by another. This type of verbal abuse is disruptive to the class and demeaning to peers.

INTERVENTION: During the problem identification interview with the junior high school resource room teacher, the consultant determined that there were three students during a specific period each day who exhibited negative verbal behaviors toward their peers. The teacher was asked to collect baseline data on their behavior, which was discussed at the problem analysis interview. They averaged twenty-five negative verbal remarks per period; the range was from fifteen to forty-one. The teacher and consultant jointly designed a DRL intervention in which the class could earn reinforcement for five or fewer negative remarks in a period. When this criterion was achieved, it was then reduced to three or fewer negative remarks in a period. The reinforcement for each student was dependent on group performance, an interdependent group contingency. The results of the intervention were determined using a changing-criterion design and reviewed at the problem evaluation interview. Negative remarks were reduced to an average of 2.5 per day during phase 1 and 2.6 during phase 2, providing evidence for the effectiveness of the intervention.

COMMENTARY: The results of this study suggest that behavioral consultation can be used successfully in junior high school settings. There is considerable evidence to support behavioral intervention, and this case study illustrates that it can be implemented by the teacher without direct service from a consultant.

Of note is the interdependent group contingency, a behavioral approach that seems particularly suited to adolescents. Peer pressure is used in a constructive way in this study.

Informal teacher comments indicated that the reduction in negative remarks toward peers also seemed to decrease movement of students in the classroom and result in more cooperative behavior.

SOURCE: Zwald, L., & Gresham, F. M. (1982). Behavioral consultation in a secondary class: Using DRL to decrease negative verbal interactions. *School Psychology Review, 11*, 428–432.

Peer Monitors to Reduce Negative Interaction

AUTHORS: B. Susan Dougherty, Susan A. Fowler, and Stan C. Paine

PRECIS: Reducing negative and aggressive behavior toward peers by two mildly retarded boys, using a modification of the RECESS program to involve peers as the change agents

INTRODUCTION: Aggressive behavior toward peers frequently occurs in settings where there is limited adult supervision, such as a yard or a playground during recess. When adults are not available to provide contingent intervention, there is some evidence that peers may be trained to assume this role. In this study peers were trained to monitor recess activities in order to reduce negative and aggressive behavior toward other children. The effects on the children who were monitored as well as on the children who served as monitors were assessed.

INTERVENTION: The RECESS program (Reprogramming Environmental Contingencies for Effective Social Skills) is a treatment package developed by H. M. Walker and colleagues to remediate negative and aggressive behavior in playgrounds (Walker, H. M., Street, A., Garrett, B., Crossen, J., Hops, H., and Greenwood, C. R. *RECESS: Reprogramming Environmental Contingencies for Effective Social Skills.* Center at Oregon for Research in Behavioral Education of the Handicapped). The components of the program used in this study included individual and class social skills training and a daily and weekly reward system. While the program was originally designed for adult intervention, it was modified in this study for peer-mediated intervention.

Two mildly retarded boys, ages nine and ten, were selected for participation in the study because of their aggressiveness toward peers as well as their oppositional and noncompliant behavior, particularly during recess on the playground. Their special education classmates (nominated by teachers or the subjects) served as monitors; in one case, one of the subjects served as monitor for the other. Observations were made during three recess periods: morning, lunch (noon), and afternoon.

The initial intervention was implemented by an adult who withdrew points from the boys for negative behavior and gave them bonus points for exemplary behavior. Time out was implemented when they lost all their points, and they were given rewards such as a small group activity for a fixed number of points. They accumulated daily points for a weekly class reward as well. Following this adult-mediated intervention, one peer monitor took over for each recess period and carried out the same token program with occasional prompts from the adult. The monitors also received small rewards. A final phase of the study allowed the subjects to monitor themselves. Follow-up occurred three months after intervention.

Using a multiple-baseline-design across recess periods, the rates of negative behavior for both boys were lower when the token program was implemented by the adult and by the peer monitors than during baseline. At follow-up in a new playground at the beginning of the new school year, one student had a relatively low rate of negative interactions, but the other student's negative interactions were higher than during the intervention. Positive interactions increased for the first boy and remained stable for the second boy. Additionally, the negative interactions for three of the children who were appointed as monitors decreased to near zero rates.

COMMENTARY: This study clearly demonstrates that children can successfully serve as behavior change agents to modify aggressive interactions of their peers. Further, this role appears to have beneficial effects for them as well. Using peers allows teachers and other adults to play a more supervisory role in behavior change, freeing them for more academic pursuits.

Additional work needs to be done to examine the importance of having an adult intervene first before introducing the peer monitors. What is the importance of the order of the interventions? Could self-monitoring have been successfully implemented first? Also, the peer monitors did not implement the points, fines, and rewards as did the adults. Peers were less likely to withdraw points and more likely to award bonus points, suggesting that response cost procedures may be a component they cannot handle successfully.

Finally, this study has implications for generalization. If peers can be used to modify behavior, interventions may be introduced in many more settings, leading to potentially greater generalization.

SOURCE: Dougherty, B. S., Fowler, S. A., & Paine, S. C. (1985). The use of peer monitors to reduce negative interaction during recess. *Journal of Applied Behavior Analysis, 18,* 141–153.

Using Mediation to Resolve Student Disputes

AUTHORS: Tony Graham and Paul C. Cline; Moses S. Koch

PRECIS: Students trained as mediators to deal with conflicts between other students

INTRODUCTION: Mediation is an alternative form of conflict resolution that has been used widely in the legal profession and in community matters. Mediators do not solve problems, but they aid others in arriving at their own solution. Mediation differs from negotiation, which does not have the assistance of the mediator.

In recent years schools have begun to adopt mediated dispute resolution in dealing with certain students' aggressiveness toward their peers.

Preliminary results reveal that physical harassment and disruptive behavior were reduced in settings that used mediation. The authors of these two articles discuss the potential usefulness of this approach, citing some case examples.

INTERVENTION: Introducing mediation into a school system involves training teachers in the process; parents should also be made aware of the basic skills taught including communication, reasoning, listening, logical thinking, civic consciousness, and sense of responsibility. Students volunteer or are nominated to be mediators; those selected are trained. The training may take as little as a day in middle school or several days in a high school setting. Training might include establishing a minicourse as part of the social studies curriculum or having an after-school club. Types of peer aggressiveness that have been amenable to student mediation include fighting, name calling, and disagreements. It is not used in more serious incidents involving drugs or weapons. Also, it should be used only with student-student conflicts.

Mediators participate only when asked to do so by the students; rules of the mediation process are (1) tell the truth, (2) do not interrupt, and (3) agree to work sincerely on the problem. The mediator goes through a series of steps with the students including airing grievances and identifying the main features of the dispute. Brainstorming is used to generate alternate solutions, and the best one is selected by the disputants.

COMMENTARY: Mediation is an approach that has only recently been instituted in schools. Although preliminary indications are that it decreases peer aggressiveness, virtually no research has been done to provide support for the efficacy of the process.

One advantage cited is that mediation frees the teacher from dealing with behavior problems, allowing more time for academics. It seems that considerable training would be necessary for the students to be effective in their role, however, and that teachers would have to be very involved in the process. Still, with good training and rotating the role of mediator, a number of students would be able to participate and improve their own communication skills.

Estimates of cost include the initial contract for teacher training and a quarter- or half-time coordinator chosen from the school faculty. This is a relatively modest expenditure.

SOURCES: Graham, T., & Cline, P. C. (1989). Mediation: An alternative approach to school discipline. *The High School Journal, 72,* 73–76.

Koch, M. S. (1988). Resolving disputes: Students can do it better. *NASSP Bulletin, 72,* 16–18.

Cognitive-Behavioral Interventions and
Teacher Consultation with Aggressive Boys

AUTHORS: John E. Lochman, Louise B. Lampron, Thomas C. Gemmer, Steve R. Harris, and Geoffrey M. Wyckoff

PRECIS: Anger-coping groups using cognitive-behavioral and social problem-solving training reduce aggressive classroom behavior and increase perceived social competence in fourth through sixth graders

INTRODUCTION: The anger-coping program used in this study has been successful in reducing children's disruptive-aggressive off-task behavior in classrooms and at home. In prior studies a greater number of sessions (18) and the inclusion of a goal-setting procedure were found to augment the reductions in children's aggressive behavior; the inclusion of a self-instruction training component did not improve the subjects' behavior. This anger-coping program is based on a social-cognitive model of anger arousal that assumes that aggressive children perceive hostile intentions from others at a greater level than they actually exist, that they place responsibility on peers for conflict, underestimate their own level of aggressiveness, and do not expect to resolve problems through nonaggressive means. Their deficient social problem-solving strategies are targeted for remediation in this program. In this study a new component, structured consultation with teachers with emphasis on behavioral management and on students' problem-solving skills, was introduced to facilitate generalization to the classroom setting.

INTERVENTION: The thirty-two fourth-, fifth-, and sixth-grade boys in this study were identified by their teachers and through a teacher checklist as the most aggressive and disruptive in their classrooms. The boys were placed in one of three groups: (1) anger-coping condition, (2) anger-coping condition with teacher consultation, or (3) untreated control. The eighteen-session anger-coping intervention took place in the schools weekly; each session lasted for forty-five to sixty minutes and had two leaders—a guidance counselor from the school and a staff member from the community guidance clinic. The content of the sessions included establishing group rules and contingent reinforcement, teaching self-statements to inhibit impulsive behavior, identifying problems, and social perspective-taking with actual social problem situations. Dialoguing, discussion, and role-playing were used. Additional activities included showing videotapes of children becoming aware of their own physiological arousal when they became angry, using self-statements (e.g., Stop, Think), and having the boys plan and make their own videotape with a problem they chose.

The two group leaders also participated in the teacher consultation component, which involved about six hours in one- or two-hour sessions.

The major emphasis of the meetings was dialogue practice, which has six steps: (1) identify the problem, (2) explore the motivation for the child's actions, (3) help the child assume the perspective of the other in the problem situation, (4) help the child generate solutions and likely consequences, (5) help the child evaluate the possible solutions and select one, and (6) encourage the child to try out the solution and discuss how it worked.

Results of the study corroborate prior findings that training in coping with anger improved the boys' disruptive-aggressive behavior in the classroom as well as their perceived competence in both treatment groups, as measured by a behavior observation schedule, a teacher checklist, and a perceived competence scale. There was no additional effect from the teacher consultation component.

COMMENTARY: Anger-coping training has been shown repeatedly to modify the behavior of aggressive boys. The success of the intervention in this case is facilitated by a joint effort between the school and the community guidance clinic. The groups were school-based, allowing for ease of participation by the boys.

Surprisingly, the addition of a teacher consultation component did not appear to be a cost-effective procedure. The authors suggest that while teachers participated in the consultation sessions, there was no measure of teacher involvement or verification that a change in teacher behavior occurred. Greater support from school administration might enhance such an effect in the future.

SOURCE: Lochman, J. E., Lampron, L. B., Gemmer, T. C., Harris, S. R., & Wyckoff, G. M. (1989). Teacher consultation and cognitive-behavioral interventions with aggressive boys. *Psychology in the Schools, 26,* 179–188.

Additional Readings

Batsche, G., & Moore, B. (1989). Bullying. *Communiqué: National Association of School Psychologists.*

This handout contained in the *Communiqué* was prepared for professionals to use with parents and faculty. It provides easily understood information on the bullying problem, including how bullying is learned (both home and school factors) and why some children become victims. It also recommends specific actions that should be taken in the home and at school to respond to a bullying problem and supports early intervention. The interventions are practical and include both punishment of bullying behavior through removal of privileges rather than physical punishment and suggestions for schoolwide responses, such as buddy systems, cooperative learning, and big brother–big sister programs.

Brown, J. E. (1986). The use of paradoxical intention with oppositional behavior in the classroom. *Psychology in the Schools, 23,* 77–81.

The use of a paradoxical strategy requires the teacher to encourage or demand the inappropriate behavior from the child. If the child continues to behave inappropriately, he or she is complying with the teacher's request. If the child ceases the behavior so as not to comply with the teacher, the objective has been realized.

Two case studies in the article illustrate the use of paradox with eight-year-old boys who were acting aggressively toward their peers.

Carlson, C. I. (1987). Resolving school problems with structural family therapy. *School Psychology Review, 16,* 457–468.

The structural family therapy approach was applied in two case studies with youngsters experiencing multiple school problems, including aggressive peer interactions or poor peer relationships. In each case a family assessment was conducted; this involves determining the structure of the family, family alignments, flexibility, social supports, and the home-school relationship. Interventions were implemented through a series of family or family-school meetings and included such strategies as strengthening the parental boundaries and/or power hierarchy and redirecting the school's scapegoating of the family.

Kettlewell, P. W., & Kausch, D. F. (1983). The generalization of the effects of a cognitive-behavioral treatment program for aggressive children. *Journal of Abnormal Child Psychology, 11,* 101–114.

A group of forty-one children attending a summer day camp affiliated with a residential treatment center were identified as displaying excessive physical or verbal aggressiveness toward their peers. The treatment group received cognitive-behavioral training twice weekly for ninety minutes and a thirty-minute individual session weekly. Behavioral rehearsal procedures and self-instruction training were used in the group sessions. The treatment group improved from pretesting to posttesting on several of the twelve outcome measures including improved interpersonal problem-solving skills and a decrease in being disciplined for fighting. Aggression toward peers was not reduced.

McConnell, S. R. (1987). Entrapment effects and the generalization and maintenance of social skills training for elementary school students with behavioral disorders. *Behavioral Disorders, 12,* 252–263.

Children with behavioral disorders are often aggressive toward their peers and have difficulty interacting with others. Even after social skills training, they are often still rejected by their peers. This article discusses the importance of entrapment to facilitate behavior change. Entrapment refers to the process by which a child's social behavior comes under the control of naturally occurring reinforcers. The author suggests emphasis on teaching children to exhibit behaviors that will be naturally reinforced by their peers, thus increasing the likelihood that they will recur. Intervention guidelines targeting the peer group are provided in this article. Three standardized programs—RECESS, PEERS, and ACCEPTS—are discussed.

Shure, M. B., & Spivack, G. (1988). Interpersonal cognitive problem solving. In Richard H. Price, Emory L. Cowen, Raymond P. Lorion, & Julia Ramos-McKay (Eds.), *14 ounces of prevention: A casebook for practitioners* (pp. 69–82). Washington, DC: American Psychological Association.

This preventive program teaches children there is more than one way to solve an interpersonal problem. The emphasis is on *how* children think rather than on *what* they think. Children with adjustment problems often do not consider consequences and alternative ways to achieve a goal; as a result they often resort to aggressive, impulsive, and/or withdrawn behavior. Interpersonal cognitive problem-solving skills (ICPS) are used to facilitate their interpersonal adjustment.

The preschool and kindergarten program described was implemented over four months in daily twenty-minute sessions led by the teacher. Children work in groups of six to ten students. The curriculum includes sessions on language, thinking and paying attention, identifying how people feel, and problem solving. The concepts taught are used in real classroom situations as well. Results indicate that children trained by teachers improved their ICPS skills and reduced their overimpulsive and inhibited behavior. Their prosocial behaviors increased. Gains were maintained at one- and two-year follow-up. This program appears to improve the coping strategies of high-risk children, resulting in decreased aggression toward peers.

Tattum, D. P., & Lane, D. A. (Eds.). (1989). *Bullying in schools*. Stoke-on-Trent, England: Trentham Books.

This book provides a comprehensive look at bullying in England and Scandinavia. The prevalence and nature of bullying at different school levels (junior, middle, and high schools) is presented and interventions for each setting are provided. There is general agreement that dealing with bullying on an individual basis is an insufficient response; it is necessary to involve parents and the whole school in the intervention. The emphasis is on making school a safe place for students. The articles in this volume appear to be very applicable to American society as well.

Further Reading

Dubow, E. F., Huesmann, L. R., & Eron, L. D. (1987). Mitigating aggression and promoting prosocial behavior in aggressive elementary school-boys. *Behavior Research and Therapy, 25,* 527–531.

Prejudice

Prejudice refers to attitudes or opinions about people that are formed without just basis because the people belong to a specific racial, religious, ethnic, or other group. Prejudiced individuals often make oversimplified generalizations about a group of people. Actions that result from prejudice include avoidance, exclusion, and verbal and/or physical abuse.

Several recent surveys provide evidence for the continued existence of racial and anti-gay prejudice among adolescents. In one survey, junior and senior high school students polled about their biases against a variety of minorities reacted most negatively to homosexuals, with animosity toward gay men and lesbians held constant across race and ethnicity (Governor's Task Force on Bias-Related Violence, 1988). A 1990 survey (Louis Harris and Associates, 1990) found that in tenth through twelfth grade, one in four students say they have been the target of racial or religious bias. Forty-three percent of students had witnessed some acts of bias violence in their schools. The prevalence of anti-gay violence and harassment in junior and senior high schools ranged from 33 percent to 49 percent in several recent studies. Further, prejudice is not limited to adolescents. It has been reported in four- to seven-year-olds as well (Aboud, 1988). The way children understand and deal with bias varies with their age and developmental level.

Although prejudice exists against many groups, the intervention studies in the literature are focused exclusively on racial and ethnic prejudice. These show that, in general, neither proximity brought about by desegregation nor increased knowledge about other groups leads automatically to a reduction in prejudice. The studies suggest a number of conditions that promote prejudice reduction. These include equal group status, cooperative interdependence, support by those in authority, and knowledge that group behavior is unsupportive of stereotypical beliefs. The studies presented here provide interventions consonant with these conditions. The reader should note that research findings about one target of prejudice have not been shown to generalize to all instances of prejudice (Walton, 1987).

One particular prejudice — homophobia, or hostile reactions to lesbians and gay men — appears to be of increasing concern in schools. There are virtually no articles describ-

ing anti-gay intervention strategies for school-age populations, but some work has been done on responses to college-level anti-gay prejudice and is listed in the section on additional readings. Finally, despite many anecdotal reports of prejudice against youngsters with handicaps, there has been very little literature on combating this pervasive school problem.

References

Aboud, F. (1988). *Children and prejudice.* New York: Basil Blackwell.

Governor's Task Force on Bias-Related Violence. (1988). *Final report.* (Available from Division of Human Rights, 55 W. 125th St., New York, NY 10027.)

Louis Harris & Associates. (1990). *High school students' attitudes on human rights: Community activity and steps that might be taken to ease racial, ethnic, and religious prejudice.* (Study No. 902054. Prepared for the Reebok Foundation and the Center for the Study of Sport in Society, Boston, MA.)

Walton, J. R. (1987). Children and prejudice. In A. Thomas & J. Grimes (Eds.), *Children's needs: Psychological perspectives* (pp. 431–441). Washington, DC: National Association of School Psychologists.

Effects of Cooperative Learning on Interethnic Contact

AUTHORS: David W. Johnson and Roger T. Johnson

PRECIS: Interethnic contact increased and attitudes improved as a result of cooperative learning experiences in the classroom

INTRODUCTION: The placement of students from different ethnic groups in the same classroom does not necessarily result in positive interaction or attitudes toward each other. In fact, students may become more prejudiced or rejecting of minority students after school desegregation. A number of studies have shown that cooperative learning experiences, compared with competitive and individualistic learning experiences, promote more constructive interethnic relations. Cooperative experiences may facilitate a mutual attraction among members of a group. This study extends these findings using observational and behavioral measures of interpersonal attraction and measures of transfer to noninstructional situations.

INTERVENTION: Students from two innercity fourth-grade classes were placed in cooperative or individualistic learning conditions. The sample of fifty-one students included eleven minority students (nine black, one American Indian, one Hispanic). There were four students, one a minority, in each of the cooperative groups; the groups were balanced for sex and ability. Under the cooperative learning condition the students worked together as a group on one assignment daily with instructions that all members of the group should contribute and master the material. Praise and reward was for the group as a whole. The students in the individualistic condition worked alone, did not interact with other students, and were praised individually.

Each group was assigned a separate classroom. The four teachers who participated were well trained in both instructional procedures. The social studies curriculum unit used by all children was on Indian life-style and culture and was carried out for sixteen days at fifty-five minutes a day.

The findings clearly show that cooperative learning experiences, compared to individualistic ones, promote more interethnic interactions during both instructional and free time as well as more cross-ethnic giving and receiving of help. Attitude measures also show that students perceive the interactions as encouraging academic work and friendships.

COMMENTARY: This well-designed study addressed a number of shortcomings of prior studies in this area. Improvements included random student assignment, highly trained teachers who were rotated across conditions, verification of the implementation of treatments, and behavioral observation. Of particular note, the relationships established during cooperative learning groups do generalize to free time, free choice situations. This finding has implications for many schools where more traditional, individualistic, and competitive instructional methods are being used. The intervention appears to be a cost-efficient procedure that would require training of teachers to implement. This study demonstrates improvement of interethnic relationships among fourth-grade students. Perhaps instruction using cooperative learning procedures could be started in an even earlier grade.

SOURCE: Johnson, D. W., & Johnson, R. T. (1981). Effects of cooperative and individualistic learning experiences on interethnic interaction. *Journal of Educational Psychology, 73,* 444–449.

Peer Tutoring to Increase Interethnic Relations

AUTHORS: Patricia Rooney-Rebeck and Leonard Jason

PRECIS: Using cooperative group peer tutoring to improve interethnic relations among young children

INTRODUCTION: Cooperatively structured settings have been shown to be effective in promoting social interactions. Characteristics of cooperative settings that reduce prejudice include encouragement of interethnic contact by authorities and some degree of intimacy in the contact, perhaps through the sharing of common objectives. Peer tutoring is a cooperative teaching method that has benefited students on behavioral and academic indices. This study employs a peer tutoring technique with first and third graders to prevent or reduce the early signs of prejudice.

INTERVENTION: A cooperative group tutoring session was added for half an hour twice a week to the class schedule of first- and third-grade youngsters in an innercity parochial school over an eight-week period. The children were placed in six-person (first grade) or four-person (third grade) groups of mixed ethnicity, sex, and academic ability levels. Students in each grade were black (15 percent), white (35 percent), and Latino (50 percent). The first-grade class was compared to a control second-grade class and the third-grade class to a control fourth-grade class; neither control received any intervention.

The students tutored each other in pairs within the group and switched at least once during the half hour from "teacher" to "student." Math equations and reading words were practiced during the sessions. Cooperation was emphasized by having team names and a team reward contingency for weekly quiz performance. For example, a student contributed six points to the team total for a perfect quiz paper. Following the quizzes, award ribbons were awarded to teams, not individuals, and team points were displayed on a chart in the classroom.

Direct observation of interactions in the first-grade peer tutoring and second-grade control group revealed that both the number and percentage of expected interethnic interactions at playtime were higher for the peer tutoring group. Interestingly, blacks had more interethnic interactions than had been anticipated, while Latino and white first graders showed the expected levels of these interactions. The sociometric measures also showed that the first-grade peer tutoring group chose more other-ethnic children for playmates and workmates at the end of the study. These findings were not replicated for the third- and fourth-grade students.

COMMENTARY: It appears that the establishment of common objectives in a cooperative peer tutoring situation increased the interethnic associations for first graders but not for third graders. The authors comment that third-grade students have a longer history of competitive classroom activities and may have found it more difficult to develop cohesive and interdependent groups. The third graders needed to be reminded to help each other while the first graders were still using their group name eight months after the study was completed. This suggests that early experiences of cooperative situations, even as limited as the one in this study, may help reduce prejudice.

SOURCE: Rooney-Rebeck, P., & Jason, L. (1986). Prevention of prejudice in elementary school students. *Journal of Primary Prevention, 7,* 63–73.

_____

Using Dramatic Plays to Reduce Prejudice

AUTHORS: Beverly J. Gimmestad and Edith de Chiara

PRECIS: Four plays about ethnic groups and related classroom activities increase knowledge and reduce prejudice

INTRODUCTION: Simply increasing children's knowledge about other ethnic groups does not necessarily reduce prejudice toward them. The goal of this study was to use specially prepared plays and activities about the heritage and life-styles of four groups—blacks, Puerto Ricans, Jews, and Chinese—to increase children's knowledge and improve their attitudes toward these groups. The plays were developed under the auspices of the Family Theatre of the Henry Street Settlement and represent the first plays or theater productions of this type available for children.

INTERVENTION: Students from ethnically mixed fourth- through sixth-grade classes read each of the plays and discussed the content including the sequence of events, the theme, main characters, and economic, political, and sociohistorical factors that contributed to the events. In other related activities the children conducted follow-up research on the contributions of the ethnic group to U.S. society, acted out scenes to foster intragroup cooperation, and described similar events or feelings the groups had experienced. The children in the control group were not exposed to the plays in their classes. Knowledge and attitude tests were used to measure changes from pre- to posttesting.

Results showed that the students in the experimental group had greater knowledge about black, Jewish, Puerto Rican, and Chinese cultures than did the students in the control group and that this knowledge increased with grade level. On the Bogardus Social Distance Scale, which measures the distance children put between themselves and members of each ethnic group, there were statistically significant gains for the experimental group, but these were mostly attributable to fourth graders and toward the black ethnic group.

COMMENTARY: The development of these plays seems to be an important contribution to materials dealing with prejudice. They are available from the director of the Family Theatre for use in elementary schools. It is difficult to determine, however, what aspect of the intervention was responsible for the results. The authors stress that the post-play activities included many small group assignments with heterogeneous groups of children. Since the posttests were given after all activities were completed, it is not possible to separate the reading of the play from the accompanying curricular materials. Nonetheless, these findings suggest that the use of the dramatic plays may be useful for reducing prejudice.

SOURCE: Gimmestad, B. J., & de Chiara, E. (1982). Dramatic plays: A vehicle for prejudice reduction in the elementary school. *Journal of Educational Research, 76,* 45–49.

A Panel of Disabled Persons to Change Children's Attitudes

AUTHORS: Marcia S. Kierscht and Mary A. DuHoux

PRECIS: Use of an informal presentation by a panel of physically disabled adults to change third graders' attitudes toward the disabled

INTRODUCTION: Children with handicaps have often been the target of teasing, taunting, and in some cases, prejudiced remarks from their peers. Reducing prejudice toward youngsters with handicaps is especially important with the move toward mainstreaming in regular classrooms. Acceptance by peers can facilitate the adjustment and, hopefully, the learning of these special youngsters. This study uses a panel presentation by physically disabled adults to create positive attitudes toward the handicapped.

INTERVENTION: The third-grade students who participated in this study were assigned to either intervention or control conditions. The intervention was a forty-minute informal presentation by a panel of four physically disabled adults about their experiences, their social and family lives, others' attitudes toward them, and their interests. One of the male panelists was blind, one had cerebral palsy, and one had lost a leg. The female panelist was in a wheelchair because of arthritis. After their presentation the panel answered student questions. The control group observed a forty-minute slide presentation on travel. The Children's Attitudes About the Disabled scale was given to all children before and after the intervention. This scale measures the extent to which the disabled are perceived as different.

Results indicate that only the children in the intervention condition had more favorable attitudes after the intervention. Neither socioeconomic level nor sex of student affected the results.

COMMENTARY: The positive findings of this study on attitude change are encouraging. A one-time presentation involving interaction between children and physically disabled adults led to more positive attitudes among the children toward the disabled. Of course, much more information is needed regarding follow-up after several weeks and months and also whether this attitude change translated into behavior change in the form of less-prejudiced behavior toward peers. Perhaps a series of panels with the same or different participants to encourage greater sharing of information and communication would be useful.

The authors suggest that the panel members dispelled stereotypic images of the disabled because they had occupations, social lives, and interests, and therefore were not perceived as so different from the nondisabled. It would be interesting to see whether a panel of disabled students would influence student attitudes as well.

SOURCE: Kierscht, M. S., & DuHoux, M. A. (1980). Preparing the mainstream: Changing children's attitudes toward the disabled. *School Psychology Review, 9,* 279–283.

Additional Readings

Anti-Defamation League of B'nai Brith (1985). *A World of Difference* (823 United Nations Plaza, New York, NY 10017).

A World of Difference is a national education project to increase awareness of prejudice and to fight ethnic, religious, and racial bias. The heart of the campaign is an intensive teacher training program aimed at eliminating prejudice; it allows participants to confront their own biases as well as to learn how to use the teaching techniques and lesson plans included in the teacher-student resource guide. The training program includes curriculum materials, videotapes, and support manuals, and the campaign has utilized prime-time television, corporate sponsorship, and community cooperation. In the schools participating in the program, teachers receive a minimum of a day of training. They receive a three-part resource guide containing (1) material written by local writers that reflects the state's diversity and problems; (2) a section on prejudice, discrimination, scapegoating, and racism; and (3) articles, bibliographies, and resources. Thus, *A World of Difference* training is tailored to the specific needs of a school or district. Classroom practices, instructional strategies, and infusion of multicultural education are included in the training. Information about this program is available from the Anti-Defamation League of B'nai Brith, Department JW/AWOD, 823 United Nations Plaza, New York, NY 10017.

Berrill, K. T. (in press). Organizing against hate on campus: Strategies for activists. In Kevin T. Berrill & Greg Hereck (Eds.), *Hate crimes: Understanding and responding to violence against lesbians and gay men.* Newbury Park, CA: Sage.

This article provides a list of strategies to use in response to anti-gay and other hate-motivated attacks on college campuses. The list suggests support for the victims and documentation of incidents. Guidelines for administrators on counteracting bigotry and harassment are also given.

To overcome prejudice that leads to violence, education is cited as the only known method. Suggestions raised in this article may be useful for middle and high school settings as well.

Blanchard, F. A., Lilly, T., & Vaughn, L. A. (1991). Reducing the expression of racial prejudice. *Psychological Science, 2,* 101–105.

This article describes two experiments. After overhearing comments that were antiracist, neutral, or more accepting of racism, female undergraduate students were asked their opinions on how their college should respond to anonymous racist notes. They responded publicly in the first experiment and privately in the second experiment. Results indicate that the students exposed to strong antiracist opinion expressed more strongly antiracist opinions than those who heard statements more accepting of racism. This finding was true for both public and private responses.

Damico, S. B., Bell-Nathaniel, A., & Green, C. (1981). Effects of school organizational structure on interracial friendships in middle schools. *Journal of Educational Research, 74,* 388–393.

Interracial friendships of students in two team-centered schools were compared to those of students in three traditionally structured schools. The results indicated that white students who attended team-centered schools reported having significantly more black friends than white students attending traditionally organized schools. No difference was seen for black student ratings of white and black friends regardless of the organizational structure.

Derman-Sparks, L., & the A.B.C. Task Force (1989). *Anti-bias curriculum: Tools for empowering young children.* Washington, DC: National Association for the Education of Young Children.

This book presents principles and methods for incorporating an anti-bias curriculum into early childhood programs. It looks at racial and cultural differences, disabilities, and gender identity from the perspective of young children and suggests activities that can be used to learn about the topics. General information on creating an anti-bias environment and working with parents is also provided along with an extensive list of resources.

Froschl, M., Colon, L., Rubin, E., & Sprung, B. (1984). *Including all of us: An early childhood curriculum about disability.* New York: Project Inclusive, Educational Equity Concepts.

This early childhood curriculum guide is nonsexist and multicultural and incorporates both fictional and actual role models of children and adults with disabilities.

Harbeck, K. M. (Ed.). (in press). Homosexuality and education. *Journal of Homosexuality, 22.*

This special issue presents a series of articles that examine people's attitudes and actions with respect to homosexuality in schools and the influences that perpetuate these beliefs. Many gay and lesbian educators and students remain "invisible" because of the hostility they experience. While interventions for homophobia are not specifically addressed, a number of the authors discuss the importance of approaching homophobia in schools through the education of faculty and staff as well as students.

Hunter, J., & Schaecher, R. (1987). Stresses on lesbian and gay adolescents in schools. *Social Work in Education, 9,* 180–190.

The authors briefly describe an intervention with lesbian and gay adolescents who experienced harassment and violence in school and then became chronic truants. The New York City Board of Education and the Institute for the Protection of Lesbian and Gay Youth jointly started the Harvey Milk School, an off-site educational program for these students.

Pate, G. S. (1988, April/May). Research on reducing prejudice. *Social Education,* 287–289.

This article summarizes research on prejudice-reduction efforts. The approaches discussed are audiovisual strategies including film, drama, and television; special materials such as multiethnic readers; and teacher education. In addition, there are sections on cognitive approaches, cooperative learning approaches, human relations training, and direct approaches. Finally, schoolwide conditions that influence prejudice are briefly discussed. A monograph elaborating on this article is published by the Anti-Defamation League of B'nai Brith.

Serdahely, W. J., & Ziemba, G. J. (1985). Changing homophobic attitudes through college sexuality education. In John P. DeCecco (Ed.), *Bashers, baiters and bigots: Homophobia in American society* (pp. 109–116). New York: Harrington Park Press.

Undergraduate college students were exposed to a homosexuality unit within a sexuality course; they read a chapter on homosexuality and participated in two, dyadic role-playing situations. In both situations the student assumes the role of a gay person; one role-play involves telling parents about one's homosexuality, and the other telling one's best friend (same sex and heterosexual). The rationale for this approach was that role-playing would assist the learner in developing empathy.

Students were given a homophobia questionnaire at the beginning and end of the ten-week semester. Results indicate that students with high pretest homophobia scores who were exposed to the unit had significantly lower homophobia scores at posttest than did the control group.

Thompson, C. (1990). *A guide to leading introductory workshops on homophobia.* Cambridge, MA: Campaign to End Homophobia.

The goal of the Campaign to End Homophobia is to abolish it through education. This guide outlines a series of introductory workshops on homophobia targeted at an adult and young adult audience. It provides very specific factual information on lesbian, gay, and bisexual people and homophobia, and includes clear directions on how to conduct the workshops. It also prepares the leader for the diversity of the participants. All or some of the workshop sessions could be used with faculty, staff, and/or parents in a school district to inform and educate. It would probably be appropriate for high school students as well.

Uribe, V. (1990). *Project 10 handbook: Addressing lesbian and gay issues in our schools* (2nd ed., chapter 9: "Homophobia—What it is and who it hurts"). Los Angeles, CA: Friends of Project 10.

This is a resource guide for faculty, staff, and parents of adolescents (see also pp. 55–57 on gender identity problems). This chapter defines homophobia and describes three types: overt homophobia, institutional homophobia, and societal homophobia. Leadership by administrators to secure equity for students and to provide all a safe environment is seen as essential for reducing homophobia.

Further Reading

Aboud, F. (1988). *Children and prejudice.* New York: Basil Blackwell.

Governor's Task Force on Bias-Related Violence. (1988). *Final report.* (Available from Division of Human Rights, 55 W. 125th St., New York, NY 10027.)

Phinney, J. S., & Rotheram, M. J. (Eds.). (1987). *Children's ethnic socialization: Pluralism and development.* Newbury Park, CA: Sage.

Walton, J. R. (1987). Children and prejudice. In A. Thomas & J. Grimes (Eds.), *Children's needs: Psychological perspectives* (pp. 434–441). Washington, DC: National Association of School Psychologists.

Organizations

Anti-Defamation League
Department of Campus Affairs
823 United Nations Plaza
New York, NY 10017

Campaign to End Homophobia
P.O. Box 819
Cambridge, MA 02139

Educational Equity Concepts, Inc.
114 East 32nd Street
New York, NY 10016

National Gay and Lesbian Task Force
1734 14th Street NW
Washington, DC 20009-4309

National Institute Against Prejudice and Violence
31 South Greene Street
Baltimore, MD 21201

6

━━

Relationships with Adults

━━

The development of trust between a child and his or her world is the first stage of psychosocial development described by Erikson (1963). Consistency, continuity, and sameness of experience foster trust between child and parent as the child learns to see the world as safe and dependable. As the child grows older, a trusting relationship with parents is generalized to relationships with other adults such as relatives, teachers, and neighbors. Just as with peer relationships, competence in dealing with adults is necessary for a child's successful adjustment. When care of the child by the adult is inadequate, inconsistent, or negative, however, a disturbed relationship may result.

This chapter examines disturbed relationships with adults that occur when there is child maltreatment and conflictive family situations, and when adults use deception and/or coercion to lure youngsters into cults. In all cases, disturbed relationships with adults have an effect on children's academic and/or social-emotional behaviors in school.

Several related articles describing interventions for defiant and noncompliant behaviors, signifying a disturbed adult-child relationship, can be found in Chapter One of this book.

Reference

Erikson, E. H. (1963). *Childhood and society* (2nd ed.). New York: Norton.

Child Maltreatment

Child maltreatment refers to a number of different adult behaviors toward children. Both abusive behavior (acts of commission) and neglect (acts of omission) result in harm to children. Physical injury, psychological or emotional abuse, sexual abuse, and neglect of necessities such as failing to seek medical care for a sick child, feeding children inadequately, and leaving children unattended are all examples of maltreatment.

There are several models that attempt to explain the etiology of child abuse and neglect. Some focus attention on the pathological characteristics of the parents to explain maltreatment. Others focus on societal factors that encourage abuse, or the interactions between family members. Whatever the etiology, however, it is clear that children who have been abused or neglected are more likely than other children to have school behavior and academic problems. Long-term consequences for such children may include lower intelligence and achievement and poorer social relationships; they are at greater risk for delinquency and suicide attempts. Studies have shown that they are placed more frequently in special classes or institutions and more often require special services. The most frequent victims of physical abuse and neglect are children five years old and younger; though statistics vary, the average age of the sexually abused child is around eight, with most abuse beginning before the age of twelve. The implications of these figures is that there is a clear need for school professionals to have knowledge of assessment and intervention strategies for abused children.

The interventions in this section fall into two categories: primary prevention and treatment. As you will see, most of the prevention programs are focused on child sexual abuse. There is concern by some authors about whether prevention programs damage healthy adult-child interactions by making children fearful or by frightening caring adults. Treatment of abused children generally requires out-of-school intervention, but school professionals are in a position to provide additional services to these youngsters.

Prevention of Sexual Abuse Through
Film and Behavioral Skills Training

AUTHORS: Sandy K. Wurtele, Debra A. Saslawsky, Cindy L. Miller, Scott R. Marrs, and Jerry C. Britcher

PRECIS: Behavioral skills training, alone and in combination with a film, increases knowledge about sexual abuse for elementary school youngsters.

INTRODUCTION: One response to the large number of children who are sexually abused by adults has been the development of primary prevention programs. The focus of many of the school programs is similar because of evidence that the majority of abusers are adults known to the child, such as relatives or friends of the family, who first attempt to develop a relationship with the child and then abuse him or her without use of force but through enticement. Thus, children must be taught to recognize that such situations are inappropriate, resist the inducements, escape from the situation, and tell someone about the incident. Two ways of teaching these personal safety skills — a commercially produced film (*Touch*) and a behavioral skills training package — are compared in this study. The film uses symbolic modeling; the behavioral approach involves actual skill performance.

INTERVENTION: Participants were children in kindergarten, first grade, fifth grade, and sixth grade; they were randomly assigned to one of four groups: film, behavioral skills training, combined film and behavioral skills training, and control conditions. The children in the film group saw a thirty-five-minute film that depicted abusive incidents with children modeling a four-part response that included saying "No," yelling for help, getting away, and telling someone until they were believed. This was followed by a fifteen-minute discussion with the children on feelings, what they had learned, and a review of the actions to take if they were ever in a similar situation.

The fifty-minute behavioral skills training (BST) program focused on similar self-protective skills such as identifying one's "private parts," knowing good and bad touches, and learning verbal and motor responses such as saying "No," telling someone, and getting away. Children were first instructed; however, then the behaviors were modeled, rehearsed, shaped, and reinforced when correct. Hypothetical situations were presented and the children were able to practice what they would say and do. The combined group received a combination of the film and shortened BST training. The control group discussed unrelated topics such as self-concept and values.

Two measures of outcome were used after the intervention and at three-month follow-up: the Personal Safety Questionnaire, which assesses knowledge about sexual abuse, and the "What If" Situations Test, which assesses the actions of a child in a potential abusive situation. The results revealed that both the BST alone and the combined film and BST groups had greater knowledge about abuse than did the control group; the older children had more knowledge than the younger children. With regard to skill attainments, there was some tentative support for greater skill level in the BST group.

COMMENTARY: The effectiveness of the BST program in increasing children's knowledge is clearly documented, but translation into action is necessary. In another study reported in the additional readings section (Wurtele, Marrs, and Miller-Perrin, 1987) superior skill acquisition was reported for kindergarten children in a participant modeling condition (similar to the BST program in this study) as compared to a symbolic modeling condition. Thus, active practice modified the children's behavior. It seems that the results of this study might have been more clear-cut with a longer training period. A one-time intervention should be strengthened with follow-up practice and booster sessions to promote maintenance of skills. Of course, it is impossible to evaluate what a child would do in an actual situation.

A sensitive and well-trained leader seems essential for a program like this. Probably someone on staff could be trained to deliver this service to all children in a school.

The authors comment on the importance of having parent approval of sexual abuse prevention programs. Parent concerns included potential harmful effects, such as nightmares or fear of physical affection from family and friends. By addressing these issues and others before implementation, parent support was assured, and there were reports that family discussion on the topic was facilitated.

SOURCE: Wurtele, S. K., Saslawsky, D. A., Miller, C. L., Marrs, S. R., & Britcher, J. C. (1986). Teaching personal safety skills for potential prevention of sexual abuse: A comparison of treatments. *Journal of Consulting and Clinical Psychology, 54*, 688–692.

Educational Programs to Prevent Child Sexual Abuse

AUTHORS: Deborah J. Tharinger, James J. Krivacska, Marsha Laye-McDonough, Linda Jamison, Gayle G. Vincent, and Andrew D. Hedlund

PRECIS: A review of school sexual abuse prevention programs that looks at the nature of the programs, empirical research findings on effectiveness, and unintended consequences of the programs; provides guidelines for effective program implementation

INTRODUCTION: The authors begin by relating the etiology of child sexual abuse to prevention efforts. A widely accepted model by Finkelhor suggests four preconditions that must be met before sexual abuse can occur. The first three preconditions relate to the molester's motivation and ability to overcome internal and external inhibitions. The fourth precondition is that the potential offender must overcome or undermine the resistance of the child. Prevention programs are aimed at this fourth factor; it is assumed that a child who is aware, assertive, and empowered will be better able to stand up to a molester.

Several concerns are raised by the authors regarding these programs. They suggest that it may not be appropriate to empower children to prevent sexual victimization, that this may contribute to self-blame if they cannot prevent or stop abuse, that there may be unintended side effects such as fear and anxiety, and that it is unfair to put the burden on the child. Further, many of these programs focus inaccurately on threats from strangers rather than family, and sexual abuse education often occurs in isolation without the broader perspective of sexuality education. While there is evidence of increased knowledge from participation in these programs, there is virtually no evidence that these programs prevent children from being abused.

INTERVENTION: Despite the stated limitations of child sexual abuse prevention programs, these programs are one type of temporary effort to decrease abuse; however, long-term changes in societal conditions supporting abuse are necessary. The authors present comprehensive guidelines for deciding to implement a school prevention program. First, the practitioner must determine that a program is desired by assessing the support of parents, community, and school persons. School staff need to be informed, and school policy must be delineated with clear lines of communication in the case of disclosures. Decisions about the nature, content, and length of the program can be made by a committee (with school, parent, and community representation) that reviews materials including books, films, and packaged curricula. It is very important to match the materials to the developmental level of the students. The authors recommend teaching concepts such as body knowledge, secrets, and using a support network; they stress that sexual abuse is not the child's fault or responsibility. They do not support the use of empowerment concepts, such as saying no and being assertive, particularly with younger children. The program should be implemented over a period of time using sound instructional principles. The adults leading the programs should be well trained and available to provide ongoing support. Special consideration must be given to children who are handicapped or disabled as they are thought to be at greater risk for sexual abuse. Evaluation of all programs is encouraged.

COMMENTARY: This is a very thought-provoking article that stops to consider the issues involved in the effort to prevent child abuse. Rather than jumping on the bandwagon of prevention, the authors question some of the assumptions underlying the programs and recognize that, for example, empowerment of children stems from an approach used with victims in rape crisis centers and battered women; it may not be appropriate for vulnerable children. They caution school personnel to make a reasoned decision about the use of these programs. Some evidence does suggest an increase in children's disclosure of previous or ongoing abuse after participating in these programs, and schools should further document these preliminary findings.

The importance of a broad-based intervention involving community and families is emphasized and seems critical to the success of the intervention. The one-time workshop is criticized as being irresponsible. Ongoing discussion within the framework of sexual education is essential.

An extensive list of materials reviewed for this article is included in the references and is an excellent resource for practitioners. There are materials for young children, adolescents, parents, and mental health professional and teachers or group leaders.

SOURCE: Tharinger, D. J., Krivacska, J. J., Laye-McDonough, M., Jamison, L., Vincent, G. G., & Hedlund, A. D. (1988). Prevention of child sexual abuse: An analysis of issues, educational programs, and research findings. *School Psychology Review, 17,* 614–634.

Bibliocounseling as a Child Abuse Prevention Strategy

AUTHOR: Sheila K. Hollander

PRECIS: Children's books that increase awareness of abuse used as an important component of a school district's health and safety program

INTRODUCTION: Books are frequently used as tools to educate children on topics that are sensitive or difficult for adults to discuss. Bibliotherapy refers to guided reading whereby books help children learn more about themselves and find solutions to problems. Generally, this therapeutic use of books occurs after a problem has arisen. This article discusses bibliocounseling, which is the use of literature prior to the occurrence of a problem, as a preventive approach to child sexual abuse.

Most school districts nationwide have developed policies on child abuse prevention and reporting. Many have now implemented educational programs on child sexual abuse as well based on the assumption that an aware child will be a safer child. The author provides guidelines for the successful incorporation of literature into an educational program.

INTERVENTION: The article offers a number of suggestions for school professionals implementing bibliocounseling. It is very important that any program on sexual abuse be jointly planned by parents and school personnel; when they are involved in designing the program, parents are more likely to be supportive of such an effort and may carry it over into the home.

When the books are selected, the selector should keep in mind their age appropriateness and the children's level of maturity. An annotated list of books targeted from preschool to high school is provided in this article. Some of the books are to be read with an adult; others present hypothetical situations a child might face. One of the difficulties in writing such books is that the adult abuser is often an ordinary appearing individual, often an authority figure in the child's life rather than a "dirty old man" or stranger as the abuser is often inaccurately portrayed. Many of the books focus primarily on how to deal with strangers, a limitation of the literature. Developing awareness of potential abusers who are family members or friends without undermining the child's trust in others is a delicate task.

Books, pamphlets, and other materials may be used as a follow-up to a speaker, and students should be given specific information about where to find them so that shy youngsters do not have to ask for them. It is not good practice simply to place them in a class library without some introductory discussion. Role-playing of vignettes from some of these books to enact preventive situations may be appropriate.

The author emphasizes strongly that these materials should be used as part of a larger educational program to broaden and reinforce children's awareness; they are not to be used in isolation.

COMMENTARY: This article gives school professionals very practical and useful information. Because of the sensitivity of the topic, establishing parent involvement right from the start is important in setting the collaborative nature of this preventive intervention. Further, the program facilitates the education of staff and parents through joint planning and cooperative decision making.

The bibliography listed is current and provides the reader with good resources. The purchase of the books appears to be the main monetary expenditure involved. Perhaps fund-raising by relevant parent groups can help defray some of the costs.

SOURCE: Hollander, S. K. (1989). Coping with child sexual abuse through children's books. *Elementary School Guidance and Counseling, 23,* 183–193.

Prevention of Sexual Abuse with the Help of Spiderman

AUTHOR: James Garbarino

PRECIS: Elementary school children who read a special issue of *Spiderman* comic dealing with sexual abuse displayed increased knowledge about abuse

INTRODUCTION: A special issue of *Spiderman* comic dealing with sexual abuse was prepared and distributed nationwide. The two stories in the comic concern molestation of a boy by a teenage female babysitter, and a girl who runs away from home because she is being sexually molested by her father and her mother does not believe her. In each story the incidents are reported with support from others and the children receive help. This study addresses children's response to this comic both in terms of how much they learned from reading it, and what, if any, damaging effects it has.

INTERVENTION: Seventy-three children in second, fourth, and sixth grade read this comic book after school on their own time; many reported reading it more than once. Each child was individually interviewed by a person of the same sex and asked ten multiple-choice questions about the comic. Six of the questions concerned knowledge about sexual abuse or the response to it; the remaining four questions covered minor details of the situation. The children were also asked about how the comic made them feel, that is, whether it caused worry or fear.

Results revealed that the children did well on all the multiple-choice questions, with both boys and girls averaging over 75 percent correct answers on the questions related to sexual abuse. Boys were more than twice as likely to have read *Spiderman* prior to this intervention, and girls seemed uncomfortable with the idea of reading *Spiderman* because it was seen as male-oriented. However, this did not seem to have affected the knowledge they gained.

With the exception of the fourth-grade students, one-third or fewer of the children said the comic made them feel worried or scared. About 50 percent of the fourth graders, boys and girls equally, reported this concern. Some evidence suggested that fourth graders who discussed the comic with their parents worried more than those who did not discuss it. The author noted that some parents may be uncomfortable discussing abuse and convey their anxiety to their children.

COMMENTARY: It is recommended that the *Spiderman* comic be one part of a comprehensive and ongoing prevention program. The importance of parent involvement is underscored by the speculation that some parents conveyed their discomfort to the children, causing them to worry and be fearful. A collaborative effort between parents and school practitioners is essential for successful implementation. Although the program created anxiety in some children, the author feels it is a very inexpensive means to reach millions of children and parents.

In addition to this comic, a second edition of *The Amazing Spiderman* comic dealing with emotional abuse of children has been developed. Copies of the comics can be purchased through the National Committee for Prevention of Child Abuse, 332 South Michigan Avenue, Suite 950, Chicago, IL 60604.

Although no evidence is available concerning behavior change resulting from this intervention, there is an anecdotal report about a child who participated in the study. At the end of the interview he volunteered that he had an experience like the one in the comic with a teenage neighbor. He indicated that he would have had a better idea of what to do if he had read the comic before this incident, and he would have told his mother.

SOURCE: Garbarino, J. (1987). Children's response to a sexual abuse prevention program: A study of the *Spiderman* comic. *Child Abuse and Neglect, 11,* 143–148.

Peer Social Initiations for Maltreated Preschoolers

AUTHORS: John W. Fantuzzo, Alex Stovall, Daniel Schachtel, Cynthia Goins, and Robert Hall

PRECIS: Using a peer-initiation intervention to increase positive social behavior of maltreated preschoolers

INTRODUCTION: Child maltreatment affects the socioemotional development of young children. Such toddlers and preschool children are often socially withdrawn. They do not initiate social interactions and may be unresponsive to the overtures of others. If these behaviors remain untreated, the likelihood that they will have social adjustment problems as adults is greatly increased. The intervention selected for these maltreated youngsters is initiation of social contact with them by their higher-functioning peers in order to increase the frequency of their own responses and initiations.

INTERVENTION: Six children, ages three and four, participated in this study at a special center for maltreated children. Four of the children were selected because they were extremely socially withdrawn. Two children with relatively high social functioning (confederates) were trained as peer social initiators for the withdrawn children. There were four twenty-minute training sessions in which the confederates were taught how to approach their classmates through demonstration and role-playing. At first, a coach in the room helped the initiator, then a device in the child's ear was used to prompt the initiations. Eventually, almost no prompting was necessary. These confederates received verbal praise and tangible reinforcers after each session.

During the baseline period a confederate and two withdrawn children were brought to the playroom and given free-play time. The confederates made a minimum of ten positive social initiations during the intervention phase. Then there was a return to baseline and a follow-up two weeks later.

Positive social responses and initiated behaviors by the target children were recorded in the playroom and in the regular classroom by an observational system and by teacher interviews.

All four children increased the frequency of their positive social behavior during intervention, with eight to nine more interactions from baseline to treatment. These gains were maintained at follow-up. Their initiation behaviors as well as their response to initiations increased. Similarly, teachers reported changes in behavior for both the maltreated children and the confederates, with more positive social behaviors in the classroom by all students. This result indicates some generalization from the playroom, where the intervention took place, to the classroom.

COMMENTARY: This peer-mediated treatment provides benefit to teacher, withdrawn youngsters, and confederates. It improved the social behavior of all the children involved and did not require extensive teacher time. It appears to be a practical strategy since these social behaviors are reinforced naturally. The authors suggest that because maltreated children have a history of troubled adult relationships, peer strategies may be more effective with this population.

SOURCE: Fantuzzo, J. W., Stovall, A., Schachtel, D., Goins, C., & Hall, R. (1987). The effects of peer social initiations on the social behavior of withdrawn maltreated preschool children. *Journal of Behavior Therapy and Experimental Psychiatry, 18,* 357–363.

═══

Counseling with Sexually Abused Children

AUTHORS: Jerry Downing, Stephen J. Jenkins, and Gary L. Fisher

PRECIS: Using psychodynamic and reinforcement-based counseling to change behavior in sexually abused children

INTRODUCTION: This study provides the opportunity to examine the behaviors of sexually abused children after different one-year counseling interventions. It addresses in a preliminary fashion whether one theoretical approach was more effective in dealing with sexually abused children than another. Through naturally occurring circumstances, the four participating therapists fell into one of two categories: psychodynamic orientation or reinforcement theory-based.

INTERVENTION: Twenty-two children from five elementary schools were referred for counseling to one of four therapists by a government agency.

There was confirmation that most of these children (over 90 percent) had been molested by a nonbiological relative who resided with them.

Two approaches to treating sexually abused children and their families were followed. The counselors using a psychodynamic approach focused on relieving the children's guilt and building positive self-concepts. The usual format was to see the parents for several sessions, then to have individual sessions with the child and additional parent meetings when needed. The therapist provided a warm and supportive environment in which family members could explore traumatic events; they attempted to build up the family unit. The therapist's advice to the school was to limit pressures on these children, to show understanding of the impact of the abuse, and to allow for their acting-out behavior while these issues were being worked out in therapy. Sessions were weekly over a one-year period.

The counselors using a reinforcement theory orientation worked primarily with parents to improve the childrearing atmosphere. The focus of treatment was on the child's positive behavior in the present and future with less attention to the past abusive events. Generally, the parents met with the therapist weekly, five or six times, and then about once a month at parent request. These counselors instructed the school to treat the children like their classmates and to ignore inappropriate behavior whenever possible. Clear and firm consequences for disruptive behavior were used.

At the end of the one-year intervention period the occurrence of a number of behaviors was reported and compared to pretreatment levels. Children receiving both treatments had fewer sleep problems and reduced sex play with others; in the reinforcement theory counseling group, however, these behaviors were eliminated completely. Neither treatment orientation was able to reduce the level of sexual self-stimulation; enuresis declined in the reinforcement group by about half, but was minimally reduced in the psychodynamic treatment group. Similarly, general misbehavior decreased in both groups, but the decline was greater in the reinforcement group. Relations between the parents and school were more positive at the conclusion of treatment for those in the reinforcement group.

COMMENTARY: While this is not an empirically rigorous study, the preliminary information it presents should be of interest to school professionals. Both counseling conditions resulted in behavior improvement in all areas except sexual self-stimulation. The reinforcement approach showed greater and more immediate behavior change. Schools are generally more responsive to quick, visible results, and this may explain why relations between parents and schools in the reinforcement group were so cordial as compared to those in the psychodynamic group. These findings highlight the need for close collaboration between the counselor, family, and school, and the necessity for demonstrating change to maintain the support of the school.

Because of the nature of the outcome measures, it is not possible to ascertain whether the slower approach and focus on discussing feelings and meaning used in the psychodynamic type of counseling will eventually result in better long-term adjustment. The authors suggest that a combination of the two approaches incorporating behavior change and time to explore feelings might be appropriate.

SOURCE: Downing, J., Jenkins, S. J., & Fisher, G. L. (1988). A comparison of psychodynamic and reinforcement treatment with sexually abused children. *Elementary School Guidance and Counseling, 22,* 291–298.

Consultation for Teacher Interventions with Sexualized Children

AUTHORS: Barbara R. Slater and Mary M. Gallagher

PRECIS: Information and specific classroom interventions for teachers working with sexualized children, provided by a consultant model

INTRODUCTION: Sexualized behavior is the result of sexual abuse and may include masturbation, sexually explicit verbalizations, exposure, sexualization of teacher-student or peer relationships, and expression of pseudomature sexual needs. These behaviors are inappropriate and interfere with the functioning of the child as well as the classroom. Ongoing intensive psychotherapy or counseling is recommended for these youngsters in almost all cases. Within the school setting, however, it is still necessary for the teacher to respond to these disruptive behaviors. The authors present a consultation approach for providing information and intervention techniques for teachers working with sexualized children. They suggest that three consultant models are appropriate for different aspects of this work. The mental health model of consultation is effective for providing information, the organization-development model of consultation works best for altering classroom environment, and the behavioral model of consultation facilitates direct changes in behavior and peer interactions.

INTERVENTION: Consultation with teachers when children are not present is focused on providing them information on characteristics, needs, and treatment of sexually abused children. Specifically, children who have been abused have not been allowed to develop an independent identity or an ability to control their own behavior; they also cannot communicate effectively. These are all characteristics that are important in school adjustment. The children have a lowered self-concept and need success and acceptance. This information, presented verbally and in printed format, should emphasize that the child is never responsible for the abuse. The aim of the consultation is to change the belief system and attitudes of teachers and staff and to help them overcome their own anxiety.

Classroom environment modifications and direct teacher-child intervention may also be implemented through consultation. Some examples of classroom modifications include separating children who seem overstimulating to each other, and decreasing free time, increasing structure, and focusing attention so that children do not have time to fantasize about the abuse. By reframing and redirecting the sexualized behavior, the teacher accepts the behavior but views it in a more positive manner. For example, the authors relate a case where a child touches other children's genitals; rather than calling him bad, they suggested the teacher reframe the behavior by saying the child is seeking attention and provide another way of getting it (for the first child to tap the shoulder of the child whose attention he wants). Sometimes personal teacher characteristics such as dress style must be altered. The authors describe one situation in which a teacher wearing high heels, form-fitting skirts, and heavy perfume triggered sexual responses in several of the children. Her daily wardrobe was changed to pants and flats with minimal or no perfume. The teacher should be taught safe touch techniques, based on the nature and extent of the child's abusive experiences. Examples of direct teacher-child interventions, such as labeling emotions, providing safe outlets for anger, and activities of which the child can feel in control, are presented as well.

COMMENTARY: This article is filled with excellent, practical strategies for working with sexualized children. The emphasis is on sharing this information with teachers and those in the frontlines who are working on a daily basis with these youngsters through consultation. The point is carefully made that the interventions are in addition to intensive outside treatment and that coordination between the school and the outside therapist will facilitate a more positive school experience for the children involved.

SOURCE: Slater, B. R., & Gallagher, M. M. (1989). Outside the realm of psychotherapy: Consultation for interventions with sexualized children. *School Psychology Review, 18,* 400–411.

Additional Readings

Brassard, M. R., Tyler, A. H., & Kehle, T. J. (1983). School programs to prevent intrafamilial child sexual abuse. *Child Abuse and Neglect, 7,* 241–245.

According to these authors, the school is the logical place for preventive and educational programs on incest. Some specific recommendations made to maximize the impact of these programs include obtaining support of local parent-teacher organizations and providing programs separately for parents and children. Additional programming at the appropriate developmental level of the participants in areas such as sex education and the rights of parents and children is also suggested.

Cosentino, C. E. (1989). Child sexual abuse prevention: Guidelines for the school psychologist. *School Psychology Review, 18,* 371–385.

This article offers school professionals three levels of programming in relation to child sexual abuse: prevention before the occurrence of sexual abuse, early detection and intervention, and treatment and remediation for sexually abused children and their families. Guidelines to provide support within the school are presented. The author suggests, for example, that the school professional maintain contact with the outside therapist, refrain from touching a child who has been abused, and provide reminders that the child is likable to support his or her self-esteem.

Crumbley, J. (1985). Child and adolescent maltreatment: Implications for family therapy. In Marsha P. Mirkin & Stuart L. Koman (Eds.), *Handbook of adolescents and family therapy* (pp. 255–271). New York: Gardner.

Child maltreatment from a family therapy perspective means viewing the family system as dysfunctional and involving various subsystems including the extended family, the abusive family, and siblings in the treatment. Both structural and contextual approaches are recommended and may include developing clear boundaries between subsystems, identifying parent roles and responsibilities, providing effective disciplinary procedures and other childrearing information, and clarifying appropriate expectations for the child.

Culp, R. E., Little, V., Letts, D., & Lawrence, H. (1991). Maltreated children's self-concept: Effects of a comprehensive treatment program. *American Journal of Orthopsychiatry, 61,* 114–121.

This study compared measures of self-concept in maltreated preschool children who were enrolled in a day treatment program and those who were not. The children in the program attended daily for six hours; parent counseling and education services were available as well. Results indicate that the treated group of children viewed themselves as having higher cognitive competence, peer, and maternal acceptance than those in the untreated group. Improvements were also noted on a standardized developmental assessment test.

Garbarino, J. (1987). What can the school do on behalf of the psychologically maltreated child and the community? *School Psychology Review, 16,* 181–187.

Garbarino discusses the role of the school in preventing psychological maltreatment of children including terrorizing, rejecting, isolating, ignoring, and corrupting them. Schools should monitor the mental health of children, provide a psychologically positive climate, and offer individual as well as environmental interventions in conjunction with community agencies. Four case studies are presented illustrating possible responses to different types of maltreatment.

Harvey, P., Forehand, R., Brown, C., & Holmes, T. (1988). The prevention of sexual abuse: Examination of the effectiveness of a program with kindergarten-age children. *Behavior Therapy, 19,* 429–435.

Kindergarten children participated in a sexual abuse prevention program, Good Touch-Bad Touch, which met for three half-hour sessions. Basic information about abuse and ways to avoid and report abuse were presented using storybooks, games, film, and songs. Teaching procedures included modeling, rehearsal, and social reinforcement. At a three-week posttest and at a seven-week follow-up, the children in the program had more knowledge of abuse prevention and acted with greater skill in simulated scenes involving sexual abuse than a placebo control group. The varied nature of the training seemed to contribute to the effectiveness of the intervention with these young children.

Reppucci, N. D., & Haugaard, J. J. (1989). Prevention of child sexual abuse: Myth or reality. *American Psychologist, 44,* 1266–1275.

This thoughtful critique of sexual abuse prevention programs emphasizes the complexity for children of repelling and reporting abuse. It suggests that the content of many programs may deal with one aspect of abuse but not others. A number of programs are reviewed, and there appears to be some limited support for their effectiveness. Recommendations are made for evaluation of programs to determine whether they produce any adverse effects on children's positive relationships or any unusual fears or worry in the children.

Vernon, A., & Hay, J. (1988). A preventative approach to child sexual abuse. *Elementary School Guidance and Counseling, 22,* 306–312.

This article describes a sexual abuse prevention program developed for elementary school children in a small rural school district. Other programs reviewed were found to be too costly, too narrow, or too short term, most consisting of a one-time presentation. The components of the program included awareness of body parts and touch, decision-making strategies, assertive communication skills, whom to go to for help, and self-acceptance and acceptance of feelings.

Vevier, E., & Tharinger, D. J. (1986). Child sexual abuse: A review and intervention framework for the school psychologist. *Journal of School Psychology, 24,* 293–311.

The authors present guidelines for school intervention with child sexual abuse. The framework proposes seven functions for school professionals: establishing themselves as resources and educating faculty and staff; responding to disclosure of abuse; detecting and evaluating possible indicators of abuse; reporting suspected abuse; consulting with teachers to provide indirect service; providing direct service through, for example, group counseling; and implementing prevention programs.

Wurtele, S. K. (1987). School-based sexual abuse prevention programs: A review. *Child Abuse and Neglect, 11,* 483–495.

This article reviews sexual abuse prevention programs targeted at elementary school-age children. Most of them use varied components that may include printed materials, theatrical performances, lecture/discussion, and audiovisual materials. The content, length, and audience and trainer characteristics are summarized for the reader. The author expresses concern that so few studies on the efficacy of these programs have been done.

Wurtele, S. K., Marrs, S. R., & Miller-Perrin, C. L. (1987). Practice makes perfect? The role of participant modeling in sexual abuse prevention programs. *Journal of Consulting and Clinical Psychology, 55,* 599–602.

Kindergarten children were assigned to either a participant modeling or a symbolic modeling sexual abuse prevention program. In the participant modeling group the children were taught self-protective skills through modeling and actively practicing the skills; in the symbolic modeling group, they watched others perform the skills and did not have the opportunity to rehearse them. Children in both groups increased their knowledge of sexual abuse, but the children in the participant modeling group demonstrated greater skill in handling potential encounters. This result supports the notion that active practice may guide behavior during an actual situation.

Running Away

The number of runaways rose substantially during the 1960s and 1970s and is now at record levels. Over one million children under the age of eighteen run away annually, and boys and girls seem to be equally represented in this population. The number of runaway youngsters from single parent or divorced families is much higher than in two-parent families.

Although there are varied conceptualizations of running away, it is generally defined as a child's leaving the home of a parent or guardian for more than one night without parental consent. Runaways are youngsters who voluntarily leave home; throwaways are those who are forced out by their parent(s).

Many complex factors contribute to running away behavior; however, the most widely reported cause is a conflict-ridden family situation. In most cases, a child is running from one or both parents and away from an intolerable situation. Over three-fourths of adolescent runaways report that they have been physically abused, and many are psychologically abused. Reports of disengagement from their families are common; these youngsters feel their family involvement is minimal and describe insensitivity of parents and poor communication with them. Running away is a means of coping with seemingly insurmountable family problems. It is not a normal or productive adolescent behavior but rather an escape from a stressful environmental situation. The premature separation of these children from home and family puts them at high risk for later problems. Interventions for this multifaceted problem include counseling, family therapy, and prevention.

Designing Treatments for Runaways

AUTHORS: James D. Orten and Sharon Kelts Soll

PRECIS: Presentation of a typology of runaways that links the classes of the behavior with specific treatment recommendations

INTRODUCTION: The classification system described by the authors places runaways into categories based on two criteria. First, the degree of alienation between the home and the child is assessed using clinical judgment. This is determined by the general quality of family relationships such as the emotional relationship between the parent and child, the type and duration of the problems, and the degree to which the family participates in nonproblem activities together. The second criterion is the degree to which running away behavior is internalized as a response to stressful situations. This is measured by how often youngsters have run away from home or other similarly stressful situations such as school (that is, truant behavior). These criteria are clearly related to each other.

INTERVENTION: Three classes of running behaviors are presented on a continuum. For first-degree runners there is minimal alienation between the home and the child, and they have run away only once or just a few times; psychological independence from their families has not been achieved. The two subtypes in this category are walkaways and fugitives. Walkaways are fairly well adjusted and in their mid-teens. This one-time running away is generally seen as a learning experience. Unlike walkaways, fugitives are somewhat younger; they feel rejected, powerless, and frightened; they are highly vulnerable. What happens to them on the street helps determine their future path. If they become a member of the street culture, further alienation may occur, whereas finding support and comfort in a well-run shelter or home of a friend provides a better prognosis. Intervention for these first-degree runners is aimed at reconciliation or reunion with their families in family therapy sessions.

There is considerable alienation between second-degree runners and their families. They are ambivalent about returning home and have run away several times. Common problem behaviors exacerbating this situation may be drugs or pregnancy. Treatment for these youngsters revolves around first determining whether they should return home or to a foster care institution or independent living situation. This decision should be made by the parents and the child, and there should be continued connections with the family if the child moves out. When reunion is the choice, some form of structure, perhaps probation, should be considered to prevent recurrence of the running away behavior. Family treatment is recommended.

The alienation between the third-degree runner and the family is strong. These hardened runaways are usually sixteen or older and have lived on the streets for a year or more with little or no family contact. They are resistant to treatment, and intervention should focus on independent living and life planning, again with parent involvement. Often a restrictive treatment setting will be necessary.

COMMENTARY: This typology is a useful way for school professionals to view runaway behavior. Certainly, there are a number of classification systems, but Orten and Soll use a rather broad system so as not to oversimplify or overcategorize. They focus on the family-child relationship, a view that supports the most recent findings about runaway behavior.

SOURCE: Orten, J. D., & Soll, S. K. (1980). Runaway children and their families: A treatment typology. *Journal of Family Issues, 1,* 249–261.

School Counseling for Runaway Adolescents

AUTHORS: Phyllis Post Kammer and Dieter Schmidt

PRECIS: Characteristics of a school counseling relationship that counters the alienation and distrust of runaway teens

INTRODUCTION: Although family conflict has been described as a major factor in runaway behavior, stress in school may contribute to precipitating this behavior as well. Research shows that adolescents who run away often perform poorly in school and may have serious school problems such as truancy and drug or alcohol abuse. Often runaways who return to school do not receive support to facilitate understanding of their behavior or their readjustment. This article provides guidelines for the school professional in working with runaways.

INTERVENTION: Early intervention, at the time of the first runaway episode, is recommended. The initial step is to establish a personal relationship with the runaway that acknowledges the family and school difficulties experienced by the adolescent. School problems are often the source of family conflicts, and academic failure may be used in retaliation against the parents. These issues must be explored in the counseling situation. This relationship does not preclude an outside referral for individual or family therapy and providing knowledge of community resources for runaways. A comprehensive knowledge of the facilities and services provided will help increase the likelihood that the students will follow up.

In addition to individual counseling, a peer listener program may be developed. Training peers in listening skills and knowledge of adolescent issues helps prepare them to provide appropriate support. The aim is to lessen the feelings of alienation and loneliness experienced by the runaways. This would be most appropriate for a first-time runaway. Another way of promoting a sense of belonging is to establish support groups for runaways and others with varied adjustment problems. Membership in such a group would facilitate bonding with other students when the runaway returns to the school.

COMMENTARY: An individual counseling relationship, peer listeners, and support groups are all supportive measures that require time and no monetary outlay. They are accepted interventions in the school, and all three can be used with a variety of problems other than runaways. The major focus of all these strategies is to increase younsters' feelings of belonging and acceptance to prevent further episodes of running.

The importance of this article is to remind school professionals not to neglect runaways on their return to school and to establish a link between the school and community agencies and resources.

SOURCE: Kammer, P. P., & Schmidt, D. (1987). Counseling runaway adolescents. *The School Counselor, 35,* 149–154.

Family Therapy for Runaway Adolescents

AUTHOR: H. Charles Fishman

PRECIS: A case example of family therapy that helps parents to be firm and to provide options to their runaway adolescent daughter

INTRODUCTION: Runaway teenagers view their homes as unsupportive. Often they complain that parents are too strict, but from a systems viewpoint the problem may result from a parent conflict triangulating the child. That is, the parents focus their attention on the teen's behavior and avoid addressing their own problems. The goals of the family therapist in this case are to delineate clearly the parents' and the adolescent's issues. The parents must assume their responsibilities as executives in the family and then present options for the daughter. The case described below presents the treatment for such a family.

INTERVENTION: The fifteen-year-old daughter in this affluent family is the third of five children. She had left home several months prior to the therapy after refusing to obey her parents' rules and was now living with a boy. The therapist describes the parents as two individuals in crisis without a marital relationship. The father is depressed and experiencing a midlife crisis, and the mother is faced with an empty nest and finding her way into the work force. From a systems perspective, their daughter's running away is focusing their attention on her and deflecting attention from their own problems.

The first step in the therapy was for the parents to learn to negotiate between themselves in order to exercise executive or parental functions. They were held back by fear of what their daughter might do if they asserted themselves. Each one attempted to maintain the homeostasis of the system, and it was very difficult for the therapist to get them to discuss bringing the daughter home. They behaved at the extremes, vacillating from rigid enforcement of rules to very indulgent behavior. The therapist needed to help them create an environment of compromise. Once they were united in their communication, they were then able to negotiate with their daughter. Although the daughter fought coming home, this is viewed as a healthy response that validates her feelings and independent thinking.

COMMENTARY: The parents in this system were empowered and assumed the responsibilities of parenting. The goal of transforming the family into a caring place where children abided by limits, but were also listened to, was attained. This allowed the daughter to return to a new family context.

For school professionals it is important to recognize that the adolescent runaway is escaping from an intolerable family situation and sees no alternative. Intervention with the family is essential, and if it occurs outside the school, close contact should be maintained with the therapist so that school support is consonant with the therapeutic goals.

SOURCE: Fishman, H. C. (1988). The runaway adolescent: A therapy of options. In H. C. Fishman, *Treating troubled adolescents: A family therapy approach* (pp. 59–80). New York: Basic Books.

Improving Communication in the Families of Runaways

AUTHOR: Richard P. Barth

PRECIS: Training in communication and problem solving to resolve parent-child conflict in the case of an adolescent runaway

INTRODUCTION: One of the major goals when runaways return home is to lessen the possibility of their running away in the future. Yet, because family change occurs slowly, the adolescent often finds conditions unchanged on his or her return. There is evidence that parents of nonrunaway youth have better communication and problem-solving skills than parents of runaways. Thus, in this case study, the family is trained in communication and problem solving to help them resolve conflict. The training can be carried out in any setting (for example, foster home, shelter, home, school) and with varied family members.

INTERVENTION: In the case study presented here, the fourteen-year-old male arrived at a shelter after running away from home. He, his mother, and his sister had moved in with his uncle's family and his grandmother nine months earlier after his stepfather deserted the family. He began cutting school, was grounded at home, and was threatened with a beating, at which time he fled the house. Once he was at the shelter, a therapist initiated a series of sessions to train the family in communication and problem solving.

There are six basic stages in family communication and problem-solving training: defining the situation; assessing the family and the ecology; teaching communication skills; choosing and defining the problems on which to work; discussing, evaluating, choosing, and planning solutions; and implementing solutions. The stages occur sequentially; each one is recorded on worksheets. Defining the situation refers to establishing a task-focused relationship. Assessment addresses the specific problems that led to the runaway behavior, and a checklist of varied problems can be provided for each member of the family to fill out. Before dealing with the problem identified during assessment, the family is taught communication skills. They are asked to discuss a neutral topic, and then they analyze family members' speaking and listening skills. This is followed by a debriefing. Six communications skills are introduced: praise, paraphrase, I-statements, partial agreement, staying on topic, and asking for information. Giving and receiving appreciation and criticism are emphasized.

When choosing and defining a problem, all family members must agree. After this step they generate potential solutions, and then evaluate each one. The solution is recorded, and they develop and implement a plan. Continued monitoring or troubleshooting may result in modifications of the plan.

In this case study, the six-step procedure was followed. Before tackling the major problems of the teenager's talking back and skipping school, the family received communication skill training through demonstration, rehearsal, and homework assignments. Once they defined the problem behavior, they decided on the consequences for its occurrence as well as rewards for good behavior. It is important to note that the therapist always asked the family to consider what might go wrong with any plan they chose to implement and how they might contribute to its failure or success. After three weeks the boy returned home and went back to school.

COMMENTARY: This case describes a first-time runaway from a stressful but not chaotic situation; these conditions increased the likelihood of a positive outcome. The goal was to change the child's social ecology as quickly as possible.

The intervention is structured and goal focused and can be implemented in or out of the school setting. The family is taught skills that are applicable to any number of family problems and not limited to runaway behavior.

SOURCE: Barth, R. P. (1986). Running away. In Richard P. Barth, *Social and cognitive treatment of children and adolescents: Practical strategies for problem behaviors* (pp. 353–394). San Francisco: Jossey-Bass.

Additional Readings

Deni, J. R. (1987). Children and running away. In A. Thomas & J. Grimes (Eds.), *Children's needs: Psychological perspectives* (pp. 493–499). Washington, DC: National Association of School Psychologists.

This comprehensive review article on running away provides information on etiology as well as intervention. A number of useful actions for school personnel are suggested in addition to counseling and therapy and include the use of crisis and help lines to provide information, working with the juvenile court system, prevention programs for parents and children, and strategies to cope with daily life stresses. Telephone numbers for hot lines are provided.

Janus, M. D., McCormack, A., Burgess, A. W., & Hartman, C. (1987). *Adolescent runaways: Causes and consequences.* Lexington, MA: Heath.

This book reports on a study of Canadian runaways. It details their perceptions of and reactions to their families and the presence of abuse in their background. Interventions are discussed in the concluding chapters of the book. The authors describe three basic tasks in dealing with the runaway: assessing for possible reconciliation with the home, preparing for independent living, and maintaining health. Sample interview questions are provided and difficulties in establishing communication are discussed.

Lappin, J., & Covelman, K. W. (1985). Adolescent runaways: A structural family therapy perspective. In M. P. Mirkin & S. L. Koman (Eds.), *Handbook of adolescents and family therapy* (pp. 343–362). New York: Gardner Press.

This chapter challenges us to reconsider whether all runaways are irrevocably alienated from their families and whether removing the child from the family is the best course of action. Adolescent running is viewed as a symptom of a family facing change. The family must restructure itself as it contends with adolescence and the issues of separation and individuation.

Using a structural perspective, the authors identify four characteristics of family functioning that contribute to the runaway process. The first three are a dysfunctional generational hierarchy, triangulation of the adolescent runaway, and conflict avoidance; these are all necessary for runaway behavior to occur, but they must be accompanied by the fourth, parental collusion in the runaway process. Case examples of treatment are presented.

Manov, A., & Lowther, L. (1983). A health care approach for hard-to-reach adolescent runaways. *Nursing Clinics of North America, 18,* 333–342.

Runaway adolescents have the same basic health care needs as all adolescents, but they may have other needs as a result of their living circumstances. In addition to general health complaints, they may manifest pregnancy, venereal disease, alcohol abuse, and medical problems that are consequences of abuse and incest. This article presents a five-part approach for health care providers when these youngsters ask for health care.

Miller, A. T., Eggertson-Tacon, C., & Quigg, B. (1990). Patterns of runaway behavior within a larger systems context: The road to empowerment. *Adolescence, 25,* 271–289.

The authors present a case study and the results of a survey of a sample of adolescent runaways who were living in residential treatment. They found that teenagers do not run away for the same reasons, and that running away may be considered a solution rather than a problem to these youths. They suggest that no residential treatment be started until the youth, the family, and the professionals agree on the "house rules." A treatment plan based on the severity of the behavior must involve all professionals including police, court personnel, and others. Generally, treatment should not be focused on the running away behavior but rather on the ambivalence or lack of direction of the teenager.

Morgan, O. J. (1982). Runaways: Jurisdiction, dynamics and treatment. *Journal of Marital and Family Therapy, 8,* 121–127.

This article views running away as a family problem that should be treated with a family therapy approach. Interventions should be locally controlled, voluntarily activated, community based, and readily accessible. The author recommends against continued use of the "status offender" designation.

Wheeler, M. (1986). Runaway prey: Reaching the homeless teen. *UCLA Social Welfare, 2,* 10–15.

This article briefly describes the Runaway Adolescent Pilot Project developed jointly by the University of California, Los Angeles (UCLA), School of Social Welfare and the Los Angeles County Department of Children's Services. A house in the community serves as an intake center and has nine carefully chosen caseworkers. Immediate needs of the adolescent are assessed first — that is, food, shelter, or medical attention. Once the teen has decided to avail him- or herself of assistance, long-term services will be provided.

Cult Membership

In recent years there has been an increase in the number, size, and influence of cults. A cult is considered destructive when it is a closed system or group whose members have been recruited deceptively and lose their independence of thinking and feeling by remaining in the group. Destructive cults encourage extreme dependency and focus on the importance of group interests. The group frequently has a charismatic leader who claims to have special powers or abilities.

Four types of cults have been identified by the Cult Awareness Network: religious, therapy or pseudotherapy, political, and commercial. Adolescents are particularly vulnerable because of their stage of development and the stresses in their lives. Increased involvement of adolescents in cults, and in Satanism and the occult, in particular, has required school professionals to become more aware of cults. Generally, participation in cults results in changes in an individual's behavior and school performance as well as social withdrawal. Thus, the adolescent experiences disturbed relationships both with adults in the form of submission to a leader and with peers.

The interventions that have been suggested for cult membership include prevention, deprogramming, psychotherapy, ego structuring, and cognitive restructuring. Most of these treatments occur outside the school, and there is very limited published information on school intervention.

A Problem-Solving Approach to Cult Involvement

AUTHORS: Joan Carol Ross and Michael D. Langone

PRECIS: A problem-solving model to help parents select an appropriate strategy to help their child

INTRODUCTION: This book is written for parents who suspect or know that their child is in a destructive cult. Changed behavior in the child reported by parents includes secretiveness, a change in vocabulary or speech patterns, emotional changes such as distancing, a shift in friends and activities, diminished academic performance, rejection of secular goals, and extreme commitments. Although these do not necessarily mean there is cult involvement, they suggest that further investigation is necessary. Three problem-solving approaches are presented as intervention strategies: taking over, laissez-faire, and learner-helper.

INTERVENTION: The authors advocate the learner-helper intervention approach for most parents. This involves gathering information and accepting the possibility that it may be necessary to change their own views and behavior in order to help their child.

Five different responses to children in a cult are discussed, with cautions that there is no one correct approach. The first four are distancing yourself from the child and cult involvement, approving of the cult and looking for the good in it, tolerating but disapproving of the cult, and rescuing and deprogramming the child.

The authors generally use the fifth response—promoting voluntary reevaluation—whenever possible. It is described as a noncoercive strategy with the goal of motivating a member to assess the cult critically by stimulating his or her critical abilities through parent-child communication. One of the aims of this response is to help the child make an independent choice between the cult and the noncult world. The importance of parent-child contact, rapport, and communication is emphasized.

In order to establish rapport, parents must learn communication skills. They are taught listening, responding, asking questions, and controlling emotional reactions. Parents also learn how to overcome barriers produced by the cult such as anti-parent propaganda and fear of deprogramming.

Guidelines are provided as to when and how to let the cultist make the critical choice of whether to leave the cult.

COMMENTARY: This book appears to be a very valuable resource for parents and school personnel. It provides an objective set of guidelines but recognizes the time-consuming and emotionally draining experience that parents will go through. On the positive side, the authors view the actions taken as open-ended and flexible, based on information, and most important as respecting the autonomy and integrity of both child and parents as much as possible.

School personnel will benefit from understanding how parents are feeling and responding to the cult involvement of their child. Also, schools should not expect quick change but rather be prepared for a lengthy process. The authors stress repeatedly that there is not one correct approach and that the level of involvement must first be assessed as well as the resources and limitations of the parents.

SOURCE: Ross, J. C., & Langone, M.D. (1988). *Cults: What parents should know*. Weston, MA: American Family Foundation.

Preventive Education on Cultism

AUTHORS: Andrea Bloomgarden and Michael D. Langone

PRECIS: A live presentation by an ex-cult member and a videotape of such a presentation change high school students' attitudes about cults

INTRODUCTION: Interventions directed at cult members are generally grouped into four categories: deprogramming or trying to get the cult member to think critically about his or her situation, legislation to remove members from the cult, voluntary counseling, and preventive education.

This study addresses the area of preventive education through a comparison of four types of presentations to high school students. The authors acknowledge the paucity of empirical support for prevention and the difficulties of determining what to teach, where to teach, and who should teach.

INTERVENTION: High school students between the ages of sixteen and nineteen participated in this study. They were assigned to one of five one-time presentations: a live talk by an ex-member of the Unification Church; a videotape of the ex-cult member's talk; a film titled *Moonchild,* which portrays the conversion and deprogramming of a young man who joined the Moonies; a twenty-minute filmstrip called *Cults: The Appeal, the Danger,* which was followed by a twenty-minute discussion led by an expert on cults; and a no-treatment control.

The pre- and postintervention questionnaire asked about the students' experiences with cults, their ideas of what features identify a cult, and their attitudes toward people who join cults. There were also several hypothetical scenarios describing manipulative techniques used for recruitment and questions about how likely someone would be to accept the invitation and give in to the pressure.

Looking at behavior in the scenarios, students in the short filmstrip and both the live and videotaped ex-cult member interventions showed change, suggesting less willingness to comply with manipulative techniques. The *Moonchild* film and both ex-cult member interventions were most effective in teaching students to distinguish between a harmless and harmful cult. The control group was less sympathetic to people who joined cults than were students in the *Moonchild* or ex-cult member conditions, a finding that is viewed as a failure to acknowledge their own vulnerability to cults. It is common to blame the victim rather than to recognize that cults have the ability to manipulate an average person.

COMMENTARY: The presentation by the ex-cult member and the videotape of the presentation resulted in the most attitude change. Certainly, the "live" model is a very powerful figure, but it is less clear why the videotape worked as well. Perhaps it was the nature of the presentation, structured around a social psychological perspective; according to the authors, this made it more consonant with the nature of the questionnaire.

Despite its limitations, the study is interesting because it raises a number of questions on how best to approach prevention. Consideration must be given to the goal of the intervention: Is it attitude change, behavior change, or informational? Also, what level of active participation — for example, discussion — will result in change? The authors recommend against "scare" programs, which they see as possibly having a reverse effect on those who are susceptible to cults.

SOURCE: Bloomgarden, A., & Langone, M.D. (1984). Preventive education on cultism for high school students: A comparison of different programs' effects on potential vulnerability to cults. *Cultic Studies Journal, 1,* 167–177.

Additional Readings

Bard, E. M. (1991, June). Devil worship: Fact or fantasy. *Communiqué* (publication of the National Association of School Psychologists, Washington, DC), p. 23.

This article discusses the involvement of adolescents with Satanism and the occult in schools. It provides a set of procedures to follow when school professionals must determine the level of involvement of a teenager with the satanic belief system. These procedures are not unique to this problem — that is, interviewing the student, parents, and teachers; reviewing school records; and studying drawings the student has made — but the professional is looking for evidence of religious content or conflict, themes of subjugation and violence, and themes of good versus evil.

Dumont, L. E., & Altesman, R. I. (1989). *A parent's guide to teens and cults.* Washington, DC: Psychiatric Institutes of America Press.

This helpful guide to cults is written for parents who are concerned about their children's cult involvement. A chapter on leaving the cult discusses several interventions including prevention, voluntary departure, deprogramming, legal recourse, and psychotherapy. The authors emphasize the importance of the family in rescuing the child.

Eichel, S.K.D., Eichel, L. D., & Eisenberg, R. C. (1984). Mental health interventions in cult-related cases: Preliminary investigation of outcomes. *Cultic Studies Journal, 1,* 156–166.

This study reports on cases of college-age cult-involved individuals seen at the Re-Entry Therapy, Information and Referral Network. The interventions used were varied and included consultation with mother or family, voluntary and involuntary deprogramming, psychotherapy, and individual reentry therapy. Positive outcomes were reported for 67 percent or ten of fifteen cases.

Galanter, M. (Ed.). (1989). *Cults and new religious movements.* Washington, DC: American Psychiatric Association.

The Committee on Psychiatry and Religion of the American Psychiatric Association prepared this report on cults and new religious movements. This comprehensive work presents current information on the impact of cult membership, group function and social control, and the legal and social issues related to cults. There are several chapters that deal with intervention issues including psychotherapy with cult members, consultation and treatment of families of cult members, deprogramming of cult members, and options for legal intervention.

Halperin, D. A. (1987). Psychoanalysis and cult affiliation: Clinical perspectives. *Cultic Studies Journal, 4,* 25–37.

The author presents variations in psychoanalytically oriented treatment for individuals at different stages of cult involvement. Before commitment to a cult group is made, the goal of treatment is to have the family help the individual reconsider affiliation. Once commitment is made to a cult, lines of communication with the family should be maintained, and the individual is encouraged to look at personal changes that have occurred in him or her with cult membership. Those leaving a cult need to regain personal autonomy and confront problems associated with cult membership. A number of case examples are provided.

Zimbardo, P. G., & Hartley, C. F. (1985). Cults go to high school: A theoretical and empirical analysis of the initial stage in the recruitment process. *Cultic Studies Journal, 2,* 91–147.

This article describes a theoretical model of cult recruitment that stresses a reciprocal relationship between cult recruiters and potential recruits.

The four-phase model includes (1) precontact variables, such as background characteristics and knowledge structure of both the potential convert and the recruiter, (2) initial (recruitment) contact variable, and (3) developed (indoctrination) contact variables, or situational factors, such as face-to-face or media presentation; the final phase in the model is (4) conversion.

An empirical investigation described in the article identifies eleven variables that distinguished high school students who had been approached by recruiters from those who had not had any contacts with a recruiter. Further, fifteen variables were associated with students who would consider further invitations from cults. These results have implications for preventive work with high school students.

Resources

American Family Foundation
P.O. Box 336
Weston, MA 02193
(617) 893-0930

Cult Awareness Network
2421 W. Pratt Boulevard, Suite 1173
Chicago, IL 60645
(312) 267-7777

7

━━━━━━━━━━━━━━━━━━━━━━━━━━━

Health Management

━━━━━━━━━━━━━━━━━━━━━━━━━━━

Many children attend school each day with physical or health disabilities. These include chronic illnesses such as diabetes, asthma, headaches, epilepsy, and cancer; communicable diseases such as acquired immune deficiency syndrome (AIDS), hepatitis, measles, mumps, and tuberculosis; orthopedic problems; neurological disorders such as Tourette syndrome; and head injury. It is estimated that 2 percent of school children in this country have a chronic illness severe enough to interfere with their daily activities.

Some medical illness results in a high rate of absenteeism, leading to uncompleted schoolwork and missed opportunities to socialize with other youngsters. Those children who can attend school regularly may have restrictions placed on their participation in social and educational activities. Often, their physical or emotional energy is limited because of their treatment; this condition may adversely affect their academic performance. Families are affected as well, and the financial burdens may be onerous.

The school nurse or other medical professional works with staff, family, physician, and community agencies to supervise the health needs of the child in the school setting. Once proper medical management has been assured, the school can play an important role in increasing a student's functioning level by helping the child manage his or her illness. Interventions may include health education programs, self-management training, and behavioral strategies.

Acquired Immune Deficiency Syndrome (AIDS)

Recent data suggest that the number of AIDS cases is increasing, although it is a low-incidence disease among children. Most of the young children who acquire the virus do so from a parent at birth or through blood transfusions. As youngsters approach adolescence, however, their risk increases as this is the period of exploration of their sexuality and often, a time of drug experimentation.

AIDS is a communicable disease caused by a virus. In the past, the most successful intervention for communicable diseases has been immunization. Until a vaccine is developed to prevent this disease, however, the three main approaches to intervention in the schools will be prevention programs to reduce or eliminate high-risk behaviors, health-promotion programs to encourage and reinforce appropriate health-enhancing behaviors, and intervention on psychological issues with students who are HIV (human immunodeficiency virus) positive.

Very limited information is available on the difficulties faced by children with AIDS, and knowledge about other diseases is not easily generalizable to AIDS. These children not only face their own death but are stigmatized, and often ostracized, by others. Further, the families usually have very great supportive needs. Adolescents with AIDS may also be at high risk for suicide.

Educational Programs to Prevent AIDS

AUTHOR: Gary B. Melton

PRECIS: Effective prevention programs for AIDS to increase the personal salience of the risks, provide training in problem solving to help teenagers make their own decisions, and institute environmental changes necessary to help modify behavior

INTRODUCTION: Preventing infection by the human immunodeficiency virus (HIV) is of great urgency for adolescents as experimentation with sex and drugs generally begins during the teenage years. Over half of all teenage girls have had sexual experiences by the age of eighteen, and this number is greater for minority group adolescents. Of the fifteen- to nineteen-year-olds who are sexually active, many use condoms initially; but then condom use declines dramatically. Also, intravenous drug use, though occurring in only a small group of adolescents, is most prevalent in late adolescence and early adulthood.

This article addresses the need to focus on the prevention of AIDS in adolescents and identifies factors that are likely to affect the success of a prevention program. Differing life-styles of "normal" youth and "antisocial" youth are considered.

INTERVENTION: The aim of a prevention program is to decrease the frequency with which teenagers engage in behavior that may result in HIV infection. While providing information about AIDS is critical, it is not sufficient. The article suggests a two-pronged approach that includes discouraging risky behavior and promoting healthy behavior.

In general, teens have neither experienced negative effects from risky behavior nor have they observed it in others. The risk of HIV infection is largely invisible to them. In order to modify their behavior, teens must be convinced that the risks are real and that they apply to themselves. This can be done by giving téens more personal experiences of risks—perhaps hearing a speaker with AIDS, perhaps visiting a hospital—and by teaching them risk assessment to increase the "cognitive availability of risks and decrease the attractiveness of short-term benefits of risk-taking behavior" (p. 407).

The promotion of healthy behavior involves increased knowledge and accessibility of information. For example, there is evidence that teens lack information about AIDS in general, and about sexuality and the use of condoms in particular. Having information, however, will not change behavior; it is necessary for these young people to increase their skills as well. The author suggests, for example, that they be provided specific information about sexual practices that increase the risk of AIDS, the proper use of condoms, and the means of obtaining them. They should have decision-making exercises, problem-solving materials, and rehearsal of behavior in high-risk situations.

Another means of promoting healthy behavior is through the manipulation of the environment. For example, to decrease psychological barriers to the effective use of condoms, they might be distributed in accessible settings and/or be subsidized to reduce or eliminate cost. Similarly, access to sterile needles might be increased.

In general, a comprehensive prevention program must teach teenagers skills in risk assessment, decision making, and assertiveness in social situations.

COMMENTARY: This thought-provoking article gives a realistic appraisal of the developmental issues that impinge on prevention during the adolescent years. It is clear that a "just say no" prevention campaign for high-risk behavior is not appropriate for junior and senior high school students. Short-term benefits are too real and long-term consequences too far removed.

The author emphasizes the importance of applying psychological knowledge to these programs and not just supplying information. He acknowledges the shortcoming of providing this type of prevention program only in the schools and encourages working with community centers to reach minority and dropout teens.

SOURCE: Melton, G. B. (1988). Adolescents and prevention of AIDS. *Professional Psychology: Research and Practice, 19*, 403–408.

Multidisciplinary, Multistrategy Programs for AIDS Prevention

AUTHORS: Diane DeMuth Allensworth and Cynthia Wolford Symons

PRECIS: A multidisciplinary, multiple intervention approach including instruction, environmental support, media, role modeling, and social support for preventing infection with the human immunodeficiency virus (HIV) in schools

INTRODUCTION: The authors take the nine factors identified by Walberg to increase students' affective, behavioral, and cognitive learning and apply them to developing a health education program with specific focus on acquired immune deficiency syndrome (AIDS). These factors are grouped into three categories: (1) aptitude, which consists of ability, development, and motivation/self-concept; (2) instruction, both amount and quality; and (3) environment—that is, home, classroom, peers, and television. The research findings in these areas are taken into consideration and the authors present a model of AIDS-prevention strategies for schools.

INTERVENTION: This prevention model is provided in a grid in the article with the individuals and settings across the top and the strategies along the left. The individuals who should be involved in prevention in the school include administrators, health educators, classroom teachers, librarians, school nurses, guidance counselors, school psychologists, physical educators, coaches, parents, peers, and community members. All of these individuals will be using varied strategies that include environmental change, media, direct intervention, policy change, role-modeling, social support, and direct instruction.

An example of environmental change made by the classroom teacher might be to implement policies regarding body fluids, to model acceptance of HIV-infected students, and to display posters on AIDS prevention. The nurse might implement a primary care clinic that includes reproductive health care services and might make condoms easily available. The faculty work room might have materials available to raise AIDS awareness. Teachers or librarians might use media such as information in the student newspaper or AIDS-prevention videos. The community might develop public service announcements for radio or television or advocate discussions of AIDS on a local radio station.

The authors suggest that when a specific message is repeated, it is more likely to be internalized. Thus, they advocate multiple interventions that provide consistent and continuous messages using many channels (school, home, community, and media) and disseminated by numerous agents, including parents, peers, and professionals.

COMMENTARY: This article provides a theoretical model rather than a tested intervention, but it is based on research evidence about learning. It considers the developmental level of the child and what we know about quality instruction, both with regard to content and time needed to learn. It stresses the importance of systemwide intervention that involves home, school, and community. Certainly, support is more likely when everyone is involved and there is collaborative decision making and planning. Such an intervention does not put the burden on one individual and affirms the need to use social and environmental supports.

SOURCE: Allensworth, D. D., & Symons, C. W. (1989). A theoretical approach to school-based HIV prevention. *Journal of School Health, 59,* 59–65.

Consultation in Pediatric AIDS

AUTHOR: Margaret L. Stuber

PRECIS: Specific psychotherapy issues related to pediatric AIDS using case examples

INTRODUCTION: Certain issues faced by those treating children with AIDS are similar to issues in treating childhood cancer; others, however, are specific to AIDS and include infectivity, delayed onset of symptoms, and public fear and blame. This article presents a series of cases that provide a sample of issues that a school consultant might face.

INTERVENTION: The therapeutic issues in the first case arise from the confirmation that a white, middle-class four-year-old is HIV positive as are both his parents. A major issue is attribution of blame, that is, how did the first parent become infected? The alternatives — homosexual or heterosexual contact outside the marriage, intravenous drug use, or infection through contaminated blood products — may have varying degrees of blame associated with them. The emotionally difficult task of working with three fatally ill people may be alleviated by a collaborative approach in which one therapist works with the couple while another focuses on the child. Support for each other as well as for the teachers and other school professionals, doctors, and nurses working with this child and family is essential.

A second school-related case describes a bright six-year-old girl who is HIV infected from a transfusion as a premature newborn. The parents would like her to continue to attend school. The author recommends that a developmentally appropriate explanation be given to this youngster: that her illness is serious, that treatment is necessary, that doctors will continue to try to get rid of it, and that she will be told if it is getting better or worse. The role of the therapist or consultant is to help the family and school deal with the expected anger, frustration, and fear of the child. Play therapy approaches are suggested, and reentry to school is encouraged.

Another case deals with a Hispanic adolescent who, despite pretest counseling, is overwhelmed when he receives a positive HIV test result, probably as a result of transfusions for leukemia. His talk of suicide must be addressed and followed up as the risk of suicide is high among people with AIDS. Ethnic issues may also play a role, including fear that his social group will reject him or that professionals working with him may make assumptions based on his background that are inaccurate.

COMMENTARY: These examples provide a glimpse of the complex issues that school professionals must consider when working with pediatric AIDS patients in school. They are relevant not only in a therapy or counseling situation but also in the way faculty and staff relate to children within the school milieu.

Consultation, workshops, or educational programs for all school faculty using case examples might sensitize professionals to some of the issues. The inservice training should probably be done within a general framework rather than as a response to a single child's illness. Perhaps a discussion of AIDS could be provided within a presentation on medical disorders and their effects on children.

SOURCE: Stuber, M. L. (1990). Psychiatric consultation issues in pediatric HIV and AIDS. *Journal of the American Academy of Child and Adolescent Psychiatry, 29,* 463–467.

Additional Readings

Amer-Hirsch, W. (1989). Educating youth about AIDS: A model program. *Children Today, 18,* 16–19.

The Girls Club of New York has developed AIDS awareness workshops that provide information and skills aimed at preventing AIDS to a largely minority audience. It is presented in four weekly one-hour sessions. In addition to basic lecture information, age-appropriate activities are used including designing posters for preteens, word-finding games and spelling bees using AIDS-related words, writing, and game show simulations. The older children participate in debates and have problem-solving and role-playing exercises. In one activity students assess the risk of various behaviors, and then they discuss and rate them. Evaluation showed that participants had improved knowledge about AIDS and more accepting attitudes toward people with AIDS.

Belfer, M. L., Krener, P. K., & Miller, F. B. (1988). AIDS in children and adolescents. *Journal of the American Academy of Child and Adolescent Psychiatry, 27,* 147–151.

This article discusses clinical interventions for AIDS victims focused on the child, adolescent, and system. For younger children, issues associated with chronic illness are applicable; these children need support to lessen the impact of the stigmatization. A critical issue with adolescents is to reach the poor minority child who is at great risk. Child psychiatrist extenders such as peer counselors are suggested as possibly being more accessible and acceptable to these teens. Finally, the needs of the family system cannot be underestimated in AIDS cases nor can the feelings of staff caring for these patients.

Black, J. L., & Jones, L. H. (1988). HIV infection: Educational programs and policies for school personnel. *Journal of School Health, 58,* 317–322.

This article provides a series of recommendations for handling students infected with HIV as well as information that should be included in HIV/AIDS education programs. Guidelines for implementation emphasize that the scope and content of the HIV education should be consistent with parental and community values and should be jointly developed with community participation. An AIDS unit should be one component of health instruction and the instructor should have special training.

Centers for Disease Control and Center for Health Promotion and Education. (1988). Guidelines for effective school health education to prevent the spread of AIDS. *Journal of School Health, 58,* 142–148.

The guidelines were developed to help school personnel teach students how to avoid HIV infection. They recommend that the scope and content of a program be locally determined. A school district policy should be developed with representation from the community. The curriculum should be within a comprehensive school health education program and should be developmentally appropriate.

DiClemente, R. J., Boyer, C. B., & Mills, S. J. (1987). Prevention of AIDS among adolescents: Strategies for the development of comprehensive risk-reduction health education programs. *Health Education Research: Theory and Practice, 2,* 287–291.

The authors recommend that information about AIDS be presented within the context of sexually transmitted diseases using a variety of communication strategies such as role-playing, discussion, and videotapes. They emphasize the importance of teacher education as teachers will often be the ones to deliver the information. In particular, the inservice training should include a personal assessment of values and attitudes toward sexuality and specifically homosexuality. The authors suggest that the training for students be mandatory.

DiClemente, R. J., & Houston-Hamilton, A. (1989). Health promotion strategies for prevention of human immunodeficiency virus infection among minority adolescents. *Health Education, 20,* 39–43.

This article focuses on risk-reduction programs with black and Latino adolescents because minority youngsters see themselves as less at risk of HIV infection and have more misconceptions about the transmission of the disease. The authors recommend that activities such as decision-making exercises, cognitive rehearsal of self-protective behaviors, and assertiveness training be used to increase self-efficacy. The importance of providing AIDS instruction in the home, school, and community is emphasized.

Dorman, S. M., Small, P. A., & Lee, D. D. (1989). A cooperative learning technique for AIDS education. *Journal of School Health, 59,* 314–315.

This article presents an innovative teaching strategy, the TEAM PACK cooperative learning technique, for HIV education. It is appropriate for high school students of average and above-average reading ability and can take one or two fifty-minute class periods. This activity would be one component of an existing unit on AIDS. Students are heterogeneously placed in groups of four and given a TEAM PACK, four copies of an information sheet, and the role-play scenario. Different members of the group have answers to different questions and must share the answers with the others, creating interdependence. They then role-play an AIDS-related scenario making decisions based on the information they have shared. At the end of the class the groups are brought together for discussion.

Flora, J. A., & Thoresen, C. E. (1988). Reducing the risk of AIDS in adolescents. *American Psychologist, 43,* 965–970.

The authors suggest that information about AIDS prevention efforts can be drawn from effective health programs in other areas such as smoking prevention. These interventions include information and practice of skills to resist pressures to engage in risky behavior, practice in recognizing high-risk situations, discussion and practice of arguments to counter risky behavior, and active participation as peer leaders or by role-playing throughout the prevention program. The materials must be focused on specific subgroups and identify gender, ethnic, and racial similarities and differences.

Fulton, G. B., Metress, E., & Price, J. H. (1987). AIDS: Resource materials for school personnel. *Journal of School Health, 57,* 14–18.

This useful review article covers basic information about AIDS, school policies regarding attendance for children with AIDS, hot line numbers, relevant organizations, and audiovisual materials for possible use in the schools.

Miller, L., & Downer, A. (1988). AIDS: What you and your friends need to know — A lesson plan for adolescents. *Journal of School Health, 58,* 137–141.

High school students' knowledge of AIDS and their attitudes toward people with AIDS were tested. Based on the results of this pretest, a fifty-minute AIDS lesson plan was designed that included lecture, a videotape, a scripted slide presentation, and discussion and writing. Students were post-tested one week and eight weeks after the lesson. Changes in knowledge and attitude were seen for those who had the AIDS lesson.

Chronic Illness

More children are attending school with chronic health problems than ever before. Medical advances have led to improved survival rates for children, which means that their long-term health care needs must be considered. While the negative impact of chronic illness on school performance, social development, and school attendance has been established, until recently schools have not actively intervened in children's health management.

Asthma is the most common chronic disease in childhood and is on the rise around the country. Over 4 percent of children (approximately 2.7 million) under the age of eighteen suffer from asthma. A recent study indicated that it is the leading cause of days lost from school and results in 200,000 hospitalizations annually. About one-third of the afflicted youngsters have some limitation in activity.

McNabb, Wilson-Pessano, and Jacobs (1986) identified critical self-management competencies for children with asthma that are applicable to other chronic health problems as well. These four competency areas — prevention, intervention, compensatory behaviors, and external controlling factors — provide a framework for school-based actions. For example, competency in prevention (behaviors that help to avoid an asthmatic episode or to prevent occurrence of symptoms, such as avoidance of allergens or controlling emotions that trigger attacks) can be taught through school-based programs; similarly, children can learn compensatory behaviors that demonstrate adaptation to the condition, such as seeking peer support. Health education programs and self-management strategies are two approaches appropriate for management of chronic illness in school settings.

Reference

McNabb, W. L., Wilson-Pessano, S. R., & Jacobs, A. M. (1986). Critical self-management competencies for children with asthma. *Journal of Pediatric Psychology, 11,* 103–117.

A Health Education Program
to Improve Asthma Management

AUTHORS: David Evans, Noreen M. Clark, Charles H. Feldman, Jill Rips, Deborah Kaplan, Moshe J. Levison, Yvonne Wasilewski, Bruce Levin, and Robert B. Mellins

PRECIS: Children who participated in an asthma health education program in school, Open Airways, had reduced symptoms of asthma, improved asthma management skills, and improved school performance

INTRODUCTION: Programs to prevent the occurrence of illness are far more common in schools than those that help children manage chronic illnesses. Yet, a chronic illness like asthma can interfere with school life, and there is a need to provide education to children with asthma. Open Airways is an asthma self-management program, originally developed for parents and children in health care settings, that was adapted for use in elementary schools to address this need. This child-centered program is focused on teaching the child without requiring parent attendance at sessions.

INTERVENTION: The study took place in twelve urban elementary schools where students were primarily from low-income families. Two hundred thirty-nine children between the ages of eight and eleven, diagnosed as having mild asthma, were assigned to the health education program or a control group.

The Open Airways program consisted of six sixty-minute sessions for eight to twelve students. The topics discussed were (1) basic information and feelings about asthma, (2) how to recognize and respond to symptoms of asthma, (3) using asthma medicines and deciding when to seek help, (4) how to keep active physically, (5) identifying and controlling triggers to asthma symptoms, and (6) handling problems related to asthma at school. The goal of the program was for children to become self-managers by recognizing their asthma symptoms and initiating appropriate management steps whether or not the parent was present; they were encouraged to give information to parents and help them make management decisions as well. Components of the training included skill practice in class and at home, games to practice decision making, role-play, and physical and artistic activities. Behavioral principles were applied including positive reinforcement for use of skills in the home environment, modeling, practice, and rehearsal of new skills.

Results indicate that children who participated in the program increased the number of actions they took to manage asthma, increased their self-efficacy index scores, provided more information about their asthma symptoms to their parents, and increased their influence on parental management decisions to a greater extent than did control children. When eleven academic grades were examined at follow-up, program group children had greater increases than the control group. No differences were found in school attendance.

COMMENTARY: This well-designed study shows that a health education program not only improved the health status of children with mild asthma but also improved the general quality of their lives. They were taught to be better collaborators in family decision making and increased the social support they received in the classroom in addition to improving their academic performance.

The results suggest that children as young as eight years old are capable of taking the initiative and acting to control their own health behavior. The program was carried out within the school day, without parent attendance and over a relatively short period of time. It did not require taking children to an agency after school, which is much more complicated logistically. It seems that programs like this could be developed for other chronic illnesses and have great potential for widespread use. The Open Airways program is now being distributed by the American Lung Association (1740 Broadway, New York, NY 10019) and through local association chapters throughout the country.

SOURCE: Evans, D., Clark, N. M., Feldman, C. H., Rips, J., Kaplan, D., Levison, M. J., Wasilewski, Y., Levin, B., & Mellins, R. B. (1987). A school health education program for children with asthma aged 8–11 years. *Health Education Quarterly, 14,* 267–279.

Self-Help Relaxation for Chronic Headaches

AUTHORS: Bo Larsson, Lennart Melin, Majleen Lamminen, and Fivi Ullstedt

PRECIS: Adolescents with chronic headaches who met for five weeks of relaxation training improved on all measures of headache activity

INTRODUCTION: Chronic tension and migraine headaches occur frequently in childhood and increase during adolescence, especially in girls. Research with adults has established the effectiveness of biofeedback and relaxation training in treating headaches, but only limited work in this area has been done with children and adolescents. The focus of treatment when using these approaches is on decreasing body tension that causes the headache. Other interventions to reduce headaches have attempted to alleviate psychological stressors by teaching children coping skills, but these have had more equivocal results.

INTERVENTION: The students in this study ranged in age from sixteen to eighteen and suffered from recurrent headaches with a frequency of at least once a week. The thirty-six students were randomly assigned to one of three conditions: self-help relaxation, problem-discussion condition, or self-monitoring. The self-help relaxation group met for a total of three hours over a five-week period. Relaxation procedures included using four audiotapes (10–15 minutes each) supplemented with a manual. The students were taught to differentiate a relaxed from a tense state and to relax in response to a cue word. They practiced this rapid relaxation technique at home and at school. Personnel involved were the school nurse, who monitored the use of the audiotape, and a therapist, who met with the students three times in a small group. Students in the problem-discussion condition met for a total of seven hours in a therapist-led group; they focused on psychological conflicts in the students' daily lives and how to deal with them. They used role-play and discussion. The self-monitoring group was a control condition.

The study included a baseline period, five weeks of treatment, posttreatment, and follow-up after five months. Results indicate that the self-help relaxation group was significantly more improved on all headache activity variables than the other two groups. The variables included headache frequency, headache-free days, headache duration, and peak headache intensity. This finding held for the pretreatment–follow-up interval. In fact, the improvements for the self-help relaxation group were more pronounced at five-month follow-up than immediately after treatment.

COMMENTARY: The self-help relaxation training employed in this study is a low-cost approach using minimal therapist assistance. Because of the emphasis on self-management through use of tapes, the amount of adult supervision required was limited, and students were active participants in their own treatment. Students were able to meet in small groups during the school day rather than going for treatment after school. Further, the dropout rate from the self-help relaxation group was low, suggesting that it is an appropriate and/or appealing approach for adolescents. Of course, greater adult involvement might be needed for younger students.

There were differences in the expectancies of students in the self-help relaxation and problem-discussion group in that the latter group had lower expectancy of treatment improvement and satisfaction; therefore, discussion of psychological stressors cannot be ruled out as an intervention strategy. Relaxation training for chronic tension and migraine headache appears to have potential utility for use in schools.

SOURCE: Larsson, B., Melin, L., Lamminen, M., & Ullstedt, F. (1987). A school-based treatment of chronic headaches in adolescents. *Journal of Pediatric Psychology, 12,* 553–566.

Additional Readings

Corley, D. L., Gevirtz, R., Nideffer, R., & Cummins, L. (1987). Prevention of postinfectious asthma in children by reducing self-inoculatory behavior. *Journal of Pediatric Psychology, 12,* 519–531.

    Asthmatic children between the ages of four and eight who suffered from frequent respiratory tract infections were randomly assigned to one of two conditions: treatment through differential reinforcement of other behavior (DRO) and contingent education or a placebo control. The purpose of the treatment was to reduce hand to eye and nose contacts, which cause viral infections (self-inoculatory behavior) as well as the number and severity of their asthma attacks. Parents and children in the treatment group received eight forty-five-minute sessions of training in DRO and in contingent education that included feedback, instructions, reprimand, reasoning, modeling, practice, and positive reinforcement of appropriate behaviors. Results indicate that the nonaversive behavioral procedures used reduced self-inoculatory behavior, infection, and asthma.

Engel, N., & Mascari, A. (1992, November). Initiating an asthma/allergy support group for elementary school children. *Communiqué* (a publication of the National Association of School Psychologists), 28–29.

    This article describes a biweekly support group for children ages eight to twelve who had asthma and allergies. The group opened with an activity designed to develop a sense of trust. Topics were selected to increase student awareness and feelings of security and to encourage students to talk about their symptoms. Relaxation training was included in each meeting. Some decrease in absenteeism was noted, and the group leaders reported that students were able to change their behaviors to avoid certain environmental conditions.

Sallade, J. B. (1980). Group counseling with children who have migraine headaches. *Elementary School Guidance & Counseling,* 87–89.

    Three counseling strategies were used to help elementary-aged children suffering from migraine headaches: education in and monitoring of diet, relaxation exercises, and client-centered support. Each treatment was delivered for six weeks. Frequency of headaches was decreased only during the relaxation treatment.

Tourette Syndrome

Gilles de la Tourette syndrome is a neurological disorder that is characterized by multiple motor and vocal tics, with onset between ages two and sixteen years. Tics are involuntary movements of muscle groups and uncontrollable vocal sounds or words. Motor tics include eye blinking, facial twitching, and shoulder shrugs; vocal tics include barking, grunting, sniffing, and repeating words, sometimes obscenities. Tics may wax and wane or disappear totally for a period of time. Children must demonstrate both motor and vocal tics for at least a year to be diagnosed as having Tourette syndrome. Transient tic syndromes, a tic or involuntary movement that lasts less than a year, reportedly occurs in about 25 percent of children. Although Tourette syndrome is still a low-incidence disorder, it is seen with increasing frequency, perhaps because of greater efforts to publicize it.

Because of the age of the children with Tourette syndrome, the school is often involved in both diagnosis and intervention. There is considerable variation in behavior of children with Tourette syndrome, and difficulties may arise in such areas as writing and simple motor acts, attention and concentration, hyperactivity, visual-spatial perception, math computation, and speech and language. Thus, this chronic syndrome may have a direct effect on cognitive tasks, an indirect effect if the child tries to inhibit tic behavior, and social/emotional effects resulting from isolation and rejection such as low self-esteem, anxiety, or depression.

Medication is usually the treatment of choice for Tourette syndrome; the drug haloperidol (Haldol), for example, suppresses the tics for many children. The side effects of the medications may also affect their behavior in school. The articles that follow present several behavioral strategies that have been effective in reducing or eliminating tics. Several of the other readings provide suggestions for classroom management of Tourette syndrome youngsters.

Assertiveness Training to Reduce Facial Tics

AUTHOR: Irwin J. Mansdorf

PRECIS: Assertiveness training used in a self-instruction format to reduce facial tics in a ten-year-old boy

INTRODUCTION: In this case study, the ten-year-old boy, Ron, had had facial grimacing tics for a period of nine months prior to treatment. Several years earlier he had also had a period of high tic activity, which had been somewhat amenable to counseling, but the tic behavior was never eliminated. As no organic disorder was diagnosed, behavioral assessment was carried out. His mother kept a diary of daily events that revealed when Ron's tic activity increased. These situations were then reenacted in the therapeutic setting, with observations made of Ron's reactions. Also, the youngster was asked to report what he was thinking at the time.

The assessment revealed that when Ron had to act in an assertive fashion, such as volunteering in class, saying he did not like to do something, or asking to participate with a group of his peers, his tic activity increased.

INTERVENTION: The treatment was directed at training Ron to be more assertive rather than at reducing his tic activity. In weekly one-hour sessions Ron was taught assertive responses to threatening or challenging situations. For example, if he was teased, he learned not to be submissive and just accept the harassment. Using self-instruction, he rehearsed positive self-statements, such as "I can say just what I want to say." In addition, his parents were advised to ignore tic activity and praise him in non-tic situations.

Tic activity was measured using a global daily rating by Ron's mother on a scale of 1 (absence of tic activity) to 10 (constant activity). Tic activity was also recorded during the first ten minutes of the training session. Ron did not know his tic activity was being monitored. Results indicate that tic activity in the home decreased markedly during the fourth week of treatment, and continued to decline with ratings of 1 for weeks 8, 9, and 10 and at three-, six-, and twelve-month follow-up. Tic activity in the treatment sessions declined suddenly in the fifth week and was eliminated by week 8 with similar long-term maintenance.

COMMENTARY: By observing that social anxiety preceded high levels of tic activity, the therapist could treat Ron's anxiety rather than focusing directly on the tic behavior. Thus, Ron was not asked to suppress behavior; rather, he learned new assertiveness skills. Emphasis was on increasing positive behaviors, not reducing negative ones.

Training did not immediately reduce Ron's tic activity. About five weeks elapsed before a dramatic decrease was seen. This finding is important for those using this intervention. Once Ron became comfortable with his new skills, he had less need for the tic activity.

The author reports that he has used assertiveness training in several cases of Tourette syndrome. This treatment would have to fit the behavioral characteristics of the child and should not be used without assessment of behavior preceding tics.

SOURCE: Mansdorf, I. J. (1986). Assertiveness training in the treatment of a child's tics. *Journal of Behavior Therapy and Experimental Psychiatry, 17,* 29–32.

Hypnotherapeutic Techniques for Tourette Syndrome

AUTHORS: Daniel P. Kohen and Pamela Botts

PRECIS: Relaxation and mental imagery used in conjunction with medication to reduce tic activity in four children

INTRODUCTION: Hypnotherapy refers to the use of relaxation/mental imagery to bring about an alternative state of consciousness. The Tourette syndrome children in the case examples presented in this article were experiencing complex chronic tics that were exacerbated by stress and that proved embarrassing and isolating. Medication alleviated some of the physical symptoms, but the children needed further assistance with the psychological and behavioral problems of Tourette syndrome. The use of self-hypnosis skills emphasized self-control of symptoms by the children.

INTERVENTION: The four case examples presented were children between the ages of six and ten diagnosed as having Tourette syndrome and referred for treatment. Three of the four youngsters were on haloperidol, and all had motor and vocal tics.

The self-hypnosis intervention involved having the children develop heightened concentration on a particular idea or image. They were told that they could teach their inner mind to "help change the way tics come, are experienced, and go away" (p. 228). The process involved first pretending or imagining such things as their favorite place, something fun, or going somewhere special. Children chose their own images and were guided by the therapist. Deepening or intensification of the relaxation/mental imagery was facilitated through progressive relaxation and/or focusing on different sensations. The goal throughout the self-hypnosis was to encourage internal control and give the children a personal sense of control.

Each case involved somewhat different approaches. With one youngster, peripheral temperature biofeedback was used and metaphors to control movement were selected that fit into the child's imagery. For example, one child was the pilot controlling the movement of a plane. For several of the youngsters, the image of an internal STOP sign was employed.

Three of the children learned relaxation/mental imagery at the first visit; the fourth learned it soon afterward. All of the youngsters were given a personal audiotape with their own images and metaphors for movement control and used it for practice at home. The number of sessions for these youngsters varied and was determined by the specific needs of the family and child.

In three of the four cases there was reduced tic activity very soon after the relaxation/imagery exercises were initiated. This improvement was maintained at follow-up two years later. Medication was reduced and discontinued for two of the children and not started for a third. In the fourth case, despite initial improvement, the family did not return for treatment after the third session and follow-up was only by telephone. Improvement was maintained until a psychiatric hospitalization for Tourette syndrome three years after the last visit.

COMMENTARY: The rationale behind this type of therapeutic approach is that it gives children the "power" to control their behavior. They have this skill with them, for example, in times of stress and are able to use it without adult assistance. This ability, in turn, increases their sense of self-esteem, which is often quite poor in these youngsters.

The authors also suggest that the use of imagination is a natural process for children and something that they can understand. This makes the intervention appealing and motivates youngsters to participate.

It is not clear why the self-hypnosis is successful in improving Tourette syndrome symptoms. According to the authors, whether the relaxation is simply a coping strategy or actually results in the blockage of dopamine receptors has not been discovered.

SOURCE: Kohen, D. P., & Botts, P. (1987). Relaxation-imagery (self-hypnosis) in Tourette syndrome: Experience with four children. *American Journal of Clinical Hypnosis, 29*, 227–237.

Additional Readings

Azrin, N. H., & Peterson, A. L. (1988). Behavior therapy for Tourette's syndrome and tic disorders. In D. J. Cohen, R. D. Bruun, & J. F. Leckman (Eds.), *Tourette's syndrome and tic disorders: Clinical understanding and treatment* (pp. 238–255). New York: Wiley.

This comprehensive chapter reviews behavior therapy procedures that have been found to reduce the frequency of tics in Tourette syndrome and other tic disorders. The procedures include massed negative practice, contingency management, relaxation training, self-monitoring, and habit reversal. The authors recommend an interdisciplinary approach to Tourette syndrome treatment with medical and behavioral procedures.

Dedmon, S. R. (1986). Helping children with Tourette syndrome to cope in the classroom. *Social Work in Education, 4,* 243–257.

   This article stresses the role of the school social worker in working with teachers when a child with Tourette syndrome is in the classroom. The preferred classroom described is one that is minimally distracting (e.g., fewer windows, simple decor, less noise). Suggestions for daily routines include the use of a tape recorder for note taking, providing a handwritten copy of directives, and allowing the child time for physical movement during the day. Support to strengthen coping behaviors of the child and partnerships with parents and teachers are recommended.

Hagin, R. (1984). *Tourette syndrome and the school psychologist.* Bayside, NY: Tourette Syndrome Association.

   This small, useful pamphlet written for school psychologists provides valuable information for all school professionals. A section on educational consultation gives a range of strategies that might prove helpful to Tourette youngsters in areas such as attention, side effects of medication, interpersonal problems, and specific cognitive tasks. Strategies that address the direct effects of tics on skilled motor activities such as handwriting include buddy systems for note taking, oral responses to tests, and tape recorders in lecture classes.

   The Tourette Syndrome Association also publishes other helpful pamphlets including *Serving Clients with Tourette Syndrome: A Manual for Service Providers* (Abbey S. Meyers, 1984) and *Coping with Tourette Syndrome in the Classroom* (Judy Wertheim, 1982).

Organization

Tourette Syndrome Association
41-02 Bell Blvd.
Bayside, NY 11361
(718) 224-2999

Traumatic Head Injury

A traumatic head injury is an insult to the brain caused by an external force such as an automobile accident, a fall, an athletic injury, or an assault. Head injury is seen more often in boys than girls, and most children who experience head trauma have only mild injuries. Many more youngsters who have moderate or severe head injury will survive and return to school because of improved medical care. While all head-injured youngsters need to be followed carefully, those with traumatic head injury require extensive intervention to facilitate recovery.

Severe head injury generally results in impairment in physical and cognitive abilities, and there may also be disturbances of behavioral or emotional functioning, temporary or permanent. Any combination of physical, cognitive, or emotional symptoms may have negative educational consequences. Even mild forms of head injury can have an effect on a child's ability to concentrate or remember. The school, particularly the teacher, may provide useful information about the child's academic performance and behavior prior to the injury. The goal of treatment is to remediate dysfunction and/or compensate for its effects.

Reentry into school for these youngsters will involve extensive planning as they do not fit the traditional categories of mentally retarded, learning disabled, or emotionally disturbed. Such factors as their developmental history, the sudden onset of the disability, and the range and nature of their cognitive, physical, and emotional states distinguish them from other exceptional children (Begali, 1987).

Reference

Begali, V. (1987). *Head injury in children and adolescents.* Brandon, VT: Clinical Psychology Publishing.

Compensatory Strategies for Head-Injured Students

AUTHORS: Sally B. Cohen, Colleen M. Joyce, Kathy Weider Rhoades, and Dianna M. Welks

PRECIS: Compensatory strategies that focus on cognitive and social deficits recommended for head-injured students

INTRODUCTION: The educational needs of head-injured children vary dramatically depending on the level of recovery of the student. This article focuses on educational programming of youngsters in a long-term rehabilitation center, but the basic approach is applicable to a child returning to a public school as well. The emphasis is on the importance of linking educational assessment and prescriptive teaching, that is, finding out where learning has broken down in order to know where teaching should begin.

INTERVENTION: The three goals of school programs for severely head-injured students are thought organization, critical thinking, and social skills. Initially, emphasis is on helping students process information rather than on making academic progress. The authors recommend strategies that assist students to clarify, organize, remember, and express information. The strategies are employed in three stages. First, the teacher uses the strategies to structure the environment or the students' behavior. For example, the teacher might minimize visual distractions for a student by placing his or her chair facing an undecorated wall. Next, the teacher cues the student to perform this behavior when appropriate. Finally, the student uses the strategy independently.

Compensatory strategies for cognitive problems in a classroom setting such as attending, following directions, memorizing, sequencing, and generalizing are presented. Examples of cognitive problems are students' inability to retain information they have heard or read or to remember where to go. Some of the strategies suggested are (1) including pictures or visual cues with oral information, (2) using visual imagery, (3) using verbal rehearsal, (4) limiting the amount of information presented initially, (5) having the student take notes or tape information, and (6) using a logbook to record assignments.

Compensatory strategies for behavioral and social problems in the classroom such as disorientation; difficulty with transitions, beginning, or ending an activity; impulsive responses; and asking for help are also reviewed. Examples of strategies for facilitating transitions from one activity to the next include providing verbal cues, walking through the transitions with the student, referring to printed or pictorial schedules, and using other students to cue transition behaviors. The authors stress that the strategies can be used interchangeably for a variety of problems.

COMMENTARY: This article offers important information for those school professionals working with head-injured students. The strategies listed are very comprehensive and can be implemented easily in the classroom at little or no cost. They can also be shared with parents so that there is continuity between home and school.

In addition to the strategies listed, the authors discuss a number of considerations for planning a program. For example, school professionals must be aware of typical developmental patterns so that expectations for a head-injured child are appropriate. Also, they must be aware of the child's developmental history prior to the injury.

SOURCE: Cohen, S. B., Joyce, C. M., Rhoades, K. W., & Welks, D. M. (1985). Educational programming for head injured students. In M. Ylvisaker (Ed.), *Head injury rehabilitation: Children and adolescents* (pp. 383–409). San Diego, CA: College-Hill Press.

Microcomputers in Cognitive Rehabilitation

AUTHORS: Robert T. Kurlychek and Ann E. Glang

PRECIS: Using microcomputers and electronic games to treat brain-injured persons

INTRODUCTION: Cognitive rehabilitation of persons with traumatic head injury involves remedial training to reverse deficits in areas such as memory, perception, and concept formation. Advances in microcomputer technology have made the computer a potentially useful tool in cognitive rehabilitation. Advantages of computer use include precision of presentation, flexibility with regard to a patient's particular level of ability and deficits, immediate feedback and corrective messages (interactive capabilities), and intrinsic appeal, which can increase motivation.

INTERVENTION: The authors describe some of the software used in cognitive rehabilitation. The programs emphasize training in areas such as attention and orientation, visual perception, and memory abilities.

One commercially available system, COGREHAB, has a series of nine programs designed to improve perceptual and memory abilities. In one of the programs visual information processing—which includes anchoring at the margin, scanning horizontally, identifying words within the perceptual span, and monitoring the periphery—is assessed and trained using word lists. The words are presented in different formats on the screen and the student's speed of reading is measured. Another program in this series assessing memory displays a number of words one at a time; the person is then asked to recall words, starting with the last two words; each successive recall increases in difficulty.

Videogames have also been used in training. Lynch (1982, see "Additional Readings") categorized them into four groupings to address different deficits. These are verbal/mathematic games, memory games, spatial-perceptual motor games (requiring vigilance, quick reaction time, and visual tracking), and table games that may require strategies and understanding of rules.

This chapter is descriptive and reports that there is very limited controlled research on the effectiveness of microcomputer and videogame training and as yet very limited support. Some preliminary evidence suggests that videocomputer games have resulted in improvement in children's eye-hand coordination, attention, reaction time, letter perception, and visual scanning.

COMMENTARY: With microcomputers, level of difficulty can be adjusted based on responses, the delay of time between a stimulus and response choices, and the nature of the feedback. This flexibility makes computers appealing for use with the head-injured population. Further, the numerous repetitions often necessary in training can be done on the computer and relieve the therapist or teacher to carry out other duties.

Although little or no evaluation has been done with brain-injured populations, in the area of special education, computers have been used in remediation for a number of years. Of interest is the question of whether treatment should be focused on readiness skills as described above or on academic skills. This chapter deals broadly with the brain-injured population and not specifically with head-injured children; however, it needs to be explored further for school application.

SOURCE: Kurlychek, R. T., & Glang, A. E. (1984). The use of microcomputers in the cognitive rehabilitation of brain-injured persons. In M. D. Schwartz (Ed.), *Using computers in clinical practice* (pp. 245–256). New York: Haworth Press.

An Interdisciplinary Team
Approach to Treatment of Head Injury

AUTHOR: Vivian Begali

PRECIS: An interdisciplinary approach used in the public school system to work with head-injured students

INTRODUCTION: The reentry of students into school following moderate or severe head injury is an extension of a lengthy and difficult rehabilitation process that they have undoubtedly endured prior to their return. Professionals must actively prepare for the return to school rather than waiting until the children are physically present. The interdisciplinary approach recommended by the author is characteristic of the rehabilitation process that occurs in hospitals; in schools it involves school psychologists, speech pathologists, learning specialists, social workers, counselors, the school nurse, teachers, and parents.

The intervention plan is dependent on the student's stage of recovery at the time of reentry. Those in the early stage of recovery require sensory and sensorimotor stimulation. This might include use of colorful objects and audiotapes of familiar voices or songs, or shapes and colors to sort. Children within the middle stage of recovery require highly structured environmental adjustments and systematic retraining of cognitive functions such as attention and short-term memory. The late stage of recovery focuses on the child's developing independence and adaptability within more normal environments; school systems are most likely to have students reentering at this stage.

INTERVENTION: Remediation can be approached in several ways. First, efforts can be made to improve or strengthen the areas of the student's underlying neuropsychological weaknesses. Second, an approach that utilizes strengths and circumvents the deficiencies is often used. Generally, however, a mixed strategy combining the first two approaches has been found most effective and appropriate for schools. Recently, a fourth remedial approach, compensatory training/functional adaptation, has been used when no further progress seems to be occurring. This involves finding or developing an alternate way to achieve "an otherwise unobtainable goal" (p. 118). Compensatory techniques might include external aids, such as timers, alarm systems, and tape recorders, or internal procedures, including auditory rehearsal or sign language.

Treatment strategies for cognitive deficits are discussed with emphasis on the late stage of recovery. In the context of classroom instruction and cognitive retraining, task analysis, systematic and structured programs, individualized plans, and compensatory training are recommended teaching practices. Simultaneous sensory "bombardment" is not recommended for most head-injured youngsters; rather, direct instruction through the child's most intact sensory modality should be used. Approaches to memory improvement include internal strategies such as mnemonics, verbal strategies, and visual imagery. External aids such as lists, diaries, and notebooks are helpful. Reality orientation therapy to relearn and maintain important information is also suggested. Language retraining approaches include stimulation therapy, operant conditioning, melodic intonation therapy, and visual communication therapy.

Additional sections of the chapter cover behavior management and socioemotional issues in the classroom. An extensive table of selected physical, cognitive, behavioral, and psychosocial interventions is presented with references to the original study or source of the information. One particularly interesting intervention is videotherapy, which gives head-injured youngsters immediate visual and audio examples of their behavior. It can be used, for example, to develop or improve interpersonal strategies or reduce annoying behaviors by showing examples of the behaviors to the youngsters.

COMMENTARY: This chapter synthesizes a vast amount of information about treatment of children with traumatic head injury when they return to school. It provides a number of interesting treatment alternatives that vary in the amount of effort and time needed as well as in cost effectiveness.

The importance of a team working together and carefully planning the interventions is emphasized. Further, close collaboration with parents is an essential component. This chapter makes clear that coordinating reintegration efforts with the referring rehabilitation center or hospital is essential.

Finally, school personnel will find that head-injured students generally require more services — evaluations, programs revisions, relearning, and behavior management — because of the frequently changing nature of their condition.

SOURCE: Begali, V. (1987). Treatment rationale and strategies for the educational setting. In V. Begali, *Head injury in children and adolescents* (chap. 9). Brandon, VT: Clinical Psychology Publishing.

Additional Readings

Blosser, J. L., & DePompei, R. (1989). The head-injured student returns to school: Recognizing and treating deficits. *Topics in Language Disorders, 9,* 67–77.

Students returning to school after head injury will display a wide variety of behaviors. The article provides a table that lists types of cognitive-communicative deficits, skills that can improve or compensate for each deficit, and specific resources and materials. General classroom interventions suggested are encouraging students to reread directions more than once, asking students to repeat instructions verbatim, verifying comprehension of directions by asking students to restate them using other words, asking students to proofread assignments, and inviting students to ask questions for clarification.

Lynch, W. J. (1982). The use of electronic games in cognitive rehabilitation. In L. E. Trexler (Ed.), *Cognitive rehabilitation: Conceptualization and intervention* (pp. 263–274). New York: Plenum.

This is an early article advocating the use of videogames in cognitive rehabilitation. The author suggests that videogames can be used to measure and train sensory functions such as visual detection and motor functions such as speed, dexterity, or coordination. Videogames provide measures of alertness as well, such as reaction time. Advantages are that videogames are highly objective in both evaluation and scoring and that they provide immediate and consistent feedback.

Savage, R. C., & Carter, R. (1984, November–December). Re-entry: The head injured student returns to school. *Cognitive Rehabilitation, 2,* 28–33.

This article is a summary of work by the Head Injury/Stroke Independence Project in Vermont on the reentry of head-injured students into their former school systems. Specific guidelines are provided for parents on how to facilitate the process of reentry. The suggestions include training teachers about head injury, setting up the student's individual education program, and considering social-emotional issues. The roles of various school personnel are discussed, and the importance of parents taking an active role in the reentry is emphasized.

Szekeres, S. F., Ylvisaker, M., & Holland, A. L. (1985). Cognitive rehabilitation therapy: A framework for intervention. In M. Ylvisaker (Ed.), *Head injury rehabilitation: Children and adolescents* (pp. 219–246). San Diego, CA: College-Hill Press.

Cognitive rehabilitation is presented as an interdisciplinary effort to treat communication, behavioral, and psychosocial deficits as well as deficits in processes such as attention, perception, memory, and reasoning. General principles of treatment are presented for early, middle, and late stages of recovery. This chapter provides a framework for pediatric cognitive rehabilitation.

Name Index

Subject Index